LENINISM
UNDER
LENIN

MARCEL LIEBMAN

LENINISM UNDER LENIN

Translated by
BRIAN PEARCE

MERLIN PRESS
LONDON

First published in Great Britain 1975
© Editions Du Seuil, 1973
English translation © 1975 by Jonathan Cape Ltd
First published in paperback in 1980
The Merlin Press Ltd
3 Manchester Road
London E14

ISBN 0 85036 261 x

Printed in Great Britain by
Whitstable Litho Ltd, Whitstable, Kent

Contents

Acknowledgments

I wish to thank my friends Michel Caraël, Jean-Marie Chauvier, Monty Johnstone, Roland Lew and Ralph Miliband, who have been kind enough to read this book in manuscript, either in full or in part, and whose comments and criticism have been most helpful. I am also grateful to Tamara Deutscher, who has compared some of my quotations from the French version of Lenin's work with the original texts. None of those mentioned, of course, bears any responsibility for the ideas set out in this book.

M.L.

Translator's Note and Bibliography

For this English edition the author has substantially shortened and to some extent revised his original text, so that readers comparing the two versions will find discrepancies between them. The endnote (and footnote) references have necessarily been affected and therefore renumbered. To enable the reader to find his way about the literature on which the author draws, a complete bibliography has been compiled.

The author's principal source is the writings of Lenin, as published in the fourth edition of the *Collected Works*. His quotations were taken from the French version of this edition, and it was to this version that the volume and page numbers in his references applied. Quotations and references have been taken for this translation from the English version of the fourth edition, published in Moscow between 1960 and 1970 (and distributed in Britain by Lawrence and Wishart).

The author has used Russian works only where these are available in Western languages. For this translation references are given to English-language translations of these works, wherever available, and, wherever not, to the Russian originals—except in the cases of the books by Kritsman and Martov, which are well known in the West in their German versions.

Where only one work by a particular author is referred to in this book, the reference gives only the author's name. References to different works by the same author are distinguished by the use of short titles. Works referred to can be identified with the aid of the following list.

Abramovitch, R., *The Soviet Revolution, 1917–1939* (Allen and Unwin, London, 1962).

Angress, W., *Stillborn Revolution: the Communist Bid for Power in Germany (1921–1923)* (Princeton University Press, Princeton, 1963).

Anweiler, Oskar, *Die Rätebewegung in Russland, 1905–1921* (Brill, Leyden, 1958).

Aron, Raymond, *Democracy and Totalitarianism* (Weidenfeld and Nicolson, London, 1968).

1*

Arshinov, P. A., *Istoriya Makhnovskogo dvizheniya, 1918–1921* (Gruppy Russkikh Anarkhistov v Germanii, Berlin, 1923).

Avrich, Paul, *Kronstadt 1921* (Princeton University Press, Princeton, 1970). Short title: Avrich, *Kronstadt*.

Avrich, Paul, *The Russian Anarchists* (Princeton University Press, Princeton, 1967). Short title: Avrich, *Anarchists*.

Avtorkhanov, A., *The Communist Party Apparatus* (Regnery, Chicago, 1966).

Baechler, J., *Politique de Trotsky* (Colin, Paris, 1968).

Balabanoff, Angelica, *My Life as a Rebel* (Hamish Hamilton, London, 1938).

Baron, S. H., *Plekhanov: the father of Russian Marxism* (Routlegde, London, 1963).

Berkman, A., *The Bolshevik Myth: Diary 1920–1922* (Hutchinson, London, 1925).

Berlau, A., *The German Social-Democratic Party, 1914–1921* (Columbia University Press, New York, 1949).

Black, C. E., ed., *The Transformation of Russian Society: Aspects of Social Change since 1861* (Harvard University Press, Cambridge, Mass., 1960).

Borkenau, Franz, *World Communism* (University of Michigan Press, Ann Arbor, 1962).

Braunthal, Julius, *History of the International (1914–1943)*, 2 vols (Nelson, London, 1966, 1967).

Broué, Pierre, *Le Parti bolchevique* (Minuit, Paris, 1963). Short title: Broué, *Parti*.

Broué, Pierre, *Révolution en Allemagne (1917–1923)* (Minuit, Paris, 1971). Short title: Broué, *Révolution*.

Bukharin, N., and Preobrazhensky, E., *The A B C of Communism* (Penguin, London, 1969).

Bunyan, James, *Intervention, Civil War and Communism in Russia, April–December 1918* (Johns Hopkins Press, Baltimore, 1936). Short title: Bunyan, *Intervention*.

Bunyan, James, *The Origin of Forced Labor in the Soviet State, 1917–1921* (Johns Hopkins Press, Baltimore, 1967). Short title: Bunyan, *Origin*.

Bunyan, James, and Fisher, H. H., *The Bolshevik Revolution, 1917–1918: Documents and Materials:* Hoover War Library Publications No. 3 (Stanford University Press, Stanford, 1934; reprinted 1961).

Cammett, J. M., *Antonio Gramsci and the Origins of Italian Communism* (Stanford University Press, Stanford, 1969).

Carr, E. H., *The Bolshevik Revolution, 1917–1923* (Macmillan, London, 1950–53).

Chamberlin, W. H., *The Russian Revolution 1917–1921*, Vol. I (Macmillan, London, 1935).

Chambre, Henri, *Le Marxisme en Union Soviétique* (Seuil, Paris, 1955).

Cohn-Bendit, D. and G., *Obsolete Communism; The Left-Wing Alternative* (Penguin, London, 1969).

Dan, T., *see* Martov.

Daniels, R. V., *The Conscience of the Revolution: Communist Opposition in Soviet Russia* (Harvard University Press, Cambridge, Mass., 1960). Short title: Daniels, *Conscience*.

Daniels, R. V., *Red October: the Bolshevik Revolution of 1917* (Secker and Warburg, London, 1968). Short title: Daniels, *Red October*.

Daniels, R. V., 'The State and Revolution: a case study in the transformation of Communist ideology', in *American Slavic and East European Review*, Vol. XII, no. 4 (February 1953). Short title: Daniels, 'The State and Revolution'.

Degras, Jane, ed., *The Communist International (1919–1943): Documents*, Vols. I and II (Oxford University Press, London, 1956 and 1960).

Deutscher, Isaac, *The Prophet Armed* (Oxford University Press, London, 1954).

Deutscher, Isaac, *The Prophet Unarmed* (Oxford University Press, London, 1959).

Deutscher, Isaac, *The Soviet Trade Unions* (Royal Institute of International Affairs, London, 1950).

Deutscher, Isaac, *Stalin* (Oxford University Press, London, 1961).

Dewar, Margaret, *Labour Policy in the U.S.S.R. (1917–1928)* (Royal Institute of International Affairs, London, 1956).

Dobb, Maurice, *Soviet Economic Development since 1917* (Routledge, London, 1951).

Engels, Friedrich, *Anti-Dühring* (Eng. trans.) (Foreign Languages Publishing House, Moscow, 1954).

Erickson, John, 'The Origins of the Red Army', in Pipes, *Revolutionary Russia*, q.v.

Fainsod, Merle, *How Russia Is Ruled*, Revised Edition (Harvard University Press, Cambridge, Mass., and Oxford University Press, London, 1963).

Fainsod, Merle, *Smolensk under Soviet Rule* (Harvard University Press, Cambridge, Mass., 1958).

Fauvet, J., *Histoire du Parti Communiste Français*, Vol. I (Fayard, Paris, 1964).

Fay, Victor, ed., *La Révolution d'Octobre et le Mouvement ouvrier européen* (E.D.I., Paris, 1968).

Fedotoff-White, D., *The Growth of the Red Army* (Princeton University Press, Princeton, 1944).

Ferro, M., 'Pourquoi Février? Pourquoi Octobre?', in Fay, q.v.

Ferro, M., *The Russian Revolution of February 1917* (Routledge, London, 1972). Short title: Ferro, *February*.

Fischer, G., 'The Intelligentsia and Russia', in Black, q.v.

Fischer, Louis, *The Life of Lenin* (Weidenfeld and Nicolson, London, 1964).

Fischer, Louis, *The Soviets in World Affairs* (Constable, London, 1930, reprinted 1951). Short title: Fischer, *Soviets*.

Fisher, R. T., *Pattern for Soviet Youth: A Study of the Congresses of the Komsomols (1918–1954)* (Columbia University Press, New York, 1959).

Fitzpatrick, S., *The Commissariat of Enlightenment* (Cambridge University Press, Cambridge, 1970).

Footman, David, *Civil War in Russia* (Faber and Faber, London, 1961).

Fotieva, L. A., *Iz Vospominaniy o V. I. Lenine* (Politizdat, Moscow, 1964).

Frank, Victor S., 'Lenin and the Russian intelligentsia', in Schapiro and Reddaway, q.v.

Fülöp-Miller, René, *The Mind and Face of Bolshevism* (Putnam, London and New York, 1927).

Getzler, I., *Martov* (Cambridge University Press, Cambridge, 1967).

Geyer, Dietrich, *Lenin in der Russischen Sozialdemokratie: Die Arbeiterbewegung im Zarenreich als Organisationsproblem der revolutionären Intelligenz, 1890–1903* (Böhlau, Cologne, 1962).

Golikov, G. N., *Ocherk istorii velikoy oktyabr'skoy sotsialisticheskoy revolyutsii* (Gospolitizdat, Moscow, 1959).

Gorky, Maxim, *Lenin*, ed. Zeman (University Texts, Edinburgh, 1967).

Gorky, Maxim, and others, *History of the Civil War in the U.S.S.R.*, Vols I and II (Lawrence and Wishart, London, 1937 and 1947). Short title: Gorky, *History*.

Guérin, Daniel, *Anarchism: from Theory to Practice* (Monthly Review Press, New York, 1970).

Haimson, Leopold H., *The Russian Marxists and the Origins of Bolshevism* (Harvard University Press, Cambridge, Mass., 1955).

Hammond, T., 'Leninist authoritarianism before the Revolution', in Simmons, q.v.

Haupt, Georges, and Marie, Jean-Jacques, *Makers of the Russian Revolution* (Allen and Unwin, London, 1974).

Hill, Christopher, *Lenin and the Russian Revolution* (English Universities Press, London, 1947).

Humbert-Droz, J., *Mémoires de Lénine à Staline: dix ans au service de l'Internationale Communiste (1921–1931)* (La Baconnière, Neuchâtel, 1971).

International Labour Office, *Labour Conditions in Soviet Russia* (Harrison, London, 1920).

Joffe, Adolf, *The Last Words of Adolf Joffe* (Lanka Sama Samaja Publications, Colombo, 1950).

Kaplan, F., *Bolshevik Ideology and the Ethics of Soviet Labor, 1917–1920 (The Formative Years)* (Philosophical Library, New York, 1968).

Katkov, George, *Russia 1917: the February Revolution* (Longman, London, 1967).

Kautsky, Karl, *Nationalstaat, Imperialistischer Staat und Staatenbund* (Fränkische Verlag, Nuremberg, 1915).

Kautsky, Karl, *Der Weg zur Macht*, 2nd edition (Buchhandlung 'Vorwärts', Berlin, 1910).

Kayurov, V. N., 'Shest' dnei fevralskoy revolyutsii', in *Proletarskaya Revolyutsiya*, No. 1 (13), 1923.

Keep, J. L. H., 'October in the Provinces', in Pipes, ed., *Revolutionary Russia*, q.v.

Keep, J. L. H., *The Rise of Social-Democracy in Russia* (Oxford University Press, London, 1963). Short title: Keep, *Rise of Social-Democracy*.

Kennan, George, *Russia and the West under Lenin and Stalin* (Hutchinson, London, 1961).

Knyazev, S. P., and Konstantinov, A. P., eds., *Petrograd, October 1917; Reminiscences* (Foreign Languages Publishing House, Moscow, 1957).

Kochan, Lionel, *Russia and the Weimar Republic* (Bowes and Bowes, Cambridge, 1954).

Kollontai, Alexandra, 'Avtobiograficheskiy ocherk', in *Proletarskaya Revolyutsiya*, No. 3, 1921.

Kollontai, Alexandra, *The Workers' Opposition in Russia* (Workers' Dreadnought, London, 1921).

Kool, F., and Oberländer, E., eds., *Arbeiterdemokratie oder Parteidiktatur*, (Walter, Olten, 1967).

Kopp, Anatole, *Town and Revolution* (Thames and Hudson, London, 1970).

Kritsman, L., *Die Heroische Periode der grossen russischen Revolution* (Verlag für Literatur und Politik, Vienna and Berlin, 1929, reprinted by Verlag Neue Kritik, Frankfurt, 1971).

Krupskaya, N. K., *Reminiscences of Lenin* (Foreign Languages Publishing House, Moscow, 1959).

Labry, R., *L'Industrie russe et la Révolution* (Payot, Paris, 1919).

Lane, David, *The Roots of Russian Communism* (Van Gorcum, Assen, 1969).

Lazitch, B., *Lénine et la IIIᵉ Internationale* (La Baconnière, Neuchâtel, 1951).

Lefebvre, H., *Dialectical Materialism* (Cape, London, 1968).

Lefebvre, Henri, *La Pensée de Lénine* (Bordas, Paris, 1957).

Lefebvre, H. and Guterman, N., *Introduction aux 'Cahiers sur la dialectique' de Lénine* (Gallimard, Paris, 1967).

Lenin, V. I., *Polnoye sobranie sochineniy* (Fifth Edition of Lenin's Collected Works), Vol. XLV (Gospolitzdat, Moscow, 1964).

Lewin, Moshe, *Lenin's Last Struggle* (Faber and Faber, London, 1969).

Liebman, Marcel, *The Russian Revolution* (Cape, London, 1970).

Löwy, A. G., *Die Weltgeschichte ist das Weltgericht* (Europa Verlag, Vienna, 1968).

Lozovsky, A., *The Trade Unions in Soviet Russia* (All-Russia Central Council of Trade Unions, Moscow, 1920).

Lukács, G., *History and Class-Consciousness* (Merlin Press, London, 1971).

Lukács, G., *Lenin* (Eng. trans.) (New Left Books, London, 1970).

Lunacharsky, A. V., *Revolutionary Silhouettes* (Allen Lane, London, 1967).

Luxemburg, Rosa, *Rosa Luxemburg Speaks*, ed. Waters (Pathfinder, New York, 1970).

Luxemburg, Rosa, *The Russian Revolution*, ed. Wolfe (Workers' Age, New York, 1940).

Marie, Jean-Jacques, *Les Paroles qui ébranlèrent le monde: anthologie bolchevique 1917–1924* (Seuil, Paris, 1967).

Martov, L. (with Dan, T.), *Geschichte der russischen Sozialdemokratie* (Dietz, Berlin, 1926).

Marx, K., *Selected Essays*, trans. Stenning (Leonard Parsons, London, 1926).

Marx, K., and Engels, F., *Articles from the 'Neue Rheinische Zeitung', 1848–49* (Eng. trans.) (Progress Publishers, Moscow, 1972).

Marx, M., and Engels, F., *Selected Correspondence* (Eng. trans.) (Foreign Languages Publishing House, Moscow, 1956).

Marx, M., and Engels, F., *Selected Works in Three Volumes* (Eng. trans.) (Progress Publishers, Moscow, 1969).

Meijer, J. M., 'Town and Country in the Civil War', in Pipes, ed., *Revolutionary Russia*, q.v.

Meissner, B., *Das Parteiprogramm der K.P.d.S.U., 1903–1961*, 3rd edition (Verlag Wissenschaft und Politik, Cologne, 1965).

Meyer, Alfred G., *Leninism* (Praeger, New York, 1962).

Miliband, Ralph, 'Marx and the State', in *The Socialist Register* (Merlin Press, London, 1965).

Nettl, J. P., *Rosa Luxemburg* (Oxford University Press, London, 1966).

Nove, Alec, *An Economic History of the USSR* (Penguin, London, 1972).

Odom, William E., 'Sverdlov: Bolshevik Party Organiser', in *Slavonic and East European Review*, Vol. 44, no. 103 (July 1966).

Pannekoek, Anton, *Lenin As Philosopher* (New Essays, New York, 1948).

Pannekoek, Anton, *Pannekoek et les Conseils Ouvriers* (E.D.I., Paris, 1969).

Parti Socialiste (*S.F.I.O.*), *XVIIᵉ congrès national, tenu à Strasbourg (25–29 février 1920*), verbatim report (L'Humanité, Paris, 1920).

Parti Socialiste (*S.F.I.O.*), *XVIII° congrès national, tenu à Tours (20–26 décembre 1920*), verbatim report (L'Humanité, Paris, 1921).

Pervuy legal'ny Peterburgsky Komitet bolshevikov v 1917 g: sbornik materialov i protokolov (Gosizdat, Moscow and Leningrad, 1927).

Pietsch, W., *Revolution und Staat: Institutionen als Träger der Macht in der Sowjetrussland (1917–1922)* (Bundesinstitut für Ostwissenschaftliche und Internationale Studien, Cologne, 1969).

Pipes, Richard, *The Formation of the Soviet Union: Communism and Nationalism, 1917–1923* (Harvard University Press, Cambridge, Mass., Revised edition, 1964). Short title: Pipes, *Formation*.

Pipes, Richard, ed., *Revolutionary Russia* (Harvard University Press, Cambridge, Mass., and Oxford University Press, London, 1968).

Plamenatz, John, *German Marxism and Russian Communism* (Longman, London, 1961).

Ponomarev, B., and others, *History of the Communist Party of the Soviet Union (Bolsheviks*), (Eng. trans.) (Foreign Languages Publishing House, Moscow, 1960).

Pospelov, P. N., and others, *V. I. Lenin* (Eng. trans.) (Foreign Languages Publishing House, Moscow, 1965).

Possony, S., *Lenin: the Compulsive Revolutionary* (Regnery, Chicago, 1964).

Poulantzas, Nicos, *Political Power and Social Classes* (New Left Books and Sheed and Ward, London, 1973).

Preparing for October: the Sixth Congress of the Bolshevik Party, August 1917 (Modern Books, London, 1933).

Price, M. Philips, *My Reminiscences of the Russian Revolution* (Allen and Unwin, London, 1921).

Protokoll des II Weltkongresses der Kommunistischen Internationale (Carl Hoym, Hamburg, 1921).

Protokoll des IV Weltkongresses der Kommunistischen Internationale (Carl Hoym, Hamburg, 1923).

Protokoly tsentral'nogo komiteta R.S.D.R.P.(b), avgust 1917–fevral' 1918 (Institut Marksizma-Leninizma, Moscow, 1958).

Pyatnitsky, O. A., *Memoirs of a Bolshevik* (Martin Lawrence, London, 1933).

Rabinowitch, A., *Prelude to Revolution: The Petrograd Bolsheviks and the July 1917 Uprising* (Indiana University Press, Bloomington, 1968).

Radkey, O., *The Elections to the Russian Constituent Assembly of 1917* (Harvard University Press, Cambridge, Mass., 1950). Short title: Radkey, *Elections*.

Radkey, O., *The Sickle under the Hammer* (Columbia University Press, New York and London, 1963). Short title: Radkey, *Sickle*.

Ransome, Arthur, *Six Weeks in Russia in 1919* (Allen and Unwin, London, 1919).

Raskolnikov, F. F., 'V yul'skie dni', in *Proletarskaya Revolyutsiya*, No. 5 (17), 1923.

Reed, John, *Ten Days That Shook the World* (Modern Books, London, 1928).

Reisberg, A., *Lenin im Jahre 1917* (Dietz, Berlin, 1957).

Rigby, T. H., *Communist Party Membership in the USSR, 1917-1967* (Princeton University Press, Princeton, 1968).

Rosenberg, Arthur, *A History of Bolshevism* (Oxford University Press, London, 1934; reissued 1939).

Rosmer, Alfred, *Lenin's Moscow* (Pluto Press, London, 1971).

Rosmer, Alfred, *Moscou sous Lénine* (Pierre Horay, Paris, 1953): original of preceding item, with preface by A. Camus.

Rubel, M., *Karl Marx: essai de biographie intellectuelle* (Rivière, Paris, 1957).

Sadoul, Jacques, *Notes sur la révolution bolchevique, oct. 1917-jan. 1919* (reprint of 1919 edition: Maspero, Paris, 1971).

Schapiro, Leonard, *The Communist Party of the Soviet Union*, 2nd edition (Eyre and Spottiswoode, London, 1970). Short title: Schapiro, *Communist Party*.

Schapiro, Leonard, *The Origin of the Communist Autocracy* (Bell, London, 1955; Praeger, New York, 1965). Short title: Schapiro, *Origin*.

Schapiro, Leonard, and Reddaway, Peter, eds., *Lenin: The Man, the Theorist, the Leader* (Pall Mall Press, London, 1967).

Schwarz, S. M., *The Russian Revolution of 1905* (Chicago University Press, Chicago, 1967).

Serge, Victor, *L'An I de la Révolution* (Maspero, Paris, 1971): original of *Year One* (see below).

Serge, Victor, *Mémoires d'un révolutionnaire* (Club des Editeurs, Paris, 1961). Short title: Serge, *Mémoires*.

Serge, Victor, *Memoirs of a Revolutionary* (Oxford University Press, London, 1963): Eng. trans. of preceding item. Short title: Serge, *Memoirs*.

Serge, Victor, *Vie et mort de Trotsky* (Amiot-Dumont, Paris, 1951).

Serge, Victor, *Year One of the Russian Revolution* (Allen Lane, London, 1972).

Sharapov, G. V., *Razreshenie agrarnogo voprosa v Rossii posle pobedy oktyabr'skoy revolyutsii (1917-1920 gg.)* (Izd. V.P.Sh. i A.O.N., Moscow, 1961).

Shlikhter, A. G., 'Iz vospominaniy ob Oktyabr'skoy revolyutsii', in *Proletarskaya Revolyutsiya*, no. 8, 1922.

Shlyapnikov, A. G., *Semnadtsatiy god*, 2nd edition, Vol. I (Gosizdat, Moscow, 1924).

Shub, David, *Lenin*, revised edition (Pelican, London, 1966).

Simmons, Ernest J., ed., *Continuity and Change in Russian and Soviet Thought* (Harvard University Press, Cambridge, Mass., 1955).

Sobolev, P. N., and others, *History of the October Revolution* (Eng. trans.) (Progress Publishers, Moscow, 1966).

Soria, Georges, *Les 300 Jours de la Révolution russe* (Robert Laffont, Paris, 1967).

Sorlin, Pierre, *The Soviet People and their Society, from 1917 to the Present* (Pall Mall Press, London, 1969).

Souvarine, Boris, *Stalin* (Secker and Warburg, London, 1939).

Stalin, J., *Works* (Eng. trans.) (Foreign Languages Publishing House, Moscow, 1952–55).

Stawar, André, *Libres essais marxistes* (Seuil, Paris, 1960).

Sukhanov, N. N., *The Russian Revolution, 1917* (Oxford University Press, London, 1955).

Ter Hoeven, P. J. A., *Charisma en politieke vernieuwing* (Samsom, Alphen aan den Rijn, 1971).

Trotsky, L. D., *The First Five Years of the Communist International*, Vol. I (New Park Publications, London, 1973).

Trotsky, L. D., *The History of the Russian Revolution* (Victor Gollancz, London, one-volume edition, 1934). Short title: Trotsky, *History*.

Trotsky, L. D., *On Lenin* (Harrap, London, 1971).

Trotsky, L. D., *My Life* (Grosset's Universal Library, New York, 1960).

Trotsky, L. D., *Nashi politicheskie zadachi* (R.S.D.R.P., Geneva, 1904).

Trotsky, L. D., *The New Course* (New Park Publications, London, 1956).

Trotsky, L. D., *1905*, trans. Bostock (Allen Lane, London, 1972).

Trotsky, L. D., *Nos tâches politiques:* French translation of *Nashi politicheskie zadachi*, with appendices (Pierre Belfond, Paris, 1970).

Trotsky, L. D., *'Permanent Revolution' and 'Results and Prospects'* (New Park Publications, London, 1961). Short title: Trotsky, *Results*.

Trotsky, L. D., *Stalin* (Hollis and Carter, London, 1947).

Trotsky, L. D., *The Stalin School of Falsification* (Pioneer Publishers, New York, 1937).

Trotsky, L. D., *Terrorism and Communism* (Ann Arbor Paperbacks, University of Michigan Press, 1961).

Ulam, A., *Lenin and the Bolsheviks* (Fontana, London, 1969).

Voline [i.e., Eikhenbaum, V. M.], *Nineteen-Seventeen* (Freedom Press, London, 1954).

Voline [i.e., Eikhenbaum, V. M.], *The Unknown Revolution: Kronstadt 1921, Ukraine 1918–1921* (Freedom Press, London, 1957).

Vovelle, M., *La Chute de la Monarchie (1787–1792)* (Seuil, Paris, 1972).

Walter, Gérard, *Histoire du Parti Communiste Français* (Somogy, Paris, 1948).

Weber, Max, *From Max Weber: Essays in Sociology*, ed. Gerth. H. H., and Mills, C. Wright (Routledge, London, 1957).

Weber, Max, *The Theory of Social and Economic Organization*: trans. of Part I of *Wirtschaft u. Gesellschaft*, by A. M. Henderson and Talcott Parsons (Free Press of Glencoe, Chicago, 1964). Short title: Weber, *Theory*.

Wolfe, Bertram D., *Three Who Made a Revolution* (Beacon Press, Boston, 1955).

Yaroslavsky, E., *Kratkie ocherki po istorii VKP (b)*, Part II (Gosizdat, Moscow and Leningrad, 1928).

Zetkin, Clara, *Reminiscences of Lenin* (International Publishers, New York, 1934).

Introduction

Fifty years after the death of one of the men who did most to shape the world of today, everyone interested in Lenin is confronted with a body of writing about him that, though abundant, is to a very large extent sterile. This lamentable situation in the field of political and historical research is doubtless due to the very nature of the task that Lenin undertook. Since in the last analysis he had no other aim but to overthrow society as we know it, and since the struggle he began has not yet ceased to produce its effects, the subject continues to be surrounded by acute controversy and intense feeling. By taking sides on Lenin and Leninism a writer is not only declaring his view in an academic dispute but also, very often, proclaiming a *political* choice he has made, in relation to *political* conflicts. This is why social conditioning and ideological climate have proved especially influential in this connexion, and have been reflected in the crude Manicheism that is characteristic of the bulk of historical and sociological writing about Leninism.

It is all too obvious that the teachings of the founder of Soviet Russia have become in that country the object of a cult that is hardly favourable to serious study. Quotations such as this one, taken from *Pravda* of October 31st, 1963, could be multiplied *ad infinitum*: 'The radiant genius of the great teacher of the working people of the whole world, V. I. Lenin, lights up mankind's road as it advances towards Communism.' Or the dedication of a quasi-official biography published by the Institute of Marxism-Leninism in Moscow to 'the wisest and most far-sighted of men of our time'.[1] There is no need to dwell upon this phenomenon of sacralization, aimed at transforming a subversive theory into a system serving to justify a particular established order.

Dogmatism such as this is usually ascribed to the negative features of an all-powerful state machine, which obliges all cultural forms to serve its immediate political ends. It might be deduced from this view that in countries where greater freedom of investigation and expression prevail, and where the virtues of ideological pluralism are continually being asserted, the historical approach to Leninism, profiting by the abilities of talented Sovietologists and intelligent academics, would produce results of a very different kind. The truth of the matter is unfortunately most disappointing. In many ways Western writing on Lenin and Leninism is not so much the opposite of Soviet writing on this subject as a mirror-image of it, in which the prejudice shown, albeit with more subtlety and elegance, is hardly any less marked. I will say nothing about the frequent errors of method, projecting into the past phenomena that belong to the present, and endowing Leninism and Lenin's Russia with characteristics that made their appearance only in subsequent periods.* I will also say nothing about the tendency shown even by writers considered as reputable and serious to attribute as a matter of course the whole of Lenin's political activity to purely cynical motives: the artificial and mechanical nature of such an approach hinders analysis and distorts the conclusions drawn.†

It is worth while, though, querying the legitimacy of the methods sometimes resorted to, where Lenin is concerned, by writers whose academic standing is high and who in some cases enjoy considerable prestige. By Professor Kaplan, of Michigan University, who, in a book about the conditions of the Russian workers during the first years of the Soviet régime, while describing throughout his four hundred pages their sufferings and miseries, almost ignores the civil war that devastated the country — and, when he does mention it, says that the Bolsheviks were making war on the workers.[2] By George Katkov, author of a work on the revolution of February 1917, and engaged in research at Oxford University, who says that in order to understand Lenin's attitude in 1917 we need to resort to 'psychiatric analysis'.[3] By Professor Adam Ulam, of Harvard, who attributes to Lenin the idea that 'socialism has but little to do with the workers'.[4] Or by the American historian James Bunyan, whose occupation as an archivist might suggest a special degree of serenity, and yet who — in a book, which is nevertheless a valuable one, on the civil war in Russia — devotes a long chapter to the 'Red terror' and not one paragraph to the 'White terror'.[5] Or by Professor Alfred Meyer, to whom we owe an important commentary on Leninism, but for whom Lenin's political practice was based on a 'deep-seated hostility towards everything that exists'.[6] And, finally, by Professor Leonard Schapiro, one of the most eminent of Sovietologists, who in his learned history of the Communist Party of the Soviet Union comes close to suggesting that Lenin acted, before the revolution of 1917,

* Thus, in his book on the Russian civil war, the American historian James Bunyan writes, in connexion with the events of 1918, about the 'huge machinery of Soviet propaganda', whereas, in fact, at that time the Soviet regime was extremely weak (Bunyan, Intervention, p. 482).

† Thus, Oskar Anweiler ascribes Lenin's acceptance of the Soviets to purely tactical considerations (Anweiler, p. 265), and Richard Pipes, ignoring all proofs to the contrary, reduces to the same motivation Lenin's 'liberal' policy towards the non-Russian nationalities (Pipes, The Formation of the Soviet Union, p. 36).

as accomplice to a *provocateur* in the service of the Tsarist police.*

For my part I do not lay claim either to neutrality or to complete impartiality. I do not hide my socialist beliefs, nor do I regard these as unrelated to the analysis that I make of the phenomenon of Leninism. Convinced, however, that it is not enough to keep silent about mistakes in order to cause them to disappear, or to evade difficulties in order to resolve them, I have been inspired by the sentence that Isaac Deutscher put at the beginning of his biography of Trotsky: 'Free from loyalties to any cult, I have attempted to restore the historical balance.'[7]

Another preoccupation that is absent from nearly all works on Lenin and Leninism has affected my approach, namely, not to separate the doctrine from the historical setting in which it arose and developed. An analysis of Leninism must be a *history* of Leninism in its living evolution, and no history of Leninism can be separated from the history of the Russian revolution. Yet the biographies of Lenin, which are exclusively focused upon his personality, pay very little attention to examining his theories, while works concerned with his teachings tend to isolate them from their historical context. It is, however, not possible to understand Leninism without a close study of its involvement in the political and social setting of Lenin's lifetime. Its nature and the changes it underwent cannot be grasped unless one observes the constant pressure exerted upon Lenin's thinking by the vicissitudes of the revolutionary struggle. In particular, his policy and theories cannot be detached from the influence brought to bear on them by the activity of the masses and the reality of Soviet society. This is why this book about Leninism is also a book about the revolutionary victories of the Russian people and the earliest developments of political, economic, social and cultural life in Lenin's Russia.

Lenin was a politician who, out of concern for unity of thought and action, wrote a very great deal indeed. As a result, moreover, of his victory in 1917, a large number of his extremely numerous speeches, reports and articles were recorded and published. This provides the observer with a precious source of knowledge. True, Lenin more than once warned against too much weight being given to official documents in which his *oral* statements were reported.[8] This very circumstance, however, by justifying the caution to be observed in relation to any one quotation taken in isolation, makes all the more necessary a very extensive amount of quotation from Lenin's words. And this is none the less called for because Lenin's heirs, or epigones, have waged unending partisan struggles, or theological-style controversies, in

* Schapiro, *The Communist Party of the Soviet Union*, p. 137. The same writer, in his zeal to maintain the thesis of a profound similarity between Leninism and Stalinism, has absolutely nothing whatever to say, in his book *The Origin of the Communist Autocracy*, about the desperate struggle that Lenin waged against Stalin during the last months of his life (see the Epilogue to the present work).

which they have used quotations that were cut short too soon, or were divorced from their context. In order to be more serious it was essential to be more complete.

This book would have been longer still if it had included an attempt to survey and analyse the *legacy* of Leninism. No such attempt has been made, and this not only from considerations of length but because the Leninism of *Lenin* has a specific quality that needs to be safeguarded from the confusions that have often been introduced by commentators upon it, and deliberately fostered by the heirs of Leninism.

Leninism has long been looked at exclusively in its relation to the destiny of the Soviet Union. The debate between worshippers and scorners has amounted, very largely, to a clash between supporters of the Soviet Union and defenders of the 'free world'. But the development of revolutionary struggles all over the globe has bestowed a new significance upon Leninism. There is hardly any insurrectionary movement today, from Latin America to Angola, that does not lay claim to the heritage of Leninism. It has ceased to be merely a matter for historical study or for apologetical and quasi-religious exegesis. It serves as one of the brightest torches available to aid our observation of present-day political phenomena. Western Europe itself, which not so long ago was thought to be sunk in a doze of sluggish and cosy satisfaction, has seen the appearance since 1968 of a new Left that is radical in spirit and revolutionary in vocation, and whose obsession with Leninism—whether the reality or a mythical notion of it, and whether as something to be conformed to or something to be shunned—is now obvious. After the events of May 1968 the Paris weekly *Lutte ouvrière* wrote: 'But it is not enough simply to proclaim our determination to continue the struggle, to bring it to a successful conclusion we must draw the lessons of the past, and one of the chief lessons this spring has taught us is the need for a revolutionary party.'[9]

The crisis of the capitalist world and the crisis of the Social-Democratic and Communist organizations have indeed given topicality to this question of the 'revolutionary party', the first outlines of which were sketched by Lenin seventy years ago. The present book does not claim to offer any solution either to this problem or to that of the building of socialism. The author does not believe, in any case, that such solutions can be found in texts—not even in the writings of the greatest revolutionary of our century. But a knowledge of his work, made up of successes and failures, great achievements and glaring mistakes, can enrich the thinking of everyone who is concerned with socialist action, and can make more fruitful the efforts of all those who engage therein.

Brussels, September 1972

Part I
Leninism in opposition

1
Lenin's Party

It is hardly an exaggeration to say that Lenin's chief contribution to the political reality of our time was his creation of the Bolshevik Party, of a tool to make revolutions with—indeed, *the* tool for making revolutions. In this respect his personal contribution was much greater than that which he brought to the victory of the October insurrection (despite its decisiveness) and to the foundation and development of the Soviet state. October was the result of a concurrence of events and factors that were many and various: the world crisis set off by the war, the slough into which Russia had sunk, the collapse of the Tsarist regime, the upsurge of the masses demanding better conditions, the inability of the Provisional Government to satisfy them, the anger and exasperation left by the workers, peasants and soldiers. Among these contradictory forces, some pressing towards revolution while others strove vainly to block this trend, Leninism holds a substantial place. But Lenin did not *make* the Russian revolution. It is even debatable, as we shall see, whether he actually led it. He did, however, forge the Bolshevik Party: Leninism was embodied in the Bolshevik organization, the latter was Lenin's work, and history welded them together so thoroughly that the historian cannot separate them.

The Bolshevik *organization* was Lenin's own creation, and in this sense Leninism and Bolshevism can be seen as one. The very idea of organization occupies an essential place in Leninism: organization of the revolutionary instrument, organization of the revolution itself, organization of the society to which the revolution gave birth. Insistence on the absolute necessity of organization is to be found all through Lenin's writings and all through Lenin's career. In his first important work, *What the 'Friends of the People' Are*, written in 1894, when Lenin was twenty-four, he declared that 'organizing a socialist workers' party' constituted a 'direct task' for the Russian revolutionary movement.[1] In 1904, when the Bolshevik faction, that is, the first form of the Leninist organization, came into being, he said that 'in its struggle for power the proletariat has no other weapon but organization'.[2] During the Revolution of 1905, when the masses themselves had begun to move without the help of any party, he still affirmed: 'Unless the masses are organized, the proletariat is nothing. Organized—it is everything.'[3]

Many such quotations could be given. As for Lenin's career, right down to 1917 it was entirely devoted to giving life and substance to this *organization*, which he saw as indispensable and to which he was passionately attached. In October 1905 he wrote: 'We value our organization, embryonic though it is, and will defend it tooth and nail.'[4] And that was what in fact he did, indefatigably, the bites and scratches being sometimes distributed to left and right with, as we shall see, more generosity and vigour than restraint or scruple.

That the Russian socialist and revolutionary movement suffered, until the beginning of the twentieth century, from a total lack of organization is an undeniable fact. Lenin himself described in these words the situation that he sought to put right: 'The principal feature of our movement ... is its state of disunity and its amateur character, if one may so express it. Local circles spring up, and function in almost complete isolation from circles in other districts and—what is particularly important—from circles that have functioned and now function simultaneously in the same districts.'[5]

The consequence of this lack of organization was twofold. On the one hand, the socialist movement suffered from extreme regionalism, or even 'localism' pure and simple. Rosa Luxemburg, in her critique of Lenin's centralism, acknowledged that 'how to effect a transition from the type of organization characteristic of the preparatory stage of the socialist movement—usually featured by disconnected local groups and clubs, with propaganda as a principal activity—to the unity of a large, national body, suitable for concerted political action over the entire vast territory ruled by the Russian state' was 'the specific problem which the Russian social-democracy has mulled over for some time.'[6] The structural weakness of the socialist movement exposed its most active members to the repressive activity of the Tsarist police. A contemporary observer, reviewing his own experience, stated that, between 1895 and 1902, the average period that a Social-Democratic group survived in Moscow was, as a result of police intervention, no longer than three months.[7] The activity of the working-class movement consequently lacked continuity, and the establishment of an organization with a structure that would ensure protection against the repressive operations of the police emerged as an imperative necessity. Meanwhile, the warfare between the ruling authorities and the revolutionaries resembled, as Lenin put it, 'that conducted by a mass of peasants armed with clubs, against modern troops'.[8] Indeed, when in 1898 the first congress, held in Minsk, proclaimed the foundation of the Russian Social Democratic Labour Party, this event had no practical significance whatever, nearly all the delegates being arrested soon after the congress ended.

Autonomy that amounted to atomization, and 'craft-workshop' amateurism that made the socialist groups easy prey for the police, were the evils that the principles of party organization worked out and progressively perfected by Lenin were intended to combat. This was how Bolshevism came into being: a complex and variable reality which nevertheless, through all its variations, retained constant features that set their mark on the entire history of the Communist movement. The birth and the development of Bolshevism were historically determined in the sense that each stage was a response to the way that history unfolded, and to the surprises that it brought.

The Birth of Bolshevism

Schematizing a little, it is possible to sum up like this the first part of Lenin's career, before the 1905 Revolution: in 1895 he took part in the activities of one of those Social-Democratic groups of which there were then a number in Russia; his arrest and exile, between 1895 and 1900, were the price paid for the organizational weaknesses of the movement to which he belonged, and which, at the end of the century, found itself, especially in Petersburg, in a state of acute crisis owing to the many arrests of militants;[9] when, in 1900, he returned from exile and left Russia, he applied himself at once to the task of creating the Party organization that the revolutionary movement in his country lacked. And while the (real) foundation of the R.S.D.L.P. dates from 1903, the three years preceding this were wholly devoted by Lenin to working out his ideas on organization, and to the creation and development of an enterprise which, though apparently journalistic, was in fact the first 'sketch' for the Leninist Party.

When exiled in Siberia he had addressed to his comrades in Europe an urgent appeal declaring that 'we must have as our immediate aim *the founding of a Party organ that will appear regularly and be closely connected with all the local groups*'.[10] And again: 'Only the establishment of a common party organ can give the "worker in a given field" of revolutionary activity the consciousness that he is marching with the "rank and file" ... '[11]

It was in *Iskra* that Lenin was to develop his ideas about the requirements that the revolutionary organization must satisfy in order to acquire, at last, a degree of efficiency. As he wrote, however: 'A newspaper is not only a collective propagandist and a collective agitator, it is also a collective *organizer*.'[12]

The modest dimensions of the network of agents that *Iskra* established in Russia suffice to reveal how difficult were the tasks that the Russian socialist movement had to accomplish in order to attain real existence. The number of revolutionary militants directly linked with this network and paid by the organization was always small: about ten when the newspaper began, a dozen in 1901, thirty at most in 1903.[13] Even these figures fluctuated a lot, for arrests decimated the ranks of the 'distributors' of *Iskra*. At the end of 1902 only four were still at large,[14] and in January 1903 Lenin wrote to one of his correspondents: 'We do not know whether people are alive or not; we are compelled, simply compelled, to consider them almost non-existent.'[15]

The fact that, under these conditions, *Iskra* was able to assemble the congress that, in 1903, gave birth to the organized socialist movement in Russia shows what a weak state the latter had been in. The fact that, at this congress, the delegates from 'Iskrist' groups were in the majority bears witness, furthermore, to the effectiveness of the agitational work they had carried on among Russia's revolutionaries. This activity consisted, when the existing groups refused to collaborate and resisted all attempts at centralization, in reducing their leaders to a minority position or even in setting up dissident committees which waged ruthless struggle against the previously established ones. Martov, Lenin's principal collaborator at this time, admitted that this struggle between the 'Iskrist' agents and the opponents of centralization sometimes took the form of 'guerrilla warfare' in which 'subversive tactics' had to be employed and in which in the end 'the law of the strongest' was what prevailed.[16] So it was that the militants got their first lessons in the ruthless art of faction-fighting. In any case, these efforts were crowned with success: when the Party Congress met, in July 1903, Lenin could rightly declare that this party was being formed 'on the basis of the principles and organizational ideas that had been advanced and elaborated by *Iskra*'.[17]

It was indeed in the columns of that journal, filled by the outstanding figures of Russian Marxism—Plekhanov, Martov, Axelrod, Lenin, Trotsky—that between December 1900 and October 1903 were developed the ideas which, when systematized and perfected, were destined to form the essence of Lenin's theory of organization. This idea itself, and the need to put it into practice, was expressed first and foremost in *Iskra*. To be sure, Lenin's chief collaborators were themselves convinced—had in some cases been so long since—of the importance and urgency of the problem. Well before *Iskra*, Plekhanov had already said that 'only organized revolutionary forces seriously influenced the course of events'.[18] And Martov had been convinced since the very start of his career that 'in the code of revolutionary behaviour the demands of organizational rules and discipline should overrule all personal feelings'.[19] Plekhanov and Martov were also agreed in considering that, in the circumstances prevailing in Russia, any revolutionary, or indeed any political organization must depend for its strength upon centralization: for them, the need for cohesion and secrecy had to be given priority over the desire for large-scale recruiting.* Martov was later to abandon these principles and to criticize the work that he himself had carried out as one of the editors of *Iskra*, rejecting in his history of Russian Social-Democracy the 'centralizing and authoritarian tendencies' of that journal.[20]

Iskra employed a polemical style that was destined to enjoy a brilliant future in the Bolshevik Party, and in which Lenin was especially to excel. As Martov testified, the editors strove 'to make sure that "all that is ridiculous" appears in "a ridiculous form",' and 'to expose "the very embryo of a reactionary idea hidden behind a revolutionary phrase"'. On all sides, *Iskra*'s opponents condemned the polemical methods of this journal, which was accused, to quote Trotsky's testimony at the time, of 'fighting not so much against the autocracy as against the other factions in the revolutionary movement'.[21]

All this, though, was only by way of being an introduction—*hors d'œuvres*, so to speak. The main dish was to be cooked by Lenin himself, who, in dozens of articles and speeches, pamphlets and discussions, developed and sharpened the basic principles of Bolshevism. These amounted, in the last analysis, to two themes: the vanguard party, and centralization.

The elitist conception of the party: the proletarian vanguard
In March 1902 a fairly stout booklet was published in Stuttgart which was to mark a stage in the political history of our times. *What Is To Be Done?* is a condensation of Lenin's ideas on organization and also the most coherent exposition of the ideas of a Marxist endeavouring to create the tool by means of which to carry through a plan for revolution. It must be noted that the subjects examined in *What Is To Be Done?* were also touched on in articles, pamphlets, speeches or letters of Lenin belonging to roughly the same period, and these need to be studied along with *What Is To Be Done?*. Lenin's conviction that the revolution in Russia must necessarily be the work of a vanguard group rather than of a mass party was based not merely on the circumstances characteristic of the Russia of that time but also on the way that he conceived the relation between the working class and the proletarian party; to be more precise, it followed from his general views regarding the class-consciousness that the proletariat possessed or did not possess. In Chapter 2 of *What Is To Be Done?*, drawing lessons from the social history of his country and from the attitude of the working masses, Lenin declares that 'the "spontaneous element", in essence, represents nothing more nor less than consciousness in an *embryonic*

* ' "In despotically ruled countries, the socialist groups ... " must adopt the principle of "rigid and secret conspiratorial organization", and remain confined to "a small number of members" ' (Geyer, p. 252, quoting *Iskra* no. 5).

form', that transition from one to the other is possible, but that 'the workers were not, and could not be, conscious of the irreconcilable antagonism of their interests to the whole of the modern political and social system, i.e., theirs was not yet Social-Democratic conscious-ness'.[22] In so far as they spontaneously learn from their own ex-periences, the workers are incapable of anything more than 'trade-unionist' activity in opposition to the employers, or even merely to individual employers. Furthermore, this 'trade unionism' — typical of the British labour movement — is likely to confine itself to 'the com-mon striving of all workers to secure from the government measures for alleviating the distress to which their condition gives rise, but which do not abolish that condition, i.e., which do not remove the subjection of labour to capital.'[23]

Lenin's determined fight against *economism* was to a large extent an attack directed against the conception of spontaneity. Lenin and several others among the editors of *Iskra* rejected the theory, called by them 'economism', according to which, working-class activity being spontaneously economic, trade-union, in character, it was futile, or at least premature, to try and politicize it. 'It was best to introduce a "division of labour" into the work of opposition: the workers themselves would fight for the amelioration of their economic conditions, for potatoes, as Byelinsky had put it, while the progressive bourgeoisie, which alone showed any real interest in political and constitutional problems, fought for political democracy.'[24]

Left to themselves, the proletariat are in practice incapable, so Lenin considered, of anything more than a reaction of instinctive opposition. He denied 'that the labour movement pure and simple can elaborate, and will elaborate, an independent ideology for itself,'[25] especially since it was necessary to reckon with the influence wielded by bour-geois ideology, which 'is far older in origin than socialist ideology, ... is more fully developed, and ... has at its disposal *immeasurably* more means of dissemination.'[26] This was why 'class political consciousness can be brought to the workers only *from without*, that is, only from outside the sphere of relations between workers and employers'.[27]

Ideas such as these may strike us as pessimistic, since Marxism declares that the emancipation of the working class is the task of the workers themselves. However, socialist thinkers had never been led by this proposition to underestimate the role played by 'renegades' from the bourgeoisie, a category to which, indeed, many of themselves belonged. Rosa Luxemburg in person, while confident in the capacities of the working class for revolutionary spontaneity, acknowledged that this class, even though instinctively and spontaneously revolu-tionary, could be influenced from without. In the case of the revisionist tendencies that she vigorously opposed, this outside influence was certainly a baneful one. A revolutionary party, however, 'must work out a clear and definite scheme how to develop the mass movements which it has itself called into being ... Street demonstrations, like military demonstrations, are only the start of a battle ... The expression of the whole of the masses in a political struggle must be heightened, must be sharpened, take on new and more effective forms.'[28] Lenin would have come close to subscribing to a formulation like this, for his own conception of the spontaneity of the masses, though usually regarded as the direct opposite of Rosa Luxemburg's, was in fact less univocal and less pessimistic than is supposed. To be sure, in *What Is To Be Done?*, he denigrated the spontaneous, 'trade-unionist' consciousness of the proletariat, and even stressed the need to fight against 'this spontaneous, trade-unionist striving to come under the wing of the bourgeoisie'.[29] Lenin's criticism was directed, however, not so much towards the spontaneous *activity* of the working class as towards its *consciousness*, as being elemental, instinctive, and consequently deficient. It is important also to observe that the circumstances in which his idea was expressed probably had a certain effect on the idea itself. At the 1903 congress of the Russian Social-Democrats, Lenin himself said about *What Is To Be Done?*: 'We all now know that the "economists" have gone to one extreme. To straighten matters out somebody had to pull in the other direction, and that is what I have done.'[30]

It is necessary, therefore, to allow for the polemical purpose that inspired Lenin when he wrote his famous book. The essence of the matter nevertheless lies elsewhere. A number of passages in *What Is To Be Done?* show that the author was above all concerned to *make fully effective* the spontaneous activity undertaken by the masses. Whenever he deals with *action*, far from condemning spontaneity, he urges the revolutionary organization to assume the leadership of such movements, even affirming that 'the greater the spontaneous upsurge of the masses and the more widespread the movement, the more rapid, incomparably so, [is] the demand for greater consciousness in the theoretical, political and organizational work of Social-Democracy'.[31] Surveying the historical achievements of the Russian labour movement, Lenin noted with satisfaction that 'the upsurge of the masses proceeded and spread with uninterrupted continuity.'[32] He regretted only '*the lag of leaders* ... behind *the spontaneous upsurge of the masses*;'[33] 'the spontaneous struggle of the proletariat will not become its genuine "class struggle" until this struggle is led by a strong organization of revolutionaries'.[34] Here we see already an approach to a dialectical attempt to transcend the contradiction between the *spontaneity* and the *organization* of the proletariat.

Did Lenin not further say that what was needed was 'work that *brings closer and merges into a single whole* the elemental destructive force of the masses and the conscious destructive force of the organization of revolutionaries', that the latter had to 'come to the aid of the spontaneously rising masses' and 'direct the spontaneous movement'?[35] But the idea of independent action by the working class, so dear to Rosa Luxemburg and the Mensheviks, was certainly repudiated by Lenin.

Even though the divergence between Luxemburg's 'belief in spontaneity' and Lenin's criticism of spontaneity was not so wide as has been alleged, nevertheless Lenin did draw a clear distinction between the 'organization' and the 'movement', and thought that the activity of the masses belonged essentially under the latter heading. As a somewhat diffuse reality, the working-class movement could draw into activity a substantial section of the working class, but the revolutionary organization, and especially Social-Democracy, 'has everywhere and always been, and *cannot but be*, the representative of the class-conscious, and not of the non-class-conscious, workers'.[36] In October 1905 Lenin repeated that 'the proletariat ... is not in a position to create a party embracing the entire class—and as for the whole people creating such a party, that is entirely out of the question.'[37] Plekhanov developed the same idea, stating that a clear distinction existed between the 'class' and the 'party', the latter being called upon to exercise a veritable 'hegemony' over the former.[38]

This is the essential point. Whereas the socialist parties in the West—*mass* parties—cherished the ambition to represent the whole of the working class, Lenin considered that 'it would be ... "tail-ism" to think that the entire class, or almost the entire class, can ever rise, under capitalism, to the level of consciousness and activity of its vanguard, of its Social-Democratic Party.'[39] Things could not be otherwise, he explained, in view of 'that infinite disunity, oppression and stultification which under capitalism is bound to weigh down upon such very wide sections of the "untrained", unskilled workers'.[40] The conclusion to be drawn was clear: 'the Party must be only the vanguard ... of the vast masses of the working class ... the whole of which does not and should not belong to a "party".'[41] These ideas were undoubtedly affected by Lenin's Russian environment and the special circumstances of the revolutionary struggle that was going forward in Russia. But it is nevertheless certain—and it is important to underline this—that Lenin's theory of the relations between party and class, and his critique of 'the cult of spontaneity' have *general* application: that the ideas thus worked out did not apply, in their author's view, merely to the proletariat of Russia—only recently born and in some ways very backward—but also to the developed proletariat of Western Europe, richer as that was in experience and consciousness.*

---

* 'The history *of all countries* shows that the working class, exclusively by its own effort, is able to develop only trade-union consciousness ... ' (Lenin, Vol. 5, p. 375. My emphasis, M.L.)

So far as the Russian revolutionary movement was specifically concerned, this conception of the vanguard party was to be understood in a dual sense: both qualitatively and quantitatively. As regards quality, the Party was to be an elite formation, embracing those workers who belonged to 'the better-situated strata of the working class', who 'respond to the ideas of socialism more rapidly and more easily'.[42] In a country like Russia, especially, it went without saying that such elements could not be numerous: they were undeniably an elite. The political conditions prevailing in Russia, the autocratic and repressive nature of the Tsarist régime, the absence of any form, even the most elementary, of democratic freedom—all this ensured that it was impossible to create and develop mass parties functioning openly. Most Russian socialists willy-nilly recognized this impossibility. It was Lenin who spelt out the logical consequences: the revolutionary organization must restrict itself to *a modest size*, must be largely *clandestine*, and must be mainly composed of *professional revolutionaries*.

Socialist aims could not be attained, he declared in *What Is To Be Done?*, 'if ... we begin with a broad workers' organization, which is supposedly most "accessible" to the masses (but which is actually most accessible to the gendarmes and makes revolutionaries most accessible to the police)'.[43] The importance that Lenin accorded to this idea was one of the causes of the serious dispute between him and Martov at the congress of 1903, and so of the breach between those who were immediately named 'Bolsheviks' and 'Mensheviks'.

The Second Congress of the R.S.D.L.P., which it was hoped would consecrate the foundation of a real party, organized and united, turned out to be a congress not of unity but of division. The underlying reasons for the split that occurred are still subject to debate. Dozens of writers have examined the question, but all that emerges from their interpretations is a small number of probabilities and many hypotheses—rarely, however, any certainties. It is undeniable, though, that Lenin's concern to endow the Party that was being formed with the character of an authentic vanguard did play a determining part in the genesis of the conflict between Bolsheviks and Mensheviks. The problem at issue was that of choosing a correct and adequate definition of a Party member. Two formulations confronted each other.

Lenin's formulation stated that 'a party member is one who accepts the party's programme and supports the party both financially and by personal participation in one of its organizations'.[44] Martov's, however, said that 'a member of the Russian Social-Democratic Labour Party is one who, accepting its programme, works actively to accomplish its aims under the control and direction of the organs of the party'.[45]

What was at issue was, basically, the *size* of the Party, and, in consequence, its *nature*. Martov, recalling this controversy, said that Lenin's proposition meant 'eliminating not only many intellectuals who were in sympathy with the Party and who rendered services to it, while not being in a position ... to join an illegal organization, but also a large section of Social-Democratic workers who constituted a link between the party and the masses, but who, owing to personal circumstances, declined to join the Party'—workers who were getting on in years, or had acquired families, and also those who, because of their previous activity, had already become objects of police surveillance.[46]

For his part, Lenin never concealed his intention of restricting the membership of the revolutionary organization, and the terms of his formulation had been carefully calculated to ensure this effect. In the speech he made to the congress he blamed Martov for the 'elasticity' of his definition. 'It is just this "elasticity" that undoubtedly opens the door to all elements of confusion, vacillation and opportunism.' And he added: 'This formulation [of Martov's] necessarily tends to make party members of *all and sundry*.' For Lenin, on the contrary, 'it would be better if ten who do work should *not* call themselves party members (real workers don't hunt after titles!) than that one who only talks should have the right and opportunity to be a party member.'[47] Lenin's own definition, according to him, was aimed at setting up 'a bulwark' against invasion of the Party by 'every kind of representative of opportunism'.[48]

Martov's text was adopted by twenty-eight votes to twenty-two, with one abstention. As Lenin later explained, however, 'after Paragraph 1 of the rules had been spoilt in this way, we had to bind the broken pot as tightly as possible with a double knot'.[49] This was one of his main motives in the hard struggle he waged when the leading bodies of the Party were elected; and this struggle, which was conducted with equal ferocity on both sides, widened the gulf between those who stood for a relatively open party and those who were in favour of a more restricted and closed type of organization. The appearance of Bolshevism was thus bound up with the need, proclaimed by its founder, for a vanguard organization—in other words, the 'elite' conception of the Party.

Limited in numbers, the Party should also be mainly clandestine in character. So as early as 1899, when still in Siberia, Lenin had sent to Europe a document in which he declared that 'the traditions of the whole preceding revolutionary movement demand that the Social-Democrats shall at the present time concentrate all their efforts on organizing the party, on strengthening its internal discipline, and on developing the technique for illegal work'.[50]

In *What Is To Be Done?* he linked closely together, moreover, the question of the Party's clandestine character and that of its size:

In *form* such a strong revolutionary organisation in an autocratic country may also be described as a 'conspiratorial' organisation, because the French word *conspiration* is the equivalent of the Russian word *zagovor* ('conspiracy'), and such an organisation must have the utmost secrecy. Secrecy is such a necessary condition for this kind of organisation that all the other conditions (number and selection of members, functions, etc.) must be made to conform to it. It would be extremely naïve indeed, therefore, to fear the charge that we Social-Democrats desire to create a conspiratorial organisation. Such a charge should be as flattering to every opponent of Economism as the charge of following a Narodnaya Volya line.[51]

The number of Party members was determined by the requirements of clandestinity, and so had to be small. The quality of the membership was similarly determined: the Party must consist of men who were ready to live and act in clandestine conditions, and who were equipped to lead such an existence. The Party must be composed not of ordinary 'militants' so much as of *professional revolutionaries*.

Professional revolutionaries: they had constituted the framework of the Russian socialist movement, their ranks had been decimated by the police, the courts and the firing-squads of Tsarism, but on the soil of Russia, where the burden of tyranny aroused and nourished the thirst for freedom, the revolutionaries who were struck down were at once replaced by fighters who were equally fearless, equally heroic, and equally ill-starred. Wholly devoted to 'the cause', they had multiplied conspiracies and attempts at assassination, from the abortive effort of the Decembrists onward, inspired by the model that the anarchist Nechayev had set before them: 'The revolutionary is a marked man; he has no personal interests, affairs, or feelings, no personal connexions, nothing that belongs to him, not even a name. Everything in him is geared to a single and exclusive goal, to a single thought, a single passion: the Revolution.'[52]

Although, as a convinced Marxist, Lenin was opposed to the old revolutionary organizations of Russia, he had in many respects taken over their heritage. There was a family connexion, moreover, between him and them: Alexander Ulyanov, Lenin's elder brother, the perfect model of a professional revolutionary. Condemned to death for being implicated in an attempt on the life of the Tsar, he died after refusing to appeal to the Tsar for mercy and after telling his judges: 'There is no finer death than death for one's country's sake; such a death holds no terror for sincere and honest men. I had but one aim: to help the unfortunate Russian people.'[53] He was nineteen years old. And Lenin himself, of whom a Menshevik opponent said: 'There is no-one else who for the whole twenty-four hours of every day is busy with the revolution, who thinks and even dreams only of the revolution',[54] Lenin, too, was perfectly equipped for the life and work of the professional revolutionary.

In *What Is To Be Done?* Lenin emphasizes more than once the need to concentrate the organization of the Social-Democratic Party in the hands of professional revolutionaries: 'The struggle against the *political* police requires special qualities; it requires professional revolutionaries';[55] 'The organization of revolutionaries must consist first and foremost of people who make revolutionary activity their profession.'[56] And, more concretely, he wrote of 'our duty to assist every capable worker to become a *professional* agitator, organizer, propagandist, literature distributor, etc., etc.'.[57] A few years later, when reviewing the revolutionary events of 1905 and 1906, at the time when Bolshevism was in process of taking shape, Lenin answered the question: to what was due 'this superior unity, solidarity and stability of our Party'? 'It was accomplished,' he said, 'by the organization of professional revolutionaries.'[58]

Accordingly, the Party that would go forward to the assault upon Tsarism was to be made up of a limited number of professional revolutionaries, brought together in an organization that was clandestine or even conspiratorial. Were one to do no more than collect in this way the ideas expressed by Lenin, one would, however, deprive his thought of an aspect of major importance. Such simplification, which is often committed, is what underlies one of the charges most frequently levelled against his theory of the Party, namely, that Lenin was guilty of 'Blanquism'. His views on organizational matters, it is said, were nothing but a more or less slavish copy of the views of Blanqui, who, throughout a long political career, organized a succession of conspiracies and raids, using small groups of revolutionaries.

Actually, there was nothing 'Blanquist' about Lenin—or, at least, an essential element in his theories shows what distinguishes his conceptions from those held by the French revolutionary: namely, the need to link the Party with the masses, and, in particular, with the working-class masses. When he said that 'it is our duty always to intensify and broaden our work and influence among the masses,' for 'a Social-Democrat who does not do this is no Social-Democrat',[59] Lenin laid down for himself and for his organization a task of fundamental importance. And while the Party was to be the tool of the revolution, the role assigned to the proletariat itself in the revolutionary process was a considerable one. However solid the Party might be, however effective its methods of struggle, however clear, exalting and stirring its programme, all those qualities were meaningless except in relation to the Party's hinterland, its clientele, the milieu in which it sought recruits, its sphere of influence—to the class whose vanguard it sought to be, even more than its spokesman: namely, the proletariat. This was why Lenin as a young man devoted several essays to study of working-class conditions, and why, during the first years of his political career, he wrote numerous articles and pamphlets in which he examined, with remarkable precision and sense of the concrete, the possibilities and limitations of labour legislation.* 'A revolutionary party is worthy of its name only when it guides *in deed* the movement of a revolutionary class.'[60] Adherence to Marxism meant, of course, that the industrial proletariat was seen as being, by its position in society, the maker of the revolution. This axiom did not automatically solve all problems, though — in particular, that of the method by which it would be possible to 'push on' the activity of the masses, as Lenin expressed it.[61]

Lenin's strategic preoccupations were to become clear when, from 1905 onward, he set forth his ideas about the distinction between the bourgeois and the proletarian revolutions, the way in which one was to follow the other, and what the link was between them. When he criticized Trotsky's notion of permanent revolution† he justified his scepticism regarding the possibility of a socialist revolution in Russia by saying that 'the emancipation of the workers can only be accomplished by the workers themselves', and concluding that 'a socialist revolution is out of the question unless the masses become class-conscious and organized, trained and educated in an open class struggle against the entire bourgeoisie'.[62]

Moreover, it was because of this same concern of Lenin's that he rejected the ideas of the Socialist-Revolutionaries, and in particular their resort to terrorism, since this tactic of theirs was '*not connected in any way* with work among the masses, for the masses or together with the masses'.[63] It was not the principle of terror that he rejected, nor that of violence; but he considered that it was necessary to 'work for the preparation of such forms of violence as were calculated to bring about the participation of the masses and which guaranteed that participation'.[64]

Centralization and internal democracy

In one of his first pamphlets, written in 1897 and published in Geneva in the following year, Lenin ended thus a passage devoted to 'the tasks of Russian Social-Democrats': 'And so, to work, comrades! ... Russian Social-Democrats have much to do to ... unite the workers' circles and Social-Democratic groups scattered all over Russia into a single *Social-Democratic Labour Party*!'[65] And in 1899, in an article for a socialist paper: 'To effect this unification ... and to get rid

---

* See, for instance, his studies of the law on fines imposed on factory workers, on the laws governing the length of the working day, on the problems of handicraft industry, etc. (in Lenin, Vol. 2).

† See p. 81.

completely of narrow local isolation—such is the immediate and most urgent task of the Russian Social-Democrats.'[66]

Iskra's purpose was to bring about this gathering-together of scattered groups. Lenin's 'centralism' was, however, much more than a striving to unite: it was a conception of the relations obtaining within an organization between the 'leadership' and the 'base', between the 'centre' and the 'sections' dependent upon it, a definition of the rules of hierarchy prevailing in the organization—a whole number of elements, in fact, that bring up the question of democracy in the Party.

In what did the centralism advocated by Lenin actually consist, and what were its implications? The answer was given by Lenin himself: 'The organizational principle of revolutionary Social-Demo-cracy ... strives to proceed from the top downward, and upholds an extension of the rights and powers of the centre in relation to the parts.' In other words, basically the contrast is: 'bureaucracy versus democracy', 'centralism versus autonomism'.[67]

In itself, centralism appeared obviously necessary. Marx's doctrine favours centralism, and is clearly opposed to any federalist tendency. In the Russian socialist movement *Iskra* therefore naturally upheld and propagated the idea of centralism. In 1901, Trotsky, who was soon to offer vigorous opposition to Lenin's centralizing theories, declared that the revolutionary movement would prove to be nothing but a 'Frankenstein's monster' unless it were placed under the autho-rity of a Central Committee endowed with substantial powers. This Central Committee, Trotsky explained, 'will cut off its relations with [any undisciplined organization] ... It will send into the field ... its own detachment, and having endowed it with the necessary resources, the Central Committee will proclaim that this detachment is the local committee.'[68] Lenin himself expressed his idea less emphatically; but it corresponded nevertheless to a plan that had been carefully worked out.

So long as he confined himself to propounding principles, Lenin encountered only timid objections among his future Menshevik adversaries. The divisions that appeared at the congress of 1903, and the beginnings of fratricidal struggle within the Party, revealed the actual significance of the question of centralization. Undoubtedly, the excitement of the occasion, and personal antagonisms, contributed a great deal to the virulence of the debate; it remains true, all the same, that some people had at least an intuition of the deep implications of the controversy between supporters and opponents of centralism, or between convinced defenders of centralism and those who defended it timidly and hesitantly. What was at issue, ultimately, was the choice to be made between effectiveness and internal democracy. Lenin made himself very explicit on this point, especially after the congress, when, on the basis of the divergences that had been revealed, each camp began to give conceptual form to its views. A work that he published in 1904 is extremely illuminating in this field. In his *Letter to a Comrade on Our Organizational Tasks*, Lenin explains at length the hierarchical system that the Party must establish if it intends to put into practice the principle of centralization.

At the head of the organization there must stand a Central Committee 'embracing all the best revolutionary forces ... and *managing* all the general affairs of the party, such as the distribution of literature, the issuing of leaflets, the allocation of forces, the appointment of individuals and groups to take charge of special undertakings, the preparation of demonstrations and an uprising on an all-Russian scale, etc.'[69] In other words, the Central Committee is to guide the life of the Party not only where major decisions are involved but also in all the details of its day-to-day existence. The same principle of guidance and control* must apply at each level of the organization. Lenin lists the different committees that make up the hierarchy: centralization is pushed to the utmost degree and its most restrictive consequences are admitted. 'The committee guides the work of everyone.'[70] That such a conception implies a very strict form of discipline is obvious. Above all, by assigning all power to the executive bodies, it takes little account of the requirements of democracy, or, rather, it ignores them completely. Employing a metaphor thought up by Martov, which, while giving excessive force to Lenin's idea, serves admirably to illuminate it, Lenin declared during the congress of 1903: 'All our party rules, the whole system of centralism now endorsed by the Congress, are nothing but a "state of siege" in respect to the numerous sources of *political vagueness*.'[71]

Lenin had not waited for the congress to express his view that the Party could not afford the luxury of establishing democratic rules to govern its inner working. He explained that ' "the broad democratic principle" presupposes the two following conditions: first, full publicity, and secondly, election to all offices'.[72] Owing, however, to the demands of security, and so of clandestinity, these conditions could not be met by the Russian revolutionary movement. To call for the application of the rules of democracy in the Party was not merely utopian but also harmful; only the police would benefit.[73] Not long before the congress, Trotsky questioned Lenin about his organizational plans.

'We are the stable centre,' Lenin said, 'we are stronger in ideas, and we must exercise the guidance from here.'

* Thus, Lenin accused Martov of making impossible, through his formulation of Paragraph 1 of the Party Rules, *control* over the members of the Party (Lenin, Vol. 7, pp. 268–9).

'Then this will mean a complete dictatorship of the editorial board?' I asked.

'Well, what's wrong with that?' retorted Lenin. 'In the present situation it must be so.'*

A 'complete dictatorship' by the leadership. The expression certainly went farther than Lenin's actual conception: there was never really any question of 'dictatorship' in the Bolshevik Party before 1917. But when, during and after the 1903 congress, Lenin's old comrades-in-arms rose up against him, it was indeed the charge of 'dictatorship' that, in one form or another, they hurled against his proposals.

For example, Martov wrote in *Iskra*, when this had fallen into the hands of the Mensheviks, that Lenin's super-centralism must inevitably lead to the formation of 'a "bureaucratic, putschist organization" run by a leader and divorced from the masses.'[74] Nor was Plekhanov behindhand. Scrutinizing the prerogatives that Lenin proposed should be given to the central leading organs of the party, he declared that the congress, while supposedly sovereign, would henceforth consist only of 'creatures of the Central Committee',[75] and that Lenin's conception of centralism amounted to imposing upon Social-Democracy 'a new edition of the theory of the hero and the crowd'.[76] To which was added, almost as a logical consequence, the epithet 'Bonapartist', applied to the Bolshevik leader.[77] One of the founders of *Iskra*, Vera Zasulich, even compared Lenin to Louis XIV.[78]

These polemical exaggerations should doubtless be taken with the appropriate pinch of salt. Greater attention and weight are due, however, to the observations of Rosa Luxemburg, who denounced the 'pitiless [*rücksichtlos*] centralism' advocated by Lenin, whose thesis was 'that the Central Committee should have the privilege of naming all the local committees of the party.' She stressed the difference between the centralization that was recognized by Marxism as legitimate and indeed indispensable, and the unwarranted interpretation that, in her view, Lenin had given to this. His conception of centralization, she alleged, meant 'the absolute and blind submission of the party sections to the will of the centre'. It seemed to her that submission such as this was an essential feature of Lenin's thinking, and that what it implied in practice was that 'the Central Committee would be the only thinking element in the party'. The result would be 'the blind subordination, in the smallest detail, of all party organs, to the party centre, which alone thinks, guides and decides for all'.[79]

---

* During a certain period Lenin wanted the editorial board of *Iskra* to be made the leading body of the Party, because, being established abroad, it was out of reach of police inroads, and because in it were concentrated the most reliable ideological forces of the movement. The conversation between Lenin and Trotsky is quoted from memory by the latter in *My Life* (p. 157). The particular terms used are therefore less significant than the idea expressed.

The conferring of such extensive powers upon the Central Committee must lead to strengthening the tendency to conservatism in the party. Lenin was wrong in thinking that it would provide a 'bulwark against opportunism'. As she saw the problem, it was not possible to 'secure ourselves in advance against all possibilities of opportunist deviation. Such dangers can be overcome only by the movement itself.'[80] Rosa Luxemburg did not deny the need for a strong organization, but she believed that this would come into being in proportion as, by a continuous, parallel process, the proletariat itself developed its revolutionary activity and proceeded to set up its own class institutions. Answering her, Lenin was to say, in 1905, that her theory 'vulgarized and prostituted Marxism'.[81]

Trotsky treated Lenin's proposals no less roughly. Already at the rostrum of the congress of 1903 he had had this to say to the man who only lately had been his ally: 'Comrade Lenin ... has decided that he and he alone is "the iron hand".'[82] A year later Trotsky wrote: 'Lenin's methods lead to this: the party organization at first substitutes itself for the party as a whole, then the Central Committee substitutes itself for the organization; and finally a single "dictator" substitutes himself for the Central Committee.'[83]

This was only one dart among many others hurled at Lenin by Trotsky on this occasion. He wrote of 'Maximilien [i.e., Robespierre] Lenin', who was trying to subject the proletariat to 'a theoretical Terror', and described him as the 'leader of the reactionary wing of our Party'. Against the author of *What Is To Be Done?* Trotsky rose up in opposition to the 'régime of barrack discipline' that Lenin, it seemed to him, sought to impose upon the workers.[84]

Yet nothing about the Bolshevik organization, as it actually existed at that time, justified Trotsky in talking of dictatorship. True, the absolute necessity of the hierarchical principle was affirmed in that group, along with authoritarian centralization and what Lenin called, without beating about the bush, 'military discipline'.[85] True, there was no internal democracy in the Russian Social-Democratic Party of that time, but this fact was quite unconnected with Leninism. In their day-to-day actual political practice there was little to choose in this respect between the Bolsheviks and the Mensheviks: down to the Revolution of 1905 they both employed the same methods, in which co-option of leaders was the rule and election the exception.* For example, the Menshevik Garvi admitted that the Moscow Committee of his faction 'was built from the top to the bottom on the principle of co-option'.[86]

* When analysing the pre-revolutionary period, writers who are not at all indulgent in their attitude to Leninism agree that in practice there was no notable difference between the Mensheviks of that time and their Bolshevik opponents. Neither faction went in for democratic methods. See Ulam, p. 246; Schapiro, *Communist Party*, pp. 57–8; Keep, *Rise of Social Democracy*, p. 147; Lane, p. 209.

2*

Lenin had no occasion, during the brief period that separated the birth of Bolshevism from the first Russian Revolution, to elaborate the principles of 'democratic centralism' that were to become the Golden Rule of Communist practice. These principles, moreover, were to be affected, in their first formulation, by the twofold influence of a theoretical conception that was still in process of development, and of the modification imposed by events. In 1905, when Tsarism tottered for the first time, Leninism was still only a set of 'pointers' rather than of firm and binding rules. These owed a great deal to the circumstances that gave rise to them, and they bear the marks not only of mature reflection and gradual intellectual perfection but also of exacerbation caused by controversy and polemic. In this way, ideas that at that time only existed in a sketchy form came to assume, for their defenders and their opponents alike, the exaggerated character that they were destined to acquire in a future that was then unforeseeable.

By running so far ahead in their thinking, Trotsky, Luxemburg and Plekhanov were also, whether consciously or not, laying a bet on what the future held in store—taking their stand on a hypothesis for which reality did not yet provide support, and from which it was in any case still possible to escape. This explains the paradoxically prophetic nature of statements which owed less to critical analysis than to diatribe and denigration, and in which ill-will, rancour and spite played a bigger part than political judgment.

As for Leninism, its future remained open. The ideas set forth by Lenin, being still young, possessed the malleability and flexibility of their youth. The testing-time for which they had been prepared was, moreover, to bring a confrontation between the implications of theory and the demands of reality, and to produce the first modifications and adaptations imposed by necessity. This was the effect upon Leninism of the Revolution of 1905.

Bolshevism in 1905*

'Bloody Sunday' in St Petersburg (9 January, 1905),† when hundreds of thousands of demonstrators saw their ranks decimated by the soldiers' rifle-fire, took the Russian socialist organizations completely by surprise. The great demonstrations in Petersburg that marked the beginning of the revolutionary upsurge came up against apathy, lack of preparation, and even hostility where the socialist groups were

* On this subject see also Chapter 3, 'Lenin in 1905'.
† All dates for the period preceding February 1st, 1918, are given according to the Julian calendar then in use in Russia, which was thirteen days behind the Gregorian. Thus, January 9th in the Russian calendar of that time corresponded to January 22nd in the Western usage.

concerned — and the Bolsheviks in particular. During the months that followed 'Bloody Sunday', while the popular agitation was mounting, throughout the country, in amplitude and intensity, Lenin's followers remained reticent and hesitant in the face of some of the most striking aspects of this agitation. The progress made by the latter was such, however, and its successes, though ephemeral, so remarkable, that Bolshevism could not but fall under its influence. The Leninist organization, as shaped by the Revolution of 1905, once the importance of this movement became plain, was no longer the same as that which Lenin had worked to create. The revolution impelled Leninism to link the organization with the masses, the vanguard party with the working class.

Lenin had already been concerned about establishing this link at the time when he was laying the foundations of Bolshevism. For him, indeed, it was not a matter merely of forming an organization of professional revolutionaries whose small numbers would constitute a guarantee of homogeneity and secrecy. What had to be done in addition was to sketch out the mechanisms by which this leading nucleus could succeed in organizing, influencing and winning over the proletariat. *What Is To Be Done?* examines this problem and puts forward a plan of a very general kind in which Lenin distinguishes between the revolutionary organization properly so called, on the one hand, and on the other, a broader, more open organization, or rather series of organizations of various sorts — trade unions, friendly societies, educational associations, and so on, open to all workers, whether socialists or not, and as far as possible operating publicly and making the most of the scanty possibilities that existed for legal activity.[87] These workers' organizations constitute the link between the Party and the masses; they must be open to penetration by Bolshevik (or Social-Democratic) activists, and so to the influence of Marxism; though linked with the Party they are nevertheless not the Party.

These ideas were still somewhat abstract. Lenin made them more precise in his *Letter to a Comrade about Our Organizational Tasks*. Here he explains how he conceives the relations between the revolutionary Party organization and the mass of the workers, and gives details regarding the structure he wishes the Party to possess, and how it is to function. The local committees, themselves subject to the authority of the Central Committee, 'should direct *all* aspects of the local movement', and 'should consist of fully convinced Social-Democrats who devote themselves entirely to Social-Democratic activities'.[88] The authority of these committees is to extend over a series of technical bodies and over sections covering particular territorial areas: for example, 'propagandist groups', or 'groups for the distribution of literature', and 'district groups' serving as links between the local committee and 'factory committees'. Relations between the latter

and the local committee, and between the local committee and the
'district groups', are to be governed by the centralist principle and by a
strict hierarchical subordination, the 'district group' being, like the
'propagandist group', nothing more than a 'branch' of the local committee. Lenin repeats in this connexion that application of 'the elective
principle and decentralization ... is absolutely impermissible to any
wide degree and even altogether detrimental to revolutionary work
carried on under an autocracy'. Finally, at the 'base' are the 'factory
committees', uniting 'a very small number of *revolutionaries*, who take
their instructions and receive their authority to carry on all Social-
Democratic work in the factory *directly from the committee*'. And
Lenin emphasizes that 'every member of the factory committee
should regard himself as an agent of the committee, obliged to submit
to all its orders and to observe all the "laws and customs" of the
"army in the field" which he has joined and from which in time of
war he has no right to absent himself without official leave'.[89]

It still remained to envisage the way in which contact would be
established between the Party and the unorganized masses of the
working class. On this point Lenin merely indicates that the 'factory
committees' are to be divided into 'sub-committees', embracing
workers some of whom have joined the Party while others have not.
The composition of these sub-committees is to be more or less heterogeneous, and their size and the openness of their activity to vary in
accordance with possibilities and with the requirements of security.[90]
In this way is to be formed what Bukharin called 'the second of the
Party's concentric circles',[91] and a Bolshevik militant its 'periphery'.
The hard and homogeneous kernel becomes progressively diluted
into something nebulous; the Party's ramifications have to spread
throughout the proletariat, its roots plunge down into the working
class as a whole. The organization appears as a complex structure:
'a vertical network made up of the party organizations themselves in
a strictly hierarchical order and an equally rigid pattern of subordination; and a horizontal network of supplementary organizations,
ostensibly nonpartisan but in practice intended to execute the will of the
vertical network'.[92] It will be seen how completely this conception
emphasizes the absolute necessity of 'military discipline', and the
almost unlimited powers of the committees—first and foremost those
made up exclusively of professional revolutionaries.

The description of the Odessa organization given by the Bolshevik
Pyatnitsky is probably valid for the Russian socialist movement as a
whole in the period before the 1905 revolution. According to Pyatnitsky, the principle of co-option was applied 'from top to bottom'.

The regional committees of the large towns had divided among
[their] members the work of uniting all the Party cells of a given

district (or sub-district), and of organising new cells where there were none. The organisers of the sub-districts invited the best elements of the cells to the sub-district committees. When a member of the sub-district committee dropped out ... the remaining members co-opted another with the consent of the district committee. The district committees in turn were composed of the best elements of the sub-district committees. The city committees were formed by the union of the various groups and cells of a given city and were subject to the approval of the Central Committee. City committees had the right to co-opt new members. When a city committee was arrested as a body, the Central Committee of the Party designated one or more members to form a new committee and those appointed co-opted suitable comrades from the workers of that region to complete the new committee.[93]

Two points emerge from this account: the important role played by the committees, and the absence of any electoral procedure. This situation was characteristic of all Russia's socialist organizations down to 1905. Obviously it was bound to undergo profound changes as a result of the revolutionary events in Russia in that year. In moving from exile into Russia itself, going over from doctrinal conflicts to real struggle, from internal quarrels to an onslaught, at last, upon the class enemy, from clandestine activities to an open offensive, Bolshevism was to experience substantial alterations, and this in two spheres of special importance, namely, the linking of the Party with the masses, and inner-Party democracy.

The time for distrust was past. The great upsurge of the masses was opening new horizons before the socialist movement. Only this new climate of politics explains how it was that, in a Social-Democratic Party that had recovered its sense of unity and realized the immense resources that were at its disposal, the Bolsheviks, and Lenin in particular, now came to give a different cast to their idea of organization.

From the elite party to the mass party

In 1902 Lenin considered, as he put it in *What Is To Be Done?*, that by making the Party 'accessible to the masses' what in fact one did was to make 'revolutionaries accessible to the police'. In 1905, however, everything took on a fresh significance. Opening the Party to the masses became a necessity: this would make it accessible to the revolutionary blast, giving it a chance to keep at the head of a mass offensive ... or at least to follow this offensive. Hardly a month after 'Bloody Sunday', Lenin had realized this necessity. He wrote in the Bolshevik organ *Vpered*: 'Now the open propaganda of democratic ideas and demands, no longer persecuted by the weakened government, has

spread so widely that we must learn to adjust ourselves to this entirely
new scope of the movement.' This adaptation to events meant that
the distinction between the *organization* and the *movement*, between
the 'horizontal network' and the 'vertical network', and, finally,
between the vanguard and the working class, began to grow more
tenuous.

> We must considerably increase the membership of all Party and
> Party-connected organisations in order to be able to keep up to
> some extent with the stream of popular revolutionary energy
> which has been a hundredfold strengthened ... Recruit more
> young workers, extend the normal framework of all Party organi-
> sations from committees to factory groups, craft unions and
> student circles ... Hundreds of new organisations should be set
> up for the purpose without a moment's delay. Yes, hundreds;
> this is no hyperbole ... '[94]

This desire to bring a larger number of members into the Party was
focused upon youth in particular, and especially working-class youth.
It is important in this connexion to emphasize the extent to which
intellectual elements predominated, especially among the leaders, in
the Russian Social-Democratic *Labour* Party, and this among the
Bolsheviks as well as among the Mensheviks.* Despite certain
'ouvriériste' tendencies that showed themselves in the Menshevik
camp, Martov admitted that the leadership of the Social-Democratic
organization was in the hands of 'a special little world of intellectuals'.[95] The statistics available allow us to sustain and extend the
application of this statement, especially as regards the social composition of the successive congresses of Russian Social-Democracy
before 1914. The first of these, held at Minsk in 1898, hardly justifies
the drawing of any valid conclusions, in view of the small number of
delegates present—nine, only one of whom was a worker.[96] The
figures for the 1903 congress are more conclusive: out of the sixty-
odd delegates who took part, only three or four were workers.†
At the congress in 1905 none of the delegates present was a worker.‡
During the discussions, very useful information was given regarding
the social composition of the Bolshevik committees in Russia. The
Petrograd Committee had not a single worker among its members,
and in the Northern Committee only one out of the eight members
was a worker, while in most of the committees of the Caucasian
towns, with the exception of Tiflis, the number of worker members

---

* See Chapter 4.
† Possony, p. 94, quotes the figure 3; Wolfe, p. 230, gives 4.
‡ Krupskaya, p. 125. The Third Congress of the R.S.D.L.P. was convened by the
Bolsheviks alone and was attended only by delegates belonging to that faction.

was either very small or else zero.[97] A situation like this did not fail
to give rise to acute dissatisfaction in the ranks of the Party, which
was manifested in the course of the debates at the London congress.
Several delegates complained of the over-representation of the intelligentsia, adding that these 'committee-men' showed a distrustful attitude towards workers and avoided giving them posts of responsibility.[98]
Thus, while about 62 per cent of the Bolshevik membership in 1905
belonged to the working class,* this element is found to have been
represented less and less as one ascends the hierarchy of the organization, and is sometimes entirely missing at and above the level of the
local committee. Lenin insisted at the congress of April 1905 that the
proportion of workers in the committees be raised to 80 per cent.
Six months later he declared that 'now we must wish for the new Party
organizations to have one Social-Democratic intellectual to several
hundred Social-Democratic workers.'[99] The efforts being made by
the Bolsheviks and the Mensheviks were reinforced by the effects of
the revolutionary events themselves, and results were not lacking.
While the total numbers of the reunited Party increased markedly,
the percentage of workers in its leading organs increased in almost as
spectacular a fashion. At the congress of reunification, held at Stockholm in April–May 1906, there were 108 intellectuals to 36 workers
among the delegates. A year later, at the London congress, the
number of worker-delegates had risen to 116, or over one-third of the
total.[100] What was at least as important, however, as the social origin
of the Party's leading figures, and perhaps even more so, was the
increase in the Party's membership.

In January 1905, on the eve of the revolution, the Bolshevik organizations had 8,400 members altogether. By the spring of 1906 the total
membership of the R.S.D.L.P. stood at 48,000, of whom 34,000 were
Bolsheviks and 14,000 Mensheviks.[101] In October the total membership
exceeded 70,000, and then, despite the slowing-down of the revolutionary offensive, underwent a further increase, since, according to
the figures given at the London congress, in 1907, the R.S.D.L.P.
(leaving aside the Bundists, and the Polish and Lettish sections) had
84,000 members, of whom 46,000 were Bolsheviks and 38,000 Mensheviks.[102]

Growth such as this had a profound effect on the very nature of the
Party.† Its structure had become more flexible, and had even cracked
under the pressure of events. Moreover, the climate of comparative
political freedom, resulting from the victories of the revolution,
offered the Party opportunities for propaganda and means of spreading

* According to statistics compiled in 1922. See on this Fainsod, *How Russia Is Ruled*,
pp. 248–50.
† A Bolshevik militant who had left Moscow in the early months of 1905 said that when
he came back he 'did not recognize' the new political set-up in his district (Lane, p. 104).

its influence that had been unheard-of up to that time. The Leninist
Party, a tightly knit group of professional revolutionaries, was, in its
way, a reflection of the autocratic régime against which it fought.
When that régime was obliged to liberalize itself, the organization
that Lenin led took on a new character: one year after the outbreak of
the revolution he described this organization, for the first time, as 'a
mass party'.[103] This description did not refer merely to the number
of members, but also implied a change in the Party's structure, a new
conception of the relations between the Party and the proletariat.

In the first article that he wrote in November 1905, on his return
from exile, Lenin, examining the problem, now urgent, of 'reorganizing' the Party, wrote these remarkable words: 'Our Party has stag-
nated while working underground ... It has been suffocating underground during the last few years. The "underground" is breaking
up.'[104] He considered that while 'the secret apparatus of the Party
must be maintained,' it was 'absolutely necessary to create many new
legal and semi-legal Party organizations (and organizations associated with the Party)'.[105] Going beyond that task, however, it was
necessary to conceive the basis of the Party in a new way: 'The new
form of organization, or rather the new form of the basic organizational nucleus of the workers' party, must be definitely much broader
than were the old circles. Apart from this, the new nucleus will most
likely have to be a less rigid, more "free", more "loose" (*lose*) organization.'[106] Towards the end of 1905 a change in the structures of the
Social-Democratic movement was indeed observable: in St Petersburg and also in the provinces there appeared 'political associations'
and 'workers' clubs', in the formation of which the Mensheviks
usually took the initiative, but which the Bolsheviks also helped to
form. A new phenomenon in Russian political life, they translated
into reality the Party's desire to open itself to the masses.[107]

More than that: Lenin had thought that the proletariat's revolutionary potential needed a 'push' from without, and yet now this
pessimism was being refuted by events. Without any significant
outside 'stimulation', and in the absence of any Party organization
capable of rousing, directing and leading the activity of the masses,
the latter were developing a revolutionary movement of an essentially political character and of extraordinary scope. It was often to
be observed that the proletariat's awareness of the situation was
clearer, and in any case that it had greater boldness, than that of the
leaders who were supposed to be its guides. Drawing lessons from the
Moscow insurrection of December 1905, Lenin acknowledged that
'the proletariat sensed sooner than its leaders the change in the objective conditions of the struggle and the need for a transition from the
strike to an uprising'.[108]

This is not the only analogy discoverable at this period between

Lenin's ideas, as amended by the events of the revolution, and those that Rosa Luxemburg had expressed earlier. In March 1906 he wrote: 'Mention a period in Russian or world history, find any six months or six years when as much was done for the free and independent organization of the masses of the people as was done during the six weeks of the revolutionary whirlwind in Russia ... '[109] He declared that the general strike, which was due to the initiative of the masses, and not of any party, was also a form of organization. And he ended with an ardent eulogy of 'the organizing abilities of the people, particularly of the proletariat'.[110] Could this mean anything else but the substitution of the masses for the Party in one of its essential functions — in a sense, a rehabilitation of proletarian spontaneity?

The Party rules had formerly been conceived as a 'bulwark' against the entry into the Party of dubious elements, easy prey for opportunism. Now these fears were swept away. Raising for consideration the possibility that the Party 'would cease to be the conscious vanguard of its class,' and that, instead, 'its role would be reduced to that of a tail,'[111] Lenin said: 'Let me not exaggerate this danger, comrades,' and went on to insist that 'it would be simply ridiculous to doubt that the workers who belong to our Party, or who will join it tomorrow at the invitation of the Central Committee, will be Social-Democrats in ninety-nine cases out of a hundred.' Furthermore, he warned the Party members: 'Don't invent bugaboos, comrades! Don't forget that in every live and growing party there will always be elements of instability, vacillation, wavering. But these elements can be influenced, and they will submit to the influence of the steadfast and solid core of Social-Democrats.'[112] In June of that same year he had denounced the dangers inherent in the slogan of ' "independent activity" of the workers'.[113] A few months later, having submitted himself to learning from the experience of the revolution, and after the revolution itself had taken huge steps forward, he acknowledged the merits, occasional but fundamental, of proletarian spontaneity and initiative.

From democratization of the party to democratic centralism
The upheaval in the country in 1905 entailed an upheaval hardly less thoroughgoing in the Party. 'It will be necessary in very many cases to start from the beginning,'[114] Lenin declared in November 1905. This will to renovation found expression in the democratizing of the Party's structures and methods. As Martov testifies, 'the leaders of both factions applied themselves with vigour to getting the elective principle accepted.'[115] At the Bolshevik congress in London in April 1905, Lenin successfully moved a resolution which noted that, although 'the *full* assertion of the elective principle, possible and necessary under conditions of political freedom, is unfeasible under the autocracy,' nevertheless, 'even under the autocracy this principle

could be applied to a much larger extent than it is today'.[116] At the same time, the quasi-arbitrary powers wielded by the committees and, at the peak of the hierarchy, by the Central Committee itself, needed to be curbed, and the Party also took steps in this direction.

Lenin said, speaking of the powers hitherto accorded to the committees, that 'previous formal prerogatives inevitably lose their significance at the present time'.[117] The Bolshevik congress of 1905 declared in favour of 'the autonomy of the committees' in relation to the Central Committee, whose authority was seriously pruned.[118] Talking of the organization in Russia's capital, Lenin said:

> The St Petersburg worker Social-Democrats know that the whole Party organisation is now built on a *democratic* basis. This means that *all* the Party members take part in the election of officials, committee members and so forth, that *all* the Party members discuss and *decide* questions concerning the political campaigns of the proletariat, and that *all* the Party members *determine* the line of tactics of the Party organisations.[119]

At the head of the socialist movement in Petersburg a *conference* was placed—an elected body, meeting at least twice a month, subject to re-election every six months, and itself electing the Party Committee in the capital. Lenin said of this arrangement that it 'makes possible and inevitable the participation of the majority of outstanding workers in the guidance of all the affairs of the entire local organization'.[120] That the Party members did participate on a large scale in the discussion of major political problems, and that they took a hand in the decisions made by Russian Social-Democracy, is proved by the fact that, in the capital alone, 120 group meetings were devoted to preparing for the elections to the First Duma. The decision to boycott these elections resulted from a fairly large vote: 1,168 for the boycott, 926 against.[121] Lenin recommended that, as a general rule, a 'referendum in the Party' should be carried out where any important political question was concerned.[122]

In the Moscow organization the elective principle was likewise introduced and applied: a system of elections at different levels (factory committees, district committees, town committees) ensured the representative character of the local leadership, down 'to nearly the end of 1907'.[123] In Odessa, at a meeting of the town's Bolsheviks in October 1905, it was decided to democratize the structure of the Party organization, making use of the model provided by the German Social-Democratic Party.[124] At the same time, Lenin showed himself favourable to a 'liberal' interpretation of the right of expression in the Party, especially through the press. 'There is no question,' he declared in November 1905, 'that literature is least of all subject to mechanical adjustment or levelling, to the rule of the majority over the minority.

There is no question, either, that in this field greater scope must undoubtedly be allowed for personal initiative, individual inclination, thought and fantasy ... '[125]

It was in this period and this climate that the foundations were laid, and the main outlines drawn, of *democratic centralism*. In its origins, this reflected the *rapprochement* that had taken place during the revolution between Bolsheviks and Mensheviks: though adopted by the congress of the R.S.D.L.P. held in Stockholm in 1906, where the Menshevik faction was predominant,* it was incorporated in the Party rules on Lenin's initiative. He it was who at this congress put down a resolution stating that 'the principle of democratic centralism in the Party is now universally recognized'.[126]

What was the concrete meaning of this notion? In this connexion a statement made by Lenin in a report he gave on the Stockholm congress is especially important. He said that there was still work to be done 'really to apply the principles of democratic centralism in Party organization, to work tirelessly to make the local organizations the principal organizational units of the Party in fact and not merely in name, and to see to it that all the higher-standing bodies are elected, accountable and subject to recall'.[127] This, however, was only a first approximation. Democratic centralism had further implications. Paradoxically, perhaps, it brought into Party life a greater *autonomy* for the regional sections.† Moreover, its application 'implies universal and full *freedom to criticize*, so long as this does not disturb the unity *of a definite action*; it rules out *all* criticism which disrupts or makes difficult the *unity* of an action decided on by the Party'.[128] And again, on the same theme: 'If we have really and seriously decided to introduce democratic centralism in our Party, and if we have resolved to draw the masses of the workers into intelligent decision of Party questions, we must have these questions discussed in the press, at meetings, in circles and at group meetings.'[129] Alluding to the discussion that was then going on in the socialist movement about the opportuneness of armed insurrection and its implications, Lenin declared: 'In the heat of battle, when the proletarian army is straining every nerve, *no* criticism *whatever* can be permitted in its ranks. But before the call for action is issued, there should be the broadest and freest discussion and appraisal of the resolution, of its arguments and its various propositions.'[130]

Freedom of discussion, unity of action. What still needed to be clarified was, who was to have the power to issue these 'calls for action' which had the effect of suspending the right to free criticism?

---

* According to Schapiro (*Communist Party*, p. 73), out of 111 delegates there were 62 Mensheviks, as against 44 or 46 Bolsheviks.

† 'The autonomy of every Party organization ... must become a reality.' (Lenin, Vol. 10, p. 376).

Lenin's answer was clear: only *the Party Congress* possessed such power.*
At the same time, however, Lenin thought it was legitimate, in certain
circumstances, to 'fight ideologically against those decisions of the
Congress which we regard as erroneous'.[131] The conclusion that
followed was that the criterion distinguishing the field in which it
was legitimate to criticize and that in which unanimity was obligatory
depended on something rather vague: was the Party engaged in
action on the given issue or not? According to Lenin, it was up to the
Party congress to clarify that point.

It happened, in any case, on several occasions that the Bolsheviks
refused to put into effect decisions taken by the Central Committee
appointed by the Stockholm Congress, which had a Menshevik
majority. They argued that these decisions were not in conformity
with those of the Congress, and they invoked the principles of
democratic centralism. Thus, after the Central Committee had ruled
that 'guerrilla actions' were repudiated by the Party, Lenin openly
advised 'all the numerous fighting groups of our Party to ... undertake
a number of guerrilla actions in strict conformity with the decisions
of the Congress ... '† And on another occasion he said that 'it is clear
that if there is a new Duma campaign the Party will have to fight
against the Central Committee's Duma slogans'.[132]

The definition of democratic centralism includes one final aspect:
it implies the right to existence and to freedom of expression for a
minority in the Party. Lenin had indeed already spoken of minority
rights in 1903 and in 1904,[133] but it was from 1905 onward that he
became particularly explicit on this subject. At the Bolshevik congress
of 1905, for instance, it was resolved that 'the Minority now has the
unconditional right, guaranteed by the Party Rules, to advocate its
views and to carry on an ideological struggle, so long as the disputes
and differences do not lead to disorganization, ... split our forces, or
hinder the concerted struggle against the autocracy and the capitalists.'[134]

When the R.S.D.L.P. was reunited, the presence of Bolsheviks
and Mensheviks within the same organization gave new significance
to the problem of minority rights. These rights were defined by Lenin
in a very generous spirit. 'For there can be no mass party,' he wrote in
1907, 'no party of a class, without full clarity of essential shadings,
without an open struggle between various tendencies.'[135] Referring
to the work of the Stockholm Congress, he said that, 'strictly speaking,
these private arrangements at factional meetings are quite natural ... '[136]

---

* Lenin, Vol. 11, p. 168. Lenin wrote regarding a dispute between the Bolsheviks and
the Menshevik-dominated Central Committee: 'We abide by the decisions of the Congress
but *under no circumstances* shall we submit to decisions of the Central Committee which
violate the decisions of the Congress.'

† Lenin, Vol. 11, p. 169. For these 'guerrilla actions', see Chapter 4.

One cannot but call attention to such 'liberalism' in the way that democratic centralism was first defined.

It may be objected that Lenin's anxiety to assert and safeguard the rights of the minority was conditioned by the circumstance that at that time his Menshevik opponents enjoyed a majority in the Party. In *One Step Forward, Two Steps Back*, the work that he wrote in 1904 to explain how the split of 1903 came about, the Bolshevik leader frankly acknowledged that 'perceiving that we were in the minority ... we appealed to the Congress to protect the rights of the minority.'[137] It was, at all events, no accident that introduction of the principle of democratic centralism, its definition in a broad way, and an attempt to put it into effect occurred at the moment when Leninism, driven by events to involve itself in proletarian 'spontaneity and initiative', was brought for the first time on to that terrain for which it was destined: revolution.

Leninist sectarianism

The years 1905–7 show the extent to which the Bolshevik organization, and, more generally, the organization of the socialist movement in Russia, owed their expansion and transformation into a 'mass party' to the revolutionary outburst, with its unleashing of latent energies and the realization of hopes that had long seemed very remote.

The period beginning in 1908, which was marked by the triumph of reaction in Russia, with, first, stagnation, and then retreat and collapse of the revolutionary movement, produced the opposite effect. The advance of the revolution had raised the quasi-embryonic organization of Russian Social-Democracy to the level of a party that embraced tens of thousands of members: defeat of the revolution brought degeneration of the new-born Party into a sectarian organization.

This period of reaction is particularly important in the shaping of Leninism and Bolshevism. It was during this period, according to Lenin himself, that the Party was 'reconstructed and to a certain extent built anew'.[138] Now for the working-class movement this was a period above all of doubt and demoralization, and so of internal quarrels, desertions and setbacks. Lenin described it as 'the period of disorganization and disintegration'[139] and as 'the period of absolute stagnation, of dead calm, hangings and suicides'.[140]

Towards the end of December 1907 Lenin left Russia. This marked the beginning of a second period of exile, about which he wrote to Maxim Gorky: 'Life in exile is now a hundred times harder than it was before the revolution. Life in exile and squabbling are inseparable.'[141] In January 1908 he found himself once again in Geneva, but this time in a mood of despair. 'I have a feeling as if I've come here to be buried,' he told his friends.[142]

The decline that the Leninist organization suffered in this period cannot be understood unless account is taken of the circumstances surrounding it. Krupskaya sums them up in these words: 'During the years of reaction the number of political emigrants from Russia increased tremendously. People fled abroad to escape the savage persecutions of the Tsarist régime, people with frayed and shattered nerves, without prospects for the future, without a penny to their name, and without any help from Russia ... We had more than enough of squabbling and bickering.'[143] This time of crisis brought about complete moral collapse in the case of some of the émigrés. Describing the atmosphere that prevailed among Russian revolutionaries in Paris, about 1910, Pyatnitsky records that the exiles were not always able to earn a living. 'Some of them sank so low that they refused to look for work altogether,' preferring to live at other people's expense, resorting to trickery, swindling their compatriots or Frenchmen. 'Things went so far that not a single evening arranged by the Russian colony in aid of the émigrés' fund passed off without scandals or brawls ... '[144] 'Isolation from Russia, the engulfing atmosphere of the accursed émigré slough, weighs so heavily on one here that living contact with Russia is our only salvation,'[145] Lenin had written in 1904. After 1907, exile being now more bitter than before the revolution, the feeling of depression was heavier still.

In Russia itself matters were no better in the socialist movement. The deep crisis from which it was suffering was shown first and foremost in a steep decline in numbers, due to losses caused by exile, the massive measures of repression, and widespread loss of enthusiasm. In 1907 the Bolsheviks and Mensheviks together had 85,000 members. Recalling in 1922 the situation of the Party in the years 1908–9, Zinoviev commented that 'it may plainly be said that at this unhappy period the Party as a whole ceased to exist'.[146] In 1909 the Bolsheviks had no more than six local committees left in the whole of Russia.[147] In 1912 Lenin acknowledged that 'at present the *real* position of the Party is such that almost everywhere in the localities there are informal, extremely small and tiny Party workers' groups and nuclei that meet irregularly'.[148]

Nor was the decline only a matter of numbers. After 1907 the Russian Social-Democrats were no longer able to hold a congress. The crisis spared neither Mensheviks nor Bolsheviks, who, after their coming-together and reunification, now split once again, and this time for good. The Menshevik movement collapsed to an even worse degree than that of the Bolsheviks. The Mensheviks possessed no organization capable of withstanding the pressure of events, and became nothing more than a series of groups divided among themselves.

Many of them no longer recognized the existence of a revolutionary Social-Democratic Party, or regarded such a party as useful. They favoured replacing it by a new political formation, legal and open in character, based mainly on economic institutions and educational clubs. Those Mensheviks who did not share these 'liquidationist' views were not in a position to oppose them with either structures or an outlook of any coherence. In the words of a historian who is not at all sympathetic to the Bolsheviks, 'the Mensheviks in rejecting this notion were incapable of producing a unified and disciplined party of their own. Eventually their group was bound to dissolve into a chorus of quarrelling prima donnas.'[149]

On their part, the Bolsheviks also experienced internal divisions and fratricidal conflicts. They had their 'Otzovists' and 'Ultimatumists', forming a 'Left' wing of the Leninist organization, and their 'Conciliators', on the 'Right'.

The 'Otzovists' [from the Russian verb meaning 'to recall'] wanted the Party to break completely with the deputies who represented it in the Duma and confine itself exclusively to illegal and clandestine activities. The 'Ultimatumists' called for the Party's parliamentary group to be made more strictly subject to the Party. The 'Conciliators' favoured an attempt to unite with certain elements among the Mensheviks. None of these tendencies, however, was allowed any real rights in the Party by Lenin. On the contrary, for the first time in the history of the movement an attempt was made to impose a rigid line upon the Party and to introduce the idea that it should be monolithic in character. This development followed from an objective reality—after the period of expansion and 'opening', the Leninist organization, reverting to its initial principles, and accentuating these, was reasserting the features of centralization and clandestinity that had characterized it before the revolution of 1905. And, in the first place, stress was being laid once more—not without reason, since the Party was indeed threatened with disintegration—upon the merits of organization. 'Strengthen the organization' was the slogan issued by Lenin in July 1908, as the period of reaction got under way.[150] Whereas in 1905 the autonomy of the committees had been proclaimed, in 1909 strengthening of 'the central institutions of the Party' became a necessity once more.[151] After a period in which the 'periphery' had been expanded at the expense of the 'nucleus', the latter now seemed to be recovering all its prerogatives, while the basic committees, where in the previous period members and sympathizers had mingled, were now to be made up exclusively of members in the strict sense only.[152]

Most of these changes were not so much the result of deliberate intention or considerations of principle as of the objective conditions of the political struggle in Russia, where the régime, despite its claims to being semi-liberal, remained profoundly repressive in character.

In this situation, as in many others, Leninism showed its great flexibility. A fresh demonstration of this flexibility was given in the next
period, between 1912 and the outbreak of the First World War. This
period saw a rebirth of the revolutionary struggle, a spectacular revival
of the strike movement, and a new mobilization of the industrial
proletariat. Aware of the possibilities thus created, Lenin now emphasized on a number of occasions the need for the Party to adapt itself
to this changed situation, by expanding its activity into the legal
sphere wherever this should prove possible. Nevertheless, right down
to the eve of the revolution of 1917 the Bolshevik organization remained subject to a leadership working clandestinely, and to the rules
of conspiratorial activity.

It was in a party such as this, turned in upon itself for a long time
by force of circumstances, cut off from its working-class hinterland,
often reduced to the sluggish conditions of exile, enfeebled, split and
scattered, that sectarian tendencies developed which were destined to
set their imprint upon the subsequent history of Communism. Among
these must be mentioned first and foremost a deliberate striving to
transform the Party into a monolithic bloc. This resulted from an
attitude of strictness on two fronts—against Menshevism, and against
those tendencies within Lenin's organization whose strategy, or
merely tactics, conflicted with Lenin's own ideas.

The struggle against the Mensheviks was doubtless not lacking in
justification, since the defeat of the revolution had convinced the
Leninists that that undertaking had suffered from weakness in preparation, co-ordination and organization. Most of the Mensheviks
drew the contrary conclusion, namely, that the defeat of the attempted
revolution proved that a *reformist* policy was the right one, especially
as such a policy seemed to them to be favoured by the relaxation in
the autocratic régime.* Leninism sought to debunk such 'constitutional illusions', and denounced the habit that the Mensheviks had
acquired of 'playing at parliamentarism when no parliament whatever
exists'.[153] Furthermore, the desire of many Mensheviks to set up a new
party, unencumbered with any clandestine organization, had widened
the gulf that separated the two factions. Antagonism between them
grew more acute, without the adversaries, most of whom were in
exile, feeling obliged to reckon with the aspiration towards unity
which, in Russia, continued to inspire the socialist workers.† The
trend was towards a complete break between Bolsheviks and Menshe-

---

* On the illusory nature of the 'liberalization' of Tsarism, see Liebman, pp. 34–40.

† In a letter written in 1911 Stalin depicted the quarrels between the socialists exiled in
Europe as a 'storm in a teacup', adding that the Russian workers 'begin to look with
scorn on doings abroad'. (Souvarine, p. 128. See also Trotsky, *Stalin*, p. 133. The letter
was reprinted in *Zarya Vostoka* [Tbilisi], December 23rd, 1925. It is not included in
Stalin's *Works*). Lenin admitted in 1914 that 'the workers are tired of splits'. (Vol. 20,
p. 319.)

viks. This was consummated when, in January 1912, at a conference of his followers held in Prague, Lenin constituted his faction a Party in its own right.

This break with old comrades-in-arms—that 'Right wing' which a few years earlier Lenin had still looked on as a normal component of any working-class party—did not, however, ensure by itself the absolute homogeneity of the Leninist organization, which experienced internal tensions that the atmosphere of exile helped to exacerbate. When Lenin, after having resigned himself in November 1905 to following his Party in a boycott of the First Duma,[154] started to expound the advantages of participation in parliamentary activities, advocating that the Duma be used for revolutionary purposes, an important section of the Bolsheviks saw in this attitude of his a proof of opportunism. Uniting the 'Otzovists' and the 'Ultimatumists', and led by Bogdanov, one of the few personalities among the Bolsheviks who were capable of taking on Lenin, this section launched a vigorous offensive against the latter. He was accused of having established a 'party Tsarism', of setting up his own dictatorship, and of 'deviating towards Menshevism'.[155] This 'Leftist' tendency* held very strong positions inside Russia, possessing a majority in several centres, including St Petersburg itself.† Lenin therefore resolved to wage ruthless war against Bogdanov's followers.

The struggle culminated, in July 1909, in the expulsion of the 'Leftist' leader, but Lenin's fight against the 'Leftists' did not stop there. Recalling that he had formerly spoken in favour of the Right for different trends or tendencies in the Party to express themselves, but not being keen to allow his opponents to take advantage of such a right, Lenin declared that, far from constituting a trend they were only a 'minor group', and that 'to confuse a trend with minor groups means condemning oneself to *intrigue* in Party politics'.[156] The drive towards monolithicity also found other obstacles to crush. There was indeed some reason to claim that the 'Liquidators', who called for replacement of the existing Social-Democratic Party by an open, legal organization of a new type, had put themselves outside the camp of Russian socialism, at least as this was traditionally conceived. But Lenin did not stop there. He declared that the 'Conciliators'—those who, like Trotsky, sought to bring Bolsheviks and Mensheviks together again— also had 'nothing in common with the R.S.D.L.P.'.[157]

Having taken the path of excommunication, Lenin hurled himself along it with great fervour. Since the spirit of conciliation was not confined to the 'Trotskyists', desperately anxious to restore Party unity, he hunted down all manifestations of it that appeared among the

---

* It was in July 1908 that Lenin used the term 'Leftist' for the first time, applying it to certain Socialist Revolutionaries (Vol. 15, p. 148).

† Lenin acknowledges this in a number of places (Vol. 15, p. 431; Vol. 16, pp. 41, 65–6).

Bolsheviks themselves. Some of his followers who hesitated to copy his own intransigence towards other tendencies in Russian socialism he accused of having nothing in common with Bolshevism. Absolute homogeneity of the Party was increasingly presented as being a necessity if political struggle was to be effective. This necessary homogeneity was made to apply, moreover, not just in the realm of principles but also in that of strategy, and then in the realm of tactics as well. The spirit of unconditional conformity asserted itself more and more strictly. Thus, in 1911, Lenin ruled that 'to be a real party member, it is not enough to call oneself such, nor is it enough to carry on propaganda *"in the spirit"* of the programme of the R.S.D.L.P.; one must also carry out the *entire* practical work in conformity with the *tactical* decisions of the party.' In other words, 'a party member is one who pursues the tactical line of the party in practice'.[158] Furthermore, referring to the electoral campaign then being prepared, Lenin gave it as his view that 'only those people may be Party candidates who really carry out the policy of the R.S.D.L.P. in full, are loyal not only to its programme but also to its resolutions on tactics ... '[159]

From that time onward allusions are found more and more frequently in Lenin's writings to 'the Party line'. He increasingly contrasts those who possess *partiynost'* ('partyism'), who are 'pro-party',[160] with those who show 'anti-party' tendencies.[161] What thus emerges, in the last analysis, is a kind of 'Party patriotism' which tends to look upon the Party as an end in itself. To be sure, this allegiance to the Party organization was born and developed in circumstances that, to a large extent, serve to explain it. The advantage enjoyed by the Bolsheviks over the Mensheviks lay not so much in superior theoretical equipment as in the fact that Lenin's followers, unlike their opponents, succeeded in keeping alive, despite all failures and setbacks, and amidst the most difficult of conditions, a Party organization which, in a period of reaction and demoralization that saw the collapse of the Mensheviks, safeguarded what was essential and ensured that there would be a future for Russian Social-Democracy. Lenin was subsequently to show that 'Partyism' would not be for him an absolute imperative in all circumstances—that he would be capable of sacrificing this, when necessary, to the requirements of the revolutionary struggle. For the moment, however, in these years preceding the outbreak of the War, he became above all the 'Party man', the advocate of the Party conceived as a monolith without a single crack in it, which had to be safeguarded from all deviations. In order to ensure this safeguarding of the Party, in face of the dangers of dispersion and desertion, all methods were considered legitimate.

Already in 1907 he had been charged by the Mensheviks with employing polemical procedures that were regarded as going too far. When summoned before a 'Party court', Lenin had replied to his accusers: 'What is impermissible in members of a united party is permissible and obligatory for sections of a party that has been split. It is wrong to write about party comrades in a language that systematically spreads among the working masses hatred, aversion, contempt, etc., for those who hold other opinions. But *one may and must write* in that strain about an organization that has seceded.' And he went on to say:

> By my sharp and discourteous attacks on the Mensheviks on the eve of the St. Petersburg elections, I actually succeeded in causing that section of the proletariat which *trusts and follows the Mensheviks* to waver. That was my aim. That was my duty ... ; because, after the split, *it was necessary* ... to rout the ranks of the Mensheviks, who were leading the proletariat in the footsteps of the Cadets; *it was necessary* to carry confusion into their ranks; it was necessary to arouse among the masses hatred, aversion and contempt for these people who had ceased to be members of a united party, had become political enemies, and were trying to put a spoke in the wheel of our Social-Democratic organization in its election campaign. Against *such* political enemies* I then conducted—and in the event of a repetition or development of a split *shall always conduct*—a struggle of *extermination*.[162]

In his choice of targets Lenin from the first allowed himself a very wide field. He aimed his attacks at 'splitting' organizations, an expression that was sufficiently vague to embrace an ever-larger range of opponents. He did not hesitate from now on to describe as a 'violation of the duty deriving from Party membership' the mere attempt to bring about unification, or even *rapprochement*, between Bolsheviks and Mensheviks.[163] As for those who advocated a 'legalization' of the Party, they were to be called 'Stolypinites', the equivalent of 'Versaillais' in 1871.†

One could go on indefinitely accumulating examples of the invective indulged in by Lenin in his pursuit of what he himself called an 'implacable campaign'.[164] He went farthest of all in the treatment he inflicted upon Trotsky. Once he described the latter as 'Judas Trotsky'.[165] Though Lenin himself had sufficient sense of decency not to

---

* These 'political enemies', the Mensheviks of Petrograd, had proposed concluding an electoral agreement not merely with the non-Social-Democratic Parties of the Left but also with the Liberals, and, finding themselves in the minority at a Party conference held in the capital, had walked out. (Lenin, Vol. 11, p. 433.)

† Ibid., Vol. 17, pp. 218, 225, 241, 245, and *passim*. Lenin uses the expression 'Stolypin Labour Party', the quotation marks applying only to the word 'Labour', as though the right-wing Social-Democrats had no real links with the world of labour but were actually reactionaries who supported the autocracy and the counter-revolutionary terror associated with Stolypin.

make public the text in which this expression appears, Stalin's 'historical' dispensary showed less restraint and brought this document out of the archives, for publication in *Pravda* in January 1932, and it adds nothing to the glory of its author.

Martov, for whom Lenin had felt deep friendship, and for whom, Gorky tells us, he always retained some kindly feeling,* was also subjected to his thunderbolts. Lenin even went so far as to insinuate that Martov was, at least objectively, in the service of the Tsar's police.[166] When, however, this same Martov denounced, in the Menshevik press, the Bolshevik deputy Malinovsky as an *agent provocateur*, Lenin, who held this worker, this 'Russian Bebel', in high esteem, became furiously angry: Martov, he wrote, was 'indulging in base slander'.[167] And yet, at the time when Lenin attacked the Menshevik leader in this way, he was already aware that some at least of the 'rumours' about Malinovsky were well founded.[168]

Unrestrained in his invective—which, however, did not prevent him from declaring that 'the advanced workers ... must keep careful watch to prevent the *inevitable* controversies, the *inevitable* conflict of opinions, from degenerating into recrimination, intrigues, squabbling and slander'[169]—Lenin also carried intolerance and sectarianism to absurd lengths in this period. A few years after having had Bogdanov expelled from the Bolshevik faction, he attacked in *Pravda* the *Vpered* group to which Bogdanov belonged. The 'Leftist' leader sent the Bolshevik paper a reply, which it published in its issue of 26 May 1913. Lenin, on learning that *Pravda* had published his opponent's article, wrote to the editors a letter in which he told them that what they had done was 'so scandalous that, to tell the truth, one does not know whether it is possible after this to remain a contributor'.[170] And yet *Pravda*, in publishing Bogdanov's reply, had preceded it with a note supporting Lenin against him.†

Polemic is, of course, a classical weapon in the battle of ideas and between men in politics, and is both indispensable and legitimate. During this period of Lenin's life, however, more than any other, what we observe is not just polemic in that sense. His invective (only a few examples have been quoted from a very rich collection) was accompanied by insinuations and accusations that are all the more striking as coming from a man who had just been recommending to his followers the merits of free discussion and the broadest confrontation between ideas.* It is not Lenin alone that this behaviour of his

---

* 'The only regret he told me about was: "I'm sorry, very sorry, that Martov is not with us. What an amazing comrade he is, what a pure man!" ' (Gorky, *Lenin*, p. 46). For the concern that Lenin showed for Martov after the October Revolution, see p. 269.

† Numerous conflicts occurred between the editors of *Pravda* (which began publication in 1912) and Lenin, as the journalists tried to moderate the extremely polemical tone of his contributions and he refused to submit to this 'censorship' (Daniels, *Conscience*, p. 28).

concerns, but *Leninism*, which is more than a doctrine and a theoretical system, being also a praxis, or, to use the expression adopted by the Leninists themselves, a 'guide to action'. When a man's theories and methods become, in the movement that accepts his leadership, not merely a source of inspiration but also a code of law and a model, his failings and mistakes may also be elevated to the status of virtues. And that was what actually happened in the case of Leninism.

These various sectarian features that Leninism displayed during the last years before the War were undoubtedly consequences of the period in which they arose, and it would be artificial to try to analyse them without reference to their context. Leninism possessed Lenin's own flexibility and proved able, once the years of retreat, defeat and demoralization had been succeeded by a new revolutionary upsurge of unprecedented power, to shake off this dross. The river that during the dry season had been only mud was then once more flowing broad and full of life. But Leninism, a complex and contradictory phenomenon, was to remain marked by the after-effects of its most barren and difficult period. And when, in the period that saw revolutionary Russia withdrawing into a citadel where rich promises of future progress were mingled with so many disappointments that already left a bitter taste, Stalinism succeeded to Leninism, the new doctrine, which was not entirely made up of innovations, took over from Lenin's heritage the sectarianism that had for a few years existed as a caricatural form of Leninism.

---

* After frequently declaring that he did not impugn his opponents' motives, Lenin began systematically to present them as being allies of the bourgeoisie, whose activity had the effect, whether deliberately or not, of injecting an alien class ideology into the proletariat and serving the interests of the bourgeoisie—allegations that deprived the discussion of any meaning or usefulness. See, e.g., Lenin, Vol. 16, pp. 100, 103; Vol. 17, pp. 218, 422; Vol. 19, p. 162; Vol. 20, pp. 124, 538.

2

The policy and strategy of Leninism

Lenin and bourgeois democracy

The breach between Bolsheviks and Mensheviks occurred over a question of organization. The first controversies between them related to the structures of the socialist movement and the consequences that Lenin's centralizing ideas would entail for inner-Party democracy and for the connexion between the Party and the masses. Not until the end of 1904, and in the main not until the 1905 revolution, did the quarrel between Bolsheviks and Mensheviks spread to a new sphere, namely, the question of how to define the strategy of the revolution.

At first nothing seemed to divide Lenin's supporters from his opponents as far as this question was concerned. They shared the belief that socialism would be born from a society that had been prepared for this event by the twofold phenomenon of industrialization and bourgeois democracy. They were sure that 'only [bourgeois] rule tears up the roots of feudal society and levels the ground on which alone a proletarian revolution is possible'.[1] True, the application of Marx's *schema* to Russia gave rise to a number of questions. Was the Russian bourgeoisie strong enough to come forward as a candidate for state power? Was the Marxist prospect still valid in a country where the immense majority of the population were peasants? Would capitalism possess the same features in Russia as in Western Europe, where its dynamism had largely dispensed with state intervention? Might not the presence of a tradition of agrarian collectivism in Russia enable that country to by-pass capitalism? The adoption of Marxism by the Russian labour movement was not enough to provide a solution to these problems. But, by equipping the movement with a conception of historical development, Marxism did endow it with some intellectual certainties that were destined to have important consequences on the plane of political objectives and also of revolutionary strategy.

In the West, socialism had never repudiated the struggle for demo-

cratic freedoms which the revolutionary bourgeoisie had undertaken.
In Russia the Marxists assumed a similar attitude. Some of the values
that they wished to promote—at any rate, the freedoms that they
sought to win—were the same as those proclaimed by liberalism. In
this respect, Lenin showed himself more orthodox than original. At the
beginning of his political career he had declared his attachment to the
democratic creed, saying that 'the Russian Communists, adherents of
Marxism, should more than any others call themselves Social-Democrats, and in their activities should never forget the enormous importance of democracy'.[2]

To be sure, the Russian Social-Democrats were fighting against a
régime in which, at the end of the nineteenth century, no trace of
democracy was to be found, and opposition in Tsarist Russia still
took the form of a liberal-type constitutionalism. It is true, too, that
the West served, for many reasons, as a pole of attraction. Only
after the outbreak of the crisis caused by the First World War—and,
to a still greater degree, after the revolution of 1917—did Lenin
start to subject parliamentary and liberal democracy to ruthless
criticism. Before 1914 he was still capable of presenting America and
Britain as countries 'where complete political liberty exists',[3] and
Switzerland, Belgium and Norway as 'free nations under a really
democratic system'.[4]

Whether or not Lenin had fully considered the implications of what
he was saying, the main point is that at that time he acknowledged
that the fight for socialism in Russia was a fight for democracy and for
democratic liberties, and that he emphasized the importance, urgency
and priority of these aims.

In 1895 he had sent from prison to his comrades a draft programme
for the Social-Democratic Party then being formed. In this document
he declared that 'the struggle of the Russian working class for its
emancipation is a political struggle, and its first aim is to achieve
political liberty'. He went on to list the democratic demands of the
Russian socialists: convening of a Constituent Assembly, universal
suffrage, freedom of meeting and association, right to strike, freedom
of the press, freedom of conscience, and equality between nationalities.[5] Part of Lenin's work in that period consisted in denouncing
the Tsarist régime, describing its arbitrary methods and constantly
opposing to it the demand that the rights of the citizen be respected.[6]

The adoption of a programme like this certainly corresponded to
the immediate interests of the bourgeoisie, or at least of a part of that
class. Lenin recognized that 'to call upon the worker to fight for
political liberty would be equivalent to calling upon him to pull the
chestnuts out of the fire for the progressive bourgeoisie, for it cannot
be denied ... that political liberty will primarily serve the interests of
the bourgeoisie ... '[7] Nevertheless, taking up a series of ideas that

Marx had outlined,* Lenin put forward the reasons why the proletariat ought to wage a struggle to bring about a political system that
would serve the interests of a class that was opposed to it. He declared
that 'the worker needs the achievement of the general democratic
demands only to clear the road to victory over the working people's
chief enemy, ... *capital* ... '[8] He explained the advantages that the
proletariat would gain through the coming to power of the bourgeoisie
that exploited it: 'It is far more advantageous to the workers for the
bourgeoisie to openly influence policy than, as is the case now, to
exert a *concealed* influence.'[9] And he insisted that 'only under conditions of political liberty, when there is an extensive mass struggle,
can the Russian working class develop organizations for the final
victory of socialism'.[10] To sum up: the struggle for democracy—not
Soviet democracy, not that democracy, genuine because proletarian,
which Lenin was later to contrast with the parliamentary system, but
ordinary bourgeois democracy—was for a long time put forward by
Lenin and by Russian socialists in general as a task of prime importance. Success in the struggle would open the way to all the conquests
by the proletariat that would undermine the power of the bourgeoisie
and eventually lead to workers' power.

Although it was mainly at the outset of his career that Lenin expounded these ideas, he did not abandon them after his break with the
Mensheviks. In 1905 the programme of demands he set forth drew
largely upon them. There was no great difference in this respect between
Lenin and the Mensheviks. They parted company, however, when the
question arose of determining what the alliances were that the socialist
movement ought to conclude in order to secure these democratic
achievements. What was involved here was the problem of the relations
between the classes of society and the role assigned to each in day-to-
day tactics and in the strategy of the revolution.

The problem of alliances: Lenin and liberalism
Nobody denied that the Russian proletariat needed to find allies for
its struggle. And if in Western Europe the Social-Democratic Parties
accepted the necessity of making certain agreements with the liberal
bourgeoisie, how could it be otherwise in Russia? Isolation of the
socialist movement would reduce it to total impotence. Mensheviks
and Bolsheviks were agreed that this was obvious. Their disagreement
related to the way in which such isolation was to be overcome, and,

* [The workers] 'know that their own struggle with the bourgeoisie can only break out
on the day the bourgeoisie triumphs ... They can and must take part in the middle-class
revolution as a condition preliminary to the labour revolution'. ('Moralising Criticism
and Critical Morality' [1847] in Marx, *Selected Essays*, p. 161.) 'The best form of polity
is that in which the social contradictions are not blurred, not arbitrarily ... kept down.
The best form of polity is that in which these contradictions reach a stage of open struggle
in the course of which they are resolved.' ('The June Revolution' [1848]: in Marx and
Engels, *Articles*, p. 49.)

in particular, to the choice of allies. So long as the future Bolsheviks and Mensheviks were working together on the editorial board of *Iskra*, there seemed to be no divergence of view between them on this subject. Broadly speaking, they all recognized that an alliance must be concluded with the democratic wing of liberalism; but this must be an alliance within which the workers' party retained complete independence, and which would not hinder the Party from carrying out the task of organizing the proletariat and educating it politically. This political education consisted essentially in making the workers aware of the fundamental antagonism of interests existing between themselves and their bourgeois allies, who were not very reliable and were in any case only allies for the time being.

In 1903, at the congress that saw the split between the Bolshevik and Menshevik wings of Russian Social-Democracy, the problem of alliance with the liberals was discussed for the first time. Opposing a resolution which he regarded as being too indulgent towards the liberal bourgeoisie, Plekhanov spoke in favour of one which, without denying the necessity of an alliance with the liberals, emphasized their weakness and the need for the socialists to subject them to severe criticism.[11] Martov came close to sharing this view, considering, at this time, that while democratic liberalism would make a contribution to victory over the autocracy, leadership of the struggle must be retained by the Social-Democrats.[12] Lenin, though convinced of the need for an alliance, the exact terms of which had still to be defined, showed more plainly than anyone else an almost systematic distrust of the liberal bourgeoisie. Thus, in 1897, while affirming that 'the Social-Democrats support the progressive social classes against the reactionary classes, the bourgeoisie against the representatives of the privileged landowning estate ... ', he added immediately that 'this support does not presuppose, nor does it call for, any compromise with non-Social-Democratic programmes and principles ... '[13] Similarly, although in *What Is To Be Done?* he declared that the bourgeois democrats 'are natural and desirable allies of Social-Democracy', he also noted that 'an essential condition for such an alliance must be the full opportunity for the socialists to reveal to the working class that its interests are diametrically opposed to the interests of the bourgeoisie'.[14]

In fact, in Lenin's attitude towards even the liberal element in the bourgeoisie, distrust was definitely the preponderant feature. As long as the Russian Marxists remained united, their attitude towards the liberals seemed to form part of a common body of principles and views regarding tactics and strategy. It is significant, however, that their first political divergence, after the breach of 1903, occurred at the end of 1904, when the socialist movement had to take a stand in relation to the political campaign launched by the liberals.

3

The first setbacks suffered by the Russian army during the war with Japan were then giving rise to agitation in Russia. Reviving an old tradition of Western European politics, a large group of the bourgeoisie organized a series of banquets at which they made speeches bringing their grievances and demands to the attention of the autocracy. The whole of Russia's political life had been in a lively state since the turn of the century. The working class was becoming more militant, engaging in strikes and demonstrations, the peasantry were stirring in their turn; and the bourgeoisie were now at last starting to get together politically. Russian political life was taking on forms closer to those familiar in Western Europe. Now that, for the first time, political organizations were in being that represented the different classes of the population, and that were moved by desire for reform or revolution, the problem of alliances between them arose in concrete terms. This question was rendered the more topical owing to the initiative taken in the autumn of 1904 by the Zemstvos, institutions representing the small landowning nobility and the middle bourgeoisie,* in opening a broad political campaign which testified to the awakening of Russian liberalism as an active political force. The various trends in the socialist movement were obliged to decide what their attitude should be towards this new and important phenomenon.

The Mensheviks decided in favour of support for the Zemstvo campaign, and invited the working class to demonstrate their support for the liberals. They warned the workers to avoid doing anything that might frighten their liberal allies. The pressure brought to bear on the liberals ought therefore to be characterized by moderation and prudence.[15] Lenin came out strongly against such a line.[16] The 'inanity'[17] of the Mensheviks seemed to him all the more detestable because he believed 'an alliance of the moderate Zemstvo-ists and the government to fight the revolutionary proletariat' to be 'only too clearly possible and probable'.[18] Thus there appeared for the first time, between Lenin and his Menshevik opponents, a serious political divergence that was destined to have considerable influence, first on their tactical, and later on their strategical views.

Underlying this divergence was, in the first place, the difference in estimate made by the Mensheviks, on the one hand, and by Lenin, on the other, of the nature and potentialities of liberalism and the bourgeoisie in Russia. For Mensheviks like Theodore Dan and Vera Zasulich, an alliance between liberals and socialists was an essential condition for the struggle against the autocracy, and must dominate the policy of the working-class movement.[19] As for Martov, he had

---

* The Zemstvos were local assemblies, set up during Alexander II's reign, which possessed fairly extensive powers of self-government in the social and administrative spheres. They grew more and more political, and began to call for the autocratic régime to be made more flexible.

come, after the split in 1903, to set his hopes on the radicalization of a section of the bourgeoisie which he called 'the third element of the intelligentsia', meaning professional men and engineers.[20] He believed that the Russian bourgeoisie would take the French bourgeoisie as its model and show no less revolutionary vigour than the Third Estate of 1789 had shown in the struggle against what remained of absolutism and feudalism.* The Mensheviks took note of the turn to the Right observable among the liberals, but in their eyes, these inclinations towards agreement with an autocracy that was becoming more flexible, were, although certainly to be regretted, nevertheless only passing errors without much significance. Since Tsarism and liberalism remained in opposition to each other down to the outbreak of the World War, the Mensheviks continued to be inspired by the hope of seeing the Russian bourgeoisie launch and lead the offensive that would result in overthrow of the autocracy.

This only slightly qualified optimism on the part of the Mensheviks was opposed by Lenin with a scarcely qualified pessimism. Whereas the Mensheviks believed, despite some reservations, in the revolutionary role of the bourgeoisie, Lenin, on the contrary, declared: 'the bourgeoisie is counter-revolutionary.'[21] In the first months of the 1905 revolution he said: 'the bourgeoisie will be more fearful of the proletarian revolution and will throw itself more readily into the arms of reaction.'[22]

When, during the Zemstvo campaign, the problem of alliance with the liberal bourgeoisie came on to the agenda, Lenin warned his followers against this 'notoriously conditional, problematic, unreliable, half-hearted ally'.[23] And when, in the opening phase of the revolutionary offensive, the Russian liberals seemed to be becoming more radical, Lenin explained that this was 'in part simply because the police, for all [their] unlimited powers, cannot crush the working-class movement'.[24] Even when the Russian bourgeoisie manifested more democratic moods, Lenin's distrust of them was not mitigated. On one point his opinion remained fixed and his verdict irrevocable: the Russian bourgeoisie, lacking as it was in any dynamism whatsoever, was incapable of playing a revolutionary role. He depicted the liberals as 'flunkeys' of Tsarism,[25] and the founders of the Constitutional-Democratic Party as 'the bourgeois liberal prostitutes'.[26] He said of them, mingling contempt with indignation: 'When a liberal is abused, he says: Thank God they didn't beat me. When he is beaten, he thanks God they didn't kill him. When he is killed, he will thank God that his immortal soul has been delivered from its mortal clay.'[27]

---

* 'We have the right to expect that sober political calculation will prompt our bourgeois democracy to act in the same way in which, in the past century, bourgeois democracy acted in Western Europe, under the inspiration of revolutionary romanticism.' (Quoted in Deutscher, *Prophet Armed*, p. 119.)

No doubt it was necessary to exert pressure on the bourgeoisie, exploiting the contradictions of a situation that caused this class sometimes to protest against Tsarism and sometimes to seek to make terms with it, and to force the bourgeoisie leftward. But while Lenin agreed with the Mensheviks on that point, his agreement with them went no further. The Mensheviks, to be sure, did not propose to abstain from all and any criticism of the liberals, but what they wanted above all was to secure, in exchange for their support, promises and undertakings, to be given them by these liberals. On this aspiration Lenin commented that 'under the pressure of material class interests all pledges will go by the board.'[28] In his view, pressure on the bourgeoisie should assume quite different forms. It was necessary to engage in 'criticizing the half-heartedness' of the liberal democrats[29] and to 'relentlessly expose every false step' that they took.[30]

As the 1905 revolution progressed, Lenin subjected alliance with the bourgeoisie to conditions so strict that it was made practically impossible. When in 1906 the question of making an electoral pact with the liberals came up, Lenin said that 'temporary fighting agreements are possible and advisable at the present time only with those elements which recognize armed uprising as a means of struggle and are actually assisting to bring it about'.[31]

The fact was that the revolution had finally convinced him of the falsity of the Menshevik line and, in particular, of the hopes that his opponents still placed in the bourgeoisie. The Mensheviks tended to draw from the setbacks suffered by the revolution the conclusion that only the reformist path, the path of peaceful and gradual progress, offered any prospect of success for socialism, and that attainment of this success must depend upon a closer, firmer agreement with the liberals of the Constitutional-Democratic Party. Lenin, on the contrary, said, as early as September 1905, that 'the farther the revolution advances, the more ... liberalism exposes itself'.[32] When, after the 1905 revolution was over, Lenin reviewed its outcome and drew the lessons to be learnt from it, the verdict he pronounced upon the bourgeoisie was most severe.

> Nowhere else in the world, probably, has the bourgeoisie revealed in the bourgeois revolution such reactionary brutality, such a close alliance with the old régime, such 'freedom' from anything remotely resembling sincere sympathy towards culture, towards progress, towards the preservation of human dignity, as it has with us—so let our proletariat derive from the Russian bourgeois revolution a triple hatred of the bourgeoisie and a determination to fight it.[33]

Nevertheless, Lenin did make a distinction between 'the republican and revolutionary bourgeoisie', on the one hand, and, on the other, 'the liberal and the monarchist bourgeoisie',[34] between 'the compromising, treacherous bourgeoisie, which is obviously preparing to make a deal with the autocracy' and 'the toiling petty-bourgeoisie, who are incredibly downtrodden, who dream of an equalized division of land and who are capable of waging a resolute and self-sacrificing struggle, into which they are being driven by the whole course of events and by the whole conduct of the government.'[35]

These ideas were not merely theoretical or incidental: they assumed a quite concrete meaning, and are of capital importance in the history of Leninism. The distinction that Lenin drew between bourgeoisie and petty-bourgeoisie and, more particularly, the way he identified the latter concept with the Russian peasantry, lay at the very heart of his revolutionary strategy, which, after he had worked it out theoretically, he then applied, though in an amended version, in 1917. Between the end of the revolution of 1905 and the outbreak of war in 1914, Lenin's struggle against Menshevism became very largely a struggle against liberalism and against all tendencies towards alliance between Social-Democrats and Constitutional-Democrats. Most of the clashes that occurred between Bolsheviks and Mensheviks in this period were, indeed, due to disputes over the attitude to be taken up towards the liberal bourgeoisie and its political representative, the Constitutional-Democratic Party.

In May 1906, for example, the Mensheviks upheld the idea of a government based on the Duma—in other words, a team of ministers led by liberals. Lenin dissociated himself sharply from any such policy.[36] This controversy came to nothing, however, and was left, so to speak, hanging in the air, since Tsarism never contemplated entrusting the executive power, or even merely the administration of public affairs, to a parliamentary cabinet. The disputes between Mensheviks and Bolsheviks regarding the conclusion of electoral alliances, however, did have a practical bearing. Whereas the Mensheviks were disposed to come to an understanding with the Constitutional-Democrats so as to put forward joint lists of candidates in some constituencies, Lenin categorically rejected this tactic.[37] The conflict on this terrain between the two factions of a party that had been reunited in 1906 led to a very serious crisis in the Petersburg section of the party, and marked a decisive stage along the road to the second and this time final split.

Lenin and parliamentarism
From 1906 onwards the vicissitudes of what in Russia took the place of parliamentary life provided more and more fuel for the quarrels between Bolsheviks and Mensheviks. What they were divided about was, on the one hand, the attitude that ought to be maintained towards the parliamentary group of the Constitutional-Democrats and,

on the other, the role to be played by the group of socialist deputies
in the Duma. What was ultimately at issue was the definition of a
revolutionary policy towards parliamentary institutions, with Bolshevism and Menshevism appearing as two wholly different styles of
socialist strategy in a non-revolutionary period. The implications
inherent in the arguments exchanged by the opposing groups gave
their dispute a significance that went beyond the limits of Russian
politics.

Without ignoring or underestimating the narrowness of the limits
within which Tsarism confined the activity and competence of the
Duma, the Mensheviks considered that this assembly could constitute
the beginning of popular representation, and that it was therefore
necessary to support it whenever a conflict or a mere difference of
opinion set the Duma in opposition to the government, and to do
everything possible to increase its prerogatives.[38] At the Social-
Democratic congress held in Stockholm in 1906 Plekhanov, Axelrod
and Dan successfully moved, against the will of the Bolshevik minority,
a resolution by which the Duma, although endowed only with powers
that were very limited and often fictitious, was held to be capable of
being made to play a progressive role.[39] Later, when the Menshevik
organizations had disintegrated and a number of their leaders were
advocating the formation of a legal party, the idea arose of making the
group of socialist deputies in the Duma the political centre of a re-
organized socialist movement.[40] This was one symptom among others
of the increasing moderation and reformism of the Mensheviks,
giving expression in the Russian context to the phenomenon of
'parliamentarism' that was increasingly dominant in the European
socialist movement.

Throughout these years Lenin was continually warning against
'constitutional illusions',[41] and calling for the Party to 'explain to the
people the impossibility of achieving political freedom by parliamentary means as long as real power remains in the hands of the tsarist
government', and to show the people 'the utter uselessness of the
Duma as a means of achieving the demands of the proletariat and the
revolutionary petty-bourgeoisie, especially the peasantry'.[42] While
opposing the opportunism of the Mensheviks, Lenin was no less
opposed to the tendency frequently apparent among the Bolsheviks
to disregard the possibilities offered by the Duma to a party that
stoutly safeguarded itself against the danger of Right-wing deviation.
In general, Lenin considered that 'the ability to use parliamentarism
has proved to be a symptom ... of exemplary organization of the *entire*
socialist movement ... '[43] And although he saw the Duma as having
only 'modest importance',[44] he judged it necessary to combat vigorously all those who called for a boycott pure and simple of that
institution.

What was the 'importance' of the Duma? Lenin's ideas on the subject were those that found general expression at that time in the Left factions of the socialist parties of the West. Participation by socialists in Parliamentary activity was to serve first and foremost to amplify the party's political agitation among the workers: all the opportunities presented for socialist propaganda either from the rostrum of the Duma or in election campaigns were to be exploited to the full. Declaring that 'those seats [in the Duma] are important only because and in so far as they can serve to develop the political consciousness of the masses',[45] Lenin explained that 'the Social-Democratic Party wants to use the elections in order again to drive home to the masses the idea of the need for revolution ... '[46] The task was, in other words, to participate in the institution of Parliament only so as to carry out a debunking of parliamentarism. 'If we Bolsheviks gave any pledge at all, it was only by our assurance that the Duma was the spawn of counter-revolution and that no real good could be expected from it.'[47]

Lenin stressed that the 'primary function' of the Social-Democratic group in the Duma should be to carry on 'work of criticism, propaganda, agitation and organization,' adding that 'this, and not immediate "legislative" objectives, should be the purpose of the bills the Social-Democratic group will introduce in the Duma ... '* He thus expected nothing from the Duma itself, and when in June 1906 the Mensheviks called on the proletariat of St Petersburg to demonstrate in support of it on the day the session opened, and to organize a solidarity strike on this occasion, the Bolshevik press protested, and urged the workers not to leave work.[48]

Furthermore, while Lenin thought it possible and desirable to make use of the Duma to expand the Party's revolutionary activity, this could be done only given two conditions: that the socialist deputies be preserved from contamination by their bourgeois parliamentary colleagues (so that any agreements between Social-Democrats and Constitutional-Democrats must be forbidden), and, as a corollary to this, that the freedom of manoeuvre allowed to the socialist deputies be kept to the minimum. These militants of a proletarian organization, carrying out a mission in a sphere that was totally alien to them, were at great risk of falling under the influence of bourgeois society and even being seduced by it.

This was why Lenin opposed the Mensheviks when the latter wanted to arrange joint meetings between Constitutional-Democrat and Social-Democrat deputies.[49] He protested energetically when the Menshevik deputies decided to vote for the Constitutional-Democrats'

---

* Lenin, Vol. 12, p. 141. Nevertheless, Lenin showed some flexibility in this field, permitting the Bolshevik deputies to vote, in 1913, for proposals or bills that contributed to improving the conditions of the working class (ibid., Vol. 19, p. 424).

candidate for the Duma presidium.[50] Whereas the Mensheviks sought whenever possible to form electoral alliances with the Constitutional-Democrats, for Lenin such alliances could only be made in exceptional cases. When the fight against Right-wing candidates rendered an electoral coalition indispensable, agreement should be effected, according to Lenin, only with the parties that represented the small peasants. In some cases he even favoured making a bloc with these groups *against* the liberal candidates, so as to prevent liberals from being elected.[51]

There remained the question of the status to be accorded to the socialist group in the Duma. This was an important question, for everywhere in Europe, the Left minorities in the socialist parties were protesting against the increasing autonomy and political weight of the Social-Democratic parliamentarians, in which they saw, not without justification, a first symptom of integration into the institutions of bourgeois democracy. From this standpoint, the dispute between Bolsheviks and Mensheviks reproduced that between Right and Left trends in the labour movement as a whole. Aware of the danger, Lenin supported, against the views of the Mensheviks, a motion passed by the London congress of 1907 providing that the Party's Central Committee be empowered to give 'directives' to the Duma group.[52] The conflict between Mensheviks and Bolsheviks thus acquired a new dimension. Between 1906 and 1914 Lenin fought with tenacity to ensure that the parliamentary group be brought under the strictest control by the Party, justifying his attitude by saying that 'the aim of the proletarian party is not to do deals or haggle with the powers that be … but to develop in every way the class-consciousness, the socialist clarity of thought, the revolutionary determination and all-round organization of the mass of the workers. Every step in the activity of the Duma group must serve this fundamental aim.'[53]

Bolsheviks and Mensheviks clashed frequently on this issue. In 1908 the parliamentary group, in which the Mensheviks predominated, passed a resolution constituting itself an autonomous body in the Party. The Central Committee, in which the Bolsheviks were predominant, replied by adopting decisions that put the parliamentary group under the Party's authority.[54] The weakness of the Party at this time helped, however, to allow the socialist deputies a wide freedom of manoeuvre. Lenin never resigned himself to this situation: while his Menshevik opponents welcomed it, often seeing in it a means to bringing about legalization of the Social-Democratic organization in Russia, Lenin declared that 'the revolutionary Social-Democrats in Europe have very serious grounds for demanding this *triple* control over their members of Parliament'.[55] When, during the last years before the War, in the circumstances created by the complete split between Bolsheviks and Mensheviks, Lenin was at last in a position

to wield complete authority over his supporters in the Duma, it was
he who, so as to make control effective, wrote most of their speeches.[56]
In this way Lenin endeavoured to cut off as completely as he could the
influences by which a revolutionary party risks, in periods of relative
social peace, getting its fighting spirit blunted and turning its back
on revolution.

Bourgeois revolution and proletarian revolution

Lenin's principal contribution to socialism was, before 1917, that he
forged the instrument for revolution. He could not, however, be
satisfied with working out a theory of the Party and seeking to put it
into practice. There was also the no less necessary task of creating a
revolutionary strategy. Even if Lenin had preferred to neglect this
task, the events of 1905 would have compelled him to undertake it.

The theoretical equipment possessed by the Bolsheviks and Mensheviks was of only limited use to them in this domain. Marxism had
taught them the role to be played by the working class in the overthrow of capitalism, and had furnished them with some additional
pointers regarding the organizational and educative functions of
Social-Democracy, the need for political alliances under a régime
of bourgeois democracy, and for the establishment of a dictatorship
of the proletariat in order to carry through the transition from capitalism. It had also taught them that a bourgeois revolution must precede
the socialist one, which could be prepared only upon foundations laid
by liberal democracy and capitalist industrial development. These
generalizations had to be adapted to the conditions prevailing in
Russia. Marx himself was so well aware of the difficulty this presented
that, in a letter intended for Vera Zasulich, written in 1881, he went
so far as to say that some of the evolutionary *schemata* outlined in
Capital were inapplicable to Russia, because Russian society still
included the village commune, on the future of which Marx did not
presume to pronounce.[57]

Lenin realized that to adapt Marxism to Russia required a substantial theoretical effort. This effort on his part produced an original
strategic conception which was set forth in a thick pamphlet published
at the beginning of summer 1905, entitled: *Two Tactics of Social-
Democracy in the Democratic Revolution*, and in a number of speeches,
reports and articles of the same period.

On one point there was full agreement between the Mensheviks and
Lenin. The latter held that 'Marxists are absolutely convinced of the
bourgeois character of the Russian revolution'. And he explained
what this meant:

It means that the democratic reforms in the political system, and
the social and economic reforms that have become a necessity

3*

for Russia, do not in themselves imply the undermining of capitalism, the undermining of bourgeois rule; on the contrary, they
will, for the first time, really clear the ground for a wide and rapid,
European and not Asiatic, development of capitalism; they will,
for the first time, make it possible for the bourgeoisie to rule as a
class.[58]

But that was the full extent of the agreement between Lenin and the
Mensheviks, who considered, logically enough, that a bourgeois
revolution would be led by the bourgeoisie itself, with the working
class playing only a supporting role. It was in any case out of the
question, so Martov thought, that the working class should profit by
the revolutionary crisis in order to seize power for itself. This rule was
subject, according to him, to only one exception: in the event that the
bourgeois parties, after striking down the autocracy, should disintegrate, putting all that they had gained in jeopardy, the duty of the
proletariat would be to take the place of the defaulting bourgeoisie.
Recalling the precedent of the Paris Commune, Martov considered
that any such development must lead to catastrophe. He added,
however:

> Only in one event should Social-Democracy on its own initiative
> direct its efforts towards seizing power and holding it as long as
> possible—namely, in the event of the revolution spreading to the
> advanced countries of Western Europe ... In that event the
> limited historical scope of the Russian revolution can be con-
> siderably widened and the possibility will arise of entering on the
> path of socialist reforms.[59]

Apart from this hypothetical possibility, Social-Democrats should
confine themselves to the division of tasks and functions that Marxist
logic seemed to dictate—bourgeois power to the bourgeois parties,
proletarian opposition to the representatives of the proletariat.

But this logic was more formal in character than historical and
sociological. For while the industrial proletariat was indeed too weak
to establish socialism in Russia on its own, the liberal bourgeoisie
did not constitute, either, a social and political force capable of playing
the decisive role that Martov expected of it. The reason for this was
simple: urban economy itself occupied a very minor place in the life
of the country. The huge majority of the population of Russia was
not concentrated in the towns but scattered over the countryside.*
Even now, as the old order drew towards its close, the numerical
weakness of the bourgeoisie was striking. Between a very narrow
social elite-stratum and the great majority of the people yawned an

---

* In 1913 the population of towns with over 100,000 inhabitants accounted for no more
than 6 per cent of Russia's total population.

immense gulf. The subordination of the Russian bourgeoisie to the state contrasted with the advanced degree of independence enjoyed by the 'middle classes' in the West. To entrust to such an anaemic class the historic function of the Western bourgeoisie meant basing a strategic calculation upon a comparison that was fallacious. Lenin was right when he declared that 'the Cadets [Constitutional-Democrats] cannot lead the revolution forward, because they lack the backing of a united and really revolutionary class'.[60]

How, then, was one to solve an apparently insoluble problem, namely, the accomplishment of a *bourgeois* revolution in a country in which the bourgeoisie occupied a position in society that was at best merely secondary? How could this bourgeoisie be expected to wage a vigorous struggle against the autocracy when it was closer to the latter than to the proletariat? Lenin's reply to this twofold question consisted of two points: he drew a distinction between the upper and middle bourgeoisie, on the one hand, and the petty-bourgeoisie, on the other, ascribing democratic aspirations to the latter only; and he substituted for the idea of an alliance between the town bourgeoisie and the town proletariat that of an alliance between the latter and the mass of small peasants. That such a conception meant departing from the classical Marxist *schema* was beyond doubt, as Martov did not fail to point out. Lenin's answer was that while the petty-bourgeois nature of the peasantry would, of course, constitute an obstacle to an alliance between it and the proletariat when the task in hand was to establish socialism, this did not apply when only the bourgeois revolution was on the agenda.[61]

Lenin laid stress on the factors that made possible a bloc between workers and peasants. The latter, he explained, had every reason to support a democratic programme, since they formed the majority of the nation.[62] What they desired was nothing other than abolition of the survivals of feudalism. Russia was in a situation comparable to that in the France of 1789, but with the urban proletariat taking the place of the bourgeoisie. Whereas the Mensheviks looked on the peasantry as 'completely unorganized and terribly ignorant',[63] Lenin set his hopes on a political awakening of the peasant class. The revolution of 1905 had made possible the beginning of a *rapprochement* between revolutionary workers and peasants. True, the army, which meant the peasantry, had contributed to putting down the insurrection, but the agitation in the countryside had taken the authorities by surprise, and the Bolsheviks had made their first attempt to carry their propaganda into that milieu. In 1906 the need for a close alliance between the revolutionary movement in the towns and that in the countryside had seemed to Lenin so imperative that he made the organizing of a new insurrection dependent upon first concluding an agreement between workers' combat squads and similar groups among the peasantry.[64] In the midst of the revolutionary crisis a government newspaper had felt able to reassure its readers that 'the muzhik will help us out'.[65] This expectation proved correct. But the old régime had won only a respite. The foundations had been laid for an alliance which, in 1917, was to signify the death sentence upon Tsarism.

As early as 1905, however, Lenin had said that the Russian revolution, though bourgeois-democratic in character, would be set in motion by the proletariat, the only class 'capable of waging a determined struggle for complete liberty, for the republic ... ,' and had added that 'the proletariat can become the leader of the entire people and win over the peasantry ... '[66] Together, the two allied classes would establish a 'revolutionary-democratic dictatorship of the proletariat and the peasantry',[67] an amended version of the Marxist formula of the 'dictatorship of the proletariat'.

On this point, too, Lenin was in conflict with the Mensheviks, who contemplated forming, in relation to the liberal bourgeoisie after the latter's victory, nothing more than an opposition which, while doubtless vigorous, would accept the bourgeois order. They declined to envisage participation by representatives of the working class in a provisional government, reproducing on this question the 'anti-ministerialist' attitude of the Left in the socialist movement of Western Europe. Lenin brushed these doctrinal scruples aside, considering that the place for a revolutionary workers' party was *inside* a revolutionary government. The Mensheviks claimed that socialist ministers would be forced either to compromise themselves by association with a bourgeois policy, or to begin introducing the socialist order, thus embarking on an adventuristic course. Lenin rejected this argument. 'Some Social-Democrats, who are inclined to yield to spontaneity,'[68] might perhaps yield to such a temptation, but the Party leadership, refusing to run ahead of the possibilities of the moment, would be able to keep its head, and maintain very clearly the distinction between the democratic revolution and the socialist revolution. It was in any case impossible to put any confidence in the bourgeoisie: a provisional government would be revolutionary only if the organized proletariat were to take part in it.

This provisional government would be the executive branch of the *revolutionary dictatorship of the proletariat and the peasantry*. These views of Lenin's were bold in two respects. For the first time, a Marxist was proposing, in a practical way, to associate the peasants with the exercise of revolutionary authority:* and, also for the first

---

* The idea of alliance between the revolutionary proletariat and the peasantry in France was not entirely absent from Marx's thinking. He alludes briefly to this possibility in *The Eighteenth Brumaire of Louis Bonaparte*, where he says that the French peasants 'find their natural ally and leader in the *urban proletariat*, whose task is the overthrow of the bourgeois order' (Marx and Engels, *Selected Works*, Vol. I, p. 482).

time, this Marxist ventured to offer some pointers to the concrete meaning of the notion of the dictatorship of the proletariat, which Marx and Engels had only outlined very generally, and about which most of their disciples preferred to say nothing. These pointers were at first very vague. Having stated that one of the tasks that the people would have to accomplish was 'to "repulse together" the inevitable desperate attempts to restore the deposed autocracy', Lenin went on to say that, 'in a revolutionary epoch, this "repulsing together" is, in effect, the revolutionary-democratic dictatorship of the proletariat and the peasantry'.[69] He was hardly more explicit in his pamphlet *Two Tactics of Social-Democracy in the Democratic Revolution*, where he confined himself to saying that this dictatorship would mean 'the revolution's decisive victory over Tsarism'.[70]

Not until March 1906 do we find in Lenin's writings a description of the dictatorship that he advocated. Employing a pragmatic method, he recalled the circumstances that had seen the birth of the soviets. They had been 'set up exclusively by the *revolutionary* sections of the people: they were formed irrespective of all laws and regulations, entirely in a revolutionary way, as a product of the native genius of the people ...' Lenin added that these soviets were 'indeed organs of *authority*, for all their rudimentary, amorphous and diffuse character, in composition and in activity'. And he explained that 'they acted as a government when, for example, they seized printing plants (in St Petersburg) and arrested police officials who were preventing the revolutionary people from exercising their rights ... They confiscated the old government's funds ... '[71] Now, these 'organs of authority ... represented a dictatorship in embryo, for they recognized *no* other authority, *no* law and *no* standards ... '[72] Touching here upon an argument that he was to develop more fully in *State and Revolution*, Lenin showed that this dictatorial authority was also a democratic one. 'The new authority' was indeed a 'dictatorship of the overwhelming majority', and it 'maintained itself and could maintain itself solely because it enjoyed the confidence of the vast masses, solely because it, in the freest, widest and most resolute manner, enlisted all the masses in the task of government.'[73] Like Engels when he described the Paris Commune as 'the dictatorship of the proletariat',[74] Lenin was employing a purely empirical method in a sphere where particularly rigorous thinking was needed. History was to expose the inadequacy of such an approach.*

Nor was this the only weak point in Lenin's strategical thinking.

---

* It is noteworthy that Marx showed himself much more cautious than either Engels or Lenin on this point. Despite his eulogy of the Commune (in *The Civil War in France*) he refrained from identifying it with the dictatorship of the proletariat. See his letter of February 22nd, 1881, to Domela-Nieuwenhuis (in Marx and Engels, *Selected Correspondence*, p. 410).

He drew a sharp distinction between the bourgeois revolution and the socialist revolution. Only the former, he said, was possible in Russia. It would establish *bourgeois* democracy in that country. But how was this idea to be reconciled with his conviction that, under this system, power would in theory be in the hands not of the bourgeoisie but of the popular classes, the workers and peasants, allied *against* the bourgeoisie? Lenin, who did not overlook this difficulty, explained that the Russian revolution would be 'bourgeois in its social and economic essence'.[75] Was it to be concluded, then, that the revolution could be *bourgeois* in these two respects, and yet *anti-bourgeois* on the political plane? And, again, if the revolution was to be victorious mainly through the efforts, sacrifices and energy of the industrial proletariat, could the latter be expected to set up and show respect to a régime that was, economically and socially, bourgeois—in other words, capitalist? Was a victory of the bourgeois revolution won chiefly by the working class conceivable, given that, as Lenin himself said, this revolution would assume 'a form advantageous mainly to the big capitalist, the financial magnate, and the "enlightened" landlord'?[76] When we seek an explanation of this problem we find ourselves confronted with two hypotheses.* Either the contradiction, and consequently the flaw in the formula put forward, was not noticed by Lenin—something that seems unlikely: or else the contradiction was only apparent. In the latter event, the contradiction could be overcome through the discipline imposed upon the proletariat by the revolutionary Party. If the workers, advancing headlong, were indeed to be tempted, after overthrowing the autocracy, to go forward and establish socialism, then their Party, less ready to be carried away, less subject to *spontaneity*, and guided by keen, imperative socialist consciousness, would be able to bring them back to a more correct appreciation of what was and was not possible—to enforce what Trotsky called, not without irony, a 'quasi-Marxist asceticism'.[77] But would not such disciplinary power imply a danger of the democratic dictatorship becoming transformed into a dictatorship by the Party over the democracy? It was certainly bound up with the conception of a political organization that would guide and lead the proletariat, subjecting it to close control.

Finally, this sharp line of separation drawn between the bourgeois revolution and the socialist revolution failed to reckon with the revolutionary dynamic. Was it really possible to set limits to the revolutionary potentialities and objectives of the proletariat of a particular country by reference to the level of development of that

---

* A third hypothesis has been offered by John Plamenatz. He ascribes the contradiction purely and simply to 'folly' on Lenin's part! (Plamenatz, p. 231.) I shall not discuss this view, preferring to seek a serious explanation for a serious problem.

country's national economy, as if, in the epoch of imperialism, national economies constituted so many autarkic systems? At all events, the Mensheviks clung to Marxist orthodoxy right down to their eventual defeat: whereas Lenin, while upholding the validity of Marxism, showed himself, as we shall see, capable of both greater flexibility and greater boldness.

Lenin and permanent revolution (I)

Without formally jettisoning his overall conception, Lenin took account of the fact that the ideas about revolutionary strategy that classical Marxism provided were inadequate for the solution of an essential problem, namely, the transition from the bourgeois to the socialist revolution. Down to 1905 he had been content to separate the two revolutions by a historical phase of indeterminate length, wholly occupied by the twofold development of capitalism and of its opposite—of the bourgeoisie and of the proletariat. As soon, however, as the class struggle entered upon a period of intense effervescence, clear-cut formulas lost their clarity and doctrinal boundary-lines their rigour. The year 1905 rendered immediate the question of the telescoping of the bourgeois and socialist revolutions. Nobody saw this so well as Trotsky. Of all the outstanding socialists of Russia, he was the only one who, in 1905, showed himself able to rise to the occasion and, driven by his thirst for action, to plunge into the human tumult and become the leader and spokesman of the masses. This was only a short period, but it made the deepest impression upon him and marked him politically and intellectually.

A few weeks after his arrest, while waiting for his trial to begin, Trotsky wrote in his prison in Petersburg a series of essays, one of which, *Results and Prospects*, contains the broad outlines of his famous theory. Here he declared that 'the day and the hour when power will pass into the hands of the working class depends directly not upon the level attained by the productive forces but upon relations in the class struggle, upon the international situation, and, finally, upon a number of subjective factors: the traditions, the initiative and the readiness to fight of the workers.'[78] He also said that 'to imagine that the dictatorship of the proletariat is in some way automatically dependent on the technical development and resources of a country is a prejudice of "economic" materialism simplified to absurdity,' and concluded that 'it is possible for the workers to come to power in an economically backward country sooner than in an advanced country'.[79] Nevertheless, the victorious proletariat could not remain alone. It would have to widen the foundations of the revolution, seeking allies, especially among the peasantry, although it must keep for itself 'a dominating and leading participation' in this alliance—'the hegemony should belong to the working class.'[80] This seemed possible to Trotsky, not only owing to the weakness of the bourgeoisie but also because, despite its numerical weakness, 'the militant proletariat has nowhere acquired such importance as in Russia'.[81]

Like Lenin, and in opposition to the Mensheviks, Trotsky advocated an offensive strategy and a bold, dynamic conception of the revolution, in which the proletariat would be the driving force. Whereas, however, Lenin put forward the idea of a 'revolutionary-democratic dictatorship' in which the workers and peasants would be associated together, presenting them, implicitly at least, as more or less equal partners,* Trotsky's idea was that the proletariat should draw the peasantry in its wake. Support from the peasantry, moreover, was not needed as a prerequisite for revolutionary action: the peasantry would *follow* the offensive movement of the proletariat at a time when the peasants were still without a political organization of their own. This was why Trotsky rejected Lenin's formula of a 'dictatorship of the proletariat and the peasantry', which he considered 'unrealizable —at least in a direct, immediate sense'.[82]

What would be the function of the revolutionary ruling authority? According to Lenin, it would amount mainly to establishing bourgeois democracy and facilitating capitalist development. Trotsky, however, considered that 'it would be the greatest utopianism to think that the proletariat having been raised to political domination by the internal mechanism of a bourgeois revolution can, even if it so desires, limit its mission to the creation of republican-democratic conditions for the social domination of the bourgeoisie'.[83] The economic situation would inevitably lead to a clash between bourgeoisie and proletariat, and the state power, conquered by the proletariat, would have to take sides against the employers, and would thereby be led to adopt socialization measures. However, this socialist policy 'will come up against political obstacles much sooner than it will stumble over the technical backwardness of our country'.[84] Two features, especially, in the socialist programme would give rise to opposition from the peasantry, namely, collectivization and internationalism: and the conflict thus caused could end victoriously for the proletariat only if it were to receive 'direct state support' from the European proletariat. Trotsky added: 'there cannot be any doubt that a socialist revolution in the West will enable us directly to convert the temporary domination of the working class into a socialist dictatorship'.[85] In an article published in 1909 he returned to this idea, declaring: 'There is no way out from this contradiction within the framework of a national revolution. The workers' government will from the start be faced with the task of

---

* 'More or less', because Lenin recognized that it was specifically the proletariat that would put itself *at the head* of the entire people.

uniting its forces with those of the socialist proletariat of Western Europe.'[86] *

Commenting on these ideas in 1909, Lenin claimed that 'Trotsky's major mistake is that he ignores the bourgeois character of the revolution and has no clear conception of the transition from this revolution to the socialist revolution'.[87] Must we see in this statement a proof of Lenin's rejection of the theory of permanent revolution? According to the official Soviet interpreters of Lenin's thought there can in any case be no doubt about this rejection. The problem, however, is too important to be disposed of by means of this one very brief quotation.

What must first be noticed is the moderate tone used by Lenin when he criticizes Trotsky's revolutionary strategy: this moderation is too rare in the polemics which the two future leaders of the October Revolution were waging against each other at this time for it not to be seen as significant. Commenting on Trotsky's ideas about the role of the liberal bourgeoisie, Lenin declared, during the discussion at the London Congress of 1907, that 'Trotsky has come closer to our views'.[88] True, he added immediately that, 'quite apart from the question of "uninterrupted revolution", we have here solidarity on fundamental points in the question of the attitude towards bourgeois parties'. But Lenin's reference to the theory of permanent revolution was so brief— an allusion rather than a critique—that there is good reason to follow Isaac Deutscher when he says that 'it seems established' that it was not until 1919 that Lenin actually read Trotsky's *Results and Prospects*, of which until then he had had only partial and indirect knowledge.[89] To this can be added the statement to be found in the letter that the Bolshevik leader Joffe wrote to Trotsky before committing suicide in November 1927: 'I have often told you that with my own ears I have heard Lenin admit that in 1905 it was not he but you who were right. In the face of death one does not lie, and I repeat this to you now.'[90]

All this matters less than the ideas that Lenin himself developed during the revolution of 1905, which mark a modification in his general conception of two clearly distinct revolutions. The change is sometimes so pronounced that it is a quasi-'Trotskyist' standpoint that we find revealed in Lenin's writings of this time. Alluding to the Marxist

* The possibility that Russia might become socialist without having to pass through the phase of capitalism and bourgeois domination had been glimpsed by Marx and Engels when Russia, ceasing to be for them merely a stronghold of counter-revolution, began, thanks to its revolutionary movement, to arouse their hopes. They then contemplated the hypothesis of Russia's making a 'leap' over capitalism through modernizing the traditional village commune. This possible line of development they linked up with the outbreak of a socialist revolution in Western Europe—another instance of the close relation between Trotsky's theory and the outlook of the founders of Marxism (see Carr, Vol. II, pp. 388–91).

thesis about the bourgeois and socialist phases of the revolution,
Lenin declared in the spring of 1905: 'But if we interpret this correct
Marxist scheme of three stages to mean that we must measure off in
advance, *before any ascent begins*, a very modest part, let us say, not
more than one step, if, in keeping with this scheme and before any
ascent begins, we sought to "draw up a plan of action in the revolutionary epoch", we should be virtuosi of philistinism.'[91]

What had become, then, of Lenin's idea of the transition from the
bourgeois to the socialist revolution? In *Two Tactics* he had indicated
that the transition period could be brief, and that the Party's attitude
should be such as to actively promote this transition, its entire policy
being focused on preparing for it. Continuing his analysis, he had
added, in the same work, that there was no real breach of continuity
between the bourgeois and socialist phases of the revolution: 'the
complete victory of the present revolution will mark the end of the
democratic revolution and the beginning of a determined struggle for
a socialist revolution'.* A few months later, in a text that was published
only in 1936, describing hypothetical developments in the future, he
distinguished between the different stages in the growth of the revolution, stating that a period during which the bourgeoisie, having
become conservative, would begin to take up an openly hostile
attitude towards the revolution, would be followed by one in which,

> on the basis of the relations established ... a new crisis and a new
> struggle develop and blaze forth, with the proletariat now fighting
> to preserve its democratic gains for the sake of a socialist revolu-
> tion. This struggle would have been almost hopeless for the Russian
> proletariat alone and its defeat would have been as inevitable
> as the defeat of the German revolutionary party in 1849–1850, or
> of the French proletariat in 1871, *had the European socialist pro-
> letariat* not come to the assistance of the Russian proletariat.

He concluded: 'In such conditions the Russian proletariat can win a
second victory. The cause is no longer hopeless. The second victory
will be the *socialist revolution in Europe*.'[92] Since he seems to have
conceived the pace at which these different periods were to succeed
one another as a rapid one, and, still more, since they appear as parts
of a continuous process, this was indeed a *schema* very similar to the
one that Trotsky had worked out.

In an article of September 1905, apparently of no special importance,
Lenin wrote this typically 'Trotskyist' sentence: 'From the democratic
revolution we shall at once, and precisely in accordance with the

---

* Lenin, Vol. 9, p. 130. Again: 'The present revolution is only our first step, which will
be followed by a second; ... we must take this first step all the sooner, get it over all the
sooner, win a republic, mercilessly crush the counter-revolution, and prepare the ground
for the second step' (ibid., Vol. 9, pp. 39–40).

measure of our strength, the strength of the class-conscious and organized proletariat, begin to pass to the socialist revolution. We stand for uninterrupted revolution. We shall not stop half-way.'*

After the defeat of the proletariat and the restoration of the autocracy, Lenin seems to have abandoned the prospect of 'uninterrupted revolution' which he had glimpsed in 1905. Not until 1917 was this to re-emerge, become dominant in his thinking, and triumph as his policy.

* Ibid., Vol. 9, pp. 236–37. This same expression, 'uninterrupted revolution', was also used by Trotsky (*Results*, p. 212).

3

Lenin in 1905

It is in the course of the 1905 revolution that we can observe for the first time the flexibility of Lenin's views, the malleability of his theories, and what finally constitutes his exceptional genius as a revolutionary, namely, his capacity to grasp the meaning of events and their implications, to appreciate the dialectical potentialities* that emerge from real life, suddenly shattering *schemata* that had been thought of as established for ever. Last, and most important of all, we see Lenin's will and power to make the very most of mass movements, not out of cynical calculation but, much more fundamentally, because of a profoundly revolutionary belief in the people as the agents of their own liberation.

In order to understand Lenin's method it is not enough to analyse the far-reaching changes undergone by the structures of Bolshevism during the first Russian revolution. Historical reality must be approached more closely, the highly dialectical relationship between Lenin and his Party examined with greater attention, and the flexibility and deeply revolutionary quality of the man compared with the already conservative ponderousness and inertia of the Party apparatus, even at the time when it had only recently been formed.

The transformation of the party structures
The language of figures and the evidence of facts have shown clearly enough the extent to which the structures of the R.S.D.L.P., and of its Bolshevik faction in particular, underwent great changes during the revolutionary events of 1905 and 1906. These events, however, were not capable of bringing about unaided the changes in question. Lenin was among the most active agents in the transformation that took place, and the resistance that he encountered within his organization was vigorous. Thus, the congress that the Bolsheviks held in April 1905 was the scene of a confrontation between supporters and opponents of change, and, according to Krupskaya, some violent disputes occurred.[1] The question of the opening-up of the Bolshevik organiza-

* On Lenin and dialectics, see 'Conclusions', p. 442.

tions and committees to elements from the working class was the one that gave rise to the sharpest conflict. When delegates to the congress demanded that workers be admitted in increasing numbers to membership of the local committees, certain cadres (those whom Krupskaya calls the 'committee-men') demanded that 'extreme caution' be shown in this matter. They warned the congress against the temptation of 'playing at democracy'.[2]

In opposition to the committee-men, the advocates of change called upon the Bolsheviks to 'plunge down to the lower depths', declaring their belief that 'a social transformation of this kind would help to cleanse the atmosphere of intrigue and promote healthier relations between the leaders and the rank-and-file'. A spokesman of this 'reforming' tendency tabled an amendment by which the central committee was empowered to dissolve a local committee on the request of two-thirds of the members of its 'periphery'. Lenin supported this proposal, and tried to give it an even more *ouvriériste* character by excluding intellectual elements from the reckoning of the necessary two-thirds.[3] It was on the question of the proletarianization of Russian Social-Democracy that he intervened most strongly. When one delegate said that the criteria for admission to the committees were such that workers were in practice excluded from them, he was subjected to numerous hostile interruptions, but Lenin loudly applauded him.[4] In face of the sectarianism revealed by some participants in the congress he burst out: 'I could hardly keep my seat when it was said here that there are no workers fit to sit on the committees,' and added: 'obviously there is something the matter with the Party.'[5] Jointly with Bogdanov he put forward an amendment to the Party rules which imposed an obligation to increase the number of working-class members of the Bolshevik committees. *This amendment was rejected.*[6] If we are to believe Krupskaya, Lenin 'was not greatly upset' at this rebuff: 'he realized that the approaching revolution was bound to radically cure the Party of this incapacity to give the committees a more pronounced worker make-up'.[7] And this was what in fact happened.

From the London congress of 1905 onwards Lenin redoubled his appeals to his supporters inside Russia to take advantage of the new conditions in order to enlarge the Party organizations. The tone of these appeals tells us much about the resistance that he came up against. In a letter to a Petersburg Bolshevik in February 1905, Lenin writes: 'Be sure to put us in *direct* touch with the new forces, with the youth, with newly formed circles ... So far not *one* of the St Petersburgers (shame on them) has given us a *single* new Russian connexion ... It's a scandal, our undoing, our ruin! Take a lesson from the Mensheviks, for Christ's sake.'[8]

In the same month, in another letter to correspondents inside

Russia, he vehemently attacked the conservatism and inertia of the Bolshevik leaders there:

> You must be sure to organise, organise and organise *hundreds* of circles, completely pushing into the background the customary, well-meant committee (hierarchic) stupidities. This is a time of war. Either you create *new*, young, fresh, energetic battle organisations everywhere for revolutionary Social-Democratic work of all varieties among all strata or you will go under, wearing the aureole of 'committee' bureaucrats.[9]

When some Bolsheviks invoked the principles of *What Is To Be Done?* against its author,[10] Lenin hit out at them, declaring that 'all these schemes, all these plans of organization ... create the impression of red tape ... Do not demand any formalities, and, for heaven's sake, forget all these schemes, and send all "functions, rights and privileges" to the devil.'[11]

A large proportion of the functions, rights and privileges of the committee-men were indeed abolished, as the outcome of a hard struggle in which Lenin faced on several fronts the hesitations, reticences and fears of his comrades, and succeeded in shaking them.

Lenin, the Bolsheviks and the soviets

It was not so much surprise that marked the reaction of the Bolsheviks to the outbreak of the 1905 revolution as scepticism, incomprehension, and even sometimes outright hostility. This was especially the case in Petersburg, where the soviet enjoyed the highest prestige and made the biggest impression. Uniting delegates who represented 250,000 workers in the capital, the Petersburg Soviet was set up on October 13th, 1905, the day after the general strike was proclaimed, with the active participation of a number of Menshevik militants, who popularized the idea of the soviet among the workers. Commenting on this development, Krasikov, an outstanding Bolshevik militant in Petersburg, said: 'The Mensheviks have started a new intrigue: they're electing a non-Party Zubatovite committee.'* And Voitinsky, another prominent Bolshevik, who reports this statement, adds: 'I think that at the time almost all Bolsheviks shared this view of the Menshevik enterprise.'[12]

There was in this unfavourable reaction, which saw in the Soviet nothing but a committee of 'yellow' trade unionists, more than just a symptom of sectarianism towards the Mensheviks. In several ways the establishment of the soviets clashed with the political creed of Lenin's supporters. They were convinced—and the 'committee-men' to an

---

* The Zubatov trade unions were formed by the police with the intention of countering the progress of the labour movement.

even greater degree than the rank-and-file—of the virtues of organization, and, loyal to the ideas set forth in *What Is To Be Done?*, they felt extreme distrust of spontaneous mass movements which no party was able to control. And the great strikes of 1905 were more often than not almost entirely spontaneous in character.* Already certain that no revolution could have any chance of success unless it were firmly led by a party, the Bolsheviks looked without any sympathy whatsoever upon this new institution, which obeyed no instruction and carried out no directive, and which corresponded so imperfectly to their conception of how the masses should be organized.

The Mensheviks reacted in a diametrically opposite way, and it was no accident that the first chairman of the Petersburg Soviet, Zborovsky, and also his successor, Khrustalev-Nostar, were Mensheviks. The spontaneous nature of the movement that led to the formation of soviets made a strong appeal to them. In the two years that had followed their break with Lenin, Martov, Axelrod, Plekhanov and the rest had harshly criticized what they saw as Lenin's excessive centralism, and his advocacy of a closed and hierarchical organization. The Mensheviks had declared themselves in favour of a party that should be as large as possible and in which the workers' initiative and spontaneity should be given full play. The events of the spring of 1905 confirmed, for them, their view that the proletariat was capable of developing a large-scale revolutionary political movement without needing a disciplined, authoritarian party for this purpose. Martov had, in *Iskra*, which he edited, urged during the first phase of the revolution the forming of 'organizations of revolutionary self-government', in which the working class would try out experiments in administration, and even in government, which would serve as its apprenticeship in proletarian democracy.[13] The appearance of the soviets seemed to him and to his comrades the concrete realization of this idea, which had been criticized by Lenin, for whom conquest of state power through armed insurrection was the necessary prerequisite for any form of popular government.[14]

To be sure, wherever the soviets took on the aspect of a fighting organization, the Bolsheviks, far from holding back, entered them in large numbers, sometimes succeeding in winning control, as happened in Moscow. On the whole, however, the role played by the Bolsheviks in the soviets was 'slight and undistinguished'.[15]

In St Petersburg Lenin's supporters passed a resolution stating that the soviet was 'liable to hold back the proletariat at a primitive level of development'.[16] These prejudices survived for a long time. Thus, at a meeting of the committee of a Bolshevik organization in the capital which was held at the end of October 1905, one of the leaders called for a boycott of the Soviet by the Party because 'the elective principle

* See p. 93 for the attitude of the Bolsheviks towards these mass movements.

could not guarantee its class-consciousness and Social-Democratic character'.[17] The recommendation was not followed up on this occasion, but Bogdanov, who was then in charge of the Russian bureau of the Bolshevik organization, went even further, saying that the Soviet might become the nucleus of an *anti*-socialist party. What was necessary, according to him, was to compel the Soviet to accept the Bolshevik programme and the authority of the Bolshevik Central Committee, which would mean its absorption by the Party.[18]

Although not everyone in the Bolshevik camp shared this view, the growth of the Soviet never aroused any enthusiasm there. Often, indeed, this process inspired a mood of resignation and concern to avoid the worst. A Bolshevik witness of that time, Radin, expresses this mood: 'All we could do was prevent *possible harmful consequences in the future* and try to use the Soviet and its organization to propagate the Party's ideas.'[19] Another Bolshevik militant, a member of the Petersburg Committee, admitted that his comrades 'took fright' when they saw the Soviet expanding its activities.[20] Within the leading body that directed the Party in the capital some Bolsheviks advocated a boycott of the Soviet while others favoured 'exploding [it] from within'.[21]

On the eve of Lenin's arrival in St Petersburg, the Bolsheviks' official organ could still publish, over the signature of Gvozdev, an important article about the Soviet in which the editor of *Novaya Zhizn* declared that 'if Social-Democracy vigorously supported the Workers' Soviet as the executive organ of the proletarian action, it must now no less vigorously combat all attempts on its part to become the political leader of the working class.'[22]

About the same time Lenin, who was on the point of crossing the Russian frontier, wrote a long article for *Novaya Zhizn* under the title: 'Our tasks and the Soviet of Workers' Deputies'. In this article he dissociated himself from the views generally expressed by the Bolsheviks on the question of the Soviet. 'It seems to me that Comrade Radin is wrong in raising the question ... : the Soviet of Workers' Deputies or the Party? I think that it is wrong to put the question in this way and that the decision must *certainly* be: *both* the Soviet of Workers' Deputies *and* the Party.'[23] Contradicting the view advocated by the Bolshevik organization in the capital, Lenin further declared: 'I think it inadvisable to demand that the Soviet of Workers' Deputies should accept the Social-Democratic programme and join the Russian Social-Democratic Labour Party,' adding that the Soviet 'should be regarded as the embryo of a *provisional revolutionary government*'.[24] The Soviet, he said, ought to extend its range of activity still further and enlarge its audience, especially among the soldiers and sailors, so as to prepare the way for an alliance between the peasantry and the industrial proletariat. Finally, he refuted the argument by which the

Soviet did not constitute 'a centre solid and united enough to exercise practical leadership'[25] — in other words, the objection that their reading of *What Is To Be Done?* gave rise to in the minds of many Bolsheviks. The editors of the Bolshevik journal *refused to publish Lenin's article.*

And yet Lenin was not an unconditional defender of the soviets, and the appearance of workers' councils did not fill him with anything that could be called enthusiasm. His initial attitude expressed even that hostility and scepticism which were common to most of the Bolsheviks. When, in October 1905, the Mensheviks called on the workers of St Petersburg to elect committees in their factories — committees that were soon afterwards to become soviets — Lenin warned against 'the erroneousness of this slogan'.[26] It was the success of the soviets that helped to modify his attitude. Though he never worked out a real theory of the Soviet as an institution, he followed its development closely, and made a number of illuminating comments which together constituted a first attempt at grasping a phenomenon that was entirely new and unexpected.

In the first place, Lenin never contemplated responding to the new reality embodied in the Soviet by boycotting it — that extreme form of incomprehension and sulkiness that was manifested by many Bolsheviks. On the contrary, he considered that it was necessary to take part in the work of the Soviet, while striving to link its activities closely with those of the Party.[27] This participation in a body, the political significance of which was far from clear, by militants who were attached mainly, and in some cases exclusively, to a highly structured party, was, however, to remain something exceptional, justified only by fortuitous circumstances of 'periods of more or less intense revolutionary upheaval'.[28] This reservation was due to the weaknesses that Lenin saw in the Soviet organization, in particular its excessively dispersed character, the lack of a central authority: the All-Russia Congress of Soviets was not to come on the scene, crowning the network of soviets, until 1917.[29]

It remained the case, however, that the soviets, which originated as merely 'organs of the strike struggle', had progressively become transformed into 'organs of an uprising', and therefore the 'tremendous prestige' that they enjoyed was 'fully deserved'.[30] Lenin thus came, as we have seen, to bring together the function fulfilled by the soviets with his idea of *the revolutionary-democratic dictatorship of the proletariat and the peasantry.** It was, of course, not accidental that, in periods of revolutionary upsurge — in 1905, and, especially, in 1917 — Lenin should have concerned himself with defining the role of institutions that were very much broader than the Party organization. A Party man — indeed a man of *the* Party — he remained sensitive to the weaknesses of heterogeneous gatherings and movements that lacked

* See p. 76.

authoritative guidance. But, being a revolutionary no less, and even more, than a Party man, he appreciated the tremendous reservoir of energy, enthusiasm and creativity that the soviets contained. Consequently, he sought to reconcile these contradictory elements and to deduce an operational synthesis from them.

To a much greater extent than the other Bolsheviks—and sometimes in opposition to them—Lenin, while criticizing the 'fetishism' that the soviets inspired in their strongest supporters, nevertheless recognized in the formation of these organs a bold attempt to resolve the dialectical contradiction between the Party and the masses, transcending the narrow bounds of the formulas which he had propounded earlier. Finally, although he disagreed with Trotsky on many points, he saw in the soviets, just as Trotsky did, 'a workers' government in embryo'.[31] In this way the *rapprochements* and alliances were prepared which in 1917 were to determine the outcome of the revolution.

Lenin, the Bolsheviks, and the revolutionary activity of the masses
'A vast strike movement was in progress, some unknown tremendous wave was rising. But the Bolshevik Committee was living its own segregated life.'[32] Thus a Bolshevik witness describes the passivity shown by his organization during the decisive events of January 1905 in St Petersburg. The socialist forces were certainly weak at this time, as a result of the recent split between Bolsheviks and Mensheviks.

Agitation grew more intense in the factories of the capital and especially in the Putilov works, where the workers responded to the propaganda carried on by the priest Gapon, a strange individual in whom an *agent provocateur* was combined with an idealist, and who, having been entrusted by the authorities with a mission to be carried out among the workers, was now in the process of breaking away from his masters' control. This agitation, which developed into a mass strike, gave rise to a feeling of mistrust among both Bolsheviks and Mensheviks. When the idea was put forward and spread around that a demonstration should be held on Sunday, January 9th, to go to the Tsar and submit a petition to him, the reaction of the Socialist militants of both wings was even frankly hostile. And with good reason: how could they support a march that seemed to be conceived as a religious procession at least as much as it was to be a political demonstration? Besides, the Social-Democrats, and especially the Bolsheviks, were completely isolated in the Putilov works. 'Before January 9, the workers' feelings towards the Committee were extremely hostile. Our agitators were beaten up, our leaflets destroyed'.[33]

The Bolsheviks and the Mensheviks soon found themselves in disagreement on the attitude to be taken towards the demonstration. The former, reckoning with the state of mind of the masses, decided on a moderate line, and refrained from actually calling for a boycott of the affair. Further than that they could not go. The Mensheviks, however, issued the slogan of participation.[34] When a Bolshevik delegate tried to explain his organization's point of view to the Putilov workers, he was unable to get a hearing. Hardly had he begun his speech when he was interrupted by the workers: 'Enough, go away, don't interfere.' The would-be speaker had to take to his heels.[35]

Although it is not possible to generalize, it would seem that the Menshevik spokesmen, who were at first just as unenthusiastic as the Bolsheviks, showed themselves more sensitive to the pressure of the masses; and their organization did indeed join in the movement. The Bolsheviks, however, although at their meeting on January 8th they retracted their original decision, decided to remain together as a separate unit within the procession, not merging with the mass of demonstrators. The decision was put into practice: the Bolsheviks who in this way marched through St Petersburg on January 9th, when the revolution of 1905 broke out, numbered about fifteen.[36]

We know little regarding Lenin's attitude during these crucial days: enough, however, to observe a noticeable difference, on this question too, between his reactions and those of his supporters in Petersburg. In an article that appeared on January 11th in the Bolshevik organ *Vpered*, written shortly before 'Bloody Sunday', Lenin described the strike in the factories of the capital as 'one of the most imposing manifestations of the working-class movement'. He also refrained from criticizing the fact that the projected demonstration was intended to culminate in the presenting of a petition to the Tsar. He observed, on the contrary, that 'the primitive character of the socialist views held by some of the leaders of the movement and the tenacity with which some elements of the working class cling to their naïve faith in the Tsar enhance rather than lessen the significance of the revolutionary instinct now asserting itself among the proletariat'. And he noted that 'conscious Social-Democratic influence is lacking or is but slightly evident'.[37] There was, in fact, a great gulf between the cautious attitude of the Petersburg Bolsheviks and the passionate, already enthusiastic attention with which Lenin followed the first signs of the explosion that was imminent.

This enthusiasm was soon reinforced by the vigorous and massive reaction of the Russian proletariat to the massacre on 'Bloody Sunday'. On Wednesday, January 12th, Lenin wrote, in an article entitled 'The Beginning of the Revolution in Russia', that 'the working class has received a momentous lesson in civil war; the revolutionary education of the proletariat made more progress in one day than it could have made in months and years of drab, humdrum, wretched existence'. As regards Father Gapon, Lenin noted with satisfaction the statement he had made on the morrow of the demonstration:

'We no longer have a Tsar. A river of blood divides the Tsar from the people.'[38]

Lenin showed, moreover, a certain indulgence, perhaps even liking, where this Gapon was concerned, which contrasted with the suspicion and enmity that were the only feelings he evoked in the Leninists of the capital. One of Lenin's correspondents reproached him, in a letter dated January 1905, with being 'too lenient with Gapon'.[39] Two months later the priest went to Switzerland, to try and bring together in a new way the groups of Russian socialist émigrés. Whereas Plekhanov received him icily, Lenin showed great interest and much warmth.[40] In the presence of someone who had witnessed the revolution, and played a part in it, the doctrinal prejudices even of a man who was deeply convinced of the importance of theory could not withstand his desire for revolutionary action. Lenin urged Gapon, in order to help him acquire 'clarity of revolutionary outlook', to read the works of Plekhanov. But he had little success in this direction. As Krupskaya wrote of Gapon, 'The priest mentality blinded him.'[41]

Here are some passages from the official *History of the Communist Party of the Soviet Union* published in Moscow in 1960: 'The Bolsheviks ... called on the workers ... to go out into the streets ... in demonstration against the autocracy.'[42] 'The [London] Congress ... worked out the tactical line of the party, recognizing the organization of [an] *armed rising* as the chief and most urgent task of the party and the working class.'[43] 'In the summer and autumn of 1905 preparations proceeded apace for a general political strike. The tremendous organizational and agitational work carried on by the Bolsheviks facilitated the progress of the revolution.'[44]

This is, briefly indicated, the picture that official historians in the U.S.S.R. give of the attitude of the Bolsheviks during the revolution of 1905. It expresses and keeps alive a twofold legend: on the one hand, a flawless party, homogeneous and closely united, and, on the other, this party firm and constant in pursuit of a policy of urging the masses towards ever bolder and more revolutionary action. Neither part of the legend corresponds to the truth. The Bolsheviks did not constitute a monolithic block, and their policy was often hesitant, lagging behind the vigorous radicalism of the masses, and never serving them as a 'guide to action', the essential function ascribed to it by Lenin's doctrine. In January 1905 the Bolsheviks, to an even greater degree than their Menshevik adversaries, proved unable to foresee and direct the course of events and the movement of the masses. In the months that followed they continued to display hesitation and internal disagreement (which was inevitable) in the face of the growing size of the revolutionary upsurge. When, in August 1906, Lenin said that 'the proletariat sensed sooner than its leaders the change in the objective conditions of the struggle and the need for a transition from

the strike to an uprising,'[45] his critical reference to 'leaders' applied
particularly to the Bolshevik leaders. Later, writing of the events of
1905, he was to observe that 'the slogans of the revolutionaries ...
actually *lagged* behind the march of events'.[46] The allusion was aimed
at the slogans put forward by his own followers. To realize this it is
enough to recall the language used at the Bolshevik congress in
London by Bogdanov, the chief leader of the organization inside
Russia. Addressing delegates some of whom revealed a radical spirit
which he considered excessive, Bogdanov stressed 'the importance of
discipline for saving and concentrating the revolutionary forces,' and
called on the Party to persist in this line, 'unabashed by "unreason-
able accusations that they are slowing down the development of the
revolutionary mood of the masses" '.[47]

Were reproaches of this order actually brought against the Bolsheviks in 1905? And did their attitude during that year justify such
criticism? They were undoubtedly often to be found in the forefront
of the battle, and sometimes urged the masses to put forward fresh
demands and display renewed boldness. There were, however, a
number of occasions when Lenin's party showed itself timid and pusil-
lanimous. Evidence of this is given by the attitude that it frequently
took up in relation to the great strikes that accompanied the development of the revolutionary crisis. Without being actually hostile, the
Bolsheviks' attitude was not unconditionally favourable to this form
of action. In this matter as in so many others, the Bolsheviks did not
forget either their distrust of the 'spontaneity' of the masses or their
prejudices regarding purely 'trade union' demands. Even political
strikes were sometimes welcomed by them with mixed feelings, since
they feared that these strikes might result in frittering away the proletariat's strength and hindering the organizing of the armed insurrection. It appears that caution in this regard was especially marked in the
leading organs of the Party, and that desire for action was the livelier,
the closer the organs consulted were to the masses. Thus, when in
October 1905 the committee of the Moscow organization had to take
a decision on whether the time was ripe for a general strike, it rejected
the idea by 7 votes to 2. But when this question was discussed at a
general conference that brought together between 800 and 1,000
Moscow Bolsheviks, the decision in favour of the strike was unanimous.

In his valuable study of the revolution of 1905, S. M. Schwarz
quotes numerous accounts by Bolsheviks from which it emerges that
'in many places the Bolsheviks found themselves drawn into the strikes
and playing an active part in them despite themselves, as it were'.[48]
In some areas—Tver, for example—the Bolsheviks showed grave
misgivings, and 'some of the committee were against strike action'.[49]
It is true that the chief claim to glory possessed by the Bolsheviks of

1905 was that they launched the rising in Moscow, the most dramatic and spectacular event of that troubled year. In this case as in so many others, however, their leaders were brought to take the decision owing to pressure from the proletariat which had become irresistible. Thus, when the committee of the Moscow organization met to consider the situation, it listened to a series of statements that made clear the impatient mood of the masses. One delegate asserted that 'our workers will act themselves unless the committee calls them out'. Another reported that 'our workers are forging daggers and lances — we can't hold them back'. A third said that 'our workers are racing into battle, but have no arms'. Not long before, the head of the Party militia in the Moscow region had been against a rising. Faced now with the unanimity of this evidence, and convinced that it was impossible to keep the masses of Moscow waiting any longer, he yielded, and the Bolsheviks decided to launch the uprising. Soon afterward the Mensheviks decided to join in.[50]

At the Bolshevik congress of April 1905 the problem of armed insurrection was the subject of a long discussion, in which the delegates were far from showing a uniform degree of fighting spirit. A delegate from Saratov warned the congress against the motion that the proletarian masses were 'already armed with ideas' and only needed to have guns put into their hands. Other delegates supported this view, stating that the Party was not in a position to organize an insurrection. This tendency was a far from negligible one, and the majority had to take it into account. A resolution was passed, certainly, saying that to organize an armed rising was one of the Party's tasks; but in the listing of these tasks, those related to propaganda work were given priority, so as to appease the moderate tendency in the Bolshevik organization.[51]

It is enough, moreover, to read Lenin's writings of this period to form an idea of the resistance that he encountered among his own followers when he tried to convince them of the necessity and urgency of a resort to arms. For the founder of Bolshevism, in any case, organizing the insurrection constituted the Party's most important task. It had always figured in his code of political activity. In 1902 he had declared that the mission of the Central Committee was the 'preparation of demonstrations and an uprising on an all-Russian scale'.[52] The revolution made the fulfilment of this function a matter of urgency. In December 1904, when political agitation was mounting in the country, but as yet nobody suspected how imminent the explosion was, Lenin already foresaw that 'one of the outbreaks which are recurring now here, now there, with such growing frequency, will develop into a tremendous popular movement. At that moment the proletariat will rise and take its stand at the head of the insurrection ... '[53] On the morrow of 'Bloody Sunday' he observed, with barely concealed satisfaction: 'The uprising has begun. Force against force. Street fighting is raging, barricades are being thrown up, rifles are cracking, guns are roaring. Rivers of blood are flowing, the civil war for freedom is blazing up.'[54] Lenin strove, all through the year 1905, to convince the Bolsheviks that they must assume their responsibilities: since 'in a period of civil war the ideal party of the proletariat is a fighting party,'[55] every Party member must actively prepare for battle. This idea recurs again and again like a *leitmotiv* in the innumerable letters, articles, resolutions and reports that he wrote at this time. Lenin was now in the sphere of activity that he liked best. He was no longer merely the theoretician of organization, the craftsman and practical worker occupied with shaping the tool for revolution. At last, and for the first time, he was in the fullest sense of the word a revolutionary fighter, straining to come to grips with the enemy, at any cost, impatient to undertake the trial of strength with the old world.

This ardour and impatience of Lenin's were far from being shared by the Party as a whole. Quite apart from the Mensheviks, who were outside his influence, many Bolsheviks revealed a hesitant attitude that Lenin strove indefatigably, from his distant place of exile (he did not get back to Petersburg until the beginning of November), to overcome. At the Bolshevik congress in London he declared: 'we underestimated the significance and the inevitability of the uprising,'[56] and wanted to put on the agenda no longer just the principle of this uprising but also the working out of the practical tasks on the fulfilment of which must depend its actual launching. The appeal that he addressed on the first of May to the working people of Russia is particularly eloquent: 'To arms, workers and peasants! Hold secret meetings, form fighting squads, get whatever weapons you can … Let this year's First of May be for us the celebration of the people's uprising.' Being in favour, however, of an *organized* uprising, he added: 'Let us prepare for it and await the signal for the decisive attack on the tyrant.'[57] And it was to the leading organs and cadres of the Bolshevik faction that he then turned, for the signal to be given. To judge from Lenin's style, the response he met with does not seem to have come up to his expectations.

June 20th, 1905:
Away, then, with all doubts and vacillations. Let it be realised by one and all, now and without delay, how absurd and discreditable are all pretexts today for evading this urgent task of the most energetic preparation of the armed uprising.[58]

October 16th, 1905:
It horrifies me—I give you my word—it horrifies me to find that there has been talk about bombs for over six months, yet not one

has been made! ... Go to the youth! Form fighting squads *at once* everywhere, among the students, and *especially among the workers* ... Let groups be at once organised of three, ten, thirty, etc., persons. Let them arm themselves at once as best they can, be it with a revolver, a knife, a rag soaked in kerosene for starting fires, etc. ... The evil today is ... our senile fear of initiative. Let every group learn, if it is only by beating up policemen ... [59]

The last days of October 1905:
All delays, disputes, procrastination and indecision spell ruin to the cause of the uprising. Supreme determination, maximum energy, immediate utilisation of each suitable moment, immediate stimulation of the revolutionary ardour of the mass ... such is the prime duty of a revolutionary. [60]

Twelve years later, almost to the very day, in October 1917, Lenin was to use the same language in order to overcome resistance of the same sort among his own followers. To conclude: it was necessary for Lenin and the proletarian masses to exert a constant and increasing pressure on the leading cadres before the Party, although it had come into being in order to fight, would agree to do so. In this sphere as in many others, Lenin, using his immense power of persuasion, pressed his Party to abandon its rigid structures, to open itself up to the masses, and in particular to the workers; he pressed his Party to adopt a policy of collaboration with the soviets; he pressed it to show greater confidence in the often anarchical activity of the proletariat in revolt, and to drop the hesitancy that it often revealed in face of the development of the strike wave; finally and above all, Lenin pressed his Party to carry out its ultimate responsibility by leading the armed insurrection that was to enable the revolution to go forward.

It is true, then, in the last analysis, that the Bolshevik organization was profoundly transformed during the events of 1905. But this transformation was often effected despite the Bolsheviks themselves—despite those, especially, who had accepted most submissively the ideas and writings of Lenin. Lenin himself, however, gave in 1905 a first demonstration of that 'sense of revolution', his possession of which was to be confirmed, and its full brilliance displayed, in 1917.

4

The first results of Leninism

On the eve of the revolution of 1917 Lenin was still merely one Russian socialist leader among others, caught up in the fratricidal strife that gave occupation to *émigrés* cut off from political activity. Among all the leading socialists of Europe, however, he was the only one in whom the qualities of the theoretician were combined to such an extent with those of the practical politician—the only one to have actually created a party. Others, before and after him, busied themselves with developing the organization to which they belonged. But Lenin started from scratch in this field, and already before the revolution his work revealed an element of continuity that was characteristic of Leninism.

Lenin was already the *organization* man, and no doctrine paid so much attention as Leninism did to the demands of organization. The imperatives of centralism and discipline, of hierarchy and underground work (some of which ran counter to the most profound implications of the Marxist outlook), were for Lenin so many corollaries of a basic principle, namely, the need for a strong and vigorous organization, inspiring its supporters with loyalty and trust and its enemies with a repulsion that was mingled with fear.

A strong party does not, however, mean a rigid one. It must possess in equal measure both exceptional vigour and exceptional power of adaptation. In a bourgeois society in which the proletariat is subject to domination and its interests suffer fundamental injury, the very existence of this class being radically denied while at the same time it is continually being re-created, a society wherein the proletariat's own institutions are inevitably meagre and poor, the initiative is held, as a rule, by the dominant class. Only in periods of revolution does the proletariat break free from conditioning by this situation. Most of the time the socialist movement is in the disadvantageous position of having to reply either to the enemy's attacks or to his efforts to bring this opposition under control, to intimidate it, appease it, or seduce it. These are all so many operations, complementary or simultaneous in which the bourgeoisie takes the initiative and which the revolutionary party has to be able to answer.

To the requirements of this situation correspond two major features of Leninism, namely, the *flexibility* typical of Lenin's policy and the *discipline* imposed upon the Bolshevik organization. Lenin's flexibility comes close to being a pragmatism that seems surprising in a man almost fanatically devoted to a doctrine, Marxism, and an idea, the revolution. In reality, however, they were indispensable complements to that devotion of his, smoothing its rough edges and moderating its rigidity. Lenin's flexibility explains the fundamental contribution which he made to Marxism by 'Russifying' it, and also his constant readiness to reject 'deviations' either to Right or Left — which signified not a permanent 'centrism' on his part but rather a transition (sometimes brusque, and often skilful and, as we shall see, dialectical) from a 'Left' policy to a 'Right' one, or vice versa. The 'Russification' of Marxism consisted essentially in the perfecting of an organization adapted to the conditions of Tsarist Russia and differing profoundly from the workers' parties of Western Europe, and of a revolutionary strategy which assigned an important role to the peasantry. In this respect there was a far-reaching difference between Bolshevism and Menshevism. The latter was based not only on conviction that the Western *schemata* of social evolution must be reproduced in Russia, so that the bourgeoisie would prove to be the heir of Tsarism. It also endowed the Russian workers' party with structures and a role similar to those of the Social-Democratic Parties of Western Europe. Martov, for example, made it a reproach to the socialist movement of his country that it 'spoke too zealously in *Russian*'.[1] Axelrod defined the task of the Mensheviks as being 'to Europeanize, i.e., radically change the character of the Russian Social-Democratic movement ... and organize it on the same principles on which the European Social-Democratic party system is based.'[2] As the Bolshevik Radek put it, 'Western Europe begins with the Mensheviks.'[3] Lenin waxed ironical about this aspect of Menshevism. 'A naked savage who put on a top-hat and imagined himself therefore to be a European would look rather ridiculous.' Axelrod looked no less ridiculous 'when he puts on a top-hat inscribed "I am a European Social-Democrat".'[4]

Lenin's flexibility was thus shown first and foremost in his independent attitude to the interpretation of Marxism that was current in those days. With this went a high level of tactical sensitivity and a refusal to let himself be *imprisoned* in principles. This Lenin who was so devoted to Marxism, and so often inclined to decorate and even encumber his books and articles with innumerable supporting references to the thought of Marx and Engels, said of the Mensheviks, and not without justification, that they were 'afraid of losing the book knowledge they have learned by rote (but not assimilated)'.[5] For his part, the preoccupation that inspired him and that he often expressed in his writings was to adapt his activity to the exigencies of 'life'. In 1905 he modified to the utmost, to this end, the imperatives of clandestinity and centralism, and subordinated his principles of organization to the needs of the revolutionary struggle.

Later, after the defeat of the revolution, he carried on a bitter fight against the Mensheviks and against Bogdanov's supporters, because the former tended to concentrate all their hopes on a democratic evolution of the Duma and on the work of the socialist parliamentary group within it, while the latter refused to exploit the possibilities offered by the new institutions. Although an opponent of 'constitutional illusions', Lenin did not hesitate to commit the Bolshevik deputies to motions for improving labour legislation. On this matter as on so many others, he insisted that the Party must not be content with applying general principles but must proceed by 'carefully appraising the concrete political situation'.[6] His approach was no different as regards the structures of the Party, both open and secret. During the 'years of reaction' he never ceased to fight against the 'liquidationist' tendency of the Mensheviks, declaring that the Russian revolutionary organization must be essentially clandestine in character. He never departed from that position: but, from 1912 onwards, when he had transformed the Bolshevik faction into an entirely independent group, and its 'underground' framework seemed to him to be firm enough, he did not hesitate to develop legal activities, in the press, in social institutions and in the trade unions.

If the effectiveness of the Party called for a certain pragmatism on the part of its leader, this could not bear fruit unless the whole organization showed an equal power of adaptation, subjecting itself without friction or delay to the sometimes rather sudden changes that Lenin introduced into its political line. Such rapidity in the carrying out of decisions could be obtained only if strict discipline were to be accepted, and, consequently, if a very pronounced sense of hierarchy prevailed. The Bolshevik militant was a soldier in a formation from which quasi-military obedience was required, and the Bolshevik organization was indeed conceived by its founder as an 'army in the field'.* As Trotsky put it, 'Leninism is warlike from head to foot.'[7]

Lenin had convinced his followers of the need for such discipline. The members of his organization were not so much 'militants' as 'agents', ready at any moment to carry out the orders of their superior officers, whether these orders obliged them to change their jobs, leave their factory, their town or even their country, to take up a different form of political activity or fresh organizational task, or to engage in

---

* Lenin, Vol. 6, p. 244. In *What Is To Be Done?* he called for a 'military organization of agents' (ibid., Vol. 5, p. 515n), but this expression was omitted in the edition of 1907.

new revolutionary deeds involving incalculable risks. Many Bolsheviks were convinced that a revolutionary party must be a revolutionary army, and that the virtue of obedience was one of the chief attributes of a revolutionary socialist. Thus the Bolshevik Committee in Ufa considered in 1904 that the Central Committee ought to possess the right to dissolve by its own authority, should this seem to it necessary or even useful, any committee or any organization belonging to the Party, and similarly to deprive of his rights any individual member of the Party. In their view it was necessary to combine 'the highest degree of consciousness with absolute obedience'.[8]

To be sure, Lenin never went as far as that, and never required 'absolute obedience' from his supporters. But because he did believe in the absolute necessity of discipline and efficiency, he adopted an extremely critical attitude towards intellectuals in general, and even towards those who had joined the socialist movement. This attitude might seem strange on the part of a man who was convinced that 'without a revolutionary theory there can be no revolutionary movement,'[9] and who ascribed to intellectuals an essential role in the revolutionary struggle, acknowledging that 'the theory of socialism ... grew out of the philosophic, historical and economic theories elaborated by educated representatives of the propertied classes, by intellectuals.'[10] They it was who had the task of bringing to the proletariat, from outside, that political and socialist consciousness to which, according to Lenin, the class was unable to attain through its own experience alone. The intellectuals justified this expectation, since, after having filled the ranks of the revolutionary Populist (Narodnik) organizations, they made up a high proportion of the Social-Democrats in Russia. A biographical study of 160 leading Bolsheviks of the pre-revolutionary period whose educational background is known has shown that 79 of them had enjoyed higher education. Although among the rank-and-file the proportion of the university-educated was only 15 per cent – which is still a comparatively large proportion – among the members of the Bolshevik local committees it reached 45 per cent.[11]

Diatribes against intellectuals nevertheless figure frequently in Lenin's writings. He often attacked them in the vitriolic style he affected, speaking of 'these scoundrels' of intellectuals,[12] of 'anaemic intellectuals',[13] of the 'flabbiness ... of the intellectuals',[14] and of 'the flabby bourgeois intelligentsia'.[15]

It was not merely a question of style, however. What was involved here was Lenin's judgment on the role played by intellectuals in the socialist movement. He attributed to their petty-bourgeois social origin the defect that he mainly blamed in them, namely, their inaptitude for discipline and rejection of organization,[16] and he was continually contrasting 'bourgeois-intellectual individualism', with the 'supporters of proletarian organization and discipline'.[17] It was not only their inclination towards individualism that he denounced, moreover, but also their opportunism. It was the intellectuals, he held, who were responsible for the development of reformist trends in Russian Social-Democracy. He spoke of 'the opportunism which their mentality produces'.[18] In this connexion, too, Lenin contrasted 'the intellectual opportunist wing' with 'the proletarian revolutionary wing'.[19]

How unfortunate were those representatives of the Russian intelligentsia who had found their way in such large numbers into the socialist movement! Mensheviks and Bolsheviks blamed each other for them.[20] The former, in the person of Axelrod, accused Lenin of seeking to legitimize the domination of a proletarian party by an elite of intellectuals.[21] Trotsky, in his onslaught on Lenin, had much to say to the same effect, and depicted the Bolsheviks as 'an organization consisting of Marxist intellectuals so far as three-quarters, if not nine-tenths, of the membership is concerned'.[22] Lenin claimed that, on the contrary, at the time of the split in 1903 the opposition between Bolsheviks and Mensheviks was equivalent to one between working-class elements and intellectual elements.[23] Later, when a substantial number of Mensheviks had declared in favour of transforming the Social-Democratic Party into an open, legal organization, Lenin once again presented this 'liquidationist' tendency as a typical manifestation of the intellectual mentality.[24] I have already mentioned the efforts he made to open up his Party, and its committees in particular, to proletarians, during the revolutionary period of 1905–6. These efforts resulted in a change in the social composition of the Social-Democratic cadres. Although the proportion of intellectuals continued to be very high, among the Bolsheviks even more than among the Mensheviks workers became increasingly numerous, occupying higher positions in the organization. In 1908 Lenin noted, in a letter to Gorky, that 'the significance of the intellectuals in our party is declining; news comes from all sides that the intelligentsia is fleeing the party. And a good riddance to these scoundrels. The party is purging itself from petty bourgeois dross. The workers are having a bigger say in things. The role of the worker-professionals is increasing. All this is wonderful.'*

Leaving aside the question of Lenin's personal characteristics, this snarling attitude of his can only be understood in the light of the role that the intelligentsia had played in the Russian revolutionary movement.[25] This role had undergone a profound change since the beginning of the twentieth century. Whereas until then the very concept of

_____

* Ibid., Vol. 34, p. 379. Gorky probably reacted sharply to this letter; Lenin thought it necessary to reassure him, and wrote soon afterwards that he had 'never ... thought of "chasing away the intelligentsia" ... or of denying its necessity for the workers' movement' (ibid., Vol. 34, p. 385).

the intelligentsia had possessed a mainly subjective meaning—indicating not so much a specific position in society and a particular economic function as a certain kind of outlook—it now assumed a more and more objective meaning, in closer correlation with occupational criteria. Members of the intelligentsia became increasingly numerous in the administration and in industry and business. Before this period the intelligentsia had been characterized psychologically by a lofty idealism that kept it remote from reality, and politically by an attraction towards extremism, but now it took up new attitudes in society and in the world of politics. It showed growing interest in concrete achievements, especially in scientific and juridical associations, and in day-to-day politics, turning away from the revolutionary lures to which it had formerly been susceptible.

There was something else, though, in Lenin's attitude to the intellectuals besides a reaction to the way that large numbers of them were becoming integrated into Russian society. His antipathy to the intelligentsia was aimed not only at the new generation of intellectuals, interested in reforms and fearful of extremism. Lenin's attitude was also determined by everything that he objected to in the traditional outlook of the Russian intelligentsia, as revealed throughout the nineteenth century. His diatribes expressed 'his hatred of carelessness, vagueness, inefficiency, shilly-shallying, phrase-making, and of those endless discussions without results that were so typical of Russian intellectuals'.[26] What exasperated Lenin—the practical worker, the organizer, who devoted himself to fulfilling all the tasks of the professional revolutionary, even the most menial and thankless ones—was the propensity of Russian intellectuals, so numerous among the socialist émigrés, to lose themselves in theoretical discussions, wander among abstractions and burden themselves with a paralysing sentimentality.*

Lenin's 'anti-intellectualism' was thus not motiveless. Whatever justification it might possess, however, there were in this attitude dangers (intensified by the style of invective employed) of which Lenin—himself an intellectual, and of no mean stature—was doubtless unaware, but which the subsequent evolution of Bolshevism was to reveal in all their magnitude. In any case, Leninism contained a pernicious 'anti-intellectualism' which was the seamy side of its will to efficiency, the consequence of the character it sought to give to the Russian socialist movement: namely, that of an organization capable of carrying on a realistic policy, capable above all of waging the revolutionary battle—that is to say, in the last analysis, leading an *armed uprising* of the proletariat against Tsarism.

* Lenin ridiculed, for instance, 'the saccharine-sweet sentimentality so characteristic of our intelligentsia' (quoted by Frank, p. 30).

For that was what was ultimately at stake: Leninism and Bolshevism are a theory and a form of organization, but they are also a type of political commitment focused on the idea of battle and insurrection. In this matter Lenin's convictions were based on an objective analysis of the economic and social conditions prevailing in Russia. His interpretation of these conditions in a revolutionary sense was decisive for Lenin; and his fighting temperament did the rest.

It is impossible to understand anything about Leninism if one ignores the fact that it accords *primordial* importance to the idea of armed, organized insurrection as an indispensable, decisive form of political struggle — its highest form. From the first months that followed the 'Bloody Sunday' of 1905 Lenin delved into military literature and encouraged his followers to do the same. 'All Social-Democrats,' he wrote, '... are putting great stress on studying [military] questions and bringing them to the knowledge of the masses.'[27] Throughout the year 1905 Lenin repeatedly called upon the Bolsheviks to go over to *action*, and his instructions became increasingly precise. In an article published in *Proletary* on August 16th, 1905, he urged on them 'the stationing of patrols and the billeting of squads'.[28] In another article in the same paper (September 13th, 1905), Lenin dwelt on the need to form armed groups on a very wide scale. 'The number of such contingents of 25 to 75 men each can be increased to several dozen in every big city, and frequently in the suburbs of a big city.' Further, he demanded that they be armed 'with all sorts of weapons, ranging from knives and revolvers to bombs.' Finally, he stressed the need for serious study of 'how to put up barricades and defend them.'[29] On October 16th, 1905:

> Squads must *at once* begin military training by launching operations immediately, at once. Some may at once undertake to kill a spy or blow up a police station, others to raid a bank to confiscate funds for the insurrection ... Let groups be at once organised of three, ten, thirty, etc., persons. Let them arm themselves at once as best they can, be it with a revolver, a knife, a rag soaked in kerosene for starting fires, etc.[30]

When at last the armed rising broke out, mainly in Moscow, and ended in the defeat of the revolutionaries, Lenin, unlike the Mensheviks, who saw in this a proof of the vanity of insurrectionary methods, remained convinced of their necessity. Drawing the lessons of the revolution of 1905 a few years later, he declared: 'The revolution of 1905 was defeated not because it had gone "too far", or because the December uprising was "artificial". On the contrary, the cause of the defeat was that the uprising did *not* go *far enough*, ... that the uprising was not concerted, resolute, organized, simultaneous, aggressive.'[31]

The experience of the years 1905 and 1906 illuminates the profound difference separating Bolsheviks from Mensheviks, not only in the sphere of revolutionary strategy and in their attitudes towards the bourgeoisie but also in their style of action: the caution characteristic of the Mensheviks contrasted with the fighting spirit of the Bolsheviks, and especially with Lenin's will to struggle. Lenin was deeply aware of the contrast, and he attacked the Mensheviks on this ground as well. He ridiculed them for using the language not of political leaders but of 'archive fogeys',[32] and addressed them thus: 'Oh, you, who call yourselves supporters of the toiling masses! It's not for you to go to a rendezvous with the revolution. Stay at home; really, it will be quieter there ... '[33]

In disagreement during the revolutionary years on the question of whether the time had come for an organized general rising, the Leninists and their opponents disagreed again during the 'years of reaction', on the question of guerrilla struggle. The revolution had given birth to 'combat groups' with a wide scope of activity: organizing defence against pogroms, attacks on armouries, assassinations of spies, manufacture of bombs, and 'expropriation' operations aimed at acquiring large sums of money belonging to banks or the state treasury. As the revolutionary offensive ran out of steam, however, these guerrilla actions degenerated and came increasingly to resemble acts of banditry (forging bank-notes, selling weapons to robber bands, financial scandals, and so on). In 1906, at the Stockholm congress, Bolsheviks and Mensheviks opposed each other on the problem of this method of struggle, with the former defending guerrilla activities and the latter showing themselves more and more hostile to them. When reunified Russian Social-Democracy was led by a Central Committee with a Menshevik majority, the latter tried to put an end to the doings of the 'combat groups' and to the 'expropriations', whereas Lenin called for their continuance, thus entering into open revolt against the Party leadership.* He did certainly acknowledge that, as a result of poverty, hunger and unemployment, 'this form of struggle was adopted as the preferable and even *exclusive* form of social struggle by the vagabond elements of the population'.[34] But he remained convinced none the less of the usefulness of guerrilla actions, so great was his insistence on the need for armed struggle. After a 'military-technical bureau' had been set up by the Stockholm congress, and control of this had fallen entirely into Bolshevik hands, Lenin kept the bureau in being even though the London congress of 1907 decided in favour of dissolving it. He considered, however, that the activities of the guerrilla groups should be prepared by the Party itself and carried out under its direction, and that this form of struggle 'must be subordinated to other methods ... and must be ennobled by the enlightening and

* See p. 52.

organizing influence of socialism'.[35] Ultimately, these activities must be made to contribute to a general insurrection.

Thus, the 1905 revolution and its consequences helped to form a type of militant who was oriented no longer merely towards underground work and the acceptance of discipline and a rule of obedience, but also towards open struggle and various forms of 'direct action'. A militant of this type needed more than ever to possess courage that was proof against any trial—and also to be endowed with boldness, a mentality directed towards practical action, caring little about doctrinal or moral scruples: to be someone for whom the demands of organization were supplemented by those of warfare. Of this category of Bolsheviks Simon Ter-Petrosyan, known as 'Kamo', Stalin's comrade-in-arms in enterprises of 'expropriation', offers the most perfect example. Boris Souvarine has provided us with a striking portrait of him. The leader of a 'combat group' and responsible for some especially spectacular actions, Kamo was arrested in September 1907 by the German police, and in order to avoid being handed over to the Tsarist authorities he pretended to be mad, his masquerade being protracted for four years.

> He stamped, shouted, tore his clothes, refused food and struck his keeper. He was shut up naked in an icy cell, but did not yield ... He stood upright for four months, refused food, was forcibly fed at the expense of several broken teeth, tore out his hair, hanged himself, counting on intervention at the last moment, opened blood vessels with a sharpened bit of bone ... In order to test his pretended insensibility, needles were stuck under his nails and he was touched with red hot irons. The professors concluded that his malady was real.

Despite this, the Germans turned him over to the Tsarist police. Once again he simulated madness. Shut up in a lunatic asylum, he brought off, in August 1911, 'a marvellous escape after having spent three months in sawing through his chains and the window bars'. He met Lenin in Paris and doubtless drew from this encounter fresh reasons for hope. Having resumed his activities, he was again arrested in 1912, after a particularly audacious 'expropriation'. Four times condemned to death, he owed his life only to the amnesty proclaimed in 1913 by the Tsar on the occasion of the tercentenary of the Romanov dynasty.[36] A quasi-legendary figure in the Bolshevik movement, exceptional both in his calibre and in his tragic fate, Ter-Petrosyan nevertheless represented a type of revolutionary that was to be found in considerable numbers in the Leninist organization.

The revolution of 1905 had thus transformed quite a few 'committeemen' into heroes. To be sure, the Bolsheviks had no monopoly of such devotion and heroism. Drawn, however, by their founder into a

4*

political enterprise that was to be crowned by insurrection, and the day-to-day vicissitudes of which always involved risks of death, the Bolsheviks constituted a phalanx that united, alongside brilliant intellectuals such as Kamenev, Bogdanov, Lunacharsky and Bukharin (not to mention Lenin himself), men for whom nothing mattered any more but the demands of the revolution. From this resulted a fundamental difference between the Bolshevik organization and the socialist parties of the West—for 'the great workers' parties grew up for the most part in periods when the problem of revolution was only conceived as influencing programmes in a theoretical way rather than as something which informed all the actions of daily life'.[37] The opposite was true of Lenin's supporters.*

And this brings us back to Leninism itself, as it was on the eve of 1917, on which the time has come to conclude my observations. It was undoubtedly conditioned by its will to organize and striving for efficiency, and marked by its insistence on the merits of hierarchy and discipline, on the need for centralization of authority within the Party and subjection of the masses and all working-class institutions to Party leadership. It showed *tendencies* towards the monolithic ideal. In its organizational expression it bore the imprint of the personality of its founder and of the authority of an unchallenged leader. Let there be no misconception, however: the authority that Lenin enjoyed had nothing dictatorial about it, and if he sometimes sought to impose on his followers an attitude of unconditional acceptance, he aimed in doing this not so much at ensuring allegiance to himself personally as at obtaining unity around a theory that he believed to be correct. The history of Bolshevism before 1917 was in many ways a history of clashes and conflicts between different movements among the Bolsheviks, whose divergences were, as we have seen, public and substantial. The debates that took place at Party congresses were lively, and the resistances that Lenin encountered among his supporters were obstinate. Yet his hold upon them was strong, as many witnesses attest.†

* A document produced by a Bolshevik committee declared, for example, that 'the central organization must be made up of leaders of uniform views, and there must be no question of its including representatives of all tendencies.' (Appendix to Trotsky, *Nos tâches politiques*, p. 246.)

† The Soviet historian Pokrovsky describes as follows the power that Lenin had over him: 'There was above all his enormous capacity to see to the root of things, a capacity which finally aroused a sort of superstitious feeling in me. I frequently had occasion to differ from him on practical questions but I came off badly every time; when this experience had been repeated about seven times, I ceased to dispute and submitted to Lenin, even if logic told me that one should act otherwise.' (Quoted in Fülöp-Miller, p. 43.) Lunacharsky, who ranked among the most outstanding Bolsheviks and whose mental capacities were great, admitted that, nevertheless, when he was going to make an important speech at a congress, he submitted his draft to the Party leader. '[Lenin] attentively read through my MS. and returned it with two or three insignificant corrections—which was not surprising considering that, so far as I remember, I took [his] most precise and detailed instructions ... as my starting point.' (Quoted by Carr, Vol. I, p. 46.)

What is of greatest importance in Leninism, in the last analysis, is that, as regards both organization and strategy, it is wholly and basically oriented towards revolution, meaning the seizure of power through an armed rising. This is what gives to Lenin's work and career a coherence and unity that are lacking from those of his opponents. This is what determined increasingly, as their respective choices became clear, the difference between Bolshevism and Menshevism.

This difference was clear-cut not only because the political characteristics of Bolshevism and Menshevism diverged, from this period onwards, on some essential points, but also because, organizationally, they had cut all the ties that once bound them together. In the labour movement of the West the presence of revolutionary and reformist trends within the same parties blurred the frontiers separating these trends. Such coexistence ceased to be possible when a period of social and political upheaval opened, compelling everyone to make decisive choices. But the Western Socialists were ill-prepared to meet such a test. The need, and the outward appearance, of unity that marked their movement down to 1914 prevented the elaboration and perfection within it of a theory of action and a formula of organization oriented towards revolution and clearly distinguished from reformism. In Russia, however, although the complete break between Bolsheviks and Mensheviks certainly fostered sectarianism, Bolshevism was armed thereby, even in its sectarian phase, with a clarity, a cohesion and a cutting edge without which it would not have been able to play its role of 1917.

Unconcerned with those preoccupations about unity which almost inevitably lead to the making of compromises, Lenin was able to give a sharp outline to his doctrine, using the incisive language that he preferred and, as he often stressed, *aussprechen was ist* ('to say what is', i.e. to describe things frankly as he saw them), without having to worry about the feelings of any partners. This absence of ambiguity not only helped to separate the revolutionary trend from the reformist one, it also maintained and reinforced the distinction between the Russian socialist movement and bourgeois ideology. No doubt the weakness of liberalism in Russia limited its power of attraction: not sufficiently, though, to prevent the Mensheviks from becoming susceptible to it. Leninism, however, by its twofold opposition to bourgeois liberalism and socialist reformism, accentuated the split between the world of the bourgeoisie and that of the proletariat, in a period when Social-Democracy was weaving ever stronger bonds between them.

The concurrence of circumstances which Lenin had helped to create, and which he systematically exploited, enabled him at last to show himself in his true light: not just as a theoretician of organization and a careful practitioner of political action, but also and above all as a

revolutionary. The spirit of revolution inspired his calculations and fired his imagination. His head and his heart were alike committed to the revolution. His head, because it was thinking that led him to make his unconditional commitment to revolution, and also because it was on revolution that he counted to educate the working class.*
His heart, because 'revolutions are the festivals of the oppressed and the exploited'.[38] (Similar accents are sometimes to be caught in the writings of Karl Marx.)†

Leninism was so closely identified with revolution that Lenin resigned himself only with painful reluctance to the defeat of the revolutionary effort of 1905. In December 1906, when defeat was obvious, he was still writing: 'We shall keep to our revolutionary slogans ... —we shall make the utmost use of *all* revolutionary possibilities—we shall take pride in the fact that we were the *first* to take the path of an uprising and will be the *last* to abandon it, if this path in fact becomes possible.'[39] Only in March 1908 did he admit that reaction had won the day.[40] It is no less characteristic that already in 1910, very prematurely, he thought he could claim that 'the three-year period of the golden days of the counter-revolution (1908–10) is evidently coming to a close and being replaced by a period of incipient upsurge'.[41]

This desperate refusal to accept that the revolution had been defeated, and this persistent wish to discern, in the political and social situation, the slightest sign that might justify hope for a new outbreak are highly revelatory of the nature of Leninism. The structures that Lenin had conceived for his party were dictated by the needs of revolution: the advances recorded by his organization became possible, in 1905 and after 1912, only because the revolution had become a reality, or a hope; contrariwise, the decline of the organization, between 1908 and 1912, reflected the triumph of the counter-revolution, of which it was the result. Georg Lukács was right, therefore, when he wrote: 'Lenin's concept of party organization presupposes the fact—the actuality—of the revolution.'‡ In the face of current criticism of Leninism it is important to stress that, while Lenin was, in some ways, dominated by the idea of organization, this was organization *in the service* of the revolution. And what is true of 'Lenin's concept of party organization' is equally true of Leninism as a whole.

In Lenin's implacable, necessary, clear-sighted struggle against the Mensheviks, which was so often marked by unfairness, in the attacks

---

* Lenin speaks of the 'tremendous educational and organizing power' of the revolution, 'when mighty historical events force the man in the street out of his remote corner, garret or basement and make a *citizen* out of him.' (Lenin, Vol. 8, p. 564.)

† 'For the workers, their revolutionary activity is the greatest joy of their life.' (Marx, *Arbeitslohn*, December 1847, quoted in Rubel, p. 286.)

‡ Lukács, *Lenin*, p. 26. Again: 'the Leninist form of organization is indissolubly linked with the ability to foresee the approaching revolution' (ibid., p. 29).

he hurled against them, so legitimate and politically intelligent and yet frequently so crude, there was at bottom, perhaps, not merely political passion but also an element of sadness. 'I am hurt by this degradation of the most revolutionary doctrine in the world,'[42] he once said, referring to his opponents on the Right in the Social-Democratic movement. Lenin's bitterness and anger was due in part to his disappointment at seeing former comrades-in-arms, Marxists like himself, declining to keep that appointment which justified all the sacrifices consented to and all the hopes cherished—the appointment with revolution.

Part II
The Leninist revolution

Introduction

After 1912 the Russian labour movement, which had been decimated in 1906 and forced onto the defensive, in a nearly exhausted condition, demoralized and scattered, struggling desperately to keep its organizations in being, now experienced a fresh upsurge. Strikes and demonstrations became frequent, the latter reaching their highest point in July 1914, when St Petersburg bristled with barricades and Russia seemed on the eve of new revolutionary convulsions. From Poronino, near Cracow, Lenin followed the developing situation, and compared it to that of January 1905.* Was the 'rendezvous with revolution' about to take place?

On the contrary—war broke out, interrupting the proletarian offensive and replacing for a time the confrontation of classes by that of nations. Europe was swept by a wave of patriotic fervour to which most of the socialists who had been internationalists only the day before now gave themselves up with complete abandon. The threats they had uttered against the bourgeoisie and imperialism were forgotten.

This bankruptcy of the International made a very big impression on Lenin, and influenced Leninism profoundly. All Lenin's actions were thenceforth dominated by the will to break with social-patriotism. The final years of his exile, spent in Switzerland, were devoted to industrious preparation for this break. They are of considerable importance in the development of Leninism. Between 1914 and 1917 Lenin began applying himself to new problems. Almost entirely cut off from the Russian socialist movement, which the war had in any case disorganized and weakened,† he concentrated his studies and his efforts in fresh directions. It was in this period that he studied the question of imperialism‡ and gave more thorough attention to the

---

* In a draft for an article written between July 28th and 31st, we find these notes:

July days in 1914 vs. January 1905
1. gonfalons—barricades
2. Gapon—illegal Social-Democratic organization

(Lenin, Vol. 41, p. 335.)

† 'The most pressing question now is the weakness of contacts between us and leading workers in Russia', wrote Lenin in the autumn of 1916 (ibid., Vol. 35, p. 235).

‡ See p. 187.

questions of nationalism and of the right of nations to self-determination.*

Furthermore, and most important of all, it was during the First World War that Leninism and its founder acquired an *international* dimension. The breakdown of international relations in the European socialist movement and the retreat or realignment effected by the chief personages of the movement obliged those who would not accept the triumph of social-patriotism to come forward and take their place. At the same time, the restrictions on freedom of action and expression that were imposed in the belligerent countries cut down the role that some of the socialists living in those countries—Rosa Luxemburg, for example—might otherwise have played. Neutral Switzerland was one of the rallying centres of the minority trends which, after the catastrophic surprise of August 1914, strove to recover from their initial setback. Among these trends, the extreme Left wing found a leader in the person of Lenin. Already a model of intransigence in his fight against the Mensheviks, he now became even more intransigent still and made this attitude his platform. When the European socialists who were opposed to the war held their first conference, in September 1915, at Zimmerwald, Lenin gathered round him those few delegates who could not rest satisfied with the relative moderation of the majority of the participants. To the desire for conciliation shown by the latter, Lenin opposed his determination to cut the links with all shades of patriotism, and the class collaboration this entailed. From that moment onwards he devoted himself to a task of all-European scale: the establishment of a new International—in other words (and without Lenin's perceiving at the time all the implications of this), the creation of the world-wide Communist movement.

What is paradoxical is that Lenin attained in this way a higher standing than before at a moment when his isolation was almost total. To be sure, not a few Russian socialists were against the war. But among them were hardly any who were prepared to adopt Lenin's extreme conclusions: even among the Bolsheviks there were not many who dared to proclaim Lenin's principle of revolutionary defeatism, which, not content merely with repudiating the patriotic wave, affirmed that 'there cannot be the slightest doubt that, from the standpoint of the working class and of the toiling masses of all the nations of Russia, the defeat of the tsarist monarchy ... would be the lesser evil.'[1] On the international plane his hatred of 'centrism'†

---

* See p. 271.

† The 'centrism' that Lenin constantly attacked during the war was capable of assuming a number of forms. It could mean, for instance, desiring a reconciliation between patriotic socialists and anti-war socialists, or it could mean calling for a 'peace without annexations or indemnities', whereas, according to Lenin, no 'democratic peace' was possible without a revolution, and the latter, not any 'peace programme', ought to be the socialist reply to the war.

and contempt for pacifism were no better calculated to bring support or even sympathy Lenin's way.* At the Zimmerwald conference even the Spartakists refused to side with him.[2] Lenin's isolation was so complete that he began to take a close interest in the problems of the Swiss labour movement and to occupy himself actively in organizing its Left wing.

These activities, engaged in for lack of opportunity for anything better, were unable, however, to safeguard him against the doubts that during these dark years of his life sometimes filled Lenin with bitterness. Gnawed at by what he called the 'corrosion' of *émigré* life,[3] at the end of 1916 and the beginning of 1917 Lenin was not far from losing heart. 'The revolutionary movement grows extremely slowly and with difficulty,' he wrote to Inessa Armand on December 25th, 1916. In an almost resigned way he added: 'This has to be put up with.'[4] And soon afterwards he declared, in a public lecture: 'We of the older generation may not live to see the decisive battles of this coming revolution.'[5]

That was said on January 22nd, 1917. A month later, Tsarism collapsed, and the triumph of the proletariat of Petersburg opened before Leninism, Russia and the world a period of upheavals and hopes that had been totally unexpected.

---

* Fundamentally, Lenin considered, in February 1915, that 'at the present time, the propaganda of peace unaccompanied by a call for revolutionary mass action can only sow illusions and demoralize the proletariat, for it makes the proletariat believe that the bourgeoisie is humane, and turns it into a plaything in the hands of the secret diplomacy of the belligerent countries. In particular, the idea of a so-called democratic peace being possible without a series of revolutions is profoundly erroneous' (ibid., Vol. 21, p. 171). In September 1916 he wrote: 'an oppressed class which does not strive to learn to use arms, to acquire arms, only deserves to be treated like slaves' (ibid., Vol. 23, p. 96). Convinced as he was of the legitimacy of some wars, especially revolutionary ones, Lenin also lashed out at 'the mawkish snivellers who are afraid of war' (ibid., Vol. 21, p. 253), and spoke of 'the whole infamy of pacifism, its whole staggering banality' (ibid., Vol. 43, pp. 609–10).

1

The Party of the Revolution

Lenin and the Bolshevik Party in 1917

The Bolshevik Party was at this time, formally speaking, only five years old, and three of these years had been war years, when the internationalist line of Lenin's supporters had driven the Party deeply underground and incapacitated them from taking advantage of opportunities for legal work. Clandestine and persecuted, the Bolsheviks had been deprived of their political leaders inside Russia, through the arrest and exiling of Kamenev, Ordzhonikidze, Stalin and Sverdlov. The Party's weakness was such that the Petersburg Committee* found itself unable in January 1917 to bring out a leaflet on the occasion of the anniversary of 'Bloody Sunday'.[1] This failure tells us much about the state that Bolshevism was in when the year 1917 opened. It was to be a year when Bolshevism underwent a complete metamorphosis. In a few months the numbers of the Bolsheviks would be increased by more than tenfold,† while their methods of action would be changed, their political platform transformed, their strategy reversed — and then they would win power and shake the world.

But the year 1917, the year of the Russian proletariat's struggle against the bourgeoisie, was also the year of Lenin's struggle to free his Party from the grip of an orthodoxy and cautiousness that threatened to paralyse it just as they were paralysing its Menshevik and S.R. rivals. Renewing the efforts he had made in 1905, Lenin had once again to take up arms against those supporters of his who — often in the name of Leninism itself — were hindering the Party's march to power. It was then that Leninism came to flower, as a fully revolutionary doctrine. It was then that, violently shaken and almost battered by its own founder, the Bolshevik Party became the party of the revolution.

* In 1914 the Russian Government had changed the 'German-sounding' name of the capital to Petrograd. The Bolshevik Committee, however, reacting against this example of anti-German chauvinism, decided to keep to the old name.

† See p. 158.

The Bolsheviks before Lenin's return: a Menshevik-tending party

The Bolshevik militants were not inactive, of course, in the revolution of February 1917. From the first days of the popular agitation they closely followed the course of events and took part in them. But they were unable to take the lead in the movement, or even to put forward a clear programme of action and precise aims capable of winning the support of the most conscious and radical of the demonstrators.

After the exiling of the principal leaders, the Party inside Russia was led by the Russian Bureau of the Central Committee, made up of Shlyapnikov, Molotov and Zalutsky. Shlyapnikov, who had been in contact with Lenin by letter before the outbreak of the revolution, figured as the principal leader of the Party. In his reminiscences of the February days, V. N. Kayurov, a member of the Bolshevik committee in the industrial district of Vyborg, on the outskirts of Petrograd, tells us that, during the first days of the insurrection, they 'received absolutely no guidance from the leading organs of the Party. The Petrograd committee had been arrested, and Comrade Shlyapnikov, representing the Central Committee, was unable to give [them] directions for future activity.'[2] And Sukhanov, in his invaluable reminiscences, confirms and extends the relevance of this remark. Recording a meeting that took place on February 25th, at which representatives of the Bolshevik Party were present, he notes that 'their flatfootedness or, more properly, their incapacity to think their way into the political problem and formulate it, had a depressing effect on us'.[3]

Lacking a vigorous and clear-sighted leadership, the Bolsheviks of the capital had reacted to the first workers' demonstrations with much reserve, and even with a suspiciousness that recalls their attitude in January 1905. They were somewhat isolated in the factories where they worked, 'carrying on a desperate struggle ... against the Mensheviks and S.R.s'.[4] Representatives of the Party strove, on February 22nd, to calm down the working women who were getting ready to celebrate 'Women's Day', on the morrow, in a particularly militant way. Kayurov remembers thus this significant episode of the February days: having been sent to a meeting of working women, 'I explained the meaning of "Women's Day" and of the women's movement in general, and when I had to talk about the present moment I endeavoured first and foremost to urge the women to refrain from any partial demonstrations and to act only upon the instructions given by the Party Committee'. The temporizing slogans of the Party were not followed, however, as Kayurov learnt with 'astonishment' and 'indignation'. 'I was angered by the behaviour of the strikers,' he later related: 'in the first place they had obviously ignored the decisions taken by the Party's district committee, and then by me. The previous evening I had called on the working women to show restraint and discipline—and now, out of the blue, there was this strike.' After some discussion, however, the Bolsheviks decided to support the strike which had begun in this way, and to try to extend it.[5]

The day after that, February 24th, half of the proletariat of Petersburg, about 200,000 workers, were on strike, and street demonstrations were becoming ever larger and bolder. On February 25th there was a general strike and an insurrection, with the first shedding of blood. On that day, 'the Bolsheviks were the main organizers of the strikes and parades',[6] and it was they too who raised the question of setting up a Soviet.[7] But, also on that day, the Bolshevik leaders, when appealed to for arms by the demonstrators, refused to issue them. Shlyapnikov, who was mainly responsible for the refusal, considered that 'a rash use of arms thus supplied could only harm the cause'.[8]

In the evening of February 26th the first mutinies occurred among the troops, heralding the imminent downfall of Tsarism. Among the Bolshevik leaders, however, as Kayurov records, 'some comrades made sceptical comments and wondered whether the time had not come to call on the masses to end the strike'.[9] In general, in the opinion of Marc Ferro, a careful and illuminating historian of the revolution of 1917, at this time 'the Bolsheviks had little confidence in this movement, which they had not entirely incited, but only followed, because it was alien to the method of armed insurrection which alone, according to them, could succeed'.[10]

The spread of the mutinies sealed, on February 27th, the fate of Tsarism, and candidates for the succession emerged in the afternoon of that day, in the shapes of the Provisional Committee of the Duma and the Petrograd Soviet. It was only on February 27th that the Bolshevik organization published its first leaflet.* This leaflet declared that 'the job of the working class and the revolutionary army is to create a provisional revolutionary government which will lead the new régime, the new republican régime'. It was said that a constituent assembly must be convened, 'on the basis of direct, equal and secret universal suffrage'.[11] This document was of interest from two angles: it took up again the formula that Lenin had shaped during the revolution of 1905, calling for the formation of a provisional revolutionary government, and it made no mention of Soviets, towards which some of the Bolsheviks seemed not to have lost their former distrust.

That same day the Leninist leaders in Petrograd returned a twofold refusal to the demonstrators who applied to them: they declined, for lack of sufficient copies, to give leaflets to workers who asked for these, and they again sent away empty-handed those who asked for weapons.[12]

This hesitation and reserve, in which caution was mingled with

* Only comparatively recently did a Soviet historian prove that this leaflet came out on February 27th and not on February 26th, as had previously always been alleged (Ferro, *February*, p. 47).

scepticism, is easily understandable. The beginnings of revolutions, and especially of mass movements which bring into action against the established order, at first uncertainly, great numbers of people driven by resentment and anger, and later by enthusiasm, always ignore the directives issued by organizations and the expectations of revolutionaries. This general truth applies to the case of Russia in 1917 as well, even though there existed in the Tsarist empire a political party which had assumed the mission of preparing a people's insurrection, all the tactics and operational rules of which were concentrated towards this end.

That the Bolsheviks should have been taken by surprise by the February events is thus in conformity with the logic of social dynamics. One might at least, though, have expected them to reveal a certain aptitude for adapting themselves to the events taking place, a readiness to guide the activity of the crowds, show them the implications of their success and give them a clear awareness of the new possibilities— a will and power to carry on an independent policy, preventing the victory won by the proletariat from being exploited by a bourgeoisie which had played no part in the action. Yet, as long as Lenin was still absent from the scene, the Party's leaders proved incapable of framing a policy that was clearly different from that of its Right-wing Socialist opponents. On the contrary, despite the radicalism and dissatisfaction of many Party members, there was a tendency for the Bolsheviks to accept the platform of the Mensheviks and S.R.s, or at least not to challenge it. This failure of independent leadership was all the more serious because the Mensheviks and S.R.s were deferring to the bourgeoisie and leaving the latter to form the provisional government. There was no room for any illusions about the intentions of this government, representing the interests of a class which had just demonstrated its counter-revolutionary spirit.

The Provisional Government originated in the provisional committee of the Duma which, at the moment when the revolt was winning substantial victories but Tsarism had not yet surrendered, had given itself a title that revealed its philosophy and programme: 'Committee for the Re-establishment of Order and Relations with Public Institutions and Personages.' One of its most prominent members was Mikhail Rodzyanko, former Speaker of the Duma, who, in his own words, contemplated the possibility of Nicholas II's abdication with 'unspeakable sadness', and who had, only the day before, advised the Tsarist authorities to use fire-hoses to disperse the demonstrating crowds.[13] His friend and colleague Shulgin, a prominent figure in the 'Progressive Bloc',* who was doubtless endowed with greater energy, pointed out that 'if we do not take power, others will take it for us,

* A coalition of moderate parties in the Duma which, during the war, called on the Tsar to form a government 'enjoying the confidence of the nation'.

those rotters who have already elected all sorts of scoundrels in the factories'. He wished machine-guns had been available to him, to deal with the mob.[14]

For their part, the ministers Milyukov and Guchkov did everything they could to preserve the monarchy, despite the agreement they had just made with the representatives of the Soviet, providing that the question of the form of state should be settled by a constituent assembly. The attitude of these front-rank members of the Provisional Government towards the revolution was especially characteristic, the former considering, when the crowds moved against the Taurida Palace on February 27th, that they should be resisted, and the latter acknowledging, after the February days which had brought to power the political group to which he belonged, that 'we have been beaten by Petrograd'.[15]

The leaders of the Soviet who had negotiated with the political leaders of the Russian bourgeoisie about the formation of the Provisional Government were quite well aware of what their feelings were. One of the Soviet leaders, Sukhanov, a Left-wing Menshevik who was very influential during the first weeks of the revolution, considered that on February 27th 'the leaders of the Progressive Bloc stubbornly continued their refusal, not only to adhere to the revolution, not only to attempt to lead it, but even to acknowledge it as an accomplished fact'.[16] On March 7th, however, *Rabochaya Gazeta*, the Menshevik organ in the capital, wrote: 'Members of the Provisional Government, the proletariat and the army await your orders to consolidate the revolution and make Russia a democracy.'[17]

What led the moderate socialists to surrender power to the bourgeoisie, although only the masses had fought for the victory of the revolution, and the property-owning classes were in utter disarray, was a series of considerations of an ideological and political order. At the moment when the Soviet was formed in Petrograd and when its leaders—who in practice were self-elected—handed over legal authority to the bourgeois parties, it was not out of the question that there might be a backlash by the reactionary forces. The streets of Petrograd were in the hands of the people, but it was still possible that the front and the provinces might turn against the capital. How would the bourgeoisie react if that should happen? In order to rescue it from the temptation to ally with Tsarism, would it not be best to persuade the bourgeoisie to take power itself? Accordingly, the Soviet delegates yielded power to the bourgeois parties—without, as they did so, being certain that the latter would accept the gift being offered them.[18]

Other factors also played a part: more profound ones, of a doctrinal nature. The men who at that moment held the country's fate in their hands belonged to the variant of European socialism which, although concerned for the interests of the proletariat and sincerely devoted to its cause, had never believed in the possibility of entrusting political power to this class. Such a development seemed to them to be conceivable only after a long period of preparation and education. The sentiments of these Social-Democrats in relation to the bourgeoisie were a mixture of hostility and respect, in which the respect often outweighed the hostility. The Menshevik Potresov expressed a belief common to many socialists in Russia and the West when he declared that, 'at the moment of the bourgeois revolution, the [class] best prepared, socially and psychologically, to solve national problems, is [the] bourgeoisie'.[19] In reality, despite all proclamations of faith in socialism, many socialists believed that the bourgeoisie would continue, for an indefinite period, to be the necessary and almost natural wielder of political and social authority. As for the proletariat, if Sukhanov was to be believed, 'isolated as it was from other classes, [it] could create only fighting organizations which, while representing a real force in the class struggle, were not a genuine element of state power'.[20]

This almost deferential attitude towards the bourgeoisie was backed, in the case of many Russian Marxists, by theoretical arguments which finally stifled any radical inclinations they might entertain. Loyal to Marxist orthodoxy, they considered that, when Tsarism lay in ruins, economic, social and political power ought as a matter of course to pass to the bourgeoisie, whose reign would constitute the necessary prelude to socialism.

The moderation shown by the Mensheviks and their S.R. colleagues was therefore quite understandable. But what was the matter with the Bolsheviks, who, for years on end, had been denouncing the opportunism of their rivals, their indulgent attitude towards the bourgeoisie, and their blameworthy weakness in relation to the Liberals? Surely one might have expected a very much more critical, bold, demanding attitude on their part? For years Lenin had worked to convince them of the lifelessness, duplicity and conservatism of the Russian bourgeoisie. If the moderate leaders of the Soviet were inclined to put their trust in the Liberals, they ought, in so doing, to have provoked the wrath and aroused the virulent opposition of the Bolsheviks of the capital. Yet the Leninist leadership showed no sign of wrath or virulence, and indeed put up no serious opposition at all to the Right-wing policy of the leaders of the soviets.

When the principle that was to govern for a certain period the relations between the Provisional Government and the Petrograd Soviet was being decided, the Executive Committee of the latter body spent a long time deciding upon it. Some members were in favour of delegates from the Soviet entering the Government. The majority, however, headed by the Mensheviks Chkheidze and Sukhanov, were for a line of non-participation and conditional support. Sukhanov tells us that, during this discussion, 'as far as I remember, not one voice was raised against it on behalf of a democratic régime. Yet there were present at the meeting from the very beginning the official Bolshevik Zalutsky and the unofficial one Krasikov, and a little later Shlyapnikov, who was going about here and there on party business, presented the new Bolshevik representative Molotov to the Ex.Com.'[21] This attitude was confirmed at other meetings of the same body, in which the Bolsheviks had eleven representatives or sympathizers out of the total of thirty-nine members.[22]

This line-up with the Right-wing socialist parties and acceptance of a government that was conservative in tendency was not approved of by everyone in the Bolshevik organization in Petrograd. When, however, the young Molotov, acting in the name of the Bureau of the Central Committee, put before the Petersburg Bolshevik Committee, which was by far the most important of the Party bodies functioning in Russia, a motion criticizing the Provisional Government, denouncing its counter-revolutionary policy and calling for its replacement by a democratic government, he was rebuffed. The Petersburg Committee passed, on the contrary, a motion in which it undertook to refrain from attacking the Provisional Government 'so long as "its actions correspond to the interests of the proletariat and of the broad democratic masses of the people" '.[23]

This document is dated March 3rd, 1917.* Two days later, *Pravda* began to appear again. Under the control of the Bureau of the Central Committee, and Molotov in particular, representing at that time the Left wing in the Party, the official Bolshevik organ revealed a more critical attitude than that of the Petersburg Committee towards the Provisional Government. Nevertheless, in the issue of March 10th, it was possible to read an article in which Olminsky declared that 'the [bourgeois] revolution is not yet completed. We live under the slogan of "striking together". In party affairs, each party for itself; but all as one man for the common cause.'[24]

An end was put to this uncertain policy when, on March 12th, Stalin and Kamenev, returning from Siberian exile, arrived in Petrograd and took over leadership of the Party. As the only members of the Central Committee present in the capital they were able to give a more definite character to the Party line. But the bias that they introduced was markedly Right-ward.

On March 14th, two days after the return of the two leaders, *Pravda* sounded the keynote. Stalin published there a short article in which he called on the workers to rally round the Soviets because 'the rights won must be upheld so as to destroy completely the old forces and ... further advance the Russian revolution.'[25] There was nothing in

---

* Two days later Molotov returned to the charge, but the Petersburg Committee again rejected his anti-Provisional-Government proposal (Rabinowitch, p. 35).

this article that implied the slightest criticism of the conciliatory leadership of the Soviet, and of the Provisional Government. In the same issue Kamenev wrote an editorial in which he asked: 'what purpose would it serve to speed things up, when events were already taking place at such a rapid pace?'[26] Next day he took up his pen to comment on a call by the Soviet in which Kerensky's Russia assured the world that it would 'proudly defend its freedom' and 'would not retreat before the bayonets of the aggressors'. Lenin's lieutenant, inspired by this martial language, rose to the occasion. 'When army faces army,' he wrote, 'it would be the most inane policy to suggest to one of these armies to lay down its arms and go home. This would not be a policy of peace but a policy of slavery, which would be rejected with disgust by a free people.'[27] Stalin approved the terms of the Soviet manifesto and said that what was needed was 'to bring pressure on the Provisional Government to make it declare its consent to start peace negotiations immediately'. In the meantime, it was 'unquestionable' that 'the stark slogan "Down with the war!" ' was 'absolutely unsuitable as a practical means'.[28]*

These statements were very variously received by public opinion. According to Shlyapnikov, 'the whole of the Tauride Palace, from the members of the Committee of the Duma to the Executive Committee, the heart of revolutionary democracy [i.e., the moderate majority in the Soviets, M.L.], was full of the news—the victory of the moderate, reasonable Bolsheviks over the extremists'.[29] On the other hand, some of the Bolshevik militants were indignant at the tone adopted by the editors of Pravda. The Petersburg section even called for Kamenev's expulsion, and in the Vyborg quarter Stalin's expulsion was demanded as well.[30]

The Bolsheviks held their first national conference on March 29th in Petrograd, with fifty-eight organizations represented. It became apparent that while the policy of Kamenev and Stalin was criticized by the Left in the Party, the latter also contained elements that were even more cautious, conciliatory and moderate than the leadership. The radical elements put forward in opposition to the 'centrist' line a conception that was unambiguously revolutionary and internationalist. 'The Russian Revolution,' they declared, 'can secure for the people of Russia a maximum of democratic liberties and social reforms only if it becomes the point of departure for the revolutionary movement of the West European proletariat against their bourgeois governments.' It was necessary to prepare for a struggle against the

* What was published in Pravda was extremely interesting, but of no less importance was what was not published there. When Alexandra Kollontai brought to Petrograd, in the last days of March, the two first of Lenin's Letters from Afar (see p. 127), the editorial board hesitated for several days before publishing only one of them—and then suppressed the passages in which Lenin opposed any agreement with the Mensheviks (Reisberg, p. 101).

Provisional Government. A Workers' Red Guard was the means that they urged to this end, and they hailed the Soviets as the 'embryo of revolutionary power'.[31]

The Party leadership had to reckon with this Left tendency. During the conference it amended the views it had hitherto upheld, separating itself from a definitely Right-wing tendency which called for the strict application of a policy of national defence.[32] Stalin introduced the discussion with a report in which he essentially declined to take up a line of opposition to the Provisional Government. The latter, he said, 'has in fact assumed the role of consolidator of the conquests of the revolutionary people,' and he went on to declare that 'we need to gain time by holding back the process of rupture with the middle-bourgeois strata, so as to prepare ourselves for struggle against the Provisional Government.' Furthermore, 'we must give our support to the Provisional Government in so far as it is consolidating the steps forward taken by the revolution, while regarding as inadmissible any support for the Provisional Government in so far as it acts in a counter-revolutionary way.'[33] This abstruse language served, without challenging the tactics followed up to that time by the Party's leading group, to disarm the suspicions of the Left-wing delegates. In the resolution passed by the conference, the Party declared unanimously for exercising 'vigilant control' over the Provisional Government and for support of the Petrograd Soviet, whose Menshevik and S.R. orientation was left uncriticized.[34]

This care to avoid conflict with the moderate socialists was accompanied by a desire on the part of many delegates to re-establish unity between Bolsheviks and Mensheviks. While the Right-wing element were unconditionally for reunification, Stalin contented himself with supporting the idea of talks with the Mensheviks, saying that 'unity is possible on the basis of the Zimmerwald–Kienthal line'.* The conference set up a commission entrusted with the task of negotiating with the Mensheviks and studying along with them the possibility of healing the split in Russian Social-Democracy.[35] At the end of March, the Left-wing Menshevik Sukhanov noted, regarding Kamenev's political behaviour, that 'all the actions of the then leader of the Bolshevik party had [a] kind of "possibilist", sometimes too moderate character'.† Kamenev represented the 'centre-right' tendency which continued to dominate the Bolshevik Party even when the euphoria of the first days of February had had time to disperse. Then Lenin arrived in Russia, to turn the Party face about, putting an end to Bolshevik 'possibilism' and compelling the adoption of a revolutionary line.

* Lenin, however, had regarded the platform of these two conferences as quite inadequate, owing to its 'centrist' character, and that already in 1915 and 1916.

† Sukhanov, p. 257. 'Possibilism' was the name given, at the end of the nineteenth century, to an extremely moderate tendency in the French socialist movement.

*Lenin reconquers the party**

On March 30th (Western calendar) Lenin wrote: 'You can imagine what torture it is for all of us to be sitting here at such a time.'[36] His impatience was caused by the difficulties that were put in the way of the Russian socialist *émigrés* who were trying to get back home, by the isolation in which he found himself, and by the meagreness of the information that reached him from Russia.† Lenin knew enough, though, to realize that his supporters were not acting as he would have wished. He wrote of the 'epidemic' of 'excitement' that he feared must now be prevailing in Petrograd.[37] And there were indeed considerable differences, obvious contradictions, not to say actual incompatibility, between the standpoint of the Party leadership in Russia and that of Lenin during the last weeks of his exile.

Whereas the Bolsheviks in Russia were supporting, through the votes of their delegates at the national conference in Petrograd, Stalin's formula according to which the function of the Provisional Government was to consolidate the conquests of the February revolution, Lenin declared, peremptorily: 'Our tactics, no trust in and no support of the new government.'[38] Some days previously he had written, in a draft for his celebrated *April Theses*, about 'the deepest distrust' that he felt for the new rulers of Russia.[39] He accused the Provisional Government of having 'wrested [power] from the proletariat',[40] and denounced the political and social character of the new ministry, which he saw as representing 'the class of capitalist landlords and bourgeoisie'.[41] He pointed out that the Provisional Government's first declaration kept silence on the main economic and social problems, and concluded that this Government would be *'unable* to avoid collapse'.[42] Its incapacity was especially plain where peace was concerned: it 'cannot give the people peace, because it represents the capitalists and landlords and because it is tied to the English and French capitalists by treaties and financial commitments'.[43] And while Lenin's supporters in Petrograd sought to bring pressure to bear on the Provisional Government to initiate negotiations between the warring powers, Lenin himself considered that 'to urge that government to conclude a democratic peace is like preaching virtue to brothel-keepers'.[44] The root of the matter lay in two points. First, according

* In this section I deal only with Lenin's relations with the Party, the resistance and opposition that his radicalism came up against. Lenin's revolutionary strategy is only touched upon, being analysed in the next chapter.

† 'From Russia—nothing, not even letters!!' (Lenin, Vol. 43, p. 615). 'News is exceptionally meagre' (ibid., Vol. 35, p. 297). He had only inadequate materials on which to base his important *Letters from Afar*. Writing a foreword to his second letter on March 21st (Western calendar), he noted: 'The principal document I have at my disposal of today's date is a copy of that most conservative and bourgeois English newspaper *The Times* of March 16th, containing a batch of reports about the revolution in Russia' (ibid., Vol. 23, p. 309).

to Lenin, 'he who says that the workers must *support* the new government in the interests of the struggle against tsarist reaction ... is a
traitor to the workers ... ':[45] yet this was, broadly speaking, the line
of the Bolshevik leaders in Petrograd. Second, according to Lenin,
one of 'the immediate tasks of the revolutionary proletariat in Russia'
was 'to find the surest road to the next stage of the revolution, or to
the second revolution, which must transfer political power from the
government of landlords and capitalists ... to a government of the
workers and poorest peasants':[46] yet the Bolshevik leaders on the spot
were thinking only of 'consolidating' the gains of February.

The divergence was no less marked as regards the attitude to be
taken up towards the leaders of the Soviet. Lenin supported, of course,
the setting up of soviets in Russia,[47] but this support implied, for
him, no indulgence towards the policy being followed by the most
important Soviet, that of the capital, and still less towards the moderate
socialist parties which dominated it. Finally, while the Bolsheviks'
national conference was promoting talks with a view not merely to
closer relations with the Mensheviks but actual unification with
them, Lenin declared firmly that 'the main thing now is not to let
oneself get entangled in stupid "unification" attempts'.[48] There
could be no question of any *rapprochement* with the Mensheviks or
the other parties.* Attacking specifically the Menshevik leader
Chkheidze, the first chairman of the Petrograd Soviet, who was nevertheless not a representative of the Right wing among the Mensheviks,
Lenin declared that 'any rapprochement with ... Chkheidze and Co.
is, I am deeply convinced, *harmful* for the working class, *dangerous*,
inadmissible.'[49] The Party's duty was, on the contrary, to carry on
'the most stubborn, the most highly principled, the most pressing and
most merciless struggle against' the Chkheidze tendency. Going over
to outright threats, Lenin continued: 'And I personally will not
hesitate for a second to declare, and to declare in print, that I shall prefer
even an immediate split with anyone in our Party, whoever it may be,
to making concessions to the social-patriotism of Kerensky and Co.
or the social-pacifism and Kautskianism of Chkheidze and Co.'†

The disagreement between Lenin and the Bolshevik leadership
inside Russia was profound and general in character, their ideas on the
problems of peace and national defence being no less divergent.
Whereas Kamenev and Stalin followed a tactic that was close to
'defencism', Lenin had nothing but contempt for such an attitude.
He declared strongly that the war had not ceased, and could not

---

* On the other hand, Lenin was in favour at this time of contacts being made with the
'Leftist' Bolsheviks of the *Vpered* group, and desired to see them back in the Party (ibid.,
Vol. 35, pp. 304–5).

† Ibid., Vol. 35, p. 310. Even on the eve of his departure from Switzerland Lenin declared himself against any political *rapprochement* with Martov, although he was then in
contact with the latter in connexion with plans to return to Russia (ibid., Vol. 35, p. 302).

cease, to be imperialist on Russia's part, as long as the Provisional Government, as then composed, was still in power.[50]

In the last analysis, all these political disagreements were derived from a more important cause. Lenin saw differently from his chief supporters the fundamental problem that faced the Russian labour movement in 1917, and which was bound up with the very nature of the revolution in progress. The entire tactic adopted by the Bolshevik leaders in Russia, with its caution, moderation and concern for unity with the Mensheviks, reflected a belief that the Bolshevik leaders shared with the Right-wing Socialists. As they saw it, the fall of Tsarism was the first victory in the bourgeois revolution, which must be followed up by other successes, and in this way consolidated, without there being any question of going beyond the limits of such a revolution and undertaking socialist tasks. 'The coming revolution must be only a bourgeois revolution,' said the Bolshevik Olminsky, for example, adding that 'that was an obligatory premise for every member of the party, the official opinion of the party, its continual and unchanging slogan right up to the February revolution of 1917, and even some time after.'[51] *Pravda* of March 7th, 1917—even before Kamenev and Stalin had given it a still more Right-wing orientation —stated that 'of course there is no question among us of the downfall of the rule of capital, but only of the downfall of the rule of autocracy and feudalism'.[52] This was a view that Lenin himself had shared for a long time and that only the revolution of 1905 had caused him to doubt, without, however, leading him to replace it with a sufficiently well-defined new view.* But now, when the masses had just repeated, with greater success, their feat of 1905, Lenin again detached himself from the clear and simple notion of the two revolutions, bourgeois and socialist, profoundly distinct from one another, with only the former a matter for the present moment.

To be sure, Lenin did not categorically renounce this traditional distinction. He regarded it as being still valid, stating in the first of his *Letters from Afar* that the proletariat 'can and will proceed, first, to the achievement of a democratic republic... and then to *socialism* ...';† but already the distinction was being mentioned by him only in order to introduce the possibility of going over from the bourgeois revolution to the socialist revolution. This idea of going over from one revolution to the other became central to Lenin's thinking as early as March 17th (Western calendar), when he wrote the draft for his *April Theses*. There he spoke of the need to establish in Russia 'a workers' government that relies, first, on the overwhelming majority

---

* See p. 76.

† Lenin, op. cit., Vol. 23, p. 308. In the same period, writing to Inessa Armand, Lenin described as a 'theoretical "oddity" ' any refusal to distinguish between 'the first and the second revolution, or the first and the second stage' (ibid., Vol. 35, p. 306).

of the peasant population ... and, second, on an alliance with the revolutionary workers of all countries in the war ... ' He declared that 'the revolutionary proletariat can ... only regard the revolution of March 1 [14] as its initial, and by no means complete, victory on its momentous path.' He called on the proletariat to 'fight for a democratic republic and socialism', and gave it as his view that the need for 'full victory in the next stage of the revolution and the winning of power by a workers' government' could be 'brought home to the people in an immeasurably shorter time than under ordinary conditions'.[53]

In his first *Letter from Afar* Lenin showed that the problem was a concrete one. Not only did 'the peculiarity of the present situation' consist in this '*transition* from the first stage of the revolution to the second', but it was the duty of the working class to '*prepare the way for* [*its*] *victory in the second stage of the revolution*'.*

In his third *Letter from Afar* Lenin took a further step by suggesting that the transition from the first to the second stage in the revolution was perhaps already being accomplished.† At the same time he touched upon the question that was to form the central theme of *State and Revolution*, defining the task of the proletariat as the 'smashing of the state machine',[54] and even considered that this process was already going on.[55]

Would the Leninists in Russia prove capable of accepting, or even of understanding, such an idea? Lenin himself was dubious about this. He contemplated the necessity of undertaking 'systematic work on a party of a *new* type'.[56] On April 3rd, when he returned to Petrograd, it was to this task that he applied himself.

Historians have often described the triumphant welcome that the Bolsheviks gave their leader during the night of April 3rd–4th, 1917. From the accounts of eye-witnesses, and in particular from Sukhanov, we get an impression of great enthusiasm. This enthusiasm was doubtless genuine. But it should not be concluded that the renewed contacts between the Party and its founder in a Russia liberated from Tsarism were marked by political harmony as well as warm feeling. As soon as he reached the Party headquarters, when the public demonstrations and official ceremonies had hardly finished, during this same night of April 3rd–4th, Lenin got down to serious matters, namely, discussion of the political problems of the moment and study of the grave differences that divided him from his followers. As soon

---

* Ibid., Vol. 23, pp. 306–7. Almost at the same time Lenin wrote to Alexandra Kollontai: 'What is now on the agenda is ... preparation for the conquest of power by the *Soviets of Workers' Deputies*' (ibid., Vol. 35, p. 298).

† 'Comrade workers! ... In the more or less near future (perhaps even now, as these lines are being written) you will again have to perform the same miracles of heroism [i.e., as in February, M.L.] to overthrow the rule of the landlords and capitalists ... ' (ibid., Vol. 23, p. 323).

as this first meeting was over, another was held, at which were present, in accordance with the decisions taken previously, both Bolsheviks and Mensheviks who were eager to prepare the way for reunification of the R.S.D.L.P. Lenin attended this meeting too.

While the public reception given to Lenin by his friends was a scene of triumph, matters proceeded differently behind the doors of the Party meeting. Sukhanov, who, although a Menshevik, was able through his connexions to be present at this Bolshevik gathering, gives this account of his impressions.

> I shall never forget that thunder-like speech, which startled and amazed not only me, a heretic who had accidentally dropped in, but all the true believers. I am certain that no one had expected anything of the sort. It seemed as though all the elements had risen from their abodes, and the spirit of universal destruction, knowing neither barriers nor doubts, neither human difficulties nor human calculations, was hovering around Kshesinskaya's reception room[57] above the heads of the bewitched disciples.[58]

Sukhanov also emphasizes Lenin's 'complete intellectual isolation, not only among Social-Democrats in general but also among his own disciples'.[59] A Bolshevik who was present recalled in her reminiscences that Lenin's speech 'produced on everyone a stupefying impression. No one expected this. On the contrary, they expected Vladimir Ilyich to arrive and call to order the Russian Bureau of the Central Committee and especially Comrade Molotov, who occupied a particularly irreconcilable position with respect to the Provisional Government.'[60] Instead, Lenin did not merely support the Left wing of the Party: as Shlyapnikov put it, he showed himself 'more Left than our Left'.[61] Krupskaya said to a friend: 'I am afraid it looks as if Lenin has gone crazy.'[62]

The views that Lenin expounded in his first two speeches, provoking gibes from his adversaries and consternation among his supporters, have become famous under the title of the *April Theses*. In them he put forward a series of ideas that he had already expressed in his *Letters from Afar*. He attacked the Provisional Government, towards which his listeners were tolerant, rejected the idea of unity between Bolsheviks and Mensheviks, reasserted the need to work for 'a republic of Soviets of Workers', Agricultural Labourers' and Peasants' Deputies throughout the country, from top to bottom,'[63] and gave some indications of what his programme of economic changes would be: 'nationalization of *all* lands,' and 'the immediate amalgamation of all banks in the country into a single national bank, and the institution of control over it by the Soviet of Workers' Deputies'.[64] Lenin saw that 'the specific feature of the present situation in Russia' consisted in the fact that they were '*passing* from the first stage of the revolution —

5

which ... placed power in the hands of the bourgeoisie—to its *second* stage, which must place power in the hands of the proletariat and the poorest sections of the peasants.'[65] There was, to be sure, a reassuring side to Lenin's speech. He stressed that it was 'necessary with *particular* thoroughness, persistence and *patience* to explain' all this, and that that must be the Party's role so long as it remained in a minority.[66] But such reassurances counted for little in comparison with the revolutionary prospect that Lenin had suddenly revealed, together with the many and severe criticisms he addressed to his supporters.

In the first important speech he made after his return, Lenin said that 'our mistake is that we have not exposed revolutionary defencism* to the full'. This failure was all the more serious in that 'revolutionary defencism is betrayal of socialism'. It was necessary, he said, to 'admit our mistake'. Elaborating the errors of the Party, he noted that 'even our Bolsheviks show some trust in the government. This can be explained only by the intoxication of the revolution. It is the death of socialism.' He blamed his friends because, instead of exposing the Provisional Government they demanded that it give a series of undertakings, which merely meant sowing illusions about this government. '*Pravda* demands of the *government* that it should renounce annexations. To demand of a government of capitalists that it should renounce annexations is nonsense, a crying mockery ... ' As for the prospect of reuniting in a single party with the Mensheviks, this amounted to 'betrayal of socialism'. And Lenin's criticisms were accompanied by a threat: 'You comrades have a trusting attitude to the government. If that is so, our paths diverge. I prefer to remain in a minority.'[67] Finally Lenin raised the question of the Party itself and, if not of its existence, at least of its title.†

The theme of the 'old Party' and, more particularly, of 'old Bolshevism' and the 'old Bolsheviks', recurs frequently in Lenin's speeches and writings in the period following his return to Russia. Lenin levelled a series of reproaches at those whom he called the 'old Bolsheviks'. He considered, for example, that Kamenev's 'old-Bolshevik' formula that 'the bourgeois revolution is not completed' was 'obsolete'. 'It is no good at all. It is dead. And it is no use trying to revive it.'[68] He criticized them also for their unwillingness to go beyond the formula of the 'revolutionary-democratic dictatorship of the proletariat and the peasantry,' which he himself had put forward at the beginning of the 1905 revolution. Anybody who still held to that idea, Lenin wrote, 'should be consigned to the archive of "Bolshevik" pre-revolutionary antiques (it may be called the archive of "Old

---

* Lenin gave the name 'revolutionary defencism' to the thesis according to which, after the success of the February revolution, Russia should wage a patriotic war of defence against Germany.

† See p. 161.

Bolsheviks")'.[69] At the Petrograd conference of the Bolsheviks*
he said that 'the trouble with us is that comrades have wished to remain
"old" Bolsheviks'.[70] Kalinin, who felt that he was one of those whom
Lenin was getting at, replied to these attacks by appealing to Lenin's
own theories. 'I belong,' he declared, 'to the old school of Leninist
Bolsheviks, and I think that the old Leninism has by no means shown
itself inapplicable to the actual situation. I am astounded that Lenin
should denounce the Old Bolsheviks as a hindrance today.'[71]

However, Lenin persisted in his attack on 'those "old Bolsheviks"
who more than once already have played so regrettable a role in the
history of our Party by reiterating formulas senselessly *learned by
rote*'.[72] He emphasized the point that seemed to him of capital importance: 'Old Bolshevism should be discarded.'[73] Devoting himself
to a struggle to overcome it, he at first met with a number of setbacks.
He was, at the start, almost completely isolated, at least in the leading
circles of the Party. On April 4th, records Alexandra Kollontai, 'I
was the only one to stand up for Lenin's view against a whole series
of hesitant Bolsheviks'.[74] Two days later, Lenin took part in a meeting
of the Bureau of the Central Committee where he was criticized by
Kamenev, who accused him of 'judging the situation to be like that
in 1871, whereas we do not yet have behind us what was accomplished in 1789 and 1848'.[75] This meant raising once more the
problem of the character of the revolution that was going on: was it
bourgeois or socialist? Shlyapnikov, though belonging to what was
usually regarded as the Left tendency in the Party, also criticized
Lenin's theses, some of which, he considered, were lacking in 'practical
sense'. In general he blamed Lenin for 'trying to force the pace' and
thought he should be 'restrained'.[76]

The next day, *Pravda* published a modified, softened version, edited
by Lenin himself, of his speech on the night of April 3rd–4th.† In the
preamble to the article, he wrote of 'these personal theses of mine'.[77]
On the following day, Lenin's 'personal theses' were answered in an
editorial by Kamenev. He began by mentioning that Lenin's ideas
had been agreed to neither by the editors of *Pravda* nor by the Bureau
of the Central Committee, and added: 'As for Lenin's general *schema*,
it seems to us unacceptable, in so far as it proceeds from the assumption that the bourgeois democratic revolution is finished and counts on
the immediate conversion of that revolution into a socialist revolution.'[78]
The polemic continued in the subsequent days in the columns of the
Bolshevik journal.

Meanwhile, Lenin had suffered an important defeat in the Petrograd
Committee. On April 8th a Right-wing Bolshevik, S. Bagdatyev,

* See p. 132.
† The differences between the speech and the article are very marked. The latter is given
in Lenin, op. cit., Vol. 24, pp. 21–6, and the former in Vol. 36, pp. 434–43.

presented there a report in opposition to the *April Theses*. The debate
did not proceed easily for Lenin. Commenting on how it ended, a
Soviet historian says that 'the discussion did not immediately result in
approval of Lenin's theses'.[79] This is putting it mildly. In fact, Lenin's
resolution was defeated by thirteen votes to two, with one abstention.[80]
In the provinces the Bolshevik organizations often reacted similarly.
In Moscow and Kiev the local Bolshevik committees rejected Lenin's
theses.

The date April 14th marks a turning-point in Lenin's struggle. At
the conference of the Bolshevik organizations in Petrograd which was
held on that day he at last overcame his opponents, and succeeded in
getting his views approved, by thirty-seven votes to three. Kamenev
tried to restore the situation by putting forward an amendment in
which he attacked the 'disorganizing consequences' of the slogan
'Down with the Provisional Government!' but this was rejected by
twenty votes to six, with nine abstentions — which shows that resistance
to Lenin's ideas was still strong.[81] It was decided to reconsider the
general problem of the Party's policy at a national conference to be
held in the capital on April 24th. Lenin opened the debate at this
gathering. Dzerzhinsky, however, one of the most prominent delegates,
speaking in the name of 'many'* who 'did not agree in principle with
the theses of the spokesman', demanded that the conference nominate
a co-reporter who would represent the viewpoint of 'the comrades
who have along with us experienced the revolution in a practical
way'.[82] Although obviously aimed against Lenin, the proposal was
accepted by the conference, and Kamenev was entrusted with the
task of presenting a second report. In this he declared that 'it is too
early to say that bourgeois democracy has exhausted all of its possibilities', stressed the need for co-operation between the petty-bourgeoisie and the proletariat, and concluded by saying that the Party
should organize ' "control" by the revolutionaries over the actions of
a necessarily bourgeois government'.[83]

The April conference was a decisive success for Lenin. One of his
motions stated that 'the passing of state power in Russia to the
Provisional Government, a government of the landowners and capitalists, did not and could not alter the character and meaning of the
war as far as Russia is concerned'.[84] This motion, which ran counter
to the defencist standpoint hitherto upheld by Kamenev and Stalin,
was adopted unanimously by those present, apart from seven who
abstained from voting.[85] A second resolution written by Lenin
declared that 'the Provisional Government, by its class character, is
the organ of landowner and bourgeois domination'. The Party was

---

* According to Golikov, p. 112, the conference was attended by 133 delegates with
voting powers plus 18 with consultative powers. Trotsky (*History*, p. 340) gives the
figure 149, and Carr (Vol. I, p. 83) gives 150.

warned that 'extensive work has to be done to develop proletarian class-consciousness,' since 'only work of this nature can serve as a sure guarantee of the successful transfer of the entire state power into the hands of the Soviets of Workers' and Soldiers' Deputies'.[86] Rejecting all variants of 'support' for the Provisional Government and also of 'control' over it, the conference thus rallied to the slogan of 'All power to the Soviets!' which was to inspire the offensive of the proletarian masses all through the spring of 1917. This second resolution of Lenin's was adopted unanimously with the exception of two votes against and eight abstentions.[87]

In yet a third field Lenin scored an important victory over the adherents of the conciliationist line that the Party had followed up to that time, namely, on the question of the independence of the Bolshevik Party and its relationship with the Mensheviks, a matter on which he felt strongly. A resolution declared that 'the parties of the Socialist-Revolutionaries, Menshevik Social-Democrats, etc., have, in the great majority of cases, adopted the stand of "revolutionary defencism", that is, support of the imperialist war', and concluded that 'unity with parties and groups which are pursuing such a policy is absolutely impossible'.[88] This resolution was passed unanimously except for ten abstentions.[89]

The discussion and voting on a resolution 'on the current situation' nevertheless demonstrated that opposition to Lenin's policy was still substantial. This resolution did indeed state that, 'operating as it does in one of the most backward countries of Europe amidst a vast population of small peasants, the proletariat of Russia cannot aim at immediately putting into effect socialist changes;' but it linked the current situation in Russia with that prevailing in 'the more developed and advanced countries,' where 'the objective conditions for a socialist revolution, which undoubtedly existed even before the war, have been ripening with tremendous rapidity as a result of the war'. And Lenin, the author of this resolution, claimed that 'the Russian revolution is only the first stage of the first of the proletarian revolutions which are the inevitable result of the war'. As regards Russia more specifically, the resolution stressed again that it was impossible for the working class to 'keep its activities within limits acceptable to the petty-bourgeoisie,' and pointed to 'the urgency of taking a number of practical steps towards socialism for which the time is now ripe'.[90] This amounted to saying, or at least to suggesting, that it was possible to begin the process that would lead the Russian revolution from its bourgeois into its socialist phase, and clashed head-on with one of the theses most firmly embedded in the minds of the Party's Right wing, among the supporters of 'Old Bolshevism'. The numbers of this latter group remained large: Lenin's resolution was passed, but only by 71 to 39, with eight abstaining.[91]

Lenin's victory, an historic feat with decisive consequences, was certainly attributable to his extraordinary personality, for the standing he enjoyed among the Bolsheviks did not alone account for it. Sukhanov, an astounded observer of Lenin's successful efforts, was unable, in those crucial weeks, to hide the admiration he felt for Lenin's 'amazing force' and his 'superhuman power of attack'.[92] But other factors also played a part. In particular, the fact that, beginning in April 1917, the Bolshevik Party was reinforced by a steady and large-scale influx of new members.* This influx had the effect of crushing the nucleus of 'old Bolsheviks' who claimed to be guardians of Leninist orthodoxy, submerging them under the weight of new members who had been radicalized by the revolutionary events and were not paralysed by the principles of that orthodoxy. At the same time, the weakness and conservatism shown by the Provisional Government, its manifest inability to improve the economic situation prevailing in Russia, dissipated the illusions about it and the confidence in it that had at first been felt by part of the proletariat and by some of the Bolsheviks.

One last point deserves comment. Throughout these weeks, Lenin reiterated that a Bolshevik conquest of the soviets could be accomplished only through patient efforts of explanation and persuasion, with the exercise of 'great care and discretion'.[93] Many Bolsheviks who in April 1917 gave their support to Lenin's theses were therefore able to think of the overthrow of the Provisional Government, and with it of the bourgeoisie, as a long-term business that did not imply any immediate risks for the Party, and to be confident that Lenin himself would soon become aware of the tremendous difficulties involved. When, a few months later, they saw the issue of overthrowing the Provisional Government put by Lenin on the order of the day, presented as an immediate task, they tried again to 'hold him back'. Once more, in the weeks leading up to the October insurrection, the Party's founder was to be obliged to conquer it.

The party of insurrection

At the end of April 1917 Lenin had emerged as the champion of a policy that can be summed up as follows. The Provisional Government, representing the interests of the capitalists and landlords, was to be combated with maximum energy, so as to bring about the transfer of power to the soviets. This struggle, which was essentially revolutionary in character, had, however, to employ legal methods. The situation in Russia was an exceptional one, in which it was possible to envisage a *peaceful* conquest of state power.

The events of May seemed to justify this view of how the revolution would develop. The popularity that the Provisional Government had

* See p. 158.

enjoyed in March did not survive the revelation of its shortcomings: the frequent demonstrations, usually peaceful but sometimes rowdy, and always on a large scale, were increasingly directed against the Government's policy, and showed how discredited it was becoming. Lenin's strategy, the correctness of which was now apparent to a growing number of his associates, nevertheless stumbled against one obstacle: it was based on the slogan 'All power to the Soviets!' which gave it summary and popular currency among the workers—but the soviets themselves seemed not at all desirous of taking power. They were dominated by a very solid majority of Mensheviks and S.R.s who supported the Provisional Government and had no thought of challenging it. This circumstance showed the increasing gap between the radicalization of the masses and the ever more pronounced conservatism of the soviets as an institution. This constituted another factor in favour of the only party that refused to discredit itself by a mediocre and ineffectual policy made up of precarious agreements and patched-up compromises. But since time was in this way working for the Bolsheviks, it seemed pointless to try and force the pace of events.

On June 9th the Bolsheviks found themselves having to call off a peaceful demonstration in which their Petrograd supporters were intending to demand that the Government resign. The Right-wing majority in the soviets had banned the demonstration, without giving any valid justification for its decision. The Party protested, but it submitted; and this submission aroused discontent among some of its members, increasing the tension already growing within the Party.* Lenin was led by this episode to re-examine his strategy. Had not the condition on which it was based, namely, the respect for political freedoms in a Russia that was 'exceptionally free', now been called in question?

The decisive turn was not made, however, until the 'July days', when nearly a million demonstrators, whom the Party had not succeeded in restraining, marched through the streets of Petrograd, bringing the Government to within an inch of collapse, and sowing panic among the Mensheviks and S.R.s. The disorders that followed produced hundreds of casualties, and the Bolshevik Party, although it had been reluctant to head a demonstration that the Party leadership had not wanted, was nevertheless declared responsible. With half-hearted support from the Soviet majority, the Provisional Government launched a policy of repression against the Bolsheviks. To avoid arrest, Lenin had to leave the capital and take refuge in Finland, numerous leading members of the Party were thrown into prison, and the Bolshevik organization was reduced for a few weeks to a semi-underground existence. Lenin at once drew the most radical conclusions from this new and apparently disastrous situation.

* See p. 150.

On July 10th he wrote an article in which he abandoned the strategy he had pursued since the start of the February revolution. He declared that 'All hopes for a peaceful development of the Russian revolution have vanished for good. This is the objective situation: either complete victory for the military dictatorship, or victory for the workers' armed uprising.' Lenin emphasized this point: 'Let us have no constitutional or republican illusions about a peaceful path ... '*

There is nothing to show that Lenin himself believed in July 1917 that it would become necessary in the very near future to organize and carry through an armed rising. The possibility of going over to a practical execution of his ideas depended on the progress of rebellious feelings among the masses – and July and August saw a slowing down of the process of radicalization that had marked the spring of 1917. A certain mood of discouragement among the proletariat was intensified by the crisis that the Bolshevik Party itself was undergoing. Between July 10th and the beginning of September Lenin said no more about the problem of insurrection. He devoted himself, in his Finnish retreat, to writing *State and Revolution*. Then, in the last days of August and the first days of September, the action of the Petrograd proletariat, now already organized and led by the Bolsheviks, contributed decisively to the defeat of Kornilov's attempted *coup d'état*. On September 1st the Petrograd Soviet passed a resolution moved by Lenin's supporters, and on September 5th the Moscow Soviet did the same – events that heralded the imminent downfall of the majority hitherto dominant in the popular institutions, and the conquest of the latter by the Bolsheviks. On September 9th leadership of the Soviet of the capital passed to the Bolsheviks, with Trotsky's election as chairman. Almost immediately, the Moscow Soviet followed suit. At the same time, discontent and agitation grew in a number of cities: disorders broke out, for example, on August 30th and September 1st in Astrakhan and Tashkent. Finally, and most important, a powerful movement of unrest began to sweep over the countryside, which had so far remained relatively peaceful.

It was in these circumstances that Lenin suddenly launched an offensive in the Party which was to result, after six weeks of determined struggle, in the uprising and seizure of power. With two letters written between September 12th and 14th, Lenin called on the Party to begin concrete preparation and practical organization under the slogan of armed insurrection as an immediate objective.

The first of these letters of Lenin's began: 'The Bolsheviks, having obtained a majority in the Soviet of Workers' and Soldiers' Deputies of both capitals, can and *must* take state power into their own hands.'

* Lenin, Vol. 25, pp. 177–8. The article was published on July 20th, with cuts and alterations that slightly modified its significance. For the original version see ibid., Vol. 41, pp. 440–43.

Though it was not yet a matter of fixing the actual day or hour for the rising, the event of which Lenin spoke was nevertheless to be regarded as imminent: he explained 'why ... the Bolsheviks [must] assume power ... *at this very moment.*' It was necessary to 'consider how to agitate for this without expressly saying as much in the press'. And he ended: 'It would be naïve to wait for a "formal" majority for the Bolsheviks. No revolution ever waits for *that.*' Finally: 'History will not forgive us if we do not assume power now.'[94]

In his second letter Lenin went still further. He explained at length why it seemed to him that victory was assured, and cleared up some aspects of the general problem of the insurrection. He confirmed that it was a matter of 'the immediate transfer of all power to *revolutionary democrats headed by the revolutionary proletariat,*' and offered a first sketch of a plan for the rising, a plan which he himself regarded as merely approximate.[95]

These letters of Lenin's were received by the Central Committee when it met on September 15th in a mood of consternation and even panic. Bukharin describes in his reminiscences of this episode the atmosphere that reigned at the meeting. 'We gathered and — I remember as though it were just now — began the session ... When I entered, Milyutin came suddenly to meet me and said: "You know, Comrade Bukharin, we've received a little letter here." ' The letter was read: 'We all gasped. No one had yet put the question so sharply. No one knew what to do. Everyone was at a loss for a while. Then we deliberated and came to a decision. Perhaps this was the only time in the history of our party when the Central Committee decided to burn a letter of Comrade Lenin's.'[96] The Bolshevik leadership also decided to instruct its members who were active in the Party's Military Organization and its Petrograd Committee to 'take measures to prevent any demonstrations in the barracks and factories'.[97] Bukharin, who at that time was on the Left of the Party, gives these reasons for the Central Committee's attitude: 'Although we believed unconditionally that in Petersburg and Moscow we should succeed in seizing the power, we assumed that we could not yet hold out, that having seized the power ... we could not fortify ourselves in the rest of Russia.'[98]

The reaction of the Bolshevik leaders to Lenin's letter is easily understood. The July days and the repression organized by the Provisional Government had had serious effects in the Party, which went on being felt for several weeks. After months of successes, the Party had suffered its first setback, and one that almost ruined it. Lenin was in hiding, along with Zinoviev, while several other leaders, including Trotsky, Lunacharsky and Kamenev, were in prison. The Bolshevik press had been reduced to a semi-clandestine existence, and hundreds, even thousands of the Party's members and sympathizers had been arrested. In his notes of that time Sukhanov thought he

5*

was entitled to record that 'the July events had destroyed Bolshevism'.[99]

He was wide of the mark. But scepticism, misgivings and discouragement had indeed overcome some of the Bolsheviks in July and at the beginning of August. To take one example, the executive of the Party branch in one of the largest iron and steel works in the Petrograd area resolved by sixteen votes to four, with four abstentions, to declare itself independent of the Party and to remain so until a new Central Committee had been elected.[100]

The July defeat did not shake only the middle cadres of the Party, but its top leadership as well. Zinoviev, for example, who until then had always supported Lenin's views, was among those affected, and this was why he opposed the October insurrection right down to the moment of victory. The Party's Military Organization, which had been set up in order to co-ordinate and centralize the activity of the Bolshevik soldiers, and which in June and July had constituted a Left 'pressure-group' in the Party,* now lost much of its verve and confidence. One of its most outstanding leaders, Nevsky, explained later that, 'schooled in the bitter experience of the July days', they could not bring themselves to support Lenin's line of 'immediate uprising'.†

By September the breach had been filled up, the Party's decline checked. But was it possible seriously to contemplate hurling the Bolshevik forces into an attempt to seize power when they had only just recovered from so grave a crisis? On September 15th it was by a reflex of self-preservation that bore all the signs of wisdom that the Bolshevik leaders decided to ignore Lenin's instructions. On September 21st this same prudence caused the Central Committee to decide (on second thoughts) that the Bolshevik Party would take part in the work of the 'Provisional Council of the Russian Republic' (the 'Pre-Parliament'), which the Government, seeking to provide itself with the legitimate foundation that it so cruelly lacked, wanted to transform into a representative assembly to serve in place of a parliament. Three days later, the Party leadership passed a resolution 'on the current situation and the tasks of the proletariat' in which only a brief allusion was made to the 'transfer of power' to the soviets, and nothing whatever was said about the means whereby this was to be effected.[101]

Thus, more than a fortnight after Lenin had called on his lieutenants to put armed insurrection on the order of the day, nothing had yet been done to bring this aim nearer accomplishment. Realizing that this delay was an expression of the Central Committee's refusal to

* See p. 155.

† Daniels, *Red October*, pp. 99–100. Right down to the day of the rising, and even when it had begun, the worrying memory of the July defeat affected many Bolsheviks. One of them, who was assigned to take over the Telephone Exchange, records that even on October 24th, 'the bitter experience of the July days did not give us complete confidence in victory' (ibid., p. 142).

prepare for a rising, Lenin lost patience. He sent a letter to the Bolshevik I. T. Smilga, as chairman of the Regional Committee of the army, navy and workers of Finland, and then another jointly to the Central Committee, the Moscow Committee, the Petrograd Committee, and the Bolshevik members of the Soviets of Petrograd and Moscow. In doing this he was resorting to an exceptional procedure which he was to employ several times in this period, short-circuiting the Central Committee in order to address himself to wider levels of the Party, closer to the rank-and-file.

In his letter of September 27th, Lenin stated that 'the general political situation' was causing him 'great anxiety'. Whereas 'the government has an army, and is preparing systematically ... We are only passing resolutions. We are losing time.' He considered that 'the Party must put the armed uprising on the order of the day. Events compel us to do this ... I am afraid that the Bolsheviks forget this ... [which] may prove criminal on the part of the party of the revolutionary proletariat.'[102]

On September 29th Lenin wrote an article, entitled 'The Crisis Has Matured', in which he analysed the situation nationally and internationally. He took the view that, on the one hand, 'a *peasant revolt* is developing'—and he had always considered that the revolt of the countryside was a decisive factor on which the fate of the revolution depended—and, on the other, that 'we are *on the eve of a world-wide revolution*'. This analysis was followed by stern warnings to his friends: 'there is not the slightest doubt that if the Bolsheviks allowed themselves to be caught in the trap of constitutional illusions ... [they] would most certainly be *miserable traitors* to the proletarian cause.' In a postscript not intended for publication he added: 'What, then, is to be done? We must *aussprechen was ist*, "state the facts", admit the truth that there is a tendency, or an opinion, in our Central Committee and among the leaders of our Party which ... is *opposed* to taking power immediately, is *opposed* to an immediate insurrection.' And he went on to say that 'that tendency, or opinion, must be *overcome*. Otherwise, the Bolsheviks will cover themselves with eternal *shame* and *destroy themselves* as a party. For to miss such a moment ... would be *utter idiocy*, or *sheer treachery* to the German workers ... It would be sheer treachery to the peasants.'[103]

All Lenin is in these lines—feverish, ardent, indignant: the Lenin who, as theoretician and practitioner of revolution, had put the revolutionary Party together almost by hand, like a craftsman, had dreamed, imagined, conceived and prepared—twenty-four hours a day, as his Menshevik opponent Dan had said—this rendezvous with the revolt of the masses and the people's uprising. All Lenin is here—a Lenin who now, in his Finnish exile where he was stifling, as he had stifled in exile in Switzerland, England, Poland, France and Germany,

knew that only a few dozen kilometres separated him from the scene
of operations, from which, nevertheless, he was so remote: a Lenin
who felt that his supporters, whom he had only a few months before
persuaded that the proletarian revolution was possible, were now
drifting away from him again, dragging their feet and retreating, and
that they were going to miss the opportunity that had been looked
forward to by a whole generation of revolutionary Marxists. Anger
and fear together took hold of Lenin; in those days and weeks he
seethed with as much passion, and more, as in twenty years of passionate fighting and violent polemics. The revolution was *there*, at the
muzzles of the guns of the workers of Petrograd, at the tip of Lenin's
pen.

After the admonitions, the calls to action, and the untiringly repeated scoldings, now came the threat:

> In view of the fact that the Central Committee has *even left un-*
> *answered* the persistent demands I have been making ... , in view
> of the fact that the central organ is *deleting* from my articles all
> references to such glaring errors on the part of the Bolsheviks as
> the shameful decision to participate in the Pre-parliament ... ,
> I am compelled to regard this as a 'subtle' hint at the unwilling-
> ness of the Central Committee even to consider this question
> [i.e., of insurrection], a subtle hint that I should keep my mouth
> shut, and as a proposal for me to retire.

And Lenin ended: 'I am compelled to *tender my resignation from the
Central Committee*, which I hereby do, reserving for myself freedom
to campaign among the *rank and file* of the Party and at the Party
Congress. For it is my profound conviction that if we ... let the present
moment pass, we shall *ruin* the revolution.'[104]

On October 1st Lenin returned to the charge in a brief letter in
which the ceaseless repetition of a formula seems almost to suggest
obsession: 'procrastination is becoming positively *criminal*': 'under
such circumstances to "wait" would be a crime': 'delay is criminal':
'to wait would be a crime to the revolution'.[105]

This letter urged that the insurrection be begun in Moscow, where
the Bolshevik Left was stronger than in Petrograd, but Lenin's appeals
met with no greater echo there than in the capital.[106] In Petrograd the
Bolshevik Committee held an important meeting on October 5th at
which one of its members, Volodarsky, declared that, 'amid the
present ruinous conditions, it would be hard for us to take power,'
adding that 'if we ... were to go to war against imperialism the army
would not follow us ... We should come to power at a moment when
all enthusiasm was completely dead in the army, which would not be
willing to wage a revolutionary war. It seems to me that we, as a
party of real revolutionaries, cannot take power just in order to hold

it for only a month or two.' And Lashevich, a member of the Bolshevik Military Organization, who spoke after him, said: 'Certainly, power is coming closer to us: that is a fact, and we must take power ... But must we take power *now*? I think we ought not to force the pace of events.'[107] Many of the Bolshevik leaders, and not the least important among them, wanted to wait until the Second All-Russia Congress of Soviets, which was to open on October 20th. They were sure that, thanks to their election successes, the Bolsheviks would, with the support of their allies the Left S.R.s, have such a majority at the Congress that the Provisional Government could be removed in the name of 'Soviet legality'. If necessary, armed force would be used, but in any case the call to action should be issued by the soviets, with their Bolshevik majority, and not by the Party. Among others, Trotsky, who was convinced that the Bolshevik organization by itself did not possess sufficient authority to be capable of mobilizing the masses, was in favour of such a plan.[108] Lenin, however, rejected the idea very firmly, seeing in it a last vestige of 'legalism'.

So far, the discussion between Lenin and his lieutenants had been conducted by letter. Things could not go on like this any longer. On October 7th Lenin, disguised as a mechanic, returned to Petrograd and took up lodgings secretly in the working-class quarter of Vyborg, where he was to remain hidden until the eve of the insurrection, his movements being subject to the orders and authorizations of the Central Committee.

On October 8th he issued a fresh call for insurrection, addressing it once more, over the head of the Central Committee, to a wider audience, namely, the Bolshevik delegation to the Congress of Soviets of the Northern Region. In this appeal he analysed the international situation and the rural upheaval, declaring that 'The growth of a world revolution is beyond dispute.' And then the phrases that had become customary with him flowed once more from his pen: 'The situation is such that, in truth, delay would be fatal'; 'we must not delay and permit Kerensky to bring up more Kornilovite troops'.[109]

For the first time since his flight from Petrograd in July, on October 10th Lenin was brought face to face with those who must be described as his opponents in the Central Committee. He expounded his thesis in favour of an almost immediate insurrection, considering that only 'the technical aspect' of the problem still required attention. 'That is the crux of the matter. Nevertheless we ... are inclined to regard the systematic preparation of an uprising as something in the nature of a political sin.'[110] Lenin's speech was followed by discussion, and voting on a resolution which stated 'that an armed uprising is inevitable and the time for it is fully ripe,' in consequence of which 'the Central Committee instructs all Party organizations to be guided accordingly and to discuss and decide all practical questions ... from this point of view.' With numerous members of the Central Committee absent, this resolution was passed by ten votes to two.[111]

At first sight it might seem that the voting gave Lenin complete victory, with the question of the uprising settled politically and only 'the technical aspect' remaining to be dealt with. Events were to show, however, that a basic disagreement relating not to the form to be taken by the insurrection but to the question as to whether the moment was ripe for an insurrection at all, continued to prevail within the Bolshevik Party. Proof of this was provided the very next day, when Kamenev and Zinoviev, who were the two who had voted against the resolution, sent a joint letter to the Party's leading bodies. They set forth their interpretation of the situation, in opposition to Lenin's, denying that the Party had behind it 'the majority of the people of Russia' or 'the majority of the world proletariat'. In the country itself the army was still, as they saw it, outside Bolshevik control, and as for the working class in the West, that showed no disposition as yet to revolt against imperialism. According to Kamenev and Zinoviev, 'only the awakening of the revolution in Europe could compel us to seize power without hesitation'. Furthermore, they considered that 'the enemy's strength is greater than it seems,' while the masses gave little sign of being ready to fight. The Party was on the upgrade again and was making remarkable progress—progress that would be interrupted 'only if the Party were, in present circumstances, to take the initiative in an insurrection, whereby it would expose the proletariat to the blows of the entire united counter-revolution, backed by the petty-bourgeois democrats.'* It is clear that, if they had regarded the resolution passed the day before by the Central Committee as the expression of a finally settled decision, these two Bolsheviks of the old school would not, defying all the rules of democratic centralism, have taken such a step. In any case their letter had immediate consequences. The text, or at least the gist of it, was circulated not only within the Party but also outside, and the Menshevik and S.R. leaders, thus made more aware of the dissensions that were weakening their opponents, at once decided to put off from October 20th to 25th the meeting of the Second Congress of Soviets. They hoped thereby to see disunion spread more widely in the Bolshevik ranks, and Lenin's radicalism defeated.[112]

On October 15th the Bolshevik Committee in Moscow refused to set up a 'military revolutionary committee' with the practical task of organizing the insurrection.[113] The next day saw another meeting of the Petrograd Committee, at which delegates of the Central Committee were present. Bubnov opened the discussion on behalf of the leadership. Far from taking as read the decision to go over at once to organiz-

---

* The text of Kamenev and Zinoviev's letter is given in *Protokoly*, pp. 86–92.

ing the insurrection, he said that the rising should not take place until the meeting of the Constituent Assembly, at the end of the year.

This point of view, which Lenin would certainly have described as 'temporizing', was nevertheless regarded as excessively bold by a number of those present. Nevsky, one of the principal leaders of the Bolshevik Military Organization, took up a particularly pessimistic attitude. (Later, he was to admit that this body 'moved sharply rightward when it was faced with the prospect of an immediate insurrection'.) He said: 'we must first organize the masses.' Kalinin, the future head of the Soviet state (or rather, the future first Soviet dignitary under Lenin and then under Stalin), showed himself both shrewder and more circumspect. He acknowledged that the decision of October 10th was politically obligatory, and took the Party to the brink of insurrection. 'But we do not know when this will become possible ... Perhaps in a year's time, we don't know.'

Nineteen delegates from the various districts of the capital spoke one after the other. Among them, only a minority of eight declared themselves in favour of a rising. And even they did not all indicate the date when they thought it should take place.[114]

Would the Central Committee at last assume the responsibility of leading an insurrection, within a few days of the assembly of the Congress of Soviets? On October 16th there was another meeting of the Party leadership, reinforced by members of a number of important Party bodies: the Executive Committee of the Petrograd Committee, the Bolshevik Military Organization, delegates from the trade unions and the factory committees, and a number of other local militants. Speaking after Lenin, Kamenev and Zinoviev expounded their argument afresh, denying that the resolution of October 10th was binding on the Party.

Another member of the Central Committee, Milyutin, spoke in the same sense: 'We are not ready to strike the first blow. We are not capable of overthrowing the Government and arresting its members in the period that lies immediately ahead of us.' A representative of the Petrograd Committee summed up in these words the opinion of his Committee: 'We are not ready to begin such an action.' And Joffe, a member of the Central Committee, said: 'It is wrong to say that the problem is now merely a technical one: today the moment for insurrection still needs to be examined from the political standpoint.' The reports given by the delegates from the localities about the attitude of the masses in Petrograd provided only a confused idea of the political climate that prevailed in the capital: optimistic impressions alternated with much less optimistic ones—and the latter were certainly more numerous.

When the final resolution was voted on, two texts were put before the meeting. The first was from Lenin's pen. It called on 'all organizations and all workers and soldiers to make all-round, energetic preparations for an armed uprising', and expressed 'its complete confidence that the Central Committee and the Soviet will indicate in good time the favourable moment and the most appropriate methods of attack'. The second text was written by Zinoviev. In laconic style it confined itself to ruling that, 'while work of reconnaissance and preparation must not cease, no action is permissible before the Bolshevik fraction in the Congress of Soviets has been consulted'. When Lenin's motion was first put to the meeting it was adopted by twenty votes to two, with three abstentions. The fate of Zinoviev's resolution showed, however, that opposition to Lenin's standpoint continued to be strong; it was rejected by fifteen votes to six, with three abstentions. Finally, Lenin's motion was passed by nineteen to two, with four abstentions.[115] Lenin had won again. But he had still not succeeded in laying down a definite date for the rising.

The tendency that wanted to wait upon events had certainly suffered a defeat, and it was this that Kamenev showed he understood when he proceeded to offer his resignation from the Central Committee;* but for Lenin the struggle, which he saw as still undecided, had to continue to be fought out inside his Party. On October 17th he took up his pen again, and wrote a 'Letter to Comrades'. Once more he denounced 'the heroes of "constitutional illusions" and parliamentary cretinism,' and offered his supporters the example of the German revolutionaries who 'under devilishly difficult conditions, having but *one* Liebknecht (and he in prison) with no newspapers, with no freedom of assembly, with no Soviets, with *all* classes of the population ... incredibly hostile to the idea of internationalism ... started a mutiny in the navy with one chance in a hundred of winning.' Indignantly, Lenin pointed out how disgraceful it was that 'we, with dozens of papers at our disposal, freedom of assembly, a *majority* in the Soviets, we, the best situated proletarian internationalists in the world, should refuse to support the German revolutionaries by our uprising.' And, as before, he warned: 'in insurrection, delay is fatal.'[116]

Nevertheless, the Party still hesitated. On October 17th a conference of the Petrograd Bolshevik Committee and the Military Organization was held, with delegates present from the different districts of the capital. In principle, the purpose of the meeting was to convey to some 150 Bolshevik cadres the decisions that had been taken the previous day by the Central Committee. A friend of Trotsky's, Chudnovsky, was the first to speak. He rejected the idea of an insurrection before the meeting of the Soviet Congress. He was supported by Volodarsky, Ryazanov and Larin. Podvoisky and Nevsky admitted that the Bol-

---

* *Protokoly*, p. 105. Kamenev had already offered his resignation once before, when the Bolsheviks decided to leave the Pre-Parliament, but no notice seems to have been taken of this.

shevik Military Organization, whose spokesmen they were, was reluctant to give support to the idea of a rising. Another member of the
Military Organization then spoke. He declared against a rising, but
his speech was interrupted by Sverdlov. 'The decision of the Central
Committee on the uprising has been made. I am speaking here in the
name of the Central Committee and I will allow no one to reconsider
a decision that has been made. We have not gathered to set aside a
decision of the Central Committee, but to consider how we ought to
carry it out.' This vigorous language had the effect of reducing opponents to silence, and the gathering passed a motion approving the
policy of the Central Committee.[117]

As for carrying out this decision and the technical arrangements for
the insurrection, nothing was ready yet on October 17th—only a week
before the seizure of power. On that day Lenin met the leaders of the
Bolshevik Military Organization, Nevsky, Podvoisky and Antonov-
Ovseyenko, together with Rakovsky. According to Podvoisky's
account, 'everyone was agreed on postponing the insurrection for
several weeks'. Everyone, that is, except Lenin. It is important to
emphasize the degree of unpreparedness of the Bolshevik organization
as a whole, at a date so close to the meeting of the Congress of Soviets.
It was only on the afternoon of October 24th, the day before the actual
insurrection, that the Military Revolutionary Committee entrusted
with the leadership of the insurrection appointed a sub-committee
with responsibility for drawing up a final and precise plan.[118]

On October 18th Kamenev and Zinoviev made a final attempt to
counter the plan for an insurrection. Maxim Gorky's paper *Novaya
Zhizn*, which was extremely hostile to the Bolsheviks, had in its issue
of the previous day alluded to the letter that the two opponents of
Lenin's policy had addressed to the Party on October 11th. On
October 19th Kamenev published in this paper a statement in which he
revealed the divisions within the Bolshevik leadership. He referred to
the 'protest' made by Zinoviev and himself 'against our Party's
intention to take the initiative in the very near future in some armed
rising'.[119]

Lenin reacted, in a 'Letter to Bolshevik Party members' (and not
merely to his colleagues on the Central Committee), with great anger
against the publication of Kamenev's 'strikebreaking' letter. Associat-
ing Zinoviev with Kamenev in this matter, he wrote: 'I declare outright that I no longer consider either of them comrades and that I will
fight with all my might, both in the Central Committee and at the
Congress, to secure the expulsion of both of them from the Party.'[120]
The next day he declared to the Central Committee: 'If that is tolerated, the Party will become impossible, the Party will be destroyed ...
There can and must be only one answer to that: an immediate decision
of the Central Committee' to expel Kamenev and Zinoviev.[121]

However, the Party did not expel the 'strikebreakers'. On October 20th the Central Committee considered Lenin's letter. Stalin took the view that 'expulsion from the Party is not a recipe, and we must keep the unity of the Party intact'.[122] What was involved here was not so much a concern for unity on Stalin's part as a degree of political solidarity with the men whom Lenin looked upon as strike-breakers. In the Party organ which he was chiefly responsible for, he had published a communication from Zinoviev wherein the latter had alluded to an article in which, without actually giving his name, Lenin had argued against him. Stalin had accompanied this contribution by Zinoviev with an editorial note in which he said that 'the sharp tone of Comrade Lenin's article does not alter the fact that we remain in solidarity as political comrades' — still comrades, that is, with those whom Lenin wanted to expel from the Party.

On October 24th, Lenin addressed a final letter to the members of the Central Committee. Written in a style that was perhaps not so much menacing as moving, the letter began thus: 'I am writing these lines on the evening of the 24th. The situation is critical in the extreme. In fact it is now absolutely clear that to delay the uprising would be fatal. With all my might I urge comrades to realize that everything now hangs by a thread; that we are confronted by problems which are not to be solved by conferences or congresses (even congresses of Soviets), but exclusively by peoples, by the masses, by the struggle of the armed people.'[123]

At the moment when Lenin wrote this letter he was unaware that the die had at last been cast. But it was doubtless no accident that the spark which exploded the powder-magazine of Petrograd was struck by the Provisional Government and not by the Bolshevik revolutionaries. During the night of October 24th–25th the ministers decided to take action against their enemies, and ordered that the offices of two Bolshevik papers be sealed up. The general staff of the insurrection reacted to this measure. That night the revolutionary forces moved into battle at last, settling the fate of the Provisional Government and of bourgeois Russia.

At that moment, Lenin was still biting his nails in the flat in the Vyborg district that was his hiding-place. He had several times asked the Central Committee for permission to go to the Smolny Institute, where the Petrograd Soviet and the Military Revolutionary Committee had their headquarters. Not being anxious to create difficulties for themselves by the presence of such a compromising personage, the Central Committee had refused. At last, defying discipline, the cardinal virtue of Bolshevism, its founder, escaping from the vigilance of his landlady, wrote these words in a note he left for her, the last he was to put on paper before the conquest of power: 'I am going where you did not want me to go. Goodbye.'[124]

It is useless to ask what would have happened in Russia if, in 1917, there had not been a party like the Bolshevik Party, and in it a man like Lenin, with as determined a revolutionary will as his, as persuasive and effective a leader as he was. Without wishing to underestimate the weight of economic conditions in deciding the course of political and social evolution, one must take account of the evidence: when, acting in the 'direction of history', that is, in the narrow margin that social reality allows to human freedom, an individual possessing exceptional powers intervenes, then facts, institutions and states may all find themselves turned topsy-turvy. The pace of events is accelerated, and the impossible, or what has been thought to be impossible, suddenly becomes reality. Historical necessities, crouching for the moment in the shadows, doubtless await, impassive and patient, the moment for taking their revenge, as indeed happened in Russia. But what has been achieved nevertheless remains: in this case, the mightiest of modern political upheavals, achieved by Lenin, who, as we shall see—relying upon the masses, and sometimes urged on by them; opposed by a coalition of states and of the conservative forces in Russia; fighting against the hostility of some and the inertia of others, often against the leadership of his own Party—drove his country forward onto the road of socialist revolution.

Metamorphosis of the Bolshevik Party

An historical survey of the activity of the Bolshevik Party in 1917 confirms something that the first part of this study had enabled us to perceive, namely, that the relation between Lenin and *his* party was often a difficult one, involving conflict, and rarely harmonious. It is important to show that this was especially so in the year and in the event that decided Russia's fate, thereby establishing for ever the position of Leninism in history.

'The position of Leninism' means here, to a large extent, that of the Leninist organization, the revolutionary party consecrated by the October victory as *the party of the revolution*. If Leninism and the Leninist organization became for a substantial section of the working-class movement a guide, an ideal and a model, this was due, it is clear, to the fact of their triumph in 1917. It was the triumph of Bolshevism that caused it to become a focus of attention everywhere, whether in a spirit of hatred or one of enthusiasm, of repulsion or of devotion. In the case of Bolshevism a socialist party had successfully carried out, for the first time in history, a proletarian revolution. Was not the secret of this victory to be found in the specific structures that were characteristic of Bolshevism, the organizational conceptions it had elaborated? The history of Bolshevism, from its very beginning, thus became, through the victory of October 1917, the source of inspiration and guidance for a whole generation (at least) of revolutionary militants. This history was seen as a unified whole, as though a single *schema* and a single process of conditioning had shaped the Bolshevik Party, as though history had carried out upon it and through it a task that was continuous and linear. The Party that triumphed in 1917 was identified with the Party that from 1903 to 1914, and during the First World War, had prepared the way for this triumph. The merits of this Party were projected into the past and attributed to the underground organization — closed, conspiratorial, centralized, disciplined and homogeneous — that Lenin had founded and developed between 1903 and 1906 and in the dark years of the 'period of reaction'. The taking of power by the Russian proletariat in 1917 appeared as the practical, and therefore irrefutable, proof of the virtues of clandestinity, conspiratorial methods, centralization, discipline, and homogeneity (not to speak of monolithicity). Yet this view is not entirely correct. For historical analysis shows that in 1917, in the course of the revolution that made of Bolshevism a universal model, the Leninist organization underwent profound transformations, a kind of metamorphosis that makes it dubious, even false, to identify, without qualification, the Party of the revolution, the Party that 'made' the October revolution, with the Party that prepared the way for it under the Tsarist régime.

It was indeed a metamorphosis that occurred. Reduced in 1910 to a membership that was certainly less than 10,000, and in February 1917 numbering no more than 20,000, the Party saw its membership increase thereafter more than tenfold.* Having been obliged by force of circumstance to organize in a not very democratic way, or even in a basically anti-democratic one, the Party opened itself in 1917 to the life-giving breeze of democracy. The rules of underground work, though they did not wholly vanish, became less important than the methods of public discussion. The monolithic character that Lenin had tried to give the Party during the last pre-war years disappeared completely, yielding place to a variety of tendencies that were in many ways mutually contradictory. The right of these tendencies to exist and develop, proclaimed in theory in 1905-6 but denied in practice during the years of reaction, now became a reality. The requirements of discipline and 'absolute obedience' faded away, and, at the same time, the rigid centralism that was a corollary of this discipline and hierarchical spirit declined, under the influence of a thousand tumultuous, ungovernable pressures. In other words, 1917 saw the birth of a new, or renovated, Party, which had broken with its original conditioning and transcended this in a dialectical way,† a Party that

---

* See p. 158.
† On the role of dialectics in Leninism, see the concluding chapter of the book, p. 442.

opened itself at last, and very freely, to the irruption of the masses onto the political scene.

Democracy in the Bolshevik Party

Throughout the year 1917 the Bolshevik Party never looked like a monolithic party and never sought to conceal the fact that it was not such a party. There existed, on the contrary, a great diversity of opinions within it, and the disagreement between the various tendencies was publicly known. How, then, was the Party able to claim to unite its members around a tactic and a strategy that were common to all? Confronted with an unexpected situation, with many and sudden changes and a dynamic the pace and scope of which might take by surprise the boldest and most optimistic of revolutionaries, the Bolshevik leadership would have been hard put to it to impose monolithicity. At every level of the hierarchy, even in the Central Committee itself, tendencies clashed in decisive debates. On the outcome of these debates depended not merely the line of the Party's day-to-day policy but the very fate of the revolution. The Bolshevik organization, from which Lenin had sought, when it became an independent formation (in 1912), to exclude every factor of division, thus possessed a Right wing and a Left wing, with, between them, several 'Right-centre' and 'Left-centre' shades of opinion.

The Bolshevik Right, the moderate, conciliatory, cautious, reformist tendency in the Party, we have already seen at work, constantly striving to restrain the impetuosity of the masses, to master their impatience and, inside the Party itself, to 'hold Lenin back'. Dominant until the leader's return to Petrograd, this wing never yielded to his authority, although this became strengthened by the course of events, and it opposed right down to the eve of the seizure of power Lenin's plan for armed insurrection. The disagreement between this wing and Lenin (and the eventual majority in the Central Committee) turned upon a fundamental problem, namely, whether it was possible to 'go over' from the bourgeois to the proletarian revolution.

The presence of leaders of front-rank importance, including Kamenev, in this moderate and temporizing tendency in the Bolshevik Party seemed to endow it with special cohesion. Yet it needs to be pointed out that 'moderatism' and opportunism were not concentrated in an organized group in the Party. What was involved here was both a trend and an outlook: a trend led by prominent members of the Central Committee, and an outlook that showed itself at certain moments in Bolsheviks who, on other occasions, sometimes of decisive importance, were close to Lenin.

What was true of the 'moderate' trend in the Party was even truer of its 'Leftist' wing, owing to the lack, in this case, of outstanding leaders, or merely of members of the Central Committee who were prepared to undertake the leadership of this tendency. To be sure, Lenin himself, when he came back from exile to Petrograd and in the weeks immediately following, played such a role. Once he had beaten the Right wing, however, and put an end to the conciliatory policy followed by the Party up to that time, he went over, as we have seen, to a more cautious line. A more radical tendency, desirous of crossing swords immediately with the Provisional Government, and acting to overthrow it, then separated off to the Left of Lenin.

During April 1917 the 'Left' tendency in the Party expressed itself with vigour. The Petrograd masses, indignant at the conservative and imperialist policy that Milyukov continued to follow as Russia's Foreign Minister, came out into the streets of the capital and voiced their hostility to the Provisional Government. The Petrograd Soviet called for an end to this demonstration, which was turning into a riot, and the Bolshevik Central Committee supported this decision. The Party leadership had been subjected to strong pressure by militants who wanted to hasten the course of events and bring down the Provisional Government. This was the case with several members of the Bolshevik Military Organization, entrusted with co-ordinating and promoting Party activities in the army. One of these, Nevsky, who played a highly important role all through the year 1917, speaking in the name of the Military Organization, called publicly for an armed mobilization. In the Petrograd Committee of the Party other 'Leftists' voiced the same demand.[125]

The June days[126] were preceded in the Party by a clash between Right and Left, with the latter urging that an armed demonstration be organized and the former hesitating to encourage the masses to advance, and in any case ruling out the possibility of violent action. The Bolshevik Military Organization again appeared as a bastion of the Left.[127] When the leaders of the Soviet forbade the demonstration, the Central Committee bowed to this ruling. The reactions caused by their decision revealed, if revelation was needed, the persistence of a 'Left' trend among the Bolsheviks. Some militants tore up their Party cards. The Bolshevik representative in Kronstadt acknowledged that those moments 'were among the most unpleasant of his life', with the crowd, sometimes led by Bolshevik Party members, violently expressing its anger and resentment.[128] The Petrograd Committee did not hesitate, either, to express its dissatisfaction. Zinoviev and Lenin tried to appease their critics, but were not always successful.[129]

It can be shown that in the events leading up to the July days the 'Left' Bolsheviks were especially active,[130] and for this reason the defeat that the Party then suffered was by some laid at their door. According to the memoirs of one of the 'Leftists', it was even proposed to hold a Party 'trial' of them. The idea was not followed up, among other reasons because Lenin was against it. Whereas among many

Bolsheviks condemnation of 'Leftism' was fast becoming a regular thing, Lenin showed a great deal of understanding in relation to this phenomenon. There could be no question of subjecting the Leftists, he considered, to any pressure or repression. On the contrary, it had to be appreciated that 'he who takes no risks does not win; without defeats there can be no victories.'[131] Finally, an unnamed member of the Party's Military Organization expressed correctly the state of mind of its toughest members, those who charged the leadership with timidity, when, speaking in a discussion on the eve of the June crisis, he said: 'It is time we remembered that we represent not only socialism, but, it should also be added, *revolutionary socialism*.'[132]

One last observation needs to be made. It seems that this 'Left', or 'Leftist', tendency was stronger among the rank-and-file than among the leaders of the Party, and that it found expression with greater vigour whenever a question, having first been considered by the Central Committee, was then discussed in a wider circle of members, with less well-known militants taking part. Referring to the problem that the Bolshevik Party had to face regarding participation in or boycott of the Pre-Parliament, Trotsky notes, in his history of the revolution, that 'the deeper down this question went into the party, the more decisively did the correlation of forces change in favour of the boycott',[133] that is, in favour of the Left. This observation has a wider implication and reflects a reality that is not peculiar to the year 1917 or to the Bolsheviks: the closer one gets to the rank-and-file and the masses, the greater (in a revolutionary period, at least) is the desire for direct action, the more radical the feeling, outweighing those considerations which cause leaders, on grounds, often justified, of 'realism', to weigh carefully the risks of an undertaking, study its chances of success and, above all, seek to preserve what has already been won.

And so the Bolshevik Party was divided, during the year in which it took power, between a cautious wing that preferred to wait upon events and a wing that was mainly characterized by its will to attack, with a number of intermediate shades of opinion separating them. It is not enough to note this coexistence of different trends: we must see what kind of relations obtained between them, and how they were dealt with at the top of the Party hierarchy. Their existence dispensed with any official 'permission': it was an accomplished fact, part of the reality of revolutionary Russia and of the Party. At the Bolsheviks' national conference in April 1917 Lenin said that 'it would be advisable *openly* to discuss our differences'.[134] In September, when he expected an extraordinary congress of the Party was going to be held, he wanted '*all* elections' within the Party to be conducted around the question of support for versus opposition to participation in the Pre-Parliament.[135] This confrontation of tendencies appeared, as Trotsky mentions, to an increasing extent at every level of the Party: 'Almost all the local organizations formed into majorities and minorities.'[136] Indeed, all the major choices and great decisions that the Party had to take in 1917 were always subjected to discussion and a vote.

This happened when Lenin returned to Russia and it was a matter of deciding the Party's conception of the revolution: was it a purely bourgeois revolution, or did the question of going over to the socialist revolution arise at once with the abolition of Tsardom? The important extent of the difference of opinion among the Bolsheviks was reflected in the sharpness of the debates and in the size of the minority votes: 71 to 39, with 8 abstentions, when the principal resolution was voted on at the April conference.* More examples could be given. In June the question as to whether the Party should organize a demonstration directed against the Provisional Government was debated and settled not by the Central Committee or the Petrograd Committee but by a large, informal gathering at which three resolutions were voted on, one after the other: by 58 to 37, with 52 abstentions, the meeting noted the masses' desire to give expression to their will in a street demonstration, and by 47 to 42, with 80 abstentions, it declared that the proletariat of the capital would demonstrate even if the Soviet were to forbid this.[137] A procedure of the same kind was followed in September when it became necessary to decide whether or not to boycott the Pre-Parliament: it was not the Central Committee but a broader grouping, the Bolshevik delegation to the Pre-Parliament, that, reversing the decision originally taken by the Central Committee, decided by 77 to 50 to reject the idea of a boycott.† Certainly, the question of insurrection was, for obvious reasons, discussed by the Central Committee, and it was within this body that the majority and the minority were defined and counted: but participation in these meetings of the Central Committee was on several occasions 'enlarged', and representatives of the rank-and-file were associated with the ultimate decision.

All these votes showed that a strong minority, the numbers of which fluctuated but which was always there, existed among the Party cadres, and there was never any question of excluding this minority from the *executive* organs of the Party. The idea that these organs must, for reasons of efficiency, be marked by strict political homogeneity and therefore composed exclusively of members of the majority, had not yet entered into Communist practice. Whenever the Bolsheviks had to elect their leading bodies, a more or less proportional representation of the different tendencies was guaranteed. This occurred when the Central Committee was elected at the national conference of April 1917. The Committee comprised nine members,

* See p. 133.
† See p. 138.

five of whom belonged to what was then the majority trend in the Party (Lenin, Zinoviev, Stalin, Sverdlov and Smilga), while four represented the moderate wing (Kamenev, Nogin, Milyutin, Fyodorov).[138] In order that Kamenev might be elected Lenin had to make a public statement declaring that the presence in the Central Committee of the leader of the Right wing would be 'very valuable' for the Party.[139] This Right tendency was relatively less numerous in the Central Committee that was elected at the Party Congress held in August 1917, after the first phase of radicalization of the masses and the Party, but, even so, out of twenty-one members it could count on a group of six more or less avowed 'Right-wingers': Dzerzhinsky, Rykov, Milyutin, Nogin, Kamenev and Zinoviev. While the Central Committee was a deliberative body, it was also, in the absence of a Political Bureau, an executive organ which was called upon to put into effect the Party's policy, as decided at congresses and conferences. In October, within a few days of the insurrection, the Bolsheviks decided to form a smaller body, a political bureau (the origin of the 'Politburo' that was to become so famous), charged with the responsibility, in those days of decision, for day-to-day leadership of the Party, and, consequently, of the insurrection. To this bureau were assigned Lenin, Trotsky, Stalin, Sokolnikov and Bubnov—but also Kamenev and Zinoviev, those determined opponents of the armed rising and chief representatives of the minority.*

This desire to associate the minority with the deciding and application of Party policy is to be seen in other ways: the presence of 'minority' members in the Bolshevik press organs,[140] and the practice of providing for a 'minority report', giving a representative of the 'opposition' an opportunity of expounding the latter's view in thorough fashion at important Party meetings. At the April Conference, for example, Kamenev was able, along with Lenin, but taking the opposite line, to open the debate on general policy,† and Pyatakov was allowed to present a counter-report criticizing Lenin's views on the national question.[141]

This was not the only change that the Party experienced in 1917. After having proclaimed—in different historical circumstances—the need for discipline and for hierarchy, the Party saw these principles brushed aside. They were unable, any more than was monolithicity, to survive the new mood. Absolute respect for decisions taken by higher authorities gave way to a less formal and centralistic conception of organization. The example was set by Lenin himself when, on several occasions, including those of greatest importance, he interpreted in a very flexible way the prerogatives of the Central Committee, and did

* *Protokoly*, p. 86. Actually, the role played by this first political bureau was a very minor one.

† See p. 132.

not shrink from addressing himself to organs that were closer to the rank-and-file, without using the leadership as his channel of communication. This was notably what happened, as we have seen, during the weeks preceding the October insurrection, when he directed some of his letters not merely to the Central Committee but also, at the same time, to the Petrograd Committee, the Moscow Committee, and the Bolshevik fraction in the Congress of Soviets of the Northern Region, and when some of his messages were transmitted directly to meetings of militants in the capital.*

In the ranks of the Bolshevik Party in 1917 there was little question of obedience, and still less of 'absolute obedience'. The Central Committee's authority often came up against serious resistance, and even organs which, being based in the capital itself, were under the direct influence of the Party leaders, showed a spirit of independence. This was the case with the Petrograd Committee, which, owing to its location and numbers, was the most important organization in the Party. In May 1917 the Bolsheviks of Petrograd demanded the right to have their own paper, independent, or at least autonomous in relation to the organ of the Central Committee (*Pravda*), which they regarded as timorous and conservative. Lenin opposed this demand, which he saw as 'wasteful and harmful'.[142] So as not to clash directly with those who put it forward, however, he proposed a resolution providing a series of guarantees of freedom of expression for the Petrograd organization.[143] Despite his desire to be conciliatory, this resolution was rejected by 16 votes to 12.[144] Although he reiterated his view that 'the decision of the Petrograd Committee's Executive to establish a *special* newspaper in Petrograd is utterly wrong and undesirable,'[145] he proved unable to overcome the opposition of the Petrograd Bolsheviks. At a conference of the organization in the capital the decision to publish a special paper of their own was confirmed by 51 to 19, with 16 abstentions.[146] The Central Committee did not accept defeat and, at a meeting in August, decided that 'for the moment' the Petrograd Committee could not have a 'separate organ'.[147] Soon afterward, however, the Bolshevik organization in Petrograd informed the Central Committee that it had 'decided to set up a shareholding company to acquire a press and ... publish an organ of its own.'[148] The events of September, and even more those of October, prevented this decision from being put into effect.

If the Petrograd Committee had considerable influence in the Party, the role played by the very radical Military Organization was no less important. While carrying out its task in the army, this organization waged a struggle, sometimes very sharp, against the Central Committee, in order to preserve the *de facto* autonomy which it enjoyed. This struggle became harder after the July events, when the

* See p. 141.

setbacks suffered by the Bolsheviks caused a certain reaction to set in against the 'Leftists'. Until that time the Military Organization had been able to endow its paper, *Soldatskaya Pravda*, with a style and even a policy that were distinctive, and sometimes markedly different from those of *Pravda* itself. Thus, during the first days of July, while the Party's central organ was calling upon the workers to remain calm, *Soldatskaya Pravda* declared that 'the time has come not to sleep but to act'.[149] This attitude on the part of the Military Organization and of some of the members in charge of its paper was, after the July defeat, severely condemned, and the Central Committee decided to put an end to the virtual autonomy that *Soldatskaya Pravda* had enjoyed. The decision brought about a crisis in relations between the Central Committee and the Military Organization, which refused to obey it. Stalin informed the Military Organization that, once a decision had been taken by the Central Committee, 'it must be carried out without discussion'. The central bureau of the Military Organization decided that such a point of view was 'unacceptable', and 'demanded the immediate normalization of relations between the two organizations'. The Central Committee retreated somewhat, stating that the Military Organization's central bureau 'cannot constitute ... an independent political centre', authorizing publication of a special paper by this body, but deciding to establish 'temporary supervision' over the editorial board.[150]

The instructions and even the orders of the Central Committee were not always carried out any better when they were addressed not to such powerful organizations as these, but to a small group of individuals. Thus, there was the case of a certain number of Bolsheviks (some of whom had only recently joined the Party, which weakened their position) who wrote for the paper called *Novaya Zhizn*, edited by Maxim Gorky. This paper upheld views that were close to the 'Left-Menshevik' platform, and often showed hostility to Bolshevik policy. Towards the end of August the Central Committee decided to 'order these Party members to inform the editorial board of their refusal to continue writing' for *Novaya Zhizn*. The Bolsheviks concerned asked to be allowed to 'settle this matter on their own'. In the face of this reaction, the Central Committee decided to look at the question afresh, and then 'proposed' to the Party members that they 'withdrew their signatures'—which did not imply that they must cease to write for Gorky's paper. This concession was not enough to make the Bolshevik writers for *Novaya Zhizn* give up their resistance, and the Central Committee proceeded to retreat still further, proposing to have a general talk with the editors of the paper.[151]

This relaxation of discipline is easily explained. Whereas before the revolution the Bolshevik militants had been subject only to the pressures of their central leadership, they now found themselves in an unprecedented situation which had been created *by the masses*. The pressure exercised by the latter upon the Bolshevik cadres was sometimes so strong, and so contrary to that of the Central Committee, that these cadres were led to ignore the policy that the Party leadership had decided upon. This happened, for example, during the July days. At the start of the evening of July 3rd, the secretary of the Bolshevik Committee in the Putilov works, disregarding the orders he had been given to preach calm to the workers, was carried away by the feverish atmosphere prevailing in the plant, and called on the workers to go into action.[152] At almost the same moment the two chief Bolshevik delegates in Kronstadt found themselves faced with a crowd impatient to settle with the Provisional Government and march on Petrograd. One of the delegates, Raskolnikov, had just been talking on the telephone with Kamenev, who, in the name of the Central Committee, had ordered him to damp down the ardour of the workers and sailors of the great naval base. His partner, Roshal, far from obeying, delivered an inflammatory speech. Raskolnikov pointed out to him that he was going against the orders of the leadership. 'And what if the party does not act?' he asked. 'Don't worry,' Roshal replied, 'we will compel them to do so from here.'[153]

What was left, in this great upheaval, of the initial values and *schemata* of Bolshevism, and in particular of the rule of centralization that Lenin had introduced? Not very much. As we shall see,* the Bolshevik central organization was weak and poorly adapted to the tremendous increase in the Party's activities and membership. To these technical factors were added the desire manifested by the local and regional organizations to enjoy a wide freedom of judgment in deciding their policy. Furthermore, communications, and especially the postal service, were very defective in the Russia of 1917. The Central Committee, after acknowledging at its meeting on August 31st that 'hitherto, for purely technical reasons, the work of the Central Committee has been mainly concentrated on Petersburg,' decided to establish a body of 'travelling representatives', to be dispatched to the Bolshevik organizations in the provinces.[154] These efforts do not appear to have been very fruitful, partly as a result of resistance put up by the local committees. They sometimes opposed the formation of a regional authority which would link them more closely with the Central Committee, so jeopardizing their freedom of action.[155] It is no less significant that in this Leninist party, one of the basic principles of which was centralism, a number of local sections maintained down to the beginning of the autumn of 1917 committees in which Bolsheviks and Mensheviks sat side by side. It was only in September that the Bolsheviks in such important centres as Taganrog, Simferopol, Vladivostok and Tomsk decided to break their organic ties with the Mensheviks,

* See p. 279.

and this separation did not take place in Omsk and Irkutsk until October.[156]

This tendency towards *de facto* autonomy reflected a general feature of the country's political life. The Soviet institution was itself characterized by a high degree of decentralization. In the Petrograd area, for instance, 'the workers of the Bolshevik fortresses of Vyborg, Narva, Schluesselburg, Kronstadt, and especially the twelve boroughs of the capital ... each made up an autonomous soviet jealously independent of the Petrograd Soviet.'[157] In the provinces the situation was no different.

If these centrifugal forces, though active, did not prevent the Bolshevik Party from maintaining a degree of cohesion and unity that contrasted with the increasingly divided state of the other Socialist parties, it was due to the general line of its oppositional policy and to the authority enjoyed by its leader. This being so, it is important not to mistake this authority of Lenin's for some form of personal dictatorship. Here, too, one can all too easily project features belonging to a later phase of history back into a period which knew them not. Lenin the Party leader of 1917 was no personal dictator, and did not even enjoy unchallenged authority. Between the February and October revolutions his policy was almost continuously under attack from opponents within the Party, and this occurred without any beating about the bush. In April, Kamenev openly described Lenin's theses as 'unacceptable'.[158] In June, after the Central Committee's decision to call off the demonstration against the Provisional Government, Lenin found himself vigorously attacked by the rank-and-file. During a sharp discussion, A. I. Slutsky, a member of the executive of the Petrograd Committee, said of Lenin and Zinoviev: 'they did everything to undermine our organization by cancelling the June 10th demonstration.'[159]

In fact Lenin was obliged—and especially with regard to the most important episode of the year 1917—in order to fight against the temporizing tendency that predominated in the Central Committee and held back the October insurrection, to appeal to audiences broader than the Central Committee, which could bring pressure to bear to impose the decision that Lenin was unable on his own to persuade that body to take.

Opening-up and 'de-Bolshevizing' the party

The challenging within his own organization of the leader who had been thought unchallengeable, the criticism of the founder of Bolshevism and chief creator of the Bolshevik Party, were due to other factors besides the political transformations caused by the revolutionary events of 1917. If the spirit reigning in the Party underwent profound change, this also resulted from the fact that the composition of the

Party was subjected in that year to a veritable upheaval, which affected it at every level, from the bottom to the topmost leadership.

Party membership increased considerably. On the eve of the fall of Tsardom it numbered 23,600.[160] The national conference held in April revealed that membership had grown in a few weeks to 79,204.[161] The events of the spring and the way that the Bolsheviks reacted to them produced a fresh influx of members. The report presented by Sverdlov to the Sixth Party Congress, held in August, showed that in Petrograd there were now 41,000 members, as against about 15,000 in April; in the Moscow region there were 50,000, as against 13,000; in the Urals there were 24–25,000, as against 15,000; and in the Donets Basin there were 15,000, as against 5,500. 'These figures are minimum figures,' said Sverdlov, indicating that the total membership of the Party now numbered 240,000.* The numbers continued to grow during the weeks leading up to the October insurrection.[162] Sukhanov, describing the progress achieved by the Bolsheviks in September 1917, wrote in his memoirs that their 'army' was 'growing hour by hour'.[163] At the Central Committee meeting of October 16th, Sverdlov said that 'the growth of the Party has reached gigantic proportions: at the present time it must be estimated at 400,000 at least'—and the minutes add that he 'produced proof' of this.[164] The writer who has most systematically studied the evolution of Bolshevik Party membership nevertheless regards the figure of 400,000 as slightly exaggerated, and thinks that Sverdlov adduced it in order to demonstrate the Party's strength and in this way to support Lenin's argument in favour of insurrection.[165]

These figures must indeed not be taken too literally. Lenin acknowledged in September 1917 'the absence of any statistics concerning the fluctuation of the party membership ... ',[166] and it is hardly likely that the Party secretariat, with its tiny staff,† would have been in a position to follow and record the rapid growth of the organization. It remains clear, however, that the increase in Bolshevik membership in 1917 was so great that, at the time of the October revolution, of every twenty members, only *one* had been a member of the old organization, only one had been formed in the hard school of the closed, conspiratorial and centralized organization of the Tsarist period. The others had come to Bolshevism only in the period of its expansion and transformation.

This transformation was, moreover, not merely quantitative in character, nor did it affect only the rank-and-file. At the top, too, the

---

* *Preparing for October*, pp. 31–2. Lenin (Vol. 25, p. 260) confirms this figure, which is also given in Gorky, *History*, Vol. I, p. 300. In his book on *The Communist Party of the Soviet Union*, p. 173, L. Schapiro gives the figure 200,000, based on statistics published in the U.S.S.R. in 1958.

† See p. 279.

Party had experienced an injection of new blood. Among these new leaders the most distinguished was Trotsky. During the war Lenin had attacked him virulently because he did not share Lenin's ideas about 'revolutionary defeatism', and also because he was reluctant to break all links with the centrists. On several occasions Lenin had called Trotsky a 'Kautskian', a most inappropriate epithet, which was the worst insult in Lenin's vocabulary.[167] In February 1917, only a few days before the revolution, he uttered a judgment on Trotsky in which hatred was mingled with scorn, writing in a letter to Inessa Armand that Trotsky was 'always true to himself — twists, swindles, poses as a Left, helps the Right, so long as he can ... '[168] Trotsky's return to Russia, and the role that he at once began to play in the Soviet and as a mass agitator helped to open Lenin's eyes very quickly to the merits of his adversary and to the latter's revolutionary attitude. Within a very brief period the old quarrels between them were buried. Trotsky did not join the Bolshevik Party until August, but already in May Lenin had proposed to the Central Committee that he be entrusted with the chief editorship of a new popular paper which Lenin thought of launching. It was the Central Committee, less flexible than Lenin, and more disposed to cherish old grudges, that rejected this idea.[169]

At the end of September 1917, in a document addressed to the Bolsheviks of Petrograd, Lenin defended Trotsky, writing: 'First, upon his arrival, Trotsky at once took up an internationalist stand; second, he worked among the *mezhraiontsi* for a merger [with the Bolsheviks]; third, in the difficult July days he proved himself equal to the task and a loyal supporter of the party of the revolutionary proletariat.'* As soon as he had officially joined the Party, at the Sixth Congress, Trotsky was elected to the Central Committee, and, in September, to the editorial board of *Pravda*.†

His position in the Bolshevik Party was the stronger because he had not entered it quite alone. He belonged in 1917 to a socialist group which, though not numerous, was extremely active and played an undoubted role in the movement: the *mezhraiontsi* ('inter-district' group) had since 1913 brought together those revolutionary militants who, like Trotsky, hoped to reunite Bolsheviks and Left-wing Mensheviks. Some Bolshevik 'Conciliators' had joined this group. Though much more radical than the Mensheviks, they were critical of Lenin's organizational conceptions, and reproached the Bolshevik Party for its sectarian attitude and authoritarian tendencies. After the July days, most of the *mezhraiontsi*, who numbered 4,000 in Petrograd,

---

* Lenin, Vol. 41, p. 447. Not surprisingly, this document was not published in the U.S.S.R. until 1962.

† Deutscher, *Prophet Armed*, p. 288. Not long before, the Central Committee had, by 11 votes to 10 and against Lenin's wish, rejected this appointment.

joined the Party, and it was decided that the period of their membership of the 'inter-district' organization should be regarded for purposes
of seniority as equivalent to the same period spent in the Bolshevik
Party itself.[170] The difficulties that arose during the negotiations were
due to the hesitation shown by some of the *mezhraiontsi* who were
still suspicious of the Leninists: Trotsky himself, however, came out
strongly for unification, declaring that Lenin's Party had, through the
effects of the revolution, become 'de-Bolshevized'.[171]

A de-Bolshevized party. Later on, when anxious to present himself,
in his struggle with Stalin, as an unconditional Leninist, and to take
upon himself the whole heritage of the dead leader, Trotsky, yielding
through tactical calculation or political weakness to the growing
orthodoxy and the cult of Lenin, was to refrain from ever taking up
again this thesis of the 'de-Bolshevized party'. And yet, although
schematic, perhaps apologetical in purpose, and certainly undialectical, this thesis of the 'de-Bolshevization' of the Bolshevik Party as a
result of the February revolution of 1917 and all through its most
turbulent and most triumphant phase has much to be said for it. The
contribution made by the past, by the dozen years that Lenin and his
followers had devoted to building the Party, did not of course evap-
orate in 1917—far from that. But if Bolshevism in its original form
meant, above all, on the organizational plane, centralism, discipline
and the 'Party spirit', then the formula of 'de-Bolshevization', whatever
its shortcomings, does indeed illuminate the process of genuine transformation that Lenin's Party underwent in the great revolutionary
period opening with the fall of Tsardom in February 1917.

The thesis of 'de-Bolshevization' has been carried to its most
extreme consequences by the American historian Robert Daniels,
who writes that 'it was on the lines of this new division [defencism *v.*
internationalism]—not according to pre-1914 loyalties—that the
Bolshevik party took shape and struck for power in 1917.'[172] This
view, although it has the merit of bringing to the forefront one of the
most important and most significant phenomena of the Russia of 1917,
goes too far. Pierre Broué is more exact and closer to the truth when
he claims that 'the Bolshevik Party of 1917 ... was born of the con-
fluence in the Bolshevik stream of the independent revolutionary
streams constituted by the "inter-district" group and a number of
internationalist Social-Democratic organizations which had until
then remained outside Lenin's Party.'[173] Karl Radek wrote of the
importance of these 'streams' and 'rivulets' which joined the Bolshevik
river during the revolution.[174]

This influx enriched the Party, bringing to it some of those who were
to become its most admired and effective leaders. It is not sufficient,
in order to show this, to mention the leading Bolsheviks who obtained
their initial experience elsewhere than in Lenin's Party—among the

Mensheviks, as with Alexandra Kollontai or Chicherin, or in small independent groups, as in Trotsky's case. The general staff of the revolution was also made up to a large extent of men who had at different periods of their careers opposed Lenin, either within the Bolshevik faction itself or else in one or other of the Left or Right groups, 'Ultimatumists' or 'Otzovists' on the one hand, 'Conciliators' on the other, which had hived off from it.* If we consider these 'heretical' Bolsheviks we find that they constituted an appreciable element in the new leadership of the Party. An analysis of the official biographies of fifty-two of the most important Bolshevik leaders who distinguished themselves during the revolution shows, for example, that twenty-three of them—almost half—had in one way or another fought against Lenin's policy in the past.† Analysis of the record of the members of the Bolshevik Central Committee elected at the Sixth Congress in 1917 shows, moreover, that out of its twenty-one members this was true of nine.

Lenin understood perfectly that *this* Bolshevik Party was profoundly different from the Bolshevik organization as it had existed before the revolution. He understood it so well that he called, on his return to Russia, for a change in the Party's name, for it to abandon the title 'Social-Democrat' and become the 'Communist Party', thus cutting the terminological cord that bound it to the past.[175] His proposal evoked no response from among his followers. He repeated it at the national conference in April, without success.[176] 'We are loth to cast off the "dear old" soiled shirt ... But it is time to cast off the soiled shirt and to put on clean linen.'[177] Not until March 1918 did the Bolsheviks agree to drop the old name of the Party, consecrating in this way a metamorphosis that helped to make Russia the first workers' state in history.

---

* See p. 55.

† Haupt and Marie. These biographies were composed by the subjects themselves, when they were questioned, during the 1920s, about a past that they were still at that time in a position to describe in a serious way.

6

2
Revolutionary Strategy

On March 2nd, 1917, Nicholas II abdicated. Some Liberals turned towards his brother, the Grand Duke Michael, appealing to him to become Regent. This attempt to save the Romanov dynasty failed, however, as Michael declined the perilous honour that was offered him. The news of the Tsar's abdication and that of his brother's refusal to take over were announced simultaneously to the people of Russia. In Petrograd the response was an outburst of joy. In the midst of the crowd that was cheering the people's victory, a prominent S.R. whispered to a friend: 'Now it is finished.' But a woman bystander who heard this remark commented, 'in a very low voice': 'You are wrong, little father. Not enough blood has flowed.'[1]

The reason given by this anonymous and casual observer was crudely put, but her view that the revolution was not over and done with was a sound one. Lenin would have seen in it a proof of popular wisdom and an example of proletarian determination. It was, in any case, this correct idea, namely, that the revolution had not been completed, that inspired all his activity throughout 1917. His tactics and strategy were based on conviction that the fall of Tsardom merely meant the *beginning* of the revolution, and that a process of conquest had been started which must, however unpredictable the ultimate outcome, carry the Russian revolution forward beyond both its national frontiers and its bourgeois framework. Lenin's entire approach was guided by this principle. But his tactical plans and his strategic conception evolved as the dynamic of the revolution progressed, some features becoming sharper while others were modified, resulting in variations that only an abstract view of history can cause one to overlook.

'You are wrong, little father. Not enough blood has flowed.' And, indeed, less than two months after the fall of Tsardom, many workers were out in the streets demanding the resignation of the Provisional Government whose very existence had symbolized, a short time before, their victory over Tsardom. Even more significant, these demonstrators, numbering hundreds of thousands, were attacking, indirectly at least, the soviets themselves, which supported the bourgeois government. Blood flowed once more, with numerous victims falling beneath the bullets of the Government's defenders in the streets of Petrograd. During the spring the growing radical and discontented mood of the masses found expression in various ways: demands, backed by ever wider support, for workers' control;* an already noticeable loss of confidence in the moderate socialist parties; a spectacular increase in membership of the Bolshevik Party; a crisis in the army, reflected in a growing number of deserters; finally and generally, exacerbation of a political climate in which dissatisfaction simmered into an anger, that constantly threatened to boil over, against everything that hindered the revolution's advance. In June this pressure was already so vigorous that even the Bolsheviks, although their radicalism frightened all rival groups (except the anarchists), were nearly overwhelmed by it, and were accused of excessive moderation by their more impatient supporters. In July popular impatience attained its climax, and also its anti-climax, with the routing of tens of thousands of sailors, soldiers and workers, and a wave of repression directed against the Bolshevik Party and against the proletariat itself.

The situation thus created did not last for long. The Right-wing forces were unable to profit by their momentary advantage. The military offensive that they launched resulted, through its failure, in political recovery by the Bolsheviks. The latter were largely responsible for the crushing of Kornilov's attempted *coup d'état*. When the soviets were obliged to call on the militant proletariat of the capital to repulse the reactionary onslaught, Lenin's followers were enabled to reorganize themselves and complete the arming of the Red Guards. From September onwards the Bolsheviks emerged again, and more than ever, as a rising political force. Setbacks followed one after another for the Provisional Government and its friends: not surprisingly, those parties which, with ever greater hesitation and anguish, supported the Provisional Government, saw their followers melt away.

Already before the July days the Mensheviks had lost the ascendancy they had possessed among the working class of Petrograd during the first weeks of the revolution. When the leadership of the Soviet sent delegates into the factories to call on the workers to remain calm, they could no longer rely on the moderate socialist spokesmen, as these had lost all their audience in the popular quarters of the capital.[2] The defeat suffered by the Bolsheviks in July had given the Mensheviks hope of recovery, but the Petrograd municipal elections of August 20th shattered their illusions. The election campaign proved disastrous for them: they received only 5 per cent of the votes. While solidly established in ministerial office, they had practically lost their positions as representatives of the people. This situation was confirmed

* See p. 203

in September by the municipal elections in Moscow, where the Mensheviks won only 4 per cent of the votes. As an organized force, if not as an ideology, Menshevism was melting away. In the 'two capitals' the only organization that had ever rivalled the Bolsheviks for the allegiance of the working class had more or less ceased to count. As for the S.R.s, they had lost everything that linked them with the revolutionary populism of the Tsarist period. After February 1917 the S.R. Party became more and more obviously a bourgeois party: as Marc Ferro puts it, 'people became S.R.s in order to make a career of the Revolution.'* The tragedy of the Mensheviks and the S.R.s, reformist parties both, was that they turned their backs upon reforms, sacrificing these to the twofold constraint of alliance with a conservative bourgeoisie and pursuit of the war.

The discredit that struck the Mensheviks and the S.R.s also reflected the complete unpopularity and powerlessness into which had now sunk a Provisional Government that only a few months earlier had seemed the standard-bearer of all the people's hopes. The consequence was that Russia became a country without a central leadership, a huge vacuum in which power was not being wielded by anyone. The liberal solution had collapsed impotently, while the reactionary effort led by Kornilov had proved incapable of substituting itself for a half-hearted bourgeois democracy. This double defeat of the bourgeoisie put Lenin in an entirely new situation; and, in September, armed insurrection became a question for the immediate future.

History shows few examples of such profound changes taking place in so short a time. In February, the fall of Tsardom, after only a few days of popular demonstrations; then the establishment of a bourgeois authority enjoying the support of the workers' parties—but wasting within a few weeks the huge reserve of popularity and general trust that it enjoyed; the rapid growth of a party whose leader had been still treated in April with ridicule on account of his 'extremism'; increasing impatience on the part of the proletariat, shaking off the tutelage of an essentially revolutionary institution, the soviets, which a few months of existence had sufficed to render conservative; the check to the Bolshevik advance in July, with Lenin forced into exile once more—'the July events had destroyed Bolshevism,' wrote Sukhanov[3] ...; then, at last, from September onwards, with agitation and disorder sweeping over the countryside, the Bolsheviks, mounting over the ruins of the reactionary offensive, started along a road that was to lead them, in fewer than fifty days, to the seizure of power. Less than eight months was needed to pass from survivals of feudalism to the antechamber of socialism. How could Lenin possibly, amid such a whirlwind as this, have laid down a rigorously defined policy and carried through a precise plan? On the contrary, we see in his line

*Ferro, *February*, p. 229. For the S.R. party see mainly pp. 243–6.

of conduct a number of turns, which, however, do not affect its strategic coherence as 'transition from the bourgeois revolution to the socialist revolution'. The mere manifestation of his will to bring about that transition, in the first days — perhaps the first hours — that followed the announcement of the fall of Tsardom, was a flash of genius that decided the fate of the revolution. This determination of Lenin's defined and decided the continuity of Leninist policy throughout the year 1917. But once the possibility of a victory of the socialist revolution had been glimpsed, and once the plan outlined that would make progress in that direction feasible, the way that events developed brought hesitations, and necessitated gropings and manoeuvres in which we are able to see a Lenin bold but flexible, daring yet circumspect even in his daring; a Lenin who, while clinging firmly to one idea, took care in all circumstances to observe reality, to examine every factor governing the realization of this idea, so as to cope with the manifold surprises and snares and false hopes that made up the history of the revolution.

From February to July 1917: a peaceful revolution?
It is important to see the variations in tactics within the strategically constant framework of Lenin's revolutionary policy in 1917.

As has been said, throughout March and most of April, Lenin stood on the extreme Left of the Party, fighting for recognition of the *idea* that it was possible and necessary to transcend the purely democratic phase of the revolution. Lenin's isolated position in his own organization during the first weeks of his return to Russia testified eloquently enough to the boldness of his stand. His attitude in the next phase, the 'April days', proves, however, the extent to which his 'extreme' attitude was combined with a prudence and cool-headedness that set a certain distance between him and the most radical elements of the Petrograd masses.

Despite demonstrations in which hundreds of thousands of workers and soldiers participated, many of them armed, despite the slogan 'Down with the Provisional Government!', taken up by tens of thousands of voices, Lenin refused to make a move towards insurrection. When the Petrograd Soviet ordered the workers to call a halt to their movement, Lenin put before the Central Committee of his Party a motion stating that 'the resolution of the Petrograd Soviet of April 21st banning all street meetings and demonstrations for two days must be unconditionally obeyed by every member of our Party'.[4] This same motion explained that 'the slogan "Down with the Provisional Government!" is an incorrect one at the present moment because, in the absence of a solid (i.e., a class-conscious and organized) majority of the people on the side of the revolutionary proletariat, such a slogan is either an empty phrase, or, objectively, amounts to attempts of an adventurist character'.[5] A few days later, during the April conference, Lenin said: 'all we wanted was a peaceful reconnoitring of the enemy's forces; we did not want to give battle. But the Petrograd Committee turned a trifle more to the left, which in this case is certainly a very grave crime.' And Lenin, who, at this same conference, had just succeeded in establishing, in conflict with Kamenev and his supporters, a Left-wing point of view, added: 'At the time of action, to go "a trifle more to the left" was wrong ... Had we deliberately allowed such an act, [I] would not have remained in then Cetral Committee for one moment.'[6]

Finally, while this first trial of strength was taking place between the revolutionary proletariat and the bourgeoisie, Lenin remained faithful to the tactic that he had advocated ever since his return to Russia. Based on the conception of a *peaceful* passing of power to the soviets, it was summed up in three points which Lenin repeatedly stressed: (1) the need to win a majority, (2) the need to persuade and explain, and (3) renunciation of violent methods. In one of the first articles that he published in *Pravda* after his return to Petrograd, he declared that 'to become a power the class-conscious workers must win the majority to their side ... We are not Blanquists [wrongly given as "Blancists" in the *Collected Works* translation], we do not stand for the seizure of power by a minority.'[7] On another occasion Lenin wrote that 'only by taking—with the support of the majority of the people—the whole power of the state into its own hands, will the revolutionary proletariat, together with the revolutionary soldiers, create, in the shape of the Soviets of Workers' and Soldiers' Deputies, a government ... which will alone be capable of quickly putting an end to the war ... '[8] Quotations of a similar kind could be multiplied.[9] None of these passages, nor the whole lot taken together, has prevented some apparently very serious critics from stating, as does, for example, John Plamenatz, that Lenin made a 'proletarian' revolution without greatly caring what the workers thought![10]

The majority of the working class could, moreover, only be won by means of explanation and persuasion. This task of persuading and explaining, over and over again, was the task that the leader of the Bolshevik Party put before his supporters in the spring of 1917. When expounding his *April Theses* he said, speaking of the 'broad sections', that 'it is necessary with particular thoroughness, persistence and patience to explain their error to them, to explain the inseparable connexion existing between capital and the imperialist war, and to prove that without overthrowing capital *it is impossible* to end the war by a truly democratic peace, a peace not imposed by violence'.[11] This task of explanation was presented as what 'all our work should be focused on'.[12] This 'pedagogical attitude'[13] was not just window-dressing. In the course of a stormy discussion that took place inside the Party itself, Lenin passed over a note to an old Bolshevik militant, Lyudmila Stal, who had just lost her temper, in which he advised her, benignly, 'not to speak so vehemently ... We must explain and clarify. We must persuade: we have to win a majority among the workers.'[14]

The employment of such means clearly ruled out any resort to violence. Lenin frequently stressed this, stating, for example, in *Pravda* of April 15th, 1917: 'We not only have not been guilty, directly or indirectly, of any threats of violence against individuals, but, on the contrary, we have always maintained that our task is to *explain* our views to all the people.'[15] On a number of occasions he emphasized that it was not for the revolutionary proletariat to take the initiative in violence. For instance: 'Our Party will preach abstention from violence ... as long as the capitalists have not started using violence against the Soviets of Workers', Soldiers', Peasants', Agricultural Labourers' and other Deputies ... Our Party will fight against the profound and fatal error of "revolutionary defencism" solely by means of comradely persuasion.'[16]

When he thus put forward, for the first time, the prospect of a peaceful conquest of state power, Lenin based himself on two considerations. He referred, in the first place, to the inadequately developed political consciousness of the Russian masses, saying that 'a gigantic petty-bourgeois wave has swept over everything and overwhelmed the class-conscious proletariat ... ; that is, it has infected and imbued very wide circles of workers with the petty-bourgeois political outlook;' and adding: 'An attitude of unreasoning trust in the capitalists ... characterizes the politics of the *popular masses* in Russia at the present moment.'[17] This situation could be corrected only through the tireless effort at 'fraternal persuasion' which Lenin urged upon his followers. Such an effort could be made, and a peaceful road to socialism be then opened, because, as a result of the democratic victory won in February, 'nowhere else is there such freedom as exists in Russia'.[18] In circumstances like these it seemed to Lenin that 'any thought of civil war would be naïve, senseless, preposterous.'[19]

The attitude that Lenin maintained during the April days was thus, while quite an exceptional one during his career, in conformity with the forecast, inherent in the tactic he advocated, of a relatively slow development of the Russian revolution. The events of June helped to modify this cautious estimate. At the beginning of the month the Bolshevik leaders found themselves subjected to vigorous pressure by the Party's Military Organization and by the Petrograd Committee, which urged them to put themselves at the head of a street demonstration that was being called for by a large number of soldiers in the capital.[20] The Bolshevik leadership held a meeting on June 6th at which two tendencies made themselves felt. One, headed by Kamenev, Nogin and Zinoviev, declared against the demonstration, whereas the other, to which Lenin belonged, wanted the Party to organize it. Some even went further, demanding that the demonstration be armed. Nevsky, one of the leaders of the Bolshevik Military Organization, said, for instance, that a peaceful demonstration would be 'unimposing' and 'amateurish'.[21] It was decided to reconsider the situation at a larger meeting. With two hundred 'cadres' present the decision was then adopted, by an overwhelming majority, for the Party to take the lead in the demonstration. Nevertheless, the line decided upon was a fairly cautious one, since the idea of an *armed* demonstration was rejected.

On the eve of the day when the demonstration was to take place, the executive of the Petrograd Soviet resolved to ban it. The Central Committee at once decided to flout this ban. One of its members, Smilga, went so far as to propose 'that they should not hesitate to seize the Post Office, telegraph, and arsenal if events developed to the point of a clash'.[22] Whereas Zinoviev and Kamenev remained hostile to the very principle of the demonstration, Lenin's view was that they should allow events to proceed and act in accordance with what might occur.[23] Then, during the night of June 9th–10th, the All-Russia Congress of Soviets, meeting in full session, added its ban to the Petrograd Soviet's ban on the demonstration. Summoned in haste, five members of the Central Committee had to take an immediate decision. Kamenev, Zinoviev and Nogin were for calling the demonstration off. Sverdlov and Lenin abstained from voting, and the moderate tendency carried the day.[24]

Throughout this episode Lenin's attitude seems to have been again a hesitant one. Though not sharing Kamenev's extreme caution, he also separated himself from the 'Leftist' line of Smilga. Nor does he seem to have thrown the full weight of his authority into the scales. When, some days later, the Central Committee had to justify its attitude in face of strong criticism by Party militants, Lenin did not conceal the ambiguity of his position. Although he affirmed that 'the cancellation [of the demonstration] was absolutely necessary,' at the same time he acknowledged that 'the dissatisfaction voiced by most comrades over the cancellation of the demonstration is quite natural ... '* Furthermore, he observed that: 'today the revolution has entered a new phase of its development ... The workers must clearly realize that there can now be no question of a peaceful demonstration ... the proletariat must reply by showing the maximum calmness, caution, restraint and organization, and must remember that peaceful processions are a thing of the past.'[25]

---

* Lenin, Vol. 25, p. 79. Lenin's speech ended on a similarly apologetic note: 'The Central Committee does not want to force your decision. Your right, the right to protest against the actions of the Central Committee, is a legitimate one, and your decision must be a free one' (ibid., p. 81).

During the weeks that followed, the overall situation in the country underwent a series of changes the importance of which did not escape Lenin. There was, in the first place, the increasing popularity of his Party, which was spectacularly revealed on June 18th, in the course of a demonstration which, organized by the Soviet, had turned out in a way that embarrassed the moderate socialists. Above all, during the month of June the premises on which Lenin's calculations were based were undermined in two ways. The Russian bourgeoisie proved strong enough to oblige the Provisional Government to launch a military offensive which the entire Left had denounced, and the soviets offered only derisory resistance to this disastrous action. At the same time, relations between the Bolsheviks and the 'Government socialists' gravely worsened. On the morrow of the decision taken by the Bolsheviks to bow to the orders of the Congress of Soviets and call off their demonstration, the Menshevik minister Tsereteli denounced the Bolsheviks as 'evil plotters', and the Menshevik newspaper wrote, 'It is high time to unmask the Leninists as criminals and traitors to the Revolution.'[26]

Lenin could not leave this unanswered, and on July 1st he declared that the Mensheviks had begun 'to serve the capitalists', adding that 'if the Mensheviks and Socialist-Revolutionaries had not been betraying the revolution and supporting the counter-revolutionary Cadets, power would have been in the hands of the Executive Committee [of the Soviets] since early May'.[27] This was not just a rhetorical phrase: it recognized the existence of a new political situation. Since the beginning of May the Mensheviks and S.R.s had given up their role of respectful opposition and external support to the Government. They were now sitting in the Cabinet. Did not this collaboration within the same Government between the liberal bourgeoisie and the parties that held the majority in the soviets rule out the prospect of a gradual transfer of power *to the soviets, specifically*, which had underlain Lenin's tactics since the overthrow of Tsardom? The July days removed Lenin's last doubts on this point.

The outbreak of the crisis was preceded by a period of increasing tension during which the influence of the anarchists had markedly grown in Petrograd.* In the last days of June agitation had mounted in some of the regiments stationed in the capital, which were now threatened with dispatch to the front. The workers, on their part, were demanding ever more insistently an increase in wages. The Government was in a state of crisis owing to the resignation of the Constitutional-Democrat ministers. These were the conditions in which there arose the idea of an armed demonstration calling for the resignation of the Provisional Government and for the soviets to take power. I have mentioned how cautiously the leaders of the Bolshevik Party

* See p. 197.
6*

received the plan for a demonstration.* Undoubtedly their attitude is to be explained, to some extent at least, by Lenin's absence: through illness or fatigue, the Bolshevik leader had withdrawn to the country. But it is also true that this absence of Lenin's itself had political significance: if Lenin had believed at that time that the situation could be exploited so as, perhaps, to seize power, he would certainly have remained in the capital. His state of health would have constituted no obstacle to this, since he returned to Petrograd at once during the night of July 3rd–4th, as soon as he judged his presence there indispensable. The Central Committee then decided, cancelling its previous decisions, to put the Party at the head of a demonstration that it had not been able to prevent,† while striving to keep this demonstration organized and peaceful in character. On the morning of July 4th, Lenin addressed thousands of soldiers, workers and sailors from the balcony of the Central Committee's headquarters. As the American historian Rabinowitch writes, this speech did not meet the expectations of those who heard it, and 'many of them were evidently disappointed'. Lenin's appeal to the demonstrators to remain calm ignored their desire to settle accounts there and then with the rule of the bourgeoisie.[28] His role in the July days seems to have been confined to this somewhat cautious speech. He then devoted himself to organizing the retreat of the Bolsheviks when the Government unleashed its campaign of repression against them. On July 6th the Bureau of the Petrograd Committee discussed whether to call a general strike in the capital to protest against the terror to which the revolutionary vanguard was being subjected. When Lenin was consulted, he rejected out of hand a proposal which he rightly saw as unrealistic.[29]

Finally, from the place of refuge to which the course of events had obliged him to withdraw, Lenin expressed the view that, like the events of April and June, the crisis had shown 'revolution and counter-revolution becoming more acute, and the middle elements being eliminated for a more or less extensive period'.[30] Looking back later on, he considered that the Party could not have acted differently, for 'at that time Petrograd could not even have taken power physically, and had it done so, it could not have retained power politically ... '[31] His opinion coincides in essentials with that of Trotsky, as expressed some years after the revolution: 'the Bolsheviks could have seized the power in Petrograd at the beginning of July. But if they had done so they could not have held it.'[32]

In the last analysis, while this episode shows a reluctance on Lenin's part to follow the movement of the masses and an unwillingness finally to give up a line of action that had for some time seemed to him

* See p. 135.
† I shall discuss later the relations between the revolutionary masses and the Bolshevik Party, as these were revealed by the July days: see pp. 198–200.

doubtful, it was of decisive importance in determining Lenin's subsequent tactics. The July defeat and its consequences led him to make an agonizing reappraisal—or, if it be thought that *violent* struggle for the conquest of power constitutes, in a sense, the classic Leninist line, to go back to the norm of Leninism. Less than a week after the dispersal of the demonstration, Lenin declared: 'All hopes for a peaceful development of the Russian revolution have vanished for good. This is the objective situation: either complete victory for the military dictatorship, or victory for the workers' armed uprising.'[33] Accordingly: 'Let us gather forces, reorganize them, and resolutely prepare for the armed uprising.'[34]

This tactical turn was an amazingly bold one to make in the circumstances of the time. Having underestimated both the revolutionary potential of the masses and the readiness of the moderate socialist parties to obstruct it, Lenin deduced, sharply and clearly, the consequences of his mistake. The organizer of the Bolshevik Party then applied himself to a new task, which no Marxist had as yet tackled in a concrete way—preparing for insurrection and the practical seizure of power.

Leninism and insurrection

Though they were practical workers in the field of revolution, and even of armed insurrection, when circumstances made this possible, Marx and Engels constructed no theory of insurrection. It was to this meagre source, however, that Lenin turned as soon as he had decided that organization of armed struggle for the overthrow of the Provisional Government had become an urgent task.

'Now, insurrection is an art quite as much as war or any other, and subject to certain rules of proceeding ... ,' said Engels. These rules ('plain and simple') he set out as follows:

> Firstly, never play with insurrection, unless you are fully prepared to face the consequences of your play ... Unless you bring strong odds against [the forces opposed to you], you are defeated and ruined. Secondly, the insurrectionary career once entered upon, act with the greatest determination, and on the offensive. The defensive is the death of every armed rising ... Surprise your antagonists while their forces are scattered, prepare new successes, however small, but daily ... Rally thus those vacillating elements to your side which always follow the strongest impulse ... Force your enemies to a retreat before they can collect their strength against you; in the words of Danton, the greatest master of revolutionary policy yet known: *de l'audace, de l'audace, encore de l'audace!*'[35]

Lenin gave no more systematic thought to the art of insurrection than this. Despite, however, the absence of any thorough study on his part of the problems presented by armed revolt, we find in his writings a number of illuminating observations that relate not so much to the practical problems to be solved as to the *political* conditions that make possible and necessary the resort to force in order to take power. The most important of these observations is certainly that which defines the fundamental distinction between Leninism and any form of Blanquism: 'Victory for the workers' armed uprising is only possible when it coincides with a deep mass upheaval ... '[36] For Lenin it was clear that 'insurrection must rely upon a revolutionary upsurge of the people,' that it must 'rely upon that *turning-point* in the history of the growing revolution when the activity of the advanced ranks of the people is at its height.'[37] Again: 'If the revolutionary party has no majority in the advanced contingents of the revolutionary classes and in the country, insurrection is out of the question'[38] — although, of course, 'it would be naïve to wait for a "formal" majority for the Bolsheviks'.[39] This was why, in the situation that prevailed in Russia in the autumn of 1917, Lenin saw it as necessary for the Bolsheviks to win the majority in the Soviets of Petrograd and Moscow.[40]

This condition—support for the forces of the insurrection on the part of the masses, coincidence between the revolt of the vanguard and the offensive movement of the masses—was in its turn the resultant of a combination of circumstances which together made up a *revolutionary situation*, a state of political and social disequilibrium the constituent elements of which were many and complex, but which Lenin reduced to this twofold proposition: '*Our victory is assured*, for the people are close to desperation, and we are showing the entire people a sure way out.'[41]

'The people are close to desperation.' Let us see to what extent this formula applied to the Russian masses in autumn 1917. If hopeless apathy is meant, clearly that was not the case, but quite the contrary, since the new element which in September 1917 exerted a decisive influence on Lenin's calculations was the revolt of the countryside, spreading over the land 'like a broad river'[42] and constituting 'the most outstanding fact of present-day Russian life'.* The general strike of the railwaymen which broke out in September, in a sphere where the trade-union organization was still under Menshevik influence, showed that as winter approached the proletariat was growing more and more exasperated. The strike spread to the postal service, and Lenin regarded this dual phenomenon as being 'of immense importance from the general economic, political and military point of view'.[43] The country as a whole seemed on the brink of collapsing into chaos.

* Lenin, Vol. 26, p. 197. Lenin went so far as to say that, given the peasants' revolt, 'all other political symptoms, even were they to contradict the fact that a nation-wide crisis is maturing, would have no significance whatsoever' (ibid., p. 79).

'September and October were particularly ominous months. In the cities, civil war seemed to be coming. It was impossible to go out alone at night. Armed bands clashed in the streets.'[44] To cope with the increasing anarchy a government was needed that was ready to use its strength. However, 'the army no longer really existed'.[45] Above all, the popularity of the Bolsheviks was growing fast, and Lenin referred to this when he declared: 'the crisis has matured.'[46] What underlay this development was the lamentable failure of the June offensive at the front, together with the Government's inability to promote a policy of peace: the people's lassitude was turning into anger. In Petrograd itself the hatred of the garrison for the Provisional Government was nourished by the threat constantly held out to it that the regiments stationed in the capital would be sent to the front. On October 21st the majority of these regiments announced through their delegates that they would no longer take orders from the Provisional Government but only from the Petrograd Soviet.[47] Finally, Lenin mentioned the 'exceptional importance' of the role played by the national question in Russia.[48] In this field too the inability of the Provisional Government to satisfy the demands of the non-Great-Russian peoples was glaringly obvious. This was especially true in relation to the Ukraine's desire for autonomy and to Finland's desire for independence, which Kerensky refused to satisfy, so that a hot-bed of agitation was kept in being close to Petrograd for the Bolsheviks to profit from.

All these factors did not, strictly speaking, show that the Russian people were 'close to desperation', as Lenin claimed. But the fact that, so soon after the fall of Tsardom, only a few months after experiencing the euphoria of that liberation, the people were forced to resort to strike after strike in the towns, and in the country to individual or collective attempts to improve their conditions forcibly, provides sufficient proof of their angry mood and of the precariousness of their situation. Awareness of their misfortunes was coupled with conviction that these were not inevitable. There was a party whose existence saved the proletariat from the pit of desperation: the Bolshevik Party. The differences of opinion that existed within this Party did not prevent it from presenting the image of a coherent force rejecting the conformities, taboos, obsessions and myths in which the bourgeois and moderate socialist parties were bogged down. Unlike their rivals, for whom there could be no question of introducing social reforms so long as the war lasted, or of making any serious effort to end the war, the Bolsheviks said: we want reforms, and we want peace*—and both are possible. In contrast to their rivals, who were frightened by the way the masses were 'overwhelming' the institutions of government, the Bolsheviks sided, willy-nilly, with this process.

* See p. 188.

While everyone else denounced disorder, *they* denounced, first and foremost, resistance to change and an attitude of resignation. Whereas the moderate socialists clung to their hope of a 'democratic peace' that the Western Allies would favour, or at least permit, Lenin's supporters called on the Russian people to count on nobody but themselves in the struggle for peace, and to go forward in this struggle with all the greater resolution. The prospect thus offered—bread, land, peace—was expanded to cover all Europe when Lenin declared that the Russian proletariat was not isolated, and discovered in Germany and Italy 'indisputable symptoms that we are on the eve of a world-wide revolution'.*

On October 16th Lenin expressed his view thus: 'The situation is clear: either a Kornilovite dictatorship or the dictatorship of the proletariat and the poorest strata of the peasantry.'[49] There were two paths that Russia could follow, and two only, so that a *revolutionary* choice seemed to the masses possible and even inevitable. Here was an additional factor in the *revolutionary situation* that Lenin had observed, and to some degree created: compromise solutions were impossible, the middle parties had faded into the background, policies of conciliation had been discredited or shown to be bankrupt. On the morrow of the July days Lenin had pointed to 'the complete and final bankruptcy of the S.R.s and Mensheviks and the present majority in the soviets'.[50] This bankruptcy, along with that of the Provisional Government, was, indeed, one of the outstanding features of the situation that prevailed in Russia on the eve of the October rising. It provided the conditions for this rising to occur and to succeed. As for the soviets, or rather, their central leadership, which had long constituted a screen between the masses and the Provisional Government, they were no longer capable of fulfilling this function. The Central Executive Committee was reduced to engaging in manoeuvres to delay the opening of the Second All-Russia Congress because it realized it had lost its majority to the Bolsheviks. In the capital the C.E.C.'s authority counted for nothing since the Petrograd Soviet had elected an extreme-Left 'Bureau' and made Trotsky its chairman. It was this local Soviet, dominated by the Bolsheviks, that now led the dance, beneath the baffled gaze of the helpless Mensheviks and S.R.s.

Lenin or Kornilov, then. But the outcome of the struggle depended not only on the respective strengths of the adversaries, but also on the moment chosen to go into action: 'Insurrection must rely,' said Lenin, 'upon that *turning-point* in the history of the growing revolution when the activity of the advanced ranks of the people is at its height, and when the *vacillations* in the ranks of the enemy ... are strongest.'[51] He noted in this connexion that 'the beginning of the

* Lenin, Vol. 26, p. 74. On the problems of the world revolution, see pp. 359–65.

proletariat's civil war has revealed the strength, the class-consciousness, deep-rootedness, growth and tenacity of the movement. The beginning of the bourgeoisie's civil war has revealed no strength, no class-consciousness among the masses, no depth whatsoever, no chance of victory.'[52] In addition, the successes of the Bolsheviks at the elections, together with the decline, or even collapse, of their opponents, testified to the dynamism of the former and the lifelessness of the latter.

Between July and October electoral support for the moderate socialist groups—the Mensheviks and S.R.s—fell in Moscow from 70 per cent to 18 per cent.[53] The bourgeoisie turned towards the Constitutional-Democratic ('Cadet') party, whose criticism of the February revolution and of the weakness of the Provisional Government was the most virulent and whose links with military circles were most notorious. As for the Provisional Government itself, its impotence was obvious. It banned the Bolshevik press, yet could not prevent the Party from bringing out its organs afresh, under changed names. When the Government banned Maxim Gorky's paper, *Novaya Zhizn*, the editorial board imitated the example of the Bolsheviks, and though the paper had no party or other organization behind it, the Government did nothing.[54] Not democratic enough to inspire sympathy, it was too anaemic to inspire fear.

What seems clear today, however, was not so clear at the moment when Lenin was insisting on the necessity of insurrection. He was, moreover, fully aware of the precarious character of the advantages enjoyed by the Bolsheviks. Their superiority might not last long, and the masses might not continue indefinitely ready for action. Not long before the insurrection the working class was far from burning with zeal for the fight. The Central Committee noted on October 10th that the masses were manifesting 'absenteeism' and 'indifference' probably owing to the fact that they were 'tired of talk and resolutions'.* In his *History of the Russian Revolution* Trotsky confirms this impression, recognizing that 'there was a certain depression in the Petrograd proletariat as a result of waiting too long. They were beginning to feel disappointed even in the Bolsheviks.'[55] All the same, the revolutionary vitality of the Petrograd masses ought not to be underestimated. Sukhanov, a Menshevik observer who was distressed and yet fascinated by the spectacle of the mobilization of the working class, has left us a description of the enthusiastic meetings that were held in the capital during the last days of the Provisional Government.[56] On this point too Trotsky gives confirmation: 'All Petrograd, with the exception of its upper strata, was one solid meeting. In those auditoriums, continually packed to the doors, the audiences would be entirely renewed

* *Protokoly*, p. 85. The same idea is expressed in Lenin's 'Letter to Bolshevik comrades', October 8th (Lenin, Vol. 26, p. 184).

in the course of a few hours.'[57] In fact, the information that the Bolshevik leaders received concerning the state of mind of the Petrograd proletariat was contradictory in character.

The final moves had not yet been made, and the time factor was therefore of great importance. The equilibrium that had been established might be overthrown between one day and the next, and so it was essential not to 'let the present moment pass'.[58] This was why Lenin did his utmost to force his party to go into action, repeating *ad nauseam* that any delay could prove fatal.* This was why, not content with stating his views on the political conditions for the insurrection, Lenin sought to hasten its actual outbreak, expressing views on the technical aspect and going into details about the execution of the political decision.

Several times the Bolshevik leader put before the Central Committee a relatively precise plan for the seizure of power. Thus, on September 13th, he wrote to the Party centre:

> We must at the same time, without losing a single moment, organise a *headquarters* of the insurgent detachments, distribute our forces, move the reliable regiments to the most important points, surround the Alexandrinsky Theatre,† occupy the Peter and Paul Fortress, arrest the General Staff and the government, and move against the officer cadets and the Savage Division those detachments which would rather die than allow the enemy to approach the strategic points of the city; ... occupy the telegraph and the telephone exchange at once, move *our* insurrection headquarters to the central telephone exchange and connect it by telephone with all the factories, all the regiments, all the points of armed fighting, etc.[59]

On September 29th he urged that the revolt begin in Petrograd, Moscow and the Baltic Fleet, adding that the Bolsheviks had at their disposal '*thousands* of armed workers and soldiers in Petrograd who could *at once* seize the Winter Palace, the General Staff building, the telephone exchange and the large printing presses'.[60] His last set of detailed instructions is dated October 8th: 'Our *three* main forces—the fleet, the workers and the army units—must be so combined as to occupy without fail and to hold at any cost: (a) the telephone exchange, (b) the telegraph office, (c) the railway stations, (d) and above all, the bridges.'[61] He also urged that 'the most *determined* elements (our "shock forces" and *young workers*, as well as the best of the sailors) ... be formed into small detachments to occupy all the more important

---

* See p. 141.

† The Alexandrinsky Theatre was the seat of the Pre-Parliament: it moved soon after this to the Marinsky Palace.

points and to *take part* everywhere in all important operations, for example: to encircle and cut off Petrograd; to seize it by a combined attack of the sailors, the workers, and the troops.' They should 'form detachments from the best workers, armed with rifles and bombs, for the purpose of attacking and surrounding the enemy's "centres" (the officers' schools, the telegraph office, the telephone exchange, etc.). Their watchword must be: "Better die to a man than let the enemy pass!" '[62]

These were, of course, only very general guide-lines, not amounting to a plan, in the strict sense, for the insurrection. Lenin was not actually at the head of the general staff entrusted with carrying out this plan. Though remote from the command posts and centres of co-ordination, Lenin nevertheless strove to keep in contact with the men chiefly responsible for the enterprise, and when he met them he showed great concern for detail and an acute critical sense.[63] As for his own ideas, what is interesting in them is above all that they reveal Lenin's concern to grasp the problems of the insurrection in an all-round way, in their political-strategic, technical, and ideological aspects. He put before his Party a many-sided objective: conquest of the centres of political decision-making and state authority (the Winter Palace, where the Provisional Government was, together with the seat of the Pre-Parliament and the headquarters of the General Staff); conquest of the focal points of technological and strategic power (the railway stations, the telegraph and telephone centres, the bridges ensuring communication between the centre of the capital and the working-class districts, and the barracks); conquest, finally, of certain means of exercising ideological power, namely, the printing presses, control of which was important for waging the propaganda battle. In other words, despite the curtness of Lenin's observations and recommendations, he showed how up-to-date was his understanding of the problem of insurrection, how fully his conception took account of a number of the most vital implications of the task of seizing and wielding power. All these positive aspects stand out even more clearly if we compare, for example, the action of the Bolsheviks in October 1917 with that of the Spartakists in Berlin in January 1919.

One question, at least, still remained to be settled, however; that of the instrument to which the organization of the rising was to be entrusted. Because Lenin was passionately keen to take immediate advantage of a situation that he regarded as favourable, he fixed the date of the rising *before* the meeting of the All-Russia Congress of Soviets. He declared explicitly that the 'apparatus' for the seizure of power consisted of 'the soviets and the democratic organizations', adding that, 'to be successful, insurrection must rely not upon conspiracy and not upon a party, but upon the advanced class'.[64]

The task of preparing for the insurrection was entrusted to a body set up on October 9th by the Petrograd Soviet, the Military Revolutionary Committee. Although it co-operated closely with the Bolshevik Military Organization, this committee had a distinct status of its own. Its composition was not cut-and-dried. At the outset it comprised sixty-six members, of whom forty-eight were Bolsheviks, fourteen Left S.R.s and four anarchists.[65] Trotsky belonged to it *ex officio* as chairman of the Petrograd Soviet, but its nominal chairman was an S.R. named Lazimir—a fact that seemed to make the Military Revolutionary Committee independent of the Party, though this independence was more formal than actual. It does not appear, however, that Lenin wished to make the M.R.C. a mere tool of the Party. In his view, it was to be 'a non-party insurrectionary body which has full power and is connected with all sections of the workers and soldiers'; and he added that 'there must not be the slightest hint of dictatorship of the Military Organization [of the Bolshevik Party] over the Military Revolutionary Committee'.[66] Was the Party, the organizer of the revolutionary vanguard, to retire into the background at the moment of the seizure of power?* What needs to be emphasized is that Leninism owed its victory to a rising the general orientation of which was socialist, not Blanquist. True, the forces engaged were quite small. Estimates of the numbers of the Red Guards of Petrograd vary: some sources give the figure 23,000,[67] while others speak of 12,000;[68] in his classic work the American historian Chamberlin mentions 20,000 Red Guards ready for action in the capital.[69] In addition to these there were the purely military units involved. The forces actually committed to battle were even smaller still. Trotsky speaks of 'a few thousand Red Guards, two or three thousand sailors ... a score of infantry companies.'[70]

Was 'October', then, a *coup* carried out by a handful of fighters, a mere few thousands of soldiers, sailors and workers, who made up by the boldness of their action for the apathy of the masses? The methods used by Lenin and his followers were too much unlike the great episodes in the history of modern revolutions for the opponents of Bolshevism and Communism not to find in them what they regard as decisive arguments—and, indeed, the overthrow of the Provisional Government does not seem to have been a deed accomplished by the proletariat, but rather by a vanguard acting in the latter's name.

Actually, the proletarian revolution that the October insurrection really was cannot be understood if it be isolated from its context, from the antecedent events that explain it, the long 'road to October' marked by the 'days' of April, June and July, of which, first, the growth of the Bolshevik Party, and then its will to take power, were merely the

---

* The Central Committee set up during October a 'military revolutionary centre' consisting of five of its members. But the role played by this organ (in which Stalin participated) was quite negligible.

results. The Bolsheviks' victory in October 1917 was only the military phase of a phenomenon that was essentially political. As Trotsky observes, moreover, 'The military leadership proved incomparably weaker than the political.'[71]

It is not to be denied that the armed actions undertaken by the victors of October when the Provisional Government fell were marked by features of clumsiness, or, to employ Trotsky's expression, 'failings'.[72] It could hardly have been otherwise, since the implementing of the plan for the rising bore many signs of improvisation. Only on October 24th, during the afternoon, a few hours before the rising was to begin, did the M.R.C. appoint a sub-committee to be responsible for arresting the members of the Provisional Government. And the M.R.C. itself, formed on October 9th, held its first meeting only on the night of October 19th–20th. Undoubtedly the delays in the preparation of the uprising were partly due to the Bolsheviks' desire to take the enemy by surprise, and Trotsky showed in this matter a skill that was all the more remarkable in that it was necessary to surprise the enemy while at the same time maintaining a high level of enthusiasm and will to action in the Bolshevik ranks—to prepare an attack on the Provisional Government that would look like a defensive action. Nevertheless, the operations carried out in Petrograd on October 24th, 25th and 26th owed their success above all to another factor that was fundamentally political in character, namely, the extraordinary weakness of the Provisional Government. Only Stalinist legend-making was capable of creating the myth of an uprising that was perfectly conceived, perfectly worked out and perfectly executed, down to the last detail.*

The October uprising was not merely the outcome of a *political* victory which had itself been won only through a process that included many false steps. As it developed, the rising revealed the same essentially political features. The way in which the Bolsheviks went about capturing the Fortress of Peter and Paul, one of the principal strategic points in the capital, is significant from this standpoint. On October 23rd the leaders of the insurrection learned that the garrison of the fortress refused to recognize the authority of the Military Revolutionary Committee. Antonov-Ovseyenko proposed to send in a revolutionary battalion to disarm the garrison and take its place. Trotsky, however, urged that, instead of this risky operation, a more typically Bolshevik and *socialist* method be employed, that of political agitation.

---

* 'No insurrection in history was carried out with such organization, co-ordination and careful preparation as the October Socialist Revolution ... ' (Gorky, *History*, Vol. II, p. 298). 'Such organization and co-ordination, precision and mutual assistance had never been achieved in any previous insurrection or revolution (Ibid., p. 179.) This organization, co-ordination, precision, etc., did not prevent Kerensky from escaping from a city that was already practically in the hands of the Bolsheviks.

He went in person to the fortress, called a general meeting of the soldiers, addressed them, won them over, and persuaded them to pass a resolution announcing their readiness to overthrow the Provisional Government.[73]

While the military preparation of the rising left much to be desired, its political preparation, during the last few days and hours before it began, was intense and exemplary. The regiments stationed in the capital rallied to the insurrection after listening to fiery speeches by Bolshevik delegates; the great meeting-halls of Petrograd, such as the Modern Circus, were never empty, and Bolshevik speakers (Trotsky outstandingly) used them to maintain or revive the revolutionary ardour of the workers, sailors and soldiers. The whole of October was, in Petrograd and in the provinces alike, a period of ceaseless political activity: the soviets of the various regions assembled in conferences and congresses; the Bolshevik Party, which had been obliged to postpone an extraordinary congress fixed for the end of the month, did the same.* In October 1917 the permanent revolution took concrete form in a permanent debate. And if the masses took no direct part in the insurrection, this was, in the last analysis, because there was no need for them to do so. Their rallying to the Bolsheviks' policy had been able to find other means of expression, appropriate to the proletarian and democratic character of the enterprise, and to socialist tradition.

The workers, sailors and soldiers who patrolled the streets of Petrograd in October 1917, occupied strategic points and stormed the Winter Palace, were *carrying out a mandate* the existence of which was proved by numberless demonstrations and resolutions, frequent elections, and the thousand-and-one ways that the will of the masses found to express itself. In other words, Lenin's tactic of insurrection, while adding something new to socialist practice, was itself fundamentally inspired by socialist practice. Uniting word and deed, adding a determination to take power 'here and now' to the long-standing socialist ideal, it made of the latter a reality such as socialists had until then only dreamed of.

Lenin and permanent revolution (II)
On the eve of the fall of Tsardom, Leninist strategy was perfectly

---

* October 11th, congress of soviets of the Northern Region; October 13th, congress of soviets of Yekaterinburg district; October 16th, congresses of soviets of Vladimir province, the Volga region, Minsk, and Siberia; October 17th, congress of soviets of Tver province and regional conference of soviets of the South-West, October 18th, congress of soviets of Ryazan province.

October 1st, conference of Bolsheviks of Petrograd province; October 2nd, end of Bolshevik conference for Nizhni Novgorod province, opening of regional congress of Bolshevik organizations in the Caucasus; October 5th, regional conference of Bolshevik organizations in Byelorussia and on the Western Front: October 6th, Bolshevik provincial congress in Samara; etc. (Gorky, *History*, Vol. II, p. 56).

unambiguous in the minds of most Bolsheviks. Based upon distinguishing between the bourgeois and the socialist revolutions, it fixed
the task of the proletariat as taking the place of the defaulting bourgeoisie in order to establish a liberal democracy, and taking part, to
this end, in a revolutionary government that would embody a dictatorship of both the proletariat and the peasantry.* The few observations
made by Lenin in 1905 and 1906 which, departing from the 'classical'
schema set forth in *Two Tactics*,† pointed towards the road that the
Russian revolutionary movement was really destined to travel, had
hardly attracted any attention among Lenin's followers: and, indeed,
their significance was not really apparent until it was illuminated by
the events of 1917.

The world war had a profound effect on Lenin's ideas in the field of
revolutionary strategy, as in so many others. At first, of course, he
reaffirmed his previous views on the necessarily bourgeois-democratic
character of the aims of the revolution in Russia;‡ but the prospect was
a different one in Western Europe, since 'in all the advanced countries
the war has placed on the order of the day the slogan of socialist
revolution ... '[74] Soon Lenin was to link together the upheaval that
he foresaw taking place in backward Russia as a democratic revolution
with the socialist revolution he foresaw in industrialized Europe (and
perhaps the U.S.A. as well). By October 1915, this connexion was made
in his mind. 'The task confronting the proletariat of Russia is the
consummation of the bourgeois-democratic revolution in Russia
in order to kindle the socialist revolution in Europe.'[75]

One month later, while reasserting his conception of the 'revolutionary democratic dictatorship of the proletariat and the peasantry',
Lenin ended an article with a conclusion which, heralding the strategy
that he was to apply in 1917, had a clearly 'Trotskyist' flavour to it:
'The proletariat will at once utilize this ridding of bourgeois Russia
of tsarism and the rule of the landowners, not to aid the rich peasants
in their struggle against the rural workers, but to bring about the
socialist revolution in alliance with the proletarians of Europe.'[76] He
had returned to the possibilities glimpsed in 1905 and 1906—with an
important difference, however: the necessarily international and
internationalist character of the Russian revolution, which Lenin had
till then almost ignored, was strongly emphasized. On the eve of his
departure from Western Europe to go back to Russia, Lenin repeated,
in his 'Farewell Letter to the Swiss Workers', that 'the objective circumstances of the imperialist war make it certain that the revolution

---

* See p. 76.
† See p. 82.
‡ 'Since Russia is most backward and has not yet completed its bourgeois revolution,
it still remains the task of Social-Democrats in that country to achieve the three fundamental conditions for consistent democratic reform, viz., a democratic republic ... ,
confiscation of the landed estates, and an eight-hour working day' (Lenin, Vol. 21, p. 33).

will not be limited to the *first* stage of the Russian revolution, that the revolution will *not* be limited to Russia'.[77]

Once more, action absorbed Lenin completely. He interrupted his activity as organizer of the Party and the revolution, as publicist and journalist, only when, exiled in Finland, he ended his work on *State and Revolution*, in which problems of strategy are not touched upon. These problems were thus never dealt with by Lenin in a systematic way, and historical analysis has to base itself on a mass of scattered passages from speeches, reports and articles that were composed in relation to events of a kind capable of overturning the best established *schemata*. These passages taken as a whole are full of approximations, repetitions, contradictions—since their author had never had an opportunity to make a synthesis or theoretical elaboration such as Trotsky subsequently undertook in his book *Permanent Revolution*. From an analysis of Lenin's writings, together with the events with which they were interwoven, a number of points emerge which together sum up Lenin's revolutionary strategy in 1917.

(1) The fall of Tsardom led Lenin at once to consider that Russia was entering a period of history which made possible, not socialism itself, but a *transition to socialism*. Socialism could not be 'achieved in Russia directly at one stroke, without transitional measures';* such measures, however, would constitute an advance towards socialism, the abolition of the autocracy having been a 'by no means complete victory'.[78] It was now necessary for the proletariat to 'prepare the way for [its] victory in the second stage of the revolution':[79] so that the distinction between the two stages, bourgeois and socialist, of the revolution, lost its sharpness, became blurred and hazy, with an 'extremely original ... *interlacing*' of the period of the 'rule of the bourgeoisie' with that of the dictatorship of the proletariat and the peasantry.[80]

(2) Lenin indicated his preference for concrete measures, none of which, considered separately, meant the transition to socialism, but which together amounted to 'gradually' taking 'decisive steps ... towards the overthrow of capitalism.'[81] By meeting many popular demands they would help to keep up and hasten the dynamic of the revolution.

This was the case with the economic programme defended by the Bolsheviks between February and October. It included 'nationalization of the syndicates, i.e., the largest monopolistic associations (sugar, oil, coal, iron and steel, and other syndicates)'[82] as well as of

* Lenin, Vol. 23, p. 341. Again: 'Operating as it does in one of the most backward countries of Europe amidst a vast population of small peasants, the proletariat of Russia cannot aim at immediately putting into effect socialist changes' (ibid., Vol. 24, p. 311).

banks and insurance companies,[83] 'publication of all the fabulous profits ... which the capitalists are making on war supplies',[84] abolition of commercial secrecy,[85] introduction of universal labour service,[86] and a series of measures for state control of the economy made necessary by the country's disastrous situation.* In this programme, however, there was a point of special importance, namely, the establishment of 'workers' control', by which the soviets or the 'workers' committees' would exercise, at the level of the individual factory and also at regional and even central levels, supervision over the activity of commercial and (especially) industrial enterprises.†

If Lenin did not regard it as opportune for his Party to adopt a socialist economic programme, this circumspection was even more necessary with regard to the Party's *agrarian* programme, in order to realize the indispensable alliance between the proletariat and the peasantry. The Bolshevik agrarian programme envisaged mainly the 'nationalization of *all* lands in the country, the land to be disposed of by the local Soviets of Agricultural Labourers' and Peasants' Deputies'.[87] During the first months that followed the February revolution Lenin, without committing himself to precise demands, showed preference for measures tending towards collectivization and, in conformity with Marxist doctrine, expressed very definite reservations about the régime of small-scale landownership.[88] This meant running counter to the aspirations of the huge majority of the Russian peasantry and their desire to bring about *division* of the land in the immediate future.

During August 1917 Lenin became aware of the large number of 'imperative mandates' held by peasant deputies to the Soviet — Russian and modern equivalents of the *cahiers* of the French States-General of 1789 — in which the petty-bourgeois demands of the Russian peasantry were forcibly expressed. Reading these documents led Lenin to make his ideas on agrarian questions more flexible. At the end of August he wrote: 'The peasants want to keep their small farms ... Fine. No sensible socialist will differ with the peasant poor over this ... The crux of the matter lies in political power passing into the hands of the proletariat. When this task has taken place, everything that is essential, basic, fundamental, in the programme set out in the 242 mandates will become *feasible*.' And, to justify himself, Lenin added: 'We are not doctrinaires. Our theory is a guide to action, not a dogma.'[89]

Thus, while a phase of the revolution was unfolding which Lenin saw as a transition towards socialism, the Bolshevik Party was led to

---

* Lenin called for 'control, supervision, accounting, regulation by the state, introduction of a proper distribution of labour-power in the production and distribution of goods' (ibid., Vol. 25, p. 324).

† Ibid., Vol. 24, pp. 23 and 521–2; for the 'workers' committees', see pp. 332–5.

support a policy which, inspired by the spontaneous action of the peasant masses, far from tending in the direction of the 'advance to socialism' that Lenin spoke of, tended to strengthen the petty-bour-geois structures of the country. This was the price that Lenin was ready to pay in order to obtain the indispensable help of the peasants. He had already, in contrast to all the other parties, given approval and encouragement to the agitation and revolt in the countryside. Whereas the moderate socialists preached calm and patience to the peasants, Lenin called on his followers to spread the slogan: 'Seize the landed estates,'[90] while advising the peasants to do this in an orderly way and without impairing the supply of foodstuffs to the town population.[91] The peasantry ignored this advice, but did not fail to note the support being offered them by the Bolsheviks. In order to cement an alliance that was still uncertain and precarious it was necessary, however, to go further along the road of concessions. Lenin took this road dis-creetly at first, and later in spectacular fashion, when, on the day that the Bolsheviks seized power, he decreed the division of the big estates into separate holdings: the advance to socialism was marking time, but the revolution, by winning the support of the countryside, made a big step forward.[92]

(3) The formula, devised by Lenin, of the 'revolutionary-democratic dictatorship of the proletariat and the peasantry' encapsuled the strategic programme he had worked out at the beginning of the 1905 revolution. It implied an association between partners more or less on a footing of equality. Already in March 1917, however, he was affirming the need to establish a 'workers' government', which would emerge from the seizure of power during the second phase of the revolution, thus emphasizing the primacy of the proletarian forces in relation to the peasant movement, and making it clear that the bloc of 'revolutionary-democratic' classes must be 'headed by the revolu-tionary proletariat'.[93] This change of viewpoint led him to recognize in April that there could no longer be any question of establishing a 'revolutionary-democratic dictatorship of the proletariat and the peasantry', this being a formula that was 'behind the times', 'a theory of yesterday', which he regarded as 'now meaningless'.[94] In this way a new *rapprochement* took place between the strategy advocated by Lenin and the conception held by Trotsky, who had been readier to ascribe the 'leading' role to the proletariat.*

And, indeed, while in April 1917, at the Party's national conference, Lenin was still rejecting the idea of calling for the establishment of the dictatorship of the proletariat, a demand which he blamed for 'skip-ping over the petty-bourgeoisie', a dangerous and impracticable line to take,[95] the radicalizing of the revolution during the spring and the

* See p. 79.

resumption of the revolutionary offensive after the setback in July caused him to modify his views. In September he declared: 'Our Party, like any other political party is striving after political domination for itself. Our aim is the dictatorship of the revolutionary proletariat.'[96] At the beginning of October he modified this formula slightly, by speaking of 'the dictatorship of the proletariat and poor peasants',[97] but without basically altering it. Meanwhile, it had figured prominently in *State and Revolution*, which he had finished writing not long before.*

(4) As has been said, Lenin considered that the victory of February 1917 meant the completion of the bourgeois phase of the revolution, an idea which aroused numerous and serious objections among the Bolsheviks themselves. Yet a series of popular demands—political, or economic and social—still had to be satisfied, which in no way implied going beyond the bourgeois framework of the revolution. This situation, so different from the clear-cut *schemata*—with the bourgeois revolution plainly differentiated from the socialist one— that continued to dominate the minds of so many Russian Marxists, obliged Lenin to devise corresponding formulas regarding state power. While still in Switzerland he called on his supporters to remember the slogan once put forward by Marx, and 'smash' the existing machinery of state,[98] adding—ten days after the fall of Tsardom—that this process of smashing was already under way.[99] In other words, the state machine that he wanted to see smashed was not Tsardom but the régime that was arising upon the ruins of Tsardom, and that everyone expected would take the form of a bourgeois-liberal democracy. Lenin formally rejected the latter and called on the Bolsheviks to revise that part of their programme which declared in favour of a 'parliamentary bourgeois democracy'.[100]

What was to be put in its place? Lenin suggested a series of formulas intended to describe a somewhat vague system which, while no longer one of domination by the bourgeoisie, was not yet one with proletarian hegemony. He spoke of 'a really democratic workers' and peasants' republic',[101] of 'a more democratic workers' and peasants' republic',[102] even simply of 'a people's republic'[103] or 'a democratic republic'.[104] But was it possible to define the state that was being born, without referring to that revolutionary institution which dominated the Russian scene in 1917? Lenin therefore spoke of 'a republic where all state power ... belongs wholly and exclusively to the Soviets ... '[105] and of 'a more democratic workers' and peasants' republic, in which ... parliamentary representative institutions will be gradually replaced by Soviets of people's representatives,'[106] all these vaguely outlined

* See p. 191.

state-forms serving, as he saw it, to 'make possible the least painful transition to socialism'.[107]

Contradictions were not lacking, however, in the ideas that Lenin set forth in 1917, and the magnitude and rapidity of the changes taking place are sufficient to account for them. There was the contradiction between desire to urge the revolution onwards towards socialism and the obligation to satisfy the petty-bourgeois aspirations of the peasantry. There was the contradiction between rejection of the once-defended concept of the 'revolutionary democratic dictatorship of the proletariat and the peasantry' and, on the other, the fundamental concessions made to the peasantry by a proletariat to which Lenin nevertheless ascribed the leading role. It was a strange 'dictatorship of the proletariat' that prepared and inaugurated its reign by sacrificing its own programme to the non-socialist and even anti-socialist aspirations of the peasantry.

There was the contradiction, too, on the political plane, between the continually repeated assertion that all power must belong to the soviets and the hardly less frequent acknowledgment of the legitimacy of the Constituent Assembly—the convocation of which the Provisional Government, despite its promises, kept putting off. Logically, Lenin saw the power that would organize the transition to socialism embodied in the soviets created by the February revolution. They did indeed signify a sharp break with the bourgeois parliamentary institutions whose value Lenin denied. As a general rule, however, Lenin spoke throughout 1917 in favour of 'universal, equal and direct suffrage',[108] which was contrary to the mode of election of the soviets.

While advocating the establishment of a Soviet state,* Lenin, in accord with the Party programme and with the platform of demands regularly defended by the Party leaders, put forward the convening of a Constituent Assembly as a normal and necessary revolutionary demand.†

These gropings, hesitations and vaguenesses would certainly have resulted in confusion and incoherence if Lenin had not, in order to surmount them, set before the Russian revolution a prospect that reduced the scope of the contradictions within it—namely, the prospect of an extension of the Russian movement to the advanced industrial world, which he saw as ready for the victory of socialism. In this field Lenin relied upon some certainties that were at once reassuring and uplifting. The first was a view that the socialist movement had formulated, before the war, in the person of its most authoritative

---

* 'We want a republic where all state power, from the bottom up, belongs wholly and exclusively to the Soviets of Workers', Soldiers', Peasants' and other deputies' (Lenin, Vol. 24, pp. 373–4).

† See, e.g., Vol. 24, pp. 99, 348; Vol. 26, p. 20. For statements in favour of convening a Constituent Assembly, see, e.g., Sukhanov, pp. 550 and 552; *Protokoly*, p. 88; Daniels, *Red October*, p. 69; Reed, p. 25.

spokesman on matters of doctrine. Had Karl Kautsky not, as early as 1910, thought fit to assert that in Europe 'there can no longer be any question of a premature revolution, since the proletariat has obtained from the existing political institutions all the strength they can give it'?[109] The world war was seen by Lenin as precipitating the arrival of a great social crisis. He had analysed the causes of this war in his book *Imperialism*, the purpose of which was to show that 'the war of 1914–1918 was imperialist ... on both sides'[110] and an inevitable consequence of 'the highest phase of capitalism'. Whereas Kautsky thought that imperialism could lead to co-operation between great financial monopolies,[111] Lenin, on the contrary, thought that in the imperialist epoch 'the struggle for the territorial division of the world becomes extraordinarily sharp', and that 'capitalism's transition to the stage of monopoly capitalism, to finance-capital, *is connected* with the intensification of the struggle for the partitioning of the world'.[112] More generally, this same monopoly capitalism 'intensified all the contradictions of capitalism'.[113]

On this question Lenin's scientifically based convictions corresponded to the demands of his political faith. From both sources it followed that 'imperialism is the eve of the socialist revolution'.[114] August 1914 had shown the fallacy of the view that imperialist war would immediately be 'answered' by revolutions in all the countries concerned. But the wear and tear of war had led in due course to a reappearance of pacifist radicalism, with Karl Liebknecht as its standard-bearer and the organization founded at Zimmerwald as its rallying-point. The agitation among the working class and in the army that developed in Germany, especially during the spring of 1917, convinced Lenin that, after the reactionary interval beginning in 1914, history was at last finding its true path again, and the revolution resuming its forward march. Furthermore, both the general evolution of society and the institutional innovations made necessary in the belligerent countries by the operation of a war economy finally persuaded Lenin that 'capitalism in its imperialist stage leads directly to the most comprehensive socialization of production'.[115] Industrialized Europe was on the threshold of socialism.

In October 1917, striving to convert the Central Committee to the idea of an uprising, he stressed this point again and again. On October 1st: 'In Germany the beginning of the revolution is obvious';[116] on October 8th: 'the growth of a world revolution is beyond dispute';[117] on October 15th: 'by acting at that moment the Bolsheviks would have all proletarian Europe on their side'.[118]

The struggle between Left and Right among the Bolsheviks was ultimately centred on this problem: Lenin, in any case, believed that the Party's strategy must be determined by it. Had he not declared, when opening the April conference: 'The great honour of beginning the revolution has fallen to the Russian proletariat. But the Russian proletariat must not forget that its movement and revolution are only part of a world revolutionary proletarian movement, which in Germany, for example, is gaining momentum with every passing day. Only from this angle can we define our tasks.'[119] The Right-wing Bolsheviks did not disagree. But whereas Lenin, during the crucial October weeks, staked on the spread of the revolution over the world, and in Europe in particular, the moderate and cautious trend in the Party expressed scepticism, denying that 'the majority of the international proletariat' supported the Bolsheviks.[120]

Lenin did not confine himself to declaring his confidence in the international socialist revolution. He advocated a policy which, in his view, would help it on and hasten its coming. The peace programme that he upheld in Russia, from April 1917 onwards, was governed by this aim. He was concerned not only to satisfy the aspirations of the Russian people but also to throw a bridge between the proletariat of Russia and the proletariat of the West. Even before his return to Petrograd, in his 'Farewell Letter to the Swiss Workers', Lenin had sketched out the main features of his plan for internationalizing the revolution. The Russian socialist movement, once in power, would announce its peace proposals. Being fundamentally and unconditionally democratic, these could only be rejected by the imperialist governments. Revolutionary Russia would then 'be forced to wage a revolutionary war against the German—and not only the German—bourgeoisie'.[121] In April he added something else: '*In the event of the German, British, French and other capitalists declining such a peace, we would ourselves start a revolutionary war, and call upon the workers of all countries to join us.*'[122] And he drew this conclusion: 'the war which the capitalist governments have started can only be ended by a workers' revolution'[123]—more precisely, by workers' revolutions 'in several countries'.[124]

It is true that, as time passed and the Bolshevik Party drew nearer to power, Lenin's certainties gave way to more cautious estimates. At the beginning of September he said that it seemed to him unlikely that the capitalist governments would reject a democratic peace. If, however, they did, then Russia would indeed be obliged to wage a revolutionary war, which 'would bring even nearer the inevitable workers' revolution in the advanced countries'.[125] This cautious view that proletarian Russia *might* be able to get by without a revolutionary war was accompanied by a strong dose of optimism, since, according to Lenin, there were 'ninety-nine chances in a hundred' that a democratic peace proposed to the imperialist states would be accepted by them.[126] Whatever reply they might give to the armistice proposals that the Soviet Government, once established, would address to each of them, the stir caused by this proposal would have the effect of enhancing both the popularity of the Russian revolution among the European masses and the revolt of the Western proletariat against capitalism.[127] Through the channel of the fight against the war a concrete link was thus established between the Russian vanguard and the West-European rearguard of the world revolution.

The concept of *offensive* internationalism, the recognition of proletarian hegemony over the peasantry, and, along with this, the will to begin the struggle for socialism immediately, all marked a decisive *rapprochement* between Trotsky's theories of permanent revolution and Lenin's strategy of 1917. The Party did not fail to perceive this. If we are to believe Trotsky, 'in the leading group of the party ... they accused Lenin of Trotskyism during the month of April. Kamenev did this openly and with much insistence.'[128] When Trotsky had joined the Leninist organization he found an opportunity to develop his views in the Party press, and so *Pravda* of September 7th, 1917, carried an article ending with these words: 'A permanent revolution versus a permanent slaughter: that is the struggle, in which the stake is the future of man.'[129] According to André Stawar, who is hardly to be suspected of indulgence towards Trotskyism, 'Trotsky became within a few months the most authoritative of the leaders, after Lenin, casting into the shade the experienced members of the Party's general staff; his theory of permanent revolution ... came to occupy for a certain period the place of honour in the Party's ideology.'* Lenin was not the only one to fall under Trotsky's influence, and, more specifically, to apply Trotsky's views on revolutionary strategy. Already before 1917, during the first years of the war, men like Bukharin and Radek had not concealed their sympathy for the theory of permanent revolution.[130] The events of 1917 drew into the wake of this theory an ever larger number of followers, conscious or otherwise, who constituted the Party's Left wing and set a decisive imprint upon its policy.

---

* Stawar, p. 141. André Stawar (pseudonym of Eduard Janus) was one of the great men of Polish Communism. The *Small General Encyclopedia* published in 1959 by the State Scientific Press in Warsaw described him as 'a foremost representative of Marxist criticism'.

3

Leninism and revolutionary democracy

Shortly before the October insurrection Lenin wrote: 'We must draw the masses into the discussion of this question [of whether or not to boycott the Pre-Parliament, M.L.]. Class-conscious workers must take the matter into their own hands, organize the discussion, and exert pressure on "those at the *top*" [i.e., of the Bolshevik Party, M.L.].'[1] Around the same time he declared that 'insurrection must rely not upon conspiracy and not upon a party, but upon the advanced class ... Insurrection must rely upon a *revolutionary upsurge of the people*.'[2] Some months earlier, when he first put forward the *April Theses*, Lenin had said: 'We don't want the masses to take our word for it. We are not charlatans. We want the masses to overcome their mistakes through *experience*.'[3] He had moved a long way from the ideas expounded in *What Is To Be Done?*, a long way from the conception of organization that he had imprinted upon Bolshevism during its formative years. It was the events of 1905 that had begun to shake those ideas.* In 1917 the 'revolutionary upsurge of the people' produced the same effect, but with tenfold strength, resulting from the victories won in battle against the bourgeoisie. The theory of the Party that Lenin had worked out proceeded from the assumption that only the most conscious of the workers, themselves enlightened by intellectuals who had broken with their class, were capable of 'imparting consciousness' to proletarian political activity. But the way the revolution actually developed led Lenin to affirm that ' "the country" of the workers and the poor peasants ... is a thousand times more leftward than the Chernovs and the Tseretelis, and a hundred times more leftward than we are.'[4] While the radicalism of the proletariat was greater than that of the Bolsheviks the latter did not always make up for their inferiority in this respect, and their comparative caution, by a clearer awareness of the aims and potentialities of the revolution that was in progress. A large section of the leadership

* See pp. 50, 86.

and many of the cadres viewed with extreme reluctance the prospect of a socialist revolution: all the 'old Bolsheviks', in particular, were dead against it. Once again, and more than ever before, the relations between the Party and the proletariat, between the proletariat and its own vanguard, and, within the latter, between the rank-and-file and the leadership, were called in question. This revision resulted in Lenin's developing an original and remarkably bold new conception of the role of the state and of the social revolution.

The state and revolution: libertarian Leninism

Lenin finished writing *State and Revolution* during the weeks that he spent in enforced exile in Finland. This work bears the twofold mark of theoretical thinking which Lenin had begun before the 1917 revolution and of the influence that the latter event did not fail to exert on the author's thought—an influence that is also observable, and even more plainly, in his other writings of the period, especially in an essay concluded a few weeks before the October rising, *Will the Bolsheviks Maintain Power?*, to which I shall return.

The theoretical purpose of *State and Revolution* is that of defining the concept of the state. Analysis of this concept had been begun by Marx and Engels: but what they bequeathed was a line of thought rather than a finished system—a line of thought, moreover, that was not free from ambiguity, especially as regards relations between state and class and, most particularly, as regards the relative independence of the former from the latter.* Lenin, for his part, confines himself to asserting that 'the state is a special organization of force: it is an organization of violence for the suppression of some class'.[5] 'The state is an organization of violence.' Obviously, this proposition reduces the role of the state to an element which, though essential, is somewhat simplified: it excludes any reference or even allusion to a whole range of functions and mediations that the state fulfils—functions and mediations which do not, of course, cancel out the character of constraint (itself a form of violence) that is inherent in political power, and, in particular, in state power. Lenin's proposition, though curt, is nevertheless not abstract in the sense that it is not 'outside history': on the contrary, it results from Lenin's interpretation of the quite specific conditions of Europe at the beginning of the twentieth century. Capitalism in its monopolistic stage was in itself a synonym for imperialism, which implied a certain militarization of society. This tendency had been intensified by the war, which brought with it the abolition of many democratic freedoms, and interference

---

* Some illuminating observations on the question of the autonomy or dependence of the state in relation to the class, as analysed by Marx and Engels, will be found in Poulantzas, pp. 279 ff. See also Miliband for a useful restatement of the ideas of Marx and Engels on these matters.

by a state that was more repressive and violent than ever in many spheres of economic, social and political activity.

This is why Lenin offers in *State and Revolution* a particularly critical analysis of bourgeois democracy. Although he had never studied this systematically, he had nevertheless drawn attention to its advantages and shown himself appreciative of the possibilities it gave the working class to prepare for the overthrow of capitalism.* In 1917, however, he wrote that 'to decide once every few years which member of the ruling class is to repress and crush the people through parliament — this is the real essence of bourgeois parliamentarism, not only in parliamentary-constitutional monarchies but also in the most democratic republics'.[6] And the institutions of these bourgeois-democratic régimes were always accompanied by a bureaucratic administration which was tyrannical and parasitic.[7] It necessarily followed that the revolution must pursue 'the aim, not of improving the state machine but of smashing and destroying it'.†

There was nothing here, so far, that was not in conformity with Marxist doctrine. Lenin was faithful to the classical teaching that, on the ruins of the state thus abolished, a dictatorship of the proletariat would be erected, the need for this having been proclaimed already in the programme of Russian Social-Democracy in 1903. In *State and Revolution* Lenin said that 'a Marxist is solely someone who *extends* the recognition of the class struggle to the recognition of the *dictatorship of the proletariat*'.[8] He further declared that 'the dictatorship of a *single* class is necessary not only for every class society in general, not only for the *proletariat* which has overthrown the bourgeoisie, but also for the entire *historical period* which separates capitalism from the "classless society", from communism'.[9] He thus reaffirmed the provisional nature of the régime of proletarian dictatorship; but at the same time he acknowledged that this provisional régime might last a long time. There was no need to be unduly worried about it, though, since this dictatorship of the proletariat should mean 'an immense extension of democracy, which, for the first time, becomes democracy for the poor, democracy for the people, and not democracy for the money-bags ...' And Lenin summed up as follows the new system that the victorious people's revolution would introduce: 'Democracy for the vast majority of the people, and suppression by force, i.e., exclusion from democracy, of the exploiters and oppressors of the people.'[10] Lenin was no more explicit than this, the eulogistic references that he made to the Paris Commune[11] being in general only of an allusive nature. It must be emphasized that *State and Revolution* is an un-

---

* See p. 63.
† Lenin, Vol. 25, p. 409. This formulation, taken from Marx and Engels, is also found in an article written by Bukharin in 1916 and known to Lenin (see Daniels, 'The State and Revolution', pp. 26–7).

finished work, the writing of which was interrupted at the end of the summer of 1917 so that the author might engage in less theoretical activities and prepare for the imminent coming of the State that would be born from the revolution.

The Soviet state, and the entire experience of actually building socialism, was thus provided with a doctrinal birth-certificate which had been hastily drawn up and left unfinished. In particular, the book that Lenin wrote on the eve of the conquest of power shows glaring weaknesses where one of the most important and most difficult problems is concerned, namely, that of the dictatorship of the proletariat. In view of the transformations that this concept was destined to undergo, it is surprising to see how lightly Lenin dealt with it: as an abstraction derived from an analogy with the dictatorship wielded by the bourgeoisie under capitalism. It would be unfair and pedantic to blame the author of *State and Revolution* for the shortcomings of a book written in the circumstances of 1917 in Russia. All the same, here was a book that needed to be completed and developed, since, as it stood, it was silent about, or else overlooked, or even dodged, the gigantic problems that the building of socialist society must necessarily encounter. Such analysis was all the more needed because Lenin, advancing beyond the realm of classical Marxism, ventured in *State and Revolution* into the unknown and dangerous territory in which criticism of society gives way to constructive work.

Lenin did not confine himself to saying that, once the bourgeois state had been broken and swept away, the dictatorship of the proletariat must be set up in its place. He added that this process was inseparable from the Marxist concept of the *withering away* of the state: that the withering away of the state, and so of all political authority, *begins with* the victory of the proletarian revolution and advances steadily in step with the building of socialism. Where Engels ventured only a general statement,* Lenin was precise and committed himself decisively. The State that emerges from the proletarian revolution 'begins to wither away immediately',[12] so that 'it is no longer a state in the proper sense of the word'.[13] Lenin speaks of it as a 'semi-state',[14] a 'non-political state',[15] and adds, regarding the Paris Commune, which he takes as his model, that it '*was ceasing* to be a state since it had to suppress, not the majority of the population but a minority (the exploiters)'.[16] Since this last description corresponds to the definition of the dictatorship of the proletariat that Lenin gives, we can see that in his view, the victorious revolution initiates an original situation, one in which the political system is already in part not a

* After the overthrow of the power of the bourgeoisie, wrote Engels, 'State interference in social relations becomes, in one domain after another, superfluous, and then dies out of itself; the government of persons is replaced by the administration of things, and by the conduct of processes of production. The state is not "abolished". *It dies out*' (Engels, *Anti-Dühring*, p. 389).

state system. Here we have a formulation which, even though some-what vague, possesses an unmistakably libertarian, anarchist-tending flavour.*

In *State and Revolution* Lenin elucidates the process whereby political authority—defined as a complex consisting of the repressive power of the army and the police, on the one hand, and, on the other, the administration—withers away and disappears from history. As regards the purely repressive aspect of the state, Lenin believes that it will progressively fade away, 'for the suppression of the minority of exploiters by the majority of the wage-slaves of *yesterday* is com-paratively so easy, simple and natural a task that it will entail far less bloodshed than the suppression of the risings of slaves, serfs or wage-labourers ... And it is compatible with the extension of demo-cracy to such an overwhelming majority of the population that the need for a special machine of suppression will begin to disappear.'[17] It remains true, however, that 'democracy is ... an organization for the systematic use of *force* by one class against another, by one section of the population against another.'[18] Violence, on the one hand; on the other, an attenuation of repressive activity by the state. Must we not conclude from this that it is *the people themselves*, the armed *proletariat* who, without any mediation, will take in hand the defence of their interests and organize themselves independently of any state structures—certainly of any military apparatus in the strict sense? Lenin does not say so explicitly, but the vagueness of his observations does not rule out such a 'libertarian' interpretation of his ideas.

Abolition of the traditional army goes along with rapid erosion and fundamental transformation of the state's administrative machinery: 'The *mass* of the population will rise to taking an *independent* part, not only in voting and elections, *but also in the everyday administration of the state*. Under socialism *all* will govern in turn and will soon become accustomed to no one governing.'[19] Here the 'libertarian' tone is especially marked, even though Lenin is careful to repudiate 'anarchist dreams',[20] and defends himself against the charge of utopianism. He considers, however, that 'capitalist culture has *created* large-scale production, factories, railways, the postal service, telephones, etc., and *on this basis* the great majority of the functions of the old "state power" have become so simplified and can be reduced to such exceedingly simple operations of registration, filing and checking that they can be easily performed by every literate person ...'[21] Emphasizing the point, he declares that 'the development of capitalism ... creates the *pre-conditions* that *enable* really "all" to take part in the administration of the state ... Given these *economic* preconditions, it is quite possible, after the overthrow of the capitalists and the bureaucrats, to proceed immediately, overnight, to replace them in the *control* over production

* On relations between Lenin and the anarchists, see pp. 261–3.

and distribution, in the work of *keeping account* of labour and products, by the armed workers, by the whole of the armed population.'[22]

At the same time, Lenin recognizes that the proletarian state will not be able to do without the services of the former administration immediately. Nevertheless, these functionaries—whose pay will not exceed that received by the workers—will be 'simply carrying out our instructions'.[23]

Elsewhere Lenin was to show less ingenuousness. Speaking, at the beginning of October 1917, of the problems that the proletariat would have to solve after its victory, he admitted that they would be difficult ones, and went on:

> We are not utopians. We know that an unskilled labourer or a cook cannot immediately get on with the job of state administration ... [But] we demand an immediate break with the prejudiced view that only the rich, or officials chosen from rich families, are capable of *administering* the state, of performing the ordinary, everyday work of administration. We demand that *training* in the work of state administration be conducted by class-conscious workers and soldiers and that this training be begun at once ...[24]

Whatever may be said of the difference between the *carrying-out* of administrative tasks by all citizens and their *training* to carry them out, and whatever may be said regarding the flimsiness of some of Lenin's ideas, one cannot but note the deeply democratic inspiration behind these ideas—and this is what I am mainly concerned to emphasize. It is true that the running of an advanced industrial society, the only kind of society that is ripe for socialism, cannot in fact be reduced merely to operations of supervision and recording that can be accomplished by applying the rules of elementary arithmetic. But it is also true that the Social-Democracy with which Lenin was severing all ties had too easily resigned itself to accepting as inevitable the inferiority of the working class.

A *democratic* inspiration lies at the heart of Lenin's vision at this time, and gives it its 'immoderate' character. This is the mark of the period, suddenly imprinted upon the Marxist *schema* in such a way as to stress its most optimistic features. Let us see how it shows through in Lenin's thinking, and even in his normally rather dull style. Under the impact of the revolution, of the masses who are rising up and overthrowing the old world, winning victories that had hitherto been thought unattainable, Lenin's language becomes suddenly more vivid. In order to speak of the people's capacities, their victories, their merits, and the possibilities that are opening before them, Lenin's style attains, for the first time, a sort of lyrical quality.

Thus, for example, in his pamphlet *Will the Bolsheviks Maintain Power?*:

We have not yet seen ... the strength of resistance of the proletarians and poor peasants, for this strength will become fully
apparent only when power is in the hands of the proletariat, when
tens of millions of people who have been crushed by want and
capitalist slavery see from experience and *feel* that state power has
passed into the hands of the oppressed classes, that the state is
helping the poor to fight the landowners and capitalists, is *breaking*
their resistance ... Only then, for every *ten thousand* overt and
concealed enemies of working-class rule ... there will arise *a
million* new fighters who had been politically dormant, writhing
in the torments of poverty and despair, having ceased to believe
that they were human, that they had the right to live, that they
too could be served by the entire might of the modern centralised
state, that contingents of the proletarian militia could, with the
fullest confidence, also call upon *them* to take a direct, immediate,
daily part in state administration.[25]

And again:

When every labourer, every unemployed worker, every cook,
every ruined peasant sees, not from the newspapers, but with his
own eyes, that the proletarian state is not cringing to wealth but is
helping the poor, that this state does not hesitate to adopt
revolutionary measures, that it confiscates surplus stocks of
provisions from the parasites and distributes them to the hungry,
that it forcibly installs the homeless in the houses of the rich, that
it compels the rich to pay for milk but does not give them a drop
until the children of *all* poor families are sufficiently supplied, that
the land is being transferred to the working people and the
factories and banks are being placed under the control of the
workers and that immediate and severe punishment is meted out
to the millionaires who conceal their wealth—when the poor see
and feel this, no capitalist or kulak forces, no forces of world
finance capital which manipulates thousands of millions, will
vanquish the people's revolution; on the contrary, *the socialist
revolution* will triumph all over the world, for it is maturing in all
countries.[26]

Bolsheviks and anarchists

It is not enough to speak of a basically democratic inspiration. This
great fervour, this profound confidence in popular initiative and
striving for total liberation makes one think of anarchism. Such a
reaction is not new. As we have seen, on the very day that he returned
to Russia, when he first set forth his *April Theses*, Lenin was accused
of having abandoned Marx for Bakunin. This reproach is found

repeatedly in Sukhanov's memoir.[27] Lenin did indeed repeat several times in the course of 1917: 'we are not anarchists'.[28] But whereas in 1905 he had approved of the Petrograd Soviet's refusal to admit the anarchists, against whom he himself had argued harshly,* during the months that led up to October 1917 he abstained from public attacks on them. Addressing the Third Congress of Soviets, meeting in January 1918 in Petrograd, Lenin was to go so far as to say that 'at that time, in the period of a radical break-up of the bourgeois system, the concept of anarchism was finally assuming concrete features', adding that 'while some anarchists spoke of the Soviets with fear, because they were still influenced by obsolete views, the new, fresh trend in anarchism was definitely on the side of the Soviets ...'[29]

These reflections were merely the consequence of events themselves, of the tremendous revolutionary wave which in its broad sweep had brought about a *rapprochement* between many Bolshevik and anarchist militants. Members of Lenin's Party regularly attended the anarchist meetings that were organized in Petrograd, responding to invitations they received from the libertarian groups.† The Bolshevik Committee in the capital was obliged to pay attention to this situation. It refrained from forbidding attendance at such meetings, and merely advised Bolsheviks to be present only in their individual capacity and not to take part in any voting.[30] One member of the Petrograd Bolshevik Committee, recalling his memories of the revolution, wrote that 'the Anarchist-Communists worked arm in arm with the Bolsheviks'.[31]

Contact between anarchists and Bolsheviks was not made at rank-and-file level only. The Bolshevik leader Raskolnikov, who played an important role at the Kronstadt naval base, tells us that he 'carried on very sharp discussions with the Anarchist leader (Bleishman), but on the whole our relations with them [i.e., the anarchists, M.L.] were friendly'.[32] When the Kronstadt sailors elected delegates to the Second All-Russia Congress of Soviets, in the weeks preceding the October insurrection, their chief representative, Yarchuk, was chosen with official support from the Bolshevik group.‡ From June 1917 onwards the Party 'united with the Anarchists every time they quarrelled with the coalition', and 'concluded agreements with them ... about the administration of local affairs'.[33]

* 'A wide gulf separates socialism from anarchism', for 'the philosophy of the anarchists is bourgeois philosophy turned inside out. Their individualistic theories and their individualistic ideal are the very opposite of socialism' (Lenin, Vol. 10, p. 73).

† Two main trends were to be distinguished among the Russian anarchists. One, relatively moderate, was based on the 'Anarchist-Syndicalist Propaganda Group', while the second, represented by the Federation of Anarchist-Communists, was more disposed to collaborate with the Bolsheviks. See on this subject Avrich, *Anarchists*.

‡ In his memoirs a leader of the Bolshevik group in the Kronstadt Soviet justifies this support as follows: 'Yarchuk's theoretical considerations were of no practical importance to us—the important thing was to have a man who would not waver at the decisive moment ... ' (Knyazev and Konstantinov, p. 120).

The anarchists did not hide their surprise or their satisfaction at the way the Bolsheviks were changing. Their organ in Kharkov, for example, wrote: 'Since the time of the [February] revolution they have decisively broken with Social Democracy and have been endeavouring to apply anarcho-syndicalist methods of struggle.'[34] One anarchist leader, returning to Petrograd during the summer, expressed his conviction that Lenin had overcome his Marxist errors and was now intending to establish in Russia an anarchist régime based on destruction of the state.[35] Voline, in the highly anti-Leninist work that he wrote about the revolution, in a period of hostility between Communists and anarchists, acknowledged that in 1917 Lenin and his Party 'arrived at an almost libertarian conception of the revolution, with almost Anarchist slogans'.[36] Suspicion and conflict continued to arise, of course, and, despite the 'new course', Bolshevism did not cease to inspire much distrust among Russian anarchists. But it was no accident that the armed detachment which, in January 1918, carrying out the orders of the Government led by Lenin, dispersed the Constituent Assembly, so setting the revolution finally on the 'Soviet' path, was led by a sailor named Anatoly Zheleznyakov, whose anarchist affiliations were well known.[37]

The power of revolutionary spontaneity

Was this *rapprochement* between Bolsheviks and anarchists founded on a misunderstanding? Are we to believe, with Voline, that the 'libertarian' utterances of Leninist propaganda were 'only slogans',[38] just a stratagem intended to trick a too trusting people? Is it not nearer the truth to say, with Daniel Guérin, that 'in so far as it was an authentic revolution, taking its impulse from the bottom upward and spontaneously producing the organs of direct democracy, it presented all the characteristics of a social revolution with libertarian tendencies'?[39] And if this was the case with the Russian revolution, could it be otherwise with the doctrine and the Party which, despite hesitation, and sometimes internal tension, took the lead in this movement, the 'impulse' for which came 'from the bottom'? This point is of capital importance: Lenin's confidence in the action of the masses, in their 'initiative', which made them 'a hundred times more to the Left' than his own Party, resulted from this movement impelled 'from the bottom' — the movement which was undoubtedly, for Lenin, the great revelation of 1917. For Guérin is wrong when, analysing the spirit of the Leninism of that period, he alleges that 'there would be Soviets, to be sure, but under the control of the workers' party, a party whose historic task it is to direct the proletariat'.[40] Was it really by an oversight that in *State and Revolution* Lenin hardly mentioned the Party?

Yet it is a fact, and one of the highest importance, that the 'role of the Party' is practically absent from the great social and political project that Lenin drew up on the eve of the conquest of power.* What we see here, above all, is the growing role of the masses themselves, of Soviet (and not Bolshevik) power, of various forms of direct democracy. It is difficult to avoid the conclusion that this outlook was based on what Lenin had learnt—correctly or not—from the upheaval in which he figures both as spectator and actor; difficult to overlook the fact that, when he outlined the theoretical foundations of the proletarian state, Lenin had just been devoting weeks to convincing his Party—a party that was more than reluctant, being sceptical and sometimes angry and hostile—of the need for a 'second revolution'; difficult not to take into account the circumstance that the man who in September declared that 'to be successful, insurrection must rely not ... upon a party, but upon the advanced class ..., upon a *revolutionary upsurge of the people*,'[41] was engaged in a fresh struggle with many of his own followers, who were showing themselves reluctant and sceptical, even angry and hostile, at the prospect of an armed rising.

During the demonstration of July 3rd, 1917, the minister Chernov tried to address the crowd, in order to call on them to disperse. At that moment a worker came up to the S.R. leader, shook his fist, and shouted in his face: 'Take power, you son-of-a-bitch, when it's given to you!'[42] Neither the S.R.s nor the Mensheviks, bogged down as they were in their attempt to collaborate with the bourgeoisie, were willing to accept power, which they would not have known what to do with. The Bolsheviks, however, did not refuse power. But while it was certainly a deed of revolutionary audacity to accept this gift, it must be emphasized that the outcome of the revolution in Russia was the result of a dialectic so complex that one is equally justified in saying that the Leninist Party seized power by the October insurrection *and* that the vanguard of the masses forced the Party to adopt an attitude towards the conquest of power which these masses alone manifested with constancy and persistence.

For, while it is true that the Bolshevik organization was an indispensable instrument for the seizure of power, it is no less true that it was the masses themselves that urged the Party forward, and that the Party busied itself for a long period with holding back this pressure, which it regarded as dangerous. It is important to establish this fact, if we are to understand the significance that Lenin, in the midst of the

* The Party found a place in the important essay written by Lenin at the end of September 1917, *Will the Bolsheviks Maintain Power?* Despite, however, what the title seems to suggest, the place accorded here to the Bolshevik organization in the new political cal structures outlined by Lenin is only a modest one. Lenin alludes to the '240,000 members of the Bolshevik Party' when he discusses the future machinery of state. According to him, however, this machinery will actually be formed by drawing not only the million voters who support the Party but also 'the working people, ... the poor, into the daily work of state administration.' This is the 'magic way' on which Lenin counts to solve the problem (Lenin, Vol. 26, pp. 111–12).

battle, ascribed to the relation between the Party and the masses, and the meaning of this quasi-libertarian Leninism that developed in such a surprising way as the October revolution drew nearer.

Describing the attitude of the Bolshevik Party towards the revolutionary masses during the crises of April, June and July, Lenin said in October, that 'then it was a matter of *spontaneous excitement* which we, as a party, either failed to comprehend (April 20th) or held back and shaped into a peaceful demonstration (June 9th and July 3rd)'.[43] This moderating role played by the Party was shown, as we have seen, from the very first days of the revolution. In April the Party instructed the workers and soldiers of the capital to submit to the Soviet's ban on their demonstration.* A month later events repeated themselves. The popular effervescence did not die down, and the Bolsheviks continued with their delaying role all through June: 'We have to play the part of the fire-hose,' confessed the Vyborg Committee,[44] while the Bolshevik leader Podvoisky, although regarded as being among the most radical, acknowledged at the Sixth Party Congress, held in August, that 'we were forced to spend half our time calming the masses'.[45] We have seen how, during the July days, the Party leadership plunged into the popular movement only under pressure and after trying to prevent its outbreak. And when, in September, the countryside was swept by disturbances, and the resistance put up by the proletariat of Petrograd to Kornilov's *putsch* had displayed its fighting spirit, a member of the Bolshevik Committee of Petrograd repeated during an important discussion: 'Our task is to hold the masses back.'[46] If we are to believe the report made to the Party's Central Committee by Lomov, the situation was much the same in Moscow. Speaking at the C.C. meeting on October 3rd, he said: 'The masses are demanding that some definite steps be taken. Everywhere we are maintaining a waiting attitude.'[47] When Lenin said, in connexion with the boycott of the Pre-Parliament,† that 'class-conscious workers must take the matter into their own hands and ... exert pressure on "those at the top",'[48] he was thus merely hoping that an essential feature of the revolutionary dynamic would continue to operate and become general at a decisive moment. It is the upsurge of the masses that subjects institutions and parties, even the most radical, to a pressure to which the latter counterpose the relative inertia of their structures, the relative caution of their leaders, and the rigidity of their programmes. This impulse from 'below' is the driving force of revolution.

This decisive pressure was kept up for months. Its long duration was a symptom and result of the radicalization of the masses, and there can be no doubt that Lenin, who had always counted on a radicalization of the socialist movement, must have been profoundly

* See p. 165.
† See p. 138.

impressed by it. This spectacular process had the effect of transforming
the liberals of yesterday into partisans of a military dictatorship, and
the Soviet born of the revolution into a conservative institution. How
could Lenin have remained unaffected by this upsurge of the masses
themselves—these 'elemental', 'dark' forces, condemned by the
moderate socialists, which for Lenin constituted the driving force of
the revolution?

The radicalization of the people was accompanied, moreover, by
their politicization: intense activity, initiatives of every kind, passionate
interest in the fate of the revolution and in all the incidents of day-to-
day politics, keen participation in the discussions, debates and
demonstrations that continually took place in the capital, and not
only there. As Marc Ferro puts it, 'the citizens of the new Russia,
having overthrown Tsardom, were in a state of permanent
mobilization'.[49]

Permanent mobilization indeed: 'All Russia ... was constantly
demonstrating in those days. The provinces had all become accustomed
to street demonstrations. And in Petersburg too, in those same days,
the "over-forties" and the women were demonstrating—in general,
everyone was demonstrating who wasn't too lazy!' Sukhanov tells us.[50]
There were frequent and immense parades of supporters of peace and
supporters of war, the latter including groups of disabled soldiers who
filed past in thousands one day in order to proclaim their support for
'war to the end'. Besides the organized and peaceful demonstrations
there were many of a different kind—tumultuous, ardent, violent,
anarchical, drawing in hundreds of thousands, even millions of
participants—the succession of these demonstrations marking the
advance of the revolution. In addition to the demonstrations there
were meetings, debates and conferences that brought together substantial masses of people. 'What a marvellous sight,' wrote John
Reed, 'to see the Putilov factory pour out its forty thousand to listen
to Social Democrats, Socialist Revolutionaries, Anarchists, anybody,
whatever they had to say, as long as they would talk!'[51]

This liberation of speech burst forth all over the place, producing a
state of continuous discussion. 'The streets in those days,' wrote
Krupskaya, 'presented a curious spectacle: everywhere people stood
about in knots, arguing heatedly and discussing the latest events.
Discussion that nothing could interrupt!' Krupskaya goes on:

The house in which we lived overlooked a courtyard, and even
here, if you opened the window at night, you could hear a heated
dispute. A soldier would be sitting there, and he always had an
audience—usually some of the cooks or housemaids from next
door, or some young people. An hour after midnight you could
catch snatches of talk—'Bolsheviks, Mensheviks ...' At three in

7*

the morning: 'Milyukov, Bolsheviks ...' At five—still the same
street-corner-meeting talk, politics, etc. Petrograd's white nights
are always associated in my mind now with those all-night
political disputes.[52]

John Reed confirms the picture she draws: 'Every street-corner was a
public tribune. In railway-trains, street-cars, always the spurting up
of impromptu debate, everywhere ...'[53] The bourgeois press fulminated,
one liberal paper writing: 'In the midst of this terrible war, the country
is turning into one great debating society, one great festival.'[54] There
was intense, insatiable curiosity regarding all political questions. 'At
every meeting, attempts to limit the time of speakers [were] voted
down.'[55]

The politicization of the masses was also shown in the profusion of
political publications and the success they enjoyed: 'All Russia was
learning to read, and *reading* ... In every city, in most towns, along the
Front, each political faction had its newspaper—sometimes several.
Hundreds of thousands of pamphlets were distributed by thousands
of organizations, and poured into the armies, the villages, the factories,
the streets ...'[56] John Reed describes his experience with the soldiers
at the front: 'We came down to the front of the Twelfth Army, back of
Riga, where gaunt and bootless men sickened in the mud of desperate
trenches; and when they saw us they started up, with their pinched
faces and the flesh showing blue through their torn clothing, demanding eagerly, "Did you bring anything to *read*?"'[57]

This desire to learn was accompanied by an irrepressible will to go
over from words to deeds and take in hand the management of public
affairs and the power to make the great decisions. The model for Soviet
democracy and, still more, the model for the direct democracy that
we see depicted in *State and Revolution*, was found by Lenin in the
spectacle presented by revolutionary Russia. Committees sprang up
everywhere—workers' committees, peasants' committees, housewives'
committees: committees for factories and quarters, committees of
soldiers, Cossacks and sailors. In the industrial quarters, in the big
blocks crowded with working-class families, there were house committees which tried to regulate the details of communal life. Jules
Destrée, a Belgian 'patriotic' socialist who was in Russia as an
improvised diplomat, tells how, while travelling from Petrograd to
Moscow by a very slow train, the people sharing his compartment
had formed a 'travelling committee' before they reached their
destination![58]

The creation of the soviets themselves was part of this phenomenon.
They sprang up everywhere because 'any segment of the population
which thought it was being discriminated against would make up an
independent Soviet'.[59] This explains not only the growing number of

soviets but also the desire for autonomy, or even independence, that animated each one of them—the Soviets of the capital, for instance, where each quarter had its own, and all were jealous of their freedom of action and decision as against the Soviet of Petrograd as a whole. In general, 'each community, each group, each minority was likely to form itself into an autonomous body and bargain on equal terms with the Government and other revolutionary bodies'.[60] The 'factory committees', hardly less important than the soviets, expressed the same desire for 'self-management'. They made their appearance in the first days of March in the largest industrial enterprises of the capital, without any party or trade union having a hand in them. It was these committees that issued the call for 'workers' control': completely spontaneous in character, they could truly be described as having been 'born of the storms of the revolution'.[61]

It may be objected that the high proportion of abstentions* during the municipal elections of May and June 1917—the first free elections to be held in Russia—seems to qualify or even contradict this picture of politicization. However, Marc Ferro, a close observer of Russian social life in the revolutionary period, sees in this 'abstentionism' an expression of the attachment of the Russians of 1917 to *direct* democracy. For them 'the question was not one of being better governed, or of choosing another form of being governed, but of being self-governing. Any delegation of power was excoriated, any authority unbearable'.[62]

And, whatever the liberal press might say, all this was not 'just talk'. From this immense, continuous process of discussion emerged the force that inspired the revolution, and the general line that dictated its course. This anonymous deliberation, expressing the political life of the masses, was the source, moreover, of some of the most important creations and most decisive events of the Russian revolution. In particular, this was the case with the famous 'Order Number One' which freed millions of soldiers from the omnipotent authority of the military hierarchy and destroyed the spirit of submission and arbitrariness that prevailed in the army. Sukhanov tells us how this vital document originated. In a corridor of the Taurida Palace, the home of the Duma, he saw the Menshevik leader Sokolov seated at a table surrounded by soldiers. It was at the dictation of these men that this leader wrote out the famous proclamation, for which no other group of persons bears responsibility.[63]

This overshadowing of the leaders by the masses is typical of other, no less important episodes of the revolution. Thus, according to Marc Ferro, 'in the peace campaign the initiative did not come from the leading organizations—except for two or three minority notes from the Bolsheviks or Anarchists—but from the workers of the capital and

* Abstentions amounted to 40 per cent (Ferro, *February*, p. 321).

the provinces'.[64] The slogan of 'workers' control', which concentrated in itself some of the most heartfelt aspirations of the industrial proletariat, was not launched by a party, an organization or a paper, but arose from the very depths of the working class, assembled in the 'factory committees'.[65]

The spontaneous activity of the masses was deployed with particular force and effectiveness at the time of the attempted *coup d'état* by General Kornilov, when 'hundreds of thousands and millions of workers, soldiers and peasants rose up in arms, for defence and for attack, against the class enemy'.[66] A hostile witness, the governor-general of Petrograd, described how, in order to put the city in a state of defence, 'thousands of workers ... by their irreplaceable, personal labour achieved in the course of a few hours a colossal task which without their help would have required several days.'[67] Trotsky tells how 'the district soviets were drawing more closely together and passing resolutions: to declare the inter-district conferences continuous; to place their representatives in the staff organized by the Executive Committee [of the Soviet]; to form a workers' militia; to establish the control of the district soviets over the government commissars; to organize flying brigades for the detention of counter-revolutionary agitators'.[68] The clerks and technicians of the postal and telegraphic services undertook to disrupt the enemy's communications; the printing workers (who often had to improvise) took charge of the printing, and immediate distribution, of a mass of papers and leaflets; in the arms factories the workers, by working up to sixteen hours a day, manufactured quantities of weapons for the defence of Petrograd, in the shortest possible time. Kornilov's troops were in no position even to attack Petrograd, because the railwaymen had seen to it that the lines leading to the capital were thoroughly disorganized. These same railwaymen followed up their technical achievement by feats of political agitation, demoralizing the enemy forces and separating the soldiers from their officers.

Such, in broad outline, and illustrated by only a few of its manifestations, was the activity of the Russian proletariat in 1917. Confused and anarchical in many ways, it possesses, seen in retrospect, an exemplary clarity, for it reveals, in innumerable details and in its general tendency, the way that the revolution was overtaken by itself, how the frameworks conceived by strategists and the limits laid down in programmes were overwhelmed: here we see, quite simply, permanent revolution come true.

Is it not easier to grasp the meaning of *State and Revolution* in the light of this upsurge of the masses, this power arising out of chaos, this will that imposes itself upon institutions and parties, this spontaneous and yet self-organizing revolt, this activity that is both destructive and effective, subversive and constructive? The source of the book's democratic inspiration lay in the impression of strength and authority that was made not by a party but by a class. Is it not easier in this light to understand the confidence with which Lenin proclaims that 'no forces of world finance-capital ... will vanquish the *people's* [my emphasis, M.L.] revolution' and that 'the *mass* of the population will rise to taking an *independent* part, not only in voting and elections, *but also in the everyday administration of the state*'?

The source of the 'Leninist utopia' is to be found not only in the philosophy of Marxism, in its will to liberate man, emancipating him from the constraints of wages, labour and matter—it is situated also in all the popular and spontaneous conquests of the year 1917 in which it was not so much Bolshevism that triumphed as the proletariat, and in which the latter succeeded in setting its mark upon the former.

The party of the proletariat

There is one last point to be established before closing our account of the year 1917. The Bolshevik Party had no need, any more than its leader, to *stimulate* the masses between the revolution of February and that of October. The Party's historical merit lies elsewhere. It organized their upsurge in several decisive situations, it reinforced their offensive by endowing their action with a political outlook, and, above all, it took upon itself leadership of a popular movement which ran counter to all slogans—including, sometimes, those of the Bolsheviks themselves—and paid no heed to any *schemata*—including, to some degree, the Leninist ones as well. The historical merit of Bolshevism and Leninism, at any rate so far as the task of carrying out the revolution is concerned, lies in their having recognized in the upsurge of the masses —those whom the moderate socialists saw as 'elemental', 'blind', 'dark' forces, dangerous to society—a tremendous power for social liberation. This was why, in the course of 1917 in Russia, the masses and the Party came together, why the proletariat largely identified itself with an organization that had become, for the first time, *its own* organization. The terms of the relation between class and party, between the guided class and the guiding party, the class that is led and the party that leads, were reversed, the Bolshevik organization having at last agreed to submit itself to the revolutionary proletariat.

In the last analysis, what I have called 'libertarian Leninism' was made possible because the traditional mediator between the masses and power, in other words, the Party, the revolutionary organization, while becoming reinforced—and on what a scale!—ceased to be, in relation to these masses, an external body, an organ imposing itself as leader. An extraordinary osmosis took place between the industrial proletariat of Russia and the Bolshevik Party—an interpenetration to which history knows no equivalent, and the symptoms of which it is important to define.

The remarkable increase in the membership of the Party* is the first of these symptoms. The recorded influx of several hundred thousand new members, despite the lack of an adequate Party machine, is a proof of popularity that is certainly without precedent in the history of political parties. And this influx took place under a régime that was fundamentally hostile to the Bolsheviks, who were denounced by the greater part of the press and by the Government as agents of Germany, and many of whose leaders were, after July, either on the run or locked up. Furthermore, this increase in membership was effected among the proletariat: 'almost all the newcomers were workers', writes P. Sorlin.[69] Since the working class of Russia numbered, on the even of the World War, hardly more than three million,[70] the numerical significance of the Party's increased membership is apparent. In addition to these hundreds of thousands of workers who actually joined the Party there were many sympathizers who, in the turmoil of the time, gave support to the Party without formally joining it.

The Party's popularity can be measured by other data as well, such as election figures. In this connexion it is necessary to point out that the electoral criterion reflects only imperfectly the strength of the revolutionary parties. One of the leaders of the Bolshevik Military Organization observed on the eve of the July days that 'in the question of an uprising in the streets, the majority of regiments will follow us, but in ordinary situations—as in elections to the Soviets, etc.,— leadership is not in our hands'.[71]

Even so, Lenin's Party recorded, all through the year 1917, remarkable and almost constant election successes. Whereas at the beginning of the revolution it had only small representation in the Petrograd Soviet, by May the Bolshevik group in the workers' section of that institution possessed almost an absolute majority.[72] One month later, during the first conference of the factory committees of Petrograd, three-quarters of the 568 delegates expressed support for the Bolshevik theses.[73] Yet it was only at the end of the summer that the Leninists reaped the full harvest of their policy of opposition to the Provisional Government. In the Petrograd municipal elections in June the Bolsheviks received between 20 and 21 per cent of the votes; in August, when the Party was still suffering from the consequences of the July days, it received 33 per cent.[74] In Moscow in June the Bolsheviks had received a little over 12 per cent of the votes.[75] In September they won an absolute majority, with 51 per cent of the votes.[76] That their grip was especially strong among the working class is clear from the advance of their representation at the factory-committee conferences. In Petrograd, by September, there were no more Mensheviks or S.R.s present at the regional meetings of these bodies, their places having been taken by Bolsheviks.[77]

* See p. 158.

Once again, though, these figures, however revealing, tell only part of the truth—the most 'objective' part no doubt, but perhaps the least significant. The reality of the Bolshevik advance, as it was actually experienced, is to be sought, perhaps, not so much in the language of figures as in the testimony of their opponent Sukhanov, describing the atmosphere that prevailed in Russia in the last days of September 1917: '... the Bolsheviks were working stubbornly and without let-up. They were among the masses, at the factory-benches, every day without a pause. Tens of speakers, big and little, were speaking in Petersburg, at the factories and in the barracks, every blessed day. For the masses they had become *their own people*, because they were always there, taking the lead in details as well as in the most important affairs of the factory or barracks. They had become the sole hope ... The mass lived and breathed together with the Bolsheviks.'[78]

It is certainly true that such condensed formulations take too little account of important details. The Bolsheviks did not constitute a homogeneous group; willingness to *follow* the masses often failed them, and their radicalism was cut across and countered by tendencies of a different sort. We must get closer to reality and go beyond these approximations, penetrating the complex network of the Bolshevik party structures. When we do this we see that the closest link with the proletariat was effected at the lowest level, and, as has been mentioned, some difficulty was met with in ensuring that its results were felt at the peak of the hierarchy. The case of the Bolshevik Military Organization is interesting from this standpoint. Composed of soldiers who had joined the Bolsheviks, it directly recorded the pulsations coming from the army. Whereas the main central bodies of the Party—the Central Committee and the Petrograd Committee—were free from direct pressure by the workers and soldiers (and became even freer as the Party's membership increased), the Military Organization, born of revolutionary events and developing as these events developed, was more exposed to the radicalizing effect of popular exasperation. This was why it functioned as a transmission belt, bringing to the Party the pulsations emanating from the masses. When, in moments of crisis, the Military Organization called on the Central Committee to take up a more combative and daring attitude, its leaders drew their arguments from the pressure brought to bear upon them, and more directly still upon the Bolshevik delegates in the barracks, the militants who were in contact with the soldiers and shared their life.

Among the industrial workers, direct contact with the masses was achieved through organs that had arisen spontaneously from the revolution, namely, the factory committees. It is significant that the Bolsheviks were strong in these committees—much stronger than in the trade unions. The latter figured in the chaotic situation of 1917 as labour-movement organizations that had already become tradition-

ridden. This was why Bolshevik representation became preponderant
in the factory committees before the Party was able to go forward to
take over the trade unions. At the beginning of July, when the factory
committees were already following the line of the Bolshevik Party, the
Mensheviks still controlled 55.5 per cent of the mandates at the national
conference of the trade unions, as against 36.4 per cent held by the
Bolsheviks.[79]

This was a general phenomenon: the strength of the Bolsheviks lay
mainly in those institutions that were most recent in origin, least
structured, and closest to the masses. More precisely, they grew
predominant wherever the difference between the working class and
an institution, economic or social, which was supposed to represent it
became obliterated, in a period in which the revolutionary crisis, the
upheaval in men's minds and the rapid progress of radicalization
called in question the very idea of 'representativeness'. This was true,
especially, of the institution which more than any other symbolized the
conquests of the revolution—the Soviet. Its leadership underwent a
rapid process of institutionalization and 'bourgeoisification'.[80] The
soviets' power of initiative, the life that still breathed in them, their
revolutionary potential, were all concentrated to an increasing extent
in the *local* soviets, those of the municipalities or of particular parts of
towns. It was at the level of these more popular bodies that Bolshevik
penetration took place most quickly and powerfully. When, through
frequent elections and the genuine revocability of mandates, identification between the masses and some deliberative and executive body
became closer and closer, Bolshevism made itself felt by the numerical
strength of its representation and the acceptance of its overall policy.

Here, finally, lies the significance and explanation of Lenin's
conversion to a 'libertarian' variety of socialism—the meaning and
origin of the profoundly democratic message of the Leninism of 1917.
The men and women whom he called upon to govern *independently*,
and to whom he wished to see entrusted the conduct of public affairs,
were the same working men and women who had succeeded in
breaking through the innumerable forms of conservative conditioning:
the prestige of the bourgeoisie; trust in the leaders of the revolution;
the moral authority of the new régime—that of Kerensky, more or
less republican and more or less democratic; fear of the army and
scepticism in relation to the peasantry; the inclination to delay, and
in some cases even the pusillanimity, of the Bolshevik Party itself.

Whether or not democracy and people's power exists is not an
abstract question. On the contrary, it is born of political and social
practice, when the activity of the masses bursts forth and expands,
and their will is expressed and put into effect—more precisely, when
this is the activity of a class which, through its place in society, its
role in the economy and its cohesion, and through the Party tha

genuinely represents it, constitutes an irrefutable force in the present and a definite potentiality for the future. This was the case with the Russian proletariat of 1917. It was then that the working class broke with the established authorities and threw them out; then that this class, becoming ever more demanding, ceased to show respect to those whom it had adopted as leaders and guides; then that this class left the latter with no choice but to follow it or to resign. Overthrow of the centuries-old monarchy; creation of the Soviet, of the soviets, of factory committees, peasants' committees, committees for quarters, regiments and villages; revolt against the moderate line preached by the Mensheviks and S.R.s; overwhelming of the Bolshevik Party; spontaneous organization of resistance to the reactionary forces; rebellion of the once apathetic countryside—this was the reality of revolutionary democracy, leading tens of millions of people, in this improbable Russian scene, to make gestures, take up attitudes, initiate and organize actions which gave expression, less confusedly than appears at first sight, to their collective will.

By continually showing flexibility, frequently withdrawing into the background, and sometimes even repudiating itself, the Leninism that existed before the revolution ensured its democratic triumph of 1917.

Part III
Leninist Russia

Introduction

We shall now proceed to build, on the space cleared of historical rubbish, the airy, towering edifice of socialist society. A new type of state power is being created for the first time in history, a power that the will of the revolution has called upon to wipe out all exploitation, oppression and slavery the world over ... From now on all the marvels of science and the gains of culture belong to the nation as a whole, and never again will man's brain and human genius be used for oppression and exploitation.[1]

Thus spoke Lenin shortly after taking power.

This limitless ambition was matched by only very limited resources. In solving the innumerable problems confronting them, the Russian Communists* could look for no help from their doctrines. Building socialism was, as their leader put it, 'something new, unprecedented in history and cannot be studied from books'.[2] It was all the harder a task because the principal builders had until that time specialized – and with what zeal and talent! – in purely 'subversive' activity, entirely devoted to the destruction of the old order. What revolutionary activity now required, however, Lenin explained, was not dash and enthusiasm so much as 'day-by-day, monotonous, petty and workaday effort'.[3] What had to be done now was 'to crawl on your belly in the mud'.[4] In the mud because, as he was often to have occasion to repeat, all that was available for the accomplishment of the task of construction was the inadequate resources of Russian society – material that was faulty in a great many ways. The victors of October soon found that they had to reckon with this circumstance.

'It is a million times easier to defeat the resistance of counter-revolution than to succeed in the sphere of organization.'[5] And, indeed, the armed resistance put up by the bourgeoisie had been derisory in Petrograd. In Moscow, even, it had lasted only one week. Following up this armed resistance which had proved ineffective, there came, however, sabotage by the old machinery of government

---

* I shall henceforth use the expressions 'Bolshevik' and '(Russian) Communist' indiscriminately, although it was not until March 1919 that the Party adopted the name 'Communist'.

and the professional strata, and this went on for many weeks. The Bolsheviks had to fill the gaps thus created. But all that Stalin, for example, who was in charge of an important department, the People's Commissariat for the Affairs of the Nationalities, had at his disposal for his 'services' was a small table and two chairs in a room in the Smolny Institute that was already occupied.[6] In this country of peasants the vital People's Commissariat for Agriculture was no better endowed. When the head of this department began work he found that his office lacked even a table. He managed, however, to borrow one from Lenin's office.[7]

These were the circumstances in which the work of building Soviet Russia began—and they were to be made progressively worse by the ruin caused by the civil war, foreign intervention and the blockade. In July 1918, Lenin said: 'The people are like a man who has been thrashed within an inch of his life.'[8] In January 1919: 'The hungry masses are exhausted, and [their] exhaustion is sometimes more than human strength can endure.'[9] In December 1919: 'We are suffering from a desperate crisis':[10] 'a [further] scourge is assailing us, *lice*, and the typhus that is mowing down our troops ... *Either the lice will defeat socialism, or socialism will defeat the lice!*'[11] In December 1920 he spoke of 'the frightful conditions ...';[12] in April 1921 of 'the desperate situation'.[13] In June 1921 he said: 'No country has been so devastated as ours.'[14]

Thus, after the years of oppositional activity and the months of revolutionary offensive, Leninism came to power under conditions that were as unfavourable as they could possibly be for the carrying out of its tasks.

1

The State

Reality and limits of Soviet democracy

Libertarian Leninism, continued and concluded

The description that Lenin had given, in advance, of the Soviet régime went beyond the limits of political institutions. This 'democracy which *for the first time* becomes democracy for the poor ... for the vast majority of the people'* was not to consist merely of an upheaval in the electoral system or even of the conquest of state power by the soviets. The victory of the revolution was to entail a complete transformation in public life, with the entire people acquiring real citizenship through participation in decision-making and administration. In other words, and fundamentally, there was to be a progressive withering away of all political coercion, expressed in the disappearance of '*a special machine* of suppression', and the rapid building of an administration carried on by the people themselves;† and this was what Lenin had put before his followers as the *immediate* aim of their efforts. This was to be what Soviet democracy meant. A Utopian prospect? Not at all, replied Lenin, for 'much that seemed impossible to our narrow, old, bureaucratic forces will become possible for the millions, who will *begin to work for themselves* ...'[1]

The year 1917 had seen the masses of Russia, and the proletariat in particular, launching offensive after offensive and piling up success upon success. The initiatives from 'below' — the creation of the soviets and factory committees, the development of new demands, 'workers' control' — had provided Lenin not only with the 'libertarian' inspiration of his new conceptions but also with the quasi-Trotskyist orientation of his revolutionary strategy. This was how Russia had moved towards the October revolution. The latter did not mark in all respects a break between two worlds. The months that preceded it were months of popular offensive; but those that followed were not months of settling down and consolidation. On the contrary, many similarities

---

* See p. 192.
† See p. 194.

are to be observed between the two phases. Both belong to the same historical movement and form part of one and the same dynamic of conquest.

The autumn had seen in Russia's countryside increasingly stormy actions by peasants in revolt. The decree on land proclaimed by the new Bolshevik authority, on the very day of its inauguration by the All-Russia Congress of Soviets, abolishing landlordism and introducing division of the land,* did not put an end to the peasants' movement. Practical application of the decree took place in an anarchic way and was carried through by the peasants themselves. As Carr points out, the way the land was distributed 'depended on the collective will of the peasants concerned'.[2] Furthermore, the actual appearance of the first agricultural enterprises of a collective character, although this was desired by the new Government, was due to local initiatives.[3] And while the setting-up in June 1918, of the 'Committees of Poor Peasants'† resulted from a governmental decree, its actual implementation owed a great deal to the spontaneous intervention of the masses of demobilized soldiers who were returning to their villages.[4] In general, the drawing-up of laws and decrees by the new authority was as a rule only symbolic in character, or, rather, it served merely propagandist aims, since the Bolsheviks were without the means of making their legislative decisions effective. Lenin was to acknowledge this later, at the Eleventh Party Congress, in 1922.[5]

The activity of the demobilized soldiers continued the activity they had carried on within their regiments before the Bolshevik conquest of power. The Bolsheviks were unable to count on the General Staff of the old army to put through their peace policy, and, in face of the refusal of the high command to begin armistice negotiations, they called on the soldiers themselves to elect committees in order to arrange a cease-fire with the enemy units directly opposite them.[6] The phenomenon of the multiplying of committees which was such a feature of the Russian army between February and October thus continued throughout the winter, enabling the Bolsheviks to record important successes at the elections held to renew the already existing committees.[7] Although the Party had a direct hold on the working class, the situation was similar in the industrial towns. The achievements of the proletariat in those centres in the course of the winter of 1917–18 resulted from local initiatives and spontaneous actions. This was the case, for instance, with the establishment of workers' control over a number of enterprises—the decree legalizing this control merely approved a situation for which, though it had been foreseen and fostered by the Government, the latter was not directly responsible.‡

* See p. 438.
† See p. 238.
‡ See p. 332.

However, the workers were not content merely to take over the running of a number of separate factories. They urged the Soviet Government along the road of nationalization of industry, which at this stage formed no part of its economic programme. In the first months after the seizure of power, the Bolshevik leadership (and Lenin first and foremost), being aware of the limited possibilities of backward and isolated Russia, had no intention of socializing the country's economy. Gropingly, the latter was moving towards a type of 'mixed' economy in which a constructive collaboration would be attempted between the proletarian state and the more conciliatory of the Russian capitalists.[8] This policy came up against a twofold stumbling-block: resistance by the employers, on the one hand, and, on the other, the impatience of the workers. Application by the latter of their methods of 'workers' control' finally convinced the managers of Russia's factories that no form of collaboration with the new ruling authority was practicable. 'Workers' control' was answered by lock-outs, which in turn were answered by 'punitive' nationalizations, these being decided on sometimes by the central Government, sometimes by the local soviets, sometimes by the workers of the particular enterprise concerned. Of the five-hundred-odd enterprises that were nationalized before June 1918 (when a general nationalization measure was applied to Russian industry), about four hundred were taken over as a result of local initiatives that the central Government had vainly striven to hold back or divert.[9] In this sphere as in others, in the spring of 1918 as throughout the year 1917, it was the masses that continued to impose their will; their dynamic upsurge had not yet exhausted itself.

Many examples could be quoted to show the spontaneous emergence of popular tribunals in Petrograd and, in general, the initiative of the masses in the administration of justice, in the sphere of housing, or in that of education.* Writing in early 1919 the British journalist Arthur Ransome noted that 'in every district there are housing committees to whom people wanting rooms apply'.[10] In November 1917 the Council of People's Commissars had in fact called on citizens to 'solve the housing crisis by taking their own measures', and had given them 'the right to requisition, sequestrate and confiscate premises'.[11]

In the field of public education and culture, the People's Commissar in charge was guided by the same principle. In his first official address, on October 29th, 1917, after noting that 'the labouring masses thirst after education', he went on to declare that 'the government cannot give it to them, nor the intelligentsia, nor any force outside themselves ... The people themselves, consciously or unconsciously, must evolve their own culture.' The Commissar, Lunacharsky, concluded that 'the independent action of ... workers', soldiers' and peasants'

* See p. 326.

cultural-educational organizations must achieve full autonomy both in relation to the central government and to the municipal centres.'[12]

Politically, too, this period was a continuation of the preceding one, without any breach of continuity, at any rate so far as progress by the Communists was concerned. In November 1917 Martov himself had to admit that 'almost the entire proletariat supports Lenin'.[13] When General Krasnov attempted, in the last days of October, to reconquer the capital at the head of counter-revolutionary forces, John Reed watched the tens of thousands of workers leaving the factories for the front: 'They rolled along torrent-like ... the revolutionary proletariat defending with its breast the capital of the Workers' and Peasants' Republic!'[14] The British journalist Philips Price saw the same spectacle and testified to the same enthusiasm.[15]

Once this crisis was over, there was, of course, no longer any occasion for the stormy demonstrations that had helped to bring the Bolsheviks to power. The more peaceful processions that succeeded them nevertheless proved that the revolutionary morale of the masses remained high. This was shown by the mass participation in the day of support for the negotiators at Brest-Litovsk that was organized by the Petrograd Soviet. Despite the cold of late December, hundreds of thousands of workers, Red Guards and soldiers marched past, from dawn to dusk.[16]

Finally, and most important, the Bolsheviks' seizure of power was followed by the *spreading all over Russia of the Soviet phenomenon*, which did not really take place until *after* October 1917. A circular issued by the People's Commissariat for Internal Affairs, dated January 5th, 1918, declared that the local soviets were thenceforth invested with all the powers held by the former administration, and added: 'The entire country must be covered with a network of new soviets.' Their number did indeed increase in spectacular fashion, especially in the countryside, where they had hardly existed at all before the October insurrection.[17] In the towns the soviets inevitably functioned by way of delegation, and the large mass of electors had to be represented by elected delegates. In the rural areas, however, the soviets practised direct democracy, which was more in accordance with the philosophy of the new régime.[18] Everywhere the attempt was made to do away with the distinction between legislative and executive functions and to make individuals take part in the application of decisions they had taken jointly.[19] Tens of thousands of workers became members of the state machine, with the Bolshevik Party transforming itself into a recruiting authority for the purpose and showing very special zeal in the work.[20] It is in the light of all this that Alfred Meyer, in his classic work on Leninism, speaks of the first months of the Soviet régime as 'the honeymoon of the Revolution'.[21]

For Lenin, in any case, the revolutionary idyll seemed to be still in progress. We find in his writings of this period the same 'libertarian' accents, the same wholly democratic inspiration as in those of before October. Addressing the Second All-Russia Congress of Soviets, at the very moment of the Bolshevik seizure of power, he declared: 'We must allow complete freedom to the creative faculties of the masses.'[22] Throughout November he made many similar statements. Thus: 'Creative activity at the grass roots is the basic factor of the new public life ... Socialism cannot be decreed from above. Its spirit rejects the mechanical bureaucratic approach; living, creative socialism is the product of the masses themselves.'[23] And, in an appeal to the population published in *Pravda* of November 6th (19th), 1917: 'Comrades, working people! Remember that now *you yourselves* are at the helm of state. No one will help you if you yourselves do not unite and take into *your* hands *all affairs of state* ... Get on with the job yourselves; begin right at the bottom, do not wait for anyone.'[24]

At the end of December 1917 Lenin wrote an article (not published in his lifetime) entitled 'How to organize competition', which is very similar in inspiration to *State and Revolution*. 'One of the most important tasks of today, if not the most important,' Lenin wrote in this article,

is to develop [the] independent initiative of the workers, and of all the working and exploited people generally, develop it as widely as possible in creative *organisational* work. At all costs we must break the old, absurd, savage, despicable and disgusting prejudice that only the so-called 'upper classes', only the rich, and those who have gone through the school of the rich, are capable of administering the state and directing the organisational development of socialist society.

And, as in *State and Revolution*, he declared that 'every *rank-and-file* worker and peasant who can read and write, who can judge people and has practical experience, is capable of organizational work'.[25]

When the Third All-Russia Congress of Soviets assembled, in January 1918, the way Lenin addressed the delegates showed that the 'honeymoon' was not yet over, by a long chalk. 'Very often,' he said, 'delegations of workers and peasants come to the government and ask, for example, what to do with such-and-such a piece of land. And frequently I have felt embarrassed when I saw that they had no very definite views. And I said to them: you are the power, do all you want to do, take all you want, we shall support you ...'[26] To this he added a glowing tribute to 'the work of the masses themselves' and their 'creative activity'. 'Look wherever there are working people, look among the masses, and you will see organizational, creative work in full swing, you will see the stir of a life that is being renewed and hallowed by the revolution.'[27]

Two months later, Lenin explained to the delegates to the Seventh
Party Congress that 'what our revolution is doing is not accidental ... it
is not the product of a Party decision but ... a revolution that the
masses themselves create by their slogans, their efforts.' He emphasized
that 'socialism cannot be implemented by a minority, by the Party.
It can be implemented only by tens of millions when they have learned
to do it themselves.'[28]

What was happening, in these circumstances, to the 'withering away
of the state', that almost libertarian notion which Lenin had put on the
quasi-immediate programme of the Bolshevik Party in *State and
Revolution*? In January 1918, addressing the Congress of Soviets,
Lenin said that 'we really have a organization of power which clearly
indicates the transition to the complete abolition of any power, of
any state. This will be possible when every trace of exploitation has
been abolished, that is, in socialist society.'[29] At the Party Congress in
March 1918 he began his address by declaring that 'since the working
people themselves are undertaking to administer the state and establish
armed forces that support the given state system, the special government apparatus is disappearing, the special apparatus for a certain
form of state coercion is disappearing'.[30] Replying to a speech by
Bukharin, however, he also said: 'At present we certainly uphold the
state.'[31] Lenin went on: 'Just when will the state wither away? We
shall have managed to convene more than two congresses before the
time comes to say: see how our state is withering away. It is too early
for that. To proclaim the withering away of the state prematurely
would distort the historical perspective.'[32]

Lenin was to present this 'withering away' on a number of subsequent occasions as an objective of the revolutionary movement,*
but he would no longer make the beginning of this process coincide
with the accession of the proletariat to power. Quite the contrary, in
fact. Without saying it in so many words, Lenin more than once
suggested that, as the class struggle *grew more intense* with the seizure
of power by the proletariat, what took place was a strengthening of
the state rather than its 'withering away'. Thus, in an address of May
1919: 'It is precisely after the bourgeoisie is overthrown that the class
struggle assumes its acutest forms. And we have no use for those
democrats and socialists who deceive themselves and deceive others

* See, e.g., Vol. 27, pp. 156, 272, 408. In one of the documents adopted by the First
Congress of the Communist International, in March 1919 (written by Bukharin), the
following statement appears: 'As the resistance of the bourgeoisie is broken, as they are
expropriated and changed gradually into a working stratum, the proletarian and dictatorship disappears, the state withers away, and, with the state, classes themselves' (Quoted in
Degras, Vol. I, pp. 19–20). In 1920 Trotsky was to allude to this same phenomenon of
'withering away': 'With the final triumph of the social revolution, the Soviet system will
expand and include the whole population, in order thereby to lose the characteristics of a
form of state, and melt away into a mighty system of producing and consuming co-
operation' (Trotsky, *Terrorism and Communism*, p. 107).

by saying: "The bourgeoisie have been overthrown, the struggle is all over." The struggle is not over, it has only just started ...'[33] In his 'Greetings to the Hungarian Workers', written at the end of the same month, he said: 'The abolition of classes requires a long, difficult and stubborn *class struggle*, which, *after* the overthrow of capitalist rule, *after* the destruction of the bourgeois state, *after* the establishment of the dictatorship of the proletariat, *does not disappear* (as the vulgar representatives of the old socialism and the old Social-Democracy imagine), but merely changes its forms and in many respects becomes fiercer.'[34]

Nevertheless, Lenin stressed that the October revolution had brought into being a 'new type of state', which, moreover, had been 'created by the masses of the people'.[35] In the same statement, made in March 1918 to the Seventh Party Congress, he added: 'Soviet power is a new type of state without a bureaucracy, without police, without a regular army, a state in which bourgeois democracy has been replaced by a new democracy, a democracy that brings to the fore the vanguard of the working people, gives them legislative and executive authority, makes them responsible for military defence and creates state machinery that can re-educate the masses.'[36] To the same gathering he defined the tasks and characteristics of this new state system: to bring about the 'union and organization of the working and exploited masses'; to 'educate every member of the working population for independent participation in the management of the state'; to achieve the 'union of legislative and executive state activity', with 'fusion of administration with legislation', and the 'creation of an armed force of workers and peasants, one least divorced from the people'; finally, to ensure 'more complete democracy, through less formality and making election and recall easier.'[37] What seemed to Lenin quite incompatible with the new régime was the formalism and bureaucracy typical of bourgeois democracy. In this connexion he declared, in *The Immediate Tasks of the Soviet Government*, written and published in this same period: 'The socialist character of Soviet, i.e., *proletarian*, democracy, as concretely applied today, lies first in the fact that the electors are the working and exploited people: the bourgeois is excluded.* Secondly, it lies in the fact that all bureaucratic formalities and restrictions on elections are abolished; the people themselves determine the time and order of elections, and are completely free to recall any elected person.'[38]

Two themes predominate in Lenin's statements regarding Soviet democracy, in this period at least. It is, he says, an 'immeasurably higher and more progressive form of democracy than bourgeois parliamentarism,'[39] and it is meaningless without effective participation by the masses in administrative work: 'Our aim is to draw *the whole of*

---

* On the election arrangements under the new Soviet system, see p. 348.

the poor into the practical work of administration, ... to ensure that *every* toiler, having finished his eight hours' "task" in productive labour, shall perform state duties without pay.' Lenin concludes that 'the transition to this is particularly difficult, but this transition alone can guarantee the final consolidation of Socialism'.[40]

'The transition to this is particularly difficult.' Was there not here a new note, differing from Lenin's exaltation, not so long before, of the spontaneous activity of the masses and of their *already acquired* qualities, their aptitude, helped by revolutionary fervour, to provide, there and then, the cadres for a people's administration? To be sure, in this same period, in March 1918, Lenin had felt it necessary to tell the Party Congress that 'the bricks of which socialism will be composed have not yet been made'.[41]

The turning-point of Brest-Litovsk

Between the perhaps disillusioned realism—disillusioned so soon?— of that last statement: 'the bricks of which socialism will be composed have not yet been made', and Lenin's earlier enthusiastic description of the virtues and capacities of the revolutionary masses, the difference is marked. This difference does not point to any contradiction in Lenin's ideas but to the complexity of the facts and of the dialectical development of the revolution. For while the dynamic of the revolution was still ascending and the people's conquests were advancing, deepening and becoming consolidated, with Soviet democracy, vigorous and creative, giving proof of its reality, factors of dissolution were already present and growing, and, in the very midst of victory, the germs of defeat were already planted.

There has been much discussion about the chronological limits of Soviet democracy. Lenin's death or, to take an earlier date, his illness and withdrawal from political activity, have provided easy reference-points to those with a penchant for striking contrasts and didactic *schemata*. Albert Camus, in his preface to Alfred Rosmer's *Moscou sous Lénine*, was among the many who submitted to this facile interpretation of events. 'Wonderful times,' he wrote, about the period between the October revolution and Lenin's death: 'wonderful times, when the world seemed to be starting anew, when history was at last beginning afresh, on the ruins of an empire.'[42] Writers no less well-disposed than he towards the October revolution, but more careful, such as Pierre Broué and Isaac Deutscher, acknowledge that at the end of the civil war, or at least by the spring of 1921, Soviet democracy had for some time ceased to function. Actually, the process of break-down of this democracy had begun in a period when it still seemed in good health—and when, moreover, it was still not inconceivable that the revolution might recover its initial vigour and resume its forward march.

The winter of 1917–18, which saw the conquest of power and the triumph of the proletariat, was also a winter of misery and economic disorganization. Beginning then, in that period of victory and hope, we see the first manifestations of the phenomenon which dominates the first years of the Soviet régime: the progressive weakening of the Russian working class, a loss of strength and substance that was to end in its almost complete 'de-classing' and, in a certain sense, its temporary disappearance from the scene.

It is true that, in the spring of 1918, Soviet democracy was alive and was really, as we shall see, the dictatorship *of* the proletariat. But the Soviet historian Sobolev tells us that, in April 1918, 265 out of the 799 industrial enterprises in Petrograd were closed down, and in the city's large-scale industry taken as a whole less than half of the workers were still at work.[43] In the spring of 1918 the total population of the capital numbered no more than one-and-a-half million, as against two-and-a-half million a year previously. The economic collapse and the threat from the German Army had led to the dismantling of many factories. In Moscow in the same period the population had fallen from two million to one-and-a-half.* To this was added the scourge of famine. In February and March 1918 most parts of Russia were receiving only 12 or 13 per cent of the amount of bread officially 'provided for' by the Food Commissariat. In April this amount fell by half. In the industrial centres the workers went for several days without getting their bread-ration.[44] And at the beginning of 1918 this ration was only 50 grammes per day in the capital.[45] Already the black market had become, despite the exorbitant prices demanded, the chief means of keeping alive.[46] Towards the end of April, Jacques Sadoul, an observer well-disposed towards the régime, wrote this description of the situation in Moscow, which a month before had been made the capital of Soviet Russia:

> In the districts away from the centre, frightful poverty prevails. There are epidemics of typhus, smallpox, children's diseases. Babies are dying *en masse*. Those one sees are weak, fleshless, pitiful creatures. In the working-class quarters one too often passes poor, pale, thin mothers, sadly bearing in their arms, in a little coffin of silver-painted wood, looking like a cradle, the tiny lifeless body that a small quantity of bread or milk would have kept alive.[47]

The loss of the Ukraine as a result of the draconian provisions of the

---

* Pietsch, p. 88. Leonid Krassin, one of the principal organizers of the Soviet economy, speaking at the end of 1918 of 'the almost complete destruction of the industry of Petrograd', blamed the 'panic fear' that had taken hold of the authorities at the beginning of the spring (Carr, Vol. II, p. 193).

peace of Brest-Litovsk,* the interruption in commercial exchanges between town and country, and the catastrophic state of transport, all contributed to this disaster. The consequences for the working class were extremely serious. Speaking at the Seventh Party Congress, Bukharin described in alarming terms what he called, as early as March 1918, 'the disintegration of the proletariat'.[48]

The expression used by the leader of the 'Left Communists', the chief critic of the Government's policy,† was perhaps polemical. In any case it revealed perfectly the new climate, much altered for the worse, which we find reflected in the writings and speeches of Lenin. There is a noticeable, though imprecise, dividing line between his extreme optimism and 'democratism', in the first months following the October victory, and his loss of this mood, between the exaltation of the 'creative work' of the masses, the 'organizational work' they were carrying out,‡ and that disillusioned statement: 'the bricks of which socialism will be composed have not yet been made'.§ It was not that, after this change of lighting, with the shadows now preponderating over the well-lit patches, the latter had wholly vanished. For a very long time afterwards—indeed, to the end of his life—Lenin upheld some of the views set forth in *State and Revolution*. In August 1918, for example, he wrote in his *Letter to the American Workers* (the context makes his statement, therefore, something of an apologia): '*For the first time*, not the minority, not the rich alone, not the educated alone, but the real people, the vast majority of the working people, are *themselves* building a new life, are *by their own experience* solving the most difficult problems of socialist organization.'[49] And the same note was sounded in the winter of 1918–19, in the draft programme that he prepared for the Eighth Party Congress.[50]

Long since, however, emphasis had been laid on the difficulties encountered in democratizing the state and its administration, and so in the creation of Soviet democracy. What had seemed on the eve and on the morrow of October to be about to be realized, almost present, was increasingly shifted to the status of an ideal to be attained, or an aim to be achieved. Whereas in November 1918, on the first anniversary of the capture of power, Lenin could still write: 'Now all workers, not just the leaders and advanced workers, but great sections of workers, know that they themselves, with their own hands, are building socialism and have already laid its foundations'[51]—this optimism being perhaps connected with the solemnity of the occasion, as well as with the euphoria caused by the outbreak of the German revolution**—one month later his tone was more modest and more

* See p. 346.
† See p. 288.
‡ See p. 219.
§ See p. 222.
** See p. 363.

realistic. Writing in December 1918 and January 1919 about the tasks of the trade unions, Lenin acknowledged that, as regards 'the construction of socialist society', 'the very essentials are not yet guaranteed', and that 'the main body of working people are still not playing a big enough part in the construction'.[52] And in a pamphlet published in March–April 1919, *Achievements and Difficulties of the Soviet Government*, Lenin observed that 'the organization of proletarian influence over the rest of the population, the creation of a new mass environment', constituted 'an immensely difficult task, the fulfilment of which will require decades'.[53]

Not such a long period as that was needed for Lenin's departure from his optimism of 1917 to become observable. He had begun by exalting the possibilities – and, more than that, the already established capacities, the already realized potentialities – of the entire proletariat and peasantry. But in an important work, *The Immediate Tasks of the Soviet Government*, written in March–April 1918, Lenin drew for the first time a distinction *within* the proletariat, stressing 'what prolonged and persistent efforts must be exerted by the best and the most class-conscious workers and peasants in order to bring about a complete change in the mood of the people and to bring them on to the proper path of steady and disciplined labour.'[54]

He was finished, for the time being, with exaltation of the proletariat as such, of the people as a whole, of the working class hailed as a single entity, of the peasantry praised as an undifferentiated mass. More and more frequently, and very soon in a quite systematic way, Lenin began to single out the 'advanced workers', who alone were still worthy of trust, and to denounce the harm done, in the ranks of the proletariat itself, by the vestiges – or resurgences? – of the petty-bourgeois spirit and the capitalist mentality. In May 1918 he was already appealing to the 'class-conscious and advanced workers', declaring that 'the country and the revolution can be saved only by the mass effort of the advanced workers', and emphasizing that 'we need tens of thousands of advanced and steeled proletarians, class-conscious enough to explain matters to the millions of poor peasants all over the country and to assume the leadership of these millions ...'[55] They were not so very numerous, either, those advanced workers. 'We know how small is the section of advanced and politically conscious workers in Russia,'[56] said Lenin in a speech on May 23rd, 1918. They were even getting fewer, apparently, since, at the beginning of June 1918, he admitted that 'the number of waverers and despairers in our ranks is growing';[57] and a few weeks later, addressing the Fourth Conference of the Trade Unions, he denounced those workers who 'are abandoning the working class and deserting to the side of the bourgeoisie'.[58] Soon it would be a matter of 'safeguarding the interests

8

of the working *class* against the few, the groups and sections of workers who stubbornly cling to capitalist traditions.'[59]

We are here, of course, running ahead of the situation as it was in the spring of 1918, when circumstances forced Lenin to make a change in his evaluations and appreciations which was at first hardly perceptible, but which facts themselves would cause to become increasingly accentuated. In the spring of 1918 we are still a long way from that statement, the truth of which had not struck Lenin during the 'honeymoon of the Russian revolution': 'There never has been, and never can be, a class struggle in which *part* of the advanced class does not remain on the side of the reactionary forces.'[60] As early as May 1918, however, at a time when this theme was quite new for Lenin, he was commenting that 'when the worker became the vanguard leader of the poor, he did not thereby become a saint. He led the people forward, but he also became infected with the diseases of petty-bourgeois disintegration.'[61] At that moment Lenin still had a long way to go before making the invitation he addressed in February 1920 to the organs of the Cheka, to direct 'revolutionary coercion' against 'the wavering and unstable elements among the masses themselves'.[62] But he was also already a long way from the enthusiasm and euphoria aroused in him by the offensive of 1917 and the October victory.

This disillusionment, this pronounced return to 'realism', this comparatively sudden awareness of everything that separates the desirable from the possible, and the possible from the actual, was due not only to the events that were taking place in Russia — an economic and social crisis and a civil war. Attentive study of Lenin's writings and declarations, careful research into the origins of this 'turn' with a view to an attempt to give it a date, lead us to a fairly definite conclusion. It is in the signing of *the peace of Brest-Litovsk* that the principal — though certainly not the only — cause of the phenomenon must be sought. Was it accidental, indeed, that it was on February 24th, 1918, the day after that on which the German armies, halted by the peace negotiations which had now been broken off by decision of the Party's Central Committee, resumed their march into Russia — that it was then that Lenin said: 'Hitherto the revolution has proceeded along an ascending line from victory to victory; now it has suffered a heavy defeat'?[63] Was it accidental that, the same day, Lenin reflected: 'It may be that the respite needed for an uprising of the masses will take no little time'?[64] That, defending the signing of the peace treaty with Germany to the Party Congress of March 1918 he said: 'We must be prepared for extraordinary difficulties, for extraordinarily severe defeats'?[65] Or that, in the same speech and in relation to the same subject, he urged the delegates to 'abandon illusions for which real events have punished you and will punish you more severely in the future. An epoch of most grievous defeats is ahead of us'?[66]

This was the moment when a theme first appeared which was to dominate Lenin's speeches for years thereafter: 'One must know how to retreat.'[67] This theme found expression also in his pamphlet of March–April 1918, *The Immediate Tasks of the Soviet Government*: 'In order to go on advancing successfully *in the future*, we must "suspend" our offensive *now*.'[68] At this moment, too, Lenin attacked the 'Leftism' of some of his comrades—whereas all through 1917 and in the weeks immediately following the conquest of power, he had been systematically attacking *the cautious and conciliatory trend* among the Bolsheviks.

Lenin's differences with the 'Left' were not confined to matters of foreign policy, although that point was the decisive one. The logic of his 'realism' led Lenin to change the main direction of his fire. He became, as we shall see, the defender of 'state capitalism',* and recommended increasingly not the merits of initiative but the need for discipline, output, productivity and order, as imposed from above upon a proletariat which, though still loyal to the Soviet régime, was being increasingly undermined so far as its physical resources were concerned.† On all of these matters he clashed with the 'Left Communists'.[69] This was the consequence of the first defeat suffered by Bolshevism since its accession to power. Significantly, this reverse— the first, but also the most decisive, the one that was to prove, despite all hopes and all efforts, irreversible—was suffered on the plane of the international strategy of Leninism, the plane of *the world revolution*.

All that was to follow, followed from this: the isolation of the Russian working class, abandoned to its own resources, and therefore to *want*; and, as a corollary, the decline and degeneration of that Soviet democracy the birth of which we have watched, and the death agony of which must now be described.

Degeneration of the soviets

The régime created by the October insurrection took several months to surround itself with a constitutional framework. The very drawing-up of a constitution seemed, indeed, to the new régime to be something contrary, by its formal and juridical nature, to a living and dynamic conception of the revolution. It would be better, in any case, it was thought, if the form to be taken by the new state were *not* fixed by law, especially as the national setting to which it was confined for the moment, and which determined some of its features, would certainly be transcended, with the help of the world revolution, in the very near future, so that many legislative arrangements would be rendered inoperative.

The soviets became the depositories of legitimacy and sovereignty.

* See p. 337.
† See p. 345.

In particular, it was the local soviets that were treated in the constitution as the foundation of political authority. They it was, indeed, that embodied most authentically the *spontaneous action of the masses*, of which the constitution was, said the new leaders, only a pale and imperfect translation into juridical terms.[70] Nevertheless, in their distribution of powers, the makers of the constitution assigned a relatively large share to the central authority, represented by the All-Russia Congress of Soviets, and, between sessions, by the All-Russia Central Executive Committee of this Congress. Despite this granting of extensive powers to the centre (together with the right to define these powers and, if necessary, to extend them), the intentions so expressed were not successfully translated into reality. The initial phase of the Soviet régime was a period of almost unrestricted autonomy of local bodies. Animated by intense activity, the local soviets, which continually grew in numbers, showed themselves jealous in safeguarding their own authority.

Thus, one of the members of the 'collegium of the People's Commissariat for Internal Affairs',* speaking in 1918, declared that 'the municipal and village soviets acknowledge no authority but their own, or, if they do acknowledge another authority, this happens only when the decisions issuing therefrom bring them some advantage'.[71] The Deputy People's Commissar for Finance said that, despite the important powers ascribed to the central authority in respect of fiscal matters, 'the local soviets do as they please, and, as the old saying has it, are even capable of changing a man into a woman, or vice versa'.[72] Lenin looked upon this situation very philosophically, seeing it as 'a disease of growth' which was 'a quite natural phenomenon'.[73] It led, however, to some odd situations. Over very large areas autonomous authorities arose which felt themselves in no way bound by the Central Government's decisions. Thus, the regional Soviet of Siberia, although constitutionally subordinate to the All-Russia Congress of Soviets, to which it sent representatives, refused to accept the treaty of Brest-Litovsk, which the central Soviet authority had ratified, and announced that it was still in a state of war with the Central Powers.[74] Even greater absurdities sometimes appeared in the economic sphere. In April 1918 it was reported that oil from Baku was not reaching Moscow until it had been taxed by all the various regional soviets located along the route.[75] This was the brief period known in the history of Soviet Russia as the *oblastnichestvo*—the 'period of regionalism'.

Not until the autumn of 1918 did these 'basic' authorities start to disintegrate rapidly. What ended them was not so much the will of the central authority as the exigencies and consequences of *the civil war*.

---

* So as to make the system more democratic, each People's Commissar, whose function was equivalent to that of a Minister, was surrounded by a 'collegium' responsible for helping and supervising him.

Until then the power of the soviets, especially on the local plane, had been almost undivided, and in any case greater than that of the Bolshevik Party.* Within a few months this power now collapsed. The White Terror was partly responsible for this, of course, since victories by the counter-revolutionary forces were usually accompanied not only by the massacring of large numbers of Communists but also by extermination of the most active members of the soviets, and in any case, by suppression of the latter. More paradoxically, however, the soviets also fell victim to the organization that was specially charged with the struggle against the 'Whites'—the Cheka.

The Cheka (short for 'Extraordinary Commission'—itself short for 'Extraordinary Commission for Combating Counter-Revolution and Sabotage') was set up by a decree of December 7th, 1917. The rapid spread of the civil war from the end of the summer of 1918 onwards resulted in this purely repressive institution being endowed with considerable powers, in face of which the soviets had to accept a minor role. On August 28th, 1918, the headquarters of the Cheka actually instructed its local agencies to refuse to submit to any interference by the soviets: on the contrary, it was these local agencies that were to impose *their* will upon the soviet bodies. They succeeded in doing this in the many areas that were affected by military operations.[76] The institutions that competed in authority with the Cheka were no longer the local or regional soviets but the new administrative institutions born of the civil war. Among these, the 'Military Revolutionary Committee of the R.S.F.S.R.' and the 'revolutionary committees' that represented it in the localities held an important position.[77] Furthermore, in accordance with a process of ever-greater compelling power, bureaucratization entailed the multiplying of commissions, committees and organs of all kinds, which often overlapped each other. Thus, the end of November 1918 saw the creation of the 'Council of Workers' and Peasants' Defence', which soon virtually took the place of the Government itself. This body, while having no concern with military operations as such, was entrusted with solving the supply problems of the Red Army, and started a process of militarizing the whole of public life, again at the expense of the soviets, or of what was left of them.[78]

The 'de-Sovietization' of political life developed quickly, and made itself felt at the centre as well as at the local level. The All-Russia Congress of Soviets, which was supposed to meet every three months, and whose frequent gatherings—October 1917, January, March and July 1918—reflected the intense activity of the soviets during the first few months of the new régime, began to space out these occasions over longer intervals. From the end of 1918 they became annual, and

* See p. 279.

also acquired an increasingly academic character. The Central Executive Committee of this Congress had been conceived as a permanent, or quasi-permanent, body. However, it did not hold a single meeting between July 14th, 1918, and February 1st, 1920—though decrees continued to be issued in its name. In general, the *militarization* of the whole of public life had suppressed the soviets as really functioning bodies. What obtained was what Bukharin and Preobrazhensky, the authors of the semi-official *ABC of Communism*, called 'a militarist proletarian dictatorship'.[79]

Born from the spontaneous activity of the masses, organized so as to perpetuate this activity and give it the broadest and freest expression, by the second half of 1918 the soviets had lost their drive and their animation. Where they still existed, their life was due much more to the activity of their executive organs than to that of their deliberative bodies, which had become lethargic. Kamenev admitted this when he addressed the All-Russia Congress of Soviets in December 1919: 'Individual members busy themselves with purely technical matters ... Plenary meetings are held only rarely, and when the deputies do meet, this is only to listen to a report or to a few speeches.'[80]

Lenin himself acknowledged, addressing the Eighth Party Congress in March 1919, that 'the Soviets, which by virtue of their programme are organs of government *by the working people*, are in fact organs of government *for the working people* by the advanced section of the proletariat, but not by the working people as a whole'.[81]

Was this not, in effect, the death certificate of the most original and really democratic institution thrown up by the Russian revolution? To be sure, neither the Communist leaders, nor the Party activists, nor the Soviet cadres, resigned themselves to this situation. This was seen when, as the civil war seemed to be nearing its end, voices were raised on all sides to call for the re-establishment of the soviets in their full rights. The demand for 'revival of the soviets' occupied, for example, an important place in the discussions that took place at the meeting of the All-Russia Congress of Soviets, already mentioned, held at the end of December 1919. The Menshevik Martov was the chief spokesman for this demand, but he was supported by some Communist delegates, who succeeded in passing a resolution calling for the power of the soviets to be strengthened.[82] The Central Executive Committee of the All-Russia Congress now resumed its activities, after a long hibernation, and assembled in February, May, June and September 1920, each of these sessions lasting a week. With the return of peace and the passing of the threat of counter-revolution, many local soviets reappeared in the countryside, and the Soviet Government announced its intention of giving up some of the prerogatives it had usurped and restoring the rights of the Central Executive Committee, which under the constitution of 1918 was supposed to supervise the activities of the People's Commissars.[83] Moreover, in 1920 elections to the soviets re-acquired some of the freedom that had been characteristic of them at the outset. The Mensheviks took part in increasing numbers, and their leader, Martov, acknowledged at the beginning of 1920 that, except in Petrograd, 'where "Zinovievite" elections were held in the old manner,' the return to more democratic methods was general, and often worked to the advantage of the candidates of his party.[84]

The hopes that supporters of Soviet democracy were able to entertain at that moment were not, however, destined to be realized. The worsening of the economic and social situation had done too much damage throughout Russia to make possible any return to the starting-point. Counter-revolution flared up again, moreover, with the Polish attack on Soviet Russia and the offensive of the Whites under Wrangel. Finally, and above all, the crisis of the autumn of 1920 and the winter of 1920–21 brought the collapse of all such hopes. With the revolt of the countryside against the Soviet régime, increasing discontent among the working class, the fierce determination of the Communists to remain in power despite their unpopularity, and, last but not least, the ruined state of the economy, the demoralization of the people, the increasing isolation of a devastated country and an exhausted nation, the very basis for a revival of the soviets was no longer present.

For this to become possible a new period of revolutionary advance would have had to begin. But the introduction of the New Economic Policy (N.E.P.) signified the very opposite. Soviet democracy, born of the upsurge of the masses and the Bolshevik victory, had, as a result of defeats and isolation, finally ceased to exist.

The coming of the monolithic state

The interpretation offered by most historians of Russian Communism possesses the merit, if not of truthfulness, at least of clarity. Convinced of the basic Machiavellianism of the founder of Russian Communism, and of the servile submission of his supporters, they see in the beginnings of the Soviet régime the apparent justification of a familiar and banal thesis: Lenin, the man of Organization and of the Party, had in view only the triumph of his faction. Identifying socialism with the rule of the vanguard, Lenin—clever, crafty and free from all scruples —spoke in a democratic way when that was needed, relied, when this seemed useful, upon the spontaneous action of the masses, pretended to be converted to the libertarian philosophy of the soviets, and even allowed himself to borrow some slogans from the anarchists. When, however, by means of tactical subtleties and tricks against which the pathetic naïvety of his opponents proved helpless, Lenin had gained power, he hastened to throw off the disguise that he had assumed. After reproaching the Provisional Government for failing to convene the Constituent Assembly, and then, having allowed it to meet, observed with chagrin that the results of the election constituted a repudiation of Bolshevism, Lenin dispersed the Assembly. After proclaiming his devotion to democratic freedoms, he lost no time in stifling them, and after announcing his intention of establishing a Soviet and socialist régime, he made haste, not content with installing his own Party alone in power, to prohibit and persecute the other socialist parties. So rapid, almost immediate, a disavowal of the Bolshevik programme by the Bolsheviks themselves, and by Lenin of his own ideas, must surely prove, by the irrefutable testimony of facts, that the Leninist doctrine, a totalitarian plan, *necessarily* had to give rise, once victorious, to a totalitarian state—and Leninism and Stalinism were really one and the same.

To quote Leonard Schapiro, a well-known supporter of this view: 'The malignant figure of the General Secretary, Stalin, has become only too familiar in its portrayal by disappointed oppositionists, defeated by the apparatus which he controlled. But it was Lenin, with their support, who equipped him with the weapons, and started him upon his path.'[85] Raymond Aron says the same thing: 'In the case of the Soviet régime, the monopoly of the party and of ideology [in other words, totalitarianism, M.L.] is the essence itself of Bolshevism ...'[86]

Facts are of decisive importance in judging the nature of Leninism—so decisive that it is indispensable to examine them with very close attention and, refusing to be satisfied with half-truths, to study the actual circumstances that presided over the degeneration of the Soviet régime and the coming of the Bolshevik monolith and Soviet totalitarianism. Was Leninism responsible for this process, or was Leninism itself among its victims? This is, in a sense, what all the argument is about.

The Constituent Assembly and its dissolution

The convening of a Constituent Assembly figured in the programme of all the Left parties in Russia, and especially in that of the Social-Democrats, Bolsheviks included. While they did not make it the axis of their propaganda, since they mobilized themselves and the masses in the name of Soviet power ('All Power to the Soviets!') Lenin's supporters and Lenin himself had, between February and October 1917, presented the convening of a Constituent Assembly as one of the aims of their activity. On October 25th, at the moment of the seizure of power, Lenin told the delegates to the Second All-Russia Congress of Soviets that 'the Soviet government ... will ensure the convocation of the Constituent Assembly at the time appointed.'[87] The Council of

People's Commissars itself acknowledged, through Lenin, its provisional character, 'until the Constituent Assembly is convened'.[88]

During the first weeks following the insurrection Lenin had occasion to confirm these assurances.* The elections did indeed take place: they were held on and after November 12th, 1917, in an atmosphere of great freedom.† The first results that came in confirmed the verdict of elections held previous to the October rising, and favoured the Bolsheviks; but when the results arrived from the provinces they did not support the optimistic impression thus given. As they came to hand they revealed more and more clearly the great success won by the Socialist-Revolutionaries, and especially by their Right wing. In the end, the Assembly was made up as follows: S.R.s, 299 seats; Ukrainian S.R.s, 81; Left S.R.s, 39; Bolsheviks, 168; Mensheviks, 18; Constitutional-Democrats, 15; the remaining 83 seats being divided among small parties, mostly non-Russian nationalists.[89]

The opponents of the Soviet régime thus enjoyed a comfortable majority in the Assembly, and the Bolshevik Government found itself confronted with a dilemma which the Party's Central Committee was obliged to discuss at its meeting on November 29th. To judge by the minutes, the discussion was very confused. Though Lenin was present, he took no part in this discussion, which came to no decision, so great was the uncertainty and irresolution among the Bolsheviks.[90] Their disappointment was all the greater because they had entered with zeal, and sometimes with real enthusiasm, into the election campaign, in which the Party militants had shown tremendous activity.[91]

The moderate Socialist parties—the S.R.s and Mensheviks—called for the Assembly to be convened at once; they saw it, and not the soviets, as the sole legitimate depository of sovereignty. The bourgeois politicians carried on agitation, former ministers in the Provisional Government striving vainly to bring about on their own a meeting of members of the Assembly. Finally, the first counter-revolutionary forces, which were starting to gather in the south of Russia—especially the 'Volunteer Army', concentrated in the Don region—included only a single point in their meagre political programme: all power to the Constituent Assembly.[92]

The Bolsheviks were still divided. They had already formed their elected deputies to the Assembly into a parliamentary group, and this group had chosen a bureau, consisting of Kamenev, Rykov, Ryazanov, Larin, Milyutin and Nogin—all of them important figures known for their 'moderate' outlook. They were, as a whole, in favour of allowing the Assembly to meet, and, doubtless, of respecting its rights. On December 11th the Central Committee discussed the question afresh,

---

* E.g., on November 8th, 1917, in connexion with the powers to be given to the local soviets (Lenin, op. cit., Vol. 26, p. 299).

† See, generally, for the question of the Constituent Assembly, Radkey, *Elections* (on the free nature of the elections, see Chapter 4).

and Lenin proposed that the bureau of the Bolshevik group in the Assembly—described as 'the Right-wing tendency'—be dissolved. He was unsuccessful, the Central Committee preferring not to vote on his resolution.[93] The Central Executive Committee of the All-Russia Congress of Soviets decided soon afterwards that the Constituent Assembly should meet on January 5th, 1918, but Lenin almost at once revealed the reasons behind his attitude of distrust towards the Assembly: his 'Theses on the Constituent Assembly', written on December 12th, were published in *Pravda* of December 26th. For the first time, explicitly at any rate, he stated that the imminent confrontation of the two bodies, the Constituent Assembly and the Congress of Soviets, and the possible clash between them, was nothing less than a confrontation and clash between classes, with the proletarian institution facing the bourgeois one.[94] To this fundamental conception he added arguments relating more closely to the circumstances in which the Constituent Assembly had been elected. It could not reflect in its composition, he claimed, the split that had taken place between the Right S.R.s, hostile to the Soviet Government, and the Left S.R.s, who had decided to support the new régime. The election had taken place, too, before the people, especially those in the rural areas, had really become aware of the October revolution, or at least of what it implied. Finally, the beginning of counter-revolutionary action, and so of civil war, had made it impossible to observe normal electoral procedures. Lenin declared that the slogan 'All power to the Constituent Assembly!' had become '*in fact* the slogan of the Cadets and the Kaledinites [the followers of the "White" General Kaledin, M.L.] and of their helpers'. He concluded that 'the Constituent Assembly ... must inevitably clash with the will and interests of the working and exploited classes which on October 25th began the socialist revolution against the bourgeoisie. Naturally, the interests of this revolution stand higher than the formal rights of the Constituent Assembly ... '[95]

When the Constituent Assembly met, on January 5th, 1918, with the Right S.R. Chernov in the chair, it was invited by the Bolshevik group of deputies to ratify the principal measures taken by the Soviet Government, which amounted to acknowledging its legitimacy. The motion put down to this effect was rejected by 237 votes to 138. The Bolshevik and Left S.R. deputies then walked out of the Assembly, never to return. The debates went on all through the night of January 5th–6th. Soon after five in the morning, the commander of an armed detachment, the anarchist Zheleznyakov, carrying out the Government's instructions, ordered the Assembly to stop working—'because the guard is tired', he explained. Without attempting to resist, the members of the Assembly dispersed. They were never to reassemble, a decree of the Soviet Government having dissolved the Constituent Assembly.[96] The reaction of public opinion, especially of its most active element, showed great indifference to what had occurred, though on January 5th the Bolsheviks had briskly dispersed a large demonstration in support of the Assembly. It was to be the last of its kind.

The question of the fate meted out by the Soviet Government to the Constituent Assembly, the only assembly freely elected by universal suffrage that Russia ever knew, can be considered in a number of ways. The first of these is to state, absolutely, that there is no democracy without consultation of the citizens as a whole and respect for the will of the majority that emerges from this. If this point of view is accepted, it means *ipso facto* condemning the attitude of the Russian Communists, and of Lenin in particular. If, however, one chooses a different approach, refusing to adopt an absolute, and therefore *abstract*, judgment, certain observations have to be made regarding the political and social forces that clashed with each other on the occasion of and in connexion with the meeting of the Constituent Assembly. From this standpoint, no doubt is possible: the industrial proletariat and the masses it led were *against* the Constituent Assembly and for the soviets; the bourgeoisie and the conservative or reactionary elements were, on the contrary, against the soviets and *for* the Constituent Assembly. On the former of these propositions the testimony of Oskar Anweiler, the chief Western historian of the soviets as an institution, is all the more convincing because his attitude is not one of indulgence towards the Bolsheviks. He is quite categorical: 'The Soviets were seen by the masses as "their" organ, and it would have been impossible to mobilize them against the Soviets in the name of the Constituent Assembly.'[97]

Socially, supporters and opponents of the Constituent Assembly also present another kind of differentiation. At the elections to the Assembly the Bolsheviks received massive votes not only in the industrial towns but also in those country districts and sectors of the front that were near urban centres. It was also observed that, in the countryside, the Bolsheviks obtained their best results in the villages and localities situated along the railway lines—wherever, in fact, the communications network made it possible to spread, through the agency of workers and soldiers, the message of the revolution, and, consequently, to stir up the peasants politically.[98]

The Assembly, when it met, was dominated by the huge contingent of S.R.s—who, as we shall see, were neither Socialist nor Revolutionary. This party, having lost its Left wing, represented, on the contrary, an increasingly conservative force.* It had just chosen a new president, belonging to the Left-Centre tendency, in the person of its most esteemed leader, Chernov, who had been Minister of Agriculture in the Provisional Government. But the S.R. group in the Assembly was much further to the Right than the leadership of the Party.[99]

* See p. 243.

The principal historian of the S.R. Party considers that the members of the S.R. group's steering committee in the Assembly could be 'regarded, and not without reason, as the worst enemies of the revolution'.[100] The same writer describes thus the predominant social composition of the Assembly: 'Men of prestige and experience ... experts in agronomy or administration, peasants who were looked up to by their communities.'[101] To translate and sum up, this was an 'assembly of notables' which, by its origins and aspirations, justified the hope and trust placed in it by the conservative camp. Thus, while the confrontation between the soviets and the Constituent Assembly corresponded, on the plane of principle, to the distinction between revolutionary democracy and parliamentary democracy, it signified in social and political reality the opposition between two hostile worlds: that of the bourgeoisie and its allies, and that of the proletariat and its supporters.

Finally, the question 'Soviets or Constituent Assembly?' transcends the historical and geographical limitations in which we have hitherto considered it, for it is not confined either to the year 1917 or to Russia. When we think of the great social clashes of modern times, we observe, in France and Germany as in Russia, that the revolutionary dynamic has always been blocked by the paralysing or braking force of the election mechanism, even in its democratic form of universal suffrage. This happened in 1848 in Paris, when the proletariat attacked in the streets and the bourgeoisie answered with rifle-fire—and with votes. This happened in 1871, too, when the National Assembly was able, in face of the Commune, to boast of a democratic legitimacy that the workers of Paris did not have: *they* were not representatives of the nation's sovereign will. Every time, universal suffrage crushes beneath numbers, and by virtue of that force of inertia which the revolution is in revolt against, the revolution's own *élan*.* The revolutionary is a bad voter, and the voter a poor revolutionary. This is confirmed by an event geographically and historically nearer than those mentioned to the Bolshevik revolution: the German revolution of 1918. The political and social struggle that developed amid the ruins of the Hohenzollern empire assumed the same outlines and gave rise to the same divisions as in Russia. In Berlin, conservatives who had, the day before, been staunch supporters of a semi-autocratic monarchy and a semi-feudal order, proclaimed themselves overnight republicans and democrats, supporters of 'popular sovereignty'; in other words, quite concretely, of a national Constituent Assembly.[102] The 'Freikorps' themselves, forerunners of the Nazis, made their members swear an oath of allegiance to this democratic institution.[103] And it was the Spartacists who opposed the convening of such an Assembly and countered the very principle of it with their demand for a 'democracy of councils'. In their paper, the *Rote Fahne*, they presented the Constituent Assem-

* A similar development was seen in France in 1968.

bly as 'the bourgeois solution', whereas Workers' and Soldiers' Councils were 'the socialist one'.[104]

In Russia, moreover, though the dissolution of the Constituent Assembly was actually effected by the Bolsheviks, who were in power, this deed was approved by the Left S.R.s and by the anarchists, both of which groups were alien to Leninist doctrine, but who were also in favour of very thorough-going democracy.

In the last analysis, what causes surprise is not that Lenin assumed the responsibility of dissolving the Constituent Assembly, but that he took so long in deciding to do this, and had such difficulty in identifying the terms in which the dilemma—for there was a dilemma—presented itself, namely: Constituent Assembly *or* soviets. It is simplistic to attribute Lenin's conduct in this matter to that Machiavellianism which some writers see as his second nature, if not his first. In reality, in this field as in many others, he was not guided by any previously determined strategy. In one of his last writings, reviewing the events of 1917, he acknowledged that he had been inspired by a dictum of Napoleon's: 'Napoleon, I think, wrote: "*On s'engage et puis ... on voit.*" Rendered freely this means: "First engage in a serious battle and then see what happens." Well, we did ... '[105] In January 1918 he told the congress of Russia's railwaymen: 'We had not acted according to plan.'[106] In 1917 Lenin had, indeed, committed himself to the soviets, to restarting the revolutionary offensive, to launching a fresh assault by the proletariat upon the positions of the bourgeoisie—in fact, he had opted, as we have seen, for 'permanent revolution'. But when he did this he did not cease to be, in many respects, a man of Russian and international Social-Democracy for whom the conquests of the revolution formed part of the classic programme of demands of the labour movement—which included the securing of a *constitutional* régime in autocratic or semi-autocratic states, and of universal suffrage where the electoral law still included property qualifications.

Had Lenin, wholly absorbed in day-to-day revolutionary activity, not noticed what, today, with the hindsight of history, seems so obvious—that the very notion of entrusting power, *all* power, to the soviets, popular institutions which did not provide for the representing of all classes, ruled out any notion of making a Constituent Assembly elected by the population as a whole the sovereign organ of state power in Russia? What seems now so plain evidently seemed much less so to Lenin. He did not immediately grasp the constitutional implications of the revolutionary dynamic which, making the conquests of February look trivial, and in any case anachronistic, hurling the soviets into attack on the newly established order and the masses into attack on the soviets, the peasants into attack on the land and the workers on the factories, caused the idea of permanent revolution, conceived by Marx and Trotsky, to become the ruling principle of the

Russia of 1917. It is not accidental that we find Lenin so hesitant in characterizing the events of this period. Today it appears to us that with each leap forward made by the revolution—the struggle for Soviet power against the Provisional Government, the liquidation of the latter, the breaking of the alliance with the Western bourgeois democracies, support for workers' control and dissolution of the Constituent Assembly—the revolution, transcending its bourgeois limits, intensified its character as a *socialist* revolution. Lenin, however, hesitated on this point, groping his way, and sometimes contradicting himself.

He was later to refer to 'setting up the Soviet state system' and 'getting out of the imperialist war' as the essential preliminary 'tasks of our revolution in the sphere of socialist construction'.[107] In the period when the Constituent Assembly was dissolved, speaking in January 1918 to the Third All-Russia Congress of Soviets, he declared: 'Today, when the Soviets are in power ... there can be no question of a bourgeois-democratic revolution.'[108] Yet the question of the bourgeois revolution was so much in Lenin's mind that he often identified the transition from the bourgeois to the socialist revolution with the setting-up in June 1918 of the 'Committees of Poor Peasants', which, breaking the unity of the peasant camp, introduced the class struggle into the countryside. In *The Proletarian Revolution and the Renegade Kautsky* he asserted unequivocally that 'our revolution is a bourgeois revolution *as long* as we march with the peasants *as a whole*'.[109] And to the Eighth Party Congress, in March 1919, he said that it was 'from the moment the Poor Peasants' Committees began to be organized' that 'our revolution became a *proletarian* revolution'.[110]

These approximations and varying definitions will surprise only those who wish to see in Lenin an infallible master and omniscient planner—whether providential or diabolical—of revolutionary strategy. This he was not. He was not even the real theoretician of the revolution, but 'merely' the maker of it. And it was his absorption in practical activity that, doubtless, prevented him in 1917 from deducing theoretical conclusions from the lessons of events. Hence the *theoretical* hesitancy of his approach to the problem of the Constituent Assembly —which he made up for, and very greatly, by his boldness in practice.

The Bolshevik Party and the socialist parties

Linear *schemata* are the most alluring. Here is one example. In their thirst for power, the Bolsheviks, almost as soon as they had become masters of the situation, proceeded to eliminate their political opponents. Dealing first of all with the Constitutional-Democrats,* they

---

* The Constitutional-Democratic Party was banned on December 1st, 1917. Its papers continued to appear, though not without difficulty, until the summer of 1918 (Carr, Vol. I, p. 169).

then turned to suppress the socialist parties. Totalitarian Leninism: that is the thesis which Leonard Schapiro sums up perfectly in his classic history of the Communist Party of the Soviet Union: 'The refusal to come to terms with the socialists and the dispersal of the Constituent Assembly led to the logical result that revolutionary terror would now be directed not only against traditional enemies, such as the bourgeoisie and right-wing opponents, but against anyone, be he socialist, worker or peasant, who opposed Bolshevik rule.'[111]

'The refusal to come to terms with the socialists.' This is how the writer summarizes an important episode of the Russian revolution—the attempt, on the morrow of the October insurrection and the establishment of Soviet power, to form a broad coalition socialist government, which would have prevented Communist monolithism from appearing and developing. The question is too heavy with implications not to be looked at carefully.

One observation must be made at the outset. The history of relations between the Bolsheviks and the moderate Socialist parties does not begin in October 1917. Even without going back to the pre-revolutionary period, it must be kept in mind that divergence between the Leninists, on the one hand, and the S.R.s and Mensheviks, on the other, marked the entire evolution of events in Russia between February and October 1917: it was a complete divergence, bringing the two camps into conflict on *all* the problems of the revolution, and, in the last analysis, on the fundamental question: was it or was it not necessary to trust the bourgeoisie, allowing that class to establish its authority and, indeed, encouraging it to do so? It was because the Bolsheviks and the moderate socialist parties disagreed on this vital point that the October rising took place *against* those parties, and because of this that they did not content themselves with holding aloof from it, but denounced it, and would have crushed it if their weakness had not been as great as their disapproval and anger. Hardly had the sovereignty of the soviets, as the source of state power, been proclaimed, during the night of October 25th–26th, 1917, than the Mensheviks and S.R.s refused to recognize it, and walked out of the All-Russia Congress of Soviets—most of them never to return.

It might be concluded that this refusal and this walk-out, confirming a disagreement that related to the very nature of the new régime, must make impossible any collaboration between parties that were thenceforth each other's adversaries, despite the similarity of their titles.

Was all possibility of a compromise between Bolsheviks and moderate socialists—moderate in their socialism but not at all, as we shall see, in their hatred of Bolshevism—finally ruled out from that moment, and with it the possibility of a coalition government? An initiative taken by the railwaymen's trade union brought the question up. On October 29th, this union issued an ultimatum which was mainly aimed at Lenin's Government. The railwaymen called for the formation of a coalition including all the parties represented in the soviets: if this did not take place, they would call a general railway strike throughout the country. That same day, the Bolshevik Central Committee (with Lenin absent) met to examine the railwaymen's 'proposal'. They decided to take part in the conference that was to be held to discuss the question of a coalition, and were all the better disposed to do this because, in the words of the resolution unanimously voted by those present, they considered it 'necessary to enlarge the basis of the Government'.[112] A delegation was nominated to carry on the negotiations: significantly, it consisted of three Right-wing Bolsheviks, Ryazanov, Sokolnikov and Kamenev. The two last-named spoke at the Central Committee meeting in favour of including *all* socialist groups in the future Government, even those of the extreme Right tendency.[113] Furthermore, the Bolshevik leaders decided to enlarge the Central Executive Committee of the Soviets by adding to it delegates from 'the parties which left the Congress', this to be done on a basis of proportional representation.[114]

On November 1st the negotiators reported to their colleagues on the Central Committee on how the 'coalition conference' was going. Kamenev, Sokolnikov and Ryazanov mentioned the demand made by the moderate socialists to have the Central Executive Committee of the soviets enlarged by adding a strong contingent of *bourgeois* representatives, members of the Municipal Councils of Petrograd and Moscow, a demand which called in question the *Soviet* character of the new régime. This move by the moderate socialists caused Lenin to take a hostile line towards the conference—and all the more so because the Bolshevik delegates reported another condition laid down by the S.R.s and Mensheviks: that on no account must Lenin or Trotsky be a member of the coalition.[115] He formally proposed that the negotiations be 'suspended'. This proposal, however, was rejected by ten votes to four, and the Bolshevik delegates accordingly continued their efforts to form a coalition government.

At the next day's meeting of the Central Committee Lenin won some ground. His motion challenging 'the opposition within the Central Committee' was passed by ten votes to five. This 'opposition', whose central figure was Kamenev, had shown its hand in the Central Executive Committee of the Congress of Soviets. Kamenev was chairman of this important body. Anticipating the course of the negotiations, he had proposed that the Council of People's Commissars resign and be replaced by a coalition government. He was supported by a strong contingent of leading Bolsheviks, including Nogin, a member of the Party's Central Committee and People's Commissar for Industry and Commerce, Rykov, also a member of the Central Committee, Milyutin, People's Commissar for Agriculture, and Teodorovich People's Commissar for Food—not to mention Zinoviev, once more allying himself with Kamenev.[116] The 'moderate' tendency was thus still strong among the Party's leaders. When Lenin put down a motion declaring that 'to yield to the ultimatums and threats of the minority in the soviets means finally rejecting not only Soviet power but democracy itself, for such concessions signify fear by the majority to make use of its majority,'[117] the discussion led to an indecisive battle. The first vote showed six for Lenin's motion and six against; the second vote showed seven for and seven against; a third vote had to be taken, from which Lenin emerged as the victor by one vote— eight for, seven against.[118]

Defeated, the minority decided to leave the Central Committee, raising the slogan: 'Long live the Government of the Soviet parties!'[119] This minority included one-third of the leadership: Kamenev, Zinoviev, Rykov, Nogin and Milyutin. Several People's Commissars also resigned from their posts, so great was their desire to find a basis of agreement with the moderate socialists. Although this hope of theirs was nothing extraordinary—for, as the American historian R. Daniels points out, at the time of the October insurrection the Bolsheviks as a whole had no notion of ruling the country alone,[120] and the Left Communists themselves, despite their habitual radicalism, were in favour of a coalition, provided that the Bolsheviks held a majority in it[121]—the stubbornness of their attitude was more so. The agreement they wanted would have been possible only if the mood of the Mensheviks and S.R.s had been similar to that of most of the Bolsheviks. The marriage of convenience that they wanted proved to be out of the question, however, because the Bolshevik suitors found themselves faced only with hostility, contempt and refusal to compromise.

Speaking in the name of his Party, a Socialist-Revolutionary declared: 'For us a government with Bolsheviks participating is unthinkable.'[122] And he went on to proclaim that 'the country will not forgive them the blood that has been shed.'[123] The Mensheviks endorsed this view. On the morning of October 30th, when the discussion was resumed, the representatives of the two moderate socialist parties put forward demands that might have been more appropriate coming from victors than from vanquished. The Bolsheviks must undertake to disarm the Red Guards and to allow Kerensky's troops to enter the capital without resistance! When, however, news was received of the defeat of the anti-Bolshevik rising of the officer-cadets in Petrograd, a section of the S.R.s—but not all of them—showed greater modesty. They said they were ready to contemplate the possibility of allowing a few Bolsheviks to participate in the

Government, as individuals—this tolerant attitude not extending, however, to either Trotsky or Lenin.*

Negotiations were resumed, on this basis, on November 1st, with Bolshevik delegates present who were still ready, as we have seen, to offer the most far-reaching concessions to their interlocutors. The S.R.s admitted that it was only their military setbacks that led them to take part in the work of the conference. Next day, however, the S.R.s and Mensheviks jointly announced their decision not merely to 'suspend' the talks but to put an end to them altogether. The American historian Radkey concludes in this connexion: 'The Socialist-Revolutionary Party at the outset had taken an intransigent stand, departing from it only under the spur of disaster and even then demanding that their adversaries come round by the back way to share in power the plenitude of which they already possessed.'[124] It is hard to conceive a greater lack of realism or more complete absurdity of conduct. In fact, however, the policy followed by the S.R.s and the Mensheviks during the coalition talks was laughable only in appearance. It corresponded to a logic that the same writer has summed up very well: 'In the last analysis it was the Bolshevik commitment to the Soviet form of government which wrecked the negotiations.'[125]

That was the root of the problem. Only a minority (even though a substantial one) of the Bolshevik leadership were ready to sacrifice *the Soviet régime* to the anti-Soviet attitude of the moderate socialists. The rest were unwilling to accept such a surrender, even though they were no less desirous of widening the composition of the Government. As for Lenin, he was neither more nor less uncompromising than most of his colleagues—merely more clear-sighted. That he was not intransigent or intent on monopolizing power for his own Party is shown by his efforts to bring the Left S.R.s into the Government.† It is elsewhere than in the abortive attempt to form a coalition between the Bolsheviks and their socialist opponents that we must seek for the origins of Communist monolithism.‡

Socialist-Revolutionaries, Mensheviks and anarchists

And so, apart from the brief period of collaboration between the

* On the attitude of the S.R.s and Mensheviks during the negotiations about a coalition, see especially Radkey, *Sickle*, pp. 65–72. L. Schapiro, for whom the absence of a coalition socialist government is an important factor in explaining the régime of terror applied by the Bolsheviks during the civil war, says nothing, in his history of the C.P.S.U. (B) about the negative attitude of the S.R.s and Mensheviks. He does, however, make a brief allusion to it in *Origin* (pp. 71–2).

† See p. 256.

‡ At a colloquium held at Cambridge, Mass., on the fiftieth anniversary of the Russian Revolution, two historians, Messrs Fainsod and Geyer, neither of whom has ever shown any tenderness towards the Communists, agreed in saying that the Bolsheviks 'ostensibly favoured a coalition of socialist parties and were forced to govern alone only because the other parties refused to co-operate' (Pipes, ed., *Revolutionary Russia*, p. 217).

Bolsheviks and the Left S.R.s,* the Leninists, often against their will, concentrated the whole of state power in their own hands, with no share held by other socialist parties. Furthermore, the new régime moved towards prohibition and suppression of these parties. This attitude on the part of the Bolsheviks towards their socialist opponents, as also towards the anarchists who in some circumstances acted as their allies,† seems, indeed, to show a culpable desire for power, a fatal tendency towards monolithism.

The case of *the Socialist-Revolutionaries* is at first sight the most disturbing, since Lenin had expressed concern to base himself on the majority of the population and needed, therefore, to obtain the support of the peasantry, whose political spokesman was, traditionally, the S.R. Party. In January 1918, addressing the Third All-Russia Congress of Soviets, Lenin said: 'In Russia only that power could last for any length of time that would be able to unite the working class and the majority of the peasants, all the working and exploited classes, in a single inseparably interconnected force fighting against the landowners and the bourgeoisie.'[126]

Compared with this consideration, others, based upon the revolutionary past of the S.R. Party, might appear trivial, especially as this past, made up of struggles that were often ineffectual, though always heroic, was remote from and unrelated to the social character and political orientation of the S.R.s as they actually were when the Bolsheviks took power. We have seen how they turned their backs on the Congress of Soviets. This decision was not due merely to the fact that, in October, they had lost their majority to the Bolsheviks. It was not just the majority in the soviets that they rejected, but *the Soviet régime itself*. In September 1917 the newspaper *Izvestiya*, which they controlled, had written that 'the useful life of the soviets is coming to an end', and, a month later: 'When the autocracy and the bureaucratic régime collapsed, we created the soviets as a sort of shelter in which democracy could seek temporary refuge. Now we are about to build a more suitable edifice to replace this shelter, and it is natural that the people should move to a more comfortable home.'[127]

It was not surprising that the S.R.s should have preferred, in the autumn of 1917, to the poverty of the Soviet 'temporary shelter', the comfort of new premises—those, no doubt, which they visualized the Constituent Assembly as occupying. Everything impelled them towards such a preference, starting with their social basis, which their principal and most scrupulous historian describes like this: 'The core of the Socialist-Revolutionary Party was the rural intelligentsia: the village scribes, the children of the priests, the employees of the *zemstvos* and co-operatives, and, above all, the village schoolteachers.'[128] These

* See pp. 256–7.
† See p. 197.

typically petty-bourgeois elements soon came, as the year 1917 wore on, to line up with the Constitutional-Democrats, who themselves had become converted to a conservative and even reactionary outlook. This was the reason why the S.R.s refused, between February and October, to support the demands that had figured in their own programme since the Party's foundation, and why they opposed, sometimes violently, the attempts made by the peasantry to divide up the large estates.

> The fact is that a large segment of the Populist [i.e., S.R.] intelligentsia had become Kadets [Constitutional Democrats] without admitting it. They clung to the old S.R. label even though the old faith was gone ... The last thing wanted by these people who continued to call themselves Socialist Revolutionaries was a social revolution, for it would halt the war, jeopardize their status in life, and enrage the Kadets, to whom they looked up in worshipful admiration.[129]

In the Constituent Assembly their group was to represent 'one of the most conservative elements in Russian society'.[130] The S.R.s continued to be a peasants' party certainly, but, as E. H. Carr says, one that was concerned more specifically with the interests of the *well-to-do* peasants which they protected to the best of their ability during the distribution of land that followed the Bolsheviks' accession to power.[131]

This, then, was the Socialist-Revolutionary Party. Revolutionary before 1917, conservative between February and October, it showed itself to be counter-revolutionary from the very first days, even the first hours, of the Soviet régime. It was on October 26th, 1917, that the majority of the Central Committee of the S.R. Party resolved to undertake, forthwith, *armed* action against the Bolsheviks.* This decision, kept secret at the moment when it was taken, was made public at the Fourth Congress of the S.R. Party, held openly in Petrograd in December 1917. The carrying out of the plan was entrusted to the Party's most influential figure, Abraham Gotz, who had received more votes than anyone else in the election to the Party's central committee. It turned out very soon, however, that Gotz could not count on the S.R. activists in order to put his counter-revolutionary plan into effect. He therefore turned, first, to the Cossacks stationed in the capital, and then, when they refused to commit themselves, to the training schools of the 'junkers', the officer-cadets, who were well-known for their conservative loyalties. The cadets accepted the assurances of the monarchist Purishkevich, with whom Gotz had made a pact that was doubtless decisive in rendering armed action possible. This was the background of the rising of the officer-cadets

---

* My account of the counter-revolutionary activity of the S.R.s in the aftermath of the Bolsheviks' seizure of power is mainly based on Radkey, *Sickle*, pp. 18–39.

which disturbed the calm of Petrograd on October 29th, and which the Red Guards put down without much difficulty. Faced with this defeat, several of the S.R. leaders made their way to the front, to join forces with elements of the Army which they expected to launch an offensive against the Bolsheviks in the immediate future. The former Minister for Agriculture, Chernov, who was regarded as more to the Left than to the Right among the S.R.s, was there already, working hard to promote a speedy reconquest of the capital.[132]

I shall not trace in detail the counter-revolutionary activities of the S.R.s before and after the disssolution of the Constituent Assembly; but it is certain that the S.R.s were pioneers on the counter-revolutionary side in the launching of the civil war. In November 1917 their military commission planned to kidnap Lenin and Trotsky, entrusting this scheme to a group of officers.[133] And if the demonstration in support of the Constituent Assembly which they organized in January 1918 in the streets of Petrograd was peaceful, this was not because the S.R.s had wanted it to be an unarmed one, but merely because they had not been able to obtain arms. The plan originally conceived by the Party's leaders envisaged, on the contrary, a violent attempt to bring down the Soviet Government: 'For weeks all preparations had been made with this end in view. But by the new year it was evident that a strictly military coup could not succeed.'[134]

After the dissolution of the Constituent Assembly, the S.R.s decided to supplement their methods of action with a weapon taken from their Party's old traditions: that of individual terrorism. In the spring they hatched a plot to assassinate Lenin.[135] In June 1918 one of their men killed the Bolshevik leader Volodarsky, and, a month later, another killed Uritsky, also an important figure in the Government camp.[136] Altogether, in the civil war that ravaged the country from July onwards, the S.R.s played a very prominent role. Already in May, at their Eighth Conference, they had resolved 'to overthrow the Bolshevik dictatorship and to establish a government based on universal suffrage and willing to accept Allied assistance in the war against Germany'.[137] The S.R.s took part on a large scale in all the anti-Bolshevik governments that were set up in Russia, often predominating in them. They took part in such governments even when these proclaimed and carried out a clearly reactionary programme. This was the case, for example, with the 'Provisional All-Russia Government' formed in the autumn of 1918, whose programme was 'to develop the productive forces of the country with the help of private Russian and foreign capital, and to stimulate private initiative and enterprise'.[138]

What was left of the socialist and revolutionary past of this organization, in which its old leader Chernov, despite his hatred of the Bolsheviks, 'was horrified by the progress made by the monarchists and by the weakness of the moderate ones among us in consenting to a coalition

with the antidemocratic forces'?[139] This conversion of numerous S.R.s
to monarchism was nothing new in the autumn of 1918. Jacques
Sadoul, in a letter sent from Moscow in April of that year, summed
up in these words what had emerged from his talks with S.R. leaders:
'Without so far admitting it publicly, many of them affirm, in private
conversation, the need for a restoration of the monarchy.'[140]

It is true that a change took place in February 1919, after months of
civil war, in the attitude of certain S.R.s in Moscow and in Samara,
where they had participated in an anti-Communist Government. They
decided to seek a *rapprochement* with the Soviet régime: but their
party's Ninth Conference, held secretly in the capital, replied by denouncing these 'conciliators', who thereupon left the S.R. Party.[141]
Meanwhile, the Bolsheviks had responded to this turn on the part of a
minority of the S.R.s by re-legalizing their Party, which they had
banned in June 1918.* This gesture of toleration was to remain without
a future, however, for the waverings and hesitations of a few individual
S.R.s, amid the tumult of civil war, did nothing to alter the basic fact
that, in the conflict between classes that preceded and followed the
October revolution, the S.R. Party chose the banner of counter-
revolution, and fought for it with all the violence that was typical of
the period. The 'intolerance' the Bolsheviks showed in relation to the
S.R.s was a reply to this decisive choice made by the latter. The case
of the *Mensheviks* differs considerably from that of their S.R. allies.
They were no less anti-Bolshevik than the S.R.s but their opposition
had necessarily to take other forms, owing to their weakness and also
to the very nature of their Party.

At the moment when Soviet power was established, the Mensheviks
looked quite discredited. A party of the towns, the election results
showed that they had lost all their popularity there. A working-class
party, they had lost the support among the proletariat that they had
enjoyed in the first months following the February revolution. In
October 1917 the Mensheviks seemed to be a political formation
without any social basis. A grouping that included some eloquent
politicians and brilliant intellectuals, they seemed, in their almost
pathetic weakness, like ghosts from a world that had passed away.
Besides this weakness, which contrasted with the still firm roots possessed by the S.R.s in the countryside, another point of difference
between the S.R.s and the Mensheviks was the political character of
the latter. In many ways their Party was a grouping of genuine
moderates. Their long dispute with the Bolsheviks, since the foundation
of Russian Social-Democracy, testified to their caution and concern
for legality. After having shown, before the February revolution, that
they were very timid revolutionaries, they had proved between
February and October that they were mediocre politicians. Their defeat

* See p. 248.

was so absolute that they seemed to have no future at all before them. However, they were to discover and display in adversity that energy in which they had been so sadly lacking during their brief period in power.

During the negotiations organized by the railwaymen's union with a view to the forming of a coalition government, the Menshevik representative began by declaring that the only language appropriate for talking to the Bolsheviks was that of guns.[142] Since, however, the art of war had never been the Mensheviks' strong point, they agreed to sit down at the conference table. When the S.R.s decided to terminate the negotiations most of the Mensheviks concurred. Martov, who since his return to Russia in May 1917 had led the Left wing of the Party, and disagreed profoundly with its Right-wing leadership, condemned this attitude.

In December 1917, at an extraordinary congress of the Menshevik Party which was publicly convened in Petrograd, Martov and his group strengthened their position at the expense of the Right tendency led by Lieber. Whereas the latter called on his comrades to join in a 'fighting alliance of all anti-Bolshevik forces', Martov, after demonstrating that this extreme view was held by a minority only, secured approval for his own viewpoint, one which was so hedged about with qualifications as to amount almost to a mere muddle: approval, subject to reservations, of participation in the soviets was accompanied by a statement of loyalty to the Constituent Assembly.[143] Martov explained that it was impossible to join the anti-Communist camp, since that would mean a complete break with the working class, 'now under the sway of utopias and illusions', i.e., of Bolshevism.[144] His comrade Dan acknowledged, more prosaically, that since the attempt to overthrow the Bolsheviks 'by force of arms' had 'failed', it was now necessary to take up 'the position of conciliation'.[145]

During the winter of 1917–18 and the spring of 1918 the Mensheviks reappeared in the Central Executive Committeee of the Soviets, where they formed a very small group—half a dozen out of nearly 350 delegates. Their speakers also took part in the discussions at the All-Russia Congresses of Soviets, and on all such occasions Martov denounced with remarkable vigour the policy being followed by the Bolshevik Government. The Menshevik opposition was far from being a tame and respectful one.

The Menshevik newspapers, which continued to be published openly, even though under difficult conditions,* also attacked various aspects of Communist policy. They reproved the Soviet Government for employing officers of the Tsarist Army in the Red Army, and also the

* As had happened with the Bolshevik press after the 'July days' of 1917, the Menshevik papers were often obliged, in order to continue to appear despite measures banning or suspending them, to change their titles.

first attempts made to subject the working class to labour discipline.* In the spring of 1918 this Menshevik press was quite important, including daily papers as well as periodicals.[146] It gave support to the Party's candidates when they put themselves forward for election to the soviets—and they succeeded in getting substantial votes as the country's economic difficulties intensified. In Tambov, for instance, the Mensheviks even managed to win the majority in the town Soviet.[147] In other cases they declined to take part in elections, or were prevented from doing so by the Bolsheviks.[148]

In May 1918 the Menshevik Party held a new conference—officially and openly—at which they condemned the Allied intervention in Russia (a step to the Left) but also confirmed their devotion to the Constituent Assembly (a step to the Right).[149] The majority of the Party, except for a conservative wing which supported the counter-revolution, increasingly gave the impression of trying, in the civil war that was beginning, to remain above the battle and retain a certain neutrality. Thus, when, at the end of May, the Czechoslovak Legion in Russia, which was being transferred to the Western Front in order to continue fighting Germany, became involved in an armed clash with the Bolsheviks, the Mensheviks, on being asked by trade unionists among the railwaymen what attitude they should take up, advised them to stay neutral. When this advice was felt to be too vague, the Menshevik Central Committee explained that the neutral attitude to be maintained should be 'friendly to the Czechs and hostile to the Bolsheviks'.[150]

Whatever the difficulties experienced by Martov and his friends in deciding on a coherent policy that could rally the support of all the different tendencies among the Mensheviks, the Soviet Government took a decision of major importance in relation to them and to the S.R.s. On June 14th, 1918, a decree was issued expelling the representatives of these two parties from the All-Russia Congress of Soviets and from its Central Executive Committee, and calling on all local and regional soviets to follow this example. Communist monolithism, favoured by the 'waiting' policy of the Mensheviks and provoked by the frankly counter-revolutionary conduct of the S.R.s, had taken a decisive step forward.

After the summer of 1918, with the rapid development of the civil war, the Mensheviks found it very hard to form themselves into a comparatively homogeneous group. A series of divergences appeared among them which it was not easy to reconcile, and which their traditional lack of organization and discipline prevented them from overcoming. There were the minorities at the two extremes. One of these, led by Lieber, stood for armed struggle against the Bolsheviks,

* Carr, Vol. II, p. 111; Deutscher, *Prophet Armed*, pp. 409–10. On the labour policy of the Bolsheviks, see p. 336.

and in some cases actually participated in this struggle.[151] The Party's central committee expelled those members who took an active part in the counter-revolution, but this decision seems neither to have been applied to all the Mensheviks concerned nor to have been made effective, since the counter-revolutionary Mensheviks in outlying parts of the country continued to regard themselves as members and representatives of the Party. On the extreme Left was another minority, which advocated and practised *rapprochement* with the Soviet Government and even with the Communist Party.[152] In the centre, the majority of the Central Committee gathered around Martov, who recovered, after 1917, the stature as a leader that he had lost in the pre-October period.

Martov's attitude towards the Soviet Government, and by implication that of the majority of the Mensheviks, has been described by a perceptive and well-disposed biographer as 'semi-loyal'.[153] Paradoxically, it was after the Party had been banned that their leader drew closer to the Communist régime. His attitude, and that of his Party, during the civil-war period, were defined at a conference held by the Menshevik Central Committee in Moscow during five days in October 1918. By the final resolution the Menshevik leaders undertook to support Lenin's government in so far as it was defending the gains of the revolution, but to oppose its policy of immediate socialization, the dictatorship of the Bolshevik Party and the exercise of terror. This conversion was subject, however, to reservations so subtle that it is uncertain whether everyone concerned was capable of grasping what they implied. Thus, the conference stated that the Party was 'obliged to take the Soviet régime as point of departure in its struggle, accepting it as reality and not as a principle', while at the same time remaining faithful to 'the idea of popular sovereignty, universal suffrage and the Constituent Assembly'. The resolution expressed the hope that the situation would evolve in such a way as to make possible in the near future resumption of the struggle for the Constituent Assembly.[154]

Despite its subtlety and contradictoriness, this document, when made public, produced a good impression on the Bolshevik leaders, and they were not long in responding to it. On November 30th a decree of the C.E.C. of the Soviets — actually, of the Government — announced the 're-legalization' of the Menshevik Party. It was at this period — *but only at this period* — that the Menshevik Central Committee 'definitively' separated itself from the Party's extreme Right element, who were still actively participating in the counter-revolution.[155]

In 1919, especially in the second half of that year, the Mensheviks were thus able to make their appearance once more in the soviets, even though in small numbers only, and to defend their ideas, even though with very limited resources. As a constitutional opposition, they developed their policy in three directions: defence of 'Soviet legality' and struggle against the Red Terror; demands for measures of economic liberalization; and support for the restoration of independent trade unions and the rights of the working class. On economic matters the Mensheviks called in July 1919 for a relaxation of 'War Communism'. In a pamphlet which was circulated openly, which they had been encouraged to produce by an important Bolshevik, the economist Larin, and which they had the happy idea of entitling *What Is To Be Done?* the Mensheviks argued for a series of measures of liberalization that constituted an anticipation of the New Economic Policy.[156]

The Mensheviks chiefly made their mark, however, during 1919 and 1920, by their defence of the rights of labour and the independence of the trade unions. The comparatively strong position they held before 1918 in certain trade-union organizations and their concern to maintain this position in face of pressure and coercion which, in many instances, emanated from the new rulers, account for their policy of defence of the trade unions, which was accompanied by a striving to safeguard the working class from a worsening of its standard of living — both being concerns that accorded with the traditional Menshevik line. Undoubtedly, as a result of the Government's increasing unpopularity, and the loosening of revolutionary tension as the civil war drew towards its close, the Mensheviks recovered a certain basis among the workers. This was reflected in the gains they made in some elections to the soviets. In 1920, for example, they won 46 seats in the Moscow Soviet, 205 in that of Kharkov, 120 in Yekaterinoslav, and 50 in Tula.[157] They had an official headquarters in Moscow and published several papers legally, and at public meetings Menshevik speakers sometimes took the floor to oppose the representatives of the Bolshevik Party.[158]

At the same time, the spirit of toleration shown by the Communists must not be exaggerated. Even during the time when the Mensheviks were legal their freedom was highly precarious and subject to vexations, discriminations and methods of intimidation, in the form of arrests for brief periods.[159] Nevertheless, in the words of Martov's biographer, 'outright repressions, arrests and expulsions from Soviets were the exception rather than the rule.'[160] This toleration, with occasional lapses, was subjected to a severe test in May 1920, when Menshevik trade unionists organized a meeting in honour of a delegation from the British trade unions which was visiting Moscow. The speeches made at this meeting were critical, of course, of the Government's policy. That was in order; but what was perhaps not, and certainly looked like an act of provocation, was that the organizers of the meeting allowed their platform to be used by the S.R. leader Chernov, that veteran leader of the counter-revolution, who was wanted by the police.[161] The authorities took a month to react to this, but when they did, they reacted with vigour, arresting many Mensheviks, especially those active in the trade unions. It will be noted that this repression coincided with the Polish invasion and the renewal of the civil war, events which, in general, had a disastrous effect on the attempts to revive Soviet democracy.*

Even so, it was not until the winter of 1920–21 that the Menshevik Party was suppressed in a systematic way. The Communists' decision to do this was doubtless partly due to the important role played by their opponents in the agitation and wave of strikes that occurred in February 1921 in Petrograd, immediately before the outbreak of the Kronstadt revolt. But although this activity on the part of some Mensheviks was bound to anger and even alarm the Government, it was not the chief cause of the hardened attitude of the Communist Party. The leaders of the latter, with Lenin at their head, were made aware at that moment of how isolated they were and how precarious was their power.† In the catastrophic circumstances, both economic and political, that governed the repression of the Kronstadt revolt and the introduction of the N.E.P., they resolved to allow no more opposition from outside the Communist Party, and also to restrict it considerably inside the Party. The Mensheviks were neither the only nor the principal victims of these events, but they signified their doom, and a few weeks of systematic suppression proved enough to delete them permanently from the political map of Soviet Russia.

While, in principle, coexistence between the Leninists, as Marxists, and the *anarchists*, as anti-Marxists, was subject to serious obstacles, the evolution undergone by the Bolsheviks, and especially by their leader, during 1917, had brought about the *rapprochement* between them which has already been mentioned.‡ How would the relations thus established develop once the Bolshevik Party had come to power and thus embodied in the eyes of the anarchists the principle and reality of that state authority which they rejected, root and branch? It is unfortunately hard to give a clear picture of these relations, so far as essential matters are concerned, owing to the variety of tendencies and trends among the anarchists, which were sometimes so widely divergent that it is meaningless to call them all by the same name.

Besides the Anarcho-Syndicalists and the Anarcho-Communists, themselves by no means homogeneous in either case, there were other varieties, such as the Anarcho-Universalists, as well as a whole series of individual anarchists who are difficult to classify. On the fringe, anarchism was diluted in ephemeral, informal groupings which,

* See p. 231.
† See p. 310.
‡ See p. 279.

though not highly political, were animated, no less than the relatively organized anarchists, if not by the doctrine then at least by the philosophy, or general outlook, of 'libertarianism'. Victor Serge, who, because of his own political origins and despite having joined the Bolsheviks, kept up quite friendly relations with the anarchists, explains that 'in this environment of famine, the sincere demagogy of the libertarian propagandists was well received by the backward elements of the populace ... The anarchists themselves admitted that suspicious elements, adventurers, common criminals and counter-revolutionaries, were thriving among them, but their libertarian principles did not permit them to refuse entrance to their organizations to any man, or to subject anyone to real control.'*[162] So anarchical a situation was not one to facilitate making the distinction the Bolsheviks claimed to observe between 'ideological' anarchists and others.[163]

In addition to these fundamental differences in principles and ways of life there was another cleavage among the anarchists, caused by the special circumstances of the time and the place, separating the pro-Soviet ones from the anti-Soviet ones. The former wanted to collaborate with the new régime, if only because they saw it as a lesser evil. As for the anti-Soviet anarchists, they displayed more verbal vigour—and not only the verbal kind, as we shall see—than subtlety, calling upon the people, for example, to rise in revolt against the 'social-vampires'—i.e., of course, the Bolsheviks—who 'are drinking your blood' and alleging that 'the Bolsheviks have become monarchists'.[164] Finally, in addition to the pro-Soviet and the anti-Soviet anarchists, there were those anarchists who wanted to wage a struggle on two fronts at once.

At first, while there were some anarchists who proclaimed the necessity of preparing for 'a third and last stage of the revolution',[165] there were others who looked with sympathy on the Bolsheviks' policy regarding workers' control, and also on the Bolsheviks' attitude towards the Constituent Assembly, which they loathed as the embodiment of parliamentary democracy. The anarchists were able, in any case, to gain strength until the moment came, in April 1918, when the Government decided to launch a large-scale attack on their headquarters in Moscow, following an incident in which it was difficult to distinguish between political anarchism and the anarchism of adventurers.[166] Blood was shed, and several hundred anarchists, described by the authorities as 'criminal elements', were arrested (about a quarter being immediately released).[167] This action was received with disapproval by some Bolsheviks, who felt reluctant to suppress the anarchists who had helped 'in our hour of revolution'.[168]

---

* Serge, *Year One*, p. 214. A prominent anarchist, Alexander Gay (Ghe), admitted to Jacques Sadoul that monarchist elements had joined the libertarian movement (Sadoul, p. 296).

The Moscow events caused a number of libertarians to leave the capital for the Ukraine, which became, in a sense, the stronghold of anarchism. Even in Moscow, however, during the civil war, a fairly substantial residue of anarchists remained. According to Victor Serge, they constituted an appreciable force there in the autumn of 1918, and were planning to start an armed rising against the Soviet power.[169] While there were many pro-Soviet anarchists who co-operated with the Bolsheviks, others engaged in acts of revolt of various kinds. Some anarchists took part in the rising in Moscow in July 1918 led by the Left S.R.s,* and in September 1919, helped by S.R.s, they blew up the headquarters of the Moscow Communist Party while an important meeting was in progress, causing the death of twelve members of the local Bolshevik Committee. Over fifty people were wounded, including Bukharin.[170] On the other hand, when Yudenich's counter-revolutionary forces approached Petrograd, one month after the explosion in Moscow, some anarchists, who must have belonged to a different tendency, enlisted in the workers' forces that undertook the defence of the city.[171]

It was in the Ukraine, however, that the most important conflict took place between Communists and anarchists. Relations between the two groups included phases of precarious collaboration, based on their common hatred of the 'White' forces, which were especially strong in the Ukraine, and also phases of violent antagonism, caused by the desire for independence on the part of Nestor Makhno's forces and the determination of the Red Army command to impose upon these anarchists its own authority, which tended, in the Ukraine as everywhere else, towards centralism. The to-ings and fro-ings of the bloody struggle cannot be described here, any more than we can here examine the claim that the 'Makhnovists' revealed at certain moments in the Ukraine a 'capacity for organization' that Victor Serge confirms.[172] Their antipathy to all political parties and the fact that they banned these wherever they established their power—a ban which applied indiscriminately to both Bolshevik and non-Bolshevik organizations—did not facilitate their dealings with the Communist Government. The latter was, in any case, not at all disposed to tolerate the existence of a 'counter-authority' in the Ukraine. In November 1920 the Red Army brutally smashed what remained of Makhno's forces, putting a bloodstained close to an episode of the Russian revolution that still awaits its real historian.†

That cannot be said of the drama of Kronstadt, which the American historian of Russian anarchism, Paul Avrich, has analysed in a book in

---

* See p. 257.

† I have based my account of the struggle between Bolsheviks and anarchists in the Ukraine, for want of anything better, on the books by Arshinov and Voline, supplemented by facts taken from Avrich, *Anarchists*.

which sympathy for the cause of the rebel sailors does not interfere with either the rigour of the account given or the lucidity of the analysis made.[173] The merits of this work are not slight, since the field is one in which, to an unusual degree, passionate feelings have distorted the argument. Even today, more than fifty years after the event, Communists of various allegiances, Trotskyites of different schools, and anarchists of all colours and shades clash over Kronstadt, in controversies that are rarely conducted with honesty, are often rowdy and are always absolutely useless, as the Leninists (of both the 'Communist' and the 'Trotskyist' kind) endeavour to dodge the real problems, while the 'anarchists' fail to present them in other than emotional terms. All that can be done here is to offer a very brief and summary account, relying mainly on Avrich's book.

The attitude taken up by the Communist Government towards the Kronstadt rising cannot be understood unless the event is placed in its context. At the moment of the rising the Government's situation was really disastrous. Addressing the Tenth Congress of the Communist Party while the rising was in progress, Lenin described thus the condition of the essential, if not the only, social basis of the Soviet régime: 'our proletariat has been largely declassed' owing to the 'terrible crises'[174] and 'extreme want and hardship'.[175] In the same period he described the working class as 'uncommonly weary, exhausted and strained', adding that 'never has its suffering been so great and acute'.[176] The state of the countryside caused Lenin even more anxiety. 'The crisis in peasant farming,' he warned, 'is coming to a head.'[177]

There were, indeed, 50,000 peasants in open revolt in Tambov province alone, and in the Ukraine nearly thirty partisan detachments, some of them over a thousand strong, were operating against the Soviet power.[178] The big strikes that had broken out in Petrograd at the end of February (and, shortly before that, in Moscow itself) showed that the industrial workers were not immune to the current unrest. Finally, on the international plane the situation was far from reassuring: peace had not yet been signed with Poland, and the forces of the 'White' General Wrangel, amounting to some tens of thousands, though defeated and obliged to leave Russian soil, were still not far away, standing ready to resume the civil war should opportunity arise.

Does this mean that no other means but force was open to the Moscow Government in order to deal with the rising? This cannot be said. The Communist representatives sent to Kronstadt to restore order behaved with clumsiness and arrogance, inflaming angry feelings rather than calming them down. Was this because they felt themselves to be in a hostile and alien setting? The bulk of the Kronstadt sailors were certainly not what they had been at the time when they formed the spearhead of the revolution. Their social composition was markedly more 'peasant' than in 1917.[179] This was, indeed, why the sailors at the naval base were particularly concerned about the misery in the rural areas. As for their state of mind, this was more than ever marked by anarchistic inclinations—reluctance to submit to any authority, desire for freedom and independence, what the Bolshevik Dybenko, who knew the sailors well, having long been one himself, called their 'eternally rebellious spirit'.[180]

The uneasiness felt by the Communists is thus easily explained. Nevertheless, the charges they levelled against the rebels, whom they presented as counter-revolutionaries linked with, or manipulated by, the Mensheviks, the S.R.s and the émigré 'Whites', had little connexion with reality. The Mensheviks, constituting an opposition that was still legal, or semi-legal, refused to endorse the revolt.[181] The S.R.s, in the person of Chernov, offered the rebels their services, but these were declined for the time being at any rate.[182] As for the counter-revolutionary émigré circles, they did, it is true, prepare to launch an operation directed at the Kronstadt naval base, control of which they saw as invaluable, even indispensable, if they were to be in a position to rekindle the civil war: but there is nothing to show that the Kronstadt sailors took any part in these preparations, or that they even knew about them. After the suppression of the revolt, however, the 'Provisional Revolutionary Committee' of Kronstadt, or what was left of it, did make an agreement with the Paris 'Whites',* and its principal figure, the sailor Petrichenko, worked actively for their 'Russian National Centre' in the spring of 1921, carrying on counter-revolutionary activities on their behalf in Petrograd.[183]

What is essential is the programme of the rebellion and its ideology. The Kronstadt programme† consisted of a set of political demands supplemented by some economic ones. The rebels wanted, above all, restoration of liberties, an end to the monopoly of power held by the Communists, restoration of all rights to the anarchists, the 'Left Socialist Parties' and the trade unions, and fresh elections, by secret ballot. Freedom of enterprise should, they declared, be given back to the peasants and craftsmen.

We shall not describe the course of the battle between the Communist troops and the rebel sailors, a plebeian force in which officers played no part but which had been joined by quite a few Bolsheviks. It was a hard fight with heavy losses on both sides. The subsequent repression was severe.‡ In the last analysis we must ask ourselves, like

* On relations between Kronstadt and the émigrés, see Avrich, *Kronstadt*, pp. 106–23.
† Given in full by Avrich, *Kronstadt*, pp. 73–4.
‡ The Communists shot some of their prisoners, even several months after the end of the revolt, and many of the Kronstadt men were sent to detention camps, where they encountered relatives of theirs who had been arrested as hostages (Avrich, *Kronstadt*, pp. 211–15).

Paul Avrich: 'What government would long tolerate a mutinous navy at its most strategic base, a base which its enemies coveted as a stepping-stone for a new invasion?'[184]

The dramatic quality of 'Kronstadt' does not lie in the repression that followed it so much as in its political significance. The Soviet Government had found itself compelled to act against men who were only asking for application of the principles on which that government had based its authority, and this was happening after the close of a civil war that the Soviet Government had won. It amounted to 'defeat in victory'. Discouragement and bitterness were sown among those anarchists in Russia who, in spite of everything, had still clung to the hope of possible collaboration with the Communists.*

The *Left Socialist-Revolutionaries* offer the interesting peculiarity that they were the only party to have collaborated in government with the Bolshevik Party. The revolutionary wing within the S.R. Party did not actually secede from it until after the October Revolution. After the seizure of power the Bolsheviks invited them to enter the Council of People's Commissars.[185] Lenin showed 'surprising patience'[186] with them, offering three portfolios, including the vital one of Agriculture, but was rebuffed. When the Bolshevik People's Commissar of Agriculture, Milyutin, resigned as a result of his dispute with the Central Committee on the question of coalition,† Lenin approached the Left S.R.s again, but without any better success.[187] Eventually, however, on December 12th, 1917, agreement was reached, the Left S.R.s receiving seven People's Commissariats as against the eleven held by the Bolsheviks, and a Left S.R. being appointed deputy-head of the Cheka.

During the three months that they remained in the Government, the Left S.R.s, whose social basis was mainly the middle peasantry,[188] and whose political tendencies were somewhat akin to syndicalism, especially as regards their hostility to centralism, strove mainly to exert a moderating influence on their Bolshevik partners.[189] They were reluctant to use violent methods to combat counter-revolution.[190] The immediate cause of their departure from the Government was the signing of the peace treaty of Brest-Litovsk, to which they were, as a whole, strongly opposed. Efforts were made to overcome this divergence, which was not entirely a question of a split between Bolsheviks and Left S.R.s, since the Bolsheviks themselves were divided on the issue.‡ On February 23rd, 1918, at the crucial moment in the discussion on whether or not to sign the treaty, the Bolshevik and Left S.R.

---

* When he heard the sound of the cannonade that heralded the Bolshevik onslaught against Kronstadt, the American anarchist Alexander Berkman, an active supporter of the line of collaboration with the Communists, murmured: 'Something has died within me' (Berkman, p. 303). That was true not only of him.

† See p. 241.

‡ See p. 287.

groups in the Central Executive Committee of the Soviets held a joint meeting to seek a compromise. It is interesting to note that the anarchist members of the C.E.C. were also invited to this meeting.[191]

After their 'ministers' had resigned, the Left S.R.s continued for some time to maintain relatively friendly relations, or at any rate to continue certain forms of co-operation, with the Bolsheviks. Their representatives still sat as members of the commissions of the C.E.C. engaged in drawing up a draft of a new constitution, to supervise the 'land committees' in a number of provinces,[192] and to occupy important posts in the Cheka.[193] Alongside these overt forms of co-operation were others, more discreet, such as the organization of struggle against the German occupying forces in the Ukraine.[194] What destroyed all possibilities of agreement or compromise between the two parties was the Government's agrarian policy, especially the setting-up of the 'Committees of Poor Peasants' and the dispatch of workers' detachments into the countryside for the purpose of requisitioning foodstuffs. These measures aroused opposition not only among the kulaks but also among the middle peasants, who were the chief clientele of the Left S.R.s. The latter protested vigorously against these measures, but got no satisfaction, and this caused the final and complete break with the Bolsheviks.[195]

As true revolutionaries, the heirs and successors of the terrorist tradition of the Narodnaya Volya, the Left S.R.s expressed their opposition with the utmost violence. In July 1918 they assassinated Count Mirbach, the German Ambassador, in the hope of restarting the war between Russia and Germany, and at the same time launched in the streets of the capital a revolt against their erstwhile allies. They too had gone over to the camp of counter-revolution, and, in this direction as in so many others, all chance of co-operation between Bolsheviks and non-Bolsheviks was finally ended.*

Leninism and the opposition

If we consider what is understood today by the 'Soviet model', at least in the field of political institutions, we observe that it signifies, very largely, the one-party system. The most innovatory, or most revisionist, wing of the Communist world (the confusion of these terms having become practically inextricable in the Stalinist and post-Stalinist imbroglio) may contemplate, in its bolder moods, a revision of the concept of the single Party, redefining its role and functions in

---

* It should here be noted that, unlike what had happened in June 1918 with the Mensheviks and Right S.R.s, the Left S.R.s were not excluded as a party from the soviets in July. Even at that stage a relatively substantial section of them declared for continued co-operation with the Bolsheviks. The Left S.R.s were also spared by the wave of Red Terror that swept over Moscow in September (see p. 314). However, their political role became quite insignificant (Schapiro, *Origin*, pp. 123–6).

9

society. Never, though, does it question, in the countries where the Communists are in power, the idea, which has indeed become sacrosanct, that state power must be identified with, or at least based upon, a political organization that knows no rival. This concept of the single Party occupies such a place in the 'Soviet model', and the latter has been so easily identified with the political and institutional realization of Leninism, that it is essential to analyse with some care the historical factors that governed the emergence and consolidation, in the Soviet Russia of Lenin's time, of the single Party, the sole wielder of political power.

Faced with the situation created by the civil war directed against the bourgeoisie, which had been ousted not only from power but also, to a large extent, from political life itself as a result of the dictatorship of the proletariat, and faced with the counter-revolutionary attitude adopted by some of the socialist parties and the refusal, at first practically unanimous, of these parties to accept the legitimacy of the Soviet régime, what solution did Lenin advocate? Did he, under the pressure of events, work out a theory of political power which affirmed the need for a single proletarian party? Certainly not – if only for the simple reason that, after taking power, Lenin proved incapable, in an almost physical, material sense, of conceiving any theoretical system at all. In default of any Leninist doctrine inspired by the lonely exercise of power, we can only note that, in his writings and speeches before the revolution, Lenin had never suggested anything remotely resembling a single-Party system – and then proceed to study what he said, wrote and did in the period subsequent to October 1917. Let us recall, in this connexion, that we have seen that he opposed the entry of the Mensheviks and Right S.R.s into the Soviet Government *after* they had – not content with displaying all through 1917 their pusillanimity and inclination to side with the bourgeoisie – refused to recognize the sovereignty of the soviets, and that, in contrast to this, he showed himself anxious to add to the Bolshevik team of People's Commissars representatives of the Left S.R.s who, despite reservations, *had* accepted the new state.

It is true that monolithism does not consist only, or mainly, in keeping one's political opponents in opposition, but also, and above all, in depriving them, first, of any right to express themselves, and eventually of all possibility of existence. Now, freedom of expression was allowed to the Right S.R. and Menshevik parties by the Soviet Government for several months. It vanished when these parties were banned, in June 1918, in circumstances that have already been explained. Until then the press of the socialist (or ex-socialist) opposition had been, at best tolerated, at worst (and most often) harassed, but certainly not muzzled or suppressed. Here are some relevant facts.

The Moscow anarchist paper *Burevestnik* wrote in April 1918: 'We have come to the limit! Bolsheviks having lost their senses have betrayed the proletariat and have attacked the anarchists. They have joined the Black Hundred generals, the counter-revolutionary bourgeoisie ... Our November is still ahead.'[196] The Left Menshevik paper *Novaya Zhizn*, edited by Maxim Gorky, published between October 1917 and its suppression in July 1918 a series of highly inflammatory articles which nevertheless did not bring down upon it the thunderbolts of the state. It denounced the 'vanity of Lenin's promises ... the extent of his madness,' and described the Council of People's Commissars as an 'autocracy of savages'. Furthermore, it said: 'Lenin and his acolytes think they have licence to commit every crime,' and, regarding Lenin himself: 'He is an incurable madman, signing decrees as head of the Russian Government instead of undergoing hydrotherapeutic treatment under the care of an experienced alienist.'[197] And *to the Right* of papers like this were the organs of the Right S.R.s and the 'orthodox' Mensheviks.

All the same, we do not find in Lenin any categorical statement (let alone any theoretical reflection) about 'freedom of the press', any more than about the question of the rights of parties, and certainly nothing about either the right of an opposition press to exist, or the negation of this right. Apart from incidental remarks, thrown off in the heat of debate and of a more or less polemical nature,[198] we chiefly have from his pen on this subject a 'draft resolution on freedom of the press' written barely a week after the taking of power and not published until long after Lenin's death. According to this document, 'For the workers' and peasants' government, freedom of the press means liberation of the press from capitalist oppression, and public ownership of paper mills and printing presses; equal right for public groups of a certain size (say, numbering 10,000) to a fair share of newsprint stocks and a corresponding quantity of printers' labour.'[199] For the present, Lenin demanded restrictions on the freedom of the bourgeois press, declaring before the C.E.C.: 'We cannot provide the bourgeoisie with an opportunity for slandering us.'[200] This attitude met with vigorous opposition among the Bolsheviks themselves, and when a prominent Party member, Larin, put down a motion criticizing the restrictions imposed by the Government on press freedom, the C.E.C., although dominated by Bolsheviks, rejected it by a majority of only two.[201]

Generally speaking, Lenin linked the problem of press freedom with that of political freedom in general, relating these freedoms to the situation in the civil war,* and adopting a class viewpoint on the whole question. ' "Liberties" and democracy *not* for all, but for the

---

* 'At moments when the country is in danger, when Kolchak [has] reached the Volga and Denikin Orel, there can be no freedoms,' said Lenin in September 1920 (Vol. 42, p. 209).

working and exploited masses, to emancipate them from exploitation.'[202] There was nothing in all this that implied systematic and final banning of the opposition *socialist* press. Although the measures taken by the Bolshevik rulers during the civil war were certainly dangerous in their severity and their pragmatic character, they cannot seriously be judged in isolation from their context and without extending our field of observation to include cases other than that of the Communist Government. If we look, for example, at German Social-Democracy, which was born and developed in a climate of great freedom of expression, and which had allowed the most diverse tendencies within it to exist and even to flourish, we are surprised to see that its leaders, when they found themselves in especially serious circumstances of political crisis, paid hardly more heed to 'freedom of the press' than did the Russian Communists. During the First World War, even before they came to power, Ebert and his colleagues of the German Party leadership deprived the Left tendency, by a veritable act of violence, of the papers that it had long been in control of.[203] Once installed in state power in November 1918, these same Social-Democratic leaders did their best, during the development of the revolutionary crisis, to prevent the Spartacist and Independent Left Socialist papers from being published.[204]

The case of the German revolution of November 1918 deserves attention from the angle of this problem of freedom of the press and its use in a revolutionary period. It illustrates, indeed, the disastrous consequences for the socialist cause that can result from the existence of the big *de facto* press monopoly enjoyed by the bourgeoisie and made use of by it in crisis situations, not to mention more normal ones. As Pierre Broué observes, in his book on the German revolution:

> After November [1918], thanks to the watchword of 'freedom of the press' put about by the Social-Democrats and the forces behind them, the supplying of information remained in the hands of the enemies of the working class. While the *Vossische Zeitung, Berliner Tageblatt, Kreuzzeitung* and the rest [the very papers that were to applaud the murder of Karl Liebknecht and Rosa Luxemburg, depicting this as the providential elimination of 'criminals pure and simple',[205] M.L.] continued to appear, backed by substantial funds, the revolutionary workers' organisations, which could count on nothing but the workers' contributions, were obliged to remain silent, or to express themselves only with very inadequate means, in face of the coalition that was crushing them ... It is easily appreciated that, under these conditions, almost the entire press ... joined in orchestrating a systematic campaign to discredit the Workers' and Soldiers' Councils.[206]

The measures of prohibition and intimidation adopted by the Bolsheviks, and recommended by Lenin, certainly do not provide a *solution* to the very real problem posed by freedom of the press in a revolutionary period. To represent them, however, as proof of a deliberate striving for totalitarianism is to close one's eyes to the reality of a revolution. This amounts to advising revolutionaries to answer the massive pressure exerted by the bourgeoisie (not to mention its violence) with the Franciscan virtues of renunciation, resignation and humility.

The press is only a vehicle of opinions and interests, the means of expression of organizations, notably of political bodies, and it is Lenin's attitude to the latter that is of fundamental interest in our present context. In this connexion Lenin's attitude to the anarchists constitutes a special case. E. H. Carr considers that 'from the time of *State and Revolution* onwards Lenin always showed a certain tenderness for anarchists'.[207]

Though Professor Carr's formulation is questionable, his opinion is basically quite justified. To be sure, reiterating his previously expressed views, Lenin declared in the spring of 1918, in *The Immediate Tasks of the Soviet Government*, that 'anarchism and anarcho-syndicalism are *bourgeois* trends ... irreconcilably opposed ... to socialism, proletarian dictatorship and communism,'[208] but this statement surprises us if we compare it with numerous indulgent, complaisant or even favourable references that he made to anarchists, if not to anarchism. In January 1918 he had already spoken of 'the new, fresh trend in anarchism [which] was definitely on the side of the Soviets'.[209] It was above all in August 1919, however, in a letter to Sylvia Pankhurst, that Lenin revealed his sympathy for a certain form of anarchism: 'Very many anarchist workers,' he wrote, 'are now becoming sincere supporters of Soviet power, and that being so, it proves them to be our best comrades and friends, the best of revolutionaries, who have been enemies of Marxism only through misunderstanding, or, more correctly, not through misunderstanding but because the official socialism prevailing in the epoch of the Second International (1889–1914) betrayed Marxism ... '[210] In *'Left-Wing' Communism, An Infantile Disorder*, Lenin, again referring to the attitude of the anarchists towards socialism before 1914 admitted that 'the anarchists rightly pointed to the opportunist views on the state prevalent among most of the socialist parties'.* Acknowledging that 'the old division' between socialists and anarchists had 'proved to be outdated', since 'the working-class movement in all countries followed

* Lenin, Vol. 31, p. 34. In his 'Theses on the Tasks of the Second Congress of the Communist International' Lenin was to mention again the 'perfectly legitimate hatred of the opportunism and reformism of the parties of the Second International' that was found among the anarchists before the First World War (ibid., Vol. 31, p. 201). On the anarchists and semi-anarchists in the Third International, see p. 397.

a new line, not the line of [either] the anarchists and [i.e., or] the
socialists, but one that could lead to the dictatorship of the proletariat'.[211] Lenin quite logically called upon the anarchist workers to
join the ranks of the Third International, even considering that 'the
measure in which genuinely Communist parties succeed in winning
mass proletarian elements, rather than intellectual and petty-bourgeois
elements, away from anarchism is a criterion of the success of those
parties'.[212]

This unconcealed sympathy towards anarchism, shown in a period
when clashes with other Marxist socialist trends were, on the contrary,
becoming sharper, did not, however, suffice to ensure relatively
harmonious co-operation between the Bolsheviks and the various
libertarian tendencies. This failure resulted from the variety of such
tendencies and the very pronounced contradictions that led some
anarchists to take up a certain position *within* the Soviet order while
others, as we have seen, opposed it violently. Faced with these divergences, Lenin could only make a distinction between the 'ideological'
anarchists and the rest.* Lasting co-operation between Communists
and anarchists was also hindered by the contrast between the strength
of the former and the comparative weakness of the latter. As has been
said, the Kronstadt revolt and its suppression was to draw a line of
blood between them. It is to be observed, however, that, even in
Kronstadt, the rebels showed a certain sympathy with Lenin, whereas
they felt violent hatred for Trotsky. After the revolt had been crushed,
when the Communists recovered possession of the base, they discovered, for instance, that in the offices the rebels had occupied,
though portraits of Trotsky had been torn down, those of Lenin had
been allowed to remain.[213] Lenin took the trouble, in September 1921,
to arrange for all the better-known anarchists who had not committed acts of violence against the state to be released from prison, on
condition that they left the country at once.[214] Moreover, Lenin met
Nestor Makhno, during the summer of 1918, and showed himself
conciliatory and even friendly towards him, saying that 'if only one-
third of the Anarchist-Communists were like you, we Communists
would be ready, under certain well-known conditions, to join with
them in working towards a free organization of producers'.†

No less significant is the fact that Lenin kept in touch with Kropotkin, although the latter had taken up a patriotic attitude during the
war and supported Russia's participation in that conflict alongside the
Entente countries. The two men met from time to time, and corresponded. Lenin showed 'considerable respect' for the great anarchist
leader. The latter said that 'our aims seem to be the same' but that

* See p. 252.
† Avrich, *Anarchists*, p. 211, quoting Makhno's own account of the meeting (*Pod
udarami kontr-revolyutsii* (*aprel'–iyun' 1918 g.*), Paris, 1936, pp. 126–35).

their methods differed greatly, and proposed that he supply Lenin with reports on the injustices committed by the Soviet authorities. Lenin agreed to this, and Kropotkin sent him such reports, until his death in February 1921.*

Let mention finally be made of a number of attempts that were pursued during the civil war to bring communists and anarchists together, with a view to complete legalization of the libertarian movement. Kamenev and Alfred Rosmer took part in these moves. The anarchists were called upon to check their ranks and carry out a purge of the unbalanced and uncontrollable elements that were so numerous among them, along with some actual counter-revolutionaries. As Victor Serge records, however, 'the majority of the anarchists gave a horrified refusal to this suggestion of organization and enrolment ... Rather than that, they would disappear, and have their press and premises taken off them.'[215]

Thus, whereas Lenin's attitude towards the anarchists, immediately after the October revolution and in the first years of the Soviet régime, showed more goodwill than sectarianism, his policy in relation to the moderate socialists was one of great sternness. Here we touch upon a question of major importance—whether it was possible for the Communists to coexist with a socialist opposition that accepted the essential foundations of the Soviet régime, as did the Mensheviks, in contrast to the S.R.s. That such coexistence would inevitably have been very difficult is obvious. The civil war and the exacerbation of relations between classes and parties was bound to cause a strengthening of the extremes and threaten to ruin any tendency favouring conciliation. This was what happened with the Mensheviks. That their heterogeneity, with the presence inside the complex Menshevik 'family' of trends that were Rightist and sometimes counter-revolutionary, made worse by a long tradition of toleration and indiscipline, must have intensified these difficulties is not to be denied. Lenin was not altogether wrong when he declared that 'there is *no* definite line of demarcation' between Rights and Lefts among the Mensheviks, and that, 'although they verbally "condemn" their "Rights", even the best of the Mensheviks and S.R.s, in spite of all they say, are actually *powerless* compared with them'.[216] It remains true, however, that he did nothing—quite the contrary—to overcome these difficulties, and

---

* Shub, p. 384. Kropotkin's funeral was the occasion of a great demonstration organized by Moscow's anarchists, some of whom were released from prison for twenty-four hours so as to be able to attend. Lenin himself is said to have proposed to Kropotkin's family that he be given a national funeral, but they declined. At the funeral Alfred Rosmer delivered a speech, in the name of the Executive Committee of the Third International, in which he avoided all polemical allusions—whereas the anarchist speakers did not miss the opportunity to attack the Government. Their addresses were printed and circulated legally, in 40,000 copies. The authorities transformed Kropotkin's house into a museum devoted to his memory (Schapiro, *Origin*, p. 187; Rosmer, *Lenin's Moscow*, pp. 97 ff; Avrich, *Anarchists*, pp. 227–8).

appears to have resigned himself to them rather easily, thus obliging the Mensheviks to play the role of a less and less tolerated opposition, and progressively eliminating them from all sectors of public life.

The Fifth All-Russia Congress of Soviets, in July 1918, was the last at which the opposition was present in strength. At the next Congress, held four months later, there were 933 Communist delegates out of the total of 950.[217] Although the Mensheviks had played no part in the rising of the Left S.R.s, they suffered for it as well—and along with them, Soviet democracy. The policy thereafter followed by Leninism in power towards the Mensheviks can be summed up as follows: total subordination to the requirements of the civil war; conviction that, in such a period, neutrality is out of the question; and treatment of Mensheviks and Right S.R.s as though they were the same. The first point corresponds to an unchallengeable logic which was affirmed by Lenin on numerous occasions.[218] In face of the exigencies of the struggle against the 'Whites', he said, the distinction between Left Mensheviks and Right Mensheviks inevitably became unimportant. 'Even supposing,' he said to the Central Trade-Union Council in April 1919, 'the Menshevik Central Committee is better than the Mensheviks in Tula who have been definitely exposed as fomentors of strikes—in fact I have no doubt some of the regular members of the Menshevik Committee are better—in a political struggle, when the White guards are trying to get us by the throat, is it possible to draw distinctions? ... In two years' time, perhaps, after we have beaten Kolchak, we shall examine this matter, but not now.'[219]

Moreover, in view of the gravity of the situation in which the Communist rulers found themselves, with the ephemeral but sometimes spectacular and apparently decisive advances made by the counter-revolutionary forces, Lenin refused to allow that there could be any neutrality in the conflict. 'He who is not for us is against us.'[220]

That, in these circumstances, the Bolshevik rulers should not have been greatly disposed to welcome the subtleties of the resolutions passed by the Mensheviks, and Martov's 'semi-loyalism', goes without saying.* But this did not prevent them from taking note of the turn made by the Mensheviks in October 1918, and hailing it as a positive act, since they agreed to 'regularize' the Party's position. Lenin considered that they should 'take into account and make use of the turn'.[221] He stressed that 'many of the slogans of this struggle [against the S.R.s and Mensheviks, M.L.] have now become frozen and petrified and prevent us from properly assessing and taking effective advantage of the new period, in which a change of front has begun among these democrats, a change in our direction'. And he concluded that 'it would be ... foolish ... to insist only on tactics of suppression and terror in relation to the petty-bourgeois democrats ... '[222] In December

* See p. 249.

1918 he reaffirmed: 'We must not now turn them [the Mensheviks] away, on the contrary, we must meet them halfway and give them a chance to work with us.'[223] This joint work had definite limits, however: Lenin was agreeable, at this moment, to maintaining 'good neighbourly relations' with Mensheviks, but he added immediately: 'We are quite willing to legalize you, Menshevik gentlemen,' though 'we reserve state power for ourselves, *and for ourselves alone.*'[224] There would be, so to speak, a division of labour between Mensheviks and Communists: the latter would hold power, while the former, assuming they collaborated loyally, would be assigned *practical tasks.**

Lenin never went any further than this towards conciliation with the Mensheviks, and soon resumed an extremely severe attitude towards their Party as a whole. His severity increased as the ending of the civil war revealed the ruined state of the country and the stark isolation of the Communist Party. In March 1919 he told the Eighth Party Congress that 'the Mensheviks are the worst enemies of socialism.'[225] In December of the same year, addressing the Congress of Soviets, he accused the Mensheviks of wanting to see a return to bourgeois democracy, and exclaimed: 'when we hear people who profess sympathy with us making such declarations we say to ourselves, "Yes, the terror and the Cheka are absolutely indispensable."'[226] This meant suggesting, at least, that the terror and the Cheka might be used against the Menshevik party. Above all, with the introduction of the New Economic Policy and the all-round political crisis nothing mattered any more but coercion, unity and discipline. Unity and discipline, as we shall see, for the Communists themselves,† and coercion for the Mensheviks. In and after 1922 Lenin frequently instructed his colleagues, especially in the People's Commissariat for Justice, to intensify repression against the Mensheviks,[227] calling on the Political Bureau to wage a 'relentless struggle against' what he called 'the most dangerous *de facto* accomplices of the White Guards,'[228] and recommending that 'the application of the death sentence should be extended (commutable to deportation) ... to all forms of activity by the Mensheviks, S.R.s and so on.'[229]

What accounts for the almost entirely negative, and occasionally terroristic, attitude taken up by Lenin towards the Mensheviks is the hostility, almost repulsion, that their principal activities inspired in him. He blamed them especially for their legalism and their condemnation of the use of terror when only ruthless struggle against reaction

---

* In March 1920 Lenin advised Kamenev how to deal with Martov and Dan, who had been elected to the Moscow Soviet: 'I think you should "wear them out" with *practical* assignments: Dan—*sanitary inspection*, Martov—control over *dining rooms*' (Vol. 44, p. 350).

† See p. 302.

9*

could save the régime,[230] and, more generally, their continual uncertainty—'the spineless vacillation bringing them to serve Kolchak'[231]—
the zigzags of an unstable and wavering policy which Lenin attributed
to the fundamentally petty-bourgeois character of the Mensheviks'
social basis.[232] More concretely, the Mensheviks exasperated Lenin
by their social agitation and their readiness to encourage the workers
to go on strike to protect their immediate interests.[233] The successes they
achieved in this field testified to a recovered popularity that made them
more dangerous than they had ever been since October 1917.[234] Their
activity, carried on during a phase of retreat and setbacks, threatened
to intensify the crisis of the régime. The weakness of the Communist
Party itself, a prey to its own divisions,* tipped the scale in favour of a
policy of force; and what was left of the Menshevik party was finally
liquidated.

What is most striking, however, in Lenin's attitude, and calls for
most severe criticism, is the 'amalgam' that he kept making between
the Mensheviks and the Right S.R.s.[235] Enough has been said on the
differences between these two parties for it to be unnecessary to prove
how deeply mistaken it was to treat them as being essentially the same.
It was understandable that he should say, in November 1920, that
'the Soviet régime would *most certainly* have been overthrown if
Mensheviks, reformists, petty-bourgeois democrats had remained in
our party, or even if they had remained in any considerable numbers
in the central Soviet bodies'.[236] But to eliminate them completely
from the public life of Soviet Russia and destroy them as a party was
fatal to Soviet democracy. This destruction of the Menshevik party was
indeed one of the worst symptoms of the malady from which this
democracy was suffering. It was doubly wrong and doubly unjust to
identify the Mensheviks with the S.R.s, who had degenerated politically into enemies of the revolution. The two parties had certainly
been closely associated in 1917. On the morrow of the October revolution, however, the S.R.s markedly intensified their conservative
tendencies, and got rid of their Left wing, so that they fell into the arms
of the counter-revolution. The Mensheviks, on the contrary, made a
turn to the Left shortly after the establishment of the Soviet régime,
reducing their former Right-wing leadership to minority status and
transforming the fiercely anti-Bolshevik element into a marginal
tendency in the party. This development brought the Mensheviks
closer to their Marxist origins and caused them gradually to resume
contact with the working class.

This *rapprochement* between Menshevism and the working class
took place during a period of ebb-tide in the revolution. Being in
many ways the opposite of Bolshevism, it was not possible for Menshevism to find a social basis and a certain degree of strength except in

* See p. 290.

a period of retreat and defeat, just as Bolshevism could advance only
in a period of workers' victories and revolutionary advance. The
corollary applies, also, that Menshevism found an echo, from 1920
onwards, only in a working class that had been largely de-classed and
was in any case weakened and demoralized. These circumstances
nevertheless do not alter the fact that the Menshevik movement, in so
far as its existence was tolerated, became once more the political
voice of a *working-class* reality. Yet Lenin, in an arbitrary way,
described Menshevism as something petty-bourgeois pure and simple.
In fact, with the limited means at their disposal, and despite the
precarious conditions in which they had to act, the Mensheviks strove
to undertake active defence of the workers' material conditions.
They were behind a number of strikes that occurred, including the very
big one in Petrograd shortly before the Kronstadt rising. Lenin considered that these strikes were against the interests of the proletarian
state.* Even so, during the great debate about the trade unions that
was held in the Communist Party† he admitted that the degree of
bureaucracy that prevailed in the régime justified a policy of pressure
by the workers' own organizations. The Mensheviks, while endeavouring to defend the poor remnants of trade-union independence that
still remained, came forward to take the place of the trade unions,
now enfeebled and much bureaucratized. Their old familiarity with
trade-union activity helped them to play this role. Lenin sometimes
denounced the demands raised by the Russian workers as evidence of
an egoistic attitude at a time when the Soviet power (or what was left
of it) could be saved only by sacrifice. Faced with the rising wave of
discontent, the reaction of the Communist leaders, headed by Lenin,
was often to denounce the petty-bourgeois mentality which had evidently not disappeared, and was still doing harm. However, this argument was facile and dangerous. The Leninist rulers, backs to the wall,
never made a serious attempt to introduce any mechanism of 'social
defence' apart from the institutions of repression that operated during
the civil war. They did not really permit the working class to develop
any autonomous activity in pursuit of its own demands. In this
sphere, Lenin opted for an authoritative and even authoritarian line.

There is, however, one reservation to be made, and it is a serious
one. Lenin never depicted what he considered to be a necessity as
being either a virtue or as a really lasting system. On the contrary,
some remarks of his—incidental, certainly—allow us to assume that
the existence of a plurality of parties accorded better with his political
plans. In March 1919, addressing the Party Congress, he said that
'for a long time these [petty-bourgeois, M.L.] parties are bound to take

* See p. 341.
† See p. 344.

one step forward and two steps back',[237] and appeared to be resigned
to this. Even more clearly, he acknowledged during the discussions at
the Tenth Congress of the Communist Party, in 1921, the congress
that placed restrictions on freedom within the Bolshevik organization,*
that 'the choice before us is not whether or not to allow these parties
to grow—they are inevitably engendered by petty-bourgeois economic
relations. The only choice before us, and a limited one at that, is
between the forms of concentration and co-ordination of these
parties' activities.'[238] The formulation is vague and far from satisfactory, but it certainly does not suggest a desire to eliminate the
opposition parties once for all. One cannot discern any totalitarian or
monolithic scheme here; nevertheless, what Leninism actually *did*
contributed to bring such a development about. It banned the legal
opposition constituted by the Menshevik party—an irreparable mistake which the tragic circumstances of the civil war explain, but which
the very principle of proletarian democracy puts beyond justification.

According to Pierre Broué, Lenin was thinking, during the final
weeks of his active life, of legalizing the Menshevik party. Unfortunately, however, he gives no source for this important claim.[239]
Victor Serge alleges categorically that 'in May 1922 Lenin and Kamenev
were considering the revival of some degree of press freedom',[240]
but also gives no authority for the statement. It would seem, on the
contrary, that Lenin was in favour of strengthening repression of the
Menshevik party. Did he perhaps—as a result of the illness that kept
him away from the exercise of state power, and gave him the opportunity to discover the latter's grave imperfections—become aware,
belatedly but clearly, of the defects of increasing monolithicity? Nothing
in Lenin's last writings gives grounds for claiming this—at least so
far as what has been published is concerned—despite the considerable interest and almost prophetic quality of some of these writings.
At most one may observe that in an instruction addressed to his
secretaries in February 1923 Lenin asked for information on 'the
present situation (the election campaign, the Mensheviks, suppression,
national discord).'[241] There is not enough here for the slightest conclusion to be drawn, and any assumption based upon it, in the present
state of our knowledge, is entirely conjectural and unwarranted. It
will be observed, nevertheless, that this note was written in the very
last weeks of Lenin's active life, when he was attempting a final assault
on some especially pernicious forms of political arbitrariness. To this
must be added certain facts regarding the relations between Martov
and Lenin and how these developed during Lenin's illness.

The relations between Lenin and Martov constitute a subject that
the historian and sociologist can study only with the help of the
psychologist. We know for certain that the Bolshevik leader felt for

* See p. 302.

his Menshevik rival a degree of admiration and of friendship that was unusual for him. As the struggle between factions and parties developed, however, Lenin had come to employ unrestrained verbal violence against Martov.* Even the internationalist attitude taken up by the latter during the war—'centrist' in character, to be sure—did not suffice to shelter him from attack after attack, and neither did his opposition to the conservative policy followed by the Menshevik leadership during 1917. When virulently attacked by Martov, Lenin replied with the crudest invective, calling his opponents a 'lackey of the bourgeoisie'[242] and 'a rogue',[243] accusing him of 'refined corruption', 'hypocrisy' and 'treachery' because he had said that the civil war was dividing the working class itself.[244]

And yet Lenin's incredibly hard attitude was compatible with some ambiguous feelings. Lunacharsky, writing in 1923 at a time when the expression of any sort of sympathy with Martov was not calculated to bring approval in Soviet Russia, said that in the spring of 1917 Lenin 'dreamed of an alliance with Martov'.[245] What is certain is that Lenin showed in his last years definite solicitude for his old opponent. In October 1921 Martov, suffering from the tuberculosis that was to kill him two years later, asked permission to leave Russia in order to attend the congress that the Independent Socialist Party of Germany was to hold at Halle, to decide whether or not to join the Third International. Although Martov intended to speak, in the name of the Mensheviks, against joining the Comintern, he was given his passport. The Communist Party's Political Bureau had favoured refusal, but Lenin's personal intervention had reversed their decision.[246] Martov never returned to Russia, but settled in Berlin, laid low by his illness. (In the winter of 1919–20 Lenin had sent him the best doctor obtainable in Moscow.) Martov's biographer relates, on the authority of the memoirs of Svidersky, a former People's Commissar for Agriculture, that during Lenin's last illness he showed an 'obsession to get together with Martov: paralysed and having lost his speech, Lenin would point at Martov's books on his shelves and demand that a driver take him to Martov'.[247] The testimony of Krupskaya is doubtless more reliable, though the freedom of expression she enjoyed after her husband's death was also more limited. She records that 'Vladimir Ilyich was already seriously ill when he said to me once sadly: "They say Martov is dying too"', and takes the opportunity to mention Lenin's warm attitude towards his old associate.[248]

This incursion into the history of personal relations is bound up with one of the most serious historical problems that Leninism presents, namely, Lenin's inability to allow the existence, alongside of his own Party, of an opposition group that might have checked or prevented the growth of monolithism. Professor Carr has depicted this growth

* See p. 60.

as something that was practically inevitable,[249] but such a view reflects, perhaps, a determinism that is excessively rigid. It is true that the possibility of coexistence between a revolutionary ruling power and a diversified and flexible structure that would enable a legal opposition to the Communist Party to express itself must be subject to very grave difficulties that an historian may confuse with irresistible fatality. But Lenin had shown on a number of occasions that he did not resign himself to any fatalities. If he had realized, between 1918 and 1922, the need for a proletarian democracy to preserve, as an essential constituent, the right of opposition, would he not have striven to overcome even those obstacles that were apparently most refractory? In the last analysis Victor Serge is right when he says that 'if the revolution is to be well served ... it must be constantly on guard against its own abuses, excesses, crimes and reactionary elements. It therefore has a vital need for criticism, opposition and civic courage on the part of those who carry it out.'[250] Actually, the complete suppression of Menshevism by the Leninist ruling power had *two* victims—Russian Social-Democracy, with its ambivalent nature (bourgeois-democratic in ideology, proletarian in its basis) and also Bolshevism itself, the vitality of which proved unable to resist the ravages of orthodoxy and monolithism.

Leninism and the nationalities

In addition to all the economic and social difficulties that Russian reality placed in the way of the building of a society that broke with the old capitalist world, there was one of another sort, namely, the problem of the nationalities. At the end of the nineteenth century the Tsarist empire, excluding Finland, had a population in which the strictly 'Russian', i.e., Great-Russian, element did not amount even to half, being only 44·3 per cent.[251] The heritage from the past was especially burdensome in this field. Relations between the Great-Russians and the other peoples suffered from the systematic policy of violence and oppression carried out by the autocracy. In solving the problems produced by the cohabitation of such a mixture of peoples, the Marxists could only draw upon the resources of an internationalism that naturally tended to play down the importance of national questions. Lenin, however, did not make this particular mistake.

His writings during the last years before the First World War reveal, on the contrary, increasing interest in the national question. Stimulated by the situation he discovered in Galicia, where he took up residence in 1912, as well as by the Balkan Wars, he entrusted Stalin with writing a little work on *Marxism and the National Question*, a task for which Stalin's Georgian origin may have seemed to make him particularly suitable. It does not appear that Lenin regarded Stalin's answers to the question to have been wholly satisfactory: in any case, he still thought it necessary to write a number of articles and pamphlets himself on the matter.

Lenin's teaching on this question was largely inspired by the general principles of democracy, proclaiming 'the right of nations to self-determination', and specifying that this right implied 'the right to secede'.[252] There were two comments to be made, however. Recognition of the right to secede did not mean that exercise of this right was always to be advocated. The advisability of secession was something that the Social-Democratic Party must decide 'exclusively on its merits in each particular case, in conformity with the interests of social development as a whole, and with the interests of the proletarian class struggle for socialism'.[253] Furthermore, 'the proletariat ... assesses any national demand, any national separation, *from the angle* of the workers' class struggle.'[254] As regards his own country, Lenin thought: 'it is this Great-Russian nationalist poison that is polluting the entire all-Russia political atmosphere'.[255] In order to remedy this situation he called for 'full equality of all nations and languages', with 'no compulsory official languages', 'no encroachment whatsoever upon the rights of a national minority', and 'wide regional autonomy'.* Finally, let us note this categorical statement of Lenin's: 'Can a nation be free if it oppresses other nations? It cannot.'[256]

The outbreak of the world war and the ravages of chauvinism among the socialists themselves had the effect of strengthening Lenin's internationalist convictions, together with his hatred of nationalist excesses. Already before the war he had noted the 'defect *common* to the socialists of the dominant nations (the English and the Russians): failure to understand their socialist duties towards the downtrodden nations'.[257] At the same time, while stressing the importance of national demands and national rights, Lenin reaffirmed their conditional nature: 'The several demands of democracy, including self-determination, are not an absolute, but only a *small part* of the general-democratic (now general-socialist) *world* movement. In individual concrete cases, the part may contradict the whole: if so, it must be rejected.'†

These were the principles which, in the difficult circumstances of

---

* Lenin, Vol. 19, p. 427. At the same time, Lenin opposed the federalist solution of the problem ('Marxists are, of course, opposed to federation and decentralization, for the simple reason that capitalism requires for its development the largest and most centralized possible states' [Vol. 20, p. 45]) and also the 'national-cultural autonomy' advocated by the Austrian Marxists, since this slogan '*joins* the proletarian and bourgeoisie of *one* nation and *keeps* the proletarians of *different* nations *apart*'. Social-Democrats, Lenin held, 'do not support "national culture" but *international* culture' (Vol. 19, p. 116).

† Ibid., Vol. 22, p. 341. Lenin gives this illustration of what he means: 'To be in favour of an all-European war merely for the sake of restoring Poland is to be a nationalist of the worst sort' (ibid., Vol. 22, p. 350).

1917 and then of the civil war, Lenin tried to put into effect, clashing, in this field as in so many others, with the different outlook of a number of other Bolsheviks. The Provisional Government had shown itself no more effective where the national question was concerned than in the fields of social reform or foreign policy. It had turned a deaf ear to the demands of the Ukrainians and Finns, and its liberalism towards Poland was due less to goodwill on the part of the ministers in Petrograd than to the German armies which had torn that country from the Russian empire. The failure was complete: as a representative of one of Russia's Eastern peoples put it, 'the February revolution had brought no changes.'*

The victory of the October insurrection entailed a complete break with this attitude based on Great-Russian nationalism. On November 2nd (15th), 1917, only a few days after the Bolsheviks' triumph, a 'Declaration of the Rights of the Peoples of Russia' proclaimed the right of nations to self-determination, including the right of secession.[258] Explaining this policy and answering critics, Lenin said: 'We are told that Russia will disintegrate and split up into separate republics but we have no reason to fear this. We have nothing to fear, whatever the number of independent republics. The important thing for us is not where the state border runs, but whether or not the working people of all nations remain allied in their struggle against the bourgeoisie, irrespective of nationality.'[259]

Such democratic arrangements were not enough, however, to solve the problem of relations between now-Bolshevik Russia and the non-Great-Russian nationalities. The case of Finland provides an example. That country's independence was immediately recognized by the People's Commissars, although a bourgeois and even anti-socialist government was in power there. A revolt of the Finnish workers, near neighbours of Petrograd, brought about a civil-war situation, with very soon the appearance of two opposing authorities, one bourgeois and the other proletarian. Soviet Russia could not but accord recognition to the latter, despite the Finnish bourgeoisie's protest against 'interference' which they treated as incompatible with the right of nations to self-determination. The intervention of German forces in support of the Finnish bourgeoisie and their suppression of the Finnish workers put an end to this ambiguous situation.[260] Conflict between classes had disturbed the application in a pure and simple way of the bourgeois-democratic principle of self-determination. This difficulty was confirmed and aggravated by what occurred in the Ukraine.

Ukrainian nationalism had borne an almost exclusively bourgeois and intellectual character before the revolution, and between Feb-

* Liebman, p. 222. For a brief review of the Provisional Government's record on the national question, see Liebman, pp. 221–2.

ruary and October 1917 the Rada (the Ukrainian Central Council) never demanded anything beyond autonomy in a decentralized Russia. As soon as the civil war began, however, the Rada showed partiality in the struggle between 'Reds' and 'Whites', the latter being helped while the former were subjected to systematic hostility, and workers armed by the Ukrainian soviets were attacked by the troops of the Rada. The Rada negotiated with a French military mission with a view to an agreement that caused the Bolsheviks concern. The worsening of relations between the nationalists of Kiev and the soviets, both Russian and Ukrainian, caused Stalin to propose an important amendment to the principle of self-determination. Addressing in January 1918 the Third All-Russia Congress of Soviets, he said that this principle ought to be interpreted 'as the right to self-determination not of the bourgeoisie but of the labouring masses of the given nation. The principle of self-determination should be a means in the struggle for socialism and should be subordinated to the principles of socialism.'[261]

Since nationalist Ukraine owed its precarious existence only to the protecting presence of German forces, and, after the armistice of November 1918, to that of French ones; since the Georgian Republic, proclaimed independent in May 1918, 'in a sense, had come into being on German initiative'[262] and accepted the protection, successively, of German and of British imperialism,* and since this tutelage from outside linked these non-Great-Russian nationalities with states that were intervening in Russia on behalf of the counter-revolution, it was inevitable that the entire 'nationalities policy' of the Soviet Government should be profoundly affected. It must be added that in a number of cases the demand for independence was more a reaction against Bolshevism than an expression of genuine nationalism. The Georgian Mensheviks, for example, had been opposed before the October revolution to the idea of independence for Georgia, and between February and October had ignored the affairs of their own little country, preferring to devote themselves to the problems of Russia as a whole, in the ministries and streets of Petrograd.[263]

The solving of the problem of the nationalities was further complicated, during the first years of the Soviet régime, by other considerations, related to the outlook of the Bolsheviks themselves. Lenin's principles had not been accepted without resistance by a number of his followers. Among some of these, and especially among the 'Left' Communists, the principle of national self-determination seemed a bourgeois demand and a diversion that would undermine the unity of the proletariat, to the advantage of the class enemy. Such men as Bukharin, Pyatakov and Radek were, in this matter, much closer to

---

* When the British troops withdrew from Georgia at the end of 1919 they did so against the wishes of the Government in Tbilisi (Pipes, *Formation*, p. 217).

Rosa Luxemburg than to Lenin. In her pamphlet on the Russian revolution, Rosa Luxemburg attacked the Bolshevik nationalities policy, as imposed by Lenin upon his Party, declaring that 'the Bolsheviks, by their hollow nationalistic phraseology concerning the "right of self-determination to the point of separation," have ... supplied the bourgeoisie in all border states with the finest, the most desirable pretext, the very banner of their counter-revolutionary efforts.'[264] Luxemburgism, in the sense of this critique, had many supporters among the Bolsheviks. When the People's Commissariat for the Affairs of the Nationalities was formed, on the morrow of the seizure of power, these 'Luxemburgists' seem to have been in the majority within it, while Lenin's viewpoint was shared, among the men at the top, by Stalin only.*

There were other reasons, too, for the centralist attitude of the Bolsheviks and their reluctant, or even hostile, reaction to the national demands of the 'nationalities'. In the areas dominated by Islam, in particular, there was the atheist outlook of the Bolsheviks, which the social conservatism of many of the Islamic religious authorities tended to strengthen. In these areas, formerly colonized by Tsardom, the Great-Russians were mostly townspeople, workers, rather than countryfolk, and they constituted—as a whole, and very relatively—a privileged element in relation to the natives. And it was for the most part among these socially and economically more advanced people that the Bolsheviks found support. They were not always able, in the Asiatic setting, to get rid of 'poor white' attitudes. In January 1922 the Party's Central Committee found it necessary to exhort the Communists of Turkestan to free themselves from any 'colonist deviation'.[265] Such a deviation was able in some cases to assume the more respectable form of a sort of paternalism, of which Lenin was critical. A leader of the Tatar Republic asked him: 'Is it right to say that the Communists of the formerly dominant nation, as having a higher level in every respect, should play the part of pedagogues and nurses to the Communists and all other working people of the formerly oppressed nationalities?' Lenin replied, by telegram: 'Not "pedagogues and nursemaids", but helpers.'[266]

Finally, there were all the factors in favour of unity and centralism that emerged either from the Bolsheviks' fundamental aim or from the circumstances of the civil war. A kind of cultural standardization developed which, in some cases, conflicted with the right of self-determination and, for instance, with the principle of equality between languages, as proclaimed by Lenin and the Party programme. It was all very well for the Party to pass resolutions to that effect; the

---

* Carr, Vol. I, pp. 278–9. This writer mentions that the official journal of the People's Commissariat in question published in June 1919 an editorial in which Rosa Luxemburg's ideas on the national question were warmly approved.

'principle' stumbled against realities that doctrinal discipline was not always able to suppress. During the Party Congress of 1923, Rakovsky mentioned 'the incident of a high Ukrainian official who, as he was leaving a congress at which he had voted for a resolution asserting the equal rights of the Ukrainian language, replied curtly to a question addressed to him in Ukrainian: "Speak to me in an intelligible language."'[267]

The existence of a mentality like this, in conjunction with sometimes unfavourable objective conditions, explains why the decentralizing projects of the Soviet power were regularly hindered by the ill-will of the Communists of the 'non-Russian' areas. It was against the centralist views of the local Bolsheviks that, for example, the Autonomous Soviet Socialist Republic of the Crimea was established in 1921.[268] A year earlier, the Communists of Kazan had tried to dissuade Lenin from setting up an Autonomous Tatar Republic.[269] The Communists of Bashkiria had similarly sought to prevent an autonomous régime being formed in their region,[270] and it was the Moscow Government that obliged the Soviet authorities in Turkestan both to form an autonomous republic and to adopt a policy of collaboration with the native peasantry.[271]

Lenin's conduct in all these circumstances was to urge upon his followers the virtues of patience, moderation and understanding. In a document prepared for the discussion of the new Party programme of 1919, he wrote: 'It is, therefore, necessary to exercise special caution in respect of national feelings and to ensure the pursuance of a policy of actual equality and freedom to secede so as to remove the grounds for this mistrust and achieve the close voluntary union of the Soviet republics of all nations.'[272] Addressing the Communists of the Ukraine, he said: 'Since the many centuries of oppression have given rise to nationalist tendencies among the backward sections of the population, Russian Communist Party members must exercise the greatest caution in respect of those tendencies ... ' He told them that they 'must in every way counteract attempts at Russification'. Furthermore, 'Steps must be taken immediately to ensure that in all Soviet institutions there are sufficient Ukrainian-speaking employees.'[273]

Lenin showed a similar attitude in connexion with the problem of relations between Soviet Russia and independent Georgia. Despite well-founded grievances against the Menshevik régime in that country, the Soviet Government recognized Georgian independence in May 1920. In February 1921, however, the Red Army occupied the country and put an end to this independence. The invasion of Georgia was decided on behind the backs of Lenin, Trotsky and the Political Bureau. Shortly before the invasion began Lenin had expressed his opposition to any such move. It was Stalin who overruled him.[274] Once the occupation of Georgia was a *fait accompli*, Lenin sought to mitigate the consequences of a policy that he regarded as harmful. Writing to Ordzhonikidze, who was in charge of 'Soviet Georgia', he said: 'It is of tremendous importance to devise an acceptable compromise for a bloc with Jordania [the former president of the Georgian Republic, M.L.] or similar Georgian Mensheviks, who before the uprising had not been absolutely opposed to the idea of Soviet power in Georgia on certain terms.'[275] In a telegram to the Soviet army of occupation he called on them to 'observe particular respect for the sovereign bodies of Georgia' and 'display particular attention and caution in regard to the Georgian population.'[276]

Later, when the brutal and chauvinist attitude of Stalin and Ordzhonikidze brought about a crisis between the Russian and Georgian Communists, Lenin intervened with desperate insistence on behalf of the latter. It was through this episode that Lenin, who, though already incapacitated by illness, hurled his last reserves of energy into the battle, became aware of the extent to which the policy of Russification had developed. It was then that he launched his last anathemas against 'that really Russian man, the Great-Russian chauvinist, in substance a rascal and a lover of violence', and wrote that disillusioned sentence: 'If matters had come to such a pass ... we can imagine what a mire we have got ourselves into.'*

Can we sum up as 'a mire' the 'national' achievements of the Communists during their first years in power? At the end of the civil war they had brought together in the Russian Socialist Federative Soviet Republic about a score of autonomous entities inhabited by non-Russian populations. They were also linked by bilateral treaties with a series of republics whose independence was doubtless more formal than real, since all the Soviet structures were in fact governed by the Party, which was one and undivided, rather than by state institutions. Drawing up a balance-sheet of the 'national' policy pursued during the first years of the Soviet régime, Isaac Deutscher wrote:

> None of these [Eastern Soviet] republics was or could be really independent; but all enjoyed a high degree of self-government and internal freedom; and, under the guidance of Stalin's Commissariat [of Nationalities], all tasted some of the benefits of modern civilisation. Amid all the material misery of that period, the Commissariat helped to set up thousands of schools in areas where only a few score had existed before. Schemes for the irrigation of arid land and for hydro-electrical development were initiated. Tartar became an official language on a par with Russian. Russians were forbidden to settle in the steppes of

* See p. 422.

Kirghizia, now reserved for the colonisation of native nomads. Progressive laws freed Asiatic women from patriarchal and tribal tyranny. All this work, of necessity carried out on a modest scale, set a pattern for future endeavours; and even in its modest beginnings there was an *élan* and an earnest concern for progress that captivated many an opponent of Bolshevism.[277]

Lenin's disappointment perhaps related not so much to the results obtained as to the hopes he had cherished, and the anxieties he felt for the future. The régime established by the October revolution 'guaranteed respect for the rights of the non-Russian groups remaining within the Soviet system' and 'encouraged their languages and culture and the development of their educational system'.[278] In so doing it revealed its tremendous possibilities, but also its wretchedly limited resources.

2

The Party

Role, structure and functioning

One of the most complex problems that the Bolshevik Party had to solve after its accession to power was that of the place it should occupy in the new state. The Party's activity had been entirely directed towards the conquest of state power, and it had never given any thought to how the proletarian state should be organized. There is nothing to show that Lenin ever thought of endowing the Party with any sort of political sovereignty. When the new régime was established, nothing had been foreseen, and everything remained to be decided. To begin with, there were great difficulties, not the least of these being the weakness of the Bolshevik Party's organization. In a pragmatic and improvising way, this had to be found some place among the new Soviet institutions. A member of the Petrograd Bolshevik Committee, Yevdokimov, observed, not long before the insurrection: 'We say: "All power to the proletariat and the poor peasantry." But how is this power to be conceived, concretely? We also say: "All power to the Soviets" ... Actually, it is not possible to decide in advance what organ will wield power.'[1] It is noteworthy that the Party was not even mentioned as a possible wielder of power by this important 'cadre', who was to become a member of the Central Committee.

In the early days of the Soviet régime, the place occupied by the Bolshevik organization in the state apparatus as a whole was governed by a factual consideration, namely, this organization's extreme weakness, both locally and, even more, at the centre. In the first few weeks the Military Revolutionary Committee formed by the Petrograd Soviet, which had been the chief organizer of the armed insurrection, enjoyed greater authority than the Party, and sometimes gave the impression of seeking to rival the Council of People's Commissars.[2] The M.R.C. disappeared fairly soon from the political scene; but the Party did not gain from its disappearance,[3] since it lacked the resources to do this. In Petrograd even, the Central Committee possessed only two politically responsible secretaries and an office staff of four. This apparatus grew very slowly: in 1919 it still numbered only about fifteen people.[4] The situation was no better at the local level, where the Party possessed practically no permanent apparatus.[5] Even in 1920, when the Party, as a whole, had begun to remedy this situation, the Bolshevik organization in the province of Smolensk, with its more than two million inhabitants, had only a flimsy administrative structure, with a single typist.[6]

This weakness of the apparatus, and especially of the Central apparatus, meant that there was a yawning gap between the Central Committee and the local and regional organizations of the Party. What a Party official in Saratov said in October 1917 was doubtless true of other parts of the country as well: 'Our party committee, which was closely following the approaching dénouement, impatiently awaited the guiding instructions promised by the Central Committee. Alas! None came.'[7] There was no improvement in this respect during the first year of the Soviet régime. According to official statistics, the Party's Central Committee received regular reports in March 1919 from only three provincial organizations out of thirty-six. Of the 219 *uyezd* committees, only 52 were in regular relations with the centre, which was completely ignorant of what was going on in nearly half of them.[8] Lenin, commenting on this state of affairs at the Eighth Congress of the Party, attributed it to 'our Russian lack of organizational ability ... in all its shameful wretchedness.'[9] At the local level, the situation was exploited in order to defy almost openly the instructions of the Central Committee when these did reach their destination. Thus, when the Smolensk province committee received an order to send cadres to Moscow in order to strengthen the Party's central apparatus, it refused to obey.[10] This was the period when, in the Soviet bodies as in those of the Party, 'localism flourished'.[11]

The Bolshevik Party's structural weakness at this period is all the more apparent if it be compared with the (relative) strength of the *state* organization. At the top the contrast is striking: whereas the Central Committee had a staff no larger than ten at its disposal, the Council of People's Commissars had as many as sixty-five, even though these were still insufficient.* The problem was one not merely of quantity, but also of quality: as Leonard Schapiro observes, the best of the Party cadres had been integrated in the apparatus, both central and local, of the soviets.[12] The Bolshevik organizations were financially dependent on the help given them by the local Soviet institutions: generally speaking, such dependence was complete.[13] It was even possible for prominent Bolsheviks, such as Preobrazhensky, to suggest that the Party should dissolve itself completely in the Soviet apparatus.[14] Most

---

* These figures, for February 1918, are given by Pietsch, p. 141.

of the Communists, however, did not resign themselves to this situation, and from 1919 onwards they began demanding that the Party be re-established in its rights.

This rectification was aided by the crisis in the Soviet institutions. As the popular basis of the new régime contracted, and Soviet democracy became more formal, the Party, which, thanks to its greater cohesion, put up a firmer resistance to the social and political difficulties of the time, strengthened its authority and corrected to its advantage the imbalance that had existed previously. It became all the more necessary to define what were the Party's functions and role inside the Soviet state.

The Eighth Party Congress, in March 1919, expressed a definite view on this subject. The Party, it considered, 'must win individual political sway in the soviets and effective control over all their activities'.[15] This aim was undoubtedly achieved quite soon, by way of the formation of Communist 'cells' throughout the institutional hierarchy and in all spheres of public life. These cells brought together, in accordance with the statutes adopted in 1919, all Party members working in the numberless institutions of Soviet society and subjected them to directives from the leadership to such effect that, faced with an atomized non-party mass, they acquired a discipline and homogeneity which ensured them positions of control and dominance.[16] The authority thus acquired led Zinoviev to declare in 1920 that 'every conscious worker must realize that the dictatorship of the working class can be realized only through the dictatorship of its vanguard, that is, through the Communist Party.'[17]

The whole problem of the relations between Party and state was governed by a phenomenon that everyone took note of, namely, the increasing *fusion* of the two types of apparatus. This caused Kamenev to say, in 1920: 'The Communist Party is the government of Russia. The country is ruled by the 600,000 Party members.'[18] It was the Political Bureau of the *Party* that, during the Eighth, Ninth and Tenth Congresses of *Soviets*, appointed the commissions charged with preparing the agenda for their proceedings,[19] and there was, in general, a very great overlapping in the leading personnel of Party and state institutions. At the Party Congress of 1919, two-thirds of the delegates held office in Soviet institutions.[20]

This being the case, the privileged and leading position that the Party occupied in the state called for a re-definition of its functions. It had, first and foremost, to carry on with the task it had begun before the revolution, namely, the *organization* and *education* of the working class.[21] It had, also, to concern itself with selecting the administrative personnel of the state. There was a special Party body charged with this work, the *Orgburo* (organization bureau),* which worked in

* See p. 282.

conjunction with a special department of the Central Committee, the *Uchraspred* (section for distribution of members). It was a very active body: between February 1920 and February 1921 more than 42,000 Party members were assigned to jobs by the Orgburo.[22] Lenin defined the chief functions of the Party in power as those of 'educator, organizer and leader',[23] entrusting it also with the task of ensuring political co-ordination of the various state institutions.[24] Before arriving at this view, Lenin had begun, however, by according a much more modest place to the Communist organization. In the first months of the new régime he had not departed from that silence about the role of the Party which was a feature of *State and Revolution*. In his writings of this period much was said about the masses and about the Soviet institutions, but the Party received only casual mention.

In August 1919, however, Lenin himself said that 'the dictatorship of the working class is being implemented by the Bolshevik Party'.[25] In '*Left-Wing*' *Communism* he confirmed that 'the class dictatorship' is exercised 'under the leadership of the party'.[26] The increasing identification between the state apparatus and that of the Party, together with the undivided domination exercised by the Party in the country's political and social life, helped to render the structure of power more monolithic.

In Lenin's view, this situation had unsatisfactory consequences. Speaking in 1922 at the Eleventh Party Congress (the last he attended), he said: 'the relations between the Party and the Soviet government bodies are not what they ought to be.' His analysis of this situation was very cursory, however, as were his proposals for remedying it. He merely suggested that 'the Party machinery ... be separated from the Soviet government machinery,' and said: 'We must raise the prestige of the Council of People's Commissars', in other words, of the state as compared with the Party.[27]

The resolutions that were passed in favour of separating state and Party powers nevertheless remained inoperative. Had they been put into effect they would perhaps have helped to establish in the proletarian régime a system of separation (and mutual checking) of powers which might have made the political structure as a whole more flexible. Some Communists had vaguely thought of bringing this about, it appears, at a moment when the dangers of the situation that was emerging were not yet evident. During the discussion that the Central Committee devoted to the signing of the treaty of Brest-Litovsk, Trotsky, replying to Bukharin, said that 'the state has been obliged to do something that the Party would not have done'.[28] In 1919 the Left Communists expressed a desire to stress the distinction between state and Party: the latter, it seemed to them, had a greater concern than the former with *internationalism*, in accordance with their own inclinations.[29] The Party ought, so to speak, to play the role of conscience to the Government and the state. This 'conscience' could make itself heard, and listened to, however, only if it possessed a certain degree of independence of the state, and also some mechanisms of control over the latter. Nothing of the sort came about, however. Concentration of power became total, since there was no real institutional counterweight.*

The Bolshevik Party's accession to power confirmed the principle of centralization that was fundamental to its functioning before the revolution, even though, in fact, the local organizations had long enjoyed wide autonomy. It was to remedy that *de facto* situation that the Party Congress of 1919 stressed the need for 'the strictest centralism and severest discipline' to prevail in the Party.[30] Whereas the state was given a federal structure, the Party remained 'one and indivisible', throughout all the Soviet republics. Furthermore, although the Bolshevik organization maintained the Party congress and the Central Committee, at least in principle, in their sovereign prerogatives, at the same time it set up, under pressure of necessity, a series of leading bodies, some of which were to acquire such substantial powers as to eclipse the theoretically sovereign organs.

The *Political Bureau* was created by a decision of the Eighth Party Congress, in March 1919. Its task was to 'take decisions on questions not permitting delay'. Consisting of five members, it was to report on its activities at the two-monthly meetings of the Central Committee, to which it was statutorily (but only statutorily) subject.[31] In fact its powers rapidly increased. At the Party Congress of 1920 Lenin noted that: 'the Political Bureau adopted decisions on all questions of foreign and domestic policy,'[32] adding that 'the Political Bureau [should] deal with policy.'[33]

While the *Orgburo* was to 'conduct the whole organizational work of the Party'[34] and in particular to concern itself with the selection, appointment and transfer of administrative, and especially political, cadres, the *Party Secretariat* (created, like the *Orgburo*, in 1919) was to become an organ of prime importance. It prepared the agenda for meetings of the Political Bureau, provided the latter with the documents required for its discussions, communicated its decisions to the local organizations, and also concerned itself with the appointment of personnel.[35] When Stalin took over the Party Secretariat in April 1922, as General Secretary, he obtained control of one of the organs which, if not among the most highly respected, was certainly one of the most influential in the entire Party organization. Finally, the Control Commissions, central and local, formation of which had been recommended by a national conference of the Party in 1920, were

---

* In 1928 it was to the identification of the Party with the state that Bukharin attributed the Stalinization of the régime (Deutscher, *Prophet Armed*, p. 336).

officially set up in 1921, at the insistence of the Workers' opposition which saw in them a means of fighting against the bureaucratization of the Party. No member of a local Party committee or of the Central Committee could be a member of one of these commissions, which were nominated by local and national Party congresses and not by the Committees. The Central Control Commission was the highest court of appeal for Party members expelled in the regular Party purges.*
This body soon became, however, an instrument in the hands of the General Secretary, and, about the same time, began to work regularly with the G.P.U., which in 1922 succeeded the Cheka as the chief repressive institution.†

The evolution of the powers and operation of the Party's two 'classical' organs, the Central Committee and the congress, reflects fairly closely that of the Party in general, and the degree of democracy that existed within it. *The Central Committee*, the sovereign Party body between congresses,‡ lived an exceptionally intense life in the first months following the capture of power. It was in this body that were discussed and decided the vital questions confronting the Bolshevik Party and the Soviet state, such as the question of a coalition government and, above all, that of the Brest-Litovsk peace. As regards the latter, the role played by the Central Committee was crucial. In the course of endless discussions, through passionate debates in which tendencies opposed each other without the least beating about the bush, and in which majorities were made and unmade in accordance with the weight of the arguments brought forward, and in an atmosphere of freedom of which the life of parties *in general* offers few examples, the Central Committee of the Bolshevik Party settled the fate of Soviet Russia. At that time the frequency of the Central Committee's meetings testified to its importance. For a period of a little over three months we have the minutes of sixteen of such meetings, the minutes of a number of other meetings held in this period not having survived. Subsequently, during the civil war, meetings of the Central Committee became less frequent. There were only six between April and July 1918, and between July and November 1918 the C.C. did not meet at all. This was complained about at the Congress of 1919. Later these meetings became more regular,§ witnessing to the authority that the C.C. still enjoyed.

* See p. 306.

† On the Control Commission, see Deutscher, *Stalin*, pp. 233–4; Carr, Vol. I, pp. 196 and 212; Schapiro, *Communist Party*, p. 260.

‡ As we have seen, before the revolution, Lenin declared that, in accordance with the principles of democratic centralism, the congress and the congress alone incarnated Party sovereignty (see p. 52). He did not voice this idea again.

§ Between April and October 1919 the C.C. met six times (as against 29 meetings of the Political Bureau and 110 of the Orgburo); between April 1920 and March 1921 the C.C. met 29 times (as against 66 meetings of the Political Bureau and 102 of the Orgburo) (Pietsch, p. 153).

The Party *Congresses*, which were held annually in accordance with the Party rules, and were complemented by frequent conferences, remained important for a long time, and did not really lose importance until after Lenin's death, when, retaining only their ceremonial character, they came to fulfil a merely ritual function. The Party Congress made very rare use, to be sure, of the sovereign power that it 'legally' possessed. Decisions were taken elsewhere, in the Central Committee and the Political Bureau. Nevertheless, since the Central Committee was elected by the congress, the influence of the latter continued to be effective until the Secretariat succeeded in filling it with delegates that it had itself chosen. That situation did not come about until after 1922 or even 1923.

Down to that time the Congresses of the Communist Party continued to live up to the best traditions of the socialist movement. There was open discussion and free criticism of the Party leadership, including Lenin himself; delegates challenged each other fearlessly, and the classical procedures of Party gatherings were followed— meetings of commissions and sub-commissions, presentation of majority and minority reports,* drawing-up of composite resolutions in which shrewd editorial subtleties and wise compromises endeavoured to reconcile majority and minority, forming of tactical alliances between different trends in the organization.

The atmosphere of freedom that reigned at these gatherings had lost none of its intensity when, at the last congress Lenin attended, in March–April 1922, Antonov-Ovseyenko attacked the Bolshevik leader, accusing him of encouraging the kulaks and showing too friendly a face to foreign capitalism. Stukov also challenged Lenin personally: 'We must give other comrades the possibility of speaking freely within the Party without threatening them with damnation for saying today what Lenin said yesterday.' Kosior followed up this attack, criticizing 'the rule of force, which has nothing in common with real discipline and which is practised among us'. Ryazanov, head of the Marx-Engels Institute and *enfant terrible* of the Party, an oppositionist *par excellence*, was applauded, and not only in a humorous spirit, when he said: 'The English Parliament can do anything except change a man into a woman. Our Central Committee is more powerful—it has already changed more than one extremely revolutionary man into [an old] woman, and the number of these [old] women has increased incredibly.'[36]

At the Twelfth Party Congress in 1923, the last one held in Lenin's lifetime, Zinoviev, who saw himself as the destined successor of the paralysed leader, opened the discussion in a style that was at that time unusual but had a great future before it. 'Every criticism of the Party line,' he declared, 'even a so-called "Left" criticism, is now

* See p. 296.

tion was a concept void of revolutionary content in the industrialized Europe of the twentieth century.* For this reason, these men, who belonged to the Left trend in the Bolshevik Party, and adhered on this question to the views of the extreme Left in European socialism, found themselves preaching—or at least encouraging, or tolerating—a policy of Russification of the non-Russian nationalities, whereas Lenin, when he opposed them, was accused of fostering petty-bourgeois nationalist forces. 'Right' and 'Left' here took on meanings that were highly ambiguous and confusing.

While the Bolshevik Party had a Right that did not show itself—or, in the person of Lenin, a Right that did show itself but was not really 'Right'—there was quite definitely a Left, or rather, various Lefts, successive embodiments of a constant will to 'revolutionize' even more thoroughly both Soviet society and the outside world. The first attack of these Lefts was launched in the domain of foreign policy, on the question of signing the treaty of Brest-Litovsk with the Central Powers. This was not accidental: a link between militant revolutionary zeal and fervent internationalism is, indeed, a 'constant' in modern politics.

That the great majority of the Communists should have reacted with anger and consternation to the draconian peace proposals put forward by the German and Austrian negotiators is not a matter for surprise, especially as the international strategy of Leninism was wholly based on the assumption that world revolution was inevitable and the Bolsheviks' duty to hasten its coming.† The first meeting held by the Party after the demands of the Central Powers had become known showed the trends that existed, and their respective degrees of strength. At a meeting in Petrograd on January 8th, 1918, three conflicting points of view were expressed. Lenin proposed that the Austro-German proposals be accepted, and his motion received fifteen votes. Trotsky spoke for his policy that became known as 'Neither war nor peace', and which consisted of refusing to sign any treaty with the imperialists of Berlin and Vienna while refraining from launching a revolutionary war against them: his motion received sixteen votes. Finally, Bukharin called for the launching of a revolutionary war, and was supported by thirty-two votes.[38] The 'Left Communist' trend was born. Its strength was confirmed in the weeks that followed this first test of opinion. Thus, the Petrograd Committee of the Party supported Bukharin's line unanimously, apart from one dissentient. Later, as the dispute became more heated and the moment of final

---

* This critique of Lenin's policy on the national question is set out in Rosa Luxemburg's famous pamphlet on the Russian revolution (in Chapter III of the edition by B. Wolfe
† See p. 359.

decision drew near, the executive of this committee confirmed its attitude, and even threatened the Central Committee with a split if the Government agreed to sign the 'shameful peace'.[39] The Moscow Committee of the Party adopted the same line.[40] This opposition was strong not only in the 'two capitals' but also in the provinces—even in Siberia, where the Communist authorities refused to be bound by the treaty of Brest-Litovsk.* It could count on a constellation of leaders of fame and talent, and it was strong not only in the Party but also in the state machine. The Supreme Council of the National Economy, for example, was controlled by 'Left Communists'.[41]

What were the arguments they used in defence of their standpoint? Bukharin, their chief spokesman, mentioned some considerations of internal policy. Anxious not to break the alliance with the Left S.R.s he demanded that the latter be allowed not to sign a peace treaty which they vehemently rejected. His co-thinker Uritsky claimed that if the Germans, carrying out their threat, were to advance deeply into Russia, they would provoke a vigorous popular reaction in the rural areas, where the people's 'instinct of self-preservation', thus sharply stimulated, would make possible reconstitution of the country's defence forces and the waging of a revolutionary war.[42] Above all, however, the Left Communist group based their attitude on the absolute priority that they accorded to the world revolution as against the Russian revolution, and their belief that to sign a peace treaty with the Austro-German imperialists would weaken the international struggle of the proletariat. They favoured risking the loss of what had already been won, for the sake of what existed only potentially—the world revolution.[43] Here was a symptom of their absolute devotion to principles which they regarded as fundamental, a purism that was among the principal characteristics of this trend and which ran all through their programme.

The latter covered the building of a new society in Russia as well as the Government's foreign policy. In general, the Left Communists were for as rapid an achievement of socialism as possible, through nationalization and workers' control.† They were violently hostile to the bourgeoisie, whose 'complete ruination' they called for,[44] and, showing indifference to the wishes of the peasantry, they demanded collectivization of farming.[45] Socialism was the cause of the industrial proletariat and it was on that class alone, on 'the creativity of the workers themselves', that reliance must be placed for building the new order.[46] They challenged the entire economic policy of the Government. They denounced the regulations regarding labour discipline and output, and regarded as scandalous the defence of Taylorism

---

* See p. 288.

† The entire platform of the Left Communists is given by Bunyan and Fisher, pp. 560–564: see also Dobb, p. 92.

and one-man management that Lenin was now making.* Every concession to the old world which they had supposed abolished seemed to them inadmissible—in particular, the giving of posts of responsibility to bourgeois 'specialists'.[47]

On the more strictly political plane, the Left Communists were in favour of a workers' democracy, which meant for them a wide degree of autonomy for the soviets and the creation of a proletarian army. Recourse to the employment of former Tsarist officers and the ending of election of officers in the Red Army made them indignant.[48] Finally, the winding-up of the debate about the peace of Brest-Litovsk did not reconcile them to the Government's foreign policy: according to them, or at least to Radek, one of their most prominent spokesmen, this was such as to imply that the Government had 'decided to renounce the policy of the attack on imperialism'.[49] For their part, they called for 'a fearless foreign policy which is based on class principles, which unites international revolutionary propaganda both in word and in deed, and which aims to establish organic connexion with international socialism (and not with the international bourgeoisie)'.[50] As one of them observed, the Left Communists revived a number of ideas that Lenin himself had formerly upheld: they could claim to be the true Leninists.[51]

The agitation organized by the Left Communists was intense, enough to shake the Party's unity to a serious degree. Nevertheless, a few months sufficed to calm the uproar. The Left Communist trend disappeared—but not as the result of any disciplinary or administrative measure. Its death was more or less a natural one: the outbreak of the German revolution put an end to the controversy about Brest-Litovsk and proved that Lenin's policy had not, after all, paralysed the efforts of the German proletariat, while the introduction of 'War Communism', as a result of the civil war, satisfied the 'Left' to some extent, since Russia now seemed to be advancing with giant strides towards socialism, or even to have achieved it.

Even during the civil war there were tensions inside the Party that were sufficiently strong to give rise to an opposition trend. The 'Military Opposition', which criticized the policy followed by the leadership, and by Trotsky in particular, in Army affairs, attacked this policy openly at the Party congress of 1919, and proved strong enough to extort concessions to its members, who, united by a common enmity to the Tsarist officers serving in the Red Army, were moved by contradictory feelings, partly democratic but partly corporatist in character.[52] However, the activity of this opposition was the exception rather than the rule: faced with the threat from the 'Whites', the Bolsheviks responded with a reflex in favour of unity which helped to give their party a homogeneity and strength that contrasted with the

* On Lenin's defence of 'state capitalism', see p. 337.

divisions in the counter-revolutionary camp. It was with the end of the civil war, when the country discovered how enormous was the destruction it had suffered, and the Government became aware of the immense disorder which prevailed, that the Communist Party lost its unity, and opposition trends reasserted themselves—and with what vigour! Besides the 'Ukrainian opposition', which rose up against the Russifying tendencies of the central authority and shared Lenin's helpless hostility to all forms of Great-Russian chauvinism,* there were two groupings which attracted large numbers of discontented Party members: the one called 'Democratic Centralism', and the 'Workers' Opposition'.

The Democratic Centralism group, which originated in 1919, did not really make itself felt until the Party congress of March 1920, but did so then with a forcefulness that was to mark it until the end of its brief life. This group was mainly 'intellectual' in character, which distinguished it from the 'Workers' Opposition', but it also sometimes managed to ally itself with trade-union leaders such as Tomsky.[53] Among its chief spokesmen we find important personages like Osinsky, who had been head of the State Bank and chairman of the Supreme Council of the National Economy; Bubnov, an alternate member of the Central Committee; Sapronov, who had been secretary to the C.E.C.; and (Vladimir) Smirnov, leader of the Bolshevik insurrection in Moscow. At the congress of March 1920 the 'Democratic Centralists' made numerous and lengthy contributions.[†] They protested against 'bureaucratic centralism' and 'authoritarian centralism', and warned the Party against the danger of a 'bureaucratic dictatorship'.[‡] The Democratic Centralists, whose demands were confined to the sphere of inner-Party democracy, and whose proposals for reform always remained vague, were active in the preparation and conduct of the Tenth Party Congress. There they once again spoke about the problems of Bolshevik democracy, but their role was eclipsed by that of the 'Workers' Opposition'.

Like the Democratic Centralism group, the Workers' Opposition was founded in 1919, but, unlike the former, the latter had a proletarian basis, being wholly rooted in the trade unions, which gave it substantial strength. This became apparent especially during the winter of 1920–21 when, during the extensive Party discussion of the trade-union question,§ the Workers' Opposition made its presence

---

* On the 'Ukrainian Opposition', see Daniels, *Conscience*, pp. 102 ff. On Lenin's attitude to the Ukrainian demand for autonomy, and, in general, to the non-Great-Russian nationalities, see pp. 270 ff.

† Osinsky's speech alone occupies seventeen pages in the official report of the proceedings (in Kool and Oberländer, pp. 141–57).

‡ Ibid., pp. 128–57, where extensive extracts are given from the speeches of the 'Democratic Centralists'.

§ See p. 343.

and cohesion felt, and registered notable successes. At the conference of the Moscow Party organization held in November 1920, nearly half the delegates (124 out of 278) declared their support for the theses of the Workers' Opposition. Feeling ran so high at this meeting that the Workers' Opposition organized a separate caucus to arrange how they would vote on resolutions and candidates.[54] The Workers' Opposition was also especially strong in Samara (where it dominated the Party), in the Ukraine, and, as regards the trade-union movement, in the metal-workers' organization.* Yet at the Tenth Party Congress, in March 1921, where the existence of this faction was to be one of the central issues, it had only 45 or 50 delegates out of the total 694.[55] During the preparations for the congress, the leadership had succeeded in rallying all its forces by appealing for Party unity. And if the representation of the opposition at this national gathering was less than proportional to its strength among the rank-and-file, that is a phenomenon encountered in the life of all political parties. On one point, however, the procedure followed in the Communist Party at that time contrasted favourably with the usual practice of political organizations, including those laying claim to the greatest internal democracy. The Party leadership undertook the publishing of the platform of the Workers' Opposition in its official organ, *Pravda*, and also issued in 250,000 copies a pamphlet in which Alexandra Kollontai (who, along with Shlyapnikov, led this group) set out its ideas.†

Kollontai took up in her pamphlet a sharply 'proletarian' attitude, coming forward, in the name of the Workers' Opposition, as spokeswoman of the demands of the working class. According to her, the Russian working class was playing an ever more limited role in the life of the country, because the Soviet Government, yielding to opportunism, was trying to reconcile the interests of all classes. For its part, the Workers' Opposition was interested exclusively in protecting the interests of the industrial workers. In taking this line it distinguished sharply between state, and even Party, institutions on the one hand, and trade-union institutions on the other, seeing in the latter the *only* valid interpreter of the ideas of the working class. A genuinely proletarian régime, as advocated by the Workers' Opposition, would therefore establish a dictatorship of the trade unions.

The weakness of the pamphlet lay in the absence of concrete ideas capable of leading to an improvement in the situation and the *rap-*

---

* Daniels, *Conscience*, p. 127. The Workers' Opposition was also well represented in the miners' union. In a discussion in the Communist group in this union the Workers' Opposition's theses received 61 votes, as against 137 for Lenin's and eight for Trotsky's (Lenin, Vol. 32, p. 535, note 20).

† Lenin, Vol. 32, p. 256. An English translation of Kollontai's pamphlet was published in London in 1921, by Dreadnought Publishers, under the title *The Workers' Opposition in Russia*. A German translation is included in Kool and Oberländer, pp. 182–240.

prochement that was so badly needed between the Bolshevik leadership and the Russian proletariat. Kollontai was merely content to assert her confidence in 'the collective creative efforts of the workers themselves'. Another, and fundamental weakness in the Workers' Opposition viewpoint was the contradiction between their aspirations and the actual possibilities of the moment. Kollontai acknowledged that the country was in a state of 'complete destruction and breakdown in the economic structure'. The proletariat was the principal victim of this state of affairs. As we shall see, the de-classing, demoralization and physical degradation of the working class put out of the question any political action based on mobilizing the working masses.

The Tenth Party Congress saw a systematic attack on the Workers' Opposition and all other opposition trends,* and the imposing of a ban on their existence as organized factions. The Workers' Opposition survived this measure for a short period. At the congress of 1922 Kollontai again spoke as leader of a Left-wing minority.[56] Shlyapnikov, too, continued his oppositional activity, but incurred, as we shall see, the wrath of the leadership, and came close to being expelled from the Party. Several of the leaders of the Workers' Opposition, who were joined in this approach by some other prominent activists, appealed in 1922 to the Communist International, setting forth their grievances regarding the repressive treatment to which they were subjected. They called on the International to bring about a return to democracy in the Russian Communist Party.† Needless to say, nothing could come of such an approach. The Comintern Executive did not question the legitimacy of the action taken by the 'twenty-two', or the existence of grounds for some of their statements, but advised them to submit to the discipline of their own party.

We must now consider how Lenin reacted to these challenges to his policy. In the early months of the Soviet régime, the controversy about Brest-Litovsk gave him occasion to level certain charges against the Left Communists which became constant features recurring throughout the dialogue between Lenin and the extremist elements — rebels and impatient persons of all kinds — that appeared in the Communist Party. The Left Communists, ferocious opponents of any sort of agreement or truce with imperialism, were guilty, in Lenin's view, of an intolerable romanticism. He said that theirs was the point of view of the Polish nobleman 'who, dying in a beautiful pose, sword in hand, said: "Peace is disgraceful, war is honourable",'[57] and in this way allowed themselves 'to be carried away by a "flash" slogan'.[58] The reproach was not groundless, if we are to judge by the

---

* See p. 302.
† The text of the 'Letter of the Twenty-Two', together with the Comintern's reply, are given in Humbert-Droz, pp. 48–50.

attitude of some of the most prominent leaders of the group in question—such as Alexandra Kollontai, in particular, who confided to Jacques Sadoul that 'it would be very fine to make a beautiful end, to die fighting. Yes, that should be the line: victory or death.'[59]

This romanticism found expression, almost inevitably, in a taste for 'the revolutionary phrase', which Lenin repeatedly denounced. He defined what he meant by 'the revolutionary phrase' as 'the repetition of revolutionary slogans irrespective of objective circumstances at a given turn of events',[60] the content of the 'phrase' consisting of 'sentiment, wishes, indignation and resentment'.[61] The mistakes of the Lefts caused them to be accused of 'objectively ... *helping* the imperialists to draw us into a snare'.[62] Lenin was not afraid to polemize against them, especially as he saw in Bukharin's tendency a grave danger against which 'relentless struggle'[63] must be waged: he, personally, would carry on 'ruthless war'[64] with it. He accused the Lefts of going to 'monstrous lengths of self-deception',[65] and of 'complete renunciation of Communism in practice,'[66] and referred to their journal, *Kommunist*, as 'pseudo-Left'.[67]

At the same time, however, and despite the liveliness of the dispute, Lenin acknowledged that he was 'nine-tenths in agreement' with Bukharin.[68] This is an important element in the debate between Lenin and the Left Communists which Soviet historians regularly ignore.* Lenin frequently stressed that, unlike the Left S.R.s and the Mensheviks, the Left Communists stood on common ground with him, the ground of revolutionary Marxism, and that this circumstance gave great interest to a discussion with them.[69] He did not fail to pay homage to them as men who were inspired by 'the best, the noblest and loftiest impulses'.[70] When their leaders resigned from the Central Committee, Lenin put down a motion at the Seventh Party Congress calling on the Left opposition to resume its place in the leadership,[71] and when he accused them of 'completely disloyal and impermissible violation of party discipline'[72] this was not because of the ideas they defended but because they stubbornly refused for some time to take their seats in the Central Committee.

Until the discussion about the trade unions, during the winter of 1920–21, and the development of the influential Workers' Opposition within the Party, Lenin showed no further interest in 'Left-Wing Communism' except as it made its appearance in the Communist International.† He then attacked its anti-parliamentarism (or, rather,

---

* For example, Ponomarev writes, in the official *History of the C.P.S.U.* (B) (p. 280): 'Lenin unmasked the "Left Communist" group as accomplices of the German imperialists and the Russian bourgeoisie.' In fact, Lenin never accused the Left Communists of any complicity with the enemy. Such complicity would have ruled out solidarity between the leadership and the oppositionists, solidarity that Lenin expressed on numerous occasions. Far from accusing them of being anybody's 'accomplices', Lenin blamed them for their 'utter naïveté' (Vol. 27, p. 325).

† See p. 398.

the form that this assumed) and its anti-trade-unionism. As for the Workers' Opposition in the Bolshevik Party itself, Lenin took up an attitude to this which in some ways resembled that which he had shown in relation to the Left Communists of 1918: sharp criticism, but at the same time a call for joint action and solidarity. Since the Brest-Litovsk period, however, times had changed. The 'deviation' of Bukharin and his friends had shown that the revolutionary movement was going through *a crisis of growth*, but this could not be said in 1920 and 1921. The debate with the Workers' Opposition therefore took place in a quite different climate, and Lenin hardly took the trouble to analyse the ideas of Kollontai, Shlyapnikov and their associates, but confined himself to depicting their programme as smelling of syndicalism and anarchism, or semi-anarchism.[73] Such a programme, said Lenin, constituted 'an obvious deviation from Communism and the Party'.[74] He explained why he brought such a charge against it: the Workers' Opposition sought to deprive the Party of important prerogatives, in particular as regards administrative appointments, and to transfer these to the trade unions.[75] Furthermore, whereas Lenin had shown himself both sharp and at the same time conciliatory in his treatment of the Left Communists of 1918, he made the Workers' Opposition the first victim of the anti-democratic regulations introduced into the Party at its Tenth Congress, in March 1921.

Even in this case, however, Lenin never depicted his opponents on the Left as enemies to be struck down or to be driven out of the Party. Not only did he call on them to work with him at the peak of the hierarchy, he explicitly endorsed certain points of their programme, especially the striving to proletarianize the cadres of Party and state. In November 1920, for example, while accusing the members of the Workers' Opposition of becoming an 'opposition for the sake of opposition', Lenin admitted, somewhat in contradiction to this, that 'the opposition which exists, not only in Moscow but throughout Russia, reveals many tendencies that are absolutely healthy, necessary and inevitable at a time of the Party's natural growth'.[76] Despite the heat of the dispute and the importance of the points at issue, Lenin remained bound to his opponents by a fundamental solidarity. Even in his book on *'Left-Wing' Communism, An Infantile Disorder*, he wrote that the principal danger facing the revolutionary movement was the old and evergreen danger of opportunism, in comparison with which 'the mistake of Left doctrinairism ... is at present a thousand times less dangerous and less significant'.[77] The struggle that Lenin often waged, after the conquest of power, against all these 'Leftists' was, and remained to the end, a struggle carried on with comrades who were in error, but were never seen as enemies. There were important disagreements on tactics involved, but, in the last analysis, all concerned in these disputes were engaged in one and the same fight.

In the Brest-Litovsk period, Lenin and the Left Communists had had in common an interest in preparing for a revolutionary war against imperialism.[78] In 1921 Lenin shared with the Workers' Opposition a desire to proletarianize Soviet society. The confrontation between Leninism and sundry variants of 'Leftism' retained the character of a *family* quarrel.

Freedom of tendencies and factions

If one means by inner-Party democracy something more than a mere formality, the requirements and conditions for its realization are many, unstable, precarious and sometimes contradictory. Crisis situations and great upheavals may favour such democracy by giving Party activists the chance to break with routine and shake up the leadership, forcing the latter both to question what had hitherto been taken for granted and to cast off its own inertia, all this leading to changes in the composition of the leadership. This was what happened in the Bolshevik Party in 1917. However, there can also be crises of a different sort, producing very different results. When the structures created by a movement of a deeply democratic nature become blocked in their working through events which, far from bringing about active participation in politics by the masses, are accompanied by stagnancy among the latter, then the very source of democracy dries up. Democracy ebbs away increasingly from the institution that it had enriched. Deprived of the energy of the masses, the parties so affected surrender to routine, authoritarianism and bureaucracy. The civil war that devastated Russia between 1918 and 1920, and the economic catastrophe it entailed, were events of this negative type. The internal democracy that had animated the Bolshevik Party of 1917 was unable to survive their destructive effects. Nevertheless, the disappearance of this democracy was not at all a simple process. When some of the conditions for democracy had already vanished, others were still actively present. This was true of the free existence of tendencies and groupings, on the one hand, and, on the other, of the right to public expression of disagreements and differences of view.

Recognition of the real rights of an opposition does not, of course, exhaust the requirements for internal democracy. Alongside it there are others, the importance of which is no less great: sovereignty of the Party congress as the body that decides Party policy, and the resolutions of which are actually put into effect; possibility for the Congress to check on the activities of the Central Committee; absence of interference by the central Party bodies in the election of local and regional committees and in the nomination of delegates to Congress; free confrontation of points of view, and information for the rank and file regarding the decisions made by the leadership, together with the facts on which these decisions are based. Russian reality did not allow all of these conditions to apply, even to a limited extent. The Communists themselves acknowledged that the civil war had brought about a 'militarization' of the Party organization. Before this situation was reached, however, the Bolshevik Party had enjoyed, as Professor Carr puts it, 'a freedom and publicity of discussion rarely practised by any party on vital issues of public policy'.[79]

This was true of the discussions about the Brest-Litovsk question, when despite the importance of the issue and of the divergent views, the Central Committee, at Lenin's request, gave the Left Communists the right to make their views known through *Pravda* and to carry on agitation in the Party.[80] When the central authorities of the Soviet State discussed the drawing-up of a Constitution, the opposition trend was given a share in this work, the result being clashes between the centralizing tendency led by Stalin and those who favoured an extensive degree of autonomy for the soviets.[81] The same thing happened a year later with the settlement of the new Party programme, for on a series of questions Bukharin and Lenin upheld opposing views; they were both appointed *rapporteurs*, and a commission eventually succeeded in drawing up a document that synthesized these views.[82] Bukharin had had occasion to make known his theories, which were opposed to Lenin's on many points, in a pamphlet which was published in May 1918 in a printing of one million copies.[83] The dispute between the Left Communists and the Party leadership concerned also the direction to be given to the Soviet economy, and the two tendencies in this domain confronted each other in April 1918 in a public debate in the C.E.C., with opponents of the Bolshevik Party present. Once again, a *rapporteur* and a *co-rapporteur* were appointed, in the persons of Lenin and Bukharin. No agreement could be reached, however, and no thesis was established as a result of this discussion.[84]

These democratic procedures did not all disappear with the progress of the civil war and the 'militarization' of the Party. The central bodies did indeed assume powers not provided for in the Party rules, such as appointment of the secretaries of local organizations. But at the congress of 1919, as has been mentioned, when Lenin found himself in conflict with the views of the former 'Left Communists' regarding the new Party programme, the 'report' given by the Party's leader was challenged in a 'counter-report' given by Bukharin.[85]

In 1920 the opposition trends known as the Democratic Centralism group and the Workers' Opposition were still accorded official existence, and the Central Committee associated them closely with the work of a commission charged with reorganizing the Party.[86] At the Ninth Conference of the Party the Left trends even gained a victory which seemed, for the moment, to be decisive: as Daniels notes, the resolution passed bore a remarkable resemblance to the documents circulated by the Opposition.[87] The same historian writes: 'The fall of 1920 saw the high point of open discussion in the Communist Party and of free opposition to the leaders' authority.'[88]

Freedom of discussion was to take another—and final—step forward in the months following the Ninth Conference. The controversy about the role and place of the trade unions in Soviet society and the Soviet State gave occasion for a debate in which a number of trends opposed each other openly and, in articles and pamphlets, in meetings at every level of the Party, and also in public meetings, expounded their arguments and endeavoured to win over the majority in the ruling bodies.* True, Lenin had at first wanted to restrict the discussion to the leading committees of the Party,[89] but the division of opinion prevailing among the members of the Central Committee soon overcame this intention of his, since, according to the then accepted notion, the role of the congress and the rank and file was to 'pass judgment' on the tendencies existing among the Party leadership whenever these proved to be practically equal in strength.[90] The trade-union discussion took place at the beginning of the year 1921, in the period immediately preceding the drama of Kronstadt and the meeting of the Tenth Party Congress. The latter, in an atmosphere of crisis and defeat, agreed, however, to restrict the exercise of freedom inside the Party, to reduce the rights of the Opposition, and to suspend the working of internal democracy. Before analysing the mechanism of this decline, let us look at the attitude taken up by Lenin himself towards the problems involved in inner-Party democracy.

Always willing to enter into a vigorous argument with the Opposition, Lenin did not deny the latter, throughout the period down to the Tenth Congress, either the right or the means to defend its views. This was the case not only during the Brest-Litovsk debate, when, after the first clashes, he called for 'a meeting representing all shades of opinion and standpoints'.[91] His attitude was the same in other episodes of Party life. At the Eighth Congress, for example, Lenin called for the Opposition to be represented in the bodies charged with drawing up the new programme.[92] In doing this he merely confirmed the view he had expressed at the previous congress, when he accepted the legitimacy of 'trends', and spoke of 'sections', a 'majority' and an 'opposition' in the struggle inside the Party.[93] Representation of tendencies was regarded as normal not only in the Party Congress but also in the Central Committee, in which Lenin called for an opposition presence—the Left Communists in 1918 and the Workers' Opposition in 1921.† Representation of tendencies was also to be observed when the trade-

* On the points at issue in the trade-union debate, see p. 342. On the scope and public character of the debate, see Lenin, Vol. 32, pp. 44–6 and 70, and Carr, Vol. II, p. 223.
† For 1918, see p. 293; for 1921, see p. 301.

union organizations chose which of their leaders should be delegates to the Central Committee.*

In November 1920, addressing the Italian Communists, Lenin again spoke of the correctness of 'allowing all tendencies to express themselves'.[94] He expressed the view, at this same time, that tendencies had a natural and legitimate propensity to form themselves into factions, and listed the rights of the latter: election to the Party's leading bodies on the basis of grouping into 'two trends or factions', with votes cast being counted in the presence of 'scrutineers from both groups'. He added that 'proportional representation' seemed to him 'essential' in the election of deliberative bodies such as congresses or conferences—though not in that of executive bodies 'charged with the conduct of practical work'.[95] In January 1921, in connexion with the campaign preceding the Tenth Party Congress, Lenin said: 'It is, of course, quite permissible (especially before a congress) for various groups to form blocs (and also to go vote-chasing).'[96]

It seems clear that this attitude of Lenin's was bound up with his conviction that the 'ideological struggle' constituted a major necessity in Party life. Such struggle seemed to him necessary, at any rate, in so far as it meant 'not mutual ostracism but mutual influence',[97] because only through discussion of theoretical differences could the Communist movement forge a unity that was not merely factitious. This statement of Lenin's, made shortly before the Tenth Congress, which restricted the rights of the Opposition in the Party—a restriction never to be lifted—defines the limits that this limitation upon freedom of discussion had in the thinking of its principal advocate in the Bolshevik Party. It was as though, just before it collapsed, the Party's internal democracy, already deeply shaken, was proclaiming for the last time one of its most indispensable conditions.

The Congress of 1921 and afterwards

While, in March 1921, the Tenth Party Congress brought about, as we shall see, the downfall of inner-Party democracy, it must not be supposed that this democracy had been flourishing until that moment. That was far from true. As has been said, the Communist organization had suffered, as a result of the civil war, a process of 'militarization'. Cases of arbitrary behaviour, breaches of the Party rules, acts of coercion and, in general, irregular conduct by the Party leadership were not wanting. At the Ninth Congress, in March 1920, a long and formidable list of them had been drawn up by Opposition speakers. They had denounced transfers of Party members carried out for political reasons, and cases of internment which in some instances

* Lenin, Vol. 30, pp. 477–8. It is true that on this occasion Lenin was pleading for the representation of the 'trend that particularly insists on sensible methods', in other words, the one that supported his own views.

involved entire committees. More frequently, local organizations had seen their own executive committees replaced by 'political departments' directly appointed by the Party's central authorities.[98] A member of the 'Democratic Centralism' group alleged that the Central Committee had sent Shlyapnikov out of Russia, finding an excuse to entrust him with a mission abroad so as to prevent him from adding to the strength of the Opposition in the congress. Lenin rejected this charge, adding that, if such a measure had indeed been taken, it would have been 'infamous'.[99] In this particular instance Lenin's denials were probably justified,[100] but the system of political 'exile' (even if only very temporary exile) did certainly exist; such sympathetic observers as Victor Serge and Alfred Rosmer acknowledge that this was so.[101]

Some of the Opposition's charges of discrimination were undoubtedly contradicted, to some extent, by the mere fact that they were allowed to publish and circulate them on a large scale, and there was a certain polemical element in such allegations. Basically, however, the pertinence of this criticism was undeniable, and the Party leadership, by announcing their intention to introduce reforms and strengthen democracy, admitted both the seriousness of the situation and the shortcomings in inner-Party democracy. The Ninth Party Conference, in September 1920, in its concluding resolution, listed these shortcomings and called for a more thorough-going critique of Party institutions at all levels, together with 'rejection of any kind of repression against comrades because they have different ideas'.[102]

These shortcomings were all too real, and the Opposition's inability to suggest concrete remedies for the situation by going to the root of the problem did not in the least detract from the validity of the criticism it made. The fact that it was possible to voice such criticism at the highest level, and have it given extensive publicity, might, however, while not abolishing the evils in question, nevertheless contribute to limiting their extent. This is why the severe restriction placed on the rights of the Opposition, going so far as to challenge its very right to exist, which was decided on by the Tenth Congress, marks an important turning-point in the history of the Leninist Party. Those mechanisms of control and criticism, serving as antidotes to the features of authoritarianism that were already present in Party life, suffered in March 1921 a definitive and maiming blow.

Paradoxically, this defeat of democracy had been preceded by one of its most spectacular manifestations. The discussion about the trade-union question had not merely stirred up the Party but had shaken it, and its to-ings and fro-ings had seemed all the more disturbing in that the controversy was in many ways artificial and almost unreal.* Referring to the 'confusion' that reigned in the Central Committee

* See p. 343.

in this period, Lenin said: 'it is the first time this has happened in
our Party's history, in time of revolution.'[103] The remark is surprising
when one recalls how sharp the controversy in the Central Committee
had been in 1918 in connexion with Brest-Litovsk. There was, though,
a difference between the two episodes that justifies, in retrospect,
Lenin's equanimity during the earlier debate and his fears during the
later one. The decision that the Communists had to take during the
Brest-Litovsk negotiations had as its background a period in which
the revolution was still benefiting from the dynamism acquired in the
preceding months, whereas the trade-union discussion occurred in a
period of crisis and discouragement. Moreover, the problem raised
in 1918 by the need to end the war brought into confrontation two
tendencies that were clearly defined, representing choices that were
quite unambiguous. The trade-union discussion, however, gives the
impression of taking place in a cloudy atmosphere in which the sharpness of the statements made is due not so much to incompatibility
of the opposing views as to the explosion of passions long held in
check. Lenin was undoubtedly right when, forcing himself to 'face
the bitter truth', he declared that 'the Party is sick. The Party is down
with fever.'[104] He even went so far as to express, at the miners' congress, fear of seeing a split in the Party and concluding that in the
given circumstances the formation of new factions could have very
dangerous consequences.[105]

This was the disturbing prelude to the Tenth Congress inside the
Leninist organization itself. The gravity of the crisis in the Party
reflected that which the whole country was experiencing, and of which
the dramatic events in Kronstadt, along with the peasant revolts and
workers' strikes, proved the importance.* At the congress itself Lenin
did not give a systematic description of these circumstances, all too
well known as they were to the delegates. One year later, however,
at the Eleventh Congress, recalling the situation in Russia at the end
of the winter of 1920–21 and the dangers that had then faced the
Party, he declared:

> It is terribly difficult to retreat after a great victorious advance,
> for the relations are entirely different. During a victorious advance,
> even if discipline is relaxed, everybody presses forward on his
> own accord. During a retreat, however, discipline must be more
> conscious and is a hundred times more necessary, because, when
> the entire army is in retreat, it does not know or see where it
> should halt. It sees only retreat; under such circumstances a few
> panic-stricken voices are, at times, enough to cause a stampede.
> The danger here is enormous. When a real army is in retreat,
> machine-guns are kept ready, and when an orderly retreat degen-

* See p. 254.

erates into a disorderly one the command to fire is given, and quite
rightly too.[106]

In opening the congress of March 1921 Lenin made it plain that big
decisions were being prepared. Referring to the trade-union discussion, he said: 'We have passed through an exceptional year, we have
allowed ourselves the luxury of discussions and disputes within the
Party. This was an amazing luxury for a Party shouldering unprecedented responsibilities and surrounded by mighty and powerful
enemies uniting the whole capitalist world.'[107] While the Party
as a whole was thus reproached, it was the Workers' Opposition that
suffered the most direct and vigorous attacks. Lenin ridiculed their
'arguments about freedom of speech and freedom to criticize ... which
... constitute nine-tenths of the meaning of these speeches, which
have no particular meaning at all.'[108] He alleged that their ideas were
'an expression of petty-bourgeois and anarchist wavering in practice,
and actually ... help the class enemies of the proletarian revolution.'[109]
Criticism was this time accompanied by a threat: 'If they continue
this game of opposition, the party will have to expel them.'[110] Lenin's
attacks went so far that the delegates of the Workers' Opposition
protested, and their principal spokesmen refused to accept election
to the Central Committee, as Lenin wished. Lenin then repeated his
proposal, pointing out that the leadership had agreed that some of
the Opposition's demands, in connexion with 'developing democracy
and workers' initiative', needed to be 'examined with the greatest
care'.[111] He expressed his 'comradely confidence' in them[112] and
described their leaders' election to the Central Committee as 'the
Party's greatest expression of confidence'.[113] Finally, after a resolution specially composed for this purpose had been put down, two
representatives of the Workers' Opposition, Shlyapnikov and Kutuzov,
were elected to the Central Committee, and a member of the Democratic Centralism group was elected an alternate member.[114]

The congress had already lasted a week by this time, and it might
have been supposed that it would end on this gesture of appeasement.
Then, however, on the last day of the congress, when several hundred
delegates had already left Moscow, Lenin put down two motions, one
'on Party unity' and the other on 'the syndicalist and anarchist deviation in our Party'.[115] The former of these decreed that 'in the practical
struggle against factionalism every organization of the Party must
take strict measures to prevent all factional actions',[116] and ordered
'immediate dissolution of all groups without exception formed on the
basis of one platform or another (such as the Workers' Opposition
group, the Democratic Centralism group, etc.)'. Non-observance of
this decision of the congress would entail unconditional and instant
expulsion from the Party.[117] Finally, a clause that was to be kept from

publication provided that, in order to ensure 'maximum unanimity', 'the Congress authorizes the Central Committee, in cases of breach of discipline or of a revival or toleration of factionalism, to apply all Party penalties, including expulsion, and in regard to members of the Central Committee, reduction to the status of alternate members and, as an extreme measure, expulsion from the Party' — the last-mentioned measure to require, however, a two-thirds majority in the Central Committee.[118] This motion was passed against the negative votes of twenty-five delegates,[119] and not without Lenin making clear that the secret clause was 'an extreme measure that is being adopted specially, in view of the dangerous situation'.[120] Lenin's second motion was aimed against the Workers' Opposition, which he depicted as a 'syndicalist and anarchist deviation'. That group was condemned to disappearance when the congress resolved that 'the propaganda of [its] ideas' was 'incompatible with membership of the Russian Communist Party'.[121] This resolution was passed with thirty votes against.[122]

The decisions thus taken were of capital importance for the Party's future, and the considerations with which Lenin surrounded them make their significance plain. He defined 'factionalism' as meaning 'the formation of groups with separate platforms, striving to a certain degree to segregate and create their own group discipline'.[123] Factionalism as thus conceived is forbidden in the practice of most political organizations, whether Communist or not. Condemnation of any deviation from the Party line might seem, however, a more arbitrary measure. Lenin appears to have been aware of this, and he explained that 'by saying "deviations" we emphasize that we do not as yet regard them as something that has crystallized and is absolutely and fully defined, but merely as the beginning of a political trend of which the Party must give its appraisal,'[124] adding that 'a deviation is something that can be rectified'.[125] These explanations having no doubt proved insufficient, Lenin sought to give further reassurances, saying: 'If we find a milder term, I would propose that it be substituted for the word "deviation", and also that other parts be modified,'[126] and even addressed this proposal directly to Shylapnikov.[127]

On the other hand, Lenin's speeches included passages which, far from reassuring, were bound to arouse the liveliest apprehensions. Not only did the resolution on the Workers' Opposition go beyond the ban on factions by subjecting to the most severe sanctions the mere defence of certain opinions that were arbitrarily described as non-Communist, but Lenin even said that 'the political conclusion to be drawn from the present situation is that the Party must be united and any opposition prevented', adding: 'We want no more oppositions!'[128] Soon afterwards he added that 'the White Guards strive, and are able, to disguise themselves as Communists, and even as the most Left-wing Communists.'[129] The fact that the voting of these measures was accompanied by ringing promises about re-establishing inner-Party democracy* was not so much a proof of hypocrisy as a sign of incoherence and thoughtlessness. The resolution on Party unity itself spoke of 'criticism of the Party's shortcomings' being 'absolutely necessary'.[130] But Lenin, by adding that 'every critic must see to it that the form of his criticism takes account of the position of the Party, surrounded as it is by a ring of enemies',[131] discouraged in advance any Party members who might be tempted to follow that advice.

Does this mean—and it is a question of great importance for the analysis of Leninism—that the anti-democratic measures taken in March 1921, at Lenin's request, were definitive in character? This claim cannot be maintained. Lenin was not really explicit, to be sure, except about the clause providing for expulsion of members of the Central Committee by a two-thirds vote, which he presented as 'an extreme measure that is being adopted specially, in view of the dangerous situation'.[132] In addition, though, in his speech closing the debate on the Central Committee's work, he said: 'Comrades, *this is no time* to have an opposition', and: 'Comrades, let's not have an opposition *just now*!'† Moreover, Lenin had emphasized too strongly the objective conditions in which the congress met, with his continual references to the enemy, and these conditions were too serious, for anyone to doubt that the decisions of the Tenth Congress were anything but a response (inadequate in itself) to a *particular* situation. This situation had been defined, as we have seen, explicitly and at length, as an operation of retreat which must necessarily be regarded —unless the prospect of revolution was to be renounced for ever— as only temporary. Additional proof of this can be found in Lenin's reply to a speech by Ryazanov: in this reply he condemned as 'excessive' and 'impracticable' the wish to 'prohibit' what he called 'fundamental disagreements' from 'being brought before the judgment of the whole Party', and went on to say that it was quite possible that, when delegates were being chosen for a subsequent congress, 'the elections may have to be based on platforms'.[133]

This question resembles that relating to the origins of the single-Party system. Just as it was never consciously decided to abolish all opposition parties and make a system of the resulting situation, so the abolition of one of the essential conditions for inner-Party democracy, namely, the right of minority and opposition groups to exist, was not put forward as a matter of principle, and still less presented as an inherent feature of the Soviet régime and the theory of the Communist Party. Lenin responded to an exceptional crisis with an

* These declarations are summarized in Broué, *Parti*, pp. 158–9.
† My emphasis, M.L.: Lenin, Vol. 32, p. 200.

exceptional measure. Undoubtedly he saw the measure as something temporary: an unwise presumption, which contributed substantially to the birth and growth of sterile and authoritarian conformism in the Communist movement.

The Communists

Organized in more or less autonomous cells, grouped in sections governed by an increasingly coercive discipline, members of a Party responsible for dominating the state—who, and how numerous, were these Communists, those heirs of the movement that had overthrown the old order, who were now called upon to build, organize and administer?

Estimates of the size of the Communist Party vary from one source to another, at least as regards the first years of the Soviet régime, when the inadequacies of the Party secretariat and the independent character of many local organizations rendered any centralization of statistics impossible. The most precise and up-to-date work on the subject offers the following figures:

	Members	Candidates*	Total
1917	240,000		
1918 (March)	390,000		
1919 (March)	350,000		
1920 (March)	611,978		
1921 (March)	732,521		
1922	410,430	117,924	528,354
1923	381,400	117,700	499,100
1924	350,000	122,000	470,000[134]

The same source gives the social composition of the Communist Party as follows:

	Workers	Peasants	'White-collar' workers and others
1917	60·2%	7·5%	32·2%
1918	56·9%	14·5%	28·6%
1919	47·8%	21·8%	30·4%
1920	43·8%	25·1%	31·1%
1921	41%	28·2%	30·8%[135]

The purges of 1922 increased the proportion of workers, who, in 1923, made up 45 per cent, with 26 per cent peasants and 29 per cent 'others'.[136]

* See p. 308.

These statistics show the mass-scale entry of workers into the Communist Party. A comparison of the two tables demonstrates that there were 200,000 working-class members of the Bolshevik Party in 1917; this figure acquires its full significance if one appreciates the small size of the industrial proletariat of Russia, which numbered only about three million. After 1917 the statistics of the percentage of workers in the Party are subject, however, to reservations. Generally speaking, the data collected were based on the members' original occupations and not their *actual* occupations. Thus, for the year 1919 the statistics show 47·8 per cent of the members as workers; of these, however, over 60 per cent were working in the administrative services of the State, the Party or the trade unions, 25 per cent were serving in the Red Army, and only 11 per cent were actually working in factories.[137] Some Party members, moreover, strove to conceal their non-proletarian origins, or forged a proletarian background for themselves.[138] Nevertheless the proportion of workers continued to be very high among the members of the Party in a period when, as we shall see, the number of workers in industry suffered a steep decline.* As for the number of peasants in the Party, its increase was to be expected in a Party which, on the eve and on the morrow of the October Revolution, was practically unrepresented in the countryside, and made its real appearance there only as a result of the capture of power and acquisition of local responsibilities. To this it must be added that, broadly, the Communist Party was a party of men, and of young people. In 1922 only 7·5 per cent of members were women, and at the end of 1919 more than half the members were under thirty and less than 10 per cent were older than forty.[139]

In 1921, then, it was a party of 700,000 members—a mass party, wholly different in size, in the character of its activities and in its political functions from the former sect of conspirators, professional revolutionaries and underground militants. And yet, despite some outward appearances, the Bolshevik Party—renamed in 1919 the Communist Party (Bolsheviks)—was still profoundly different from the workers' parties of the West and the classical mass parties. The numerical aspect was irrelevant, in fact, for the Bolsheviks, after coming to power, remained loyal to certain fundamental conceptions of Leninism regarding the nature and function of the vanguard party. A distinctive feature that followed from this was mentioned by Lenin in an article published in *Pravda* in October 1919: 'Our Party ... is the only government party in the world which is concerned not with increasing membership but with improving its quality, and in purging itself of "self-seekers".'[140]

Despite its great size and completely transformed role, the Communist Party strove indeed, under Lenin's guidance, to preserve at all

* See p. 347.

costs its nature as the vanguard of the proletariat. The objective difficulties lying in the way of this were considerable, and Lenin soon became aware of them. In January 1918, speaking in the Central Committee at a time when everyone's attention was absorbed by the Brest-Litovsk debate, Lenin showed by an apparently incidental remark how much he was worried by the transformation that the Party was in danger of undergoing as a result of its conquest of power. He demanded that 'when members are enrolled we must record the date that they joined the Party: before 25 October (1917) or after — and the new members must acknowledge the necessity of the tactics that the Party found correct for carrying out the October revolution.'[141] A few months later, writing in *Pravda*, Lenin became more explicit: 'We must not accept people who try to join from careerist motives; people like this should be driven out of the Party.'[142] He was never to cease dwelling on this theme, to the very end of his life. Addressing the Petrograd Soviet in March 1919 he said: 'We threw out the old bureaucrats, but they have come back, they call themselves "commonists" when they can't bear to say the word Communist, and they wear a red ribbon in their buttonholes and creep into warm corners. What to do about it? We must fight this scum again and again, and if the scum has crawled back we must again and again clean it up, chase it out … '[143]

Clean up, chase out these unclean elements! Lenin went on to indicate to the Party members those whom this work of hygiene and sanitation should concentrate upon. In the rural districts 'people who call themselves members of the Party are often scoundrels, whose lawlessness is most brazen'.[144] He drew attention to 'the abuses committed by former government officials, landowners, bourgeois and other scum who play up to the Communists and who sometimes commit abominable outrages and acts of tyranny against the peasantry'.[145] Along with these representatives of enemy classes who had succeeded in penetrating the Party there were other harmful elements, such as 'approximately ninety-nine out of every hundred Mensheviks who joined the Russian Communist Party after 1918, i.e., when the victory of the Bolsheviks first became probable and then certain.'[146] There were also the 'bureaucratic Communists',[147] as well as 'all members of the R.C.P. who are in any way dubious, unreliable, or who have failed to prove their stability': these should be purged, too, although, in their case, 'with the right of readmission upon further verification and test'.[148]

All this shows that increased membership of the Party was not for Lenin an end in itself. In many circumstances, indeed, such increase could be dangerous. At the Ninth Party Congress, when the military situation seemed stabilized and the Soviet power consolidated, he said that 'the huge membership … our Party has attained gives rise

to a certain apprehension,' because 'the rapid growth of our Party
has not always been commensurate with the extent to which we have
educated this mass of people for the performance of the tasks of the
moment.'[149] This desire to limit the size of the Party was not turned
into an absolute rule, however. Essentially circumstantial in character,
it was dropped whenever the situation was such as to render vain the
fear of opportunist infiltration. Thus, when in the autumn of 1919 the
victories of the counter-revolutionary armies threatened the downfall
of the Soviet régime and it seemed possible that Petrograd would be
taken by the 'Whites', the Party opened its gates wide to new members: in these circumstances a Party card 'meant something approaching a candidature for Denikin's gallows'.[150] In Moscow alone, in a
single week, 13,600 new members were enrolled. Lenin commented:
'This is a huge, quite unexpected success.'[151] During these difficult
weeks, when the precariousness of Soviet power was revealed, the
Party made no less than 200,000 new members.[152] It was not only
scoundrels, opportunists and former officials seeking influence who
joined the Party.

And yet the evils of which Lenin complained and the dangers he
warned against were only too real. The day-to-day hardships, the
continual tension, the impossibility of relaxing an effort that had been
kept up for years, the gnawing hunger, the want that never loosened
its grip and the doubt that from time to time took hold of even the
best—all this could not but bring about consequences that caused
indignation among austere and idealistic Communists. At the Party
congress of March 1919 Nogin had expressed the horror he felt at
the 'drunkenness, debauchery, corruption, cases of theft and irrespon-
sible behaviour to be found among many Party officials'. 'Really,'
he said, 'at the sight of such things your hair stands on end.'[153] As for
the careerism of the more ambitious, the opportunism of the more
mediocre, and the simple 'realism' of the average citizen, they were
the unavoidable price paid for political success, a price that other
parties, with a less prestigious record than the Bolshevik Party, have
had and still have to pay, without too many scruples or too much
revulsion. For the Bolshevik revolutionaries, though, these characteristic features of human weakness were a source of surprise and concern,
as in the case of Zinoviev, who told the congress of March 1918 of
the experience of a Communist Party official who, receiving a newly
joined member of the Party and asking him to come back the next day
to collect his membership card, was given this reply: 'No, comrade,
let me have it today, I need it at once in order to get a job in an
office.'[154]

Neither the Party nor Lenin viewed this state of affairs with resignation. They sought cures that would do away with it, or at least
reduce its effects. In March 1919 Lenin told the Petrograd Soviet:

'We have passed a decision not to allow members who have been in the Party less than a year to be delegates to a Party congress,' and said of the new recruit to the Party that 'he must not be given the card until he has been tested.'[155] This procedure was to be introduced officially in December of that year: the procedure of candidature and of probationary periods during which the new member was obliged to learn the programme and tactics of the Party, and the leaders concerned had the opportunity to form an impression of his personal qualities.[156] Also advocated was re-registration of members who wanted to stay in the Party, a formality which enabled the organization to re-examine their cases,[157] and checking on Party members by non-Party workers.[158] But the method that seemed to him the most effective, and that assumed the most spectacular form, was the *purging* of the ranks of the Party, an operation which came to be carried out regularly and which, though inspired by the most legitimate of motives, was to produce some deplorable results after Lenin's death.

In 1919 the Bolshevik Party decided on the first purge of its members, so as to eliminate those who came under any of the following headings: drunkenness, abuse of power, desertion, refusal to carry out Party orders, and frequent absence without excuse from Party meetings. This purge seems to have eliminated between 10 and 15 per cent of the membership in the towns and a higher proportion in some parts of the countryside.[159] The purging operation carried out in 1921 was on an even larger scale, resulting in the elimination of a quarter of the total membership. Thirty-four per cent of those expelled suffered this penalty for 'passivity', 25 per cent for 'careerism', 'drunkenness' and 'bourgeois mode of life', and 9 per cent for corruption. Another reason quoted was 'refusing to carry out Party directions'.[160] In March 1922 Lenin, considering that, in the event of a Soviet diplomatic success at the Genoa conference,* the Party might experience a fresh influx of members, called on the Central Committee to strengthen the rules governing admissions. He had in mind a twofold aim: preventing the acceptance of unsuitable persons, and reinforcing the proletarian character of the Party. When Zinoviev proposed that the probationary period be fixed at six months for workers and a year for candidates from other walks of life, Lenin asked for an amendment: six months for workers 'who have actually been employed in large industrial enterprises for not less than ten years', a year-and-a-half for other workers, two years for peasants and soldiers, and three years for everyone else. Although he emphasized the need to lengthen the probationary period, the Central Committee rejected his proposal.[161] The criteria applied during the purge of 1921 nevertheless made possible an increase in the percentage of 'workers'— with the reservations that use of the term in this context implies—

* See p. 373.

which reached 45 per cent in 1922: two-fifths of the peasant members and more than a third of the 'white-collar' workers had been eliminated as against only one-sixth of the worker members.[162]

That membership of the Party should have enabled persons to acquire privileges over and above those of power and prestige ought not to surprise us. Material advantages often went along with the privileges of power and prestige, even though the egalitarian ideology of the first years of the régime, and the example of austerity set by most of the leaders, created an atmosphere which restricted opportunities for abuses and made those that did occur appear intolerable in the eyes of the rank-and-file.

Such material advantages as there were to be had, and even the prestige and possession of a share of authority, were in most cases of little significance in comparison with the sacrifices imposed on Communists. Formed in the underground struggle of the Tsarist period and, more frequently, in the revolutionary struggle of 1917, they had been placed in positions of political and administrative responsibility which required that they change their outlook completely. Conspirators and revolutionary activists who had become officials, commissars and officers, they struggled to find their feet in situations that were often too much for them, striving to find solutions to problems that were literally matters of life and death. The most sincere among them were perhaps more embarrassed than anything else by the need to employ methods that had little in common with their aspirations, the irritation of having to become administrators, accountants, and calculators—and, very probably, incompetent ones at that—and the frustration of feeling that, despite all their efforts, a gulf was opening between them and the masses: not only the peasant masses, moreover, but the mass of the workers as well. There were thankless missions and impossible tasks to carry out, disappointments and also substantial risks to be incurred. During the civil war, in the zones occupied by the 'Whites', Communist officials resumed their old practices of the underground struggle, becoming guerrillas and revolutionary fighters. Those of them, and there were many, who fell into their enemies' hands paid with their lives for the fearful privilege of belonging to the Party. For the tens of thousands of bureaucrats and timeservers who infiltrated the Party there were as many members, and more, who, in the administrative services, at the front and in the factories, continued to function as militants committed to the revolution. Subject to military discipline, appointed and transferred according to the needs of the war or the judgment of their superiors, running the risk of the punishments entailed by all their weaknesses and mistakes, they formed a cohort subjected to the hardest of tests: a long march which was often nothing but an apparently ceaseless marking-time. By its efforts and its victory the Leninist Party, formed to conquer power and charged with the defence and consolidation of this power, performed a feat the consequences of which were immense, setting its mark on the entire history of our time. This cohort, victorious but exhausted, was in 1921, however, an isolated party. Shlyapnikov admitted this when, during the Eleventh Party Congress, he observed, ironically: 'Vladimir Ilyich said yesterday that the proletariat as a class, did not exist [in Russia]. Permit me to congratulate you on being the vanguard of a non-existing class.'[163] Zinoviev, replying to a member of the Workers' Opposition who called for the convening of a 'congress of producers', admitted that if such a congress were to be held, 'the majority will consist of non-Party people. A good many of them will be S.R.s and Mensheviks.' And the Communist leader asked the Party member who had made this proposal: 'Should we hand over everything to them?'[164]

Exhausted by their victory, isolated and so defeated in the very midst of their triumph, victims of a calamity they had done everything to prevent—this was how the Communists appeared at the end of the civil war: guides and builders of a new society that was rich in promise but crushed by want.

3
Society

After the political forces we must now consider the social ones—
a world in which contradictory currents were confused together, a
mingling of bold innovations with old traditions, of new factors with
old influences stronger than the revolutionaries were able to imagine,
a world to which aggression from without, added to internal upheaval,
brought disorder and devastation.

Attempting to define in one chapter the nature of this society is a
venturesome task that can neither be realized satisfactorily nor yet
avoided. One must embark upon it in full awareness that only a few
features of the subject can be sketched—those that seem the most
important in relation to the social and political plans of Leninism.

The impact of the Terror

'Marxists have never forgotten that violence must inevitably accompany the collapse of capitalism in its entirety and the birth of socialist
society,' said Lenin, addressing the Seventh Party Congress in March
1918.[1] This statement was both a prediction and an objective observation. Violence had already broken out in Russia at the beginning of
the spring of 1918; but this violence was to become greatly intensified,
assuming the forms of mass-scale and systematic terror, permeating
the country's atmosphere throughout the civil war and setting its
mark for a long time upon the characteristics of Soviet society.

It would be wrong, however, to suppose that, starting from a
theoretical opinion about the role of force in history—that 'it is the
midwife of every old society pregnant with a new one', and 'the instrument with the aid of which social movement forces its way through
and shatters the dead, fossilized political forms'[2]—the Bolsheviks
proceeded to impose, immediately on coming to power, a reign of
terror directed against the old order. On the contrary, the period in
which the revolution experienced its 'honeymoon' was also a period of
relative but genuine *moderation* in the repression of counter-revolutionary elements.

It was a moderation that was sometimes reminiscent of the generosity that had occasionally accompanied the euphoria of earlier revolutionary victories. When the Red Guards captured the Winter Palace in Petrograd, the seat of the Provisional Government, they released the officer-cadets who had fought against them, requiring only that they give their word not to take up arms against the revolution any more. A few days later this same body of cadets organized an armed rising in the capital.* The Bolsheviks easily overcame them—and then once again released their prisoners.[3] General Krasnov, commanding the counter-revolutionary forces that were brought up to reconquer Petrograd, also obtained his freedom in return for a promise not to fight against the soviets again—and almost immediately joined the anti-Bolshevik forces gathering in the South.[4] In Moscow, where the insurrection had been much bloodier, the 'Whites' were treated in the same easy-going way, despite the massacre of prisoners of which they had been guilty.[5] In the provinces the taking of power by the Bolsheviks occurred, generally speaking, with very little violence.[6] Moreover, the members of the Provisional Government who had been arrested on October 26th—or at least those of them who belonged to the socialist parties†—were released, *at Martov's request*.

There were indeed, in the first months after the conquest of power and before the beginning of the civil war in the strict sense, some violent incidents in which both revolutionaries and counter-revolutionaries suffered. But the Bolsheviks endeavoured on a number of occasions to calm the fury of the crowds and restrain their excesses. Thus, in Saratov, when the members of an anti-Communist 'Committee for Salvation' were seized by demonstrators and roughly handled, the Soviet authorities succeeded in rescuing them.[7] Among the lynchings carried out by the masses, those of General Dukhonin, commander-in-chief of the army, and of the Constitutional-Democrat former ministers Shingarev and Kokoshkin, the latter murdered in their hospital beds, were particularly sensational. Dukhonin was killed despite the intervention of the Bolshevik People's Commissar, Krylenko, who implored the sailors involved to show clemency.[8] The murder of the Cadet ministers was condemned by *Izvestiya*, the official organ of the Government, as 'a blot on the honour of the revolution',[9] and Lenin demanded, in a telephone message to the People's Commissariat of Justice on the very day of the murder, that the authorities 'begin a rigorous investigation', and 'arrest the sailors guilty of this murder'.[10]

Maxim Gorky wrote in his *Revolt of the Slaves*: 'A people brought

---

* See p. 244.

† According to Carr (Vol. I, p. 152) all the ministers were set free. According to Deutscher (*Prophet Armed*, p. 336) and Schapiro (*Origin*, p. 72), only the socialist ministers benefited from this treatment.

up in a school which dwells vulgarly on the terrors of hell, tutored with blows of the fists, with rods and whips, cannot have a tender heart. A people who have been trampled down by the police will be capable in their turn of trampling on the bodies of others.'[11] Babeuf had said the same thing during the French Revolution: 'Instead of civilizing us, our masters have made barbarians of us, because that is what they are themselves. They are reaping, and will continue to reap, that which they have sown.'[12]

During the first months of their rule, the Bolsheviks, far from inflaming the anger and vindictiveness of the masses, sought to set bounds to the manifestation of such feelings. Official repression, moreover, assumed comparatively benign forms. No death sentence was pronounced during the first three months of the Soviet régime, and no official execution took place. Indeed, one of the first decrees of the new Government abolished the death penalty, which Kerensky's Government had restored in September 1917.[13] As Professor Carr notes, 'the revolutionary tradition of opposition to the death sentence weakened and collapsed only after the outbreak of the civil war and open insurrection against the Soviet régime'.[14] In July 1918, after suppressing the armed revolt of the Left S.R.s,* the Bolsheviks showed such moderation in their measures of reprisal that the German Government, whose ambassador had been killed by the rebels, protested to the Soviet authorities.[15]

The moderation of the Bolsheviks is all the more remarkable in that it contrasted in this period with the first outbursts of 'White' terror, both on a small scale, like the massacre of their 'Red' prisoners by the officer-cadets during the Moscow insurrection of October 1917, and on a grand scale, as in Finland, where between ten and twenty thousand workers were slaughtered by the counter-revolution, not including the more than two thousand prisoners who died in internment camps.[16] In Souvarine's words, 'The Cheka seized hostages; its repressive measures were still moderate, while the Whites, by their mass shootings and hangings, were sowing the seeds of inexpiable hatred and ensuring severe reprisals for themselves.'[17]

With the beginning of the civil war and foreign intervention the Bolshevik Government, yielding to the spirit of the time, itself resorted to terror. Undoubtedly it was the numerous attempts on the lives of some of their leaders that helped to overcome their last hesitations in this matter: the attempt to kill Lenin on January 1st, 1918, the murder of Volodarsky in June, the unsuccessful attempt on Trotsky's life at the beginning of August, and, at the end of that month, the murder of Uritsky and the attack on Lenin that nearly killed him, immobilizing the head of the Government for several weeks.[18]

In August 1918 Zinoviev announced in Petrograd the beginning of

* See p. 257.

the Red Terror.[19] The attempted murder of Lenin and the actual murder of Uritsky evoked an immediate response. The newspaper *Krasnaya Gazeta* wrote: 'Each drop of Lenin's blood must be paid for by the bourgeoisie and the Whites in hundreds of deaths ... The interests of the revolution demand the physical extermination of the bourgeoisie. They have no pity: it is time for us to be pitiless.'[20] Like Paris during the French Revolution, Petrograd had its September massacres, the statistics of which are hard to determine. According to official sources, 800 'counter-revolutionaries and White Guards' (otherwise described as 'hostages') were executed in Petrograd, and there were also many victims in Moscow and in the provinces.[21] The authorities sought merely to 'organize' the terror, in other words to keep it within certain bounds. Serge writes, however, 'After the September days the terror does not die away; it slackens and becomes systematic.'[22] And E. H. Carr confirms that September 1918 'marked the turning point after which the terror, hitherto sporadic and unorganized, became a deliberate instrument of policy'.[23]

Two features were characteristic of the Red Terror as it was applied during the civil war. In the first place, the forms and extent of repression were closely dependent on the military situation. When, in January 1920, the Soviet Government took account of the end of hostilities and learnt that the Western Powers were lifting the blockade of Russia, they immediately announced the abolition of the death penalty.[24] A few months later, however, the military aggression by Poland led to its re-introduction.[25] In the second place, the Red Terror, like the White, bore a distinct class character. Latsis, one of the heads of the Cheka, wrote on November 1st, 1918: 'Do not ask for incriminating evidence to prove that the prisoner opposed the Soviet either by arms or by word. Your first duty is to ask him what class he belongs to, what were his origin, education and occupation. These questions should decide the fate of the prisoner. This is the meaning and essence of Red Terror.'[26] It is true that Lenin condemned (in a document not published at the time) the 'absurd lengths' to which Latsis went:[27] the practice of taking hostages, systematically chosen from among the bourgeoisie and the aristocracy, and their execution in moments of extreme tension, or as a reprisal for measures taken by the Whites, was, all the same, inspired by the principle that the Cheka chief had propounded. This philosophy determined not only the selection of victims but also, inversely, the choice of suspects to be released. Thus, in the daily report prepared in September 1918 by one section of the Cheka we find the following entry: 'Shustov, Evdokim: a store employee, arrested for having a false permit to carry arms. Decision: because he belongs to the proletarian class, Shustov is to be released from arrest.'[28] The same report mentions numerous executions of lawyers, officers, and, in general, members of the bourgeoisie. In other cases, the Chekists were ordered to re-examine their prisoners' dossiers and give preferential treatment to those who were found to be of working-class or peasant origin.[29]

In the opposite camp, where justice was no less expeditious, its targets were regularly chosen from among the labouring classes. One White military commander, for example, ordered his subordinates not to arrest workers but to either hang or shoot them. In one of his dispatches he wrote: 'The orders are to hang all arrested workers in the street. The bodies are to be exhibited for three days.'[30]

What was Lenin's attitude in face of this outbreak of violence? Soon after the seizure of power he thought it possible to say: 'We have not resorted, and I hope will not resort, to the terrorism of the French revolutionaries who guillotined unarmed men,'[31] although according to Trotsky he also sharply criticized the decision of the Congress of Soviets to abolish the death penalty: 'Nonsense. How can one make a revolution without firing squads?'[32] Trotsky's report is probably correct, for during the first months of the new régime, Lenin did, we know, urge the Soviet authorities to show ruthlessness towards counter-revolutionaries. He reproached the workers and peasants with not yet breaking down resistance 'firmly and ruthlessly enough'.[33] He complained that 'in many cases the Soviet government ... has had the appearance not of iron but of jelly, from which socialism cannot be built.'[34] He returned to this theme again and again,[35] frequently denouncing the 'howls' and 'whinings' of the bourgeois intellectuals who wailed at the horrors of the Red Terror, and the Mensheviks who demanded that they cease.[36]

Although Lenin's motive—to defend the Soviet power against the attacks of the counter-revolution—was obvious and his logic impeccable, one is nevertheless taken aback at the wide range of targets that he proposed for the exercise of Red Terror. The latter was not merely to be aimed at counter-revolutionaries in the strict sense, but also at speculators,[37] at those bourgeois who, having tried, when Petrograd was in fear of a German attack, to get out of obligatory labour-service, were to be threatened with the death penalty,[38] and also at all persons who were found in unlicensed possession of arms.[39] Lenin declared: 'We shall be merciless both to our enemies and to all waverers and harmful elements in our midst who dare to bring disorganization into our difficult creative work of building a new life for the working people.'[40] 'Shooting for indiscipline' was to be introduced in the supply services, when these were in a state of utter disorganization during a period of famine.[41] At the time of the anti-Communist rising in Nizhni Novgorod he considered it necessary to 'shoot and deport [sic] the hundreds of prostitutes who are making drunkards of the soldiers',[42] and a few months later demanded capital punishment for 'informers giving false information'.[43] Nor is even this list complete. Lenin also threatened with death those officials of the central food-purchasing board who showed 'formal and bureaucratic attitudes to work and incapacity to help starving workers'.[44] It was necessary, he said, to 'shoot without mercy for plundering, violence and illegal requisitions on the part of the troops.'[45] There must be 'ruthless extermination of the kulaks',[46] and, furthermore, 'revolutionary coercion is bound to be employed towards the wavering and unstable elements among the masses themselves'.[47] Looking back over that period of revolutionary terror, Lenin was to epitomize its logic in these words, in April 1920: 'This is the way unity of will was expressed during the war—anybody who placed his own interests (or the interests of his village or group) above the common interests, was branded as a self-seeker and was shot.'[48]

In the face of such an apocalyptic roll of victims there is reason to ask oneself whether Lenin always weighed his words with sufficient precision. The question is more pertinent and less apologetical than may appear at first sight. There are a number of Lenin's writings in which it is obvious that some of the expressions used are not to be taken literally. Here are some examples. Writing, at the end of 1920, some notes 'on polytechnical education', he demands that a programme of 'general instruction' be compiled, including such subjects as: 'communism, history in general, history of revolutions, history of the 1917 revolution, geography, literature, etc.', and he goes on: 'If there are no such programmes yet, Lunacharsky to be hanged'[49]— Lunacharsky being the People's Commissar for Education. In a communication of July 1921 he warns two officials: 'another quarrel between you two, and we shall dismiss and jail both.'[50] Other examples of such verbal ferocity could be given.[51]

Even so, allowing for the possibility that Lenin may have permitted himself stylistic excesses that exaggerated his meaning, the responsibility he bears for the development of terror and counter-terror cannot be lightly dismissed. If the language he uses in relation to his own colleagues is sometimes metaphorical, and his threats to enemies not always to be taken literally, we nevertheless glimpse here features that tell us much about the political system that was introduced into Soviet Russia as a result of the civil war, and their gravity should not be underestimated.

At the same time it must not be forgotten that it was Lenin himself who, at the beginning of 1920, proposed that the death penalty be abolished, as soon as he felt that 'in the main the problem of the war has been solved'.[52] In the same period he explained to the Cheka that 'it goes without saying that the Soviet Government will not keep the death penalty longer than is absolutely necessary'.[53] It was Lenin, too, who in December 1921, addressing the Congress of Soviets, spoke of the need to 'reform the Cheka, define its functions and powers, and limit its work to political problems'[54]—while at the same time, as we have seen, advocating the most severe repression of Menshevik activity.* ' "What do you want?" he would ask, astonished, and cross,' Gorky tells us. ' "Is it possible to act humanely in such an unusually ferocious fight? Is there a place for kindness or magnanimity? We are blockaded by Europe, we are deprived of the help of the European proletariat, counter-revolution is creeping up on us like a bear, and we—what would you have us do? Should we not, have we not the right to fight, to resist? I am sorry, but we are not a bunch of fools".'[55] And yet it was to Lenin that Gorky, who 'was a one-man civil liberties union' turned for help in the last resort when trying to save victims of the Terror: 'Lenin was his final court of appeals.'[56] Victor Serge writes regarding the arrest of Dan and Abramovich in 1921: 'I appealed to Gorky; at that very moment he was intervening with Lenin to save the lives of the Menshevik leaders. Once Lenin was alerted they were absolutely safe.'[57] And it was at Lenin's request that Kropotkin undertook to keep him regularly informed about excesses committed by the repressive organs.[58]

A study could be made of Lenin's attitude towards the terror which would go beyond the bounds of the present work, and would need to concern itself with psychology as much as with politics. That his writings bear the imprint of the unbridled violence of the civil-war years is not in doubt. This fact gave fuel to the humanistic criticism of Leninism set forth in Karl Kautsky's *Communism and Terrorism*, and strengthened the hostility of 'democratic socialists'. There is often an element of hypocrisy in the reproach brought against the nascent Communist movement and the Bolshevik leaders that they employed methods of terror, as though the violence that broke out in Russia in those days somehow defiled an epoch of peace and progress. The Russian revolution, with the massacres of the ensuing civil war, was neither more nor less bloody than the First World War, which piled up so many corpses with the blessing of the priests of all religions, including the Social-Democratic sect. The latter did not reject violence when this served to defend the Fatherlands, but only when it was used in the service of the proletariat and socialism. One can understand Trotsky when he considers it unnecessary to justify revolutionary terror because its accusers come from among 'the organizers and exploiters of the great world slaughter'.[59] Among those who have criticized Leninism in this connexion there are indeed many who should themselves be accused rather than accusers. But there are others, too, such as Rosa Luxemburg, who, in her pamphlet on *The Russian Revolution*, warned against the demoralizing effects of terror on those who employ it: 'Against [corruption], draconian measures of terror

* See p. 265.

are powerless. On the contrary, they cause still further corruption.'[60]

This is indeed the heart of the matter. Let the moralist approve or condemn terror *per se*: the task of the sociologist or the historian is to note its consequences. Heirs already to a past of tyranny and crime raised by Tsardom to the rank of permanent institutions, the régime and society born of the October revolution were deeply marked by a fresh outburst of violence which often made a mockery of talk about socialist legality and respect for the rights of the individual—even the proletarian individual. In this way reflexes were formed, or reinforced, that were to last long after the situations that first gave rise to them. Is not the origin of the often gratuitous terror of Stalinism to be found in the largely uncontrolled and uncontrollable violence of the years 1917 to 1920? It is certainly not accidental that, of all the organs born of the civil war, one alone retained a degree of power that no attempt at reform and no change of label succeeded in cutting down: namely, the repressive institution known successively by the names Cheka, G.P.U., N.K.V.D. and M.G.B.

The weight of the bureaucracy

With the outbreak of the civil war, begun by the bourgeoisie with the backing of the imperialist powers, the launching of terror and counter-terror, and the development and omnipresence of repressive bodies, things had moved a long way from the prospects opened up by Lenin in his *State and Revolution*, wherein he had forecast that although, after the proletariat comes to power, 'a special apparatus, a special machine for suppression, the "state", is *still* necessary, ... the suppression of the minority of exploiters by the majority of the wage slaves of *yesterday* is comparatively so easy, natural and simple a task that it will entail far less bloodshed than the suppression of the risings of slaves, serfs or wage labourers ... '[61] This weakening of the repressive functions of the state was one of the conditions underlying Lenin's concept of its 'withering away'. The other condition was the progressive replacement of bureaucratic and oppressive administration by popular administration based on Soviet democracy. This was how society would advance towards socialism, under which '*all* will govern in turn and will soon become accustomed to no-one governing'.[62]

Three years after writing *State and Revolution*, Lenin was to acknowledge publicly that what had arisen on the ruins of Tsarist society was 'a workers' state with bureaucratic distortions.'[63] Between and after these dates lay his desperate struggle against the installation of a bureaucratic system, which to him represented the main enemy of democracy and socialism. The history of this struggle is essential for an understanding of Leninism.

The call that Lenin's Government issued to technicians and officials to collaborate with the new régime, when it was first established, was accompanied, of course, by a reference to 'the *leading role* of the practical organizers from among the "people".'[64] Already on November 4th, 1917, however, Lenin had acknowledged (speaking to the Petrograd Soviet): 'we do not intend, at the moment, to deprive them of their privileged position.'[65] In his pamphlet *The Immediate Tasks of the Soviet Government* he recognized that, in paying 'a very high price for the "services" of the top bourgeois experts,' the régime had made 'a departure from the principles of the Paris Commune and of every proletarian power' and added that 'this measure not only implies the cessation—in a certain field and to a certain degree—of the offensive against capital ... , it is also a step backward,' for, by consolidating established privileges, it could not but exert a 'corrupting influence ... upon the Soviet authorities.'[66]

He was already at that time speaking from experience. From December 1917 onwards the spread of Soviet institutions to areas where they had not yet struck root had the effect of bringing them into contact with many of the municipal administrations and *zemstva*, whose personnel were absorbed into the new apparatus.[67] In this way the problem arose of the relations between the Soviet power and the working class, on the one hand, and the traditional administrators on the other, the Soviet official of this period being 'as a rule a former member of the bourgeois intelligentsia or official class'.[68] The social weight of these officials was due not only to their numbers, even though, in some cases, they exceeded numerically the representatives of the proletariat in the state machine.* The cadres who came from the bourgeoisie acquired a dominant position also through their technical superiority and their 'monopoly of culture'. 'Building a machine or organizing an office, drawing up a plan or teaching in a school, all such enterprises necessitated utilizing the services of these people and, in many cases, charging them with the actual leadership.'[69]

Here was a problem of major importance. Lenin intended that the proletariat and its representatives should possess a political and social weight in conformity with the aims of the new régime. The 'specialists' drawn from the old régime must therefore be kept 'under the vigilant supervision of the proletariat', and 'no political concessions whatever' made to them.[70] At the same time, however, the workers must 'learn from them'.[71] The dilemma and the contradiction thus took this form: 'our own militant contingents of workers ... will learn from them and direct them.'[72] There was, of course, in theory, a way of overcoming the problem. Lenin expressed the hope that if the proletariat proved equal to its task, the bureaucrats of bourgeois background would be 'conquered *morally*' and 'then of themselves be

---

* According to a report made by Stalin in 1919, the administration of the Vyatka region consisted of 4,766 officials, of whom 4,467 came from the old Tsarist bureaucracy (Stalin, Vol. 4, p. 222).

drawn into our apparatus'.[73] But the task that the régime set before
the proletariat was, in the economic and social circumstances of that
time, unrealizable in practice. It was therefore necessary to face the
facts: what Lenin called at the end of 1921 the 'Soviet bureaucrats'*
did not believe in the new régime and had 'no confidence' in it.[74]
'Nine-tenths of the military experts,' wrote Lenin in *The Tax in Kind*,
'are capable of treachery at every opportunity', and the position was no
better with the non-military ones.[75]

An inquiry carried out in the summer of 1922 among 270 engineers
in the service of the Soviet state confirmed Lenin's opinion. These
officials were divided into two categories, the first comprising those
who had belonged before the revolution to the higher ranks of the
administration, and the second embracing those who had been only
'ordinary engineers' under the old régime. To the question as to whether
they were in sympathy with the Soviet state, 9 per cent of the first
category and 13 per cent of the second answered in the affirmative.†
The Soviet historian Kritsman, author of an important work on 'War
Communism', notes that in their administrative work the representatives of the old intelligentsia showed off-handedness and hostility
towards the public.[76]

Preponderant as they were both in numbers and in (relative) competence, the bulk of the bureaucrats of bourgeois origin were unwilling
to accept the proletarian leadership that the Bolsheviks at first tried
to impose upon them. The opposite relationship established itself
among the administrators. In his address to the Eleventh Party
Congress, in March 1922, the last he attended, Lenin said, with notable
frankness and plainness: 'If we take that huge bureaucratic machine,
that gigantic heap, we must ask: who is directing whom? I doubt very
much whether it can be said that the Communists are directing that
heap. To tell the truth, they are not directing, they are being directed.'[77]

And yet the Soviet Government had done much to bring about
maximum participation by workers in the tasks of management and
administration. In twenty of the most important departments of the
state economic administration, officials of proletarian origin and
delegates from working-class organizations accounted in 1918 for
43 per cent of the total, as against 10 per cent from an employing-class
background, 9 per cent technicians and 38 per cent former Tsarist
bureaucrats.[78] To this must be added the substantial position occupied

---

* Lenin, Vol. 32, p. 129. He used the contraction *sovbur*, which has also been translated
as 'Soviet bourgeois'. At the Eighth Party Congress, in 1919, Lenin spoke of 'the new
bourgeoisie which have arisen in our country ... not only from among our Soviet government employees ... but from the ranks of the peasants and handicraftsmen ... ' (Vol. 29,
p. 189).

† Kritsman, p. 233. A second question put to them related to the usefulness of the work
they were doing. In the first group 30 per cent answered that they thought their work
useful; in the second group the percentage giving this answer was 75.

in social life by working-class organizations, and especially by the trade unions.* Large numbers of workers had entered the apparatus of the Communist Party, and many more were serving in the Red Army. Lenin constantly emphasized the need to draw the masses into administrative tasks.[79] But what did these few hundred thousand workers, active as they were to the point of heroism, matter in the immense network of a monstrously swollen administration?

The increase in the number of officials had been comparatively slight during the first year of the Soviet régime. Between the first half of 1918 and the first half of 1919 their numbers rose from 114,359 to 539,841.[80] By the end of 1920, however, the Soviet machine consisted of not less than 5,880,000 officials.[81] This gigantic increase corresponded not to economic progress by Russian society but, on the contrary, to a profound crisis that brought ruin to all branches of the economy. This contrast between the growth of the administration and the decline of the country's production-capacity was especially striking in the sphere of transport. That branch of the economy employed 815,000 persons on the eve of the First World War. In 1920 the number employed in transport was 1,229,000—and this with only one-fifth the amount of traffic.[82] Proposals were often made to reduce the number of officials, but at least until the introduction of the New Economic Policy, nothing was actually done about this. In a ruined country the machinery of state served, of course, not so much to fulfil a productive function as to provide for millions of citizens, threatened with unemployment and starvation, some sort of job, however nominal, and some sort of wage, however wretched. Zinoviev, addressing the All-Russia Congress of Soviets in December 1920, said: 'We can make as many resolutions as possible but if, at the same time … tens of thousands of people press upon us in many cities, seeking to find some kind of work for themselves, we cannot by any means fight against the swelling of bureaucracy in our apparatus … '[83]

Never, perhaps, was a régime so dominated by bureaucracy headed by a statesman so hostile to this phenomenon. 'Our enemy today, if we take the enemy within, … is the profiteer and the bureaucrat',[84] he told the C.E.C. in January 1919. In the same period he complained: 'We are being ground down by red tape.'[85] It was from 1921 onwards, however, and especially in 1922, that he realized the true dimensions of the evil: 'The serious matters have been swamped in bureaucratic litter';[86] 'bureaucracy is throttling us';[87] 'All of us are sunk in the rotten bureaucratic swamp of "departments".'[88] Bureaucracy aroused in Lenin a feeling of fury that was due, perhaps, to his sense of the incapacity of the Soviet régime to wage an effective struggle against it. In December 1921 he wrote to Bogdanov: 'We don't know how to conduct a public trial for rotten bureaucracy; for this all of us …

* See p. 351.
II

should be hung on stinking ropes. And I have not yet lost all hope that one day we shall be hung for this, *and deservedly so.*'[89] He was to admit, towards the end of his life, speaking of 'our machinery of state', that 'We have not been able to study this question up to now ...'[90] He strove, nevertheless, to distinguish the principal causes of the bureaucratic phenomenon and to suggest some ways of preventing its growth.

In Lenin's view, the great weight of bureaucracy in Russia was due to the country's 'cultural underdevelopment' and in particular to the fact that 'Russia was not sufficiently developed as a capitalist country'.[91] This circumstance was naturally aggravated by the effect of the civil war. By disturbing or even destroying the relations between town and country it had smashed Russia's economic development and brought about stagnation so that the administration expanded in a situation of complete vacuum.[92] This was why the heritage from the past, in a country where state bureaucracy had always played a big role, had become even heavier and more paralysing than before.[93] Faced with conditions so hard to escape from, Lenin realized how difficult any attempt must inevitably prove to reduce the power of the bureaucratic apparatus. Addressing the miners' congress in January 1921 he said: 'We shall be fighting the evils of bureaucracy for many years to come, and whoever thinks otherwise is playing demagogue and cheating, because overcoming the evils of bureaucracy requires hundreds of measures, wholesale literacy, culture and parti- cipation in the activity of the Workers' and Peasants' Inspection.'[94] Although he was not often hesitant to employ surgical methods, he acknowledged that repression could do nothing to remedy the abuses of bureaucracy:

> You can throw out the tsar, throw out the landowners, throw out the capitalists. We have done this. But you cannot 'throw out' bureaucracy in a peasant country, you cannot 'wipe it off the face of the earth.' You can only *reduce* it by slow and stubborn effort. To 'throw off' the 'bureaucratic ulcer' ... is wrong in its very formulation ... To 'throw off' an ulcer of this kind is *impossible*. It can only be *healed*. Surgery in this case is an absurdity, an *impossibility*; only a *slow cure*—all the rest is charlatanry or naïveté.[95]

Confronted, however, with a disease the causes of which were pro- found and the symptoms of which were many and various, Lenin nevertheless recommended that all forms of treatment be used, even the harshest, not excluding surgery, although he thought this not very effective. In order to hinder the growth of bureaucracy, to reduce it somewhat, he put forward many suggestions, plans and recommenda- tions. He advised that the administrative apparatus be filled with workers.[96] He urged the setting up of a small number of 'exemplary departments', to serve as models for the rest.[97] He proposed that the press be assigned the task of keeping the bureaucracy under critical supervision.[98] He drew up regulations providing for officials to submit themselves to 'control' by the public, especially by workers and housewives.[99] His concern for detail went so far as to cause him to draw up a long questionnaire aimed at discovering the principal shortcomings in the administration and how to put them right.[100] Finally, and most important, he took the initiative in creating *Rabkrin*, the 'Workers' and Peasants' Inspection', an institution inspired by his constant preoccupation with making the administration more 'popular' in character, or at least ensuring 'popular' control over it. The members of the Workers' and Peasants' Inspection were to be elected, and were to work in it for short periods only, so as to ensure that everyone was in turn drawn into this work.[101] Despite the hopes he had built upon the functioning of this body of 'people's inspectors', Lenin admitted its failure already at the end of 1920.* In the document known as his 'Testament' he returned to the subject. 'The Workers' and Peasants' Inspection, on whom this function [checking, improving and remodelling our state apparatus] devolved at the beginning proved unable to cope with it.'[102] At that time *Rabkrin*'s staff numbered not less than 12,000, and it had become merely an extra cog in the bureaucracy that it was supposed to combat.[103]

This example is typical of the methods that were often used by the Soviet state in order to correct its own faults. When attacked by the apparently incurable disease of 'institutionitis', it tried to deal with the defects of the existing bodies by creating new ones, which did not always abolish the old bodies, but merely took their places beside them. 'I am in mortal fear of reorganizations,' Lenin acknowledged in January 1922: 'We are always reorganizing things, instead of getting on with the practical business.'[104] He seemed, however, like his colleagues, to suffer from a mania for setting up commissions. Trotsky, describing his last conversation with Lenin, during the latter's illness, tells us: 'Lenin summoned me to his room in the Kremlin, spoke of the terrible growth of bureaucratism in our Soviet apparatus and of the need of finding a lever with which to get at that problem. He proposed to create a special commission of the Central Committee ... '[105]

His helplessness was the greater, and probably he was the more consciously aware of it, in that he came up against the inertia and incompetence of a particular type of bureaucrat, the 'Communist

* 'After all, the Workers' and Peasants' Inspection exists more as a pious wish; it has been impossible to set it in motion because the best workers have been sent to the front, and the cultural level of the peasant masses is such that they have been unable to produce a sufficient number of officials' (Lenin, Vol. 31, p. 423).

bureaucrat'. Those who should have got rid of the evil contributed, on the contrary, to worsen it. Lenin pursued them with his obloquy. At the Eighth Party Congress he denounced 'the tsarist bureaucrats' who 'began to assume the colouring of communists and, to succeed better in their careers, to procure membership cards of the Russian Communist Party'.[106] These 'Soviet bureaucrats, the pampered "grandees" of the Soviet Republic',[107] were distinguished by their ' "communist" conceit',[108] their 'intellectualistic and bureaucratic complacency'.[109] This attitude was capable of causing 'a member of the Communist Party, who has not yet been combed out,' to imagine that 'he can solve all his problems by issuing Communist decrees'.[110] And Lenin urged that such Communist 'mandarins'[111] be punished 'with triple sentences as compared with non-Party people'.[112] He did whatever he personally could to counter this 'Communist conceit'. Louis Fischer tells us: 'In a dispute between a Communist powerman with no knowledge and an expert with no power, the latter lost unless the matter came to the attention of Lenin or another high-ranking unconventional party officer.'[113]

From January 1922 onwards, in the last months of his political activity, Lenin discovered that bureaucracy meant not only the conceit, complacency, abuses and authoritarianism that he had condemned, but also, on a scale he had hitherto not dreamed of, the slowness of that all-conquering 'red tape' which led Rykov to remind Soviet officials that 'labour is the relation of man to nature, and not to paper'.[114] Lenin became aware of this incompetence in one sector of the administration after another: in January he noted: 'the Central Committee apparatus is not working';[115] in February he found that the State Bank's Trading Department was 'just as sh——bureaucratic as everything else.'[116] and he concluded: 'All of us are sunk in the rotten bureaucratic swamp of "departments" ... the departments are shit ...'[117] In March 1922 he wrote that 'complete anarchy reigns' in the Commissariat of Finance.[118] At the end of 1922, during a few weeks of respite from his illness, he had occasion to observe the 'crying anarchy' existing in the administrative arrangements of the Comintern and the Profintern (the 'Red International of Labour Unions').[119] Lenin described the impressions he formed during a journey that he made, becoming aware of the dilapidated state of the railways and the muddle in their administration.

> This was the first time I travelled along the railway lines not as a 'dignitary', getting all and sundry to hustle with dozens of special telegrams but as an unknown person ... I found the railway trolleys in the worst state possible. I saw utter neglect, semi-ruin (very many things have been stolen!), total disorder, the fuel appears to have been stolen, there is water in the kerosene, the

engine running excruciatingly, stoppages on the way every minute, the traffic wretched.

And he insisted that 'this was no exception ... The whole organization was incredibly disgraceful, with complete dislocation and clumsiness.' He confessed that the experience had filled him with a sense of 'depressing hopelessness'.[120]

What made Soviet bureaucracy so absolutely intolerable was the lack of interest in their work shown by the officials. Let us consider Max Weber's description of the Prussian civil service, whose qualities constituted for him the model of an ideal bureaucracy: 'Precision, speed, unambiguity, knowledge of the files, continuity, discretion, unity, strict subordination, reduction of friction and of material and personal costs—these are raised to the optimum point in the strictly bureaucratic administration.'[121] It was Soviet Russia's misfortune that whereas her officials sometimes shared the arrogance of their German colleagues, they rarely possessed their characteristic efficiency. Thus, a régime born in a struggle for freedom and amid hopes for a libertarian society acquired, in the shape of a burdensome and authoritarian bureaucracy, what was to be one of the most lasting features of the Soviet scene.

The wave of reforms (*law, culture, teaching*)

While 'Leninist' society was marked by violence, and bureaucracy bulked big in it almost from the start, it was nevertheless too close to its revolutionary origin and its ideal of human emancipation not to show a rich diversity of achievements wrested from the old world. In a great variety of fields it demonstrated that the relation between 'reform' and 'revolution' was the opposite of that conceived by Social Democracy. It was not the fight for reforms that led up to and prepared the way for the revolution, but the revolution that opened the way to the most thorough-going reforms. The capture of power by the Russian working class in October 1971 led to numerous and substantial changes, sometimes to tremendous upheavals in the country's social life.

The Soviet régime was hardly one month old when it issued a decree that the Provisional Government had proved incapable of issuing throughout its eight months' existence: the law introducing the right to divorce, and, in particular, to divorce by mutual consent. (About the same time, civil marriage replaced religious marriage.) The Family Code of 1918 laid down divorce procedure, simplifying it to a very great extent.[122] The purpose of this reform was, in the words of one of the leading legislators of the time, to transform an institution that 'must cease to be a cage in which husband and wife live like convicts'.[123] Furthermore, the 1918 Code proclaimed, in its Article 133, the end of legal distinctions between legitimate and illegitimate children.[124] Henri Chambre considers that in the 1918 Code 'the legislator was guided by two concerns, to which everything else was subordinated: the emancipation of women and the ending of the inequality of rights between legitimate and illegitimate children.'[125]

Besides the numerous innovations in civil law there was a complete recasting of criminal law. A decree of December 7th, 1917, abolished 'all existing general legal institutions,'[126] and, having thus cleaned the board of everything inherited from the past, proceeded to introduce a wholly new conception of penal law, some features of which merely implemented traditional democratic demands, while others were harbingers of a socialist organization of justice. Punishment was no longer to bear the character of 'the expiation of an offence, or an atonement. The concept of an objective offence was firmly ruled out.'[127] Among the sources of the new legal system an important place was accorded to the ideas of 'revolutionary consciousness', the 'class-consciousness of the working people', and 'socialist consciousness'.[128] Thus, 'when deciding what penalties to impose, the Principles [of Soviet penal law, M.L.] take into account the danger to society represented both by the offender (is he or is he not a member of the bourgeoisie?) and by the offence (was it or was it not committed with a view to restoring the oppressor class to power?) ... Heavier penalties will be imposed if the answers to these questions are in the affirmative.'[129]

Finally, and most important, the new conception of law, which appeared at the moment when Soviet democracy was enjoying its fullest development, involved drawing the masses into the administration of justice. The popular 'courts', apart from those that arose quite spontaneously,[130] were from December 1917 onwards made up exclusively of *elected* judges. In February 1918 it was decided that magistrates should be appointed by the local soviets.[131] Some features were, however, retained from the 'pure democracy' that marked judicial practice in the earliest days of Soviet power, such as the selection of prosecuting and defending 'counsel' from lists of volunteers from among the ordinary people.[132]

The value of such a system of justice obviously depended on the level of the citizens who were called upon to administer it. In the large towns the results appear to have been frequently satisfactory, with the accused able to count upon the indulgence of their judges.[133] In the rural areas, however, the improvised courts handed down sentences the barbaric nature of which revealed the cultural backwardness of the peasantry. The death penalty was invoked for mere cases of theft, and sometimes carried out on the spot. The 'penal code' drawn up in a little village in Tambov province laid down that if a man struck another, 'the sufferer shall strike the offender ten times'. Elsewhere, a village woman accused of adultery (and also, to be sure, of complicity with her lover in murdering her husband) was sentenced to be buried alive. Elsewhere again, a man condemned to death had his sentence commuted to 'twenty-five blows with a rod', thanks to the intervention of a priest.[134] In the realm of justice as in others, the application of the revolution's legislation showed the extent to which the régime established by the October revolution could bear fruit only in advanced conditions, free from survivals of the Middle Ages.

If we now turn to the domain of the arts, culture and education, there is a general observation to be made about the atmosphere in which they developed. As Alfred Meyer says, in this domain 'the revolution carried with it maximal freedom of expression and experimentation'.[135] This was particularly true in literature and the arts, which flourished remarkably until quite late in the 1920s. The People's Commissariat of Education, under the enlightened direction of Anatol Lunacharsky, followed a 'policy of tolerance'[136] to the advantage of the widest diversity of schools and tendencies in the artistic and intellectual spheres, including the most contradictory. This liberal attitude aroused frequent protests among the more radical elements, the advocates of a 'new cultural October', who charged those responsible for this sector of public life with 'opportunism', on account of their easy-going and broadminded approach.[137] Lunacharsky, with Lenin's backing, strove to defend against Mayakovsky and other iconoclasts the classics of Russian literature, and of art in general.[138] The paradoxical spectacle was seen of a state cultural department defending freedom of creation against attacks from certain 'Left' artists and writers. The latter described Lunacharsky as a 'reactionary' in the columns of *Pravda*, which, thanks to Bukharin, were readily available to them. The People's Commissar replied that, whereas his detractors considered themselves 'called on to defend Party discipline in the field of poetic creativity', he considered that one of his own functions, on the basis of the office which he held, was 'the defence of the rights of free culture against Red sycophancy'.[139]

Actually, the avant-gardist zeal of many of these artists was equalled only by their ingratitude. While Lunacharsky and his Commissariat protected the various forms of classical and traditional art against revolutionary impatience and the intolerance of the modernists who wanted to consign to 'the dustbin of history' these vestiges of a drowned world, they also showed at least as much indulgence, and gave as much support, to their denigrators on the 'Left'. Specimens of highly non-traditional art were freely displayed in the streets of Moscow. Arthur Ransome describes the decorations for the first anniversary of the October revolution, still to be seen when he visited the capital early in 1919: 'Where a hoarding ran along the front of a house being repaired, the painters had used the whole of it as a vast canvas on which they had painted huge symbolic pictures of the revolution.'

And the British journalist goes on: 'Best, I think, were the row of wooden booths almost opposite the Hotel National ... These had been painted by the futurists or kindred artists, and made a really delightful effect, their bright colours and naïf patterns seeming so natural to Moscow ... '[140] The liberalism of Lunacharsky and the Soviet authorities was all the more praiseworthy because the modernism of such *avant-garde* artists did not always meet with enthusiastic approval on the part of the masses, as Ransome mentions.[141]

The relations between Lunacharsky's Commissariat and the organization called *Proletkult* also illustrate the difficulties encountered by the non-sectarian policy that was followed by the Soviet power in the realm of literature and art. Grouped in a highly structured association, with its own 'Central Committee', the partisans of *Proletkult* ('proletarian culture') considered 'that all culture of the past might be called bourgeois, that within it—except for natural science and technical skills (and even there with qualifications) there was nothing worthy of life'.[142] The *Proletkult* organization, not satisfied with the autonomy it had been accorded, demanded for itself 'full power in the cultural field'.[143] Such a demand necessarily affected its relations with the Government. The latter had at first been widely popular among the zealots of 'proletarian culture', so that they elected Lenin honorary president when they held the first All-Russia congress of *Proletkult* organizations in Moscow in September 1918.[144] However, while tolerating and even to some extent encouraging the activities of the group, the Soviet authorities sought to integrate them in the People's Commissariat of Education.[145]

This move towards a certain centralization of cultural and artistic expression, under the (very liberal) guidance of the state, was undoubtedly connected with Lenin's attitude towards artistic and cultural creativity. This was a mixture of lively hostility and relative tolerance. 'I am,' he said, 'strongly opposed to all these intellectual fads and "proletarian cultures".'[146] According to Lunacharsky, Lenin 'was very much afraid that *Proletkult* intended to occupy itself ... with the elaboration of proletarian science and, in general, with the whole volume of proletarian culture. Firstly, that seemed to him premature and a task beyond its strength. Secondly, he thought that the proletariat shut itself off from study and the assimilation of the already existing elements of science and culture by such fantasies, which were naturally for the time being precocious.'[147] In a talk with Clara Zetkin, Lenin said: 'I have the courage to show myself a "barbarian". I cannot value the works of expressionism, futurism, cubism and other isms as the highest expressions of artistic genius. I don't understand them. They give me no pleasure ... We don't understand the new art any more, we just limp behind it.'[148]

Unappreciative of modern forms of art, and acknowledging that in

this field he was 'not a competent judge',[149] Lenin was not disposed
to apply in the cultural field a rigorous line or a real censorship either.
True, he wrote to Lunacharsky: 'Aren't you ashamed to vote for
printing 5,000 copies of Mayakovsky's *150,000,000*?' But between the
'shameful' tolerance that he deplored and the rigour he seemed to be
advocating the difference was not so very great, in a period when all
publishing was beset with difficulties, since what he proposed was that
'such things' be printed in no more than ... 1,500 copies.[150] He put
down a motion in the Political Bureau directed against the theses of
'proletarian culture', but, faced with Bukharin's objections, he did
not insist that it be voted on.[151] He did, however, try to introduce
some responsible Communists into the 'art department' of the People's
Commissariat of Education, while at the same time defending the
department against some Party members who were calling for it to
be simply dissolved.[152] In general, Lenin did not like the toleration
shown by Lunacharsky towards all manifestations of *avant-garde*
culture, and the material assistance he gave them, but he nevertheless
continued to express confidence in the People's Commissar of Education in spite of the attacks often directed at him.

The development of the arts* and of literature might seem an almost
indecent luxury in a country crushed by war and poverty. With the
work of the Soviet Government in the sphere of popular education,
however, we enter a field which the Russian Marxists had always
regarded as vital. 'Were we, Communist propagandists,' asked Lunacharsky, 'ever really concerned with anything other than the education
of the people?'[153] And Lenin said: 'It takes knowledge to participate
in the revolution with intelligence, purpose and success.' This was
how he justified his putting forward of a plan for reorganizing Petrograd's public library, in which he called for an increase in the staff,
adding that 'the library's reading-room must be open, as is the practice
with *private* libraries and reading-rooms for the *rich* in civilized
countries from 8.00 a.m. to 11.00 p.m. daily, *not* excluding Sundays
and holidays'.[154] This proposal of Lenin's is dated November 1917,
when none of the vital problems of a régime only just born had yet
been solved†—a fact that shows clearly enough the importance that
Lenin accorded to questions of education. In addition to his functions
as head of the Government and principal leader of the Party he was
also chairman of the commission on reorganizing the People's Com-
missarist of Education, and followed its work from day to day.
Between 1917 and 1922 he was present, and spoke, at 'every major

---

* On the remarkable achievements and projects of Soviet architecture during the first
years of the régime, see Kopp.

† For other evidence of the close interest Lenin took in the public library service, see,
e.g. Vol. 28, pp. 451–2, and Vol. 45, p. 145.

educational conference'.[155] When, at the end of the civil war, attention was focused on the organization of the economy and on the appalling state it was in, Lenin spoke of 'raising the cultural level' as the fundamental remedy for the evils of bureaucracy.[156] Above all, he constantly reiterated the idea that it was the duty of all Party members and officials, in whatever circumstances, to *study*.[157]

Some of the innovations made by the Soviet authorities in the first years of the régime gave the impression that a regular revolution in education was being prepared. The principles of Lunacharsky and his closest colleagues were inspired by the 'progressive', non-directive methods advocated by some American and West European educationists. Other important officials in the Commissariat wanted to go further, however, and set up school communes where the children would be completely removed from a family environment.[158] The latitude allowed to local bodies in testing out new methods made possible, in this sphere as in so many others, extensive freedom to experiment. Despite the great diversity, however, it is possible to distinguish the main lines of the reforms carried out in Soviet Russia at the different levels and in the different sectors of popular education. A decree of December 10th, 1918, mobilized as 'readers' all literate citizens except those employed full-time in Soviet institutions. These 'readers' were to form themselves into groups in order to familiarize the illiterate population with all governmental decrees and the contents of Communist newspapers.[159] To complement this measure, all illiterate citizens between the age of eight and fifty were obliged to attend literacy courses arranged in the schools themselves.[160] The Government had shown its desire to popularize literature in the very first days of the Soviet régime, when a decree provided for the publication of popular editions of the works of the great classical authors, these books to be sold at cost price or, if possible, even more cheaply.[161]

Wide autonomy was allowed in the organization of primary and secondary education. Some general directives were, however, laid down by the central authorities. A decree of May 1918 introduced co-education in all schools, and, a few months later, other instructions were circulated that pursued the aims of combining school work with productive manual work and of making education both polytechnical and collective (with the formation of groups for research and reading), as well as of ensuring wide freedom of creativity for the pupils.[162] Anticipating demands that the events of 1968 were to popularize in France, and, in some cases, reforms that are still revolutionary half a century later, the leaders of Soviet education decided in October 1918 to abolish the examination system; decreed that each school be governed by a 'collective' including all workers employed in the given establishment, together with representatives of the local workers' organizations, and also of the pupils of twelve years of age and over, along with one representative of the People's Commissariat of Education; and proclaimed that 'the first aim [of the Communist nucleus in the school] is to establish a political centre ... where students may undertake the study of various political questions connected with current world events. The study should aim to develop the class consciousness of every student ... '[163] Homework was done away with, and teachers were called upon to avoid as far as possible all exercises that were mere tests of memory. The pupils were relieved of the obligation to show their teachers those marks of respect which, in the regimented educational system of Tsarist Russia, had been particularly numerous and burdensome. High-school students were explicitly urged to 'come out openly and courageously in defence of their interests'.[164] A task of profound and serious liberation of the human spirit was thus inaugurated.

At the university level the People's Commissariat also undertook pioneering work. Anticipating the criticisms made in our own time, Lunacharsky expressed indignation that the universities were 'nothing but diploma-factories',[165] and sought to remedy this state of affairs. A decree of December 1918 abolished fees for university education and opened the universities wide to new students. This decree had the result of increasing the numbers enrolled at Moscow University, in one academic year, from 2,632 to 5,892.[166] In October 1918 measures were taken to change the composition of the teaching body and to weaken the authority of the established 'mandarins'. A decree attacked the privileges of professors by depriving them of their monopoly of chairs and by allowing anyone who had given proof of competence to offer himself as a university teacher. Academic titles were abolished, and an attempt was made to subject the teaching body to regular renovation, teachers who had held their positions for fifteen years being obliged to resign, with the right to offer themselves for re-engagement.[167]

Besides the ill-will of a teaching body that was mostly conservative in outlook, the chief obstacle in the way of the plans for educational reform was the general situation in a country where, while the Government was publishing cheap books for the education of the masses, households were obliged to burn other books to keep themselves from freezing,[168] and where civil war had in many respects destroyed the foundations of culture and civilization. In January 1923 Lenin observed sadly that 'we are still a very long way from attaining universal literacy, and ... even compared with Tsarist times (1897), our progress has been far too slow.'[169] Yet the number of primary schools in 26 provinces of Russia had increased from 38,387 at the beginning of September 1917 to 62,238 in the school year 1918–19, and secondary schools had increased from 1,830 in 1917–18 to 3,783 in 1918–19.[170] This progress, limited as it was, reflected the substantial but still inadequate drive that had been carried through in a society wherein, since the great majority of the population were still illiterate, there could be no question of introducing socialism.

The proletarian society (I): freedom through workers' control

Although these reforms were important and the changes brought about in many sectors of society were bold, on the whole these were advances that the broad democratic movements had themselves been striving to achieve. They did not have the effects to be expected from a specifically proletarian revolution and the accession to power of a party representing the working class and devoted to socialism. Nevertheless, the October rising and the establishment of a constitutional order based on the soviets, and so upon the 'toiling classes', inevitably meant giving the proletariat a wholly new place in Russian society.

The first months of Soviet power showed, in fact, that the complex nature of the revolution put on the agenda a mass of demands, some of which coincided with the programme of bourgeois democracy while others went well beyond its limits. 'Permanent revolution' was far from having exhausted its effects, as the establishment of *workers' control* showed clearly enough.

The establishment of workers' control had been included in the Bolshevik Party's programme before the conquest of power, and had indeed figured prominently in the Party's propaganda.* The very day that the Bolsheviks took power, Lenin twice confirmed, before the Petrograd Soviet and before the All-Russia Congress of Soviets, that the Bolshevik Government would establish 'real workers' control over production'.[171] A few days later he drafted a decree to introduce workers' control in Soviet Russia. Lenin's draft, the main lines of which were reproduced in the C.E.C.'s decree of November 14th, provided that 'workers' control over the production, storage, purchase and sale of all products and raw materials shall be introduced in all industrial, commercial, banking, agricultural and other enterprises employing not less than five workers ... or with an annual turnover of not less than 10,000 rubles.'† It also provided for this control to be exercised either by the workers and office staff themselves or by their elected representatives, in the case of enterprises so large as to necessitate recourse to the delegation of powers. Agreement by the workers was essential before the employers could close down an enterprise or make 'any change in its operation'. The draft also indicated how the workers' factory committees were to be integrated in the new state system, providing that their decisions could be

* See p. 183.
† This restriction was omitted from the actual decree. Lenin's draft is given in Vol. 26, p. 264. The full text of the decree is in Bunyan and Fisher, pp. 308–10.

abrogated only by the trade unions and the congresses of factory committees and that both the employers and the workers' representatives were to be 'responsible to the state for the order, discipline and safety of the property. Persons guilty of hiding raw materials or products, of falsifying accounts, and of other similar abuses,' were criminally liable.

The final text of the decree arranged for a pyramid of committees to be erected, rising from the enterprises themselves to the All-Russia Congress of Factory Committees, with intermediate levels on the scale of cities, provinces and industrial regions. It linked these committees with the Soviet institutions at corresponding levels, so as to integrate them more completely in the state structure. This integration corresponded to the Soviet Government's concern about the anarchical tendencies that were increasingly dominating the country's economic life and that of individual enterprises. The decree mentioned specifically that it had been framed 'in the interests of a systematic regulation of the national economy'.[172]

While the employers' reactions could not be other than negative, and indeed were so,* the attitude of the world of labour to the legalization of workers' control was far from uniform. In particular, there was acute tension between trade-union circles and the factory committees, to which they were often hostile, with the factory committees enjoying enthusiastic support from the anarchist movements. For the latter, the factory committees, as institutions born of the revolution itself, were closer to the masses than any others. Moreover, these committees constituted, in their eyes, 'the cells of the future society', and, as the anarchists saw it, 'they, not the state, will now administer'.[173] The anarchists reacted favourably to the decree, being agreeably surprised to scent in a governmental document, of all places, a certain 'anarcho-syndicalist' aroma that was to their liking.[174] The attitude of the trade-union leaders, Bolsheviks or not, was, on the contrary, very unfavourable, and their official spokesman in the C.E.C., Lozovsky, abstained when the decree was voted on. He said: 'The workers in each enterprise should not get the impression that the enterprise belongs to them.'[175] The doubts felt by such men in relation to workers' control did not necessarily reflect authoritarian and antidemocratic tendencies on their part. Lozovsky was one of the trade-union leaders who, coming close to Martov's position, most vigorously opposed the concentration of Soviet power in the hands of the Bolsheviks alone; for his continual breaches of discipline he was even, in January 1918, expelled from the Party (he was re-admitted in 1919).

* Thus, 'the Petrograd Factory-Owners' Association decided to close down all enterprises where the workers insisted on the right of control. The All-Russia Congress of the Manufacturers' Association, held in Moscow from 7–9 December 1917, decided to close down all enterprises where workers' control assumed the form of active interference in the administration' (Dewar, p. 23).

One of the principal economists among the Bolsheviks, Larin, was no less critical of 'workers' control', and yet he was emphatic on the need to respect the freedom of the press. And Ryazanov, who, more than anyone else in these years, voiced the spirit of insubordination and desire for democracy among the Communists, expressed the view that the factory committees represented 'the separatist opposition to the reorganization of the economy on a socialist basis'.[176] The reason for this hostility to 'workers' control' on the part of some Bolsheviks was their conviction that the autonomistic character and anarchic activity of the committees that put it into effect would hinder the establishment of a planned economy, and therefore of socialism.

The defenders and opponents of workers control faced each other at the First All-Russia Congress of Soviet Trade Unions in January 1918. The trade unionists who advocated economic centralization won a victory that owed much to Bolshevik support. The resolutions passed called for the factory committees to be reduced to the status of mere agencies of the trade unions in the enterprises, and for their activities to be restricted to control in the sense of 'supervision', without any interference in management functions in the strict sense.[177] However, the Government did little to centralize the activity of the factory committees. There being no question of using force, it merely sought to operate through the trade unions, exercising persuasion in order to reduce the dimensions of economic anarchy.[178]

The actual achievements of the factory committees amounted to little or nothing. How, indeed, could it have been otherwise, given the conditions prevailing in Russia? 'Almost all of the skilled, educated workers available were working for the Bolshevik Party. So the most [the] factory committees could do was to use up the existing stocks ... They managed to provide work, somehow or other, until the spring of 1918. Then, one after another, the factories closed down.'[179] There were certainly a few examples of successful activity, as, for instance, in the Moscow textile mills, where the workers, left to themselves, managed to carry on with the work and even to make profits.[180] But these were exceptions. In general, the factory committees refused to obey the instructions they received, and, often showing a corporatist spirit, sought to form alliances with the factory-owners.[181] Sometimes even more glaring abuses were reported: the personnel of some enterprises sold off the stocks and plant and divided the proceeds among themselves.[182] The workers frequently awarded themselves large wage-increases.[183]

Some factories, resembling 'anarchist communes', lived a self-contained existence,[184] while on the railways each station was 'a sort of republic, with the stationmaster like the chairman of a Soviet, elected by his subordinates'.[185] Clearly, these conditions were not conducive to increased production. In her reminiscences Krupskaya tells how she was visited one day by a working woman who wanted a certificate from the People's Commissariat of Education: 'During our conversation I asked her what shift she was working in. I thought she was working in the night shift. Otherwise she would not have been able to come to the Commissariat in the daytime. "None of us are working today. We had a meeting yesterday evening, everyone was behindhand with her domestic work at home, so we voted to knock off today. We're the bosses now, you know."' And Lenin's wife comments: 'For early 1918 ... this was a typical case.'[186]

Such facts as these explain the efforts made by the Government and the trade unions—efforts which long remained ineffective, and in any case failed to prevent the phenomenon of workers' control from becoming widespread in the first months of 1918. The workers were certainly not always motivated by political or doctrinal concerns, but 'libertarian' aspirations were occasionally to be observed among them. Some militants were indignant at the criticism levelled against workers' control, and upheld it in the name of the 'creativeness of the masses'.[187] In the last analysis, it is not on the planes of efficiency or output that one must judge this largely spontaneous phenomenon of the taking over of the factories by the workers themselves. Such preoccupations were, as a rule, remote from the thinking of the workers in 1917 and 1918. By opening the books of the enterprises where they worked and subjecting their employers' financial and commercial activities to supervision, by taking over the management of their factories and 'occupying' them, the Russian workers sought to show, in everyday life and in the very places where they had been exploited, that their fate had been transformed—that they were the masters now. Productivity might suffer and the economy experience further setbacks, the new rulers might express their misgivings and the trade unions endeavour to bring order into this anarchy: the mass of the Russian workers clung to this 'control' and this autonomy of their workplaces, identifying it with 'the conquests of October' and the deep, living reality of the Revolution. They clung to it, and, thanks to the weakness of the central authority, they kept it alive for a long time. As late as 1920 some trade-union leaders complained, referring to the factory committees that were supposed to be subject to their direction, of the 'dual-power situation' which was hindering economic activity.[188]

Workers' control, while technically inefficient, at any rate in the circumstances of that time, and sometimes disastrous in its effects, had such deep roots in the consciousness of the proletariat that it long remained out of reach of the Government's attempts to encroach upon it. In the first months of the Soviet régime, as Paul Avrich says, 'the Russian working class enjoyed a degree of freedom and a sense of power unique in its history.'[189]

The proletarian society (II): from freedom to compulsion

This explosion of anarchy, thise sense of popular power, and this rejection of all constraint, while proving the reality of the victory that had just been won, were not calculated to consolidate it. Yet that was the task of the moment and, while awaiting the support that the international proletariat would bring to the Russian revolution,* it was necessary to overcome the economic crisis and ensure the country's food supplies, and, to this end, re-establish exchange between town and country by increasing industrial production. Once the intoxication—*es schwindelt*, 'I am dizzy,' Lenin told Trotsky on the day of the seizure of power[190]—and, perhaps, too, the *surprise* of victory had passed off, practical tasks assumed priority. Since socialism was not applicable in Russia in the immediate future, Lenin's ideas about the organization of labour revealed rigour that was more in line with managerial orthodoxy than with revolutionary enthusiasm. What was needed, he declared, was to wage 'a ruthless struggle against the [prevailing] chaos'.[191] 'In every socialist revolution,' Lenin said, 'after the proletariat has solved the problem of capturing power ... there necessarily comes to the forefront the fundamental task of creating a social system superior to capitalism, namely, raising the productivity of labour, and in this connexion (and for this purpose) securing better organization of labour.'[192] This was a gigantic task, and an extraordinary one to undertake in a society wherein capitalism had hardly shown its face and so many sectors of public life still bore traces of the Middle Ages.

Lenin called for the application of methods that were those of capitalism itself. 'The task that the Soviet government must set the people in all its scope is—learn to work.'[193] And it was from the capitalists that the proletariat had to learn.[194] This was not so paradoxical a situation as it might seem; did not Marxism teach that socialism is built upon the foundation provided by the large-scale industry developed by capitalism? Implacable logic therefore led Lenin to call for recourse to be had to the methods which capitalist large-scale industry had introduced and which, by intensifying exploitation of the workers still further, had increased their discontent and rebelliousness. In *The Immediate Tasks of the Soviet Government* written in early spring 1918, Lenin wrote: 'We must raise the question of piece-work and apply and test it in practice.'[195] He went even further, calling for the application of the Taylor system, which aroused the wrath of the 'Left Communists' and the opposition of many trade-union leaders.[196] Lenin had himself described Taylorism, in 1914, as 'man's enslavement by the machine'.[197]

Only a few months after overthrowing the power of the bourgeoisie, Leninism was inviting its followers to find their economic and social

* See p. 364.

models in capitalist Germany: 'Yes, learn from the Germans! History is moving in zigzags and by roundabout ways. It so happens that it is the Germans who now personify, besides a brutal imperialism, the principle of discipline, organization, harmonious co-operation on the basis of modern machine industry, and strict accounting and control.'[198] Germany's war economy offered a model of efficiency which impressed Lenin and caused him to praise 'state capitalism' as a system of transition to socialism. At the very moment when Russia had just effected a twofold break with the bourgeois régime—the seizure of power in October 1917 and the dissolution of the Constituent Assembly in January 1918—and the mechanism of 'permanent revolution' had thereby been freshly stimulated, Lenin said that state capitalism would be a good thing for her, because 'state capitalism is something centralized, calculated, controlled and socialized'.[199]

The German model implied emphasis on the cardinal virtues of discipline. In December 1917, in a draft for a decree on nationalizing the banks, Lenin wrote: 'The workers and office employees of the nationalized enterprises must exert every effort and adopt extraordinary measures to improve the organization of the work, strengthen discipline and raise the productivity of labour.'[200] And in March 1918 he declared that 'the primary and fundamental task' of the day was 'adoption of the most energetic, ruthlessly determined and draconian measures to improve the self-discipline of the workers and peasants of Russia'.[201] To be sure, Lenin often called for a voluntary, freely accepted form of discipline, 'a discipline of equals ... which must take the place of barrack-room discipline'.[202] He advocated—notably in his exaltation of 'Communist Saturdays (subbotniki)'*—appealing to the noblest feelings of the workers, to their political consciousness and to the moral grandeur inseparable from the building of socialism.[203] Alongside these themes, however, which were never abandoned, others appeared and became preponderant, themes prompted by the harsh realities of Russia's situation. In one of his last writings, Lenin was to speak of a 'cultural revolution', but it was not upon a revolution in manners and morals that he counted, in general, for solution of the vital problems of social life—the feeding of a population beset by famine and the revival of an industry under threat of complete paralysis. When he spoke of 'cultural revolution' he meant, principally, acquisition of technique and knowledge inherited *from the past*, by the classes that had been deprived of them. Here, in the last analysis, besides a specific response to functional exigencies, was the expression of a philosophy which, while not

---

* The 'Communist Saturdays' brought together workers who agreed to sacrifice their rest-day, devoting it to unpaid labour. The experiment did not always retain the voluntary character it had possessed at the outset (Lenin, Vol. 29, pp. 409 ff., and Vol. 30, pp. 283–288).

ruling out appeals to the idealistic elements in human nature, was rooted in a materialist view of the world, derived from a positivist interpretation of Marxism.

There was positivism indeed in a conception of economic progress and labour relations that was strictly dependent on considerations of output, order and efficiency. Resort to a 'scientific discipline' such as Taylorism claimed to bring into the factory reflected a narrowly 'industrialist' conception. Of course, the urgency of the problems to be solved, and the acuteness of the social and economic crisis that was gripping Russia offered no encouragement for experimenting with roads that were diametrically opposite to those laid down by industrial capitalism—the 'Communist Saturdays' here figuring as an exception. Nevertheless, Lenin's views revealed a certain rationalistic shortsightedness and a lack of bold imagination which led to the deliberate rehabilitation of certain forms of culture engendered by capitalism. Advocates of cultural revolution, even Marxist-Leninist ones, will not find in Lenin any solution to the problems that interest them.

The desire to put an end to anarchy and at all costs to get production going again, the stress on the need to establish labour discipline, rapidly led to measures of compulsion of increasing severity. For, although Lenin tended to think that 'iron proletarian discipline'[204] was a permanent and natural characteristic of the working class, that 'the proletarians ... seek discipline and expect order',[205] the demoralization and de-classing of the working class* were to oblige him to rely less and less upon such considerations. In May 1918, at the congress of the Supreme Economic Council, provincial speakers, one after another, denounced the pressure that was being brought to bear on the workers, especially the railwaymen. The Government's representatives, on the other hand, complained of the anarchistic tendencies that were often manifested by the railway workers, and spoke of the need for 'Americanizing the railway administration'.[206]

It was not so much an 'Americanizing' as a *militarizing* of industry that took place, and this became one of the most characteristic features of the period of War Communism. It was to a large extent imposed by circumstances, independently of the will of the Bolshevik leaders, and even encountered reluctance and opposition on the part of some of them.[207] But how could it be avoided, when the organization of the economy, and, in particular, of the labour market was being effected no longer in accordance with the laws of the market, and yet not on the basis, either, of rational, scientific planning, but, instead, under the direct compulsion of events, and by persons whose competence left much to be desired? Amid the general wretchedness and hunger, which the Government succeeded in mitigating only for certain categories of workers, in a social climate in which egalitarianism

* See p. 348.

was still the fashion, producers could be given little direct incentive, and appeals to goodwill were frustrated by discouragement and physical exhaustion. Under such conditions, resort to measures of compulsion proved unavoidable.

Trotsky came forward as the leading advocate of such measures. In December 1919 he proposed that the working class be mobilized on a military basis. This signified, in the words of an article he wrote in *Pravda* at that time, that, in existing circumstances, 'transition to a régime of universal labour service can be accomplished only by means of coercion, that is, ultimately, by the armed force of the state'.[208] At an important gathering of trade unionists he put forward a series of draconian measures that he considered should be imposed upon the working class in order to combat chaos. Only Lenin supported him, and his proposals were rejected by some sixty votes to two.[209] Finding himself unable to transform workers into soldiers, the organizer of the Red Army resolved to transform soldiers into workers. Thus arose the Labour Armies, charged with reviving production. The results achieved, however, did not correspond to the hopes that had been entertained. Willy-nilly, the trend was towards militarization of the working class. The 'work-book', or 'labour-passport', so loathed by the workers in the West in the period when it was a means of subjecting them to employers' tyranny, now reappeared in Soviet Russia. The courts were called upon to punish breaches of labour discipline, and workers who left their factories were treated as deserters: they could be given sentences of internment in labour camps.

Needless to say, methods of compulsion were resorted to most frequently in situations of urgency and distress. This happened with transport, which was in this period in a catastrophic condition. The engineers in charge forecast that unless a spectacular change for the better took place, railway transport would come to a complete standstill in the very near future. As frequently happened in such circumstances, it was to Trotsky's organizational talents that the task of recovery was entrusted. But Trotsky did not confine himself to applying rigorous measures to the railway workers. 'When the railwaymen's trade union raised objections to his action, he dismissed its leaders and appointed others who were willing to do his bidding.'[210] He saved the Soviet transport system from disaster, but in so doing he carried the logic of militarization to extremes. In this way there appeared a 'philosophy of forced labour' that fitted oddly into a system claiming to be socialistic, a doctrine that did more than merely justify measures taken under pressure of necessity—an idealizing of such measures, that transformation of necessity into a virtue in which Stalin was later to excel.[211]

Trotsky's exaggerated policy was repudiated by the Central Committee, a majority of eight (including Lenin) against six expressing

disapproval of the brisk methods to which the trade unions had been
subjected.[212] Thus opened the 'trade-union discussion' which was to
shake the Party for several months.* Already the dictatorship *of* the
proletariat had, in this sphere, been transformed into a dictatorship
over the proletariat. For, while the measures imposed upon the
Russian working class can legitimately be depicted as due to inescap-
able necessity, to which the Communist leaders were forced to submit
in spite of themselves, the extent to which the working class was
reduced to subjection can be fully appreciated only if it be realized
that this class, made to submit to most rigorous discipline, and suffering from dreadful want, was also deprived of those means of defence
that might have mitigated its woes. Means of *defence* for a working
class which had come to power by defeating the bourgeoisie? Was this
not an incongruous idea in itself? It certainly seemed so to many
ideologists of the time, whose simplistic thinking seems, with the
hindsight of history, to have been fatally ingenuous. *The ABC of
Communism*, which served as a popular textbook during the first
years of the régime, declared — artlessly or cynically? — that 'the time for
fine phrases is past, and the time for hard work has come. No longer
does it devolve upon us to fight for our rights in Moscow or in Petrograd; the working class has secured its rights and is defending them
at the front.'[213] During the first All-Russia Congress of Trade Unions,
in January 1918, a delegate said: 'it is impossible that we (the workers)
present demands to ourselves.'[214] *A fortiori*, why should the workers
take strike action when such action, 'illogical' in a workers' state
anyway, must add to the country's economic difficulties? This was
how the metal-workers' union saw the matter when, in January 1918,
it decided to forbid its members to go on strike any more.[215]

Yet there was never any formal ban on strikes during the first years
of the Soviet régime. Zinoviev even announced, in the name of the
Party, at the first All-Russia Congress of Trade Unions, that the
Council of People's Commissars had decided to make a contribution
to strike funds.[216] There was no doctrine or legislation on this matter,
only a series of statements by a number of trade-union and political
leaders, deploring any stoppage of work. Tomsky, for example, the
chief trade-union spokesman, said that it seemed to him that strikes
were pointless under a system in which it was the trade unions themselves that decided questions of wages and labour conditions.[217]
This argument would have been more convincing if the trade unions
had in fact been representative of the will of their members. However,
as was acknowledged in a motion put before the Tenth Party Congress,
signed by Lenin and by Tomsky himself, there was need to re-establish
in the trade unions a democracy that had by then disappeared from
them.[218]

* See p. 343.

Strikes remained a constant feature of social life in 'Leninist' Russia. They occurred throughout the period of the civil war. It is difficult, however, to form an exact idea of how the authorities reacted to these movements. There were cases of imprisonment of strikers for the duration of a strike. In other cases, workers who went on strike were deprived of their wages. It is certain that the Menshevik 'agitators' who were often active in starting strikes were subjected to severer treatment. But it also happened that the trade unions decided to give financial support to workers on strike, and the Government itself stepped in to suppress the abuses that had caused the strike, instead of crushing the strike itself. This occurred during a strike on the railways in June 1918, when the Council of People's Commissars published a communiqué in which it declared its intention to 'show no mercy to those agents of the Soviet Government who by thoughtless and criminal acts intensify the dissatisfaction of the toiling masses ... ', and spoke of the workers' 'just indignation'.[219] It was true, nevertheless, that the strike, that classic weapon of the proletariat, hitherto utilized and praised by revolutionaries, while not legally proscribed, was, as a rule, regarded as a form of sabotage of the economy, condemned by most of the country's leaders, and often suppressed, or at best tolerated, in a situation where its use was justified by the hardships of the workers and the tyranny of the bureaucrats.

As for Lenin himself, he took no definite stand on the question of the legitimacy or otherwise of strikes. On two occasions only did he speak out at all clearly on the point. The first was in April 1919, at a moment when the civil war was in a phase that was highly unfavourable to the Bolsheviks. He then confined himself to emphasizing the disastrous effects that any interruption of work might have on the struggle against the 'Whites', and on the conditions of the people, already suffering from want.[220] He also declared, in view of the prevailing circumstances, for repression of the current strike movements: 'Which is better,' he demanded, 'to imprison several scores or hundreds of instigators, guilty or innocent, deliberate or unwitting, or lose thousands of Red Army men and workers?'[221] In other words, he condemned certain strikes not on account of the nature of the régime but because of the necessities imposed by the civil war.

Lenin reconsidered the problem of the right to strike in the entirely new circumstances created by the introduction of the N.E.P. In a long article on 'The role and tasks of the trade unions under the conditions of the New Economic Policy', published in *Pravda* of January 17th, 1922, he declared unambiguously for the formation of strike funds,[222] justifying this line by the fact that state enterprises were now obliged to make profits, and also by the existence of 'narrow departmental interests and excessive departmental zeal', which entailed a certain conflict of interests between the mass of the workers and the management. It followed that 'the strike struggle in a state where the proletariat holds political power can be explained and justified only by the bureaucratic distortions of the proletarian state and by all sorts of survivals of the old capitalist system in the government offices on the one hand, and by the political immaturity and cultural backwardness of the mass of the working people on the other.'[223] Naturally, it was still the duty of the trade unions to concern themselves with 'averting mass disputes in state enterprises by pursuing a far-sighted policy with a view to objectively protecting the interests of the masses of the workers in all respects and to removing in time all causes of dispute'.[224]

The problem of strikes was, however, only one aspect of a more general one, that of the status of the trade unions. The important discussion on this subject took place in terms similar to those relating to the strike question: just as striking seemed absurd in a situation where the workers were in power, so independent trade unions seemed out of place where proletarian power was identified with state power. The Bolsheviks had always condemned trade-union neutrality, and advocated the establishment of close links — of political subjection and ideological subordination — between the Party and the unions. After the October revolution they spoke out against any form of trade-union independence in relation to the Government. Zinoviev had asked the Mensheviks during the First All-Russia Trade Union Congress, in January 1918: 'From what and from whom is it necessary to be independent? From your own government, from your workers' and peasants' government, from the Soviets of Workers' and Soldiers' Deputies? ... Independence from the Soviets of Workers' and Peasant's Deputies ... means independence in order to support those who fight against the workers' and peasants' government.'[225] This same congress passed a resolution according to which 'the trade unions should, in the process of the present socialist revolution, become organs of socialist power'.[226] While the idea of independence was rejected, that of integration, pure and simple, of the trade unions in the state was thus seen as something for the future — an aim to be achieved rather than an established situation. The actual place of the trade unions, there and then, among the country's institutions, remained open to discussion.

This first trade-union congress also concerned itself with defining the tasks of the trade unions in the new political and social setting. It listed a series of functions, such as ensuring respect for the laws on wages and labour conditions, and co-operative relations with 'the regulative organs of production'. In this long list, however, no mention was explicitly made of defending the workers' interests.[227] In the euphoria of the time there doubtless seemed no need for such defence. Theoretical arguments about the trade unions' place in the state ceased to seem relevant, in any case, during the civil war. At that time the trade unions were active above all in mobilizing the working class and determining wages.[228] When, however, economic problems became topical again, the discussion on the nature of the trade unions in the Soviet order was revived, and divided the Party. As we have seen, the discussion developed on the basis of disagreements that, as Lenin said, did not really exist[229]—at least if account be taken only of the resolutions placed before the Eleventh Party Congress, which had to settle the quarrel. These resolutions, however, gave only partial expression to the real views of the opposing groups, tactical considerations having caused them to moderate their statements.

Trotsky, on the one hand, and the 'Workers' Opposition', on the other, constituted the two extreme tendencies. Kollontai, Shlyapnikov and their friends demanded that the trade unions be assigned a fundamental role in administrative and economic decision-making and management. Trotsky, on the contrary, was, after his conflicts with the railwaymen's union, in favour of complete subordination of the trade unions to political authority. By calling for a 'shaking-up' of the unions he had aroused strong feeling and angered Lenin.[230] On the eve of the congress of March 1921, after forming an alliance with Bukharin, Trotsky demanded that the trade unions be transformed into 'production organs', with the 'production point of view' taking priority over the 'trade-union point of view'. In reality, this policy had been in force for a long time already, but without being proclaimed so frankly.

The extreme tendencies were separated by a 'marsh' in which people repeated generalities about the need to restore workers' democracy in the unions, while rejecting the idea of turning them into state institutions in the immediate future. Lenin was among the ten signatories of a resolution expressing this cautious attitude, which was passed by an overwhelming majority at the Eleventh Congress.[231] One might suppose from this event that Lenin's ideas on the trade-union question were identical with the vague conformism of this majority resolution. But such supposition would be mistaken. He had, during the first period of the régime, expressed agreement with the view that the unions should be gradually transformed into state institutions.[232] In the Party programme which he drafted for the 1919 congress he included a formula which the Workers' Opposition was to utilize in support of the granting of wider powers to the trade unions: according to Lenin, they were to become 'organs administering the economy'.[233] His ideas about the relations between the Party and the trade unions contained nothing that had not been established doctrine before the revolution. Owing to 'certain reactionary features, a certain craft narrow-mindedness, a certain tendency to be non-political', the trade unions had to be led by the Party:[234] although, in practice, Lenin seems to have favoured a flexible application of this rule.* In general, the trade unions were to be regarded as a 'school of communism'[235] and to serve as 'a link between the party and the unenlightened millions'.[236]

The evolution of the régime led Lenin, however, to put forward a personal and original conception of the role of the trade unions and their place in Soviet society. He made this known during the discussion about the trade unions at the beginning of 1921, but it was not given the form of a resolution during the Eleventh Congress, and, indeed, Lenin's ideas were not embodied in any of the documents put before the congress. The fact was that his view had come up against general incomprehension,[237] owing to its originality and its departure from principles that had already assumed dogmatic form. Commenting on Trotsky's theses, Lenin opposed the notion epitomized in the rhetorical question: 'Since this is a workers' state without any bourgeoisie, against whom then is the working class to be protected and for what purpose?' Lenin rejected this notion, pointing out that 'ours is not actually a workers' state but a workers' and peasants' state': the Soviet state, he said, was, moreover, 'a workers' state *with a bureaucratic twist to it*'. Because of these facts it was not possible to do without trade unions for 'protecting the material and spiritual interests of the ... proletariat': they were necessary 'to protect the workers from their state'.[238] After the New Economic Policy had been introduced, he repeated that there was 'a certain conflict of interests in matters concerning labour conditions between the masses of workers and the directors and managers of the state enterprises,' and from this the conclusion followed that 'it is undoubtedly the duty of the trade unions to protect the interests of the working people ... and constantly to correct the blunders and excesses of business organizations resulting from bureaucratic distortions of the state apparatus.'[239]

It was highly characteristic of Lenin's genius and of the dialectical character of Leninism to perceive the contradictory relationship that existed between the state and the trade unions, despite all the snares of reassuring ideology represented by the idea of 'the workers' state'. If this clear-minded approach to the trade-union question had been pursued and carried deeper, it would have led to other dogmas as well being called in question. But it is no less significant that this idea was unable to triumph in practice. When, after the close of the trade-union discussion, the many views that had been voiced in it were embodied in congress resolutions and group platforms, no place was found, in all those documents, for Lenin's idea. That formulation, so precise and so dramatic: 'a workers' state with a bureaucratic twist to

---

* See the 'Draft resolution for the Central Committee', May 1921, in which Lenin bows to the rejection by the Communist group in the trade-union congress of a resolution reflecting the viewpoint of the Party leadership (ibid., Vol. 42, p. 306).

it', was taken up by no one, though it held a wealth of content such as was to be found neither in the endlessly repeated calls for 'militarization' of labour and 'statization' of the trade unions, nor in the incantations about 'proletarian democracy' and 'workers' creativity'. Both of those remained dead letters so far as political reality was concerned.

The proletarian society (III): the poverty of the workers
In the summer of 1917 the Bolsheviks had advanced towards power under the slogan: 'Peace, land and bread!' One year later, in July 1918, the bread rations in Petrograd were as follows. For two days: 1st category,* 200 grammes; 2nd category, 150 grammes; 3rd category, 100 grammes; 4th category, 50 grammes.[240] While the civil war lasted, the food-supply position improved only momentarily, each time that the harvest was brought in. Hunger was endemic, and was one of the principal reasons for the weakening and demoralization of the working class. In 1921, shortly before the introduction of the New Economic Policy, the best-nourished category of workers were receiving rations equivalent to between 1,200 and 1,900 calories, while some transport workers had to be content with 700 to 1,000 calories per day. In the Donets basin the miners were getting half the calories necessary for normal nourishment, even though they were 'shock workers'. As for the rest ... The population of Moscow sometimes received only 60 grammes of bread to last them for two days.[241] It is not surprising, therefore, that the 'black market' flourished, representing 75 to 80 per cent of total food supplies during the civil war years.[242] The consequences of such a situation can be imagined.

Hunger was only one aspect of a general crisis. The suffering caused by cold and lack of fuel was another. People burned books and the floorboards in their flats,[243] and literally froze in their offices. One high official in Petrograd, the chairman of the Committee of State Constructions, told Arthur Ransome that the temperature sometimes fell below zero in his department, and added: 'Many of my assistants have fallen ill. Two only yesterday had to be taken home in a condition something like that of a fit, the result of prolonged sedentary work in unheated rooms. I have lost the use of my right hand for the same reason.'[244] In the sphere of public health and hygiene the situation was no less dramatic. Medicines were reserved for the army, and the doctors had nearly all disappeared, either absorbed into the army or victims of the civil war.[245] There was grave need for their services.

---

* The inhabitants of the larger towns were divided into four categories for food-rationing purposes: workers engaged in heavy manual work; workers engaged in ordinary manual work, or brain-work of an intensive nature; ordinary brain-workers; and the unoccupied.

Epidemics spread easily. Contagious diseases that had not been brought under full control at the beginning of the 20th century again spread rapidly. Between 1917 and 1922, about 22 million people contracted typhus; in 1918–1919, the official mortality for this disease was 1·5 million, and the census was probably incomplete. Cholera and scarlet fever caused fewer deaths but affected 7 or 8 million Russians. The death rate was astronomical ... and, in the country as a whole, ... doubled. The birth-rate, on the other hand, declined considerably, barely reaching 13 per thousand in the important towns and 22 per thousand in the country. Between the end of 1918 and the end of 1920, epidemics, hunger and cold had killed 7·5 million Russians; World War had claimed 4 million victims.[246]

Among the workers, in particular, the standard of living declined precipitously. In 1922 the workers' *real* wages were only 30 per cent of the pre-war level. As compared with 1913, only their housing conditions had improved, thanks to the requisitioning of bourgeois dwellings.[247] Underlying this general catastrophe was an economic crisis caused by the breakdown of commercial links between town and country—an inextricable situation in which the peasants, finding themselves unable to obtain manufactured goods in exchange for their corn, hoarded it, and did all in their power to guard it from requisition by the state or seizure by the workers, while the workers, whose ranks had been thinned out by the ravages of the civil war, were incapable, through lack of food, of getting industrial production going again. In 1920 exchange between town and country, excluding the army's needs and those of the transport workers, amounted to no more than 12 per cent of pre-war exchange.[248]

The loss of the Ukraine, as a result of the peace of Brest Litovsk, and then the civil war, had the gravest consequences, for that region accounted for three-quarters of the country's production of coal, two-thirds of its iron ore, four-fifths of its sugar, three-quarters of its manganese and nine-tenths of Russia's exportable wheat, not to mention two-thirds of all the salt extracted.[249] The Germans also occupied other portions of Russia's territory, in which, for example, the production of fuel represented 45 per cent of the total in 1913.[250] When some regions were recovered, as a result of Germany's defeat in November 1918, the civil war brought fresh destruction. Besides the extensive damage done by actual operations in Russia and the Ukraine, the civil war also cut off from Soviet Russia such precious sources of supply as Caucasia (oil) and Turkestan (cotton). Military requirements, moreover, enjoyed absolute priority. In 1920 the Red Army absorbed half of all industrial production, 60 per cent of sugar, 40 per cent of fats, 90 per cent of men's footwear, 40 per cent of soap and

100 per cent of tobacco.[251] Finally, the blockade decreed in February 1918 by the Allied Powers had completely cut the country off from the outside world.

At that moment industrial production, in a Russia reduced territorially and economically by the Brest treaty, amounted to no more than one-fifth of the pre-war figure. A few months later, Soviet Russia controlled a mere 8 per cent of the country's pre-war coal and 24 per cent of its iron ore. In 1919 the Soviet factories received only one-tenth of the fuel they needed. At the end of the civil war, the situation was as follows. Extraction of iron ore in Soviet Russia stood at 1·6 per cent and production of cast iron at 2·4 per cent of the pre-war level. In terms of gold roubles, the total value of the finished and semi-finished goods produced came to 12·9 per cent and 13·6 per cent respectively of the 1913 figures. Of the 70,000 versts of railway track in European Russia, only 15,000 were undamaged, and over 60 per cent of the country's locomotives were out of use. In some branches of industry and some regions, productivity was down to less than 10 per cent of its 1913 level, and, for the whole country, it amounted to no more than one-third of that level.[252]

One of the reasons for this collapse of production was reversion to pre-industrial techniques. Whereas in 1916 timber represented only 14 per cent of the fuel consumed in Russia, as compared with 67 per cent for coal, in 1919 the corresponding figures were 88 per cent and 3·5 per cent, and in 1920 they were 50 per cent and 36 per cent.[253] The peasants, clinging to their land and protecting their stocks of produce by means of fraud, sabotage and armed resistance, were able to withstand this catastrophe, but the very existence of the working class was threatened. In 1917 Russia had had 3,024,000 industrial workers. Between 1918 and 1922 this number declined as follows:

1918	2,486,000
1919	2,035,000
1920–1921	1,480,000
1922	1,243,000[254]

Absenteeism, moreover, was rife in Soviet industry. A police report revealed that white-collar workers in Smolensk, demoralized by hunger and cold, often worked in their offices for only one or two hours a day.[255] As a whole, absenteeism in 1920 was *sixfold* what it had been in 1913.[256] The Soviet worker, who thus often deserted the socialized factory, was sometimes reduced to pillaging it as well. This is how the Assistant Commissar of Labour described the situation in that regard in May 1921. An average worker, earning between 3,000 and 7,000 roubles a month, could not make ends meet. To do so, indeed, he would have had to earn 39,000 or 40,000 roubles a month. He was therefore obliged to supplement his income through robbery. He stole from his factory everything he could carry away: transmission belts, tools, nails ... and sold it all on the black market.[257] Faced with this menace, the trade unions could only pass indignant and ineffectual resolutions.[258] One of their principal leaders, Lozovsky, calculated that thefts from factories amounted to 50 per cent of production.[259]

Above these ruins rose the voice of Lenin. At the Second Congress of Political Education Departments in October 1921 he spoke of 'an industrial proletariat which in our country, owing to the war and to the desperate poverty and ruin, has become declassed ... and ceased to exist as a proletariat'. And he concluded: 'The proletariat has disappeared.'[260]

Was nothing left, then, of the dictatorship of the proletariat? Had the latter ever been anything but, first, a hope, and then a myth—or a mystification? Or did the frightful poverty, Russia's regression to a state akin to barbarism (cases of cannibalism were reported during the famine of 1921), the destruction of the economy and the apparent de-classing of the proletariat—did all these hide, but without suppressing, the shoots, sometimes timid, often awkward, but constantly renewed, of a new civilization, a workers' culture, a society made for the working people by their own hands?

The proletarian society (IV): reality and limits of the dictatorship of the proletariat

When, in October 1919, Lenin said that 'it was the peasantry as a whole who were the first to gain, who gained most, and gained immediately from the dictatorship of the proletariat,'[261] he was referring primarily to their material position. It is certainly true that the peasants suffered less than the workers from the economic crisis, which was principally due to the collapse of industrial production. If one considers only this fact it is possible to see in the taking of power by the Bolsheviks in October 1917 a revolution carried out by the working class for the benefit of the peasants, whose long-cherished aspiration for division of the land was realized at last. Such a view would, however, be superficial. By many signs it was apparent after October 1917 that the working class, and the working class alone, had come to power.

In the first place there were the constitutional provisions whereby the All-Russia Congress of Soviets was to be elected on a basis of one deputy for every 25,000 inhabitants in towns and one deputy for every 125,000 in the country. This was one of the original features of the Soviet régime, contrasting with many other political systems in which the rural population is ensured over-representation at the expense of the urban masses.

Over and above this feature of the constitution it was the *social climate* prevailing in Russia in the first years after the revolution that showed the position that the working class held in the new society.

The workers were sunk in poverty, to be sure, but poverty was general. In itself this did not contradict the social position won by the Russian proletariat, which brought about a reversal of values in many spheres of life. It was in Soviet Russia, and in Soviet Russia alone, that possession of a working-class origin became such an important advantage that people often invented it, so as to be able to secure good jobs in the administration or the privileges of Communist Party membership. Was it not the fact of being a worker—or, at least, of having been one —that protected a Party member against purging, and also shortened his probationary period? The same social consideration applied, as we have seen, in the penal sphere, since the penalties imposed depended on the class to which the offender belonged, being less severe for the proletarian than for the former bourgeois.

These few points are inadequate, however, to characterize the atmosphere that permeated Soviet society, in which the whole of ideology, propaganda and education, the leaders' speeches and the articles in the newspapers, the statements of Government policy and the laws themselves (whether or not these were actually enforced), all proclaimed the virtues of the proletariat, its historical mission and its sovereign rights. When the Bolshevik rulers were still hoping to reach a temporary *modus vivendi* with the capitalists, the establishment of workers' control had shown where political and social power really lay. During the civil war, when the Government was grappling with the bourgeoisie and crushing its resistance, the Russian proletariat made use of its power at the expense of the bourgeoisie. Confiscations struck hard at the former ruling class, which was obliged to give up the houses it occupied, surrendering them to proletarians, and to hand over all those signs of comfort, luxury and social prestige that had testified to its power: not only jewels, furniture and works of art but also linen, furs and warm clothes.[262] This was confirmation in everyday life, and in striking form, of what was proclaimed in the political and economic decrees that the Government issued. The new masters, in the first period of the Soviet régime, were neither the cadres of a Party that was comparatively weak and badly organized* nor the heads of a Government and administration whose authority was still uncertain, but this great mass of peasants who were taking over the land they had coveted for so long, and of workers controlling the factories where they worked, and entering in large numbers the institutions that had now become *theirs*.†

Though the crisis in food supplies aroused discontent and agitation among the workers, their protests and angry outbursts were not incompatible with a feeling of profound identification with the Soviet

* See p. 279.

† The number of workers who in this period took up strictly political appointments has been estimated at 100,000 (Sorlin p. 80).

régime. So long as the struggle against the 'Whites' was going on, the Bolshevik rulers never failed to find among the workers—harassed, worn out, hungry and shivering with cold as they were—a degree of support that often amounted to heroism. This identification between the proletariat and the Soviet régime survived initial defeats and many disillusionments, and found eloquent illustration in the Red Army.

Once this had been formed, conscription soon replaced the voluntary principle, but the soldiers were taken, for preference, from among the working class, and this system gave results that were generally satisfactory, and sometimes better than the most optimistic had expected.[263] The Red Army consisted mostly of peasants; qualitatively, however, the role played in it by workers was greater than that of these peasant soldiers. In the officers' training schools, cadets of working-class origin were very numerous, constituting 37 per cent of the total in 1918,[264] whereas conscripts whose background was bourgeois were kept out of combatant units and relegated to the rear, where they carried out supply functions only.[265] It was not admissible to put arms into the hands of members of the former ruling classes. The value of army units in battle was found to be correlated with their social composition, those with the highest proportion of workers proving to be the bravest and most reliable. Thus, one of the elite divisions had 26·4 per cent workers in it, whereas another division, whose performance was mediocre, had only 10·5 per cent. And whereas the proportion of workers in the Red Army as a whole was 15 per cent, the proportion of workers among deserters was only 4 per cent.[266]

Finally, if the Red Army emerged victorious from its struggle with counter-revolution, powerfully supported from abroad, this was, according to a Western specialist in its history, to a large extent due to its 'consciousness of newness—the sense of having created a model revolutionary force'.[267] The cohesion and class-consciousness of the proletariat contributed greatly to the strength of the army in which it played so unique a role.

While the cadres of the army, that traditional fortress of the old ruling classes, were opened to the proletariat, a similar phenomenon occurred in another sector that had until then been no less carefully protected against any plebeian intrusion, namely, the world of the universities and of culture. The *Proletkult* organization, despite the doubts often aroused by its ideology, succeeded in establishing a position among the workers, and, in intention at least, carried into the domain of the arts, literature and the theatre the political victory that the proletariat had won. The universities, too, despite the caste outlook and conservatism of the academic staff, had to accept the creation of 'workers' faculties' (*rabfaks*), which constituted a sort of introductory course for students coming directly from the working class. Inaugurated at Moscow University in October 1919, this experiment came up against ill-will on the part of the established teachers, and on that of most of the students too. The newcomers found themselves inadequately provided for, and encountered a hostile, or at best a condescending attitude from the academic staff. The Bolshevik authorities, together with some groups of workers acting on their own initiative, then set up independent 'workers' universities'.[268] Access to secondary education, another bourgeois monopoly, was widened, and its new programme, abolishing the class barrier between 'humanistic' culture and technical training, sought to give the working-class pupils instruction that would open their minds to all branches of knowledge.*

What ultimately established, even if only *a contrario*, the social hegemony of the working class was the complete de-classing of the former elites. Targets of the Red Terror, often humiliated and always suspect, the bourgeoisie only had the choice between resigned submission and abdication through voluntary exile. They surrendered their property and prestige to the pariahs of yesterday, who had become the rulers and owners of today. The disappearance of the Russian bourgeoisie was also, and above all, facilitated by the slaughter in the civil war, in which 350,000 members of the upper classes lost their lives.[269]

Upon these ruins was erected the social power of a class whose sufferings did not detract from its devotion to the conquests of the revolution. The fact that the Kronstadt revolt itself, far from rejecting the soviets, demanded that they be re-opened to the socialist parties, and that it did not depart from the ostracism of the bourgeoisie that had become *de rigueur*, showed that the proletariat still identified itself with the foundations of the régime, even in moments of defeat and revolt. The new institutions helped, moreover, to keep fresh this feeling of identification. This was the case, for example, with the trade unions, whose independence was increasingly encroached upon, to be sure, but which became mere cogs in the state machine only after 1921. Their increasing subordination was accompanied by the granting of a number of privileges, whereby trade-union officials and activists were raised, along with engineers and other specialists, to the rank of managers, administrators, and directors of economic activity. It was they who fixed the level of wages and working conditions, as well as production norms, the Commissariat of Labour merely ratifying their decisions. The staff of this Commissariat, furthermore, were practically appointed by the trade unions, which were also well represented both on the Supreme Economic Council (where 30 out of the 69 members were their delegates) and on the Central Executive

* See p. 331

Committee of the Soviets, in which trade-union delegates made up between a quarter and a third of the total membership.[270]

While the place occupied by the workers in the state structures reflected their new status, the reigning ideology confirmed their dominance in the country's social climate. Lenin called, as we have seen, for strengthened discipline, output and productivity, and advocated the employment of certain capitalist methods of industrial management.* But these appeals, inspired by desire to overcome the economic crisis, did not prevent the implantation and development of attitudes and values which, breaking with those of the bourgeoisie, reflected the traditional aspirations of the socialist movement. This was the case, for example, with the *egalitarian* tendencies that permeated the ideals and the social practice of Leninist Russia. In this matter the example was set from the top by Lenin in particular, who took the initiative in fixing the monthly wage for the highest in the land, the People's Commissars, at 500 roubles, comparable to the earnings of a skilled manual worker. Party members were obliged to pay over to the Party any income they received in excess of that figure.† This was no mere demagogic gesture. When a decision was taken in May 1918 to increase the wages of People's Commissars from 500 to 800 roubles, Lenin wrote a letter, not intended for publication, to the office manager of the Council of People's Commissars, in which he protested against 'the obvious illegality of this increase', which was 'in direct infringement of the decree of the Council of People's Commissars of November 23rd [18th], 1917,' and inflicted 'a severe reprimand' on those responsible.[271] The 'specialists' to whom the new régime felt compelled to make concessions were paid a wage 50 per cent higher than that received by the members of the Government.[272]

This pressure for equality was at first manifested in all parts of the economy. Whereas in August 1917 the ratio between unskilled and skilled workers' wages was 1:2·32, it had fallen by June 1st, 1918, to 1:1·19 and by 1920 to 1:1·04.[273] This egalitarianism clashed, however, with concern to stimulate greater production by all kinds of methods, including material incentives, and especially by introducing piece-rates. There was then observed, in a number of sectors, a growing differentiation in wages, though this was restrained by an aspiration towards equality that nobody repudiated in principle—and also by the frequent replacement of money wages by payment in kind. The fact that certain services, such as the post, public transport and electricity, were provided free of charge, also helped to limit the process of differentiation.[274] Eventually, however, the spread in wage levels came to be 1:4 or even 1:5,[275] and this increased differentiation,

* See p. 336.

† Carr, Vol. II, pp. 198 ff.; Lenin, Vol. 42, pp. 37–8. The dwelling-space at the disposal of People's Commissars was also restricted to one room for each person in the household (ibid.).

though slight in comparison with previous social contrasts and those characteristic of bourgeois society, was recognized by the authorities as a distortion of socialist principles. For Lenin, the impossibility of equalizing wages was one of the constraints imposed by the crisis and by the country's economic backwardness, and he regarded the necessity of giving specialists specially favoured rates of pay as nothing less than a setback for the revolution.[276] In the draft programme he put before the Eighth Party Congress he repeated: 'our ultimate aim is to achieve... equal remuneration for all kinds of work.'[277] *The ABC of Communism*, a popular textbook circulated by the Party, stated: 'it remains our fundamental policy to work for a system of equal pay for all.'[278] Only with the coming of N.E.P. did a spectacular differentiation in wages develop, and only much later, in the Stalin period, was this phenomenon to be presented no longer as a regrettable necessity dictated by circumstances but as something required by the proletarian (as against the 'petty-bourgeois') spirit.*

That the working class held a very important place in Soviet society is thus beyond dispute. Nothing of the kind had happened in the aftermath of the February revolution. With the coming to power of the Bolsheviks *the dictatorship of the proletariat* left the realm of abstractions to enter that of political reality. This was Lenin's view, at any rate. While speaking of a workers' *and peasants'* state, he said in December 1917 that 'it could not be expected that the rural proletariat would be clearly and firmly conscious of its own interests. Only the [urban] working class could be ... The proletariat should become the ruling class in the sense of being the leader of all who work; it should be the ruling class politically.'[279] Was the proletariat *actually* the ruling class, though? Did Soviet Russia experience in that period a system that could properly be described as 'the dictatorship of the proletariat'? Upon the answer to this question depends, ultimately, the view to be taken of the society that arose on the ruins of the old régime, and that Leninism strove against all odds to shape to its wishes in the years following 1917.

The answer is all the harder to give because the very concept of the dictatorship of the proletariat was never defined with any degree of precision. The mechanisms and structures of such a dictatorship were never described, either by Marx or Engels or by Lenin or other socialist theoreticians. Lenin confined himself, in *State and Revolution*, to expressing confidence in the political and administrative capacities of the working class, and outlining a *schema* that made plausible the Marxist prospect of the withering away of the state.† Nothing had

---

* In 1922 and 1923 the ratio between maximum and minimum rates of pay was nearly 80:1 (Dewar, p. 94).

† See p. 193.

12

been said about the methods of government that would make the
proletariat *itself* the real wielder of state power, sparing it the need to
resort to any delegation of authority. Again, in what way would this
state power be dictatorial? Did that imply the use of terror, the denial
of any political rights to the dispossessed class, the absence of any
rule of law and the reign of revolutionary 'tyranny'? The references
made by Marx, and especially those made by Engels and Lenin, to the
Paris Commune, as the first form—imperfect but authentic—of the
proletarian dictatorship are sufficient to rule out this assumption.
The dictatorship of the proletariat, while not excluding any of the
conditions mentioned, did not necessarily require their presence,
either. It was, on the contrary, something that could be defined as
broadly and vaguely as it was by Lenin in his '*Left-Wing' Communism*:
'The dictatorship of the proletariat means a persistent struggle—
bloody and bloodless, violent and peaceful, military and economic,
educational and administrative—against the forces and traditions of
the old society.'[280] Furthermore, abolition of universal suffrage, and
so of the electoral rights of the bourgeoisie, did not, in Lenin's view,
form an indispensable feature of the dictatorship of the proletariat.[281]
Marxists had used the term 'dictatorship' for domination by the bourgeoisie even though this did not exclude either the rule of law or the
existence of political freedoms which the proletariat could use in
order to prepare its own accession to power. This meant, then, that
the proletarian dictatorship could assume a variety of forms. Circumstances might cause it to appear in its severest form, with the most
draconian manifestations. But it might also produce a less rigorous
system—the *sine qua non* always being an organized leadership, or
hegemony, of society by the working class, achieved through an
arrangement of political structures and relations between classes such
that the influence formerly wielded by the bourgeoisie was transferred
to the victorious proletariat. Lenin himself, evidently accepting
this interpretation of the dictatorship of the proletariat, described in
December 1920 'the period of transition from capitalism to communism' as a period marked by 'the leadership of that class which is
the only class capitalism has trained for large-scale production'.[282]

   It still remains to define the role exercised in this dictatorial régime
by the proletariat *itself*. The deeply democratic, quasi-libertarian
character of *State and Revolution*, and the other writings in which
Lenin gives proof of the same attitude, leave no room for doubt of his
view on this point. There should be between the class 'in power' and
its exercise of power neither the obstacle of an institutionalized system
of representation nor the screen created by delegation of powers. The
proletariat was actually to govern. Arguing with Kautsky, Lenin
insisted that 'it is altogether wrong ... to say that a *class* cannot govern',
and claimed that only 'a "parliamentary cretin" ' could say this.[283]

Was it because only reactionary stupidity could account for scepticism or even doubt on this point that Lenin never took the trouble to justify an opinion the obviousness of which is nevertheless not beyond question? Or was it because the first experiences of the Russian revolution offered some support to the idea of direct exercise of power by the proletariat itself? It is certainly the case that intervention by the proletariat was, in that period, decisive and, in a sense, continuous — that the masses, paying little heed to institutional structures and mechanisms, exerted pressure, without any mediation, in the barracks and the villages, and in the factories, where workers' control appeared before the law that legalized it, and persisted without regard to official attempts to divert it. Finally, it is true that in 1917 and part of 1918 the masses constituted the most substantial force in politics, with more dynamism and effectiveness than any other factor in public life. There were too many examples of submission by the Bolshevik Party to this elemental force for it to be deniable that, in a sense, 'government' (if we ignore the formal significance of the word) was, in that period, in the hands of the proletariat itself. Amid the ruins of the Provisional Government and the bourgeoisie, in the vacuum created by the absence of a structured Soviet system and the organizational weakness of the Bolshevik Party, there was no effective force in Russia apart from the proletariat, whose 'dictatorship', barely institutionalized as yet, was alone capable of smashing the last links that bound Soviet society to the old bourgeois world.

This period did not last long, however. The dictatorship of the proletariat was an ephemeral thing that was unable to survive for long the exhaustion of the political, or even simply physical, energy of the proletariat. In August 1919 — some little time after the event, we may think — Lenin said that 'the dictatorship of the working class is being implemented by the Bolshevik Party'.[284] Softening the implications of this statement, he added at once that the Party had become 'merged with the entire revolutionary proletariat'.[285] The thesis of *identification* of the class with the Party prevented the thesis of *substitution* from raising its head. Already before this date, however, Lenin had admitted implicitly that the dictatorship of the proletariat was a thing of the past. In a pamphlet of March–April 1919, after saying that 'the socialist revolution cannot be accomplished without the working class,' he went on to say that 'only the advanced workers' could lead the rural masses, and then to acknowledge that 'our best forces have been used up, they are weary and exhausted'.[286] At the Eighth Party Congress, held in that same period Lenin observed that 'the top layer of workers who actually administered Russia during the past year ... is an extremely thin one.'[287] He also acknowledged that 'the Soviets, which by virtue of their programme are organs of government *by the working people*, are in fact organs of government

for the working people, by the advanced section of the proletariat, but
not by the working people as a whole'.[288] This admission was made in
the spring of 1919: the reality it describes had, of course, come about
earlier than that.

There was, then, no longer any question of a dictatorship of the
proletariat *as such*. Yet it was hard to give up this fiction, which was
becoming, with the passage of time and growing disappointment, the
ideological justification for the Soviet régime. On several occasions
Lenin ascribed to the proletariat functions and powers that it no longer
possessed.[289] During the discussion on the trade unions, however, when
he defined some of the most fundamental features of the Soviet
political and social order, he declared: 'The dictatorship of the proletariat cannot be exercised through an organization embracing the
whole of that class, because in all capitalist countries (and not only
over here, in one of the most backward) ... it can be exercised only by a
vanguard that has absorbed the revolutionary energy of the class.'[290]

It was at about this time that Lenin spoke of the 'de-classing' of
Russia's proletariat and even thought it possible to say that it had
'disappeared'.* The Party, which could no longer be identified with a
'de-classed' proletariat, now strove to fill a political vacuum that would
otherwise be filled by anarchy or else by the rival forces of renascent
Menshevism and reaction. Among the ruins of a proletarian dictatorship which had borrowed its forms from the upsurge of the masses
there still survived only a few signs of the social hegemony of the
working class. The suppressed condition of the bourgeoisie testified
to it, of course. The existence of a Soviet bureaucracy whose interests
were bound up with the abolition of capitalism, and in which elements
of proletarian origin held important positions, was at once the negation of proletarian rule and, paradoxically, its safeguard. Above all,
the workers, exhausted but victorious, guardians of a revolution that
they alone had saved from ruin, maintained their loyalty to what they
saw as a proletarian régime. Their very disappointments were relative
to the conquests they had realized and the fruits of which it was, in
the last analysis, the *isolation* of revolutionary Russia that had
prevented them from enjoying.

For the scene of the revolution was world-wide, and the destiny
of the Leninist undertaking was decided, ultimately, on the international plane—in the trenches and factories of the crisis-stricken
West no less than in the countryside and cities of devastated Russia.

* See p. 348.

Part IV

Leninism outside Russia

1

The Russian revolution and the world revolution

'In Russia the problem could only be posed. It could not be solved in Russia,' wrote Rosa Luxemburg in her pamphlet on the Bolshevik revolution.[1] Lenin would have fully agreed with this formulation, for the Leninist conception of the revolution is inseparable from internationalism.

Lenin said that 'only by a series of attempts – each of which, taken by itself, will be one-sided and will suffer from certain inconsistencies – will complete socialism be created by the revolutionary co-operation of the proletarians of *all* countries'.[2] The Russian revolution was thus only an episode in a larger operation: 'Only the beginning,' as Lenin put it in December 1917, of 'the world socialist revolution'.[3] 'We, the Russian working and exploited classes, have the honour of being the vanguard of the international socialist revolution ... The Russian began it – the German, the Frenchman and the Englishman will finish it, and socialism will be victorious.'[4] It is therefore not a matter for surprise that the activity of the Russian vanguard, its offensives, and the whole of its strategy, should have been subordinated to the situation of the international proletariat. The part depended on the whole, and the arguments that went on in the Bolshevik Party as to whether the October insurrection was opportune related no less to the revolutionary readiness of the Western proletariat than to the mood of the masses in Russia. The Right in the Party justified their cautious attitude by the apparent apathy of the workers in the West, while Lenin denounced the hesitations of Kamenev, Zinoviev and other leaders as amounting to refusal to bring help to the detachments of revolutionary socialism that were already active in Europe.*

The overthrow of the Provisional Government and establishment of the Soviet régime did not put an end to this discussion. The great decisions that the Bolsheviks had to take during the first months that followed the insurrection were also closely dependent on the overall

* See p. 144.

situation of the revolutionary movement. This was obviously the case with the question of the Brest-Litovsk peace. But the controversy about forming a coalition government, apparently a matter of domestic politics alone, also had an international dimension. Supporters of the coalition idea argued from the isolated position of the Bolsheviks on the world scale, giving this as a reason for reaching agreement with the moderate socialist parties. This was the line taken, for instance, by Nogin, the People's Commissar for Industry and Trade, who aroused Lenin's anger by saying: 'the West is shamefully quiet.' Lenin, in replying, declared, after praising the struggle being waged by 'the revolutionary sailors of the German navy' and by the Spartacists: 'We believe in the revolution in the West. We know that it is inevitable ... '[5] Whenever, in this period, a sceptical view was expressed regarding the revolutionary readiness of the European proletariat, Lenin hit back very sharply at such pessimism.*

The importance of this confidence of his in the revolution in the West cannot be stressed too much. A fundamental element in Lenin's revolutionary strategy, it was central to his line in 1917, and to a large extent dictated the decision to launch the decisive struggle against the Russian bourgeoisie. Looking back on that period, Lenin acknowledged this fact without the slightest ambiguity. On the third anniversary of the seizure of power he said, for instance, 'when we began working for our cause we counted exclusively on the world revolution.'[6] And at the Third Congress of the Communist International, in July 1921: 'When we started the international revolution ... it was clear to us that without the support of the international world revolution the victory of the proletarian revolution was impossible. Before the revolution, and even after it, we thought: either revolution breaks out in the other countries, immediately, or at least very quickly, or we must perish.'[7]

Thus, the Russian Communists were convinced at the outset that their seizure of power in Russia was pointless except in the context of an international revolutionary offensive. This link with the situation outside Russia was loosened only as the Soviet power became obliged to respond to internal forces and to restrict its direct activity to Russia. As Lenin stressed towards the end of his career, 'the swift and direct support of the working people of the world' was what they had 'counted on' and 'regarded as the basis of the whole of [their] policy'.[8] With remarkable consistency, Lenin saw the final victory of socialism in Russia as dependent on the spread of the revolution, and, in particular, on its spread to the advanced capitalist countries. Many quotations could be given to show this; one question to which they are highly relevant is, of course, that of 'socialism in one country', the

* See his reply to Stalin, in *Protokoly*, pp. 171–2, and to the anarchist Ghe (Lenin, Vol. 27, p. 307).

subject of controversy between Stalinists and Trotskyists. Here is a brief selection. January 1918: 'That the Socialist revolution in Europe must come, and will come, is beyond doubt. All our hopes for the *final* victory of socialism are founded on this certainty ... '[9] Again: 'The final victory of socialism in a single country is of course impossible.'[10] March 1918: 'Regarded from the world-historical point of view, there would doubtlessly be no hope of the ultimate victory of our revolution if it were to remain alone ... '[11] And again: 'At all events, under all conceivable circumstances, if the German revolution does not come, we are doomed.'[12] December 1919: 'The victory of the socialist revolution ... can only be regarded as final when it becomes the victory of the proletariat in at least several advanced countries.'[13] November 1920: 'Until the revolution takes place in all lands, including the richest and most highly civilized ones, our victory will be only a half-victory, perhaps still less.'[14]

Lenin was therefore convinced that the Bolshevik revolution, with all its 'efforts and sacrifices', was only 'an essential step towards world revolution'.[15] And the connexion between the Russian revolution and the international proletarian revolution was seen as being so close that the main stages of Soviet *internal* policy were conceived as responses to the general evolution of the revolutionary movement in Europe. In November 1917, for example, Lenin explained to the All-Russia Congress of Peasant Soviets that 'full implementation' of the law on land promulgated by the new government was conditional upon 'close alliance of the working and exploited peasantry with the working class—the proletariat—in all the advanced countries'.[16] In December 1918 he reaffirmed, in his speech to the First Congress of Land Departments, Poor Peasants' Committees and Communes, that the progress of socialization in the Russian countryside was bound up with that of the world revolution.[17] And when, after the end of the civil war, the economic crisis brought about an upheaval in Soviet policy, with the retreat of the N.E.P., he said that 'our main difficulties ... have been due to the fact that the West European capitalists managed to bring the war to an end and stave off revolution.'[18] It seems to me that the sharp decline in Lenin's optimism, with abandonment of his 'libertarian' ideas, and appearance of a sense that the period of revolutionary offensives and conquests had been followed by one of setbacks, was a direct consequence of the peace of Brest-Litovsk.* It was on the international plane that the Bolsheviks experienced their first defeat. The consequences of this defeat were to be felt in all sectors of public life in Soviet Russia itself.

The claim to be able to build a complete socialist society in a single country was thus alien to Leninism, the founder of which stated explicitly that 'in a single country ... we could not carry out the socialist

* See p. 226.

revolution completely, solely by our own efforts,'[19] and repeated at the commemoration of the first anniversary of the seizure of power that 'the complete victory of the socialist revolution in one country alone is inconceivable.'[20] This proposition was all the more valid when history had made an isolated revolutionary stronghold of a country the cultural and economic backwardness of which Lenin never stopped emphasizing.* He warned his fellow-countrymen that 'if we behave like the frog in the fable and become puffed up with conceit, we shall only make ourselves the laughing-stock of the world ... '[21] It is true that in his pamphlet on *The Tax in Kind*, published in the spring of 1921, he envisaged 'immediate transition' from the 'semi-barbarism' existing in Russia to a socialist society. 'If,' he wrote, 'we transmit electric power to every village, if we obtain a sufficient number of electric motors and other machinery, we shall not need, or shall hardly need, any transition stages or intermediary links between patriarchalism and socialism.' But he added immediately that 'it will take at least ten years only to complete the first stage of this "one" condition.'[22] And in his last article, 'Better Fewer, But Better', he wrote: 'We ... lack enough civilization to enable us to pass straight on to socialism.'[23] Actually, the criteria that Lenin defined as constituting the basis of socialist society and ensuring its superiority over capitalism, criteria relating to economic and cultural factors and also to the political process of the 'withering away of the state', were clear and imperative. They made sense only on a basis of those higher forms of civilization for which advanced capitalism constituted the necessary precondition. To imagine, moreover, that 'socialism in a single country' was feasible was to suppose that some sort of wall could be built along the frontier, cutting the 'socialist' country off from an international system in which every component was a part closely dependent on the whole. Only idealization of Soviet Russia's isolated situation, such as Lenin never indulged in, any more than he idealized the negative consequences of this situation, together with Stalin's contempt for theory, can account for the attribution to Leninism, after the death of its founder and the gagging of its best supporters, of an idea so utterly contrary to it.

The optimism of the Russian revolutionaries who saw in the initiative they had taken the prelude to a world-wide conflagration was, indeed, refuted by what actually happened. In some ways, Stalinism is merely the ideology of this defeat and disillusionment. Lenin, however, never thought of resigning himself to it. After having supposed, in January 1918, that the inevitability of the socialist revolution in Europe was a 'scientific prognosis',[24] and having said in April 1919, at the time of the Hungarian revolution, that 'now only a few months separate us from victory over the capitalists all over the

* See p. 408.

world',[25] he took account of the delay in the growth of the revolutionary movement outside Russia. This came less hard to him, perhaps, than to some others because, except on a very few occasions, he had taken care not to predict the *imminent* collapse of world capitalism. On the contrary, indeed, when some of his comrades were expecting revolution in the West at any moment, he warned: 'it is quite impossible to predict the probable moment of outbreak of revolution and overthrow of any of the European imperialist governments.'[26] This caution was the basis of his policy in 1918, and led him to accept the conditions imposed by the treaty of Brest-Litovsk. Lenin realized that the proletarian revolution would be more difficult to bring off in Central and Western Europe than it had been in Russia because 'the bourgeoisie over there is stronger and cleverer than our Kerenskys,' and also because 'over there the workers have a measure of prosperity'.[27] Convinced as he was that 'from the standpoint of the world revolution ... Germany is the main link in [the] chain,'[28] he shared the fervent joy that filled the Soviet capital when revolution broke out in that country, one year after the revolution in Russia. As Krupskaya recalls, during those days of enthusiasm 'he was continuously addressing meetings. His face beamed with joy ... The days of the first October anniversary were the happiest days in his life.'[29] He maintained, nevertheless, a certain circumspection, and the British journalist Philips Price, who met Lenin at this time and had a long talk with him, recorded that he 'was surprised to find that he did not seem to share the prevailing optimism about the imminence of the world revolution'.[30]

Western capitalism did not collapse. The German revolutionary movement suffered its first defeat in January 1919. But Lenin's confidence in the forward march of the international revolutionary movement was sustained by the progress made by the Communist International. 'The Third International ... has spread ... rapidly, moving from success to success,' he said in March 1920.[31] In spite of everything, he believed in the basic solidarity of the Western working class with the Russian revolution, and ascribed to this the highest importance, seeing in it the main reason for the failure of the imperialist intervention in Russia: 'the workers were on our side; and this fact determined the issue of the war.'[32] The mutinies that occurred in the Allied troops sent to help the Russian counter-revolution were seen by Lenin as so many proofs of the alliance between the revolutionaries in Russia and the proletariat in the West.[33] Was this emphasis on a solidarity that gave expression to proletarian internationalism intended to limit the impact that the defeat of the world revolution might have upon the minds of Russian Communists, and thereby to prevent the isolation of Russia from leading to an upsurge of nationalism? The struggle that Lenin carried on against Great-Russian chauvinism, and against the superiority complex that threatened to corrupt the Bolsheviks, provides some basis for this assumption.*

But although Lenin still thought it possible in April 1919 to depict 'international capitalism' as 'a decrepit, dying, hopelessly sick old man',[34] he was obliged, a year later, to acknowledge that 'on an international scale, capital is still stronger, both from the military and the economic standpoint, than Soviet power and the Soviet system,' adding that this was the fundamental premiss from which to proceed.[35] He confirmed this opinion in November 1920;[36] and put forward during the autumn of 1921 a view that was even more pessimistic: 'owing to the present circumstances, the whole world is developing faster than we are.'[37] He continued, of course, right down to his death, to believe that world revolution was inevitable and would come about sooner or later.[38] But experience confirmed the caution he had shown in the Brest-Litovsk period, and this caution thenceforth governed the complex strategy followed by the Soviet Government in its foreign policy,† the most important principles of which were to 'hold on' to the proletarian citadel constituted by Soviet Russia, while helping the international revolutionary movement in a variety of ways.

In January 1918, at a time when a large section of the Bolshevik leadership still firmly believed in the power of the Soviet revolution to expand abroad, Lenin had said that it was necessary to hold on in Russia until the proletariat of other countries should come to the aid of the Russian revolution. The idea that the Russian Communists could build socialism without the help of an international proletarian revolution never occurred to him. On the contrary, as the country where the revolution had been victorious came to resemble more and more a 'besieged fortress',[39] it became only a question of preserving for the world revolution 'at least a certain bastion of socialism, however weak and moderately sized',[40] and of striving to 'maintain our position until our ally, the international proletariat of all countries, grows strong enough'.[41] To 'hold on', 'maintain our position', to 'manoeuvre and retreat',[42] this was the essence of the defensive policy that was forced upon Soviet Russia, and which had to be adhered to until the coming of external help: 'holding out until we receive powerful support from workers who have risen in revolt in other countries.'[43] The idea was a simple one and was frequently repeated by Lenin, sometimes with great feeling: 'The workers of the world are looking hopefully towards us. We can hear their cry: "Hold on a little longer! ... We shall come to your aid ..."'[44] What was needed was to 'gain time ... [while] our foreign comrades are preparing thoroughly for their revolution.'[45] This was a less humble ambition, and one less easy

* See p. 276.
† See p. 368.

to achieve, than it might seem. The difficulties involved were clear to Lenin. In his last article he wrote: 'It is not easy for us ... to keep going until the socialist revolution is victorious in more developed countries ... '[46] And he asked: 'Shall we be able to hold on ... until the West-European capitalist countries consummate their development towards socialism?'[47]

Soviet Russia's response to the capitalist encirclement in which she found herself was the pursuit of a foreign policy that was flexible and cautious, but prepared to exploit all the weaknesses and contradictions in the enemy camp,* together with renewed attempts to give concrete help to the revolutionary movement in Europe. The Soviet power, as a 'torch of socialism', was to 'scatter as many sparks as possible to add to the growing flames of socialist revolution' throughout the world.[48] Declarations of support for revolutionary action by the European proletariat, and especially by the proletariat of Germany, were therefore made again and again.† These were no mere rhetorical exercises. In a letter to Sverdlov and Trotsky dated October 1st, 1918, Lenin wrote: 'We are all ready to die to help the German workers advance the revolution which has begun in Germany.'‡ As we shall see, the help given did indeed take concrete and many-sided form, demonstrating the existence of firm and close bonds of union between the Bolshevik revolution and the revolutionary socialist movement throughout the world.§

In the last analysis, the policy followed by the Soviet Government towards the outside world—the hostile world of capitalism and also the (divided) world of the international socialist movement—had no other aim but to carry further the chain of revolutionary offensive strategy, joining up with the other links in this chain that 'Russian link' which had become for the moment detached from the rest.

---

* See p. 368.
† See the resolution placed by Lenin before the Seventh Party Congress (1918): 'The socialist proletariat of Russia will support the fraternal revolutionary movement of the proletariat of all countries with all its strength and with every means at its disposal' (Lenin, Vol. 27, p. 119. See also Vol. 27, pp. 23 and 157; Vol. 28, p. 102; Vol. 29, pp. 105–6, and *passim*).
‡ Ibid., Vol. 35, p. 364. This phrase is emphasized by three lines in the margin of the latter. The need for Soviet Russia to accept the greatest sacrifices, including the greatest *national* sacrifices, recurs often in Lenin's writings (e.g., ibid., Vol. 27, p. 189; Vol. 28, p. 191).
§ See p. 379.

2

Leninist diplomacy

Lenin's foreign policy

Talking to another Party member soon after his appointment as
People's Commissar for Foreign Affairs, Trotsky defined in these
words the 'diplomatic' tasks he saw before him: 'I will issue a few
revolutionary proclamations to the peoples of the world, and then shut
up shop.'[1] This was in the heroic period of the Russian revolution,
when it was conceived as an international enterprise being carried
forward by mass offensives and proletarian fervour. The traditional
procedures of diplomacy seemed to have had their day, and even
the very idea of 'international relations' to be no longer valid. The
socialist revolution was going to spread over the whole of Europe,
bring about the collapse of capitalism, and give birth to that 'United
States of the World (not of Europe alone)' of which Lenin had written
in August 1915.[2] During the months leading up to the October insurrection he had elucidated the main lines of a strategy that should
draw the peoples of the world into the revolutionary struggle. The
Soviet power, once established, would propose to the belligerent
states a democratic peace. Since imperialism was incompatible with
such a peace, the nations (and especially the proletariat of every
nation), kindled by the Russian example, would take the path of
revolution in order to put an end to the world slaughter. As the
moment of the insurrection drew near, Lenin, without basically repudiating this bold and linear *schema*, nevertheless seemed to make it
less rigid,* and when he had actually come to power, he had to define
and improvise a *foreign policy* that was wholly centred upon the
problem of peace.

When he addressed the Second All-Russia Congress of Soviets, the
considerations attached to the important 'decree on peace' reflected
Lenin's uncertainties and hesitations. Should revolutionary agitation
be organized among the peoples in order to end the war—or should
the Soviet Government negotiate with existing governments for this
purpose? Or should it try to do both things at once? The problem

* See p. 188.

involved was one that was not confined to those particular circumstances. When triumphant Bolshevism brought proletarian Russia into the 'concert of nations', would the revolution, having become a state, choose to employ the equivocal methods that governed international relations—or would it, repudiating all conventional and routine attitudes, as the 'Left Communists' wished, commit itself to a struggle against the old world in which no diplomatic conditions would be respected? This question constituted the essential dilemma of Soviet foreign policy; and Lenin applied himself, until his departure from the political scene, to finding a dialectical answer to it.

Speaking, on the night of October 25th–26th, 1917, about the 'decree on peace', he said: 'Our appeal must be addressed both to the governments and to the peoples. We cannot ignore the governments, for that would delay the possibility of concluding peace, and the people's government dare not do that ... '[3] And he added: 'Nor must our proposal for an armistice have the form of an ultimatum, for we shall not give our enemies an opportunity of concealing the whole truth from the peoples, using our irreconcilability as a pretext.'[4] At the same time, it was also necessary to 'help the peoples to intervene in questions of war and peace',[5] especially because 'the governments and the bourgeoisie will make every effort to unite their forces and drown the workers' and peasants' revolution in blood'.[6]

The history of Leninist foreign policy begins with the negotiations at Brest-Litovsk, which opened on December 9th, 1917. Trotsky led the Soviet team, and devoted himself to dragging them out as long as possible. Lenin approved of this tactic. In a draft resolution for the Council of People's Commissars he thus summarized his views on the matter: 'continuation of peace negotiations and resistance to their speed-up by the Germans ... Propaganda and agitation on the necessity for a revolutionary war.'[7] The new Government had to prove to the Russian masses that its promise to end the war would be realized *soon*, but it was also necessary to give the Western proletariat time to strengthen itself as a revolutionary force and to enable the revolt of the peoples to get under way. This was why Lenin, while according priority to the need to make peace, kept his eyes fixed, all through the negotiations, upon Germany, where the prospect of revolution seemed confirmed by the growth of agitation for peace. On January 19th, 1918, he proposed to his colleagues in the Party's Central Committee that airmen be sent to Berlin 'to ascertain exactly what is going on in Germany'.[8] And in his polemic against the advocates of a revolutionary war to the death, and against Trotsky, who refused to sign the draconian peace imposed by Imperial Germany, it was again to the German situation that Lenin referred. When, at the Seventh Party Congress, called to discuss the problem of peace, Ryazanov described Lenin's tactics as one of 'surrendering space to gain time' (i.e., for the revolution in the West, and especially in Germany, to mature), this description was warmly approved by the Bolshevik leader.[9]

The time of respite was a time for diplomacy, made up of subtle manoeuvrings and compromises that aroused the protests of the 'Left Communists'. When, faced with the threat of a renewed German offensive, the Central Committee of the Party had to decide whether to appeal for help to the Allies, Lenin, who was not present at the discussion, sent his comrades a note saying: 'Please include my vote *in favour* of getting potatoes and arms from the bandits of Anglo-French imperialism.'[10] This laconic formula defined one of the principal elements in Soviet foreign policy as it subsequently developed—profiting from all rivalries between imperialist powers so as to increase the division between them and prevent an anti-Bolshevik alliance from being formed. The conviction that imperialism signified 'intensification of the struggle for the partitioning of the world', and that 'inter-imperialist alliances ... are *inevitably* nothing more than a "truce" in periods between wars',[11] formed the basis for a policy that was desperately anxious to play off one imperialist camp against another. In *The Immediate Tasks of the Soviet Government*, written at the beginning of spring 1918, Lenin declared that 'the only real, not paper, guarantee of peace we have is the antagonism among the imperialist powers.'[12] About the same time, he stressed that 'we shall be protected, of course, not by a paper treaty or "state of peace", but by the continuing struggle between the two "giants" of imperialism ... '[13] This was a constant in the foreign policy of Soviet Russia as practised in Lenin's lifetime.[14]

To know what were the divisions in the enemy camp, to create new ones, if possible, and to enlarge and exploit all such divisions, became elements in a total strategy which operated both directly and indirectly, resorting to all the tricks of politics, avoiding the snares and lures of revolutionary purism, and resolved to defend as long as might be needed the 'bastion of socialism' called Soviet Russia. As Lenin wrote in May 1918 to the Armenian Bolshevik Shahumyan, in Baku: 'The difficulties are immeasurable. So far we are being saved *only* by the contradictions and conflicts and struggles among the imperialists. Be capable of making use of these conflicts: *for the time being* we have to learn diplomacy.'[15]

Did this mean the negation of previously expressed views, of the conviction voiced so often that only revolution could bring peace and ensure the right of self-determination? Was this an abandonment of the methods that had brought Bolshevism to power? The more radical of Lenin's followers soon started to believe so. Their disappointment and anger added fuel to the fiery debates about the peace of Brest-Litovsk. Soviet Russia's foreign policy under Lenin did indeed include elements that were calculated to astonish and infuriate revolutionary

Communists.* Was realism, *Realpolitik*, or even *raison d'État*, taking the place of the desire to turn the world upside down? Faced at the Eighth Congress of the Party, in March 1919, with the doubts and misgivings of some activists, Lenin endeavoured to reassure them. In his 'Draft Programme' he proclaimed 'the slogan of fighting until victory over the bourgeoisie of the whole world is achieved both in civil wars at home and in international revolutionary wars'.[16] During the discussion at the congress he went further, saying: 'We are living not merely in a state, but *in a system of states*, and it is inconceivable for the Soviet Republic to exist alongside of the imperialist states for any length of time. One or the other must triumph in the end. And before that end comes there will have to be a series of frightful collisions between the Soviet Republic and the bourgeois states.'[17] Lenin went on to distinguish between imperialist wars and 'the only legitimate, just and truly revolutionary war, a war of the oppressed against the oppressors, a war of the working people against the exploiters, a war for the victory of socialism'.† The advocate of revolutionary defeatism had not become a pacifist, and, just as war was for Clausewitz the continuation of a policy by other means, so the recourse to diplomacy seemed to Lenin merely a phase in a revolutionary undertaking in which the interests of the antagonists were fundamentally irreconcilable. However, the varying tone—now more or less aggressive, now more or less conciliatory—of Lenin's statements on foreign policy was not unconnected with the evolution of relations between Soviet Russia and the outside world.

In February 1920, speaking to the C.E.C. about relations with bourgeois Estonia, Lenin said that the soviets had proved 'our ability to renounce, in all sincerity, the use of force at the appropriate moment, in order to change to a peace policy'.[18] More plainly still, he added that 'we represent the peace interests of the majority of the world's population against the imperialist warmongers'.[19] It was not accidental that these statements were made at the moment when the Western powers had just ended their blockade of Soviet Russia. The latter now needed to obtain 'essential technical aid'[20] and to begin 'an exchange of goods with the West'.[21] And Lenin claimed: 'we have shown that all governments have to lay down their arms in face of the peace policy of the Soviet Government.'[22] Was this not, in substance, the idea of peaceful coexistence, the necessity of which the Soviet Government was later to proclaim, trying to justify it in the eyes of Left critics by linking it with successes in the *struggle against* the imperialist powers? In

* See p. 373.

† Lenin, Vol. 29, p. 391. In December 1921 Lenin affirmed that 'revolutionary wars are legitimate and just—i.e., wars waged against the capitalists in defence of the oppressed classes, wars against the oppressor in defence of the nations oppressed by the imperialists of a handful of countries, wars in defence of the socialist revolution against foreign invaders' (ibid., Vol. 33, p. 132).

November 1920 Lenin expressed a similar idea when he said: 'We are in a position of having won conditions enabling us to exist side by side with capitalist powers, who are now compelled to enter into trade relations with us.'[23]

Does this mean that the policy of 'peaceful coexistence', the virtues of which were proclaimed by several of Lenin's successors and with which 'Khrushchevism' sought to identify itself, really originated in Leninist practice? This problem has figured in the controversy among the hostile brothers of the 'socialist family', and considerable attention was given to it at one stage of the Sino-Soviet conflict. The Soviet side were able to point to the undeniable fact that Lenin used the expression several times, and seems, indeed, to have been its originator. He used it first in February 1920, in an interview with an American press correspondent. On that occasion, however, he spoke of 'peaceful coexistence with all peoples; with the workers and peasants of all nations awakening to a new life ... '* The conception was also extended by him, however, to relations between states. Addressing the Ninth Congress of Soviets in December 1921, Lenin said: 'Is the existence of a socialist republic in a capitalist environment at all conceivable? It seemed inconceivable from the political and military aspects. That it is possible both politically and militarily has now been proved; it is a fact.'[24] A year earlier, in November 1920, he had already said that, as regards relations between Soviet Russia and the imperialist powers, 'today we can speak, not merely of a breathing-space, but of a real chance of a new and lengthy period of development'.[25]

If the expression 'peaceful coexistence' be taken to signify the idea that the securing of a certain balance of forces can make possible relations of a non-violent, or at least non-belligerent, character between Soviet Russia and the capitalist world, there can be no doubt that this does correspond both to Lenin's thinking and to his actual experience. It is no less certain, however, that the expression cannot be made to signify more than that, if it is to be used in the way that Lenin used it. In particular, Lenin never said that there was a serious possibility of establishing perpetual peace between the two camps. Hostilities could give way to periods of co-operation, and these periods could be more than a mere 'breathing-space', and last for a relatively long time. Fundamentally, however, these peaceful interludes could only be precarious; the hostility between the two systems was ultimately irreconcilable. Speaking in December 1920 to a gathering of activists in Moscow, Lenin expressed himself in these words: 'I said that we had passed from war to peace, but that we had not for-

---

* Ibid., Vol. 30, p. 365. The expression was also used by Trotsky, in his speech to the Eleventh Party Congress in 1922, when he spoke of 'a long period of peaceful coexistence and of businesslike co-operation with bourgeois countries' (quoted in Deutscher, *Prophet Unarmed*, p. 31).

gotten that war will return. While capitalism and socialism exist side by side, they cannot live in peace: one or the other will ultimately triumph ... This is [only] some respite from war.'[26] And a few days later he developed the same idea before the Eighth Congress of Soviets:

> We cannot for a moment believe in lasting trade relations with the imperialist powers: the respite will be temporary. The experience of the history of revolutions and great conflicts teaches us that wars, a series of wars, are inevitable. The existence of a Soviet Republic alongside of capitalist countries—a Soviet Republic surrounded by capitalist countries—is so intolerable to the capitalists that they will seize any opportunity to resume the war.[27]

In December 1921 he wrote, discussing the theses of the French Communist Party on the agrarian question: 'There is no doubt that only the proletarian revolution can and certainly will put a stop to all war.'[28]

Official and semi-official exegetes may seek as they wish to find in one or other statement made by Lenin justification for the most contradictory of policies—their work of apologia being the easier, though also the more suspect, in that it operates with a selection of quotations effected with more care than scruple. In reality, the conduct of 'foreign affairs' by Lenin's Government was inspired by considerations that particular circumstances dictated—especially, as has been said, by concern to exploit the divisions in the capitalist camp. To this must be added another and no less important factor, namely, the extension that Lenin tried to give to the international Communist movement, making it spread beyond the merely European framework to which Social-Democracy had been confined, so as to become a *world* movement—and, in doing so, to cease to be purely anti-capitalist and assume a clearly *anti-imperialist* character.

Enmity to capitalism implied attacking that system wherever it drew strength, not excluding the empires it had established throughout the world. Soviet Russia's weakness meant that she had to seek, in her resistance to the imperialist powers, to obtain the help of the colonial peoples, whom she invited to open a 'second front' against capitalism. In this way a vital link was forged between the Russian revolution and the anti-colonial revolution—the first manifestations of which Lenin observed with all the more enthusiasm as he noted the failures of the socialist revolution in the West. His report to the Second Congress of Communist Organizations of the Eastern Peoples, in November 1919, is very illuminating on this point. Lenin pointed out that 'the imperialist war aroused the East' from its slumbers, and declared that 'our Soviet Republic must now muster all the awakening peoples of the East and, together with them, wage a struggle against international imperialism'.[29]

Stating that 'bourgeois nationalism' in the colonial countries had 'historical justification', Lenin called on the Communists of the East to render it active support. He ended by affirming that 'final victory can be won only by the proletariat of all the advanced countries of the world'—but 'they will not be victorious without the aid of the working people of all the oppressed colonial nations, first and foremost, of Eastern nations.'[*]

Speaking a year later to a purely Russian audience, Lenin said that the slogan 'Workers of all countries, unite!' must now be replaced by one of more universal application: 'Workers of all countries and all oppressed peoples, unite!' Though hardly in conformity with the canons of original Marxism, 'from the point of view of present-day politics, however, the change is correct.'[30] The enormous importance that Lenin accorded to the struggle against world imperialism and revolution in the colonial countries found its last expression in one of the notes that he wrote in December 1922, during the most critical phase of his illness. In this he linked the struggle to be waged, inside the Soviet state, against Great-Russian chauvinism, with the support that this state ought to give to the colonial peoples. The note concluded with these words: 'the morrow of world history will be a day when the awakening peoples oppressed by imperialism are finally aroused and the decisive long and hard struggle for their liberation begins.'[31]

There was something paradoxical in the circumstance that this new dimension acquired by the fight against capitalism (now, with imperialism, arrived, as Lenin supposed, at its highest stage) obliged Soviet diplomacy to come to terms with bourgeois-nationalist régimes that were vigorously anti-Communist.[†] Such dealings constituted, in the Middle East and elsewhere in Asia, a kind of supplement to the policy followed by Moscow in relation to Imperial Germany and, after its collapse, the Weimar Republic.[‡] Nevertheless, in Lenin's time, the manoeuvres and subtleties of Soviet diplomacy, while not unduly hindered by concern for socialist principles, never completely lost the imprint of the latter. If we understand these principles as meaning desire to encourage the outbreak and progress of the world revolution, and defence of Lenin's ideas on the necessary role of violence as the proletarian answer to bourgeois oppression, with the need to debunk humanist and pacifist ideology, it is noticeable that

* Lenin, Vol. 30, pp. 161–2.
† See p. 379.
‡ See p. 377.

Lenin took great care never to sacrifice his doctrine to the demands of the diplomatic game. This was particularly the case in the spring of 1922, at the Genoa Conference which saw the first open confrontation between official representatives of revolutionary Russia and those of the chief capitalist states of Western Europe.

The event was one of substantial importance. The great powers seemed at last to have resigned themselves to the existence of a state based upon and devoted to revolution. Soviet Russia seemed, on her part, to have admitted that the world revolution had suffered defeat, and to be seeking, in consequence, a *modus vivendi* with the 'class enemy'. Was not the period of harsh conflict and mutual refusal to compromise coming to an end now? The care taken by Lenin in preparing for a conference at which his state of health did not allow him to be personally present proves that he fully appreciated its implications. A number of notes written by him during the preparatory period and in the course of the conference itself show how he expected the Soviet negotiators, Chicherin, Litvinov and Krassin, to operate. It was, once again, a matter of 'dividing the different countries and setting them by the ears',[32] and of completing this divisive activity by trying 'to split the pacifist camp of the international bourgeoisie away from the other, the aggressive and reactionary camp'.[33] At the same time, Lenin urged that a clear distinction be drawn between the 'bourgeois-pacifist programme' that the Soviet delegation must be ready to subscribe to, and 'a Communist programme—the only one that is in keeping with our views—(set it forth briefly)'. Lenin added, regarding the 'bourgeois-pacifist programme', that what was involved was merely 'palliatives', which might, 'under certain conditions ... serve to mitigate the present difficult situation (the only real way out of which is possible given a final break with all the principles of capitalist property)'.*

Thus, the victory of the Bolshevik revolution in Russia had added to the tasks to be performed by the Communists those of international relations and diplomatic responsibility. Despite their original hopes, they had not been able to 'shut up shop' where foreign affairs were concerned, but were, on the contrary, obliged to strengthen their apparatus for dealing with these affairs, and to diversify their methods in this sphere. It was to Lenin's credit that, in spite of this, he kept in view even in the midst of the period of retreat the priorities and basic prospects of the revolution. The conflicting pressures of momentary

---

* Lenin, Vol. 42, pp. 396–7. In a telephone communication, Lenin warned Molotov: 'Under no circumstance should such frightful words [about our conception of history being definitely based on the inevitability of new world wars] be used, as this would mean playing into the hands of our opponents. We should confine ourselves only to mentioning that the views of the Communists do not coincide with the views of such pacifists as the states we are beginning negotiations with, such statesmen as Henderson, Keynes, etc.' (ibid., Vol. 42, p. 410).

contingencies and permanent aims gave rise to a dialectical attempt on
his part to reconcile diplomatic and constructive work with continued
pursuit of the task of undermining and destroying the capitalist order.
This endeavour governed the foreign policy actually followed by the
Soviet Government under Lenin.

The foreign policy of Soviet Russia

I shall not here undertake a full analysis of the foreign policy pursued
by revolutionary Russia in the first years after the triumph of Bolshevism. My aim is a more limited one—to observe how Lenin and the
Soviet Government sought in their diplomacy both to safeguard what
had been won and also to act in such a way as to add to the dynamic
potential of the world revolution.

In the first period after the October revolution the Soviet Government was above all concerned to demonstrate to the outside world
how utterly different it was from anything ever seen before, and its
rejection of all conformism. There was then no question of submitting
to diplomatic custom, and the need for recognition or the search for
respectability had no place among the motives of the Soviet leaders.
Publication in the official press of the secret treaties between Tsarist
Russia and her Western allies, and exposure of the imperialist schemes
underlying this alliance, made plain what the new Government's
intentions were. A gesture like this was more than symbolic: a breach
with the best-established usages, it was also and above all a political
challenge which, by debunking the democratic rhetoric of the Entente
powers, strove to strengthen the will of the masses in the Allied countries for peace and revolution.

The attitude of the Communist negotiators at Brest-Litovsk followed the same line. The Austro-German diplomats were amazed
by the conduct of Radek when the Soviet delegation's train arrived
at the Brest-Litovsk railway station. High Imperial dignitaries were
present, along with the leaders of the Austrian and German armies,
and a guard of honour was drawn up on the platform. Radek, however,
unwilling to waste his time, proceeded on descending from the train
to turn his back on all those august personages and, in the most
natural way possible, to distribute revolutionary leaflets among the
soldiers of the guard of honour.[34]

Such behaviour had a serious meaning which Trotsky made it his
business to explain to the Germans. During the negotiations he said
to them: 'We members of the Russian delegation do not belong to the
diplomatic school, but consider ourselves rather as soldiers of the
revolution.'[35] The work of propaganda carried on by the Soviet
delegation assumed a number of forms, and gave rise to vigorous
protests by the leaders of the Austro-German delegation. Trotsky
replied by inviting them to carry on propaganda for *their* point of

view among the Russian troops.[36] At every turn the representatives of the Central Powers found themselves up against the Bolsheviks' refusal to conform to diplomatic procedure. When the Germans put forward the first draft of the peace treaty, they included in it the traditional formula about the purpose being 'to establish peace and friendship' between the contracting parties. Trotsky at once objected that his delegation had come to Brest not to establish 'friendship' with imperialism but only to make peace.[37] As Ulam says, some of the requests submitted by the Soviet delegates 'would strain the patience of the most courteous and affable diplomat. Could the negotiations be delayed so that the chief of the Russian delegation could go to Vienna "to confer with the Austrian workers"? '[38] When he eventually threw into the debate the unorthodox formula: 'Neither peace nor war', Trotsky merely added one last incongruity to the many that the Bolsheviks had already contributed.

The signing of the Brest-Litovsk treaty, and the slowing-down, and then stagnation, of the revolutionary offensive was not enough to convert the Bolsheviks to respect for normal usages. The exchange of ambassadors between Soviet Russia and Imperial Germany took place with more frankness than courtesy on the Soviet side. While the Bolshevik envoy refused to present his letters of credit to Wilhelm II,[39] the German envoy was met on his arrival in Moscow by an editorial in *Pravda* depicting him as 'not the representative of the toiling classes of a friendly people but the plenipotentiary of a military clique which, with boundless effrontery, kills, rapes and plunders wherever it can'.[40] Nor was such treatment reserved for the Germans. When President Wilson sent to the Fourth All-Russia Congress of Soviets in March 1918 a message such as no other Allied power saw fit to address to the new régime, the Soviet reply took the form of a message addressed 'to the people and, first and foremost, to the toiling and exploited classes of the United States of North America' expressing confidence that 'the happy time is not far distant when the toiling masses of all bourgeois countries will throw off the yoke of capital and establish the socialist organization of society'. It was, 'as Zinoviev is said to have boasted, a "slap in the face" for the American President'.[41]

Four years later, at Genoa, the Communist delegates arrived at the conference in tail-coats and top hats. The exercise of power had taught some of them good manners, and, above all, as a result of defeats and setbacks, it had taught the Bolshevik leaders the art of diplomacy and the practice of compromise. To be sure, this change was not due to developments on the Soviet side alone. The haughty attitude of the Communists, backed by their revolutionary principles, often corresponded to the unconditional hostility shown by the Western powers towards the Soviet régime. If the year 1919 was the one in which

Bolshevik Russia's foreign policy displayed its grimmest face, this was not only because certain events seemed to be bringing nearer the world revolution, but also because the great powers were then engaged in trying to crush the new régime in Russia. The Communists' attempts to improve relations with the West were rebuffed. This happened, for instance, in January 1919, when, the Western powers having decided to summon a conference of 'all organized groups exercising or attempting to exercise power in any part of former Russian territory' in order to study the situation, the Bolshevik Government sought an invitation to this conference and showed a conciliatory attitude, particularly in the matter of recognizing the debts contracted by their predecessors. They were not even favoured with a reply.[42] It has often been alleged that the Bolsheviks' refusal to accept their 'financial obligations' towards the creditors of the Tsarist Government and holders of Russian shares and bonds explains the severe attitude taken up by the Western states towards Soviet Russia. Leonard Schapiro, among others, refers to 'their refusal ... to agree to any terms of settlement of the debts of the overthrown régime'.[43] And yet, as early as January 1919, the Soviet Government officially announced that it 'does not refuse to recognize its financial obligations to creditors who are nationals of the allied Powers'.[44] Three months later, when an American diplomat, William Bullitt, paid a secret visit to Lenin, the latter told him that if the economic blockade against Soviet Russia were lifted, the Bolsheviks would 'recognize their responsibility for the financial obligations of the former Russian Empire'.[45] When, however, on his return to the U.S.A., Bullitt tried to report this conversation to President Wilson, the President declined to receive him, 'pleading a headache'.[46] Conciliatory financial offers were repeated several times subsequently, for example, at the Genoa Conference. The soviets always linked the question of recognizing Tsarist debts, and paying compensation to foreign sufferers from the changes in Russia, with the granting of credits, since without these it would be impossible for them to meet the obligations they were asked to accept.[47] They had moved a long way from the repudiation pure and simple of the debts and obligations of the old régime that was proclaimed soon after the seizure of power.

The year 1920 saw the beginning of a *détente* between the two camps. At the start of the year the Western powers abandoned their blockade, and an agreement concerning repatriation of prisoners was signed between Britain and the soviets.[48] This development was interrupted, however, by the Polish attack, which took place despite the many gestures of conciliation and offers of negotiation made by the Soviet Government during the previous months.[49] Once the Russo-Polish war was over, and once Lenin had given up the illusion he had momentarily entertained that the European revolution would receive a decisive stimulus from the successes of the Red Army on the Polish front,* the road to a relative *détente* was opened again. Soon, an important commercial agreement was arrived at between Soviet Russia and Britain; signed in London on March 16th, 1921, this bore more than merely economic significance. Constituting the first form of recognition of the revolutionary state by one of the victorious great powers, it contained, moreover, a clause by which it was agreed

> that each party refrains from hostile action or undertakings against the other and from conducting outside of its own borders any official propaganda, direct or indirect, against the institutions of the British Empire or of the Russian Soviet Republic respectively, and more particularly that the Russian Soviet Government refrains from any attempt by military or diplomatic or any other form of action or propaganda to encourage any of the peoples of Asia in any form of hostile action against British interests or the British Empire, especially in India and in the independent state of Afghanistan.[50]

Was it not the very essence of the revolutionary enterprise that was thus being repudiated, in one of its most important aspects, namely, the struggle against imperialism? And at Genoa, a year later, the Soviet delegates did not confine themselves to putting forward conciliatory proposals on the financial question. Abandoning their former diatribes against pacifist illusions, they declared themselves, in accordance with the 'petty-bourgeois democratic' programme laid down for the occasion by Lenin, in favour of a disarmament conference. They also proposed prohibition of 'the most barbarous forms of fighting' and of the 'use of means of terrorizing peaceful populations'.†

At the same time as the Soviet Government was proposing disarmament, and encountering opposition on this question from the ex-Allied powers, it was making secret arrangements to effect its own rearmament, and that of Weimar Germany. The relations that Soviet Russia entered into with the latter state provide a good illustration of the subtlety and cynicism of the diplomatic game that the Russian revolutionaries, retreating and manoeuvring, had been obliged to play. After the end of the civil war, Germany became Soviet Russia's most favoured foreign state. The thunderbolt of Rapallo revealed the resourcefulness of Soviet diplomacy. While the Genoa Conference was in session, the Soviet diplomats concluded an agreement with Germany that made them, in the words of the London *Times*, 'the arbiters

---

* It was on this occasion that Lenin, flouting the advice of Radek and Trotsky, departed from his usual caution and authorized the invasion of Poland by Soviet troops, to whom a revolutionary as well as a military task was assigned (Carr, Vol. III, pp. 209–10).

† Carr, Vol. III, p. 373; Fischer, *Soviets*, Vol. I, p. 334. In December 1922 a regional conference on disarmament was actually organized in Moscow by the Soviet Government, but proved unfruitful (Fischer, *Soviets*, Vol. I, pp. 375 ff.).

of the conference'.[51] While the Rapallo agreement was largely concerned with economic co-operation between the two countries, other
Germano-Soviet contacts of a more compromising sort were being
discreetly effected. As early as April 1921 experts from Germany's
arms industry had visited Moscow. This delegation, headed by a
Colonel, had visited, in the company of the Deputy Commissar for
Foreign Affairs, a series of Soviet factories, with a view to arranging
technical co-operation in the production of arms. This first contact,
which was approved by Lenin, produced no concrete result; but
further negotiations brought together, from December 1921 onwards,
Soviet and German military experts. Although the Berlin Government itself appears to have been kept in the dark, the Reichswehr
showed the greatest interest in these contacts. Endeavouring to escape
from the restrictions imposed on the German army by the Treaty of
Versailles, General von Seeckt and his colleagues had no hesitation
in organizing technical and military collaboration with Soviet Russia.
The latter engaged in this collaboration with equal enthusiasm. On
July 29th, 1922, a secret agreement was made in Berlin by which
training schools for German officers were established in Russia,
together with schools for aeroplane pilots, both German and Soviet.
An aircraft factory belonging to the Junkers firm was set up near
Moscow, while Krupp opened factories producing shells and tanks
in the Urals and near Kazan.[52] The spirit of 'realism' also presided
over the policy followed by Soviet Russia, from 1921 onwards, towards the United States. At a time when, under President Harding,
the Washington Government was passing through the first of those
crises of reactionary fanaticism and anti-Communist savagery that
have recurred in the U.S.A. from time to time since then, Litvinov
proposed that normal political and commercial relations be established between the U.S.A. and Soviet Russia. The Americans, of
course, refused.[53]

The Communists' doctrinal purity was subjected to severe trials in
other ways. Unlike the old Socialist International, their movement was
beginning to spread beyond Europe, and the existence of certain non-
European Communist parties gave rise, at the beginning of the 1920s,
to serious problems both for the Soviet Government and for the
Communist International. This was more particularly the case with
the Turkish and Persian Communist Parties, both founded in the
summer of 1920. The Soviet Government had to support every movement directed against the great imperialist powers, and in this way to
give real meaning to Lenin's slogan: 'Workers of all countries and
oppressed peoples, unite!' These peoples that were starting to rise up
against European (and especially British) imperialism were headed,
however, by bourgeois or petty-bourgeois leaders who had no sympathy whatever with Communism. Since it had been declared that

'the problem of the international social revolution' was insoluble 'without the participation of the East',[54] Soviet Russia offered support both to the Turkey of Kemal Atatürk and to the Persia of Riza Khan. And when the former tried to destroy the young Communist Party of Turkey, and had seventeen of its principal leaders killed, the soviets failed to react. As Professor Carr writes, 'For the first, though not for the last, time it was demonstrated that governments could deal drastically with their national communist parties without forfeiting the goodwill of the Soviet Government, if that were earned on other grounds.'[55] Regardless of all the ups and downs of the Turco-Soviet alliance, Bukharin was able to say in April 1923 that Turkey, 'in spite of all persecutions of Communists, plays a revolutionary role, since she is a destructive instrument in relation to the imperialist system as a whole'.[56]

Soviet Russia showed no less goodwill towards Persia. Just as she had renounced all claims on the Straits, so she repudiated the treaty which in 1907 had given Russia a number of privileges in the old Persian Empire. She supported the nationalist, anti-British movement led by Riza Khan. The little Soviet Republic of Gilan, established on Persia's Caspian coast after the departure of the British troops who had been intervening in Russia, received, however, no help from Moscow. The Bolshevik leaders, anxious not to spoil their good relations with the 'national bourgeois' government in Teheran, dissuaded the Persian Communists and their radical allies from marching on the capital. The requirements of an overall strategy worked out at the very centre of the world Communist movement were, already, taking precedence over every other consideration.[57]

A policy that entailed *rapprochements* and compromises with capitalist states, with a flexibility in manoeuvring that implied renunciation of the revolutionary programme and the recommending of 'palliatives' with an opportunist smell about them, and sacrifices imposed on 'brother parties' in order to strengthen bourgeois-nationalist movements that were harshly anti-communist—was this what the foreign policy of the Leninist Government amounted to, once the euphoria of its first victories had passed? What had become of the revolutionary message proclaimed across the frontiers of Russia to the proletariat of the world? Was this, then, nothing but ideological talk intended to conceal the pursuit of Russian state interests? The relations established between Soviet Russia and the German revolutionary movement are alone sufficient to correct so crude a notion.

The Soviet state was new-born when, despite its extreme shortage of means, it announced publicly its decision 'to place at the disposal of the representatives abroad of the Commissariat of Foreign Affairs for the needs of the revolutionary movement two million roubles.'[58] True, this money was to be used to weaken the German armies by

subjecting Wilhelm II's soldiers to propaganda for peace. But when
the Brest-Litovsk treaty deprived this activity of its original purpose,
the Bolsheviks' efforts did not cease. The Soviet Embassy in Berlin
played a vital role in this connexion. For the German radicals it
served as a rallying place and a centre from which they obtained
information (purchased with Russian gold from German officials),
financial help and even some arms supplies. Joffe, the Soviet diplomatic representative in the German capital, even undertook the
sending to various places in the provinces of 'propaganda experts'
charged with strengthening the revolutionary groups. Exact figures
for the amount of money put at the disposal of the revolutionary
socialists of Germany by the Soviet representatives are not available,
but that this financial help was substantial there can be no doubt.
When, on November 6th, 1918, the German Government expelled
the Soviet ambassador, the latter handed over a sum of ten million
roubles to the Independent Socialist Oskar Cohn, with instructions to
use it for the benefit of the extreme Left in Germany. Before Joffe's
expulsion, some ten Left-wing Socialist papers had been in receipt of
subsidies from the Soviet plenipotentiary.[59]

In October 1918 the first signs that an explosion was imminent in
Germany caused the Bolshevik leaders to consider by what further
means they might contribute to the downfall of the Hohenzollerns, and
even of the German bourgeoisie. On October 1st, Lenin, as has been
mentioned, wrote to Sverdlov and Trotsky: 'We are all ready to die
to help the German workers advance the revolution which has begun
in Germany.'* In the same letter he called for 'ten times more effort
to secure grain (clean out *all* stocks both for ourselves *and for the
German* workers).'[60] In the same period, addressing a joint meeting
of the C.E.C., the Moscow Soviet, and trade unionists, Lenin emphasized the same point: 'Let us resolve that every large elevator will
put aside some grain to help the German workers should they be hard
pressed in their struggle for emancipation from the imperialist monsters
and brutes.'[61] The idea of military aid to a German revolution was
also entertained: 'We had decided to have an army of one million
men by the spring; now we need an army of three million.'[62] Some
days later, the Central Executive Committee of the Soviets declared
publicly that 'Soviet Russia will offer all its forces and resources to aid
the German revolutionary government.' The statement added that it
was the duty of the workers and peasants of Russia to give food and
arms to the proletariat of Germany and Austria-Hungary in order to
help them 'against internal and external oppressors'.[63] And in fact,
at a time when revolutionary Russia was undergoing, at the start of
the winter of 1918–19, one of its most severe crises, with famine
decimating its population, the Soviet Government sent, in mid-

* See p. 365.

November, two train-loads of grain towards Germany. The new
Republican rulers of Germany stopped the convoy at the frontier and
declined to accept the delivery. While thanking the Soviet Government for its gesture, they declined help which they considered compromising. For Radek this was a second August 4th [1914] betrayal
committed by the Social-Democrats of Berlin.[64]

A few years later, economic crisis and the progress of a German Communist Party determined to launch an offensive seemed to put revolution on the agenda in Germany once more. While the German Communists actively prepared for a confrontation they thought would be
decisive, the feverish atmosphere that suddenly developed in Moscow,
and the measures taken by the Soviet leaders to come to the aid of the
Communists of Germany proved that the Soviet power was a great
deal less 'sobered down' than its diplomatic practice had suggested, and
that it was, on the contrary, ready for a new campaign of the world
revolution.

In September 1923 a number of German Communist leaders went
to Moscow to confer with the Soviet leaders and complete arrangements for an insurrection planned for the following month. They
found a city 'transformed by the revolutionary enthusiasm aroused
by the approach of the German October. The city is covered with
posters calling on Russian youth to learn German, so as to be able to
help the coming revolution. In factories, schools and universities
meetings are held daily at which passionate speeches are delivered
on the theme of aid to the German workers. Bukharin receives an
ovation from the students when he calls on them to drop their books
and take up rifles.'[65] As a historian of the Communist movement in
Germany has written, 'hard realists ... turned into sentimental
dreamers.'[66] But these were 'dreamers' who were ready to act. To
this end, two special funds were set up—one of food-grains, and one
of gold, the women of Russia being invited to donate their wedding-
rings to the latter. A survey was made to find all the members of the
Party with a knowledge of German. A politico-military organization
was formed in which not only activists of the Comintern but also
Soviet technicians took part. Even if, as Pierre Broué says, 'the number
of Russian officers and technicians sent to Germany to help the planned
insurrection' has often been exaggerated,[67] it remains true that the
German Communist leaders were reinforced for this occasion by 'the
dispatch of instructors and specialists, both foreign Communists who
had been trained in Russia in the Red Army, and also Russian Communists'.[68] The Soviet ambassador in Berlin, Krestinsky, sat in on the
committee which was in charge of the insurrection as a whole.[69]

At the moment when Lenin was withdrawing from the political
scene, the Soviet Government thus showed that the contradiction

between its revolutionary message and its 'realistic' practice did not
mean that it had given up its revolutionary aims, but that it was trying
in a dialectical way to find a synthesis between 'subversion' and 'negotiation' appropriate to the position of a workers' state cut off from the
main body of the proletarian army. That such a synthesis was hard to
find is obvious. It was possible only if *all* the different agents of Soviet
policy could succeed, despite the different conditioning to which they
were subjected, in retaining a clear awareness of their movement's
aims, and, through all the twists and turns of day-to-day politics,
remaining profoundly conscious of the priority of strategy over
tactics. It was necessary that at the top there should continue, alive
and operative, the sense of *the plan as a whole*, so that, even in periods
of repeated setbacks and protracted stagnation, sight would not be
lost of the long-term and the short-term needs, and what was vital
would never be sacrificed to what was secondary. Leninism had to
fulfil this political and ideological role, which called for political
acuteness and flexibility together with firm adherence to revolutionary
principles.* It was the task of Leninism to keep clearly in view, through
all the confusion of events, that unifying and mobilizing concept
without which the Soviet initiative would become bogged down in
sterile pragmatism and narrow nationalism.

This function could be fulfilled, however, only in so far as institutional structures served to implement it. The twofold requirements of
defence and offence, of safeguarding what had been won while keeping
the revolutionary dynamic alive, implied a dual structure of institutions which the Soviet régime endeavoured laboriously to erect. In
the first weeks following the seizure of power this had not seemed to be
necessary. That was the period when the state itself took charge of all
sectors of politics, and tried to carry out, without any differentiation,
operations that were hardly compatible with each other. While the
People's Commissariat for Foreign Affairs was entrusted with the
task of negotiating with foreign states, it was also supplied with
financial resources to be devoted to overthrowing these states. The
course taken by the Brest-Litovsk negotiations, and their culmination
in an inter-state treaty imposing upon the contracting parties the
obligation of 'mutual respect', showed that there was something lacking in this field, a gap which the Bolsheviks hastened to fill. While
Chicherin, as head of the Soviet diplomatic service, affirmed his
concern that the treaty be respected, Sverdlov, addressing the Seventh
Party Congress, in March 1918, explained to activists ignorant of
international law:

* In his book on the history of the Workers' Internationals, Julius Braunthal acknowledges, despite his anti-Communist bias, that 'Lenin ... did subordinate Russia's interests
to those of the workers as a whole, as he understood them, i.e., to world revolution'
(Braunthal, p. 261).

We shall no longer be able in our capacity as a government, as the Soviet power, to carry on the widespread international agitation which we have hitherto conducted. This does not mean that we shall engage in such agitation one jot less. But we shall now have regularly to carry on this agitation not in the name of Sovnarkom [the Council of People's Commissars] but in the name of the Central Committee of our Party.[70]

This was only a first, provisional solution to a difficult problem. The establishment in 1919 of the Third International was to make possible the perfecting of more elaborate formulations, which the increasing identification between the Soviet state and the Russian Communist Party, the Council of People's Commissars and the Central Committee, rendered indispensable. While in 1919, with the civil war and foreign intervention still going on, the Soviet Government, the Communist Party and the Comintern usually spoke the same uncompromising language, in 1920 a process of 'splitting of functions' was initiated with simultaneous development of the diplomatic apparatus of the Soviet state, on the one hand, and of the organizations of the Comintern, on the other. Already in 1919, however, Chicherin had said: 'Soviet diplomacy is defensive and it is also highly responsible, so that when we speak of the positive tasks of the Third International we cannot identify the Communist Parties with the Soviet Governments in which these parties predominate.'[71] This cryptic language was to become less and less ambiguous, and a sort of 'division of labour' to be established, between the Soviet state and the international Communist organization. Here are some examples.

In 1921 a trade agreement was made between Soviet Russia and Great Britain which included a clause forbidding the parties to engage in subversive activity against each other. Only a few months after the signing of this agreement, the Foreign Office protested to Moscow about repeated breaches of this clause. The Soviet Government replied by casting responsibility for the actions complained of by the British upon agents of the Comintern. So formalistic an argument could hardly convince, but it was nevertheless very useful in such circumstances as these.[72] A year later, the Soviet negotiators at Genoa came out in favour of a disarmament conference, and the Moscow Government itself undertook the organizing of a regional conference with this aim. Such pacific attitudes were hard to reconcile with the principles of revolutionary Marxism. While, however, the Government was occupied in strengthening Soviet Russia's position in the world by advocating military disarmament, the Third International made it its business to protect Communists against the dangers of *political* disarmament. At the moment when Soviet diplomats were talking the language of 'petty-bourgeois opportunism', the Comintern press was

proclaiming that 'disarmament is impossible so long as the bourgeoisie remain at the helm. Disarmament is impossible without the
victory of the proletarian revolution.'[73] And while Soviet Russia was
showing such great flexibility in its dealings with Germany as to enter
into co-operation with German industrialists and militarists, the
Comintern was not failing to commit its substantial resources to a
plan directly aimed at overthrowing the ruling class of Weimar
Germany.

Thus, the foreign policy of the Soviet state, by a mixture of tactical
concessions and bold initiatives, and taking advantage of the formal
separation between its own institutions and those of its international
appendage, sought, even in isolation, to undermine the capitalist
world and prepare the onslaught that would bring about its collapse.
This enterprise necessitated the working out of an overall revolutionary strategy and the creation of an instrument capable of putting
it into effect. The Bolsheviks and their allies abroad had to win over
the socialist movement everywhere, becoming the only genuine
representatives of this movement. Since the rallying of the international proletariat to the Russian revolutionary offensive, completing the victory won in 1917, could alone ensure the triumph of
socialism, Leninism added this task to all the others it had assumed.

3

The Leninist International

Since the Russian revolution was conceived as a phase in the world socialist revolution, with the Bolshevik Party figuring as only one section of a larger proletarian army, Leninism necessarily had to operate in the field of the international socialist movement. After mastering the Bolshevik Party, Lenin's revolutionary theory set itself the aim of converting and winning over the entire socialist movement everywhere.

This ambition involved more than just launching an attack on reformism, the unsuspected extent of which had been revealed by the events of August 1914. It soon led to the complete collapse of socialist unity. On the international plane, Leninism appeared to its detractors as bearing responsibility for a split the terrible consequence of which was to weaken the proletariat and help the bourgeoisie. This accusation embittered the debate between the two sections, thenceforth hostile to one another, into which the working-class movement became divided. It was also put down to the charge of Leninism that it had founded an institution which, under cover of socialist pretensions, soon became totalitarian, and which, while claiming to be an International, provided the Soviet state with an obedient instrument for deceiving the masses. Any analysis of Lenin's work must take account of these charges and consider how justified they are.

Leninism as a divisive factor

In the first months of the war, Lenin, after noting at the beginning of September 1914 'the betrayal of socialism by most leaders of the Second International',[1] predicted that there would be a split in the German Social-Democratic Party. By March 1915, however, he was seeing the problem in broader terms: 'whoever dreams of "unity" between revolutionary Social-Democratic workers and the "European" Social-Democratic legalists of yesterday, and of *today*, has learned nothing and forgotten everything.'[2] In *Socialism and the War*, written in July 1915, he expressed the view that 'a split with the opportunists and chauvinists is the prime duty of revolutionaries'.[3] At the time, he was not certain 'whether the conditions are mature for the formation of a new and Marxist International'. If they were indeed mature, then 'our Party will gladly join such a Third International, purged of opportunism and chauvinism'.[4]

While the founding of a new International was thus subject to the selection of the right moment,* Lenin nevertheless observed, in February 1916, that 'the split in the labour and socialist movements throughout the world is a fact' and that 'it is ridiculous to close your eyes to this fact'.[5] Almost at once on arriving in Petrograd he told his supporters: 'We must take the initiative in creating a revolutionary International',[6] adding that 'it is our duty to found a Third International without delay'.[7] Although he repeatedly stressed this point, even after the seizure of power,[8] Lenin had to wait until 1919 before putting his plan into operation, because the continuing world war made it impossible for relations to be re-established between the socialists of the belligerent countries.

A split in the international labour movement as it had existed before the war was thus regarded by Lenin as being, like the class struggle, both an objective fact and a necessity that would facilitate revolutionary activity in Europe. And while the latter view was subjective and open to discussion, the former was merely an observation forced upon Lenin by events to which the war had given rise. The outbreak of the war and the contradictory reactions it produced exacerbated the already difficult relations between the tendencies in the socialist movement. The Right wing in European Social-Democracy became more 'integrationist' than ever and took decisive steps in that direction, while at the other end of the spectrum the radicals became even more radical. The sense of 'the state' and their 'responsibilities' to it expressed by the former was countered by the latter with an increasingly explosive mixture of impatience, indignation and refusal to compromise. Even before 1916, well before the Russian revolution and the advance of Bolshevism had intensified the division between reformist Right and revolutionary Left, splits had occurred in the Swedish and German movements. In the latter case, the split consummated organizationally a divorce that had grown more and more obvious as the war went on. Among the Left socialists 'it became a matter of honour to hate one's own traitors the most',[9] and as for the Right-wingers, they did not shrink from joining with the conservatives in the Reichstag in voting for the withdrawal of parliamentary immunity from their own comrade Liebknecht, thus handing him over to the gaolers of Wilhelm II.[10]

* Lenin emphasized, while condemning and denouncing opportunism, 'We do not say that an immediate split with the opportunists in all countries is desirable, or even possible at present' (Lenin, Vol. 21, p. 444).

Everywhere, the tension between the opposing groups of socialists became intolerable. While fratricidal struggles were nothing new for Russian socialists, they assumed, with the outbreak of the war, an even more passionate form than previously. When the Bolshevik Krylenko, who was to distinguish himself in the October revolution, attended a lecture in Switzerland given by Plekhanov, who had become a 'social-patriot', he trembled all over and burst into tears at the exhibition of chauvinism given by the 'father of Russian Marxism', and exclaimed: 'Our time will come, you blackguards!'[11] Plekhanov himself, who admitted that he would prefer a victory of Tsarist reaction in Russia to a victory of the Bolsheviks, told Angelica Balabanoff soon after the outbreak of the war: 'So far as I am concerned, if I were not old and sick I would join the army. To bayonet your German comrades would give me great pleasure.'[12]

This was the state of affairs in the camp of international socialism when the events in Russia in 1917, together with the beginnings of the revolution in Germany, brought in new elements of hatred and division. The circumstances surrounding the fall of the Hohenzollerns and the birth of the Weimar Republic revealed the extent to which the unity of the socialist movement no longer possessed even the value of a myth. While the Spartacists tried, through the pressure of the proletarian masses, to give socialist objectives to the November revolution, the 'Majority-Socialists' showed themselves a force for social conservatism, ready to use the most violent methods in order to halt the anticapitalist offensive. They almost managed to save the Imperial system itself. This, at any rate, was true of Friedrich Ebert, who was compensated with the title of first President of the Republic for his unsuccessful zeal on behalf of the Crown. When Philipp Scheidemann, anticipating, amid the tumult of revolutionary demonstrations, an initiative from the Left, proclaimed from the balcony of the Reichstag that the monarchy was no more, Ebert, whom Bebel's death had made the principal leader of the German Social-Democratic Party, and who had only just told Prince Max of Baden that he hated revolution 'like sin',[13] turned on his comrade, his face 'livid with wrath', and told him: 'You have not the right to proclaim the Republic ... '[14]

Legalistic to the point of conservatism, counter-revolutionary to the extent that they remained for as long as possible aloof from a mass movement the object of which was to establish a republican régime they were supposed to favour 'in principle', the 'Majority-Socialists' showed as much zeal in combating the Spartacists as they had shown against France and Russia in the war. One of them, Noske, undertook the job of executioner,[15] or, as he himself put it, of 'bloodhound', by directing the repressive activities of the regular army and the *Freikorps* of the extreme Right.

Since the Social-Democratic press denounced the 'armed bandits of the Spartakusbund' and presented them to its readers as 'madmen' and 'criminals', it is not surprising that the defeat of the Spartacist insurrection led to a massacre of thousands of workers, during and after the fighting, and the murder of a number of prominent revolutionary socialists—Rosa Luxemburg and Karl Liebknecht, Leviné, Landauer, Jogiches, Egelhofer, Gandorfer, Möller, Fernbach—whose killers enjoyed unlimited toleration under a régime in which the Social-Democrats often held the levers of political command.

There was thenceforth, between Socialists and Communists, divided members of a once united family, more than a mere political difference of opinion: there was the experience of a decisive test, in which the proletarian onslaught on capitalism had at last been attempted, and in which they had confronted each other across a ditch filled with blood. And to this must be added the attitude taken up by the 'Majority Socialists' towards Bolshevik Russia. The Berlin Congress of Workers' Councils called on the Socialist Government headed by Ebert to restore diplomatic relations with Soviet Russia, which the now defunct Imperial régime had broken off. They reckoned without the already virulent anti-Communism of the new rulers. First, the latter informed the Soviet Government that a resumption of diplomatic relations must be a matter for negotiation. One of the new ministers (an Independent Socialist, regarded as being 'on the Left') urged a policy of delay. This was definitely the view of Karl Kautsky, who had become, thanks to a revolution he had not wanted, the Social-Democrats' adviser not only in theoretical Marxism but also in practical diplomacy. In the end they decided *against* re-establishing relations with the Soviet régime.[16] Furthermore, the Socialist Government of Germany refused Rakovsky, the Soviet ambassador to Austria, permission to proceed via Berlin to Vienna.[17] Later, the troops of General von der Goltz, engaged in crushing the revolutionary workers in Finland, benefited from financial aid which Ebert continued to send them.[18] In the conflict between the capitalist West and Communist Russia, the Weimar Socialists, whom the humiliation of Versailles might have given an excuse for maintaining a certain reserve, preferred to neutrality the attractions of unlimited commitment against the 'Reds'. This was, after all, logical enough: having accorded active support to the bourgeois order in Germany itself, they followed a foreign policy inspired by the same principle.

Speaking at the Second Congress (1920) of the Comintern about the trend in socialism to which the 'Majority-Socialists' of Germany belonged, Lenin said that it was 'bourgeois socialism, not proletarian socialism', and consisted of 'better defenders of the bourgeoisie than the bourgeois themselves'.[19] While sociologically incorrect, his statement was politically beyond dispute. We shall see how unsatisfactory was Lenin's attempt to explain the social basis of Right-wing

Socialism.* But the fact that this trend had objectively—and also subjectively—chosen to defend bourgeois society at a moment when this was in peril necessarily caused it to line up, during periods of intense class struggle, with the enemies of the proletariat, and especially of the revolutionary proletariat. These were the terms in which the problem of socialist unity presented itself on the eve, and on the morrow, of the October revolution.

Nevertheless, one should not underestimate the boldness shown by Lenin when he advocated drawing definitive organizational conclusions from this obvious split that had come about among socialists. Although the class struggle had cut a line of division through the socialist movement itself, by no means everyone was resigned to ratifying in institutional form the death of working-class unity. Rosa Luxemburg, Karl Liebknecht and the German Spartacists hesitated for several years to take such action, although they felt not the slightest indulgence towards the German Social-Democratic Party and its official leaders, whom Rosa Luxemburg described as 'the most infamous scoundrels the world has ever known',[20] while she spoke of the Social-Democratic organization itself as a 'stinking corpse'.[21] Even they shrank from consummating the split by taking the responsibility of creating a new revolutionary organization and quitting for ever the old socialist movement. Among the most radical of the Spartacists there was such an attachment to the old institution and such a horror of a split that they hesitated to leave the Social-Democratic Party even when the Centrists left it, or were driven out, and were preparing to form the U.S.P.D. (Independent Social-Democratic Party of Germany). At first the Spartacists considered remaining within one or other of these parties.[22]

This attitude, expressing an ideology of unity that resisted even the most violent attacks, did not end in November 1918, with the revolution. The Spartacists opposed the forming of a Communist organization and thought they might be able to win a majority in the Independent Social-Democratic Party, using normal democratic procedures to oust the Centrist leaders, whom they denounced vigorously. It was only in December, and against the will of Rosa Luxemburg, that the majority of the Spartacists decided to form a Communist Party. In a number of places in Germany a real regrouping of the revolutionary forces did not take place until March 1919.[23] By that time the radical masses had already suffered defeats from which they proved unable to recover.

From Lenin's point of view, an organizational rupture of socialist unity was not only a matter of principle, but also one of functional necessity and timeliness. His desire to create a Communist movement

* See p. 429.

free from any links with the old Social-Democratic reformism, although nourished by a feeling of disgust and indignation, followed above all from a political judgment in which realism was not sacrificed to revolutionary purism. The establishment of the Third International expressed a strategic calculation governed by rigorous logic. As soon as the evolution of capitalism into its imperialist phase, the outbreak of the world war and the development of the crisis that it engendered, along with the first successes of the Russian revolution, made it possible to suppose that the proletariat of Europe was being offered a historic opportunity that must be seized at once, the problem immediately arose of what instrument was needed for carrying out the revolution. Naturally, it was out of the question that the Second International, or the parties composing it, should act to destroy a bourgeoisie whose allies they had become. The events in Germany proved that the last efforts of which the Social-Democratic leaders were capable would be directed against the proletariat in revolt. The twofold conviction that the class struggle on the world scale had entered a phase of extreme acuteness, and that the Russian revolution was part of a wider offensive, necessarily gave rise to the desire to create an international revolutionary organization capable of really fighting the bourgeoisie to the bitter end.

Justified from the functional standpoint, such an enterprise was found to be also historically possible. 'The old socialism ... is not yet buried ... but it is already done for in all countries of the world, it is already dead,' said Lenin in March 1918.[24] In July 1919 he spoke again of 'the shameful death of the Second International'.[25] There was, of course, a certain element of polemical exaggeration in these statements. But that the international organization of Social-Democracy had emerged greatly weakened from the war was shown both by the disaffection within its ranks and by the popularity of the Russian revolution.* The ending of hostilities had hardly enabled the restoration of relations between the socialist parties to be considered possible, when that party which, of all those in Western Europe, had suffered least from the ravages of nationalism, the Italian Socialist Party, decided to *leave* the Second International. Its example was to be followed by several others. Everywhere, the big majorities which had given a Right-wing and chauvinist orientation to the Social-Democratic parties were being encroached upon by the advance of the Left and the Centre.

These changes were symptomatic of deeper disturbances, to which above all the offensive of the masses bore witness. The great strikes in Vienna and Budapest, in January 1918, had had what the Social-Democratic historian Braunthal, not disposed to exaggerate in such

* See p. 409.

matters, called 'a grandiose revolutionary flavour'.[26] When the movement was renewed, on the same scale, in Berlin, a situation existed that Borkenau, as disinclined as Braunthal to exaggeration, described as 'the biggest political opportunity of any Western proletariat'.[27] The German revolution broke out towards the end of that year. Three months later the Third International was born in Moscow — a seat that was at first regarded as only temporary. Its foundation set the seal on a split that had appeared first in the realm of ideas and then had been brought to completion in fratricidal struggles. Leninism did not provoke this split: it took full responsibility for it, however, once it had occurred, and saw in it a condition for the 'final struggle' that had at last begun, within the very citadel of capitalism, to be carried through to the abolition of capitalism everywhere.

The International and the Leftists

'If the First International predicted the future course of development and indicated the roads it would take, if the Second International rallied and organized millions of proletarians, then the Third International is the International of revolutionary realization, the International of action.'[28] Thus spoke the new organization, in the manifesto issued at the end of its first congress, in March 1919. The 'International of action' would soon define itself, with still greater precision and ambition, as 'the party of the revolutionary insurrection of the world proletariat'.[29] With no less emphasis, the new International's first president, Zinoviev, declared at its Second Congress, in July–August 1920: 'We are fighting against the international bourgeoisie, against foes armed to the teeth, and we need to have an iron organization of the international proletariat,' with 'military discipline'.[30] The task before the Communist International was, then, to carry world revolution through to the end. Its style of action, structure and mode of recruitment were determined by this task. It implied a complete break with the ways of the Second International, the strength of which had never been more than apparent, and which had drawn its prestige mainly from the brilliance as rhetoricians of its most famous leaders.

To the new tasks there necessarily had to correspond a completely new composition and recruitment. That there was no room for reformists in this fighting organization was self-evident. This obvious fact hid, however, a problem which the Third International was obliged to deal with soon after its foundation. As individuals, the Right-wing leaders were certainly not tempted by the revolutionary activities in which the Third International proposed to specialize. As members, however, of parties that were becoming radicalized, they might be brought to join an organization the aims and spirit of which were utterly alien to them. In this way there arose a question which unleashed, from 1920 onward, the most lively of controversies, namely, that about the conditions for admission to the Third International—with, as corollary, the conditions for exclusion from that body. The question was complicated by the fact that the very definition of reformism was unclear. If one had yielded to reformism during the war, did that constitute an irreparable fault? The case of Marcel Cachin, that apostle and missionary of French chauvinism* who later rallied to Communism, proved that this was not necessarily so. Again, reformism might assume a variety of forms. In the wide range of tendencies in the socialist movement, the unquestionably reformist, counter-revolutionary Right and the unquestionably revolutionary, sometimes insurrectionary, Left were separated by a vast 'marsh' inhabited by what were called Centrists. What was to be the attitude towards those numerous undecided elements the sincerity of whose socialist sentiments was not doubted, but whose aptitude for radical action was, to say the least, questionable? When the break-up of the Second International, formally reconstituted at the beginning of 1919, became a large-scale process, the problem of who should be allowed to join the Third International emerged as a highly topical one, and President Zinoviev declared that he regarded it as necessary to 'bolt the doors', because he was afraid that entry into the Comintern might 'degenerate into a sort of fashion'.[31] The famous 'Twenty-One Conditions', drawn up, as regards essentials, by Lenin himself, served the aim of preventing any such 'degeneration'.

Draconian as the conditions were that were laid down for entry into the international Communist movement, they applied, nevertheless, to organizations, not to individuals. Aimed in the main at parties that might wish to join, they informed such parties that they were 'obliged everywhere to create a parallel illegal organization which at the decisive moment will help the party to do its duty to the revolution' (third condition); to carry on systematic propaganda work in the army, directed especially against intervention against Soviet Russia or action against the colonial peoples (fourth, eighth and fourteenth conditions); to organize 'Communist cells' in the trade unions, to combat the reformist Trade-Union International and strengthen that of the 'Red trade unions', the formation of which had just been decided on in Moscow (ninth and tenth conditions). On the plane of principles, stress was laid on the obligation to propagate the idea of the dictatorship of the proletariat (first condition). 'Iron discipline' was also required (twelfth condition), together with application of the principle of strict centralization: not only must the new programmes of parties adhering to the International be submitted to the latter for approval

---

* Cachin went to Italy during the war with the task of urging the Italian socialists to support their country's entry into the war, although for Italy, more than for any other belligerent state, the war could have no aim but territorial expansion.

(fifteenth condition), but, more generally, 'all the decisions of the congresses of the Communist International, as well as the decisions of its Executive Committee, are binding on all parties belonging to the Communist International' (sixteenth condition).

The problem of individuals was hardly touched upon, and the strictness of the conditions was, in this respect, not so great as it might seem at first sight. The document did indeed lay down that 'the Communist International is unable to agree that notorious opportunists, such as Turati, Modigliani, Kautsky, Hilferding, Hillquit, Longuet, MacDonald, etc., shall have the right to appear as members of the Communist International' (seventh condition). Indirectly, however, the way the conditions were set out, far from rigidly excluding any and every reformist or Centrist from the Communist ranks, allowed it to be assumed that their continued presence in parties which had been renovated and transformed would, given certain safeguards, be permitted. The parties were indeed told that they 'must from time to time undertake cleansing (re-registration) of the membership of the party in order to get rid of any petty-bourgeois elements which have crept in' (thirteenth condition). At the same time, however, the parties were only to 'remove reformists and centrists from all responsible positions in the workers' movement' (second condition), which did not imply expulsion. And the twentieth condition, providing that the central leaderships of the parties joining the Third International must be composed, to the extent of two-thirds at least, of leaders who had been in favour, before the Second World Congress (1920), of their organization taking this step, allowed the Executive Committee of the International 'the right to make exceptions in the case of representatives of the "Centre" '.[32]

The acceptance of the Twenty-One Conditions by the Second Comintern Congress did not put an end to controversies about joining it. This was shown in December 1920 when, at Tours, the French Socialists met to decide whether or not to adhere to the Third International. A large proportion of the debate was devoted to discussing the application of the Twenty-One Conditions. The attitude of Léon Blum, who invoked doctrinal considerations and the insuperable theoretical divergences between Communism and the socialism of the *vieille maison* as grounds for his refusing to join 'Moscow' in any case, so rejecting in advance the rule of the majority, was exceptional.[33] Whereas the future head of the People's Front Government frankly assumed, on doctrinal grounds, the responsibility of ending the unity of the French socialist movement, the great majority of the delegates who were hostile to Communism used the Twenty-One Conditions as an excuse to avoid the basic issues. Instead of dealing with these problems they declared that they had been barred from entry into the revolutionary organization. Even the celebrated telegram from Zinoviev* did not, however, stop the supporters of 'joining Moscow' from assuring their Centrist friends that nothing in the Twenty-One Conditions implied excommunications based upon past errors.† In an 'Open Letter' to the workers of France and Germany Lenin had emphasized that it would be possible to arrange for exceptions to the rules, even in favour of 'Right-wing leaders', adding: 'since exceptions are expressly declared to be permissible, there can be no talk of an absolute bar against specific individuals. Consequently, there is full recognition of the need to take into account, not the past but the present, the change in the views and conduct of individuals, of individual leaders.'[34]

Actually, Lenin, despite his extreme aversion to reformism and centrism‡ and his desire to make the Third International an organization for revolutionary combat, showed greater flexibility than Zinoviev, whose tendency was more 'Leftist'. The problem of exclusions arose, moreover, in terms of which the Soviet leaders were not the sole masters. Whereas the Soviet leaders had decided that negotiations should take place, before and during the Second Congress of the Comintern, with representatives of the Centrist parties of France (the S.F.I.O.) and Germany (the U.S.P.D.), those in the countries concerned who had already joined the Comintern brought pressure to bear on its Executive Committee to refuse any kind of compromise with hesitant and conciliatory elements.§ Finally, and most important, the whole question of who was to be allowed to join and who was not formed part of a larger group of problems for which the Communist International had no ready-made solution. Fundamentally, it was a question of defining the nature of the parties that would constitute the Communist movement in Western Europe. They would, of course, be *revolutionary* organizations—hence, *inter alia*, the insistence on their getting ready for underground activity—and they would doubtless accept, provided sufficient flexibility were shown, instructions sent out from the centralized Executive Committee, i.e., from a body

* In this telegram sent to the Tours Congress the President of the Third International declared that his organization could have nothing in common with the authors of a resolution which he regarded as unacceptable, these being Paul Faure and Jean Longuet, the chief representatives of the Centrist tendency.

† Frossard, who was to become the first General Secretary of the French Communist Party, appealed to his 'friends of the Centre', saying: 'We need you.' Paul Vaillant-Couturier assured them that the rules of admission to the Comintern related only to the future, and added that 'the exclusions provided for in Moscow's articles 7 and 8 cannot be applied to any member of the Party who accepts the decision of this Congress'. The supporters of joining even put down a motion in which the Centrists were described as 'good workers for socialism' (*Parti Socialiste* [*S.F.I.O.*], *XVIII*, pp. 385, 437, 482–93).

‡ See p. 429.

§ See *Protokoll des II Weltkongresses*, pp. 277–8. At the end of 1920 Anton Pannekoek, the Dutch Leftist, was still reproaching the leaders of the Third International with 'trying to get the maximum number of opportunists to join' (letter to Mühsam, published in *Die Aktion*, March 19th, 1921: quoted in *Pannekoek et les Conseils Ouvriers*, p. 215).

that was directly subject to the influence of the Soviet Communist Party.* Over and above these generalities, however, there was the pressure of events themselves. The world revolution was taking its time; the radicalization of the masses was leading to the formation of large Centrist parties in which scarcely disguised reformists rubbed shoulders with sincere revolutionaries; the logic of political life in Western and Central Europe favoured the appearance of mass Communist parties, capable of competing with the Social-Democratic movement. Since it soon proved impossible to destroy the latter, what was now needed was to set up in rivalry to it, and wrest from it the allegiance of the largest possible number of workers. From this standpoint, the formation, after the Halle Congress† in October 1920, of the United Communist Party of Germany, was a major turning-point. Bringing together the tens of thousands of members of the Communist Party founded in December 1918 and the substantial body of former U.S.P.D. members, the United Party constituted a mass organization with a strength of some 350,000. The sectarian spirit that threatened to overwhelm the first Communist groups formed in the West was gravely shaken by this event.

That sectarianism was limited by other factors as well, in particular by the heterogeneous make-up of the first Communist parties, the ideological diversity existing among their members, and the broad freedom for tendencies that prevailed within them. Just as it is wrong to see in Leninism the cause of the split in the international socialist movement, it is wrong also to attribute to the Third International, as it developed in the first years following its foundation, the dogmatic rigidity and sergeant-major methods of Stalinism.

The ideological diversity that marked the beginnings of the Communist International was due to the fact that, although inspired and led by revolutionaries of the Marxist school, whose first political experiences had been in the 'orthodox' socialist movement, this organization succeeded in influencing a great variety of political elements. Alongside Left socialists like the Spartacists, who had long been conducting a revolutionary struggle inside parties dominated by reformism, there figured, among the first recruits to the international Communist movement, men with an infinitely less radical past, who brought with them 'the socialist tradition'. As compared, however, with its predecessor, the Communist International showed a twofold originality, in respect of its fields of recruitment: it sought, and succeeded to a notable extent, in winning members from outside Europe, and it appealed to sections of the proletariat which had until then remained outside the socialist organizations—especially the groups

* See p. 412.
† At this congress the U.S.P.D. decided by a big majority to join the Third International.

belonging to the syndicalist, anarcho-syndicalist, and even simply anarchist 'families'.

When, at the beginning of 1919, invitations to the inaugural congress of the Third International were sent out, the list of organizations whose presence was sought included the British, American and Australian sections of the 'Industrial Workers of the World', who were anarcho-syndicalists, and the 'revolutionary element' of the British Shop Stewards' Movement, which was influenced by tendencies of the same kind.[35] A few months later a circular from the Executive Committee of the Communist International declared that the new organization 'welcomes most cordially ... the anarcho-syndicalist groups, and the groups which just call themselves anarchist.'[36] The problem implicit in the presence in the international Communist organization of these heterodox elements raised its head on the eve of the Second Congress, in July 1920. An invitation having been issued to 'all groups of revolutionary syndicalists [and] the I.W.W. unions',[37] Radek, as secretary of the Comintern, questioned the correctness of this decision. Backed by the German Communist Paul Levi and the Italian Serrati, he expressed a preference for keeping these anarcho-syndicalist and anarchistic tendencies out of the Third International. Not only was his attitude not endorsed by the majority on the Executive Committee, but, as Alfred Rosmer tells us, he was reproved for it, his post as secretary being taken from him and given to Angelica Balabanoff.[38] Rosmer, who himself had a syndicalist background, says, regarding the non-Marxist revolutionaries of that period, that they were pleased with such writings of Lenin's as *State and Revolution*. In addition,

> besides these texts, in which they could find a language akin to their own, a conception of socialism which resembled their own, what particularly pleased revolutionaries from the anarchist and syndicalist traditions, and attracted them towards Bolshevism, was the merciless condemnation of opportunism. And this was not only condemnation of hardened opportunists, the social-chauvinists who had backed up their imperialist governments during the war, but also of those who stopped halfway, who criticised government policies but did not dare draw the logical consequences of their criticism.[39]

It is therefore not surprising that close links were formed between the Comintern delegates sent into Western Europe and the syndicalist and anarcho-syndicalist groups. Jules Humbert-Droz, who was sent by the Communist International to Paris to act there for several years as 'Moscow's eye', was expressly instructed to make contact with these circles—with which, in any case, he felt, as he writes, 'a great deal of sympathy'.[40] In a country like France, possessing a strong syndicalist tradition, the contribution made by this element to the Communist

Party was extremely important. Men such as Rosmer himself, Pierre Monatte, Monmousseau and Sémard, who played a prominent part in the first phase of the French Communist Party's history, came from the syndicalist movement. In Spain the Third International received in 1919 the support of the powerful National Confederation of Labour (C.N.T.), the anarcho-syndicalist body. Even in Britain, the U.S.A. and Holland many of the first sympathizers with and adherents of the young Communist parties had similar doctrinal allegiances.[41]

The question of the anarchists, anarcho-syndicalists and syndicalists forms part, however, of a larger question, that of the 'Leftists' in general, and the place they held in the Comintern in Lenin's time. The example of German Communism illustrates very well the variety of tendencies that was represented in the Communist movement. At its foundation congress the K.P.D.(S.) – the Communist Party of Germany (Spartacus League) – immediately displayed originality both on the plane of principles and on that of organization. It took an independent line towards Bolshevik policy, Rosa Luxemburg saying plainly that the working-class revolution had no need for terror,[42] and showed antipathy to the principles of organization advocated by Leninism and realized in Bolshevism. Inspired by Rosa Luxemburg's anti-bureaucratism, the founders of the Party decided to restrict the power of full-time officials and keep their numbers small, and also to limit the financial resources at the disposal of the central leadership, and weaken its prerogatives to the advantage of the local organizations.[43] The German Party also showed at once how deeply it was influenced by Leftist views that did not fit the canons of Leninism, by deciding (even against the recommendations of its best-known leaders) to boycott the elections to the Constituent Assembly, which were due to be held in February 1919.

This 'Leftism' was destined to be a feature of German Communism all through its first years. It led to the formation in April 1920 of a dissident group which under the name of the K.A.P.D. (Communist Workers' Party of Germany) brought together the anti-trade-union, anti-parliamentarian elements of the extreme Left. This development resulted from action taken by the K.P.D. leadership. Paul Levi, angered by the strength of Leftism in his organization, called for and obtained, at the Party congress held in Heidelberg in October 1919, the expulsion of those delegates who were against participating in elections and also in the trade-union movement, which they regarded as fundamentally and hopelessly reformist.[44] The K.A.P.D., set up as a rival to the 'orthodox' organization, revealed features that marked it off very sharply from Leninism. Its activist tendency came close to adventurism, and sometimes went over the brink.

Despite these divergences and incompatibilities, however, the Third International displayed for a long time great patience and tolerance in its dealings with the extremists of the K.A.P.D. Radek, who was the E.C.C.I.'s* chief specialist on German affairs, had from the first urged Paul Levi to be cautious, and had tried to prevent the expulsion of the Leftists.[45] Lenin himself intervened in the quarrel, calling for reconciliation between the two organizations.[46] Although this advice was ignored, and relations between the K.P.D. and the K.A.P.D. became increasingly hostile, the latter continued to be treated indulgently by the International. It was invited to send a delegation to the Second Congress, and in 1921 was admitted as a 'sympathizing party', which enabled it to benefit for a certain period from the Comintern's financial support.[47]

While, however, anarchistic Leftism had set up a stronghold in the K.A.P.D. it had not been entirely purged from the ranks of the 'orthodox' Party. The latter included an important extremist wing, whose principal leaders were Arkadi Maslow and Ruth Fischer. They carried on a campaign to develop in the K.P.D. the fighting spirit which, in their view, it lacked. Their theory of 'the offensive at any price', and the inevitable defeats resulting from its implementation, caused Leftism to become discredited in the International. Trotsky, speaking at the Third World Congress in July 1921, declared: 'it is our duty to say clearly and precisely to the German workers that we consider this philosophy of the offensive to be the greatest danger. And in its practical application to be the greatest crime.'[48] He had discussed the problem previously with Lenin, and the two had decided to combine in fighting at the congress against the Leftist trend. The alarm they felt at the adventuristic excesses of Leftism was not groundless. In Germany the Leftists had not been content to talk about 'all-out offensives'. In March 1921 certain Communist groups had resorted to methods of provocation in order to stimulate the proletariat to rebel; the effect had been merely to increase their own isolation.[49]

Even before 1921 Lenin had already taken a stand on Leftism, and had not confined his criticisms to its Russian representatives. The Leftists in the international Communist movement had also been rebuked. This criticism of his, however, had been fraternal, restrained and soothing. Lenin's letter to Sylvia Pankhurst, in August 1919, already quoted,† had mentioned the divergence on the parliamentary question. Lenin recognized in his message to the British militant that 'criticism of parliamentarism is not only legitimate and necessary ... but is quite correct,' and, without abandoning his own view that revolutionaries ought to participate in parliamentary activity, had expressed the conviction that 'this disagreement is so immaterial that the most reasonable thing would be not to split over it'.[50] In October 1919, in an article entitled 'Greetings to the Italian, French and Ger-

* Executive Committee of the Communist International.
† See p. 261.

man Communists,' he again referred to the systematic anti-parliamentarism of the Leftists, and repeated that he saw it as only 'a minor question'. Even though it was giving rise to sharp controversy, he commented: 'There is nothing terrible in that; it is a matter of growing pains.'[51] After 1921, however, when Leftism assumed a more virulent form, leading to actions that were all the more adventuristic in that they were out of line with the general evolution of the situation in Germany, Lenin undertook a vigorous campaign against it. The Third Congress of the Comintern was the scene of a grand attack. Nevertheless, after savaging the Leftist leaders, some of whom, such as Béla Kun, were living in exile from their own countries, Lenin hastened to send them a letter in which he said: 'It is quite natural for *émigrés* frequently to adopt attitudes which are "too Leftist",' and expressed his sympathy with 'such fine, loyal, dedicated and worthy revolutionaries'.[52] This is an important letter, confirming as it does the observation made earlier in connexion with Lenin's attitude to the Soviet 'Leftists', namely, that, while the criticism he directed at Leftism was often very sharp and his attacks upon it sometimes violent, this was always, for him, a debate which, however vigorous, was being carried on with comrades engaged in the same fight. A similar conclusion can be drawn from the work that Lenin devoted to the Leftist phenomenon and published in June 1920, on the eve of the Second World Congress, namely: '*Left-Wing' Communism, An Infantile Disorder*.

This little book deserves its fame. Here we see a polemicist whose talent, for once, avoids the lures of linguistic excess, a rigorous analyst, and a penetrating observer of politics. This is the best Lenin, the one in whom acute realism is joined with firmness of revolutionary principle. '*Left-Wing' Communism* is an exhaustive catalogue of the mistakes of the Leftists. Among these was the rigidity into which they were led by their purism. 'Doctrinaires of the revolution'[53] — *of the revolution*, and not of the counter-revolution, as the Stalinist and post-Stalinist diatribe was later to allege — the Leftists declared against all compromise, and that was 'childishness which it is difficult even to consider seriously'.[54] Lenin also denounced the sort of libertarian demagogy that was characteristic of the K.A.P.D. and which — anticipating faults that were eventually to become all too real — systematically contrasted the 'leaders' and the 'masses'.[55] His criticism of this attitude led Lenin to stress with particular firmness the need for a strong, disciplined party whose authority would withstand the debilitating consequences of the ebb in the revolutionary tide.[56]

'*Left-Wing' Communism*, then, defined by way of a critique of Leftism the relationship that should exist between the revolutionary party and the masses. While it should not 'sink to the level ... of the backward strata of the class', the Party needed to '*soberly* follow the *actual* state of the class-consciousness and preparedness of the entire class (not only of its communist vanguard) and of all the *working people* (not only of their advanced elements)'. The need for contact with the broad masses and care to avoid getting too remote from them—to 'stick close' to them just sufficiently to make them go forward, to raise their level of consciousness and radicalize them—was a matter of major importance for Lenin, and he returned to it on a number of occasions.[57] It was because they overlooked this need that the Leftists rejected any *rapprochement* with certain trends in the socialist movement that lay to the Right of the Communists. Lenin, challenging the 'purism' of the Leftists, called for a degree of 'parliamentary' support to be given to the British Labour leaders, although he knew the latter to be closer to the Churchills and Lloyd Georges than to the revolutionaries. It was, of course, Lenin explained, in a formulation that scandalized his Social-Democratic opponents, a question of supporting them 'in the same way as the rope supports a hanged man'.[58] The tactical skill of the Communists was to produce the effect—provided that they did not sacrifice their principles—of exposing to the masses, in terms of facts and not merely of speeches, the basic conservatism and helplessness of reformism.[59]

Finally, Lenin attacked the refusal by many Leftists to work in the reformist trade unions ('to refuse to work in the reactionary trade unions means leaving the insufficiently developed or backward masses of workers under the influence of the reactionary leaders, the agents of the bourgeoisie'[60]), and also their dogmatic anti-parliamentarism. Their refusal to take part in elections or to sit in Parliament resulted, according to Lenin, from their contempt or ignorance of the broad masses of the proletariat. Thus, the Communists of the K.A.P.D. considered that 'parliamentary forms of struggle ... have become historically and politically obsolete'.[61] As Lenin remarked, the German Leftists, yielding to an inclination that was typical of their kind, took their own wishes for reality; in fact, a substantial section of the proletariat still believed in the virtues of Parliament and parliamentary activity.[62] The difficulty, and the revolutionary duty, consisted in using Parliament as a platform for agitation and propaganda. The Bolsheviks had managed to do this in the old Tsarist Duma without succumbing to any illusions: Lenin foresaw, however, that it would be 'far more difficult to create a really revolutionary parliamentary group in a European parliament than it was in Russia'.[63] This was, indeed, to prove very much more difficult.

Although it lists his points of difference with the Leftists, Lenin's *'Left-Wing' Communism* never descends to diatribe. For him, the enemy was on the Right, even if there might be error on the Left. When he referred to the Bolsheviks who had been expelled from the Party in 1908 as the predecessors of the K.A.P.D. and the 'ultra-Left' trends, he acknowledged that among them there were 'many splendid revolutionaries'.[64] While criticizing the Italian Leftist Bordiga he did not fail to mention his merits.[65] Nor did Lenin despair of those Leftists whose extremism caused them to leave the Communist movement: 'Practical experience will soon teach them.'[66] If Leftism was indeed a 'disorder', it was one that 'involves no danger, and after it the organism even becomes more robust'.[67] In this work which Stalinist and post-Stalinist orthodoxy has tried to take as its breviary, the spirit of ex-communication was, significantly, quite absent. The sometimes glaring faults of Leftism did not prevent Lenin from perceiving, along with the dangers inherent in it, which incomprehension and diatribe merely strengthen, the basically healthy attitude that inspired it. Writing about the British version of Leftism and the state of mind of many young British Communists, he said, indeed: 'This temper is highly gratifying and valuable; we must learn to appreciate and support it for, in its absence, it would be hopeless to expect the victory of the proletarian revolution in Great Britain, or in any other country for that matter.'[68] The treatment inflicted on 'Leftists' by the official heirs of Leninism does indeed give grounds for feeling hopelessness in this connexion.

The use of sergeant-major methods was no more inherent in the Leninist Comintern than was monolithism.

For several years after 1920 the congresses of the Communist International were similar in character to other gatherings of the same sort. Hundreds of delegates were present and discussions took place that were often very lively. As the 'Parliament' of the international Communist movement, the congress, though the depository of sovereignty in the organization, was, while a genuine deliberative assembly, not the wielder of real power. Decisions were usually taken elsewhere, but they were passionately debated at the congress, and publicly criticized, without any attempt by the leaders to appear before the delegates as a unanimous group, still less a monolithic one. Without showing excessive respect to the authority of the Soviet Communists, strong in their prestige as successful revolutionaries, some foreign delegates attacked, for example, the excessively 'Russian' character of the *schemata* and theses presented by the leaders of the International. According to the Italian Bordiga, the Scotsman Gallacher and the Dutchman Wijnkoop, this tendency to analyse the problems of the world revolution by always referring back to the experience of the Russian revolution meant distorting the strategy of the Third International.[69] Supporters and opponents of the theses put before the congress argued with each other freely. The report on the national question presented by Lenin was opposed, for example, by the counter-report presented by the Indian delegate Roy.[70] Opponents of partici-pation in trade unions and parliamentary activities set forth their views without constraint, and the platform of the opposition in the

Russian Communist Party was circulated among the delegates by the congress organizers themselves.[71] A year later, and despite the measures taken by the Bolshevik Party against the opposition minority within it,* Alexandra Kollontai was able to criticize from the rostrum of the Third World Congress the policy being followed in Russia by the Leninist leadership, and the general atmosphere of the gathering was no less free than in 1920. The German delegation, in particular, revealed its disagreements quite openly, and engaged in what Pierre Broué calls 'a real display of dirty linen'.[72] Controversy on the position of Communism in Germany was resumed at the Fourth Congress, in 1922, which witnessed a verbal duel between Radek and Ruth Fischer.[73]

Freedom of speech and publicity of discussion existed to the same extent in the constituent national organizations. Especially forward in criticizing the executive bodies of the International and the policy advocated by the Soviet leaders were the Italian Communists Bordiga and Gramsci. The former publicly attacked the decisions of the Fourth Congress (1922) and announced his intention of circulating his views among the Communist parties without going through the channels of the international centre. This did not prevent him from being elected to the E.C.C.I. at the Fifth World Congress, in 1924.[74] As late as October 1926, Antonio Gramsci could write, in a letter addressed to the Soviet leaders, about the fictional struggles then going on among them: 'Today you are destroying your work. You are degrading, and running the risk of nullifying, the ruling function that the Communist Party of the U.S.S.R. conquered through Lenin's work.'[75] In Germany, Paul Levi wrote in the official journal of the K.P.D. in December 1920: 'There is nothing in the rules of the Communist International that obliges us to accept as a stroke of genius every decision taken by its Executive Committee.'[76] Thalheimer rejected Lenin's proposal that the K.P.D. and K.A.P.D. be reunited, and openly explained why.[77] In 1924 he argued against Zinoviev in the columns of the international Communist press, at a time when the President of the Third International was at the height of his power.[78] Open criticism of the views, and even the decisions, of the Comintern leadership was in no sense audacity in a period when this leadership required of the leaders of the French Communist Party only that they refrain from publishing their criticisms of the *decisions* taken in Moscow in the form of unsigned editorials, thereby committing the whole organization.[79]

The internal life of the Communist parties presented similar features. In Germany, as Pierre Broué writes,

> the supreme organ ... was the ... congress, which met at least once a year, and delegates to this congress were elected on the basis of preliminary discussions in which sometimes there was a battle

* See p. 301.

between tendencies that put forward their own programmes and candidates, these tendencies being allowed the widest opportunity to express their different views, including the right to address meetings of local groups in which they had not a single supporter.[80]

The K.P.D. could boast of one exploit which, from the point of view of inner-Party democracy, might well be envied by the majority of present-day political organizations. There was, indeed, no precedent for what happened at its inaugural congress. The leaders, including such impressive figures as Rosa Luxemburg and Karl Liebknecht, had come to the rostrum, one after the other, to urge the Party to take part in the elections to the Constituent Assembly; the congress delegates (with more independence than wisdom) rejected their appeal, voting 62 to 23 against participation.[81] Throughout the early 1920s the congresses of the K.P.D., faithfully reflecting the life of the Party, continued to be lively occasions. In January 1923, for example, there were many 'incidents', and the chairman had difficulty in calming the delegates and subduing the tumult.[82] The struggle between tendencies went on no less vigorously between congresses, finding expression in close votes on Party committees and controversies in the press of the Party and the International.[83] As for the French C.P., it suffered not so much from conformism, which as yet had made little progress, as from an anarchical freedom of speech which threatened to plunge the Party into a state of incoherence and paralysis. The congress of October 1922 saw bitter exchanges and violent incidents between delegates such as are usually kept offstage in better regulated parties.[84]

The free exercise of the right to form tendencies in the Comintern and its constituent parties was both cause and consequence of this freedom of discussion and criticism. Addressing himself to the workers of the West in October 1919, Lenin had said: 'The differences among the Communists are differences between representatives of a mass movement that has grown with incredible rapidity ... On *such* a basis differences are nothing to worry about, they represent growing pains, not senile decay.'[85] It was no matter for surprise, therefore, if opinions, once defined, should crystallize, giving rise to tendencies and even factions. The Executive Committee of the Comintern at first found nothing to say against this. In the report that its representative in France sent to it on May 30th, 1922, it was said that 'the Left [in the French Communist Party] ... is organized as a faction, and wishes to be in agreement on all points with the International.'[86] At that time, however, the toleration shown by the central leadership of the Comintern towards factionalism in the parties was coming to an end. Moreover, toleration resulted in this case not merely from open-mindedness and a profoundly democratic spirit, but also from Moscow's interest in being able to rely on an organized Left group, capable of opposing, within the French C.P. especially, the strong trends towards autonomy and 'moderation' which jeopardized the unity of the International and the authority of its central organization. A similar situation arose at the Fourth World Congress, in November 1922, when the leadership of the K.P.D., which was then dominated by a 'moderate' group, sought to eliminate members of the Left faction from the delegation being sent to Moscow. It was Lenin's personal intervention that ensured that the Left was able to send representatives to the congress.[87]

But already in September 1922 the President of the International had demanded in a letter to the French C.P. that the latter carry out an 'immediate and complete dissolution of all factions'.[88] This summons was the harbinger of many still sterner ultimatums yet to come. An epoch was ending, one in which tendencies, sometimes organized in factions and often taking the greatest liberties with the rules of discipline, had enjoyed extensive rights. In Germany, in particular, where a 'Right' made cautious by the setbacks suffered in the revolution, and a 'Left' made impatient by these disappointments, had succeeded each other in the leadership of the Party, majority and minority struggled with almost equal strength (votes, even on the most important questions, were often very close, resulting in weak majorities), while reports and counter-reports alternated in the proceedings of congresses.[89] However, the evolution of the Soviet Communist Party could not remain without influence upon the International and the 'brother parties'. There was already a marked contrast between the severe restrictions which since 1921 had deprived internal democracy of substance in the Bolshevik organization, and the atmosphere of freedom that continued to prevail in the Communist movement outside Russia. Lenin's disappearance from political life, and then his death, the struggle over the succession, and the sharpening of conflict between the leadership of the Soviet Party and the opposition within it, were bound to entail a gradual bringing-into-line of the other Communist parties and a degeneration of their political life.

Internationalism and Russification

'The Third International wants only members who recognize Moscow's dictatorship not only in Russia but also in their own countries,' said Karl Kautsky in 1920.[90] This polemical observation, which anticipated by several years the situation that was indeed to come about in the Comintern, took little account, as we shall see, of the realities of the time it was made. Nevertheless, it was true that, from its very foundation, the international Communist organization accorded a considerable position to the Party which held power in Soviet Russia. It could, indeed, hardly do otherwise. The Bolsheviks were in a superior position not only by virtue of their prestige as the victors of 1917 and the civil war, being the only revolutionaries who had actually overthrown the capitalists, but because they were furthermore the only party possessing the means to give a home to the Third International and supply it with adequate financial support. In proportion as the mechanism of the socialist revolution slowed down in Europe, so did the isolated situation of Soviet Russia and its Communist Party increase the fascination they exerted. Astonished admiration developed into fervent allegiance. Western socialists, weakened by the war and only too conscious of their inability to profit from the crisis caused by the prolongation, and then the ending, of that conflict, would have needed much self-confidence, even some arrogance, in order to criticize the Bolshevik revolution — triumphant and encircled, exhausted and heroic. The reformist leaders themselves, despite their reservations or even their hostile feelings, risked unpopularity when they attacked Soviet Russia. Renaudel, for example, who belonged to the Right wing in the French Socialist Party, was happy to claim in 1920 that he was 'one of those who have never written a line against Bolshevism'.[91] When, at the U.S.P.D. congress at Halle, Martov tried to dam the current that was carrying a big majority of the German Independent Socialists towards the Third International, he explained that his task was rendered very difficult by the reluctance to criticize Bolshevism that was shown not only by the German Communist Party but also by the organ of the Centrists.[92]

There were reasons enough why the Soviet leaders enjoyed unique authority in the international Communist movement, especially as it was not only their revolutionary spirit that served as a model to those who hoped one day to follow their example: their experience itself — that is, a set of 'essential features' of the Russian revolution — was often regarded as a *schema* the validity of which transcended the geographical limits in which it had taken place. Lenin went so far as to say, at the First Congress of the Comintern, that 'the general course of the proletarian revolution is the same throughout the world,' explaining his meaning as follows: 'First, the spontaneous formation of soviets, then their spread and development, and then the appearance of the practical problem: soviets, or National Assembly, or Constituent Assembly, or the bourgeois parliamentary system?'[93] If this was so, then were not the means that had enabled the Russian proletariat to conquer, the instruments it had forged in order to overcome the bourgeoisie, capable of being exported? Had not the ideas and innovations of the Bolsheviks a universal bearing? Lenin thought at first that this was indeed the case. 'Bolshevism has become the worldwide theory and tactics of the international proletariat,' he said in October 1918.[94]

What exactly was this 'theory and tactics'? According to Lenin, the main thing was the creation of the specific institutional form of the revolutions of 1905 and 1917—soviets. He told the foundation congress of the Third International that the Communists had to convince the masses in the West of 'the necessity of the Soviet system',[95] and the Eighth Congress of the Bolshevik Party, meeting in the same period, that Soviet power was *the international, world form of the dictatorship of the proletariat.*'[96] While the necessity of that dictatorship was another Bolshevik principle of general application, it might assume a variety of forms. In particular, Lenin acknowledged that 'the question of restricting the franchise is a nationally specific and not a general question of the dictatorship. One must approach the question of restricting the franchise by studying the *specific conditions* of the Russian revolution and the *specific path* of its development.'[97] Nevertheless, 'the basic forces—and the basic forms of social economy—are the same in Russia as in any capitalist country, so that the peculiarities can apply only to what is of lesser importance'.*

But what was 'basic', what was *not* 'of lesser importance'? Lenin had mentioned that, among the 'specific conditions' of the Russian revolution there were some, of the highest importance (the link between the demands of the revolution and the problem of peace; the international conjuncture created by the war and the division of the imperialist powers into two hostile camps; the enormous size of Russia; and the presence of a peasantry ready, given certain conditions, to support the action of the proletariat), which explained why it was 'easy for Russia ... to *start* the socialist revolution, but ... more difficult for Russia than for the European countries to continue the revolution and bring it to its consummation.'[98] On the other hand, despite the very great difference between the situations in Russia and in the West, Lenin considered, at the end of 1920, that *in the advanced industrial countries just as in Russia*, 'the proletariat is still so divided, so degraded, and so corrupted in parts ... that an organization taking in the whole proletariat cannot directly exercise proletarian dictatorship. It can be exercised only by a vanguard that has absorbed the revolutionary energy of the class.'[99] This meant, in fact, even if only implicitly, endowing the idea of the dictatorship of the proletariat with a significance that Lenin wanted recognized as universal and obligatory—that of a dictatorship wielded, as in Soviet Russia, by the Communist Party.

Over and above such statements as these, sometimes contradictory and often vague, the tendency to confer an international significance upon the experiences of the Russian revolution, and so upon the theories of the Bolsheviks, resulted from a series of analogies which

* Lenin, Vol. 30, p. 108. In *'Left-Wing' Communism* Lenin was to say, more cautiously, that 'certain fundamental features of our revolution have a significance that is ... international' (ibid., Vol. 31, p. 21).

did not fail to impress observers. First and foremost, there was this: when the revolution broke out in Germany—as spontaneous in its initial manifestations as had been that of February 1917 in Russia, the masses of workers and soldiers formed themselves into 'councils' (*Räte*), very similar to soviets, and made these voice their demands. Like their Russian predecessors, the German councils agreed to turn over their powers to a Provisional Government that was socially and politically bourgeois. Just as had happened in Russia after the October insurrection, Republican Germany had to decide whether to take the Soviet path or the constitutional one (power to the *Räte* or to the National Assembly?). And the extreme Left in Germany made the same choice as the extreme Left in Russia. These analogies were completed by parallels that were never more than approximate and were usually deceptive, but which offered the advantage of encouraging the illusion that what had ultimately occurred in Russia would repeat itself elsewhere. The German Social-Democrat leaders were so many Kerenskys, heralding a Lenin as yet not recognized but already present. The offensives of German reaction, such as the Kapp Putsch of March 1920, recalled those of the extreme Right in Russia, especially Kornilov's attempted *coup d'état*, which, like its 'German version', was defeated by the counter-measures of the working class. Finally, and above all, history offered the parallel, rich in promise, between the events of July 1917, in Petrograd—an abortive offensive of the masses, to bring down the bourgeoisie, preceding the successful attempt made later by the Bolsheviks—and the outbursts of revolutionary fever in Germany, chronically as ineffectual as the 'July days' had been in Russia.

The Communists were thus able to feed themselves spiritually with comparisons that seemed to lend even greater weight to the Russian example, and therefore greater credit to the Bolshevik leaders. And yet, despite an apparently rigorous logic—prestige of the Russian revolution, moral authority of its Bolshevik makers, wealth of their experience, effectiveness of their strategy, credibility of their theories, and relative strength of their means—Kautsky's remark about the International being subject to Moscow's dictatorship was, in 1920, however accurately it may have anticipated the way things actually evolved later, in no way based on observed facts. On the contrary, it was contradicted by many of the facts of that time.

The ideology of the Comintern was, in the first place, incompatible with Kautsky's allegation—that internationalist ideology which ran all through Leninism, and which implied, as we have seen, subordinating the Russian revolution to the needs of the international revolution.* This internationalism, which was drawn from the very springs of Marxism, was not shaken by the success of Bolshevism. In conformity

* See p. 359.

with Marx's doctrine, Lenin had always believed in the superiority of Western industrial society over the Russian world, which was in some ways pre-capitalist and quasi-medieval. The victory of the revolution in Russia did not modify this view of his. To Lenin, Russia remained 'a backward country',[100] not only on account of its economy but also because of the general weakness of its proletariat. 'We have always realized,' said Lenin in November 1918, 'that it was not on account of any merit of the Russian proletariat, or because it was in advance of the others, that we happened to begin the revolution, which grew out of world-wide struggle. On the contrary, it was only because of the peculiar weakness and backwardness of capitalism, and the peculiar pressure of military and strategic circumstances, that we happened in the course of events to move ahead of the other detachments ... '[101] This advanced position, moreover, was not destined to last. In *'Left-Wing' Communism* Lenin wrote that 'soon after the victory of the proletarian revolution in at least one of the advanced countries, a sharp change will probably come about: Russia will cease to be the model and will once again become a backward country (in the "Soviet" and the socialist sense)'.[102]

The absence of any Russian self-glorification was accompanied by a national humility that even tended to increase as the Soviet experience developed. In March 1918 Lenin considered that the creation in Russia of a new type of state 'has scarcely begun and has begun badly,' and he added: 'We shall show the European proletariat this truth and say, this must be done, so that they will say, such-and-such things the Russians are doing badly but we shall do them better.'[103] 'The advanced West-European workers ... will say to themselves: "The Russians haven't made a very good beginning on the job that has to be done."'[104] The misfortune was not too great, though, because the merits of the international revolution would make up for the shortcomings of the revolution in Russia: 'Perhaps we are making mistakes,' Lenin told the Eighth Party Congress, 'but we hope the proletariat of the West will correct them. And we appeal to the European proletariat to help us in our work.'[105]

Everything that issued from the working class and the revolutionary movement in the West, even if not very far in the West, seemed to find special favour in Lenin's eyes. In April 1919, for example, soon after the ephemeral conquest of power by the Communists in Budapest, he said: 'I know that we suffer from a host of defects. I know that in Hungary Soviet power will be better than in this country.'[106] And soon afterwards came this sentence, more remarkable for modesty than far-sightedness: 'Compared with Russia, Hungary was a small country; but the Hungarian revolution would, perhaps, play a more important role in history than the Russian revolution.'[107] Apparently, the disappointments encountered in building the new society in Russia had the effect of strengthening Lenin's appreciation of every hopeful development in the West.

How, indeed, could it have been otherwise when Lenin was becoming more and more aware of the shortcomings of the Soviet state and his critique of Soviet bureaucracy was growing, from 1921 onwards, increasingly virulent?* Could revolutionary Russia show the way for Europe and the world to follow when 'all of us are sunk in the rotten bureaucratic swamp'[108] and 'the state apparatus in general' could be characterized as *bad beyond description*'?[109] Could it serve as an example when it was marked by 'national' characteristics that were far from propitious to the task of building socialism—that 'truly Soviet slovenliness',[110] that 'Russian negligence',[111] that propensity to 'inefficiency',[112] that all-round incapacity which caused Lenin to say: 'You should know that a Russian has to be sworn at twenty times and verified thirty times to have the simplest thing done properly';[113] not to mention the role played by 'such a truly Russian phenomenon as bribery.'[114] The character in literature who best personified the Russian, in Lenin's eyes, was Oblomov, in Goncharov's novel of that name, who embodied at one and the same time listlessness, lack of practical sense, and the tendency to take refuge in impotent contemplation and sentimental daydreaming. Lenin raged against the 'damnable manner of the Russian Oblomovs, putting everyone and everything *to sleep*',[115] and fulminated: 'Russia has experienced three revolutions, but the Oblomovs have survived ... It is enough to watch us at our meetings, at our work on commissions, to be able to say that *old Oblomov still lives; and it will be necessary to give him a good washing and cleaning, a good rubbing and scoring to make a man of him.*'[116] Behind this near-helpless fury of Lenin's lay much bitter experience, rich in incidents of which Krupskaya gives us an example. Travelling by car somewhere on the outskirts of Moscow, she and Lenin came to a bridge, beside which stood a peasant. Lenin stopped the car and asked the man if it was safe to drive across the bridge. The peasant shook his head and replied, with a chuckle: 'I'm not so sure. It's a Soviet bridge, if I may be pardoned for saying so.'[117]

Commenting on the achievements of the Bolshevik leaders, Rosa Luxemburg wrote, in her pamphlet *The Russian Revolution*:

By their determined revolutionary stand, their exemplary strength in action, and their unbreakable loyalty to international socialism, they have contributed whatever could possibly be contributed under such devilishly hard conditions. The danger begins only when they make a virtue of necessity and want to freeze into a complete theoretical system all the tactics forced upon them by

* See p. 324.

these fatal circumstances, and want to recommend them to the international proletariat as a model of socialist tactics.[118]

This was a view which Lenin, despite his belief in the exemplary value of certain principles of Bolshevism, explicitly confirmed. Addressing the Party Congress in 1919 he said: 'It would be absurd to set up our revolution as the ideal for all countries, to imagine that it has made a number of brilliant discoveries and has introduced a heap of socialist innovations ... If we behave like the frog in the fable and become puffed up with conceit, we shall only make ourselves the laughing-stock of the world ... '[119] Again, in March 1921: 'the Russians ... are of the same clay [as other nations], and if they choose to pretend they are not, they will only look ridiculous.'[120] In March 1919 he sent a radio-telegram to Béla Kun, leader of the Hungarian revolution, warning him: 'it is altogether beyond doubt that it would be a mistake merely to imitate our Russian tactics in all details in the specific conditions of the Hungarian revolution.'[121] Undoubtedly, the conviction that there was indeed a 'Bolshevik model' for Communists everywhere to copy related much more to the revolutionary strategy that had enabled the Bolsheviks to take power than to the *schemata* for socialist construction in Russia, the shortcomings of which were freely admitted.

Once it had been agreed that the new International must be a highly centralized organization, and would have to have its headquarters in Russia, the position held in it by the Bolshevik leaders was inevitably preponderant. Lenin said in this connexion in April 1919: 'Leadership in the revolutionary proletarian international has passed for a time — for a short time, it goes without saying — to the Russians ... '[122] In this matter, however, as in some others, the temporary and provisional was to become protracted and congealed, to an extent far beyond the most pessimistic of expectations.

The *principle* of centralization seemed an indispensable condition for the success of the revolution on the world scale. This conviction was not merely a result of acceptance by non-Russians of the Leninist theory of the Party. It was based also on the lessons drawn from the experience of the First World War by all those who had been shocked by the collapse of the Second International. Was not this collapse due to the structural weakness which had made the Second International incapable of dictating its will to the parties composing it? If, moreover, one believed that the hour of revolution had struck, then the international onslaught upon capitalism must proceed in accordance with a common strategy, worked out by an organ endowed with substantial powers, and able to impose its discipline upon all sections of the proletarian army.

The Third International therefore proclaimed that there 'must, in fact and in deed, be a single Communist party in the entire world',[123] and, as a corollary, that the decisions made by its leading — i.e., central — bodies must be 'law for every Communist organization'.[124] This was the spirit in which the 'statutes' of 1920, and, still more, those of 1922–4, were drafted.

At the Second World Congress, in July–August 1920, the statutes voted by the delegates accorded substantial power to the Executive Committee, where sovereignty lay between congresses. Made up of five representatives of the country where the International had its offices, and between ten and thirteen delegates from the principal non-Russian organizations, the Executive was given, for example, the right to require member-parties to 'expel groups or persons who offend against international discipline', and itself to expel any parties which 'violate decisions of the world congress'.[125] The Executive Committee was to nominate a presidium of five members, of whom three would be representatives of the Russian Party.[126] Some delegates did not fail at the time to express the misgiving they felt at this massive presence and overwhelming representation of the 'Russian section' of the International.[127]

Two years later, the Fourth World Congress took a step that led to a further advance in centralization. A commission was appointed to draw up new statutes. These new statutes, which were adopted by the Fifth Congress (1924), strengthened the authority of the Executive Committee in relation both to the congress (which was thenceforth to be held at two-year intervals only, instead of every year, as provided in 1920) and to the member-parties. It was expressly laid down that the E.C.C.I. 'issues binding directives to all parties and organizations affiliated to the C.I. and supervises their activities ... Decisions of the E.C.C.I. are binding on all sections and must be carried out by them without delay.' The Executive Committee was given the power to annul or amend decisions taken by the congresses or central committees of the affiliated parties, and to expel members from these parties by its own direct action.*

These formal arrangements give an inadequate picture, however, of the actual relations between the central leadership of the Comintern, where the Soviet representatives played a dominant role, and the Communist parties affiliated to it. The statutes, drafted in Moscow and voted for in Moscow, reflected a spirit that did not always prevail away from the Soviet capital. The reality was in any case very much more complex than documents and regulations suggest. The implementation of the Executive Committee's decisions depended to a large

* Degras, Vol. II, p. 119. To compensate for the congress not meeting more frequently than every other year, the number of members of the E.C.C.I. was increased, and the practice of holding 'enlarged plenums' of this body was introduced. The functions of the Presidium (with seven members now instead of five) were also increased.

extent, for example, on the persons chosen to represent it at the headquarters of the brother-parties. The papers of Jules Humbert-Droz show that when the directives issued by the centre came to be presented to the organizations which were supposed to carry out the 'law' of the Comintern, the rules sometimes underwent modification, the will of the centre being applied not without some flexibility. The Comintern representative in France found himself obliged, as Jacques Fauvet expresses it, to 'put a lot of water in the wine' that he served to the French Communists.[128] Humbert-Droz considered, in any case, that his job was not so much to command as to convince, and to advise rather than direct.[129] In contact with the realities of a situation he often found it appropriate to act with a certain degree of independence. He tells us:

> I discovered that the resolutions of the world congresses and the decisions taken by the E.C.C.I. were not well known among the leaders of the Parties, and were in some instances not capable of application, and that the role of 'Moscow's eye' was not only to keep the E.C.C.I. informed but also to propose solutions to problems which were sometimes in conflict with the decisions that had been taken in Moscow without exact awareness of an always changing situation.[130]

True, not all representatives of the Comintern acted with the circumspection and flexibility of its man in France. In Germany, for example, their activity gave rise on several occasions to recrimination and criticism. Paul Levi said of them that 'they never work with the local Party headquarters, but always behind its back, and often against it'.[131] They operated as 'grey eminences' whose reports were sent to Moscow without being communicated to the local Party, and their conduct sometimes gave rise to public protests, such as the statement issued in December 1921 by some leading German Communists, denouncing 'the pernicious influence exercised by certain members of the E.C.C.I.'[132]

What did the internationalism of the Comintern actually amount to? What concrete form was taken, in the early years, by the intervention of leaders based on Moscow in the affairs of the national organizations? The most current form was public criticism of the member-parties by the E.C.C.I. The latter explained that 'unlike the Second International, the Third is not content to send congratulations and compliments to its sections. Its duty is to show them their faults and to try to correct these, by working with the parties concerned in a spirit of harmony exclusively inspired by the interests of the world revolution.'[133] The Communist parties were therefore criticized frequently and severely, and this criticism, coming as it did from the Bolshevik leaders, with their halo of revolutionary prestige, or from close collaborators with these leaders, was in itself a means of pressure that was all the more effective because some local Communist leaders, especially in Germany, were 'always ready to admit to mistakes which they do not think they have made, in order to avoid a showdown with the Comintern Executive'.[134]

If the French Communist Party was the subject, in 1922, of several discussions on the E.C.C.I., and at the world congress of that year, this was because there was being waged between Paris and Moscow what Jacques Fauvet calls a 'war of attrition',[135] the Comintern leadership summoning a representative of the French Party five times without getting any response. From the beginning, the French Communists had 'taken lightly both the 21 Conditions of the Second Congress and the 59 Theses of the Third'.[136] As for the statutes giving the E.C.C.I. the right to intervene in a Party's internal affairs, these elicited from the French Party's General Secretary a remark the brisk offhandedness of which was not calculated to smooth away the difficulties: 'When we read them we said: "Oh well, these are statutes — they'll be enforced more or less, and we'll adapt ourselves to them as best we can. Things can always be arranged somehow."'[137] Unfortunately for Frossard and those of his sort, Bolshevism did not lend itself to arrangements and adaptations such as he had in mind. Nor did the Bolsheviks accept that the Comintern should be treated with systematic hostility in a journal run by a member of the French Party.[138] What was worse, the French Communists had categorically refused to agree to the 'united front' strategy decided on by the E.C.C.I. And since the French Party added to its external indiscipline a state of internal disorder,* the central leadership of the Comintern considered that it must take action and instruct the Party to transform itself profoundly.

In June 1922, Trotsky said, addressing the E.C.C.I.: 'A new epoch must begin for the French Communists. A great change of path and of method is needed.'[139] There followed instructions that were quite unambiguous regarding the composition of the leading organs of the Party ('it is absolutely essential that more than half of the members [of the Central Committee] be workers') and the content of the Party press.[140] Subsequently, the Comintern ordered the French Communist Party to purge its ranks of Freemasons.[141]

The representatives of the E.C.C.I. abroad sometimes endeavoured to promote the appointment by the parties of leaders whose line they approved — without, however, always meeting with success in these attempts. Gramsci, for example, when approached in this way,

---

* This was how *l'Humanité* reported, for example, the atmosphere of the congress held in December 1921: 'Amid the tumult, delegates were heard trying to talk each other down. The uproar was indescribable. From opposite ends of the hall delegates were shouting replies at each other, accompanied by a chorus of cheers and protests' (Walter, pp. 74–5).

replied that he did not want to lend himself to 'intrigues' of this kind.[142] Besides manoeuvres in this style, it was even more important that major decisions committing the International as a whole were sometimes taken by the E.C.C.I. in Moscow. This happened with the tactic known as 'the united front' (even though it originated from a proposal by the German Party). Similarly, when the German Communists had to decide on the conditions to be attached to the support they considered giving to the Social-Democratic Government of Saxony, it was in the Soviet capital that their hesitations were overcome, following a discussion in which Lenin, Trotsky, Radek and Zinoviev took part.[143] A year later, the decision to prepare for a workers' insurrection in Germany was made jointly by representatives of the K.P.D. and members of the Soviet Politburo.*

Intervention by the Russian Communist leaders or by the central bodies of the Comintern was often directed at overcoming conflicts that broke out in Communist parties which fell victims to sectarianism. The German Communists were urged to find a basis of agreement with the Leftists of the K.A.P.D. and with the radical tendency among the Independent Socialists. An attempt was made to settle their conflicts amicably by arranging for the minority tendencies to be represented in the leading bodies.[144] In France the delegates of the International also sought to persuade the 'Centrist' leaders of the Party to bring some 'Left' elements into the leadership.[145] Sometimes, too, the Comintern had to damp down the ardour of Communists impatient to have done with their local bourgeoisie. The Russian revolutionaries, so often accused of 'putschism' by their Social-Democratic adversaries, tried on several occasions to press counsels of caution upon Western Communists. During the November revolution in Germany, Joffe and Bukharin, who were in regular contact with the Spartacists in Berlin, urged them to go carefully.[146] Radek took the same line with them, but in vain, in January 1919.[147] This was not a matter of a systematic attitude, but rather of concern to adapt tactics to circumstances. When, in autumn 1920, Northern Italy, especially the Turin area, was shaken by a great wave of strikes and occupations of factories, the Comintern called on the Italian workers to arm themselves, and on the local Communists to act as 'a party taking the road to insurrection'.[148] The role played by the E.C.C.I. in the action undertaken by the K.P.D. in March 1921 is still unclear. That Béla Kun, acting as representative of the E.C.C.I., and well known for his Leftist tendencies, encouraged the most 'activist' of the Communist leaders is certain; but it is not known whether he was operating, on this occasion, with an explicit mandate from the E.C.C.I., or if he was abusing the influence given him by his appointment.[149]

* See p. 381.

Lenin commented, soon after this unfortunate business: 'I readily believe that the representative of the Executive Committee defended the silly tactics, which were too much to the left — to take immediate action "to help the Russians" ... I think that in such cases you should not give in but should protest and immediately bring up this question officially at a plenary meeting of the Executive Bureau.'[150]

In this sphere as in others, there was a great deal of pragmatism shown in a situation that was still fluid. On the plane of strategy, the activity of the international Communist organization, aiming at flexibility, sometimes came near to incoherence. On the structural plane, 'Russification' was certainly increasing, favoured by objective conditions, but it was not being deliberately promoted, and did not appear inevitable. Amid the uncertain conditions of a period and a movement rich in possibilities, nothing was as yet cut and dried. The Third International, installed in Moscow, was of course subject to conditioning by its location; but its leaders themselves had originally wanted to establish it in the West, even if this meant an underground existence.[151] As Jane Degras says, 'it is clear from speeches and articles by the Russian leaders at this time [March 1919] that they had every hope and intention of transferring the seat of the Executive to a Western capital, once conditions were favourable to such a move.'[152] It took several years for this hope to fade, even though, if it had been realized, the move would have meant a weakening of Russian influence in the movement. Russian influence was subject to other checks as well, such as the German Communist Party's ambition to play an important role in determining international revolutionary strategy. That Rosa Luxemburg, at the time of the foundation of the K.P.D., was thinking of setting limits to the spread of the 'Russian model' is quite obvious.[153] Nor was there anything heretical in that, since Lenin himself regarded the development of the revolution in Germany as a priority task for the whole International, and the success of that revolution as the most important condition for victory over capitalism.* The German representative at the Foundation Congress of the Third International recorded that 'in conformity with Lenin's ideas concerning the Spartacus League', he was elected to all the congress commissions and also to its presidium.[154] At the end of 1919, despite the setbacks they had already suffered, the German Communists had still not given up their aspiration to act as guides to the revolutionary movement throughout Europe. Thalheimer said openly that 'the historical setting of Germany is closer to that of the Western countries than Russia's is,' and concluded that German experiences in the realm of tactics would be particularly valuable to Westerners.[155] In order to be fully convincing, however, Thalheimer would have needed to have

* See p. 363.

behind him some successes comparable to those achieved by the Russian Communists.

Nothing, then, had been settled for good and all, so far, in an international organization in which discipline was often more theoretical than real and the most important decisions taken might encounter, as happened with the adoption of the 'united front' strategy, opposition from the Communist parties of France, Spain, Czechoslovakia and Italy, and very marked reluctance on the part of an element within the German party.[156] Nothing had been finally settled so long as the depth of internationalist feelings helped to slow down the march of Russification, and so long as Lenin still stood at the head of the movement, keeping a watchful eye upon this trend. His address to the last congress of the International he attended, in November 1922, dealt with it. He deplored on that occasion the 'almost entirely Russian' character of the resolution passed by the Fourth World Congress, in 1921, which he said 'the foreign comrades have signed without reading and understanding'. 'I am sure that no foreigner can read it,' he added, and, 'even if they read it, they will not understand it ... And ... if by way of exception some foreigner does understand it, he cannot carry it out.'[157] In the last analysis, 'Russification' was a result of the isolation of the Russian revolution. Leninism seemed to possess sufficient theoretical resources and internationalist vigilance to keep it in check while waiting for the only event that could really put a stop to it, namely, the ending of revolutionary Russia's isolation through a spreading of that movement which constituted the very *raison d'être* of the Communist International.

Epilogue

The end of Lenin

Although paying some attention to Lenin's individual characteristics, this book has hitherto avoided a biographical treatment of its subject. In this concluding part, however, the biographical method will take over, for reasons arising from the author's very purpose, namely, to distinguish what Leninism was really about. This stands forth in tragic relief in the last months of Lenin's life, which offer the political historian a source of highly significant observations.*

There is an air of tragedy about those last months which some writer or playwright ought surely by now to have sensed and given artistic form worthy of the greatness of the subject. Lenin's career was a victorious one, of course, and tragedy finds its material in defeats rather than in victories. But Lenin's career has seemed *completely* victorious only because of the silence that for so long surrounded the last months of his life. It is necessary to penetrate beyond appearances, however—the familiar appearances of the founder of Soviet Russia, the victor of October and the civil war, the successful revolutionary and builder of a new order. This picture has political implications. The idea of 'Lenin triumphant' provides support not only for Marxist-Leninist orthodoxy but also for the views of bourgeois historiography, always disposed to see in Leninism merely a 'will to power'—Lenin, having once conquered and consolidated his conquest, is supposed to have gone to his rest in an atmosphere of glory and self-satisfaction.

That is the legend. Here are the facts.

On May 25th, 1922, Lenin suffered his first crisis of arteriosclerosis: his right hand and leg became paralysed and his speech impaired. After a long convalescence, he returned to work in the first days of October 1922. On December 13th another attack forced Lenin to retire definitively. On March 10th, 1923, after an attack that occurred three days earlier, he finally lost the power of speech. He died on January 22nd, 1924. Behind these dates and details of Lenin's health, however, lies 'Lenin's last struggle', which was a struggle not only

---

* This is what makes Moshe Lewin's book, *Le Dernier Combat de Lénine* (Paris, 1967: English translation, *Lenin's Last Struggle*, London, 1969) so very valuable.

against illness but also, and above all, for Leninism and socialism. And never did Lenin the fighter have to fight harder or in more painful circumstances.

He was kept in conditions almost amounting to seclusion. After the attack suffered on December 13th, 1922, forced him to suspend a political activity which had already been slowed down, no one was allowed to visit him, by order of the Central Committee, or rather by Stalin himself, who had been entrusted with supervision of the sick leader. 'Friends and servants are forbidden to communicate anything to Lenin concerning political life, in order not to give him cause for reflection and anxiety.'[1] As Moshe Lewin writes, 'thus began Lenin's exhausting struggle to be kept informed of what interested him, to formulate his opinions and to communicate them to the right people'.[2] He had asked for permission to dictate to his secretaries for a few minutes every day. The doctors, who worked in concert with the Political Bureau, refused this permission. Lenin retorted by threatening that, in that case, he would refuse to co-operate in any further treatment. The doctors yielded, but the Political Bureau—in other words, Stalin—specified that, although Lenin was to be allowed to dictate 'for five to ten minutes a day', what he wrote 'ought not to have the character of a correspondence and [Lenin] must not expect replies to those notes'.[3] It was under these conditions, laid down on December 24th, 1922, that Lenin dictated the few pages that are known as his 'Testament'.

Lenin's secretaries, and Krupskaya herself, were literally spied upon by the Party's General Secretary and his collaborators, and this led to an incident occurring between Stalin and Lenin's wife that will be referred to later. As one of the secretaries notes, under the date February 12th, 1923, in the joint diary that they kept during Lenin's illness, 'The fact that the doctors knew about this [the fact that their patient was 'interested in the census of Soviet employees', M.L.] upset Vladimir Ilyich. Apparently, furthermore, Vladimir Ilyich had the impression that it was not the doctors who gave instructions to the Central Committee, but the Central Committee that gave instructions to the doctors.'[4] Stalin had already asked the secretary, on January 30th, whether she had been telling Lenin 'things he was not to be told— how was it he was posted about current affairs?'[5]

The 'current affairs' in question concerned, *inter alia*, the development of the situation in Georgia, where the Georgian Communists' desire for independence had clashed with the harsh centralizing policy of Stalin and his lieutenant Ordzhonikidze.* In order to obtain the information on this matter that was being concealed from him, Lenin organized what he himself called a ' "secret" job' for his secretaries.[6]

* See p. 422.

Having asked the Political Bureau to send him a number of files, he found himself up against a persistent refusal to co-operate. On January 30th, 1923, one of the secretaries wrote in the service diary: 'Today Vladimir Ilyich sent for me to learn the answer [to his request for the files, M.L.] and said that he would fight to get the materials.'[7]

He did indeed fight, wresting information and concessions from those in control of him, and preparing, bit by bit, an immense report, which he intended for the Party congress that was soon to take place. When Lenin's secretary Fotieva gave Lenin some information, she had to do this 'as if "by clumsiness." '[8] And when, by a miracle of effort, Lenin managed to dictate some articles and notes, he had to fight again to get the Party leadership to publish the material that he sent to *Pravda*. In the Political Bureau they even discussed having a single copy of *Pravda* printed for Lenin's benefit, containing an article he wanted published but which they would have preferred not to make known to the general public.[9] This was an article sharply criticizing *Rabkrin*, the Workers' and Peasants' Inspection, which had been headed by Stalin himself, between March 1919 and April 1922. Cut off in this way from the outside world, isolated and spied upon, it was against Stalin that Lenin was waging the most furious, most desperate but also most significant of all his struggles. What was at stake was nothing less than whether or not he would succeed in changing the course being followed by the Soviet state in a number of vital areas: bureaucratic degeneration, the excessive power wielded by the future dictator, and tendencies towards oppression of the national minorities.

An apparently mild problem had given rise to the first skirmishes between Lenin and Stalin. As a result of the N.E.P., some Soviet economic leaders considered it necessary to relax the state monopoly of foreign trade, but Lenin had opposed the decisions taken on this matter by the Central Committee in October 1922. For Lenin the monopoly of foreign trade was essential in order to raise around Soviet Russia a barrier behind which she might build an economy centred upon large-scale industry and a strong proletariat.[10] Stalin, however, thought that 'a weakening [i.e., of the monopoly of foreign trade, M.L.] is becoming inevitable'.[11] Lenin formed an alliance on this question with Trotsky, who shared his views, and charged him with defending their common position. They succeeded in getting the decisions taken by the Central Committee reviewed and a complete re-examination of the problem undertaken. Lenin wrote to Trotsky: 'I consider that we have quite reached agreement. I ask you to declare our solidarity at the plenum.'[12] This joint offensive by Lenin and Trotsky was crowned with success, the measures aimed against the foreign trade monopoly being withdrawn in December 1922. Soon afterwards Lenin said, in another letter addressed to Trotsky: 'It looks as though it has been possible to take the position without a single shot, by a simple manoeuvre. I suggest that we should not stop and should continue the offensive.'[13]

Problems of even greater importance did call for vigorous intervention. There was, first of all, the question of the machinery of state, the enormous faults in which Lenin had now come to appreciate fully. The struggle against bureaucracy had been entrusted to the Workers' and Peasants' Inspection, which was headed by Stalin until he became General Secretary. In the last article he wrote, 'Better Fewer, But Better,' Lenin declared: 'The People's Commissariat of the Workers' and Peasants' Inspection does not at present enjoy the slightest authority. Everybody knows that no other institutions are worse organized than those of our Workers' and Peasants' Inspection.'[14]

On January 23rd, 1923, Lenin dictated to his secretaries a note entitled: 'How we should reorganize the Workers' and Peasants' Inspection', intended for the Twelfth Party Congress. In it he proposed that this enormous body of over ten thousand officials be reduced to a small group of three or four hundred.[15] He further indicated that these survivors of *Rabkrin* should lose their independence, becoming merely 'auxiliaries' of the Central Control Commission, which he wanted to see enlarged by the inclusion of a few dozen new members chosen among Communists of worker or peasant origin.[16] This decision, had it been carried out, would have meant the disappearance of one of those institutions upon which Stalin's growing power was founded. Lenin was thus again in conflict with the General Secretary, and in order to wage this struggle, he drew still closer to Trotsky.*

In his autobiography, Trotsky mentions a talk he had with Lenin in October 1922. Lenin said: 'Our bureaucratism is something monstrous. I was appalled when I came back to work.' And he proposed that he and Trotsky 'form a bloc' to fight against this menace, attacking its manifestations in both Party and state.[17] On one point at least, Lenin now came round to some ideas of Trotsky's that he had formerly rejected: he recognized the need to increase the powers of *Gosplan*, the organization responsible for economic planning, and in particular to endow it with wide legislative functions.[18] More generally, Lenin acknowledged the correctness of the views expressed by Trotsky when he sought, within the framework of the N.E.P., and despite the interpretation given to the latter by some other Soviet leaders, to preserve and increase the possibilities for planning and industrialization. In a letter dictated on November 25th, 1922, Lenin recommended publication as a pamphlet of the ideas that Trotsky had worked out on this theme.[19] But since the antagonism between Trotsky and Stalin was already acute, threatening, as Lenin said in his 'Testa-

---

* In his letter to Trotsky dated March 5th, 1923, one of the last to be dictated by Lenin, he ends with a subscription that was unusually cordial for him: 'with best comradely greetings' (Lenin, Vol. 45, p. 607).

ment', to bring about a split in the Party,[20] the bloc formed against bureaucracy and for an economic policy more sensitive to the need for planning and industrialization, by bringing Lenin closer to Trotsky, widened still further the gulf between Lenin and Stalin.

During the last weeks of his active life, Lenin's struggle became even sharper. The clash with Stalin assumed a more direct form, Lenin's feelings of alarm grew more precise and intense, and he threw his last reserves of strength into a battle to save the Soviet achievement from the ravages of 'Great-Power chauvinism'.

On December 30th, 1922, Lenin dictated to his secretaries a note on 'The Question of Nationalities, or of "Autonomization".' It opened: 'I suppose I have been very remiss with respect to the workers of Russia for not having intervened energetically and decisively enough in the notorious question of autonomization ... '[21] How had Lenin come to make such a confession, which was something unusual for him, and to express so strong a sense of culpability? What lay behind this development was the evolution of relations between the central Soviet Government and the republics that the non-Great-Russian national minorities had organized within the Soviet state. Before 1922 these relations had been governed by bilateral treaties linking Russia separately with Byelorussia, the Ukraine, Georgia, Azerbaijan and Armenia, and giving these republics a semblance of independence.* In 1922 these arrangements were being changed. Despite opposition from the Georgian Communists, it was proposed to create a 'Transcaucasian Federation', grouping together Georgia, Azerbaijan and Armenia. A commission headed by Stalin was engaged in working out a new constitution. According to the draft that this commission produced, the republics were to be integrated into a Russian Federation, the government of which would be that of the Russian Republic itself. Four out of the five non-Great-Russian republics opposed this plan, but their views were ignored. Lenin, who was following the matter without intervening directly, now warned the Political Bureau: 'In my opinion the matter is of utmost importance. Stalin tends to be somewhat hasty.'[22] He put forward his own plan, in opposition to Stalin's. To integration of the other republics in a Russian Federal Republic he opposed the idea of uniting all the republics, *Russia included*, in 'a Union of Soviet Republics of Europe and Asia'.[23] Realizing the threat to the non-Great-Russian nationalities that was inherent in Stalin's intentions, Lenin launched a full-scale attack against the policy being pursued by the General Secretary. In a letter addressed to the Political Bureau he made no secret of his readiness to fight: 'I declare war to the death on dominant-nation chauvinism. I shall eat it with all my healthy teeth as soon as I get rid of this accursed bad tooth. It must be *absolutely* insisted that the Union Central Executive

* See p. 276.

Committee should be *presided over* in turn by a Russian, Ukrainian, Georgian, etc.'[24]

Stalin did not flinch, however. When, during a meeting of the Political Bureau, Kamenev passed him a note mentioning Lenin's 'declaration of war', Stalin replied: 'In my opinion we have to be firm against Lenin.'[25] A few days earlier, he had already attacked Lenin's 'national-liberalism'.[26] Lenin's counter-attack, in October 1922, was vigorous, and Stalin unwillingly had to bow to the leader's views on the constitution of the Union of Soviet Socialist Republics.

There remained the question of the Georgians and their resistance to the plan for a Transcaucasian Federation, through which, and not directly, the Georgian Soviet Republic would enter the U.S.S.R., according to this plan. Stalin's pressure on the Georgians to submit became harsher, and Ordzhonikidze, his representative in Tbilisi, even resorted to physical violence against a member of the Georgian Central Committee. The latter then resigned in a body. The affair became so embittered that a commission of inquiry was appointed, with Dzerzhinsky as chairman. After visiting Caucasia in December 1922 it acquitted Stalin and Ordzhonikidze of the charges brought against them by the Georgian Communists. Lenin, however, urged his secretaries to compile, on their own, a collection of documents that would enable him to form an objective opinion on the question. Full of distrust of the official 'channels', he seems to have entrusted Rykov with a personal mission on his behalf, to go to Georgia and investigate. On December 9th Rykov reported to Lenin, and three days later he saw Dzerzhinsky in person. One of Lenin's secretaries noted that Lenin told her that what he learnt 'had a very painful effect' on him.[27]

It was this distress that produced the note on 'The Question of Nationalities', in which Lenin wrote: 'If matters had come to such a pass that Ordzhonikidze could go to the extreme of applying physical violence ... we can imagine what a mire we have got ourselves into.' And once again Lenin pointed to the man he saw as principally responsible for the situation. 'I think Stalin's haste and his infatuation with pure administration, together with his spite against the notorious "nationalist-socialism", played a fatal role here.'[28] Lenin went on to attack 'that really Russian man, the Great-Russian chauvinist, in substance a rascal and a tyrant, such as the typical Russian bureaucrat is', and 'that tide of chauvinistic Great-Russian riff-raff'.[29] Next day, dictating a further note on the same problem, Lenin saw fit to reaffirm the principles that had always guided his policy on the national question. Refusing to be content with 'an abstract presentation of the question of nationalism in general', he insisted that 'a distinction must necessarily be made between the nationalism of an oppressor nation and that of an oppressed nation, the nationalism of a big nation and that of a small nation'. And he declared that, 'in respect of the second kind of nationalism, we, nationals of a big nation, have nearly always been guilty, in historic practice, of an infinite number of cases of violence; furthermore, we commit violence and insult an infinite number of times without noticing it.' Lenin concluded that 'internationalism on the part of oppressors or "great" nations, as they are called (though they are great only in their violence, only great as bullies), must consist not only in the observance of the formal equality of nations but even in an inequality of the oppressor nation, the great nation, that must make up for the inequality which obtains in actual practice.' As regards relations with Georgia and with the national minorities as a whole, he advised: 'it is better to overdo rather than underdo the concessions and leniency toward the national minorities.'[30]

In a final note, dated December 31st, like the previous one, Lenin called for punishment of the Soviet leaders guilty of indulging in a chauvinist and oppressive policy towards the Georgians. Although 'exemplary punishment must be inflicted on Comrade Ordzhonikidze', he considered that 'the political responsibility for all this truly Great-Russian nationalist campaign must, of course, be laid on Stalin and Dzerzhinsky.'[31]

Lenin's severity in relation to Stalin was perhaps not due merely to the role the latter had played in the Georgian affair. An incident in which the General Secretary clashed with Krupskaya strengthened still further the growing animosity felt by Lenin towards his successor-to-be. Having learnt on December 22nd that Lenin's wife had agreed to take down a short letter at the sick man's dictation, Stalin subjected her, as she put it, to 'offensive language and threats'.[32] Stalin's anger was not without some basis: the letter he was blaming Krupskaya for having taken down was the one in which Lenin proposed to Trotsky that they continue the campaign they had begun together.* This incident was bound to have a sequel. On March 5th, 1923, two days before the stroke that finally destroyed Lenin's physical resistance, he wrote the following letter, which he addressed to Stalin, with a copy to Kamenev and Zinoviev:

> You have been so rude as to summon my wife to the telephone and use bad language. Although she had told you that she was prepared to forget this, the fact nevertheless became known through her to Zinoviev and Kamenev. I have no intention of forgetting so easily what has been done against me, and it goes without saying that what has been done against my wife I consider having been done against me as well. I ask you, therefore, to think it over whether you are prepared to withdraw what you have said and to make your apologies, or whether you prefer that relations between us should be broken off.[33]

* See pp. 419–20.

Stalin's tirade had been delivered on December 22nd. It is not certain that Lenin knew about it immediately. On December 24th, however, he dictated a note—the celebrated 'Testament' in which he reviewed the chief personages in the Bolshevik leadership. Regarding Stalin he wrote: 'Comrade Stalin, having become Secretary-General, has unlimited power concentrated in his hands, and I am not sure whether he will always be capable of using that authority with sufficient caution.'[34] On January 4th, 1923, he saw fit to dictate a 'continuation' to this note, devoted entirely to the subject of Stalin:

> Stalin is too rude, and this defect, although quite tolerable in our midst and in dealings among us Communists, becomes intolerable in a Secretary-General. That is why I suggest that the comrades think about a way of removing Stalin from that post and appointing another man in his stead who in all other respects differs from Comrade Stalin in having only one advantage, namely, that of being more tolerant, more loyal, more polite and more considerate to the comrades, less capricious, etc.[35]

After the 'Testament' had been written, the Georgian affair continued its course. Lenin's four secretaries formed themselves, at his request, into a 'clandestine commission' with the task of completing a dossier that was already overwhelming. On March 3rd the commission presented its conclusions. We do not know what they were. But they evidently seemed to Lenin to justify the haste with which he proceeded to open his last campaign. On March 5th and 6th he dictated three letters, one after the other, which he told his doctors were just 'business letters', but which were in fact of major importance. In the first of them he appealed to Trotsky to 'undertake the defence of the Georgian case in the Party C.C.', adding: 'I would feel at ease if you agreed to undertake its defence.'[36] On the same day he sent Stalin the letter (already quoted) in which he threatened to break off relations with him.* On March 6th he sent a 'top secret' note to the Georgian Communist leaders. This was the first such note, and also the last. 'I am following your case with all my heart,' wrote Lenin. 'I am indignant over Ordzhonikidze's rudeness and the connivance of Stalin and Dzerzhinsky. I am preparing for you notes and a speech.'[37]

As Moshe Lewin remarks, these last two days—March 5th and 6th, 1923—of Lenin's active life bore 'the character of a major struggle ... But Lenin's declining health did not allow him to live much longer in such a state of emotional and nervous tension. His illness grew rapidly more serious ... '[38] On March 6th, Krupskaya told Kamenev that Lenin had resolved 'to crush Stalin politically'.[39] The next day, March 7th, a new attack of arteriosclerosis put an end to Lenin's

* See p. 423.

active life. His political death saved Stalin's career, and meant the doom of Leninism.

Lenin's greatness lies not so much in his victories as in the way that his life ended, in almost desperate struggle. It is the fight that he put up under the conditions of his final illness that proves how genuine was his concern for democracy. Helpless in face of a Stalin with 'unlimited power concentrated in his hands', Lenin struck out at his eternal enemy, nationalistic and bureaucratic tyranny. That his own policy had sometimes helped to strengthen that enemy cannot be denied. But the fact remains: for Lenin, that 'mire' into which Soviet Russia, isolated and exhausted, proletarian in some ways but still bourgeois in others, had sunk, had to be cleared away, and its effects combated. He realized that this was an enterprise full of risks. To be sure, he still believed, at the end of his life, in the inevitability of the crisis that would bring capitalism down. But, in his last article, 'Better Fewer, But Better', dictated on March 2nd, 1923, he raised once again, without answering it, that question which had haunted him since 1918, and determined his strategy: 'Shall we be able to hold on with our small-and-very-small-peasant-production, and in our present state of ruin, until the West-European capitalist countries consummate their development towards socialism?'[40]

There is no trace in these last words of any 'triumphalist' cocksureness. But where some would see only an admission of defeat and confession of weakness, there we find also the reply of Lenin and Leninism to their detractors. In the anguish and despair of these last struggles, in the doubt and uncertainty of these last questionings, Leninism reveals its true nature, thereby confounding the legion of those who scorn it. The heroic course of 'Lenin's last struggle' does not disarm criticism of his work: but it does make plain the meaning of Leninism as a conception and outlook that are thoroughly *democratic* in character.

Conclusion

Limitations and vindications of Leninism

History sees Lenin as the founder and leader of the Bolshevik Party, the victor of October, the builder of Soviet society, and the model of a revolutionary chief and socialist statesman. It is a record that seems to justify the triumphalism of the official interpreters of his work.

At the conclusion of this study, however, it is not possible to endorse this appreciation of Lenin, the optimism of which is based on superficial evidence. We have only to recall what the fundamental aims of Leninism were: to erect upon the ruins of world capitalism and imperialism a socialist order that would be able to lead mankind towards the peaceful and harmonious realm of Communism. When Lenin left the political stage, however, the shadows were greatly preponderant over the bright places in this scene, and one cannot seriously claim that things are different in that respect fifty years after his death. Capitalism and imperialism still possess immense power for tyranny and destruction throughout the world. Communism has not been built anywhere, and in Russia itself they are very far from having established a socialist society, in which coercion would be, by Lenin's own definition, on its way out. Although capitalism, having been abolished in Russia by the October revolution, has not been restored there, and the country's economic strength has multiplied tenfold, Soviet democracy has not been realized, and the arbitrary power of the state, which Marx and Lenin attacked, as well as bureaucracy, seems more firmly established than ever.

It would be unfair to ascribe this failure to one man, and the errors in his teaching, when they had the opportunity to develop during only a brief phase in the history of the Communist movement. Nevertheless, whatever the vindications, the victories, and all the merits of Leninism, the fact remains that it failed in two main ways. It proved unable to succeed in accomplishing those two tasks that the working-class movement has to fulfil if it is not to suffer defeat, namely, to create the instrument that can strike down capitalism in the advanced industrial countries, and, on the ruins of bourgeois power, to organize and develop a socialist democracy and culture. The defenders of Leninism can, of course, invoke the tremendous difficulties of the undertaking, the specific features of the 'case of Russia', the isolation of Bolshevism as a result of the 'betrayal' by Social-Democracy, and many other equally unfavourable and equally compelling circumstances. But the facts are plain to see: the advanced industrial societies are still without the revolutionary force that can wrest power from the capitalists who hold it, and the Leninist model has never yet proved itself effective for this purpose.

This deficiency in Leninism is not unconnected with its inadequate assessments of Western society in general, and bourgeois democracy in particular. The critique of parliamentarism given in *State and Revolution* certainly helped to debunk the mechanism of government at a time when Social-Democracy, integrating itself into the parliamentary system, was bringing support and endorsement to this régime. Lenin had no difficulty in exposing the formalism of political freedoms, or their *de facto* concentration in the hands of the bourgeoisie.* But the biting accuracy of his criticism does not alter the fact that there is a contradiction in his analysis. On the one hand Lenin said that 'the most democratic bourgeois republic is no more than a machine for the suppression of the working class by the bourgeoisie, for the suppression of the working people by a handful of capitalists';[1] that ' "freedom" in the bourgeois democratic republic was actually freedom *for the rich* ... In fact, the working masses were, as a general rule, unable to enjoy democracy under capitalism.'[2] And he concluded, in his writings on 'The Revolution and the Renegade Kautsky', that bourgeois democracy is 'democracy for the rich and a swindle for the poor',[3] 'a paradise for the rich and a snare and deception for the exploited, the poor'.[4] At the same time, Lenin considered that 'it is incumbent on us to make use of the forms of bourgeois democracy',[5] adding that 'We ought not in any way to give the impression that we attach absolutely no value to bourgeois parliamentary institutions. They are a huge advance on what preceded them.'[6] On this point Lenin never made himself clear: how could the revolutionary workers' movement hope to use to its own advantage a régime in which the freedoms provided were 'only for the rich'? In the absence of a more thorough analysis, such categorical judgments ought, it would seem, to have led Lenin to the anarchistic conclusions for which he blamed the 'Leftists'.

The limitations of his thinking about Western capitalist society are also apparent in his analysis of the phenomenon of reformism in the labour movement. The extent to which this had spread had been noticed, before the First World War, by only a very few observers, the arts of rhetoric and the successes achieved in the field of organiza-

---

* See p. 192. Nevertheless, in 1913 Lenin considered 'Switzerland, Belgium and Norway' to be examples of 'free nations under a democratic system' (Lenin, Vol. 19, p. 91).

tion hiding as they did the ravages of opportunism. Lenin failed to grasp the nature of German Social-Democracy, mistaking its orthodoxy for loyalty to revolutionary Marxism,[7] and he defended the purely defensive tactics of the Centrist leadership right down to November 1910, when the Left in the German Social-Democratic Party had long since lost all illusions about the intentions of the Bebels and Kautskys.* His awakening, in August 1914, was all the more painful, and his hatred, not only of the socialists who rallied to chauvinism but also of the Centrists, was all the deeper as a result. 'The renegade Kautsky' was the chief target of this hatred, but none of the Centrist leaders escaped it.† The reformists (who in Germany took their stand indeed in the counter-revolutionary camp)‡ were thenceforth seen by Lenin as 'class enemies of the proletariat'.[8] The continued strength of reformism, belying the hope that Western social-democracy would not survive the compromises of the war years and the advance of the revolution, was attributed to the existence of a *labour aristocracy*, which Lenin analysed in a very schematic way. He affirmed that the basis for this stratum was the 'superprofit' of imperialism, 'part of which is used to bribe the top section of the proletariat and convert it into a reformist, opportunist petty-bourgeoisie that fears revolution'.[9] For a long time he saw this stratum as not numerous, even though important,[10] but in 1921 he acknowledged that 'the percentage of workers and office employees who enjoy a petty-bourgeois standard of living' thanks to the exploitation of the colonies was 'extremely high'.[11] He never went further in his analysis than to comment on the capacity for corruption possessed by the bourgeoisie and by reformist institutions.[12]

As for the Centrists, who bore very heavy responsibility for the crushing of the German revolution, Lenin described them in 1915 as 'the most dangerous opponents of internationalism',[13] because 'undisguised opportunism ... is not so frightful and injurious as the theory of the golden mean, which uses Marxist catchwords to justify opportunist practice.'[14] For several years he waged a vigorous campaign against this trend in the socialist movement, being obliged on more than one occasion to overcome the hesitations of his own followers, who were not anxious to break completely with former comrades. In July 1919 Lenin said that alliance with reformists was permissible only as 'a temporary evil in situations that were clearly not revolutionary'.[15] Was the situation like that in 1921, when he considered that the activity of 'hunting out Centrists', in which he had

---

* Lenin approved the German Social-Democrats' tactics of catching the enemy 'in the toils of his own legality' and compelling him 'to "shoot first" ' (ibid., Vol. 16, p. 311).

† E.g., Viktor Adler and Otto Bauer were described as 'rank traitors' (ibid., Vol. 30, p. 359).

‡ See p. 387.

engaged more ardently than anyone else, had gone on 'long enough', and that 'exaggeration of the struggle against Centrism means saving Centrism'?[16] Lenin was among the first and strongest advocates of the 'united front' tactic, which he supported as early as July 1921, for Germany at any rate.[17] Thus began that development of a policy through which the hostile brothers of the labour movement were to grope, intermittently, towards an often ephemeral reconciliation. Lenin cannot be held responsible for all the difficulties encountered along this road, but the problem of relations between Communists and Socialists was always bedevilled by the superficiality of the Leninist analysis of reformism. If there was one field in which Lenin did not succeed in dialectically overcoming the contradiction between an indispensable challenge and a necessary collaboration it was the field of relations between reformists and revolutionaries, which was of such great importance for the strategy of socialist victory.

At the same time, Leninism failed to solve the problems of the dictatorship of the proletariat and socialist democracy. It is even highly doubtful whether Lenin ever faced them properly. As a revolutionary force for subversion and destruction, the Bolshevik organization achieved victory nowhere but in a society very different from the one that Marxism aimed to conquer in order to build the foundations of complete Communism. This failure can be imputed to the major weakness in Lenin's own strategy: having counted, in launching the proletarian insurrection in Russia, upon the revolutionary capacities of the working class in the West and the prospects of world revolution, he found himself, in the years following the October revolution, faced with a reality that was the negation of these hopes. Were not all the disillusionments and retreats of the Soviet power, in the last analysis, so many inevitable consequences of this negation?

It is all too easy, though, armed with the wisdom of hindsight, to brandish the 'lessons of history' against those who, amid the changing uncertainties of actual life, tried to hurry forward the course of history. Such wisdom could only escape the charge of pedantry if the international revolutionary enterprise led by Bolshevism had obviously and from the very outset been condemned to defeat. In fact, Europe really did experience a period of great upheavals, with the revolution in Russia as the most spectacular and lasting example, but with revolutions in Central Europe and social crises in France and Italy also among its manifestations.

These are the terms in which a question arises, the answer to which lies at the very heart of the problematic of revolution. When the proletarian masses begin to move, and their relative passivity gives place to angry impatience; when, without the help of any party, and contrary to everyone's expectations, a great social eruption takes place and the lava from this eruption sweeps away régimes that the best observers had regarded as firmly entrenched; when, in short, the revolution becomes reality, what should be the attitude of the revolutionary party to this release of forces that are ill-controlled and hard to control? There is a great temptation, and perhaps good reason, to proclaim the popular offensive premature and adventuristic, to see in the masses an 'elemental' and 'blind' force the impulsiveness of which risks compromising achievements won by methods less spectacular, but systematic and fruitful. This was the reaction of Menshevism, not only in Russia but throughout Europe.

The attitude of Leninism was different. It recognized that, under historical conditions such as are rarely found together, the masses were 'a hundred times more "Left" ' than the most revolutionary party; that, in circumstances like these, history had chosen *for* the party and was *forcing* it to accept and follow the offensive of the masses; that this choice was not free from risk and that, even given an objectively favourable situation, the revolution was still an adventure. The choice, however, was a harshly simple one: either the revolutionary organization regarded the dangers as too great and the uncertainties too considerable, and turned its back on a popular upsurge that it deemed anarchical; or else the organization accepted the risks of revolutionary action, showing itself ready both to *follow* the offensive of the masses and to provide it with *leadership*. Prudence is undoubtedly a political virtue not to be neglected by a revolutionary party. But refusal to take the side of the proletariat when a revolution is under way brings with it a penalty that a socialist party cannot escape. If it fails to fulfil its revolutionary function at the moment when events, or, more precisely, the proletariat, have put fulfilment of this function on the agenda, it ceases to be a party of revolution. Thus, Menshevism and Social-Democracy were for a long time able to put themselves forward as parties concerned to defend the interests of the working class. But their attitude when faced with the phenomenon of revolution as a real thing put an end to an ambiguity they had long indulged in, by stripping them of all claims to stand for the socialist revolution. Leninism, on the contrary, even if committing mistakes of calculation all through 1917, acted as a force which accepted responsibility for the revolutionary function. The revolutionary may tack, may put off the decisive clash, may prepare for it with the greatest care, may arm himself with patience and prudence. But he must, in the last analysis, when the class struggle breaks out in its sharpest form, take up other arms as well, above all when the proletariat itself puts them into his hands—the arms of revolutionary combat. *This is the essential meaning of the revolutionary's political and social role.* And while Russian Bolshevism accumulated many mistakes and suffered many setbacks, Menshevism was swept away by the revolution. At certain moments of history, the last word of wisdom and realism is not to wait cautiously but to run risks and take off into the unknown.

Thus, Leninism gave back to the working-class movement a revolutionary content that corresponds to the alienated situation of the proletariat in capitalist society, and which reformist socialism had ceased to keep alive. This content is not merely a matter of using violence in the struggle against the bourgeoisie. Through all the twistings and turnings of tactics and strategy, Leninism keeps in mind an awareness that political action by the socialist proletariat has meaning and justification only if it aims at the conquest of *political power*. This is a conception that Social-Democratic pragmatism has long since abandoned: participation in governments subject to the power of the bourgeoisie (whether or not such participation is entered upon in order to serve the workers' interests) constitutes the height of its modest ambition.

The *conquest of power*, which was the main aim of Leninism before 1917, implies the existence of a revolutionary organization, to be constantly strengthened. In this field, too, the contribution of Leninism has been decisive and lasting. In some ways, the importance of the vanguard party has even become greater than in the period when Lenin set out the theory of it. The development of imperialism, monopoly capitalism, and state control over the economy has reinforced the ideological influence of the bourgeoisie over the working class, with Social-Democracy helping to make this influence more effective. As factors of differentiation increase inside the proletariat itself, *self*-emancipation by this class becomes more and more problematical. It was not accidental, after all, that Rosa Luxemburg herself, after the First World War, which had considerably strengthened the penetration of bourgeois ideology into the working-class movement, felt bound to acknowledge that 'the absence of leadership, the non-existence of a centre responsible for organizing the workers of Berlin, cannot be allowed to continue. If the revolutionary cause is to progress, if the victory of the proletariat and socialism are to be more than a dream, then the revolutionary workers must set up leading organs capable of guiding and utilizing the fighting energy of the masses.'[18]

Long years of stagnation in the development of the revolution, and the experience of the international Communist movement, have certainly illustrated the dangers inherent in excessive centralization and submission to the directives of the 'vanguard party'. It remains true that revolutionary socialism cannot avoid the necessity of organizing itself in a party capable of rebutting the ideological offensive of the bourgeoisie and preparing the offensive against a capitalism which, though powerful, is mortal. In so far as the significance of Leninism can be summed up in that sentence, it seems to be beyond doubt that, although it may have settled nothing finally, it has lost neither its actuality nor its relevance.

Leninism and Stalinism

This book ends with the death of the founder of Soviet Russia. It would, however, be possible to claim that the history of Leninism really begins at the moment when its founder died, when his doctrine became congealed into dogma, and the 'heirs of Lenin' set to work on a task of sacralization that has not yet exhausted its effects. It could also be said that study of this subsequent fate of Leninism forms part of the study of Leninism itself—indeed, that its essential nature has been revealed only as Lenin's continuators have 'developed' it. As I said at the beginning, however, the specific interest of Lenin's own activity in relation to what is called 'Marxist-Leninist' doctrine provides reason for the analysis to end with the departure of the great revolutionary leader.

A book about Lenin's policy and ideology would nevertheless be incomplete if it did not try to answer this question: despite the very real differences between Lenin and Stalin and between their respective political activities, is not Stalinism the continuation of Leninism? Does it not constitute a finished, perfected form of Leninism, its logical conclusion, and, in that sense, something perhaps more 'Leninist' than the Leninism of Lenin himself?

One can grant straight away to the critics of Leninism that the history of the bureaucratic and totalitarian degeneration of the Soviet régime does not begin with the death of Lenin, or even with Stalin's accession to important positions of authority in the Soviet state. This matter has been too fully treated in the present book for it to be necessary to recapitulate it at length. The birth of the Communist bureaucracy antedated the appearance and growth of Stalin's influence, and the same is true of monolithism—Lenin's responsibility in the latter connexion, one of crucial importance, being incontestably substantial. His assertion of the fundamental role played by the vanguard organization in preparing and consolidating the revolution, and his emphasis on the virtues of discipline, however understandable and necessary, also contained germs the growth of which produced most baneful results. It is impossible not to conclude that the origin of a phenomenon as complex as Stalinism has to be sought in a historical background containing a great variety of factors, one of which was certainly Leninism.

And yet it is hard to exaggerate the essential *differences* underlying the basic *incompatibility* of Leninism and Stalinism. Is not the latter identified with the omnipotence of bureaucratic tyranny, with the domination of a pragmatism that is often incoherent, bold strokes punctuating a highly conservative policy—and, above all, with the exercise of unlimited personal dictatorship? Yet *Lenin* strove desperately to restrict the power of a bureaucracy whose excesses conflicted both with his democratic aspirations and with his desire to give economic policy a scientific character. He tried also to make the Soviet state's policy a harmonious whole, overcoming the contradictions that arose from the variety of functions it sought to fulfil in relation to the outside world, and to put into practice the difficult demands of dialectics.* Finally, and above all, nothing was less like the dictatorial autocracy of Stalinism than the kind of authority that Lenin exercised in the Bolshevik Party and the Soviet state.

This last point is worth dwelling on. Leninism can be defined as a doctrine and practice of political centralization; as an enterprise of revolution based on the action of a vanguard; as a technique of socialist construction based on an authoritarian state, or on active participation by the people in administrative tasks. Undoubtedly it could be defined in other ways as well. Only by grossly distorting the facts, however, can Leninism be presented as a form of personal dictatorship. The question of the authority that Lenin concentrated in his hands transcends the problematic of the Russian revolution and Marxism-Leninism. Looked at in a broader context, it enables us to consider how far Weber's theory of charisma applies to the case of a socialist leader heading a popular revolution and a proletarian movement.†

Weber considers that 'in traditionally stereotyped periods, charisma is the greatest revolutionary force',[19] that it appears in a situation of apparently inextricable social crisis, and is accompanied by an extreme upsurge of radicalism. He adds that the authority of the charismatic leader is based on the support of a nucleus of loyal followers, resembling, to some extent, the vanguard party, but differing profoundly from Lenin's followers in the unconditional and irrational character of their allegiance to the leader. Despite some rather superficial analogies, the differences between the charisma that Weber analyses, on the one hand, and Lenin's personality, on the other, are, however, most striking. Whereas the charismatic authority shows complete disdain for economic considerations—'pure charisma is specifically foreign to economic considerations ... From the point of view of rational economic activity charisma is a typical anti-economic force'[20]—Lenin, on the contrary, carried his concern for economic development to the extremes of an 'industrialism' tinged with positivism.‡ Whereas the charismatic leader founds the fascina-

---

* See p. 382.

† See Max Weber's analysis of charisma in his *Wirtschaft und Gesellschaft* (English translation, *The Theory of Social and Economic Organization*), and also a useful work of synthesis by Ter Hoeven.

‡ See p. 338.

tion that he exercises upon his rejection of all and any compromise, Lenin, on the contrary, defended realism against revolutionary purism. The specifically irrational and often religious orientation of the charismatic authority contrasts with Lenin's materialism and devotion to scientific socialism. Again, and especially, nothing in Lenin's style recalls either the demagogy resorted to by the charismatic leader, or his insatiable vanity, or the carefully nourished belief in the sacredness of his mission. Finally, there is no trace, with Lenin, of the organization of any kind of 'cult of personality'.

His legendary austerity certainly fits the image that the charismatic leader sometimes tries to project; though there are few examples of a head of state, even a charismatic one, contenting himself with what Victor Serge described as 'a small apartment built for a palace servant',[21] and protesting, in a letter not intended for publication, against his being given an increase in his wages, although these were the very modest wages of a skilled worker.[22] It is, though, the exceptional simplicity and modesty of Lenin that contrasts most with the charismatic style. When head of the Soviet Government, he writes in September 1920 to the librarian of the Rumyantsev Museum a letter in which he asks permission to borrow, for one night, 'when the library is closed', some reference books that he needs. '*I will return them by morning*', he assures his correspondent.[23]

In his lifetime there was no sign of a 'cult of personality' around this man whose corpse was destined to be mummified and his ideas turned into holy scripture. There must have been great temptation to organize such a cult, as the inevitable corollary of that ideological mystification that a revolutionary régime in danger of defeat can resort to. But Lenin never lent himself to any such operation. Rejecting all ceremony, 'he entered the room, simply, as was his habit, scarcely noticed by the other comrades, who were deep in discussion'.[24] This lack of affectation displeased Stalin, to whom it seemed contrary to the requirements of dignity. Recalling, in a speech delivered soon after Lenin's death, the atmosphere of a Bolshevik congress, Stalin said: 'what ... was my disappointment to learn that Lenin had arrived at the conference before the delegates, had settled himself somewhere in a corner, and was unassumingly carrying on a conversation, a most ordinary conversation with the most ordinary delegates at the conference. I will not conceal from you that at that time this seemed to me to be something of a violation of certain essential rules.'[25]

And when the Bolshevik Party decided to celebrate Lenin's fiftieth birthday, he was not content with protesting. 'When the laudatory speeches commenced, he got up and walked out, and telephoned every few minutes from his Kremlin office inquiring when the oratory would cease so he could return to the session.'[26] An extremely critical observer of the Soviet régime notes that, in the Young Communist organization, where a cult of the leader might have made a special appeal, 'restraint [in this regard, M.L.] prevailed even in the enthusiasm of the closing ceremonies'.[27]

The sociologist will reckon with the fact that one of the men whose activity contributed most to shaping the world of today, and whose grip upon his people was considerable, eludes the canons of charismatic power. The reason for this probably lies in the fact that Lenin, while never believing in any kind of personal 'mission', identified himself, at the moments when he did most to determine history, with the will of a class. Far from making himself its master and subjecting it to his purposes, he was content to guide its activity and give expression to its power. Charisma has no place in the great conquests of socialism.

There remains the question of the dictatorial power that is ascribed to Lenin, making him, in many people's eyes, the forerunner or the harbinger of Stalinism. Certainly his authority in Party and state was enormous. But all through this book the reader can find examples of clashes between Lenin and some section — even a majority sometimes — of his followers. He often succeeded in overcoming this opposition, by a combination of his power of conviction and the pressure of facts. But he also frequently found himself in a minority, and obliged therefore to give up the policy he wished to get accepted by the Party or by the state. There was no sphere in which the 'dictator' did not have to accept defeat. During the discussion on the trade union question* he was put in a minority in the Party's Central Committee.[28] In the economic field, he twice called upon the All-Russia Trade Union Council to accept the principle of 'one-man management', and on each occasion, in January and March 1920, he 'met with a rebuff'.[29] At about the same time he put before the Bolshevik group in the Trade Union Council, jointly with Trotsky, a resolution in favour of the 'militarization' of labour. This resolution was rejected almost unanimously.[30] And when, in May 1922, he proposed to the Central Executive Committee of the Soviets that the size of the Red Army be reduced by a quarter, he was again defeated.[31]

Many such examples could be given. An incident in which Lenin came into conflict with Angelica Balabanoff illustrates the way Lenin could react to attitudes of opposition on the part of his colleagues. During the First Congress of the Communist International he passed a note to her, asking her to 'take the floor and announce the affiliation of the Italian Socialist Party to the Third International'. Angelica Balabanoff refused: it was, she considered, for the Italian Socialist Party to 'speak for themselves'. Lenin insisted: 'You have to. You are their official representative for Zimmerwald. You read *Avanti* and

* See p. 339.

know what is going on in Italy.'* 'This time,' Balabanoff tells us, 'I merely looked at him and shook my head.'[32] At the conclusion of the congress, however, she was appointed, with Lenin's approval, secretary of the Communist International.

It is hardly necessary, perhaps, to recall that on many occasions Lenin was a target of criticism, sometimes very sharp, and often made publicly, within his own Party. Such criticism came both from the most eminent Bolsheviks and from obscure Party members. It was Trotsky who, in the trade-union discussion of the autumn and winter of 1920, declared that Lenin wanted 'at all costs to disrupt or shelve' fundamental discussion of the matter,[33] and Bukharin who, in the same period, alleged that Lenin had 'dropped the line laid down by the Ninth Party Congress'.[34] It was one of the representatives of the opposition in the Party who, at this same congress, told Lenin that what he was saying was 'absolutely false',[35] and, during the congress of 1921, that the resolution he had put down regarding the Workers' Opposition was 'slanderous'.[36] At a still lower level of the hierarchy, a Communist writing to Lenin accused him, without beating about the bush, of having 'slipped up'.[37] One could go on almost indefinitely quoting instances to show that Lenin's position was, in the Communist Party and in the Soviet state, that of a leader whose authority, though substantial, constantly came up against objections, criticism and opposition, which obliged him to come to terms with his friends just as he had to with his enemies, and with reality.

What would Lenin have done?

Neither a dictator nor a charismatic leader, Lenin thus differed *absolutely*, in his methods of government, from the man who succeeded him at the head of the Soviet régime. This observation is not enough, however, to close the discussion on the relationship between Leninism and Stalinism. May one not claim that, despite the great differences and many incompatibilities, and despite everything that separates and contrasts the two men, nevertheless Stalinism, while not the same as Leninism, was the prolongation, so to speak, of the latter, and that, despite all their differences in character — temperament, aspirations, ways of thinking, moral principles, reactions in behaviour — Lenin would have been led to follow a policy very similar to Stalin's? Surely, the logic of the system, together with the constraints of the concrete historical situations, would have got the better of anyone's intentions and scruples — these latter being, as is well known, not among the chief driving forces of social evolution.

It is, of course, impossible to prove what Lenin 'would have done' in the period subsequent to his last struggle against Stalin, and his

* The Italian Socialist Party was indeed one of the first to join the Communist International.

death. Yet this circumstance need not put an end to discussion of the point. There are objective facts which entitle us to make some deductions that can rank as probabilities.

The first of these concerns one of the major episodes of Stalin's policy, the forced collectivization of agriculture. What has been called the 'second revolution' entailed the launching of a second civil war. The mass terror that accompanied it shaped the Soviet Russia of the 1930s, contributing to accentuate, sometimes to the point of absurdity, the most totalitarian features of the Stalinist system. Now, the carrying out of such a policy as this was made possible only by complete abandonment of the attitude that Lenin had systematically adopted towards the peasantry.

As we have seen, one of the decisive elements in Lenin's adaptation of Marxism was the substitution of the idea of an alliance of the working class with the peasantry for that of an alliance with the progressive bourgeoisie.* After the October revolution he showed constant concern to safeguard this alliance. The 'decree on land', proclaimed on the very day of the insurrection, by allowing the peasants use of the nationalized land on an individual basis, was both a breach of socialist principles and a major concession made to the Russian peasantry. To be sure, the Soviet Government sought in 1918 to encourage collective agricultural undertakings, but it did this on a very modest scale. At the end of the civil war, which meant the end of a period of 'War Communism' that was favourable to the most radical transformations, the situation in the countryside was marked by what was called 'middle-peasantization',[38] while the number of collective farms, never very large, was on the decline.[39] This moderate policy, hardly in conformity with the canons of Marxism, and severely criticized by Rosa Luxemburg in her essay *The Russian Revolution*,[40] gave faithful expression to Lenin's concern to conciliate the peasantry. He considered, indeed, that 'the problem of our attitude towards the middle peasants' was 'one of the most difficult problems of communist development in a country of small peasant farms',[41] and that 'the question of work in the countryside [was] now ... the basic question of socialist construction in general.'[42] Lenin saw the final victory of socialism as subject to two conditions: success of the proletarian revolution in the West, and 'agreement between the proletariat, which is exercising its dictatorship, that is, holds state power, and the majority of the peasant population'.[43] In his last writings he was to reiterate that 'in our Soviet Republic, the social order is based on the collaboration of two classes: the workers and peasants',[44] and that it was essential to 'strive to build up a state in which the workers retain the leadership of the peasants, in which they retain the confidence of the peasants ... '[45]

* See p. 75.

While Lenin called for ruthless struggle against the kulaks, he proclaimed the necessity for an agreement with the middle peasantry,[46] and this despite the aid that the middle peasants sometimes lent to the actions of the well-to-do and rich peasants.[47] It followed that the policy of agrarian collectivization had, in Lenin's view, to be based upon *example* and *persuasion*.[48] 'Nothing is more stupid', said Lenin in March 1919, 'than the very idea of applying coercion in economic relations with the middle peasant.'[49] Of course Lenin remained convinced that 'the solution lies only in socialized farming',[50] and that 'turning to collective farming' was 'the only means of restoring the agriculture that has been ruined and destroyed by the war'.[51] But what had to be undertaken in that sphere was 'a prolonged and gradual process',[52] in which 'the greatest prudence should be exercised in introducing innovations'.[53] Everything suggests that Lenin, while pursuing the aim of collectivizing agriculture, would have been careful *not* to do this at the headlong pace of the campaign Stalin began in 1929. It is almost unthinkable that he would have given this policy the form of a wave of violence that shook the very foundations of the social system and the Soviet economy, and made inevitable the rise and triumph, on the ruins of kulak power, of bureaucratic dictatorship and terroristic monolithism.

Would Lenin's concern to conciliate the peasantry have made him, in the controversies of 1925–30, a supporter of the 'Bukharin line', pro-peasant and even pro-kulak, cautious to the point of conservatism? At first one is inclined to think so, when reading the advice he lavished on his followers in his last writings. In 'Better Fewer, But Better', his very last article, with its revealing title, he wrote: 'in matters of culture, haste and sweeping measures are most harmful ... Thus, in the matter of our state apparatus, we should now draw the conclusion from our past experience that it would be better to proceed more slowly ... It is time we did something about it. We must show sound scepticism for too rapid progress, for boastfulness, etc. ... The most harmful thing here would be haste.' Finally: 'We should not stint time on building ["a really new state apparatus"], ... it will take many, many years.'[54]

If we remember, too, the tactic almost constantly recommended by Lenin to his followers, after the October revolution—to retreat and manoeuvre*—we are tempted to find in these political attitudes of Lenin's a foretaste of the Right-wing line of Bukharin, who, once having left his Leftist phase behind him, and engaged in the struggle for the succession to Lenin, advocated merely the protection of peasant interests and an extremely slow advance towards the building of socialism.

There are, however, good reasons for not resorting, where

* See p. 364.

Lenin and Leninism are concerned, to the simplistic categories of 'Leftism' and 'Right-wing Bukharinism'. It needs to be observed that at the very moment when the reverses suffered by the international revolutionary movement and the isolation of Soviet Russia were causing Lenin to advocate organized retreat, he *also* showed remarkable readiness for offensive revolutionary action. It was in the period of the Genoa conference and the Rapallo Treaty, when a *modus vivendi* was being established with Western imperialism, and Communist Russia was expressing more keenness than ever to be accepted into the 'concert of nations', and multiplying proofs of her moderation, that Lenin, addressing the Political Bureau, said in a note dated February 4th, 1922, on the subject of the fight against war, that 'only a ready and experienced revolutionary party, with a good illegal machinery, can successfully wage a struggle against war,' and called for 'the formation of revolutionary groups in the warring armies and their preparation for the carrying out of a revolution'.[55]

The attitude taken up by Lenin during the Third Congress of the Communist International, in 1921, reveals even more clearly that this readiness for revolutionary action was still present in him even when he was engaged in a hard fight against the Leftism of certain Communists, and was trying to overcome the advocates of 'all-out offensive'. During the summer of 1921, in the aftermath of the defeat of the German Communist Party's 'March action', Lenin had agreed with Trotsky to throw his whole weight into the struggle against the 'ultra-revolutionary' tendency.* But while he crossed swords with the representatives of this wing, he also argued against the Czechoslovakian Communist Šmeral, well known for his Right-wing tendencies. In one of the congress commissions, Šmeral had stressed the difficulties that the revolutionary movement would encounter in his country, and had expressed anxiety lest the Comintern drive the European proletariat into offensive action. The course of the discussion calmed his misgivings. Hardly had Šmeral expressed his satisfaction at this, however, than Lenin answered him in these words: 'Will things really come to the stage of preparation for the offensive in Czechoslovakia, or will they be confined merely to talk about difficulties? The Left mistake is simply a mistake, it isn't big and is easily rectified. But if the mistake pertains to the resolution to act, then this is by no means a small mistake, it is a betrayal. These mistakes do not bear comparison.'[56] And what matters here is not merely the emphatic nature of Lenin's statement, but also, and especially, the *moment* when it was made.

It is hard not to conclude that the policy that Lenin would have followed at the head of Soviet Russia and of the Comintern would certainly have reckoned with the substantial sources of strength that

* See p. 398.

the capitalist world still possessed, would have taken all possible steps to preserve the revolutionary movement from the temptations of adventurism and premature offensive, and would probably have continued to 'manoeuvre' and 'retreat'. But Lenin would probably also, to an infinitely greater degree than Stalin, have remained attentive to *changes* in the international situation. He would have watched keenly for more favourable political weather. Events showing that new revolutionary possibilities were on the horizon would most likely have been welcomed by him with a combination of cool appraisal and fighting spirit, in which the latter would, given certain conditions, have predominated over the former. It was in this way, for example, that Lenin greeted the social and political crisis that broke out in Italy in the autumn of 1920, giving rise to the ephemeral successes of the 'workers' councils'.

The Red Army had just been defeated in Poland, destroying the hope that a bridge would be established between Soviet Russia and the German proletariat. Everywhere else the revolutionary movement seemed to be marking time: in France, for instance, the offensives of a radicalized trade-union movement had ended in defeat and disillusion. Lenin had just written his *'Left-Wing' Communism, An Infantile Disorder*, with its fraternal but unsparing attack on Leftism.* But then, in September 1920, the action begun by the workers of Turin at the end of August took on a wider scope, leading to the occupation of numerous factories. Even though these actions failed to develop further, the country did not return to normality—the crisis persisted. It was in these conditions that Lenin wrote to the Italian Communists that 'in the present-day conditions in Italy one should *lean to the left*. To successfully accomplish the revolution and safeguard it, the Italian party must take a *definite step to the left* ... '57

Can one seriously doubt that the advance of the revolutionary movement in China, the social upheaval caused by the world economic crisis, the radicalization produced by the rise of Fascism in France and Spain, and, in the latter country, the outbreak of a civil war with revolutionary possibilities, would, no less but even more than the events of September 1920 in Italy, have caused Lenin to urge the Communist movement to 'lean to the Left', and not remain in the defensive postures in which Stalinism kept it between the wars? In other words, would Lenin not have gone along with the offensive of the masses, and given his backing to a revolutionary dynamic which, after years of retreat and stagnation, was resuming its forward march—identifying himself, as in 1917, with the development of a proletarian movement rich in democratic hopes and deadly to bureaucracies and established power-structures?

This 'revolutionary readiness' of Lenin's is only one aspect of a

* See p. 399.

larger phenomenon. It expressed a feature of Leninism that distinguishes it from and opposes it to Stalinism perhaps more than any
other. In contrast to Stalin, we see in Lenin a remarkable assimilation
of dialectical method and principle in his political praxis.

Leninism: politics and dialectics

'Dialectics ... embodied in the consciousness of a man like Lenin
becomes an art of action ... , it becomes an intelligence, a genius that
is not mystical in character, but the apogee of common sense,' wrote
Henri Lefebvre and Norbert Guterman.[58] Lenin as a dialectician, or,
more precisely, as partisan, assimilator and practician of the dialectical philosophy—there was a field for which his activity as a revolutionary, essentially concerned with politics, and his original training,
as a lawyer and an economist, had provided little preparation. And,
indeed, Lenin's first incursion into the realm of philosophy was not a
success. His *Materialism and Empiriocriticism* (1909) is a work that
smells of its author's mainly pragmatic and polemical intentions. The
way it was written reflected Lenin's concrete concerns of the time,
which were not all exclusively focused on a philosophical debate.
The latter was certainly important: the advances made in physics at
the beginning of the twentieth century were re-stating the problem
of the relations between matter and consciousness, and the explora-
tion of the infinitely small had made possible a new attack on materialism.[59] But if the controversies thus provoked had a bearing on the
political dispute between orthodox (and therefore 'materialist)'
Marxists and revisionists, Lenin does not seem to have realized that
very quickly. His book was directed mainly against the Bolsheviks
Lunacharsky and (especially) Bogdanov, who was interested in the
philosophical writings of Mach and Avenarius, seeking to find a
'third way' between materialism and idealism. In 1904 Bogdanov had
sent Lenin the first volume of his book *Empiriomonism*, and Lenin
had not only not protested, but had continued to maintain good relations with the author. What led him to declare war on the 'idealism' of
his comrade-in-arms was Bogdanov's *political* attitude. The latter
was on his way to becoming the leader of the Left wing in the Party,
and would soon have to pay for his extremism by being expelled from
it.* Concerns so remote from the very subject of the debate between
idealists, materialists and sensationalists were not calculated to produce a real contribution to the advancement of science and philosophy,
even though Lenin, with his usual thoroughness, carefully and lengthily
prepared his attack, submerging himself during a whole year in philosophical books.

Lenin's explicit purpose was simple: 'to note how *in fact* the empty,
pseudo-scientific claim to have transcended idealism and materialism

* See p. 57.

vanishes',[60] and how the 'materialist solution alone is really compatible with natural science'.[61]

For the needs of his cause, however, he identified sensationalism with idealism, and the latter with essentially religious 'fideism'.[62] His methods were extremely dubious: sometimes he attributes to Avenarius statements that he never made,[63] sometimes he fights Mach and his followers with quotations from other philosophers and men of learning who, in Lenin's view, were authorities,[64] frequently he vilifies his opponents' intentions,[65] and while, so far as this opponent is concerned, indictment sometimes takes the place of analysis,[66] Lenin shows towards Engels, 'the teacher',[67] a respect that borders on fetishism.[68] Undoubtedly, this work of Lenin's provided a rich source for 'Marxist' dogmatism.

Materialism and Empiriocriticism holds an isolated position among Lenin's many writings. After publishing it, he abandoned the philosophical field and went back to more familiar activities. Some years later, however, he returned to philosophy—in circumstances that were peculiarly unfavourable to abstract speculation, and for reasons that are not absolutely clear. In September 1914, when the outbreak of the war and the collapse of the Second International made political struggle more necessary than ever, and gave it a new dimension, Lenin buried himself in Hegel, making notes and summaries and commenting at length on that philosopher's works, especially those relating to dialectics.

Despite their often lapidary nature, these notes of Lenin's enable us to perceive the significance that he personally attributed to the principal concepts of Hegelian dialectics. I shall not list them all: the question is of interest here only in so far as it illuminates what could be called the methodological and philosophical inspiration of a political practice that was profoundly marked by dialectics. It is worth noting, however, what Lenin had to say about such concepts as movement, contradiction and the qualitative leap. These lie, as we shall see, at the very centre of Lenin's perception of some decisive political and social phenomena of his time.

Regarding movement, he wrote: 'We cannot imagine, express, measure, depict movement, without interrupting continuity, without simplifying, coarsening, dismembering, strangling that which is living. The representation of movement by means of thought always makes coarse, kills—and not only by means of thought, but also by sense-perception, and not only movement but *every* concept.' And he concludes, on this point: 'And in that lies the *essence* of dialectics.'[69] Regarding contradictions: '*Dialectics* is the teaching which shows how *opposites* can be and how they happen to be (how they become) *identical*—under what conditions they are identical, becoming transformed into one another—why the human mind should grasp these opposites not as dead, rigid, but as living, conditional, mobile, becoming transformed into one another.'[70]

And on the qualitative leap: 'What distinguishes the dialectical transition from the undialectical transition? The leap. The contradiction. The interruption of gradualness. The unity (identity) of Being and not-Being.'[71]

What is significant here is above all the concern to give the concepts of dialectics a significance in which abstraction disappears, giving place to living reality, and also the considerable importance Lenin obviously ascribed to dialectical analysis. This was so great that, despite the hostility he still felt towards Hegel's idealism,[72] he freely displayed increasing admiration for this philosopher.[73] It was perhaps to this deeper, and less 'polemical' incursion into philosophy, and this more acute awareness of the implications of dialectics, that was due Lenin's modification of his former uncompromising and dogmatic attitude towards idealism in every form. It is surprising to find in his notes this remark, which clashes with the foursquare formulations of *Materialism and Empiriocriticism*: 'Intelligent idealism is closer to intelligent materialism than stupid materialism.' Lenin adds that it would be better to speak of 'dialectical idealism instead of intelligent.'[74] Again, he writes:

> Philosophical idealism is *only* nonsense from the standpoint of crude, simple, metaphysical materialism. From the standpoint of *dialectical* materialism, on the other hand, philosophical idealism is *one-sided*, exaggerated ... development (inflation, distention) of one of the features, aspects, facets of knowledge into an absolute divorced from matter, from nature, apotheosised. Idealism is clerical obscurantism. True. But philosophical idealism is ... a *road* to clerical obscurantism *through one of the shades* of the infinitely complex *knowledge* (dialectical) of man.[75]

If, as Henri Lefebvre says, 'praxis is the starting point and the end-point of dialectical materialism', it is at the level of Lenin's political activity that we must look for evidence of his sharpened awareness and understanding of dialectics. A series of facts and episodes in his career do make possible such a confrontation of theory and praxis. It will be noticed that these are situated mainly in the latter part of Lenin's life, during and after the conquest of power, in other words, *after* the deeper study of dialectics that he undertook between 1914 and 1916.

Our first example relates to the concept of the qualitative leap. It is in this connexion that Hegel speaks of 'interruption in gradualness'.[76] Was it perhaps his awareness of the importance of this concept that made Lenin so particularly attentive to the consequences that can result from 'exaggerations', even slight and seemingly harmless ones? Writing about the employment by the Soviet administration of officials of the defunct Tsarist state, he said, for example:

> Men's vices, it has long been known, are for the most part bound up with their virtues. This, in fact, applies to many leading Communists. For decades we had been working for the great cause, preaching the overthrow of the bourgeoisie, teaching men to mistrust the bourgeois specialists, to expose them, deprive them of power and crush their resistance. That is a historic cause of world-wide significance. But it needs only a slight exaggeration to prove the old adage that there is only one step from the sublime to the ridiculous.[77]

The 'exaggeration' referred to here led some Communists to refuse to accept the employment of bourgeois officials, or to make it impossible for these officials to work. Lenin's sense of dialectics enabled him to perceive the presence in this sphere of contradictory factors: the need to employ bureaucrats, and the existence of a bureaucratic deviation and danger due to this very need.

An example taken from revolutionary action itself is the attitude taken up by Lenin during the 'April days' of 1917.* At a time when Lenin, apparently no less 'Left' than the most impatient of his supporters, had just unseated the Right-wing leadership of the Party, the demonstrations of the Petrograd masses incited the extreme Left element among the Bolsheviks to advocate a (premature) attempt to overthrow the Provisional Government. But Lenin, the 'Left' of the day before, considered that to go 'a little more to the Left would be a very serious crime'. The Party's policy would be transformed: revolutionary radicalism would become, by a mere prolongation, so to speak, of the tactic that was applied previously, something qualitatively different, a policy of adventurism.

In his *Encyclopaedia*, Hegel says that 'an object without contradictions [is] nothing more than a pure abstraction of the understanding, which maintains one of these determinations with a sort of violence and conceals from consciousness the contrary determination that contains the first one'.[78] It was Lenin's dialectical vigilance in perceiving the contradiction in an 'object' that accounts for his concern to safeguard during a particular phase of political action the possibility of going over to an opposite phase. Speaking at the Fourth Congress of the Comintern in November 1922 he said, for example, that 'all the parties which are preparing to take the direct offensive against capitalism in the near future must now give thought to the problem of preparing for a possible retreat'.[79] His attitude to the N.E.P. provides another

* See pp. 165 ff.

illustration of the same way of thinking. It was he who was responsible for introducing it in March 1921. In the year that followed, and, indeed, right down to the end of his political career, he never questioned its continuance, but went on explaining why it was necessary. In March 1922, however, he said to the Eleventh Party Congress: 'For a year we have been retreating. On behalf of the party we must now call a halt ... We have reached a new line ... '[80]

Annotating in autumn 1914 Hegel's *Science of Logic*, Lenin had written: '*Dialectics* is the teaching which shows how *opposites* can be and how they happen to be (how they become) *identical*.'[81] It is well known that the idea of the transcending (*Aufhebung*) and synthesis of these opposites is an essential feature of the dialectical theory. 'A thing that has been transcended,' said Hegel in this connexion, 'still has within it the determination from which it originates.'[82] And Lenin wrote in his notebook the elliptical formula:

aufheben = ein Ende machen
          = erhalten (aufbewahren zugleich)
supersede = terminate = maintain (simultaneously to preserve)[83]

If we seek to relate these concepts to Lenin's political activity, we notice that some of his most illuminating ideas and most important contributions to history are not unconnected with this dialectical conception of the existence of opposites and the transcending (or superseding) of them. I have already suggested that the Communist International can be seen as an original and audacious attempt to 'overcome' the contradiction between the need to safeguard the interests of the Soviet state, within the limits of the old Russia, and the need to promote the advance of the world revolution.* Lenin's realization that the régime born of the success of the Russian revolution *and* of its inability to advance beyond the national frontiers had given rise to a political and social system in which were present the two opposite realities of a tyrannical bureaucracy *and* genuine workers' power, a truly dialectical idea, found expression in that formula of the 'workers' state with bureaucratic distortion' which Lenin alone produced amid the confusion of the trade-union discussion of the winter of 1920–21.†

Finally, and most important, can we not see that one of Lenin's fundamental contributions to present-day politics results, in many ways, from a profoundly dialectical phenomenon: the transcending (or superseding, or surmounting) of two contradictory terms which act upon each other while negating each other. In this way is born 'the Third Term [which] turns back to the first term ... It releases the con-

* See p. 383.
† See p. 344.

tent of the first term, by removing from it that whereby it was incomplete, limited and destined to be negated ... Its one-sidedness is thus surmounted and destroyed ... '[84]

Let us re-read history, and in particular the history of the Bolshevik Party, equipped with this 'code'. We saw the main event of the year 1917 was the metamorphosis of the Leninist organization, the closed, hierarchically structured vanguard born of the struggle against Tsarism, and its 'transcendence' into a new party, the historical merit of which lies in its having achieved a brief but extraordinary identification with the class that it represented.* For the Bolshevik Party became in 1917 *both* the opposite *and* the continuation of what it had been before the February revolution. And what Lenin tried, dialectically, to do during the first years of the Soviet régime was to preserve what had thus been achieved. The Soviet Communist Party, having come to power, appeared both as the closed vanguard of the beginnings of Leninism and as its opposite: it opened itself to the masses, while endeavouring to retain some aspects of its original 'elitism' and to protect itself against the dangers of opportunism. This was the significance of the policy of selection, probation and purging advocated by Lenin.† And if the 'first term' in the dialectical contradiction and transcendence can be represented, in the great debate between the supporters of organization and those of spontaneity, by a Luxemburgism carried to extremes, identified with absolute faith in the self-emancipation of the masses—a line that Rosa Luxemburg herself never fully espoused—and the 'second term' by a purely elitist conception of the Party such as Blanquism incarnates better than even the earliest form of Leninism, is not the 'third term' to be found in the Bolshevik Party as it developed in the rising phase of the revolution of 1917, before and after October? At that time the Party appears as a synthesis in which we see, merged and interacting, features retained from the original Bolshevism—with its discipline, will to coherence, tendency to centralism, concern for efficiency—and the characteristics that accompany great popular movements, defying all organization from without, instructions from the top, and even the forecasts of the most revolutionary of strategists.

Whether we look at the greatest moments in the history of Leninism or at its less spectacular achievements, dialectics is seen to be the weapon used by Lenin, and used with a skill exceeding that of any of his lieutenants. That he ascribed decisive importance to it is given a final proof, if that be needed, in Lenin's own last words about Bukharin. In his 'Testament' Lenin does not stint praise of the former leader of the Left Communists: 'Bukharin is not only a most valuable and major theorist of the Party; he is also rightly considered the

* See p. 148.
† See p. 306.

favourite of the whole Party.' But Lenin adds: 'But his theoretical views can be classified as fully Marxist only with great reserve, for there is something scholastic about him (he has never made a study of dialectics, and, I think, never fully understood it).'[85]

The same might be said, with even more emphasis, of Stalin and Stalinism. Of course, the latter dressed themselves up in the finery of dialectics and made 'Diamat' the official truth of the Communist movement. But although Stalinist practice often referred to dialectics, the contradictions it contained and the successive 'leaps' by which it functioned never provided any example of a transcendence or a synthesis. Stalinist dialectics was merely the ideological cover for the ramblings of a short-sighted pragmatism. If Stalinism is Leninism *plus* administrative tyranny and *plus* bureaucratic terror, it is also Leninism *minus* dialectics. It is thus Leninism *impoverished* by being deprived of that leaven which has made of it, even in its mistakes, and in spite of its failures, one of the richest sources of inspiration in the fight for socialism, one of the most fruitful contributions to men's struggle for their emancipation.

Notes

Introduction

1 Pospelov, p. 9.
2 Kaplan, p. 371.
3 In Pipes, ed., *Revolutionary Russia*, p. 222.
4 Ulam, p. 232.
5 Bunyan, *Intervention*.
6 Meyer, p. 81.
7 Deutscher, *Prophet Armed*, p. viii.
8 Lenin, Vol. 29, pp. 87–8; Vol. 33, pp. 121–3 and 346–7.
9 Quoted in Cohn-Bendit, p. 200.

Part I: Chapter 1

1 Lenin, Vol. I, p. 294.
2 Ibid., Vol. 7, p. 415.
3 Ibid., Vol. 11, p. 320.
4 Ibid., Vol. 34, p. 346.
5 Ibid., Vol. 4, p. 321.
6 Rosa Luxemburg, 'Organisationsfragen der russischen Sozialdemokratie', in *Die Neue Zeit*, 1903–4: in *Rosa Luxemburg Speaks*, p. 115.
7 Lane, p. 99.
8 Lenin, Vol. 5, p. 442.
9 Lane, p. 66.
10 Lenin, Vol. 4, p. 218.
11 Ibid., Vol. 4, p. 224.
12 Ibid., Vol. 5, p. 22. My emphasis, M.L.
13 Schapiro, *Communist Party*, p. 39.
14 Broué, *Parti*, p. 30; Geyer, p. 340.
15 Lenin, Vol. 34, p. 137.
16 Getzler, p. 82. See also Keep, *Rise of Social-Democracy*, pp. 96 and 109, and Schapiro, *Communist Party*, p. 41.
17 Lenin, Vol. 7, p. 211.
18 Quoted in Haimson, p. 45.
19 Ibid., p. 68.
20 Martov, p. 68.
21 Getzler, pp. 47–8; Trotsky, *Nashi politicheskie zadachi*, p. 17.
22 Lenin, Vol. 5, pp. 374–5.
23 Ibid., Vol. 5, p. 387.
24 Liebman, p. 60.

25 Lenin, Vol. 5, p. 383.
26 Ibid., Vol. 5, p. 386.
27 Ibid., Vol. 5, p. 422.
28 Quoted by Nettl, Vol. I, p. 424.
29 Lenin, Vol. 5, pp. 384–5.
30 Ibid., Vol. 6, p. 491.
31 Ibid., Vol. 5, p. 396.
32 Ibid., Vol. 5, p. 396.
33 Ibid., Vol. 5, p. 446.
34 Ibid., Vol. 5, p. 475.
35 Ibid., Vol. 5, pp. 512–13.
36 Ibid., Vol. 4, p. 291.
37 Ibid., Vol. 9, p. 363.
38 Quoted in Carr, Vol. I, p. 18.
39 Lenin, Vol. 7, p. 260.
40 Ibid., Vol. 7, p. 262.
41 Ibid., Vol. 6, p. 502.
42 Ibid., Vol. 4, p. 280.
43 Ibid., Vol. 5, p. 460.
44 Ibid., Vol. 6, p. 476. My emphasis, M.L.
45 Ibid., Vol. 6, p. 244.
46 Martov, p. 84.
47 Lenin, Vol. 6, pp. 502–3.
48 Ibid., Vol. 7, p. 285.
49 Ibid., Vol. 7, p. 81.
50 Ibid., Vol. 4, p. 181.
51 Ibid., Vol. 5, pp. 475–6.
52 Quoted in Liebman, pp. 63–4.
53 Quoted in Wolfe, p. 64.
54 Dan, quoted in Hill, p. 43.
55 Lenin, Vol. 5, p. 450.
56 Ibid., Vol. 5, p. 452.
57 Ibid., Vol. 5, p. 472.
58 Ibid., Vol. 13, p. 103.
59 Ibid., Vol. 8, p. 453.
60 Ibid., Vol. 6, p. 194.
61 Ibid., Vol. 5, p. 462.
62 Ibid., Vol. 9, p. 29.
63 Ibid., Vol. 6, p. 195.
64 Ibid., Vol. 6, p. 175.
65 Ibid., Vol. 2, p. 347.
66 Ibid., Vol. 4, p. 215.
67 Ibid., Vol. 7, pp. 396–7.
68 Quoted by Deutscher, *Prophet Armed*, p. 48.
69 Lenin, Vol. 6, p. 236.
70 Ibid., Vol. 6, p. 251.

15

71 Ibid., Vol. 6, pp. 507–8.
72 Ibid., Vol. 5, p. 477.
73 Ibid., Vol. 5, p. 479.
74 Quoted in Getzler, p. 85.
75 Quoted in Geyer, p. 413.
76 Quoted by Hammond, p. 147.
77 Quoted by Keep, *Rise of Social-Democracy*, p. 141.
78 Quoted by Avtorkhanov, p. 13.
79 *Rosa Luxemburg Speaks*, pp. 116–17.
80 Ibid., p. 129.
81 Lenin, Vol. 8, p. 61.
82 Quoted by Baechler, p. 187.
83 Trotsky, *Nashi politicheskie zadachi*, p. 54 (quoted in Deutscher, *Prophet Armed*, p. 90).
84 Trotsky, *Nashi politicheskie zadachi*, pp. 74 and 95–8.
85 Lenin, Vol. 6, p. 247.
86 Lane, p. 102.
87 Lenin, Vol. 5, p. 452.
88 Ibid., Vol. 6, p. 237.
89 Ibid., Vol. 6, pp. 243–7.
90 Quoted by Broué, *Parti*, p. 63.
91 Quoted by Keep, *Rise of Social-Democracy*, p. 211.
92 Avtorkhanov, p. 3.
93 Pyatnitsky, p. 77.
94 Lenin, Vol. 8, pp. 216–19.
95 Martov, p. 135.
96 Keep, *Rise of Social-Democracy*, p. 54.
97 Schwarz, pp. 55 and 218.
98 Ibid., p. 219.
99 Lenin, Vol. 10, p. 36n.
100 Souvarine, p. 107.
101 Avtorkhanov, p. 77, and Broué, *Parti*, p. 36.
102 Keep, *Rise of Social-Democracy*, p. 288.
103 Lenin, Vol. 10, p. 99.
104 Ibid., Vol. 10, p. 32.
105 Ibid., Vol. 10, p. 29.
106 Ibid., Vol. 10, p. 34.
107 Schwarz, p. 242.
108 Lenin, Vol. 11, p. 173.
109 Ibid., Vol. 10, p. 258.
110 Ibid., Vol. 10, p. 259.
111 Ibid., Vol. 10, p. 31.
112 Ibid., Vol. 10, p. 32.
113 Ibid., Vol. 8, p. 505.
114 Ibid., Vol. 10, p. 33.
115 Martov, p. 150.
116 Lenin, Vol. 8, p. 409.
117 Ibid., Vol. 10, p. 33.
118 Ibid., Vol. 8, p. 444.
119 Ibid., Vol. 10, pp. 502–3.
120 Ibid., Vol. 12, p. 396.
121 Ibid., Vol. 10, p. 127.
122 Ibid., Vol. 11, p. 434.
123 Pyatnitsky, pp. 103–4.

124 Ibid., p. 90.
125 Lenin, Vol. 10, p. 46.
126 Ibid., Vol. 10, p. 163.
127 Ibid., Vol. 10, p. 376.
128 Ibid., Vol. 10, p. 443.
129 Ibid., Vol. 10, p. 380.
130 Ibid., Vol. 10, p. 381.
131 Ibid., Vol. 10, p. 314.
132 Ibid., Vol. 11, p. 266.
133 Ibid., Vol. 8, pp. 307, 446.
134 Ibid., Vol. 8, p. 434.
135 Ibid., Vol. 13, p. 159.
136 Ibid., Vol. 13, p. 323.
137 Ibid., Vol. 7, p. 298.
138 Ibid., Vol. 17, p. 226.
139 Ibid., Vol. 17, p. 275.
140 Ibid., Vol. 17, p. 332.
141 Ibid., Vol. 34, p. 421.
142 Krupskaya, p. 162.
143 Ibid., p. 168.
144 Pyatnitsky, pp. 177–8.
145 Lenin, Vol. 7, p. 526.
146 Quoted in Souvarine, p. 117.
147 Schapiro, *Communist Party*, p. 103.
148 Lenin, Vol. 17, p. 202.
149 Ulam, p. 256.
150 Lenin, Vol. 15, p. 153.
151 Ibid., Vol. 15, p. 448.
152 Ibid., Vol. 15, p. 354.
153 Ibid., Vol. 9, p. 258.
154 Daniels, *Conscience*, p. 18.
155 Ibid., pp. 23–5.
156 Lenin, Vol. 17, p. 271.
157 Ibid., Vol. 17, p. 217.
158 Ibid., Vol. 17, pp. 221–2.
159 Ibid., Vol. 17, p. 224.
160 Ibid., Vol. 15, p. 459; Vol. 16, pp. 159, 193.
161 See e.g., ibid., Vol. 16, pp. 100, 289; Vol. 17, p. 203.
162 Ibid., Vol. 12, pp. 425–6.
163 Ibid., Vol. 17, pp. 228, 257 ff.
164 Ibid., Vol. 17, p. 276.
165 Ibid., Vol. 17, p. 45.
166 Ibid., Vol. 17, p. 219n.
167 Ibid., Vol. 20, p. 525.
168 Wolfe, Chapter 31.
169 Lenin, Vol. 19, p. 492.
170 Ibid., Vol. 19, p. 173.

Part I: Chapter 2

1 Marx, *Class Struggles in France, 1848–1850*, in *Selected Works*, Vol. I, p. 214.
2 Lenin, Vol. I, p. 290.
3 Ibid., Vol. 15, p. 186.
4 Ibid., Vol. 19, p. 91.
5 Ibid., Vol. 2, pp. 96–7.

6 E.g., ibid., Vol. 4, pp. 402, 416, 418, and Vol. 5, p. 325.
7 Ibid., Vol. 1, pp. 293–4.
8 Ibid., Vol. 1, p. 291.
9 Ibid., Vol. 2, p. 119.
10 Ibid., Vol. 4, p. 266.
11 Keep, *Rise of Social-Democracy*, p. 185.
12 Getzler, p. 51.
13 Lenin, Vol. 2, p. 334.
14 Ibid., Vol. 5, p. 362.
15 Martov, p. 98; Wolfe, p. 281; Getzler, p. 98.
16 Lenin, Vol. 7, p. 507.
17 Ibid., Vol. 7, p. 502.
18 Ibid., Vol. 7, p. 507.
19 Deutscher, *Prophet Armed*, p. 88.
20 Getzler, p. 97.
21 Lenin, Vol. 10, p. 289.
22 Ibid., Vol. 8, p. 258.
23 Ibid., Vol. 7, p. 506.
24 Ibid., Vol. 8, p. 88.
25 Ibid., Vol. 8, p. 575.
26 Ibid., Vol. 9, p. 126.
27 Ibid., Vol. 11, p. 385.
28 Ibid., Vol. 9, p. 219.
29 Ibid., Vol. 7, p. 501.
30 Ibid., Vol. 11, p. 59.
31 Ibid., Vol. 10, p. 159.
32 Ibid., Vol. 9, p. 240.
33 Ibid., Vol. 13, p. 73.
34 Ibid., Vol. 9, p. 46.
35 Ibid., Vol. 10, p. 448.
36 Ibid., Vol. 10, pp. 483–4.
37 Ibid., Vol. 11, pp. 433 ff.
38 Wolfe, p. 523.
39 Martov, pp. 185–6.
40 Dan, in Martov, p. 235.
41 Lenin, Vol. 10, p. 218.
42 Ibid., Vol. 13, p. 129.
43 Ibid., Vol. 16, p. 35.
44 Ibid., Vol. 11, p. 145.
45 Ibid., Vol. 11, p. 416.
46 Ibid., Vol. 18, p. 384.
47 Ibid., Vol. 13, p. 42.
48 Martov, pp. 195–6.
49 Ibid., p. 212.
50 Lenin, Vol. 12, p. 162.
51 Ibid., Vol. 11, pp. 23, 310–11, 312, and Vol. 17, pp. 469, 490.
52 Ibid., Vol. 12, note 183.
53 Ibid., Vol. 15, pp. 439–40.
54 Schapiro, *Communist Party*, p. 103.
55 Lenin, Vol. 10, p. 304.
56 Ulam, p. 388; Wolfe, pp. 546–7; Pospelov, p. 204.
57 Carr, Vol. II, pp. 388–93.
58 Lenin, Vol. 9, p. 48.
59 Getzler, p. 102; Lenin, Vol. 9, p. 82.
60 Lenin, Vol. 10, p. 221.

61 Ibid., Vol. 12, pp. 464–5.
62 Ibid., Vol. 9, p. 99.
63 The Menshevik organ *Nashe Dyelo*, quoted in ibid., Vol. 11, p. 249.
64 Ibid., Vol. 11, pp. 91–2.
65 Quoted in ibid., Vol. 13, p. 118.
66 Ibid., Vol. 8, p. 539.
67 Ibid., Vol. 8, pp. 384–5.
68 Ibid., Vol. 8, p. 294.
69 Ibid., Vol. 8, p. 465.
70 Ibid., Vol. 9, p. 56.
71 Ibid., Vol. 10, p. 243.
72 Ibid., Vol. 10, p. 244.
73 Ibid., Vol. 10, p. 244–5.
74 Engels, Introduction to *The Civil War in France*: in Marx and Engels, *Selected Works*, Vol. II, p. 189.
75 Lenin, Vol. 9, p. 48.
76 Ibid., Vol. 9, p. 48.
77 Trotsky, *1905*, p. 315.
78 Trotsky, *Results*, pp. 194–5.
79 Ibid., p. 195.
80 Ibid., p. 202.
81 Ibid., p. 197.
82 Ibid., p. 205.
83 Ibid., pp. 233–4.
84 Ibid., pp. 236–7.
85 Ibid., p. 237.
86 Trotsky, *1905*, p. 317 (Article in *Przeglad Socjal-Demokratyczny*.)
87 Lenin, Vol. 15, p. 371.
88 Ibid., Vol. 12, p. 470.
89 Deutscher, *Prophet Armed*, p. 162.
90 Joffe, pp. 5–6.
91 Lenin, Vol. 8, p. 465.
92 Ibid., Vol. 10, p. 92.

Part I: Chapter 3

1 Krupskaya, pp. 126–7.
2 Keep, *Rise of Social-Democracy*, p. 210.
3 Ibid., p. 211.
4 Schwarz, p. 219.
5 Lenin, Vol. 8, p. 411.
6 Keep, *Rise of Social-Democracy*, p. 211.
7 Krupskaya, p. 127.
8 Lenin, Vol. 34, p. 296.
9 Ibid., Vol. 8, p. 146.
10 Keep, *Rise of Social-Democracy*, p. 210.
11 Lenin, Vol. 9, pp. 344–5.
12 Schwarz, p. 175.
13 Getzler, p. 108.
14 Lenin, Vol. 9, p. 184.
15 Carr, Vol. I, p. 47.
16 Keep, *Rise of Social-Democracy*, p. 231.

17 Lane, p. 88.
18 Keep, *Rise of Social-Democracy*, p. 231.
19 Schwarz, p. 179.
20 Ibid., p. 180.
21 Ibid., p. 181.
22 Ibid., p. 187. In Odessa a Bolshevik leader recorded that 'the Soviet was organized almost without my being aware of it', adding that 'the Bolshevik Committee never discussed questions connected with a Soviet' (Pyatnitsky, p. 92).
23 Lenin, Vol. 10, p. 19.
24 Ibid., Vol. 10, p. 21.
25 Ibid., Vol. 10, p. 24.
26 Ibid., Vol. 9, p. 306.
27 Ibid., Vol. 11, pp. 156–8.
28 Ibid., Vol. 12, p. 143.
29 Ibid., Vol. 10, p. 203.
30 Ibid., Vol. 11, p. 124.
31 Trotsky, *1905*, p. 251.
32 Quoted in Schwarz, p. 67.
33 Ibid., p. 55.
34 Ibid., pp. 56–64.
35 Ibid., p. 69.
36 Ibid., p. 70.
37 Lenin, Vol. 8, pp. 90–93.
38 Ibid., pp. 97–8.
39 Schwarz, p. 70.
40 Krupskaya, pp. 111–12.
41 Ibid., pp. 112–13.
42 Ponomarev, p. 88.
43 Ibid., p. 94.
44 Ibid., p. 107.
45 Lenin, Vol. 11, p. 173.
46 Ibid., Vol. 13, p. 26.
47 Schwarz, p. 133.
48 Ibid., p. 134.
49 Lane, p. 153.
50 Keep, *Rise of Social-Democracy*, pp. 248–9.
51 Ibid., p. 188.
52 Lenin, Vol. 6, p. 236.
53 Ibid., Vol. 8, p. 28.
54 Ibid., Vol. 8, p. 64.
55 Ibid., Vol. 11, p. 220.
56 Ibid., Vol. 8, p. 370.
57 Ibid., Vol. 8, p. 349.
58 Ibid., Vol. 8, p. 538.
59 Ibid., Vol. 9, pp. 344–6.
60 Ibid., Vol. 9, p. 424.

Part I: Chapter 4

1 Quoted in Lenin, Vol. 16, p. 374.
2 Quoted in ibid., Vol. 18, pp. 182–3.
3 Quoted in Carr, Vol. I, p. 40.
4 Lenin, Vol. 18, p. 184.
5 Ibid., Vol. 8, p. 288.
6 Ibid., Vol. 11, p. 142.
7 Trotsky, *The New Course*, p. 50.
8 See the document included as an appendix in Trotsky, *Nos tâches politiques*, pp. 245–7.
9 Lenin, Vol. 2, p. 343.
10 Ibid., Vol. 5, p. 375.
11 Lane, pp. 26, 47–8.
12 Lenin, Vol. 34, p. 379.
13 Ibid., Vol. 9, p. 347.
14 Ibid., Vol. 7, p. 269.
15 Ibid., Vol. 10, p. 398.
16 Ibid., Vol. 7, pp. 391–2.
17 Ibid., Vol. 7, p. 269.
18 Ibid., Vol. 7, p. 404.
19 Ibid., Vol. 9, p. 108.
20 As regards the social composition of the Menshevik and Bolshevik factions, E. H. Carr notes that the former

> found their adherents among the most highly-skilled and organized workers, the printers, the railwaymen and the steelworkers in the modern industrial centres of the south, whereas the Bolsheviks drew their main support from the relatively unskilled labour of the mass industries—the old-fashioned heavy industry of the Petersburg region and the textile factories of Petersburg and Moscow (Carr, Vol. I, pp. 40–41).

Lunacharsky points out in his memoirs the difference that there was, before the revolution, between the Menshevik and Bolshevik intellectuals. Lenin's supporters were numerous among the professional revolutionaries. 'These were largely made up of intellectuals of an obviously different type—not academic Marxist professors and students but people who had committed themselves irrevocably to their profession—revolution' (Lunacharsky, pp. 37–8). David Lane, in a book containing very useful economic and sociological data, adds that the workers who were found in the ranks of the Bolsheviks were mostly of more recent peasant origin than the Menshevik workers. It remains true that petty-bourgeois elements were more numerous among the Mensheviks, and this helps to explain the more proletarian character of the Bolshevik electorate (Lane, pp. 50 and 209). It is to be noted, too, that the average age of the Mensheviks, especially among the leaders, was considerably higher than among the Bolsheviks (ibid., p. 214).

21 Keep, *Rise of Social-Democracy*, p. 143.

22 Trotsky, *Nashi politicheskie zadachi*, pp. 37–8.

23 Lenin, Vol. 7, p. 479, and Vol. 8, p. 60.

24 Ibid., Vol. 20, p. 268.

25 See on this subject G. Fischer.

26 Meyer, pp. 79–80.

27 Lenin, Vol. 8, p. 565.

28 Ibid., Vol. 9, p. 203.

29 Ibid., Vol. 9, p. 284.

30 Ibid., Vol. 9, pp. 345–6.

31 Ibid., Vol. 18, p. 107.

32 Ibid., Vol. 9, p. 41.

33 Ibid., Vol. 11, p. 462.

34 Ibid., Vol. 11, p. 216.

35 See 'Guerilla warfare', in ibid., Vol. 11, pp. 213–23.

36 Souvarine, pp. 101–3. For a brief biography of Ter-Petrosyan see also Haupt and Marie, pp. 138–41.

37 Lukács, *History and Class-Consciousness*, p. 297.

38 Lenin, Vol. 9, p. 113.

39 Ibid., Vol. 11, pp. 360–61.

40 Ibid., Vol. 15, p. 25.

41 Ibid., Vol. 16, p. 339.

42 Ibid., Vol. 11, p. 221.

Part II: Introductory section

1 Lenin, Vol. 21, pp. 32–3.

2 Rosenberg, p. 75.

3 Lenin, Vol. 35, p. 279: 'It was interesting to see "live" people, not corroded by emigrant life.'

4 Ibid., Vol. 35, p. 266.

5 Ibid., Vol. 23, p. 253.

Part II: Chapter 1

1 Marie, p. 16, quoting Shlyapnikov.

2 Ibid., p. 37, quoting Kayurov.

3 Sukhanov, p. 24.

4 Marie, p. 29, quoting Kayurov.

5 Ibid., p. 30, quoting Kayurov.

6 Ferro, *February*, p. 37.

7 Ibid., p. 39.

8 Katkov, p. 264.

9 Marie, p. 36, quoting Kayurov.

10 Ferro, *February*, p. 40.

11 Ibid., p. 344.

12 Marie, p. 26, quoting Shlyapnikov.

13 Liebman, p. 112.

14 Ibid., p. 112.

15 Ferro, *February*, pp. 44 and 74.

16 Sukhanov, p. 38.

17 Ferro, *February*, p. 172.

18 See on this point the thoughts of one of the chief negotiators on behalf of the Soviet, namely, Sukhanov, p. 8.

19 Gorky, *History*, Vol. I, p. 122.

20 Sukhanov, p. 7.

21 Ibid., p. 108.

22 Soria, p. 76.

23 Carr, Vol. I, p. 74.

24 Ibid., Vol. I, pp. 73–4.

25 Stalin, Vol. 3, p. 1.

26 Ferro, *February*, p. 175.

27 Carr, Vol. I, p. 75.

28 Stalin, Vol. 3, p. 8.

29 Quoted in Souvarine, p. 151, and Trotsky, *History*, pp. 305–6.

30 Ferro, *February*, p. 176; Souvarine, p. 152.

31 Daniels, *Conscience*, pp. 41–2.

32 Ferro, *February*, p. 176.

33 Marie, pp. 41–2 (quoting from Stalin's report of March 29th, 1917, as given in *Voprosy Istorii K.P.S.S.*, no. 5 of 1962).

34 Rabinowitch, p. 38.

35 Reisberg, p. 103.

36 Lenin, Vol. 35, p. 309.

37 Ibid., Vol. 35, p. 299.

38 Ibid., Vol. 23, p. 292.

39 Ibid., Vol. 23, p. 289.

40 Ibid., Vol. 23, p. 287.

41 Ibid., Vol. 23, p. 303.

42 Ibid., Vol. 23, p. 323.

43 Ibid., Vol. 23, p. 288.

44 Ibid., Vol. 23, p. 334.

45 Ibid., Vol. 23, p. 305.

46 Ibid., Vol. 23, p. 340.

47 Ibid., Vol. 23, pp. 290 and 324.

48 Ibid., Vol. 35, p. 298.

49 Ibid., Vol. 35, p. 309.

50 Ibid., Vol. 35, p. 310.

51 Trotsky, *History*, p. 335.

52 Ibid., p. 335.

53 Lenin, Vol. 23, pp. 289–90.

54 Ibid., Vol. 23, p. 325.

55 Ibid., Vol. 23, p. 326.

56 Ibid., Vol. 35, p. 299.

57 The house of the ballerina Kshesinskaya was at this time the headquarters of the Bolshevik Party in Petrograd.

58 Sukhanov, p. 280.

59 Ibid., p. 288.

60 Drabkina, in *Proletarskaya Revolyutsiya*, No. 4 of 1927, quoted in Daniels, *Conscience*, p. 43.

61 Quoted in Souvarine, p. 154.
62 Abramovich, p. 30, quoting the memoirs of G. Denicke.
63 Lenin, Vol. 24, p. 23.
64 Ibid., Vol. 24, p. 23.
65 Ibid., Vol. 24, p. 22.
66 Ibid., Vol. 24, p. 24.
67 Ibid., Vol. 36, pp. 436, 437, 438, 443, 447.
68 Ibid., Vol. 24, p. 50.
69 Ibid., Vol. 24, p. 45.
70 Ibid., Vol. 24, p. 141.
71 Quoted by Souvarine, p. 156; also by Trotsky, *History*, p. 338.
72 Lenin, Vol. 24, p. 44.
73 Ibid., Vol. 24, p. 149.
74 Marie, p. 58, quoting Kollontai.
75 Golikov, p. 107.
76 Reisberg, p. 113, and Golikov, p. 108.
77 Lenin, Vol. 24, p. 21.
78 Sukhanov, p. 289: also quoted in Trotsky, *History*, pp. 326–7; Carr Vol. I, p. 81; Reisberg, p. 115; and, Daniels, *Conscience*, pp. 43–4.
79 Golikov, p. 112.
80 Rabinowitch, p. 40.
81 Ibid., p. 257.
82 Trotsky, *History*, p. 341.
83 Daniels, *Conscience*, p. 44.
84 Lenin, Vol. 24, p. 270.
85 Carr, Vol. I, p. 83.
86 Lenin, Vol. 24, pp. 274–5.
87 Carr, Vol. I, p. 83.
88 Lenin, Vol. 24, p. 294.
89 Schapiro, *Origin*, p. 39.
90 Lenin, Vol. 24, pp. 309–11.
91 Carr, Vol. I, p. 84.
92 Sukhanov, p. 290.
93 Lenin, Vol. 24, p. 312.
94 Ibid., Vol. 26, pp. 19–21.
95 Ibid., Vol. 26, p. 26.
96 Quoted in Daniels, *Red October*, p. 54. Bukharin's account is to be found in Trotsky, *History*, p. 984. See also Odom, p. 432.
97 See *Protokoly*, p. 55. The episode is described in Deutscher, *Stalin*, p. 159, and Schapiro, *Origin*, p. 57.
98 Quoted in Trotsky, *History*, p. 984.
99 Sukhanov, p. 490.
100 Rabinowitch, p. 220.
101 *Protokoly*, pp. 69–71.
102 Lenin, Vol. 26, pp. 69 ff.
103 Ibid., Vol. 26, pp. 74, 77, 81–2.
104 Ibid., Vol. 26, p. 84.
105 Ibid., Vol. 26, pp. 140–41.
106 *Pervuy legal'ny Peterburgsky komitet ...*, p. 295.
107 Ibid., p. 297.
108 Trotsky, *History*, pp. 1124–35.
109 Lenin, Vol. 26, pp. 182–7.
110 Ibid., Vol. 26, p. 189.
111 Ibid., Vol. 26, p. 190, and n. 78.
112 Daniels, *Red October*, p. 98.
113 Ibid., p. 90.
114 Ibid., pp. 90–91.
115 Lenin, Vol. 26, pp. 193–4, and n.; *Protokoly*, pp. 93–105; see also Gorky, *History*, Vol. II, p. 187.
116 Lenin, Vol. 26, pp. 202, 204, 208.
117 Daniels, *Red October*, pp. 99–100.
118 Ibid., p. 141.
119 *Protokoly*, pp. 115–16.
120 Lenin, Vol. 26, p. 217.
121 Ibid., Vol. 26, pp. 225–6.
122 *Protokoly*, pp. 106–15.
123 Lenin, Vol. 26, p. 234.
124 Ibid., Vol. 43, p. 638.
125 Rabinowitch, pp. 44–5.
126 See Liebman, pp. 178–86.
127 Rabinowitch, pp. 56–9.
128 Ibid., pp. 79–80 and 265.
129 Ibid., pp. 86–90.
130 Ibid., pp. 112 ff. and 126 ff.
131 Ibid., p. 226. This remark is also quoted by V. I. Nevsky in Knyazev and Konstantinov, p. 231.
132 Rabinowitch, p. 124.
133 Trotsky, *History*, p. 843.
134 Lenin, Vol. 24, p. 42.
135 Ibid., Vol. 26, p. 57.
136 Trotsky, *History*, p. 843.
137 Rabinowitch, p. 67.
138 Daniels, *Conscience*, p. 45.
139 Reisberg, p. 125.
140 *Protokoly*, p. 27.
141 Gorky, *History*, Vol. I, p. 188.
142 Lenin, Vol. 24, p. 543.
143 Ibid., Vol. 24, p. 545.
144 Ibid., Vol. 24, p. 553.
145 Ibid., Vol. 24, p. 554.
146 Rabinowitch, p. 155.
147 *Protokoly*, p. 4.
148 Ibid., p. 16.
149 Rabinowitch, p. 134.
150 *Protokoly*, pp. 23, 24, 25.
151 Ibid., pp. 27, 33, 36, 47.
152 Rabinowitch, p. 151.
153 Ibid., pp. 151–2.
154 *Protokoly*, p. 40.
155 On the lack of effective centralization during the events of 1917, see Keep, 'October in the Provinces', pp. 180 et seq.; also Schapiro, *Communist Party*, p. 174.
156 Gorky, *History*, Vol. II, p. 58.
157 Ferro, *February*, pp. 170–71.
158 Yaroslavsky, p. 132.
159 Rabinowitch, p. 92.
160 Schapiro, *Communist Party*, p. 172.

161 Gorky, *History*, Vol. I, p. 169;
     Golikov, p. 113; Schapiro, *Communist Party*, p. 173.
162 Schapiro, *Communist Party*, p. 171.
163 Sukhanov, p. 525.
164 *Protokoly*, p. 94.
165 Rigby, pp. 61–3.
166 Lenin, Vol. 26, p. 32.
167 Ibid., Vol. 21, p. 312; Vol. 22, p. 120;
     Vol. 35, p. 200.
168 Ibid., Vol. 35, p. 288.
169 Deutscher, *Prophet Armed*, p. 257,
     n. 2.
170 Carr, Vol. I, p. 91, n. 2.
171 Deutscher, *Prophet Armed*, p. 258.
172 Daniels, *Conscience*, p. 29.
173 Broué, *Parti*, p. 88.
174 Quoted in ibid., p. 89.
175 Lenin, Vol. 24, p. 84.
176 Ibid., Vol. 24, p. 147.
177 Ibid., Vol. 24, p. 88.

Part II: Chapter 2

1 Quoted by Ferro, *February*, pp. 76–7.
2 Sukhanov, p. 428; Liebman, p. 180.
3 Sukhanov, p. 490.
4 Lenin, Vol. 24, p. 211.
5 Ibid., Vol. 24, pp. 210–11.
6 Ibid., Vol. 24, pp. 244–5.
7 Ibid., Vol. 24, p. 40.
8 Ibid., Vol. 24, p. 185.
9 E.g., ibid., Vol. 24, pp. 145, 216, 312;
   Vol. 41, p. 433.
10 Plamenatz, p. 238.
11 Lenin, Vol. 36, p. 435.
12 Ibid., Vol. 24, p. 207.
13 An expression used in Victor Fay,
   'La tragédie des vieux-bolchéviks',
   in Fay, p. 39.
14 Quoted by Reisberg, p. 115.
15 Lenin, Vol. 24, p. 127.
16 Ibid., Vol. 24, p. 163; see also p. 201
   and *passim*.
17 Ibid., Vol. 24, p. 62.
18 Ibid., Vol. 24, p. 145; see also p. 22.
19 Ibid., Vol. 24, p. 201.
20 On the June events, see Ferro,
   February, pp. 310 ff.; Liebman,
   pp. 164 ff.; Rabinowitch, pp. 57 ff.;
   Reisberg, pp. 139 ff.
21 Rabinowitch, p. 57.
22 Trotsky, *History*, p. 453.
23 Ferro, *February*, p. 311.
24 Rabinowitch, p. 77; Reisberg, p. 77.
25 Lenin, Vol. 25, pp. 79–80.
26 Liebman, pp. 167–8.
27 Lenin, Vol. 25, p. 149.
28 Rabinowitch, pp. 184–5.

29 Ibid., p. 215.
30 Lenin, Vol. 25, p. 171.
31 Ibid., Vol. 25, p. 250.
32 Trotsky, *History*, p. 1130.
33 Lenin, Vol. 25, p. 177.
34 Ibid., Vol. 25, p. 178.
35 Engels, 'Germany: Revolution and
   Counter-Revolution', in Marx and
   Engels, *Selected Works*, Vol. I,
   p. 377.
36 Lenin, Vol. 41, p. 442.
37 Ibid., Vol. 26, p. 22.
38 Ibid., Vol. 26, p. 134.
39 Ibid., Vol. 26, p. 21.
40 Ibid., Vol. 26, p. 19.
41 Ibid., Vol. 26, p. 24.
42 Ibid., Vol. 26, p. 137.
43 Ibid., Vol. 26, p. 80.
44 Sorlin, p. 61.
45 Ibid., p. 61.
46 Lenin, Vol. 26, p. 74.
47 Chamberlin, Vol. I, p. 302.
48 Lenin, Vol. 26, p. 79.
49 *Protokoly*, p. 94.
50 Lenin, Vol. 25, p. 177.
51 Ibid., Vol. 26, pp. 22–3.
52 Ibid., Vol. 26, p. 35.
53 Chamberlin, Vol. I, p. 279.
54 Sukhanov, p. 519.
55 Trotsky, *History*, p. 1031.
56 Sukhanov, pp. 584–5.
57 Trotsky, *History*, p. 966.
58 Lenin, Vol. 26, p. 84.
59 Ibid., Vol. 26, p. 27.
60 Ibid., Vol. 26, pp. 83–4.
61 Ibid., Vol. 26, p. 180.
62 Ibid., Vol. 26, pp. 180–81.
63 Knyazev and Konstantinov, pp. 25 ff.
64 Lenin, Vol. 26, pp. 21, 22.
65 Chamberlin, p. 300.
66 Knyazev and Konstantinov, p. 39.
67 Golikov, p. 264.
68 Gorky, *History*, Vol. II, p. 208.
69 Chamberlin, Vol. I, p. 307.
70 Trotsky, *History*, p. 1074.
71 Ibid., p. 1146.
72 Ibid., p. 1142.
73 Liebman, p. 308.
74 Lenin, Vol. 27, p. 33.
75 Ibid., Vol. 21, p. 402.
76 Ibid., Vol. 21, p. 420.
77 Ibid., Vol. 23, p. 373.
78 Ibid., Vol. 23, p. 290.
79 Ibid., Vol. 23, p. 307.
80 Ibid., Vol. 24, pp. 45–6.
81 Ibid., Vol. 24, p. 36.
82 Ibid., Vol. 25, p. 329.
83 Ibid., Vol. 26, p. 65.
84 Ibid., Vol. 25, pp. 20–21.
85 Ibid., Vol. 25, p. 43.

86 Ibid., Vol. 24, p. 426.
87 Ibid., Vol. 24, p. 23.
88 Ibid., Vol. 24, pp. 169, 293, 477–8.
89 Ibid., Vol. 25, p. 281.
90 Ibid., Vol. 24, p. 72.
91 Ibid., Vol. 24, pp. 47, 72, 103–4 and passim.
92 On the agrarian policy of the Bolsheviks in 1917, see Sharapov.
93 Lenin, Vol. 26, p. 26.
94 Ibid., Vol. 24, p. 46.
95 Ibid., Vol. 24, p. 246.
96 Ibid., Vol. 25, p. 306.
97 Ibid., Vol. 26, p. 94.
98 Ibid., Vol. 23, p. 325.
99 Ibid., Vol. 23, p. 326.
100 Ibid., Vol. 24, p. 278.
101 Ibid., Vol. 24, p. 323.
102 Ibid., Vol. 24, p. 471.
103 Ibid., Vol. 41, p. 405.
104 Ibid., Vol. 24, p. 373.
105 Ibid., Vol. 24, pp. 373–4.
106 Ibid., Vol. 24, p. 471.
107 Ibid., Vol. 24, p. 471.
108 Ibid., Vol. 24, p. 472.
109 Kautsky, Der Weg zur Macht, p. 105.
110 Lenin, Vol. 22, p. 189.
111 Kautsky, Nationalstaat.
112 Lenin, Vol. 22, p. 255.
113 Ibid., Vol. 22. p. 300.
114 Ibid., Vol. 22, p. 187.
115 Ibid., Vol. 22, p. 205.
116 Ibid., Vol. 26, p. 140.
117 Ibid., Vol. 26, p. 182.
118 Ibid., Vol. 26, p. 192.
119 Ibid., Vol. 24, p. 227.
120 Protokoly, p. 89.
112 Lenin, Vol. 23, p. 370.
122 Ibid., Vol. 24, p. 165.
123 Ibid., Vol. 24, p. 419.
124 Ibid., Vol. 24, p. 420.
125 Ibid., Vol. 25, p. 315.
126 Ibid., Vol. 25, p. 315. A similar statement appears in Vol. 26, p. 25.
127 Ibid., Vol. 26, p. 63.
128 Trotsky, My Life, p. 332.
129 Ibid., p. 332.
130 Daniels, Conscience, p. 38.

Part II: Chapter 3

1 Lenin, Vol. 26, pp. 57–8.
2 Ibid., Vol. 26, p. 22.
3 Ibid., Vol. 36, p. 439.
4 Ibid., Vol. 24, p. 364.
5 Ibid., Vol. 25, p. 402.
6 Ibid., Vol. 25, pp. 422–3.
7 Ibid., Vol. 25, pp. 451–2 and 473–4.
8 Ibid., Vol. 25, p. 412.
9 Ibid., Vol. 25, p. 413.
10 Ibid., Vol. 25, pp. 461–2.
11 Ibid., Vol. 25, pp. 413–32, 441, 449–452, 461.
12 Ibid., Vol. 25, p. 402.
13 Ibid., Vol. 25, p. 463.
14 Ibid., Vol. 25, p. 397.
15 Ibid., Vol. 25, p. 438.
16 Ibid., Vol. 25, p. 441.
17 Ibid., Vol. 25, p. 463.
18 Ibid., Vol. 25, p. 456.
19 Ibid., Vol. 25, pp. 487–8.
20 Ibid., Vol. 25, p. 425.
21 Ibid., Vol. 25, pp. 420–21.
22 Ibid., Vol. 25, p. 473.
23 Ibid., Vol. 25, p. 426.
24 Ibid., Vol. 26, p. 113.
25 Ibid., Vol. 26, p. 126.
26 Ibid., Vol. 26, p. 127.
27 Sukhanov, pp. 287, 289, 526, 530, 553, 570.
28 Lenin, Vol. 24, pp. 146, 319, and passim.
29 Ibid., Vol. 26, p. 475.
30 Rabinowitch, pp. 100–102.
31 Ibid., p. 62.
32 Marie, p. 73, quoting Raskolnikov.
33 Ferro, February, p. 233.
34 Avrich, Anarchists, p. 143.
35 Ibid., p. 129.
36 Voline, Nineteen-Seventeen, p. 69.
37 Avrich, Anarchists, p. 132.
38 Voline, Nineteen-Seventeen, p. 70.
39 Guérin, p. 82.
40 Ibid., p. 87.
41 Lenin, Vol. 26, p. 22.
42 Rabinowitch, p. 188.
43 Lenin, Vol. 26, p. 210.
44 Trotsky, History, p. 521.
45 Rabinowitch, p. 112.
46 Pervuy legal'ny Peterburgsky Komitet, p. 261.
47 Protokoly, p. 74.
48 Lenin, Vol. 26, p. 58.
49 Ferro, 'Pourquoi Février? Pourquoi Octobre?', p. 13.
50 Sukhanov, p. 391.
51 Reed, p. 12.
52 Krupskaya, pp. 351–2.
53 Reed, p. 12.
54 Quoted in Liebman, p. 138 [I have changed 'feast' to 'festival'—Trans.].
55 Reed, p. 12.
56 Ibid., pp. 11–12.
57 Ibid., pp. 12–13.
58 Quoted in Liebman, p. 327.
59 Ferro, February, p. 170.
60 Ibid., p. 171.
61 The Menshevik S. Schwarz, quoted in Avrich, Anarchists, p. 141.

62 Ferro, *February*, pp. 321–2.
63 Sukhanov, p. 113.
64 Ferro, *February*, p. 193.
65 See in this connexion Kaplan, especially Chapters 2 and 3.
66 Sukhanov, p. 522.
67 Quoted in Trotsky, *History*, p. 736.
68 Ibid., p. 734.
69 Sorlin, p. 58.
70 Ibid., p. 29.
71 Rabinowitch, p. 267.
72 Reisberg, p. 133.
73 Ibid., p. 133
74 Ferro, *February*, p. 234; Sukhanov, p. 497.
75 Ferro, *February*, p. 234.
76 *Protokoly*, p. 267 (note 135).
77 Kaplan, p. 83.
78 Sukhanov, p. 529.
79 Kaplan, p. 50.
80 See Liebman, pp. 161–4.

Part III: Introductory section

1 Lenin, Vol. 26, pp. 480–82.
2 Ibid., Vol. 26, p. 459.
3 Ibid., Vol. 31, p. 454.
4 Ibid., Vol. 27, p. 101.
5 Ibid., Vol. 27, p. 430.
6 Souvarine, p. 199.
7 Marie, pp. 132–3, quoting Shlikhter.
8 Lenin, Vol. 27, p. 514.
9 Ibid., Vol. 28, p. 440.
10 Ibid., Vol. 30, p. 227.
11 Ibid., Vol. 30, p. 228.
12 Ibid., Vol. 31, p. 501.
13 Ibid., Vol. 32, p. 289.
14 Ibid., Vol. 32, p. 444.

Part III: Chapter 1

1 Lenin, Vol. 26, p. 115.
2 Carr, Vol. II, p. 46.
3 Sharapov, p. 201; Price, p. 265.
4 Sharapov, p. 161.
5 Lenin, Vol. 33, p. 303.
6 Carr, Vol. III, p. 26; Serge, *Year One*, p. 110.
7 Radkey, *Sickle*, pp. 88 and 343–4.
8 Nove, p. 54; Kritsman, p. 62; Carr, Vol. II, pp. 81–3.
9 Dobb, p. 90.
10 Ransome, p. 19.
11 Serge, *Year One*, p. 94.
12 Fitzpatrick, p. 26.
13 Quoted in Getzler, p. 172.
14 Reed, p. 149.
15 Price, p. 155.
15*

16 Ibid., p. 192.
17 Anweiler, pp. 274–5, 298.
18 Broué, *Parti*, p. 108.
19 Carr, Vol. I, p. 146.
20 Kritsman, p. 128.
21 Meyer, p. 185.
22 Lenin, op. cit., Vol. 26, p. 261.
23 Ibid., Vol. 26, p. 288.
24 Ibid., Vol. 26, p. 297.
25 Ibid., Vol. 26, p. 409 (first published, January 1929).
26 Ibid., Vol. 26, p. 468.
27 Ibid., Vol. 26, pp. 476–7.
28 Ibid., Vol. 27, p. 135.
29 Ibid., Vol. 26, p. 466.
30 Ibid., Vol. 27, p. 126.
31 Ibid., Vol. 27, p. 147.
32 Ibid., Vol. 27, p. 148.
33 Ibid., Vol. 29, p. 356.
34 Ibid., Vol. 29, p. 389.
35 Ibid., Vol. 27, p. 133.
36 Ibid., Vol. 27, p. 133.
37 Ibid., Vol. 27, p. 154.
38 Ibid., Vol. 27, p. 272.
39 Ibid., Vol. 27, p. 153.
40 Ibid., Vol. 27, p. 273.
41 Ibid., Vol. 27, p. 148.
42 A. Camus, preface (p. 12) to Rosmer, *Moscou sous Lénine*. (This preface is not included in the English translation of Rosmer's book, *Lenin's Moscow*.)
43 Sobolev, p. 392.
44 Ibid., p. 392.
45 Nove, p. 55.
46 Carr, Vol. II, p. 119.
47 Sadoul, p. 318.
48 Carr, Vol. II, p. 193.
49 Lenin, Vol. 28, p. 72.
50 Ibid., Vol. 29, p. 107.
51 Ibid., Vol. 28, p. 140.
52 Ibid., Vol. 28, p. 383.
53 Ibid., Vol. 29, p. 72.
54 Ibid., Vol. 27, p. 244.
55 Ibid., Vol. 27, pp. 395–6.
56 Ibid., Vol. 27, p. 403.
57 Ibid., Vol. 27, p. 439.
58 Ibid., Vol. 27, p. 485.
59 Ibid., Vol. 28, p. 297.
60 Ibid., Vol. 30, p. 33.
61 Ibid., Vol. 27, p. 398.
62 Ibid., Vol. 42, p. 170.
63 Ibid., Vol. 27, p. 45.
64 Ibid., Vol. 27, p. 46.
65 Ibid., Vol. 27, p. 99.
66 Ibid., Vol. 27, p. 109.
67 Ibid., Vol. 27, p. 101.
68 Ibid., Vol. 27, p. 245.
69 Ibid., Vol. 27, pp. 323–4
70 Carr, Vol. I, p. 130.

71 Quoted in Pietsch, p. 76.
72 Ibid., p. 80.
73 Carr, Vol. I, p. 132.
74 Pietsch, p. 77.
75 Ibid., p. 79.
76 Ibid., p. 94.
77 Ibid., p. 102.
78 Schapiro, *Origin*, p. 172.
79 Bukharin and Preobrazhensky, p. 240.
80 Anweiler, p. 297.
81 Lenin, Vol. 29, p. 183.
82 Pietsch, pp. 116–17.
83 Ibid., pp. 120–36.
84 Getzler, p. 201.
85 Schapiro, *Origin*, p. 361.
86 Aron, p. 194.
87 Lenin, Vol. 26, p. 247.
88 Ibid., Vol. 26, p. 262.
89 Anweiler, pp. 261–2.
90 *Protokoly*, pp. 160–61.
91 Radkey, *Elections*, p. 56.
92 Footman, p. 36.
93 *Protokoly*, pp. 160–61.
94 Lenin, Vol. 26, pp. 379–83.
95 Ibid., Vol. 26, pp. 381–2.
96 Carr, Vol. I, pp. 117–20.
97 Anweiler, p. 273.
98 Ibid., p. 262; Radkey, *Elections*, pp. 24–6, 36, 56.
99 Radkey, *Sickle*, pp. 282–7, 353–4.
100 Ibid., p. 357.
101 Ibid., p. 290.
102 Broué, *Révolution*, p. 169.
103 Ibid., p. 237.
104 Quoted in Nettl, Vol. II, p. 726.
105 Lenin, Vol. 33, p. 480.
106 Ibid., Vol. 26, p. 495.
107 Ibid., Vol. 33, p. 87.
108 Ibid., Vol. 26, p. 475: see also Vol. 33, p. 22.
109 Ibid., Vol. 28, p. 299.
110 Ibid., Vol. 29, p. 157.
111 Schapiro, *Communist Party*, p. 183.
112 *Protokoly*, p. 122.
113 Ibid., p. 123.
114 Ibid., p. 123.
115 Ibid., pp. 125, 129. The minutes of the Central Committee meeting of November 1st, 1917, cover pages 124–30.
116 Broué, *Parti*, p. 99.
117 *Protokoly*, p. 132.
118 Ibid., p. 275 (note 173).
119 *Protokoly*, p. 135.
120 Daniels, *Conscience*, p. 64.
121 Ibid., p. 65.
122 Radkey, *Sickle*, p. 66.
123 Bunyan and Fisher, p. 159.
124 Radkey, *Sickle*, p. 72.
125 Ibid., p. 69.

126 Lenin, Vol. 26, p. 456.
127 Quoted in Liebman, p. 230.
128 Radkey, *Elections*, p. 8.
129 Radkey, *Sickle*, pp. 469–70.
130 Ibid., p. 491.
131 Carr, Vol. II, pp. 47–8.
132 Radkey, *Sickle*, pp. 73–4, 88.
133 Ibid., p. 332.
134 Ibid., pp. 373–4.
135 Bunyan, *Intervention*, p. 180.
136 Fischer, *Life of Lenin*, p. 293.
137 Bunyan, *Intervention*, p. 187.
138 Ibid., p. 355.
139 Footman, p. 117.
140 Sadoul, p. 287.
141 Carr, Vol. I, p. 172.
142 Bunyan and Fisher, p. 190.
143 Anweiler, p. 270.
144 Martov, p. 311.
145 Serge, *Year One*, p. 92.
146 Schapiro, *Origin*, p. 192.
147 Anweiler, p. 289.
148 Ibid., p. 288.
149 Ibid., p. 294.
150 Footman, pp. 101–2, quoting I. Maisky, a Menshevik who went over to the Bolsheviks.
151 Ibid., pp. 103 and 112.
152 Getzler, p. 184.
153 Ibid., p. 189.
154 Martov, p. 313; on the conference of October 1918, see also Anweiler, p. 294; Getzler, pp. 186–8; and Carr, Vol. I, p. 171.
155 Getzler, p. 185.
156 Anweiler, p. 294; Getzler, p. 198.
157 Anweiler, p. 295.
158 Ransome, pp. 131–3.
159 Martov, p. 318.
160 Getzler, p. 201.
161 Schapiro, *Origin*, p. 206.
162 See also Kaplan, pp. 161–2.
163 Avrich, *Anarchists*, p. 185.
164 Ibid., pp. 186–7.
165 Ibid., p. 159.
166 Serge, *Year One*, p. 215.
167 Carr, Vol. I, p. 161.
168 Avrich, *Anarchists*, p. 184.
169 Serge, *Memoirs*, p. 75.
170 Avrich, *Anarchists*, p. 188.
171 Serge, *La Ville en danger: Petrograd, l'an II de la Révolution*, in Vol. 3 of his *L'An I de la Révolution*, p. 133. (Not included in *Year One*, the English translation of *L'An I* ...)
172 Serge, *Memoirs*, p. 121.
173 Avrich, *Kronstadt*.
174 Lenin, Vol. 32, p. 199.
175 Ibid., Vol. 32, p. 248.
176 Ibid., Vol. 32, p. 274.

177 Ibid., Vol. 32, p. 178.
178 Schapiro, *Origin*, p. 218; Broué, *Parti*, p. 153.
179 Avrich, *Kronstadt*, p. 89.
180 Ibid., p. 64.
181 Ibid., p. 125.
182 Ibid., pp. 124-5.
183 Ibid., p. 128.
184 Ibid., p. 137.
185 *Protokoly*, pp. 132, 138-9.
186 Radkey, *Sickle*, p. 148.
187 Carr, Vol. II, p. 41.
188 Serge, *Year One*, p. 263.
189 Carr, Vol. I, pp. 126-8; Radkey, *Sickle*, pp. 99-100.
190 Carr, Vol. I, p. 163.
191 Price, p. 246.
192 Ibid., p. 269; Carr, Vol. I, p. 149.
193 Ulam, p. 554.
194 Price, p. 277.
195 Dobb, pp. 104-5; Sobolev, p. 378.
196 Bunyan and Fisher, pp. 584-5.
197 Quoted in Souvarine, pp. 196-7.
198 See Lenin, Vol. 27, pp. 179, 484-5; Vol. 29, p. 534; Vol. 32, p. 506, and *passim*.
199 Lenin, Vol. 26, p. 283.
200 Ibid., Vol. 26, p. 285.
201 Broué, *Parti*, pp. 99-100.
202 Lenin, Vol. 27, p. 155.
203 Nettl, Vol. II, pp. 645, 655.
204 Ibid., Vol. II, p. 722.
205 Ibid., Vol. II, pp. 777-8.
206 Broué, *Révolution*, pp. 175-6.
207 Carr, Vol. I, p. 170.
208 Lenin, Vol. 27, p. 254.
209 Ibid., Vol. 26, p. 475.
210 Ibid., Vol. 29, pp. 561-2.
211 Ibid., Vol. 30, p. 420.
212 Ibid., Vol. 31, p. 201.
213 Avrich, *Kronstadt*, p. 177.
214 Avrich, *Anarchists*, p. 233.
215 Serge, *Memoirs*, pp. 119-20: see also Rosmer, *Lenin's Moscow*, pp. 101-102.
216 Lenin, Vol. 29, p. 557.
217 Serge, *Year One*, p. 336.
218 Lenin, Vol. 29, pp. 264, 294, 451, 557, and *passim*.
219 Ibid., Vol. 29, pp. 296-7.
220 Ibid., Vol. 29, p. 294. See also p. 278, and *passim*.
221 Ibid., Vol. 28, p. 190.
222 Ibid., Vol. 28, pp. 190-91.
223 Ibid., Vol. 28, p. 198.
224 Ibid., Vol. 28, pp. 212-13.
225 Ibid., Vol. 29, p. 181.
226 Ibid., Vol. 30, p. 233.
227 Ibid., Vol. 45, pp. 456, 458.
228 Ibid., Vol. 42, p. 408.

229 Ibid., Vol. 42, p. 419.
230 Ibid., Vol. 28, p. 463, and Vol. 29, p. 536.
231 Ibid., Vol. 28, p. 447.
232 Ibid., Vol. 29, pp. 262-3.
233 Ibid., Vol. 29, pp. 264, 296, 300.
234 Ibid., Vol. 32, pp. 361-2; Vol. 33, pp. 40-41; Vol. 45, p. 443.
235 Ibid., Vol. 27, pp. 262, 346, 428, 492; Vol. 28, p. 55.
236 Ibid., Vol. 31, p. 384.
237 Ibid., Vol. 29, p. 150.
238 Ibid., Vol. 32, p. 230.
239 Broué, *Parti*, p. 171.
240 Serge, *Memoirs*, p. 163.
241 Lenin, Vol. 42, p. 620 (note 607).
242 Lenin, Vol. 27, p. 221.
243 Ibid., Vol. 29, p. 503.
244 Ibid., Vol. 29, pp. 544-5.
245 Lunacharsky, p. 137.
246 Getzler, pp. 207-8.
247 Ibid., p. 208.
248 Krupskaya, p. 99.
249 Carr, Vol. I, p. 183.
250 Serge, *Mémoires*, p. 111. (Not included in the English translation of this book, which is abridged.)
251 Pipes, *Formation*, p. 2.
252 Lenin, Vol. 19, p. 116.
253 Ibid., Vol. 19, p. 429.
254 Ibid., Vol. 20, p. 411.
255 Ibid., Vol. 20, p. 451.
256 Ibid., Vol. 20, p. 413.
257 Ibid., Vol. 20, p. 435.
258 Serge, *Year One*, p. 109.
259 Lenin, Vol. 26, p. 344.
260 Carr, Vol. I, pp. 287-9.
261 Stalin, Vol. 4, p. 33.
262 Pipes, *Formation*, p. 211.
263 Ibid., p. 18.
264 Rosa Luxemburg, *The Russian Revolution*, p. 29.
265 Carr, Vol. I, p. 338.
266 Lenin, Vol. 36, pp. 541, 703.
267 Carr, Vol. I, p. 374.
268 Pipes, *Formation*, p. 190.
269 Ibid., p. 171.
270 Ibid., p. 164.
271 Ibid., p. 179.
272 Lenin, Vol. 29, p. 110.
273 Ibid., Vol. 30, pp. 163, 164.
274 Pipes, *Formation*, pp. 236-7.
275 Lenin, Vol. 32, p. 160.
276 Ibid., Vol. 35, p. 479.
277 Deutscher, *Stalin*, p. 244.
278 Carr, Vol. I, p. 285.

Part III: Chapter 2

1 Quoted by Pietsch, p. 28.

2 Ibid., pp. 42 ff.
3 Ibid., p. 141.
4 Broué, *Parti*, p. 128.
5 Schapiro, *Communist Party*, pp. 246–247.
6 Fainsod, *Smolensk under Soviet Rule*, p. 39.
7 Quoted by Keep, 'October in the Provinces', p. 189.
8 Rigby, pp. 68–9.
9 Lenin, Vol. 29, pp. 161–2.
10 Fainsod, *Smolensk under Soviet Rule*, p. 38.
11 Ibid., p. 6.
12 Schapiro, *Communist Party*, p. 246.
13 Ibid., p. 243; Broué, *Parti*, p. 129.
14 Schapiro, *Communist Party*, pp. 246–247.
15 Ponomarev, p. 318.
16 Carr, Vol. I, p. 222.
17 Anweiler, p. 302.
18 Pietsch, p. 147.
19 Ibid., p. 149.
20 Rigby, p. 75.
21 Meissner, pp. 122–3.
22 Carr, Vol. I, p. 229.
23 Lenin, Vol. 31, p. 367.
24 Ibid., Vol. 30, p. 459, and Vol. 31, p. 369.
25 Ibid., Vol. 29, p. 559.
26 Ibid., Vol. 31, p. 48.
27 Ibid., Vol. 33, pp. 306, 307, 314.
28 Pietsch, p. 73.
29 Ibid., p. 144.
30 Carr, Vol. I, p. 194.
31 Ibid., Vol. I, p. 194.
32 Lenin, Vol. 30, p. 444.
33 Ibid., Vol. 30, p. 467.
34 Carr, Vol. I, p. 194.
35 Deutscher, *Stalin*, p. 232.
36 Deutscher, *Prophet Unarmed*, p. 31; L. Fischer, *Life of Lenin*, pp. 588–590; Souvarine, p. 292.
37 Broué, *Parti*, pp. 180–81; Deutscher, *Prophet Unarmed*, pp. 96–8.
38 Trotsky, *My Life*, p. 382.
39 *Protokoly*, p. 176.
40 Ibid., pp. 182–3.
41 Daniels, *Conscience*, p. 84.
42 *Protokoly*, p. 170.
43 Ibid., pp. 169–71.
44 Bunyan and Fisher, p. 564.
45 Daniels, *Conscience*, p. 94.
46 Ibid., p. 85.
47 Carr, Vol. II, pp. 89–90, 97, 110–11, 114; Daniels, *Conscience*, pp. 84–6.
48 Pietsch, p. 99; Daniels, *Conscience*, p. 104.
49 Carr, Vol. III, p. 71.
50 Bunyan and Fisher, p. 563.
51 Daniels, *Conscience*, p. 79.
52 Broué, *Parti*, p. 139; Schapiro, *Origin*, pp. 239, 245.
53 Carr, Vol. I, p. 195.
54 Daniels, *Conscience*, p. 138.
55 Schapiro, *Origin*, p. 314.
56 Ibid., p. 335.
57 Lenin, Vol. 27, p. 105.
58 Ibid., Vol. 26, p. 451.
59 Sadoul, p. 181.
60 Lenin, Vol. 27, p. 19.
61 Ibid., Vol. 27, p. 21.
62 Ibid., Vol. 27, p. 329.
63 Ibid., Vol. 27, p. 40.
64 Ibid., Vol. 27, p. 64.
65 Ibid., Vol. 27, p. 83.
66 Ibid., Vol. 27, p. 348.
67 Ibid., Vol. 27, p. 81.
68 Ibid., Vol. 27, p. 306 (see also p. 110).
69 Ibid., Vol. 27, pp. 286, 343.
70 Ibid., Vol. 27, p. 36.
71 Ibid., Vol. 27, p. 151.
72 Ibid., Vol. 27, p. 202.
73 Ibid., Vol. 32, pp. 178, 197, 252.
74 Ibid., Vol. 32, p. 106.
75 Ibid., Vol. 32, p. 106.
76 Ibid., Vol. 31, pp. 422–3.
77 Ibid., Vol. 31, p. 103 (see also pp. 31 and 90).
78 Ibid., Vol. 27, p. 20.
79 Carr, Vol. I, p. 188.
80 *Protokoly*, p. 226; Krupskaya, p. 447.
81 Pietsch, p. 88.
82 Meissner, pp. 30–33.
83 Löwy, p. 111.
84 Carr, Vol. II, pp. 88–95.
85 Lenin, Vol. 29, pp. 165 and 186; Carr, Vol. I, pp. 268–9.
86 Daniels, *Conscience*, p. 116.
87 Ibid., p. 117.
88 Ibid., p. 129.
89 Lenin, Vol. 32, p. 41.
90 Ibid., Vol. 32, p. 204.
91 Ibid., Vol. 26, p. 508.
92 Ibid., Vol. 29, p. 196.
93 Ibid., Vol. 27, pp. 111, 124.
94 Ibid., Vol. 31, p. 390.
95 Ibid., Vol. 31, p. 427.
96 Ibid., Vol. 32, p. 52.
97 Ibid., Vol. 32, p. 106.
98 Daniels, *Conscience*, pp. 113–17; Kool and Oberländer, p. 137.
99 Lenin, Vol. 30, p. 466.
100 Schapiro, *Origin*, p. 228; Carr, Vol. II, p. 213.
101 Serge, *Vie et mort de Trotsky*, p. 133; Rosmer, *Lenin's Moscow*, p. 121.
102 Daniels, *Conscience*, p. 117.
103 Lenin, Vol. 32, p. 34.
104 Ibid., Vol. 32, p. 43.

105 Ibid., Vol. 32, pp. 62–3, 67.
106 Ibid., Vol. 33, pp. 281–2.
107 Ibid., Vol. 32, p. 168.
108 Ibid., Vol. 32, p. 200.
109 Ibid., Vol. 32, p. 248.
110 Ibid., Vol. 32, p. 200.
111 Ibid., Vol. 32, pp. 259–60.
112 Ibid., Vol. 32, p. 260.
113 Ibid., Vol. 32, p. 260.
114 Schapiro, *Origin*, p. 317.
115 Lenin, Vol. 32, pp. 241–8.
116 Ibid., Vol. 32, p. 243.
117 Ibid., Vol. 32, p. 244.
118 Ibid., Vol. 32, p. 244.
119 Schapiro, *Origin*, p. 319, note 16.
120 Lenin, Vol. 32, p. 258.
121 Ibid., Vol. 32, p. 248.
122 Schapiro, *Origin*, p. 319, note 16.
123 Lenin, Vol. 32, p. 241.
124 Ibid., Vol. 32, p. 249.
125 Ibid., Vol. 32, p. 251.
126 Ibid., Vol. 32, p. 259.
127 Ibid., Vol. 32, p. 260.
128 Ibid., Vol. 32, pp. 193, 200.
129 Ibid., Vol. 32, p. 242.
130 Ibid., Vol. 32, p. 243.
131 Ibid., Vol. 32, p. 243.
132 Ibid., Vol. 32, p. 258.
133 Ibid., Vol. 32, p. 261.
134 Rigby, p. 52.
135 Ibid., p. 85.
136 Schapiro, *Communist Party*, p. 239.
137 Ibid., p. 238; Rigby, pp. 80–81.
138 Schapiro, *Communist Party*, pp. 237–238.
139 Ibid., p. 237.
140 Lenin, Vol. 30, p. 63.
141 *Protokoly*, p. 193.
142 Lenin, Vol. 28, p. 61.
143 Ibid., Vol. 29, pp. 32–3.
144 Ibid., Vol. 29, p. 265.
145 Ibid., Vol. 32, p. 355.
146 Ibid., Vol. 33, p. 41.
147 Ibid., Vol. 33, p. 41.
148 Ibid., Vol. 42, p. 315.
149 Ibid., Vol. 30, pp. 485–6.
150 Rigby, p. 82.
151 Lenin, Vol. 30, p. 71.
152 Rigby, p. 87.
153 Pietsch, p. 121.
154 Ibid., p. 133.
155 Lenin, Vol. 29, p. 33.
156 Rigby, p. 73.
157 Ibid., p. 70.
158 Lenin, Vol. 33, pp. 39–41.
159 Rigby, p. 77.
160 Schapiro, *Communist Party*, p. 236.
161 Lenin, Vol. 33, p. 254; Rigby, p. 103.
162 Rigby, p. 97.
163 Deutscher, *Prophet Unarmed*, p. 14n.
164 Deutscher, *Soviet Trade Unions*, pp. 54–5.

Part III: Chapter 3

1 Lenin, Vol. 27, p. 130.
2 Engels, *Anti-Dühring*, p. 255.
3 Reed, p. 141.
4 Carr, Vol. I, p. 152.
5 Serge, *Year One*, p. 79.
6 Keep, 'October in the Provinces', p. 190.
7 Ibid., p. 199.
8 Reed, p. 244.
9 Bunyan and Fisher, p. 387.
10 Lenin, Vol. 44, p. 54.
11 Quoted in Souvarine, pp. 253–4.
12 Quoted in Vovelle, p. 125.
13 Carr, Vol. I, p. 153.
14 Ibid., Vol. I, p. 153.
15 Schapiro, *Origin*, pp. 122–3.
16 Serge, *Year One*, p. 189.
17 Souvarine, p. 221.
18 Sobolev, p. 328; L. Fischer, *Life of Lenin*, p. 293; Serge, *Vie et mort de Trotsky*, pp. 109–10.
19 Serge, *Year One*, pp. 283–4.
20 Ibid., p. 288.
21 Carr, Vol. I, p. 168.
22 Serge, *Year One*, p. 304.
23 Carr, Vol. I, p. 168.
24 Deutscher, *Prophet Armed*, p. 459.
25 Serge, *Memoirs*, p. 100.
26 Bunyan, *Intervention*, p. 261.
27 Lenin, Vol. 28, p. 389.
28 Bunyan, *Intervention*, p. 247.
29 Fainsod, *Smolensk under Soviet Rule*, p. 153.
30 Serge, *Year One*, p. 327.
31 Lenin, Vol. 26, p. 294.
32 Trotsky, *On Lenin*, p. 115.
33 Lenin, Vol. 26, p. 408.
34 Ibid., Vol. 27, p. 233.
35 Ibid., Vol. 27, p. 356; Vol. 35, pp. 352–6, 392; Vol. 44, p. 118, and *passim*.
36 Ibid., Vol. 44, p. 285, Vol. 26, p. 402.
37 Ibid., Vol. 26, p. 410.
38 Ibid., Vol. 27, p. 33.
39 Ibid., Vol. 27, p. 35.
40 Ibid., Vol. 27, p. 233.
41 Ibid., Vol. 27, p. 406.
42 Ibid., Vol. 35, p. 349.
43 Ibid., Vol. 42, p. 115.
44 Ibid., Vol. 36, p. 499.
45 Ibid., Vol. 44, p. 277.
46 Ibid., Vol. 44, p. 141.
47 Ibid., Vol. 42, p. 170.
48 Ibid., Vol. 30, p. 510.

49 Ibid., Vol. 36, p. 533.
50 Ibid., Vol. 45, p. 203.
51 E.g., ibid., Vol. 35, p. 367; Vol. 36, p. 558.
52 Ibid., Vol. 30, pp. 327, 331.
53 Ibid., Vol. 42, p. 167.
54 Ibid., Vol. 33, p. 176.
55 Gorky, Lenin, p. 39.
56 L. Fischer, Life of Lenin, p. 328.
57 Serge, Memoirs, p. 130.
58 Shub, p. 384.
59 Trotsky, My Life, p. 474.
60 Rosa Luxemburg, The Russian Revolution, p. 51.
61 Lenin, Vol. 25, p. 463.
62 Ibid., Vol. 25, p. 488.
63 Ibid., Vol. 32, p. 48.
64 Ibid., Vol. 26, p. 413.
65 Ibid., Vol. 26, p. 294.
66 Ibid., Vol. 27, pp. 248–50.
67 Anweiler, p. 276.
68 Carr, Vol. II, p. 187.
69 Stawar, p. 55.
70 Lenin, Vol. 29, p. 24.
71 Ibid., Vol. 29, p. 74.
72 Ibid., Vol. 30, p. 415.
73 Ibid., Vol. 29, p. 180.
74 Ibid., Vol. 31, p. 178.
75 Ibid., Vol. 32, p. 363.
76 Kritsman, p. 234.
77 Lenin, Vol. 33, p. 288.
78 Carr, Vol. II, pp. 183–4.
79 Lenin, Vol. 27, p. 156; Vol. 30, p. 311, and passim.
80 Serge, Year One, p. 356.
81 Pietsch, p. 137.
82 Stawar, p. 53.
83 Kaplan, p. 298.
84 Lenin, Vol. 28, p. 394.
85 Ibid., Vol. 28, p. 405.
86 Ibid., Vol. 45, p. 107.
87 Ibid., Vol. 33, p. 239.
88 Ibid., Vol. 36, p. 566.
89 Ibid., Vol. 36, p. 557.
90 Ibid., Vol. 33, p. 395.
91 Ibid., Vol. 29, pp. 178, 182.
92 Ibid., Vol. 32, pp. 351–2.
93 Ibid., Vol. 33, pp. 428–9.
94 Ibid., Vol. 32, p. 68.
95 Ibid., Vol. 35, p. 492.
96 Ibid., Vol. 30, pp. 405–6.
97 Ibid., Vol. 33, p. 337.
98 Ibid., Vol. 45, p. 498.
99 Ibid., Vol. 28, pp. 349–52, and 486.
100 Ibid., Vol. 32, pp. 383–98.
101 Carr, Vol. I, p. 226; Lenin, Vol. 30, p. 300.
102 Lenin, Vol. 36, p. 597.
103 Carr, Vol. I, p. 227.
104 Lenin, Vol. 45, p. 445.

105 Trotsky, Stalin School of Falsification, p. 73.
106 Lenin, Vol. 29, p. 183.
107 Ibid., Vol. 32, p. 132.
108 Ibid., Vol. 32, p. 142.
109 Ibid., Vol. 32, p. 141.
110 Ibid., Vol. 33, pp. 77–8.
111 Ibid., Vol. 36, p. 567.
112 Ibid., Vol. 36, p. 562.
113 L. Fischer, Life of Lenin, p. 582.
114 Bunyan, Origin, p. 83.
115 Lenin, Vol. 45, p. 450.
116 Ibid., Vol. 45, p. 478.
117 Ibid., Vol. 36, p. 566.
118 Ibid., Vol. 45, p. 519.
119 Ibid., Vol. 45, p. 599.
120 Ibid., Vol. 45, pp. 432–3.
121 Weber, From Max Weber, p. 214.
122 Chambre, pp. 61 and 69.
123 Ibid., p. 62.
124 Ibid., p. 71.
125 Ibid., p. 72.
126 Bunyan and Fisher, p. 291.
127 Chambre, p. 175.
128 Ibid., p. 173.
129 Ibid., p. 176.
130 Bunyan and Fisher, p. 288.
131 Anweiler, p. 278.
132 Bunyan and Fisher, p. 291.
133 Ibid., p. 289.
134 Ibid., pp. 290–91.
135 Meyer, p. 186.
136 Fitzpatrick, p. 288.
137 Ibid., pp. 139, 156–7.
138 Ibid., p. 125.
139 Ibid., p. 157.
140 Ransome, pp. 22–3.
141 Ibid., p. 23.
142 Fitzpatrick, p. 92.
143 Ibid., p. 92.
144 Ibid., p. 96.
145 Ibid., p. 106.
146 Lenin, Vol. 29, p. 373.
147 Fitzpatrick, p. 178.
148 Zetkin, pp. 12–13.
149 Lenin, Vol. 33, p. 223.
150 Ibid., Vol. 45, p. 139.
151 Fitzpatrick, p. 177.
152 Ibid., pp. 179–81.
153 Ibid., p. 289.
154 Lenin, Vol. 26, p. 352.
155 Fitzpatrick, p. 317.
156 Lenin, Vol. 33, p. 76.
157 Ibid., Vol. 33, pp. 78, 246, 298, 299.
158 Fitzpatrick, pp. 29–30.
159 Bunyan, Intervention, pp. 542–3.
160 Dewar, p. 69.
161 Bunyan and Fisher, pp. 595–6.
162 Bunyan, Intervention, pp. 532–3.
163 Ibid., pp. 538–9.

164 Bunyan and Fisher, p. 596.
165 Ibid., p. 599.
166 Bunyan, *Intervention*, pp. 534–5; Fitzpatrick, p. 77.
167 Bunyan, *Intervention*, pp. 534–6; Fitzpatrick, pp. 74, 85.
168 Serge, *Memoirs*, p. 116.
169 Lenin, Vol. 33, p. 462.
170 Bukharin and Preobrazhensky, p. 297.
171 Lenin, Vol. 26, pp. 240 and 247.
172 Bunyan and Fisher, p. 308.
173 Deutscher, *Soviet Trade Unions*, p. 16n; see also Kaplan, p. 163.
174 Avrich, *Anarchists*, p. 161.
175 Carr, Vol. II, p. 68.
176 Kaplan, p. 182; Dewar, p. 20.
177 Lozovsky, pp. 23–4.
178 Kaplan, pp. 172, 179, 181.
179 Sorlin, p. 65.
180 Sobolev, pp. 300–301.
181 Kaplan, p. 129.
182 Nove, p. 50; Carr, Vol. II, p. 70; International Labour Office, p. 241.
183 Labry, p. 180.
184 Price, p. 212.
185 Labry, p. 194.
186 Krupskaya, pp. 460–61.
187 Dewar, p. 19; see also Kaplan, pp. 175 and 192, and Avrich, *Anarchists*, p. 162.
188 Kaplan, p. 327.
189 Avrich, *Anarchists*, p. 162.
190 Trotsky, *My Life*, p. 337.
191 Lenin, Vol. 27, p. 200.
192 Ibid., Vol. 27, p. 257.
193 Ibid., Vol. 27, p. 259.
194 Ibid., Vol. 27, p. 296.
195 Ibid., Vol. 27, p. 258.
196 Ibid., Vol. 27, p. 259; see also Vol. 27, p. 316, and Vol. 42, p. 87; Price, pp. 282–4; Kool and Oberländer, pp. 103–104.
197 Lenin, Vol. 20, pp. 152–4.
198 Ibid., Vol. 27, p. 163.
199 Ibid., Vol. 27, p. 294.
200 Ibid., Vol. 26, p. 394.
201 Ibid., Vol. 27, p. 118.
202 Ibid., Vol. 26, p. 500; see also Vol. 27, pp. 232, 444, and Vol. 29, pp. 373, 447.
203 See, in particular, ibid., Vol. 26, pp. 404–15.
204 Ibid., Vol. 27, p. 329.
205 Ibid., Vol. 27, p. 313.
206 Price, p. 280.
207 Dewar, pp. 39–40.
208 Chambre, pp. 99–100.
209 Deutscher, *Prophet Armed*, p. 493.
210 Ibid., pp. 501–2.
211 Trotsky, *Terrorism and Communism*, p. 140.
212 Broué, *Parti*, p. 141.
213 Bukharin and Preobrazhensky, p. 316.
214 Kaplan, p. 250.
215 Dewar, p. 28.
216 Carr, Vol. II, p. 105.
217 Ibid., Vol. II, p. 202.
218 Deutscher, *Soviet Trade Unions*, pp. 48–9.
219 Bunyan, *Intervention*, pp. 165–6.
220 Lenin, Vol. 29, p. 264.
221 Ibid., Vol. 29, p. 300.
222 Ibid., Vol. 33, p. 185.
223 Ibid., Vol. 33, pp. 186–7.
224 Ibid., Vol. 33, p. 188.
225 Kaplan, p. 206.
226 Carr, Vol. II, p. 106.
227 International Labour Office, pp. 188–190.
228 Carr, Vol. II, p. 202.
229 Lenin, Vol. 32, p. 80.
230 Ibid., Vol. 32, p. 44.
231 Carr, Vol. II, p. 225.
232 Ibid., Vol. II., p. 224.
233 Lenin, Vol. 29, p. 113.
234 Ibid., Vol. 31, p. 50.
235 Ibid., Vol. 31, p. 51.
236 Ibid., Vol. 30, p. 459.
237 Stawar, p. 50.
238 Lenin, Vol. 32, pp. 24–5.
239 Ibid., Vol. 33, p. 186.
240 Serge, *Year One*, p. 250.
241 Dobb, p. 100; Carr, Vol. II, p. 242; Avrich, *Kronstadt*, p. 23.
242 Carr, Vol. II, p. 241.
243 Serge, *Memoirs*, p. 116.
244 Ransome, pp. 68–9.
245 Sorlin, pp. 77–8.
246 Ibid., p. 78.
247 Kritsman, p. 286; Dewar, p. 94.
248 Kritsman, p. 273.
249 Serge, *Year One*, p. 115.
250 Ibid., p. 199.
251 Kritsman, pp. 265 and 273.
252 Dewar, p. 37; Pietsch, p. 105; Avrich, *Kronstadt*, p. 26; Carr, Vol. II, pp. 192–5.
253 Kritsman, p. 84.
254 Ibid., p. 252; Carr, Vol. II, p. 194; Bunyan. *Origin*, p. 172.
255 Fainsod, *Smolensk under Soviet Rule*, p. 38.
256 Kritsman, p. 297.
257 Dewar, p. 80.
258 Carr, Vol. II, p. 243.
259 Deutscher, *Prophet Unarmed*, p. 7, n. 2.
260 Lenin, Vol. 33, p. 65.
261 Ibid., Vol. 30, p. 112.

262 Kritsman, p. 290.
263 Erickson, p. 248.
264 Fedotoff-White, p. 56.
265 Ibid., p. 106.
266 Ibid., p. 105.
267 Erickson, p. 258.
268 Fitzpatrick, pp. 79–80.
269 Sorlin, p. 79.
270 Deutscher, *Soviet Trade Unions*, p. 22;
    International Labour Office, pp.
    177–8; Dewar, p. 72; Lozovsky, p.
    33; Carr, Vol. II, p. 199.
271 Lenin, Vol. 35, p. 333.
272 Carr, Vol. II, p. 113, n. 2.
273 Kritsman, p. 337.
274 Carr, Vol. II, pp. 207, 260, 263.
275 Dewar, p. 31.
276 Lenin, Vol. 27, pp. 249, 250, 316.
277 Ibid., Vol. 29, p. 113.
278 Bukharin and Preobrazhensky, p. 345.
279 Lenin, Vol. 26, p. 365.
280 Ibid., Vol. 31, p. 44.
281 Ibid., Vol. 28, pp. 255–6.
282 Ibid., Vol. 32, p. 21.
283 Ibid., Vol. 28, p. 241.
284 Ibid., Vol. 29, p. 559.
285 Ibid., Vol. 29, p. 559.
286 Ibid., Vol. 29, p. 82.
287 Ibid., Vol. 29, p. 158.
288 Ibid., Vol. 29, p. 183.
289 E.g., ibid., Vol. 30, p. 129, and Vol.
    32, p. 118.
290 Ibid., Vol. 32, p. 21.

Part IV: Chapter 1

1 Rosa Luxemburg, *The Russian Revo-
    lution*, p. 56.
2 Lenin, Vol. 27, p. 346.
3 Ibid., Vol. 26, p. 386.
4 Ibid., Vol. 26, p. 472.
5 Ibid., Vol. 26, p. 291.
6 Ibid., Vol. 31, p. 397.
7 Ibid., Vol. 32, pp. 479–80.
8 Ibid., Vol. 33, p. 145.
9 Ibid., Vol. 26, p. 443.
10 Ibid., Vol. 26, p. 470.
11 Ibid., Vol. 27, p. 95.
12 Ibid., Vol. 27, p. 98.
13 Ibid., Vol. 30, pp. 207–8.
14 Ibid., Vol. 31, p. 399.
15 Ibid., Vol. 28, p. 155.
16 Ibid., Vol. 26, p. 328.
17 Ibid., Vol. 28, pp. 342 ff.
18 Ibid., Vol. 32, p. 113.
19 Ibid., Vol. 27, p. 412.
20 Ibid., Vol. 28, p. 151.
21 Fitzpatrick, Vol. 29, p. 192.
22 Ibid., Vol. 32, p. 350.

23 Ibid., Vol. 33, p. 501.
24 Ibid., Vol. 26, p. 443.
25 Ibid., Vol. 29, p. 300.
26 Ibid., Vol. 26, p. 443.
27 Ibid., Vol. 26, p. 494.
28 Ibid., Vol. 28, p. 123.
29 Krupskaya, p. 489.
30 Price, p. 345.
31 Lenin, Vol. 30, p. 418.
32 Ibid., Vol. 30, p. 496; see also Vol. 33,
    p. 145.
33 Ibid., Vol. 30, pp. 384–5, and Vol. 33,
    p. 118.
34 Ibid., Vol. 29, p. 257.
35 Ibid., Vol. 30, p. 505.
36 Ibid., Vol. 31, p. 365.
37 Ibid., Vol. 33, p. 72.
38 E.g. ibid., Vol. 33, pp. 350, 499.
39 Ibid., Vol. 28, p. 394.
40 Ibid., Vol. 27, p. 290.
41 Ibid., Vol. 27, p. 401.
42 Ibid., Vol. 27, p. 373.
43 Ibid., Vol. 27, p. 232.
44 Ibid., Vol. 28, p. 53; see also Vol. 28,
    p. 359.
45 Ibid., Vol. 32, p. 492.
46 Ibid., Vol. 33, p. 498.
47 Ibid., Vol. 33, p. 499.
48 Ibid., Vol. 28, p. 25.

Part IV: Chapter 2

1 Trotsky, *My Life*, p. 341.
2 Lenin, Vol. 21, p. 342.
3 Ibid., Vol. 26, p. 252.
4 Ibid., Vol. 26, p. 256.
5 Ibid., Vol. 26, p. 252.
6 Ibid., Vol. 26, p. 253.
7 Ibid., Vol. 26, p. 397.
8 Ibid., Vol. 26, p. 508.
9 Ibid., Vol. 27, p. 110.
10 Ibid., Vol. 44, p. 67.
11 Ibid., Vol. 22, pp. 255, 295.
12 Ibid., Vol. 27, pp. 237–8.
13 Ibid., Vol. 27, p. 29.
14 See ibid., Vol. 29, p. 315; Vol. 30,
    p. 451; Vol. 31, p. 413.
15 Ibid., Vol. 35, p. 332.
16 Ibid., Vol. 29, p. 130.
17 Ibid., Vol. 29, p. 153.
18 Ibid., Vol. 30, p. 318.
19 Ibid., Vol. 30, p. 323.
20 Ibid., Vol. 30, p. 335.
21 Ibid., Vol. 30, p. 345.
22 Ibid., Vol. 30, p. 350.
23 Ibid., Vol. 31, p. 412.
24 Ibid., Vol. 33, p. 151.
25 Ibid., Vol. 31, p. 413.
26 Ibid., Vol. 31, p. 457.

27 Ibid., Vol. 31, p. 472.
28 Ibid., Vol. 33, p. 132.
29 Ibid., Vol. 30, pp. 160–61.
30 Ibid., Vol. 31, p. 453.
31 Ibid., Vol. 36, p. 611.
32 Ibid., Vol. 42, p. 392.
33 Ibid., Vol. 42, p. 403.
34 Liebman, p. 303.
35 Trotsky, *My Life*, p. 373.
36 Ibid., pp. 364–5.
37 Fischer, *Soviets*, Vol. I, p. 43.
38 Ulam, p. 572.
39 Carr, Vol. III, p. 76.
40 Sadoul, p. 322.
41 Carr, Vol. III, p. 69.
42 Ibid., Vol. III, pp. 110–11; Fischer, *Soviets*, Vol. I, pp. 166 ff.
43 Schapiro, *Communist Party*, p. 222.
44 Carr, Vol. III, pp. 110–11.
45 Fischer, *Soviets*, Vol. I, p. 172.
46 Kennan, p. 132.
47 Carr, Vol. III, p. 374; see also Kennan, p. 204.
48 Carr, Vol. III, p. 157.
49 Ibid., Vol. III, pp. 159 and 162; Kennan, p. 168.
50 Carr, Vol. III, p. 288.
51 Fischer, *Soviets*, Vol. I, p. 335.
52 Kochan, pp. 60–61; Carr, Vol. III, pp. 362–71 and 434–7.
53 Fischer, *Soviets*, Vol. I, p. 314.
54 Resolution of the Ninth Party Congress (1919), quoted in Carr, Vol. III, p. 236.
55 Ibid., Vol. III, p. 301.
56 Ibid., Vol. III, p. 484.
57 Ibid., Vol. III, pp. 243–4, 292–3; Fischer, *Soviets*, Vol. I, pp. 429–30.
58 Carr, Vol. III, p. 18.
59 Ibid., Vol. III, pp. 76–7; Fischer, *Soviets*, Vol. I, p. 75; Broué, *Révolution*, p. 126; Serge, *Year One*, p. 326.
60 Lenin, Vol. 33, p. 365.
61 Ibid., Vol. 28, p. 103.
62 Ibid., Vol. 28, p. 103; see also Vol. 35, p. 365.
63 Bunyan, *Intervention*, pp. 151–2.
64 Carr, Vol. III, p. 98.
65 Broué, *Révolution*, pp. 721–2.
66 Angress, p. 396.
67 Broué, *Révolution*, p. 731.
68 Ibid., p. 731.
69 Angress, p. 395.
70 Carr, Vol. III, p. 72.
71 Degras, Vol. I, p. 344.
72 Carr, Vol. III, pp. 344–5.
73 Degras, Vol. I, p. 346.

Part IV: Chapter 3

1   Lenin, Vol. 21, p. 16.
2   Ibid., Vol. 21, p. 174.
3   Ibid., Vol. 21, p. 329.
4   Ibid., Vol. 21, p. 330.
5   Ibid., Vol. 22, p. 127.
6   Ibid., Vol. 24, p. 24.
7   Ibid., Vol. 24, p. 90.
8   Ibid., Vol. 26, p. 474; Vol. 27, p. 127, and *passim*.
9   Nettl, Vol. II, p. 614.
10 Ibid., Vol. II, p. 649.
11 Löwy, p. 50.
12 Baron, pp. 324, 328.
13 Berlau, p. 200.
14 Nettl, Vol. II, pp. 711–12.
15 Broué, *Révolution*, p. 236.
16 Carr, Vol. III, pp. 99–100; Trotsky, *Terrorism and Communism*, pp. 126–127.
17 Carr, Vol. III, p. 100.
18 Fischer, *Soviets*, Vol. I, p. 192.
19 Lenin, Vol. 31, p. 231.
20 *Rosa Luxemburg Speaks*, p. 423.
21 Nettl, Vol. II, p. 658.
22 Ibid., pp. 638–9.
23 Ibid., pp. 725 and 752.
24 Lenin, Vol. 26, p. 465.
25 Ibid., Vol. 29, p. 504.
26 Braunthal, p. 99.
27 Borkenau, p. 95.
28 Degras, Vol. I, p. 47.
29 Ibid., Vol. I, p. 181.
30 *Protokoll des II Weltkongresses der Kommunistischen Internationale*, pp. 13 and 69.
31 Ibid., p. 12.
32 Degras, Vol. I, pp. 166–72 (Conditions of Admission to the C.I.).
33 *Parti Socialiste (S.F.I.O.)*, *XVIII*ᵉ … . For Blum's speech, see pp. 245 ff.
34 Lenin, Vol. 31, p. 281.
35 Degras, Vol. I, p. 4.
36 Ibid., Vol. I, pp. 66–7.
37 Ibid., Vol. I, pp. 103–4.
38 Rosmer, *Lenin's Moscow*, pp. 79–80.
39 Ibid., pp. 47–8.
40 Humbert-Droz, p. 20.
41 Borkenau, pp. 167–8.
42 Nettl, Vol. II, p. 732.
43 Broué, *Révolution*, p. 94.
44 Ibid., pp. 309–12; Degras, Vol. I, p. 66; Carr, Vol. III, p. 137.
45 Degras, Vol. I, p. 66.
46 Lenin, Vol. 30, pp. 87–8.
47 Broué, *Révolution*, pp. 406 and 450–52.
48 Trotsky, *The First Five Years of the Communist International*, Vol. I, p. 329.

49 Braunthal, p. 227.
50 Lenin, Vol. 29, pp. 564–5.
51 Ibid., Vol. 30, pp. 54, 61.
52 Ibid., Vol. 45, pp. 203–4.
53 Ibid., Vol. 31, p. 62.
54 Ibid., Vol. 31, p. 37.
55 Ibid., Vol. 31, p. 41.
56 Ibid., Vol. 31, pp. 43–4.
57 Ibid., Vol. 31, pp. 58, 93.
58 Ibid., Vol. 31, p. 88.
59 Ibid., Vol. 31, p. 85.
60 Ibid., Vol. 31, p. 53.
61 Ibid., Vol. 31, p. 56.
62 Ibid., Vol. 31, p. 58.
63 Ibid., Vol. 31, p. 64.
64 Ibid., Vol. 31, p. 35.
65 Ibid., Vol. 31, pp. 65n., and 112.
66 Ibid., Vol. 31, p. 107.
67 Ibid., Vol. 31, p. 45.
68 Ibid., Vol. 31, p. 79.
69 Protokoll des II Weltkongresses, pp.
   188, 422, 435.
70 Ibid., pp. 145 ff.
71 Ibid., p. 59.
72 Broué, Révolution, p. 521.
73 Protokoll des IV Weltkongresses der
   Kommunistischen Internationale,
   pp. 82, 100 ff.
74 Cammett, pp. 165, 169.
75 Ibid., p. 181.
76 Broué, Révolution, p. 452.
77 Ibid., p. 334.
78 Ibid., p. 780.
79 Walter, p. 99.
80 Broué, Révolution, p. 606.
81 Nettl, Vol. II, p. 757.
82 Broué, Révolution, p. 650.
83 E.g., ibid., pp. 370 and 452–3.
84 Walter, pp. 103–11.
85 Lenin, Vol. 30, p. 55.
86 Humbert-Droz, p. 79.
87 Broué, Révolution, p. 559.
88 Humbert-Droz, p. 95.
89 Broué, Révolution, pp. 619, 642–3,
   668–9.
90 Quoted in Lazitch, p. 127.
91 Parti Socialiste (S.F.I.O.), XVIIᵉ … ,
   p. 363.
92 Getzler, p. 209.
93 Lenin, Vol. 28, p. 470.
94 Ibid., Vol. 28, p. 116.
95 Ibid., Vol. 28, p. 472.
96 Ibid., Vol. 29, p. 145.
97 Ibid., Vol. 28, pp. 255–6.
98 Ibid., Vol. 31, p. 64.
99 Ibid., Vol. 32, p. 21.
100 Ibid., Vol. 27, p. 291.
101 Ibid., Vol. 28, pp. 137–8.
102 Ibid., Vol. 31, p. 21.

103 Ibid., Vol. 27, pp. 133, 137.
104 Ibid., Vol. 27, p. 188.
105 Ibid., Vol. 27, p. 138.
106 Ibid., Vol. 29, p. 299.
107 Ibid., Vol. 29, p. 322.
108 Ibid., Vol. 36, p. 566.
109 Ibid., Vol. 36, p. 588.
110 Ibid., Vol. 33, p. 344.
111 Ibid., Vol. 45, p. 425.
112 Ibid., Vol. 33, p. 296.
113 Ibid., Vol. 44, p. 403.
114 Ibid., Vol. 33, p. 75.
115 Ibid., Vol. 35, p. 519.
116 Ibid., Vol. 33, p. 223.
117 Krupskaya, p. 470.
118 Luxemburg, The Russian Revolution,
    p. 55.
119 Lenin, Vol. 29, p. 192.
120 Ibid., Vol. 32, p. 278.
121 Ibid., Vol. 29, p. 227.
122 Ibid., Vol. 29, p. 310.
123 Degras, Vol. I, p. 164.
124 Ibid., Vol. I, p. 71.
125 Ibid., Vol. I, p. 165.
126 Protokoll des II Weltkongresses,
    p. 479.
127 Ibid., p. 583.
128 Fauvet, p. 44.
129 Humbert-Droz, pp. 28 and 92.
130 Ibid., p. 28.
131 Broué, Révolution, p. 495.
132 Ibid., p. 550.
133 Walter, p. 65.
134 Broué, Révolution, p. 594.
135 Fauvet, pp. 42–3.
136 Ibid., p. 40.
137 Walter, p. 101.
138 Degras, Vol. I, p. 325.
139 Walter, p. 98.
140 Ibid., p. 99.
141 Ibid., p. 120.
142 Cammett, p. 163.
143 Broué, Révolution, p. 628.
144 Ibid., pp. 498, 649–50; Degras, Vol.
    I, p. 102.
145 Humbert-Droz, pp. 103–4.
146 Löwy, pp. 106–7.
147 Nettl, Vol. II, p. 765.
148 Degras, Vol. I, p. 193.
149 Carr, Vol. III, pp. 334 ff.; Broué,
    Révolution, pp. 477–81.
150 Lenin, Vol. 45, p. 124.
151 Ibid., Vol. 42, p. 119.
152 Degras, Vol. I, p. 37.
153 Nettl, Vol. II, p. 718.
154 Lazitch, p. 107.
155 Broué, Révolution, p. 336.
156 Degras, Vol. I, pp. 307–8.
157 Lenin, Vol. 33, pp. 430–31.

Part IV: Epilogue

1 Lewin, pp. 70, 153 (quoting the 5th edition of Lenin's collected works, in Russian, Vol. XLV, p. 710).
2 Ibid., p. 70.
3 Ibid., pp. 74, 153 (quoting the same instruction as in n. 1).
4 Lenin, Vol. 42, pp. 492–3.
5 Ibid., Vol. 42, p. 484.
6 Ibid., Vol. 42, p. 485.
7 Ibid., Vol. 42, p. 484.
8 Lewin, p. 94 (quoting L. A. Fotieva, one of Lenin's secretaries, *Iz Vospominaniy*).
9 Trotsky, *Stalin School of Falsification*, p. 72.
10 Lenin, Vol. 33, p. 458.
11 Lewin, p. 37 (quoting the 5th edition of Lenin's works, in Russian, Vol. XLV, p. 548, n. 126).
12 Lenin, op. cit., Vol. 45, p. 604.
13 Ibid., Vol. 45, p. 606.
14 Ibid., Vol. 33, p. 490.
15 Ibid., Vol. 33, p. 482.
16 Ibid., Vol. 33, pp. 482–3, 491; Vol. 36, pp. 603–4.
17 Trotsky, *My Life*, pp. 478–9.
18 Lenin, Vol. 36, pp. 598–602.
19 Ibid., Vol. 45, p. 593.
20 Ibid., Vol. 36, p. 594.
21 Ibid., Vol. 36, p. 605.
22 Ibid., Vol. 42, p. 421.
23 Ibid., Vol. 42, p. 421.
24 Ibid., Vol. 33, p. 372.
25 Pospelov, p. 525.
26 Trotsky, *Stalin School of Falsification*, p. 67.
27 Lewin, pp. 58, 68 (quoting Fotieva, *Iz Vospominaniy*), and Lenin, Vol. 42, p. 484.
28 Lenin, Vol. 36, pp. 605–6.
29 Ibid., Vol. 36, p. 606.
30 Ibid., Vol. 36, pp. 607–9.
31 Ibid., Vol. 36, p. 610.
32 Ibid., Vol. 45, p. 758.
33 Ibid., Vol. 45, pp. 607–8.
34 Ibid., Vol. 36, pp. 594–5.
35 Ibid., Vol. 36, p. 596.
36 Ibid., Vol. 45, p. 607.
37 Ibid., Vol. 45, pp. 607–8.
38 Lewin, p. 98.
39 Deutscher, *Prophet Unarmed*, p. 90.
40 Lenin, Vol. 33, p. 499.

Conclusion

1 Lenin, Vol. 28, p. 458.
2 Ibid., Vol. 29, p. 312.

3 Ibid., Vol. 28, p. 108.
4 Ibid., Vol. 28, p. 243.
5 Ibid., Vol. 28, p. 414.
6 Ibid., Vol. 27, p. 146.
7 Ibid., Vol. 13, p. 161.
8 Ibid., Vol. 29, p. 104.
9 Ibid., Vol. 28, p. 433.
10 Ibid., Vol. 31, p. 193.
11 Ibid., Vol. 32, p. 456.
12 Ibid., Vol. 31, pp. 230–31.
13 Ibid., Vol. 21, p. 166.
14 Ibid., Vol. 21, p. 257; see also Vol. 22, p. 162.
15 Ibid., Vol. 29, p. 545.
16 Ibid., Vol. 32, pp. 474, 521.
17 Ibid., Vol. 42, pp. 324–6.
18 Rosa Luxemburg in *Die Rote Fahne*, January 11th, 1919, quoted in Broué, *Révolution*, p. 252.
19 Weber, *Theory*, p. 363.
20 Ibid., p. 362.
21 Serge, *Memoirs*, p. 101.
22 Lenin, Vol. 35, p. 333.
23 Ibid., Vol. 35, p. 454.
24 Zetkin, p. 29.
25 Stalin, Vol. 6, p. 56.
26 Fischer, *Life of Lenin*, p. 414.
27 R. T. Fisher, p. 36.
28 Lenin, Vol. 32, pp. 37, 45.
29 Carr, Vol. II, p. 190.
30 Deutscher, *Prophet Armed*, p. 493.
31 Fischer, *Life of Lenin*, p. 600.
32 Balabanoff, p. 239.
33 Lenin, Vol. 32, pp. 86–7.
34 Ibid., Vol. 32, p. 102.
35 Kool and Oberländer, p. 133.
36 Lenin, Vol. 32, p. 257.
37 Ibid., Vol. 35, p. 491.
38 Sharapov, p. 177.
39 Sorlin, p. 76; Carr, Vol. II, p. 168.
40 Luxemburg, *The Russian Revolution*, ed. Wolfe, Chapter 2.
41 Lenin, Vol. 29, p. 144.
42 Ibid., Vol. 30, p. 143.
43 Ibid., Vol. 32, p. 215.
44 Ibid., Vol. 33, p. 485.
45 Ibid., Vol. 33, p. 501.
46 Ibid., Vol. 27, p. 548; Vol. 28, pp. 27 and 31–2.
47 Meijer, pp. 267–9.
48 Lenin, Vol. 28, p. 346; Vol. 30, p. 200.
49 Ibid., Vol. 29, p. 211.
50 Ibid., Vol. 28, p. 175.
51 Ibid., Vol. 28, p. 344.
52 Ibid., Vol. 28, p. 346.
53 Ibid., Vol. 31, p. 339.
54 Ibid., Vol. 33, pp. 487–8.
55 Ibid., Vol. 36, p. 559.
56 Ibid., Vol. 42, p. 328.
57 Ibid., Vol. 31, p. 383.

58 Lefebvre and Guterman, p. 82.
59 See Lefebvre, *La Pensée de Lénine*, pp. 144 ff.
60 Lenin, Vol. 14, p. 73.
61 Ibid., Vol. 14, p. 80.
62 Ibid., Vol. 14, pp. 59, 63, 160.
63 Ibid., Vol. 14, p. 76.
64 Ibid., Vol. 14, pp. 94–7.
65 Ibid., Vol. 14, pp. 125, 132.
66 Ibid., Vol. 14, p. 114; see also Pannekoek, *Lenin as Philosopher*, pp. 48 ff.
67 Lenin, Vol. 14, p. 99.
68 Ibid., Vol. 14, p. 146.
69 Ibid., Vol. 38, pp. 259–60.
70 Ibid., Vol. 38, p. 109.
71 Ibid., Vol. 38, p. 284.
72 Ibid., Vol. 38, p. 294.

73 Ibid., Vol. 38, pp. 171, 189, 193.
74 Ibid., Vol. 38, p. 276.
75 Ibid., Vol. 38, p. 2.
76 Quoted in Lefebvre, *Dialectical Materialism*, p. 43.
77 Lenin, Vol. 32, p. 145.
78 Quoted in Lefebvre, *Dialectical Materialism*, p. 29.
79 Lenin, Vol. 33, p. 421.
80 Ibid., Vol. 33, p. 280.
81 Ibid., Vol. 38, p. 109.
82 Quoted in Lefebvre and Guterman, p. 85.
83 Lenin, Vol. 38, p. 108.
84 Lefebvre, *Dialectical Materialism*, p. 34.
85 Lenin, Vol. 36, p. 595.

Index